WEB 2.0
FUNDAMENTALS

WITH AJAX, DEVELOPMENT TOOLS, AND MOBILE PLATFORMS

Oswald Campesato

Kevin Nilson

JONES AND BARTLETT PUBLISHERS

Sudbury, Massachusetts

BOSTON   TORONTO   LONDON   SINGAPORE

World Headquarters

Jones and Bartlett Publishers
40 Tall Pine Drive
Sudbury, MA 01776
978-443-5000
info@jbpub.com
www.jbpub.com

Jones and Bartlett Publishers
6339 Ormindale Way
Mississauga, Ontario L5V 1J2
Canada

Jones and Bartlett Publishers International
Barb House, Barb Mews
London W6 7PA
United Kingdom

Jones and Bartlett's books and products are available through most bookstores and online booksellers. To contact Jones and Bartlett Publishers directly, call 800-832-0034, fax 978-443-8000, or visit our website, www.jbpub.com.

Substantial discounts on bulk quantities of Jones and Bartlett's publications are available to corporations, professional associations, and other qualified organizations. For details and specific discount information, contact the special sales department at Jones and Bartlett via the above contact information or send an email to specialsales@jbpub.com.

Production Credits

Publisher: David Pallai
Editorial Assistant: Molly Whitman
Production Director: Amy Rose
Production Manager: Tracey Chapman
Production Assistant: Ashlee Hazeltine
Production Assistant: Rebekah Linga
Associate Marketing Manager: Lindsay Ruggiero

V.P., Manufacturing and Inventory Control:
    Therese Connell
Composition: Lapiz Online
Cover and Title Page Design: Scott Moden
Cover Image: © James Thew/ShutterStock, Inc.
Printing and Binding: Malloy, Inc.
Cover Printing: Malloy, Inc.

Library of Congress Cataloging-in-Publication Data

Campesato, Oswald.
  Web 2.0 fundamentals with Ajax, development tools, and mobile platforms / Oswald Campesato, Kevin Nilson.
    p. cm.
  Includes bibliographical references and index.
  ISBN-13: 978-0-7637-7973-3 (pbk. : alk. paper)
  ISBN-10: 0-7637-7973-3 (ibid. : alk. paper) 1. Internet programming. 2. Web 2.0. I. Nilson, Kevin. II. Title.
  QA76.625.C36 2011
  006.7'6–dc22

2009050409

6048
Printed in the United States of America
14 13 12 11 10   10 9 8 7 6 5 4 3 2 1

Disclaimer

During the production of this book, Sun Microsystems Inc. suspended Sun Zembly on November 30, 2009. Unfortunately, it was too late to remove material referencing the program. For up-to-date information on products mentioned in this book, please go to http://web2-book.com.

*I'd like to dedicate this book
to my parents—may this bring
joy and happiness into their lives.*
—Oswald Campesato

*I'd like to dedicate this book
to my son, Andy, who sat patiently on my
back overlooking much of the work for this book.*
—Kevin Nilson

Contents

Acknowledgments

◼ OSWALD CAMPESATO

When I initially thought about writing a Web 2.0 book in 2007, I did not fully anticipate the interesting and delightful path it would take. This fabulous journey began with preliminary discussions with Dave Pallai about the viability of this book, and when I contacted Kevin Nilson (in late 2008) about his impression of the table of contents, Kevin offered to contribute several chapters. I immediately accepted Kevin's offer and never regretted making him co-author of the book.

In fact, during the past year, we revised the chapters of this book by including the Future of the Web chapter (suggested by Kevin), removing two of the original chapters, and then adding four new chapters because we were convinced that the modified set of chapters would best serve the interests and needs of our audience.

Clearly, our combined technical experience, in conjunction with Siamak Ashrafi's frequent and invaluable suggestions, enabled us to create a Web 2.0 book with content beyond the reach of an individual author. I look forward to collaborating with them on additional projects in the future.

As you can see, this is an extremely ambitious book, and we always aspired to underpromise yet overdeliver in terms of the material that we included. The contents have been reviewed by many talented people, yet I take responsibility for any errors or omissions that you might find in any of the chapters. Feel free to give us your thoughts on our website http://web2-book.com.

I'm also blessed with a highly supportive family and relatives, especially Andrea, Pietro, and Marco, who unabashedly express their admiration for my books. I feel fortunate and grateful to receive such genuine and unsolicited praise from them. Other relatives who have influenced me include Lia Campesato, whose house was like a second home for me when I lived in Milan; Elda Grisostolo, for cooking six-at-a-time quail dinners for me; and Carlo Grisostolo, for his cellar filled with cheese, wine barrels, and a plethora of multi-berried wines. My thanks also extend to Fumi Lee and Aya Shio, whose help and patience enabled me to improve my Japanese pronunciation, and to my soulmates—Laurie Dresser, Farid Sharifi, and Rajiv Lakhanpal.

I'm always grateful to the people who have supported me in my endeavors or influenced me in my life, sometimes in subliminal ways. I've found such people in many parts of the world, even in an uber-competitive place such as Silicon Valley. In particular, I want to thank all of the highly accomplished contributors who provided material for this book, most of whom are also authors, many Googlers whom I have had the privilege to meet, and various meetup organizers, all of whom are listed in the contributing authors section of this book.

Finally, I would be remiss if I did not thank Dave Pallai, Publisher; Siamak Ashrafi, Technical Reviewer; Lindsay Ruggiero, Associate Marketing Manager; Molly Whitman, Editorial Assistant; and Ashlee Hazeltine, Production Assistant, all who made valuable contributions to improve the quality of this book.

■ KEVIN NILSON

I would like to deeply thank my wonderful family for making this book possible. Without my loving wife Cathleen's remarkable support, many of my career dreams and goals would have been impossible, including this book. I was also impressed by my four-year-old son Andy's understanding when some of our playtime was limited while writing this book. Huge thanks go to my parents-in-law—the generous time they spent with my son and their unconditional love has truly been a blessing. Finally, I wish to thank my parents for sending me out of the house years ago with my head on straight and pointed in the right direction.

I also want to thank a few people for helping me overcome some technical hurdles while writing this book. On many occasions, Googler Jason Cooper was a huge help in answering questions and explaining Google® technologies and APIs. Googler Stephanie Liu has been a huge help in directing me to the appropriate resources when I had questions. Finally, I want to thank Peter Higgins and many other fine folks who helped by answering questions on the #dojo FreeNode channel.

I also want to thank the many folks who contributed content to this book. They helped raise the bar of this book and made it very unique. I greatly appreciate the time and energy they volunteered to provide amazing content. I really enjoyed working with the contributors and reading the material they provided.

Thanks to Oswald Campesato for inviting me to be a co-author of this book and for sharing his knowledge and experience. The technical feedback we have received from Siamak Ashrafi has been a huge help in making sure important details were not missed. Thanks to Oswald and Siamak for taking the time to meet with me every week to discuss the details of each chapter and help determine the most valuable topics for our readers.

Lastly, but not least, I want to thank all the readers of our book. Enjoy!

Biographies of Book Contributors

■ CONTRIBUTORS

The first section provides short biographies of the contributors who provided content for the Industry Perspective sections at the ends of the chapters or for the Start-up Innovators or Future of the Web sections (both in Chapter 18).

The second section provides information about people who provided support, such as recommendations or advice about code samples, or have contributed to the IT community in Silicon Valley. We value the contributions and efforts of all of these people!

■ Chapter Contributors

The following people contributed to the Industry Perspective section at the end of each chapter or to the Future of the Web chapter.

Andres Almiray is a Java™/Groovy developer with more than 10 years of experience in software design and development. He has been involved in web and desktop application development since the early days of Java. He is a true believer in open source and has participated in popular projects like Groovy, Griffon, and DbUnit™, and has started his own projects (JSON-lib, EZMorph, GraphicsBuilder, and JideBuilder). Andres is a founding member of the Griffon framework, and he maintains a blog at http://jroller.com/aalmiray.

Monica Anderson has a master's degree in computer science and has worked in Industrial grade AI for almost two decades. She suddenly lost faith in Classical AI and, except for two years working at Google, she has been working on what she calls "Artificial Intuition" since 2001. The Artificial Intuition website is here: http://www.artificial-intuition.com. Monica is the CEO and founder of Syntience Inc., a pure research startup in Silicon Valley. The Syntience Inc. homepage can be found here: http://www.syntience.com. Monica also runs the Bay Area AI Meetup, and its homepage can be found here: http://www.ai-meetup.org.

Siamak Ashrafi is a Bio-Computational Specialist at TDI working on finding new cancer biomarkers and drug targets, and he contributes to publications in scientific journals. He has been programing for 11 years and has been issued several patents. He competes in coding competitions using social, mobile, cloud, and web technologies. He also enjoys presenting his work at various local events. In his spare time, he attends UCSF medical seminars and Stanford surgical seminars. He is very happy with all of this, but what he would really like is to get a major surfing (as in water, not http) sponsor.

Michael Carter is an expert on highly scalable, real-time web application architectures. He is an officially recognized contributor to the W3C® HTML5 specification, particularly for his work with the WebSocket proposal. He is the founder and lead of the Orbited™ project (http://www.orbited. org), an MIT-licensed Comet™ server built for high-performance browser networking. He is currently a freelance consultant and technical lead for OS-SLine (www.ossline.org), a Silicon Valley nonprofit that provides technical and legal infrastructure to a host of open source projects, including Orbited, the browser network protocols project js.io (http://js.io) and the Python® message queue MorbidQ (http://www.morbidq.com). Michael also writes network games as the CTO of the mobile games company Xio Interactive (http://xiointeractive.com).

Stephen Chin is the founder of numerous open source projects, including WidgetFX and JFXtras, and the director of software engineering at Inovis in Emeryville, CA. He has been working with Java desktop and enterprise technologies for over a decade, and he has a passion for improving development technologies and processes. Stephen's interest in Java technologies has led him to start a Java- and JavaFX-focused blog that is targeted at early technology adopters. Stephen is also the co-author of the *Pro JavaFX Platform* book.

Andrew (Aiguo) Dong is a senior R&D manager at VMware, responsible for the development of VMware®, vCenter Lab Manager™, vCenter Stage Manager™, and next-generation cloud service management and automation product. Andrew has more than 10 years of experience in the software industry, primarily at software companies in Silicon Valley. Prior to VMware, Andrew was the founding chief architect and director of engineering at Provilla, a start-up in Data Loss Prevention (DLP) space, which was successfully acquired by Trend Micro. Andrew has a master's degree in computer science and is a co-author of a few pending patents. Andrew currently lives with his family in northern California.

Marina Fisher has worked as a web scale architect at Sun Startup Essentials for the past couple of years, and she assists start-ups in the Bay Area with architecture, scalability, and Sun™ technologies. Prior to Sun Startup Essentials, Marina was part of the Sun ISV Engineering team, which focused on SAP® solutions. She has worked in the IT industry for 12 years, and she has held various positions at Sun. Marina also spent about five years with Sun Professional Services delivering enterprise solutions to Fortune 500 customers.

Marina is the author of the book *Java EE and .NET Interoperability: Integration Strategies, Patterns, and Best Practices*, the recent Sun Blueprint "Addressing Systemic Qualities in SAMP Architectures," and she holds patent 7076762 on "Design and Redesign of Enterprise Applications."

Marina is a frequent speaker at JavaOne℠, and local meetups and also attends local start-up events. Marina currently lives with her family in the Bay Area and can be reached on Twitter at @MarinaFisher and on Facebook at http://www.facebook.com/people/Marina-Fisher/564102787.

Aleksandar (Saša) Gargenta is the technology brains at Marakana. Alexsandar is always on top of the latest software, and he is the company's radar for technology that matters.

Aleksandar is the author of Marakana's Java, Advanced Java, Spring, Hibernate, JBoss, Apache, XML/XSL, and JUnit/TestNG training courses. And if that's not enough, he is also the chief architect of Marakana Spark, the on-demand software platform that powers marakana.com and a number of other training companies. As an instructor, he's taught hundreds of classes for everyone from Apple® to Disney®, from NASA to the Department of Defense.

In his spare time, Aleksandar runs the San Francisco Java and the San Francisco Android user groups, which have over a thousand members between the two. Aleksandar holds a bachelor's degree in mathematics and computer science from the University of Waterloo, Canada. He is also a father, photographer, hiker, and race car driver.

Jennifer Glore is a staff engineer at Sun Microsystems. She has worked with Sun's ISV partners for almost 10 years, helping them adopt Sun technologies. Recently, she has been focused on MySQL®, software infrastructure, and Java.

Ted Goddard received his PhD in mathematics in 1996, answering open problems in complexity theory and infinite colorings for ordered sets, and proceeded with post-doctoral research in component and web-based collaborative technologies. Following work at Java Software and Sun Microsystems, he was a device management and XML architect at Wind River, participating in the IETF NETCONF design team. Ted currently participates in the JavaServer Faces and Servlet expert groups and is a senior software architect at ICEsoft Technologies developing ICEfaces™, an Ajax framework for JavaServer™ Faces.

Chet Haase is a senior computer scientist on the Flex SDK™ team at Adobe, focusing on animation and graphics features. He is co-author of the book *Filthy Rich Clients: Developing Animated and Graphical Effects for Desktop Java Applications.*

Tom Hughes-Croucher works at Yahoo! as senior developer and technical evangelist. He's worked in the Internet industry his entire career, with clients including huge UK brands, such as Tesco, Channel 4, and 3 telecom.

Tom has worked on several web standards including the W3C's WCAG 2.0 guidelines and the British Standard Institute's IST-43. Tom occasionally blogs at http://kid666.com and often tweets from @sh1mmer. Tom lives in San Francisco with his wife and their two cats—when he isn't out speaking on the conference circuit.

Yehuda Katz is currently employed by Engine Yard and works full time as a Core Team Member on the Rails™ and Merb™ projects. He is the co-author of *jQuery in Action* and the upcoming *Merb in Action* and is a contributor to *Ruby in Practice*. He spends most of his time hacking on Rails and Merb, but also on other Ruby community projects, like Rubinius and Datamapper. And when the solution doesn't yet exist, he'll try his hand at creating one—as such, he's also created projects like Thor and DO.rb.

Vincent Lauria is the co-founder of Lefora.com, a modern forum hosting service for communities on the web. Vincent has been actively involved with social software on the web since 2005, while also working at IBM. He's been involved with web start-ups since 1996.

Vincent is also the organizer of the 4,300 member Silicon Valley New-Tech meetup (www.newtechmeet-up.org), where Web 2.0 companies get a chance to demo their services to a group of tech enthusiasts each month. Vincent currently lives in "sometimes" sunny San Francisco and can be reached online at www.vinnie.net.

Michael Ogrinz is the author of *Mashup Patterns* (Addison–Wesley, March 2009). He is also a director at one of the world's largest financial institutions. His business focus is to identify and integrate emerging technologies into the enterprise and to create innovative and competitive solutions. A frequent industry speaker on various facets of Enterprise 2.0 as they relate to the financial industry, Michael has been instrumental in enhancing the environment at his firm through his work on user interfaces and usability, wikis and blogs, so-nets, and most recently, mash-ups.

You can read his blog at mashuppatterns.com or follow him at @mogrinz on Twitter. Michael lives with his wife, two daughters, a collection of classic pinball and vector arcade machines, and a partially completed B9 Robot in wonderfully rural Easton, Connecticut.

Angelo Rajadurai works as a technology evangelist at Sun Microsystems Inc., where he helps start-ups and Web 2.0 companies with their technical and performance-related needs. Angelo has worked at Sun Microsystems for the past 16 years and has worked in the IT industry for almost 20 years.

Angelo has worked in different groups at Sun, including Solaris Kernel Engineering, Developer Technology Evangelism, ISV Technology Office, and in other technical roles. Angelo holds patent 6978441 on a rating apparatus and method for evaluating bugs. He is also a regular speaker at JavaOne, CommunityOne, and other meetups. Angelo currently lives with his family in Massachusetts, and he can be reached on Twitter at @rajadurai and on Facebook at http://www.facebook.com/arajadurai.

Michael Van Riper has a bachelor's degree in computer science from MIT. Van has more than 20 years of experience as a software engineer in Silicon Valley. He was a core member of the engineering team at Adobe that built the award-winning Adobe® PageMill® web authoring program. Since 1999, he has focused on developing web applications in Java. He is chief web technologist at Krillion in Mountain View, California. Van leads the Silicon Valley Web JUG and the Silicon Valley Google Technology user group.

Alex Russell is a software engineer at Google, where he has contributed to the development of Google Chrome Frame. Prior to joining Google, he worked for nearly a decade building open source tools and techniques that enabled richer web interfaces, primarily by augmenting declarative mark-up with JavaScript. He lives in San Francisco with his ever-patient and supportive wife Jennifer.

Dylan Schiemann is CEO of SitePen, Inc. and co-founder of the Dojo Toolkit, an open source JavaScript toolkit for rapidly building websites and applications, and is an expert in the technologies and opportunities of the Open Web. Under his guidance, SitePen has grown from a small development firm to a leading provider of inventive tools, skilled software engineers, knowledgeable consulting services, and top-notch training and advice. Dylan's commitment to R&D has enabled SitePen to be a major contributor to, or creator of, pioneering open source web development toolkits and frameworks like Dojo, CometD, Persevere, and DWR.

Dylan regularly speaks at conferences and events, such as the Apple WWDC, the Ajax Experience, JavaOne, and Adobe MAX. He also conducts seminars and training for companies interested in leveraging the technologies of the Open Web to create highly efficient and effective web application platforms. Dylan recently authored a chapter on Comet for the book *Even Faster Web Sites*.

Prior to SitePen, Dylan developed web applications for companies such as Renkoo, Informatica, Security FrameWorks, and Vizional Technologies. He is a co-founder of Comet Daily, LLC, a board member at Dojo Foundation, and a member of the Advisory Board at Aptana, Inc. Dylan earned his master's in physical chemistry from UCLA and his B.A. in mathematics from Whittier College.

Thomas ("Tom") Tague leads the Thomson Reuters Calais initiative, spearheading strategy and product development. He also oversees the Calais developer community at OpenCalais.com, evangelizing the Calais web service and working closely with commercial and noncommercial developers alike.

Tom brings more than 25 years of solutions experience and domain expertise to Thomson Reuters. Previous roles include EVP, client solutions for Darwin Partners—which he grew to $40 million in revenue in 4 years—and co-founder and chief operations officer of Tessera Enterprise Systems, a quantitative analysis and data warehousing company he helped grow to $30 million in 5 years. He also served in senior roles at database marketing pioneer, Epsilon, and systems management company, Electronic Data Systems (EDS).

Greg Wilkins is the lead developer of the Jetty open source servlet server and the CometD framework. Greg has also contributed to Apache Geronimo™, JBoss®, ActiveMQ, DWR, and other open source projects. He is a member of the experts group for the servlet specification from the Java Community Process and is contributing to the IETF efforts to standardize the bidirectional web (Hybi). Born in Sydney in 1964, Greg graduated from Sydney University with an honors degree in computer science in 1986. Since then he has worked as developer, designer, team leader, and architect on various problem domains, including defense, telecoms, and the web. Greg is the founder of Mort Bay Consulting and the CTO/founder of Webtide.

■ Additional Content Contributors

Google employees who work with Google Wave™ include: Marcel Prasetya (software engineer), Brian Kennish (developer advocate), Kimberly White (software engineer intern), and Elizabeth Ford (CD software engineer intern). All four of them contributed in one fashion or another to the Google Wave content for this book.

Other Googlers who have been a pleasure to work with and interact with socially include Jason Cooper, Stephanie Liu, Brad Neuberg, and Fred Sauer.

■ Meetup Organizers

There are many terrific Meetups in the San Francisco Bay Area that provide venues for sharing information about various aspects of technology. Both of us attended numerous Meetups, and we'd like to bring attention to the following Meetups and their respective URLs (whose leaders/organizers are listed in parentheses):

Silicon Valley Web JUG (Kevin Nilson and Van Riper)
http://www.meetup.com/sv-web-jug/

Silicon Valley Google Technology user group (Kevin Nilson and Van Riper)
http://www.meetup.com/sv-gtug/

Silicon Valley JavaScript Meetup (Michael Carter and Kevin Nilson as Assistant)
http://javascript.meetup.com/9/

BayJax — The Bay Area Ajax and JavaScript Meetup (Michael Carter and Uri Sarid)

http://www.meetup.com/BayJax/

San Francisco Java meetup (Aleksandar Gargenta)

http://www.sfjava.org/

The San Francisco Semantic Web Meetup (Marco Neumann)

http://www.meetup.com/The-San-Francisco-Semantic-Web-Meetup/

Welcome to the Twitter meetup (Sudha Jamthe)

http://www.meetup.com/TwitterMeetup/

Facebook Application Development (Lawrence Sinclair and Sudha Jamthe as Assistant)

http://www.meetup.com/facebookmeetup/

The Silicon Valley iPhone Developers' Meetup (Tim Burks)

http://www.meetup.com/sviphone/

The Silicon Valley Flex User Group (Silva FUG) (Keith Sutton)

http://ria.meetup.com/12

East Bay Innovation Group Java SIG (Chris Richardson)

http://www.ebig.org/

Silicon Valley Web Builder (Bess Ho)

http://www.svwebbuilder.com/

Preface

WHAT IS THE GOAL OF THIS BOOK?

The goal of this book is to assist technically oriented professionals in quickly learning about the Web 2.0 landscape, after which they will be in a position to make more informed decisions about the specific technologies that they want to explore in more detail. Although this book will not make people experts in Web 2.0, we hope that readers can leverage the knowledge that they acquire for near-term opportunities and longterm career growth.

This book will examine many facets of Web 2.0 to increase your knowledge of the concepts, tools, products, and technologies that belong to the Web 2.0 landscape. The code samples in this book delve into the underpinnings of Web 2.0, and some of the code samples can be downloaded from the book's website. The knowledge that you gain from reading this book will assist you in making more informed decisions about the types of Web 2.0 applications that will be useful to you. Whether you are learning Web 2.0 for your current job, for advancing your technical career, or for projects during your personal time, you can benefit from reading this book.

YOUR TECHNICAL BACKGROUND

We wrote our book with very few technical prerequisites so that it would appeal to those with little or no experience with Web 2.0. Basic knowledge of JavaScript, PHP, and JSON is helpful for understanding the corresponding code fragments we provide. In addition, a basic understanding of Java is necessary for some of the code samples in Chapter 12. All of the required knowledge can be acquired by reading tutorials that are available for free on the Internet. After you complete this book, you will be ready to learn how to leverage more advanced technical topics (e.g., REST, SOAP, and so forth) in conjunction with Web 2.0.

■ HOW WERE THE TOPICS IN THIS BOOK SELECTED?

Technical authors try to be objective in their choice of topics that they believe will be useful and informative for their target audience. Authors are influenced by their level of expertise, technical background, and personal preferences. Therefore, computer books that contain the same subject matter (and for the same target audience) can be noticeably different in terms of their focus.

In addition, determining the depth-versus-breadth of material is particularly important for a book that discusses a highly dynamic and diverse topic such as Web 2.0. Because readers have differing interests, needs, and technical expertise, it is impossible to write a technical book that has an optimal balance of material for everyone. If you look at other technical books, they invariably choose either "depth" or "breadth" of content, which can significantly affect the size of the book's audience.

We took all of the preceding points into consideration when selecting material to cover. We also used the following criteria to verify (from the perspective of our readers) the overall robustness and utility of the Web 2.0 topics in this book:

- the major categories of Web 2.0 (as of 2009)
- the emerging trends in Web 2.0 (as of 2009)
- the technical background of the target audience
- the expertise of the authors in multiple Web 2.0 topics

Three technologies that we discuss (social networks, enterprise mash-ups, and cloud computing) are mentioned in a Gartner article that lists the top ten strategic technologies for 2009, which you can find here: http://www.esmashup.com/2009/04/gartner-identifies-top-10-strategic.html.

■ HOW IS THIS BOOK ORGANIZED?

The first chapter discusses the Web 2.0 landscape and describes the major aspects of Web 2.0 technology, which will be described in much greater detail in the remaining chapters. As a result, the detailed chapters focus on discussing substantive material without presenting high-level preamble that presents introductory concepts.

Chapters 2 and 3 have some Ajax-related dependencies, so it's a good idea to read them in sequence. Chapters 4 through 12 are "loosely coupled" in terms of technical interdependencies, which means that you can read them in a different order without a significant loss of continuity. Chapters 13 through 15 rely on material that is presented in previous chapters, so it's best for you to read these chapters after you have read Chapters 1 through 12. The final chapter discusses future trends of Web 2.0, and that material will be more meaningful if you have already read the earlier chapters.

We recommend that you first glance through the appendices to familiarize yourself with the concepts that are presented so that you will be able to understand the code fragments in this book. This approach is advantageous because you will make fewer digressions to the appendices that describe dependent concepts, which will be a more efficient use of your time as you read each code fragment in its entirety. We also recommend that you read the chapters of this book in order because that will ensure that you have the requisite knowledge for each chapter.

■ WHY DOES THIS BOOK HAVE A CD-ROM?

The CD-ROM contains three appendices that list the URLs in every chapter of this book, as well as additional URLs for further reading that we believe will be useful for you. We made this decision based on the following goals:

- to reduce the weight of the book
- to enable you to copy-paste the long, tedious, and error-prone URLs directly into a web browser

■ WILL THIS BOOK HELP ME START A WEB 2.0 COMPANY?

We certainly hope so! While we cannot make such a guarantee, we do hope that the information in this book will help you become successful in your endeavors. If you are interested in monetizing an idea for a Web 2.0 product, here are some suggestions:

- determine your target audience
- understand the needs of your target audience
- determine which products exist for your target audience
- understand which products are successful (and why)
- determine why your product will be appealing
- think of ways to market your product quickly and effectively

One surprising aspect of Web 2.0 is something that we call the "equal opportunity playing field." Some of the most financially lucrative Web 2.0 products are based on simple (some people would even say trivial) ideas that seem to require very little technical expertise. Indeed, Web 2.0 has ushered in a new era where nontechnical people can create Web 2.0 companies that can become very successful.

Look at the extensive list of Web 2.0 URLs in the appendices, and use them to gain a more detailed understanding of Web 2.0. May your search help you achieve your goals and lead you to success!

■ DO YOU ENDORSE PRODUCTS IN THIS BOOK?

Neither of us have an affiliation with any other software tools and products (open source or commercial) that are discussed in this book. We prefer not to explicitly endorse or recommend products or tools for several reasons. First, there are so many Web 2.0 tools available that it's difficult to assert that a particular tool is "the best one" in its class. Second, "the best one" depends on your specific needs, and therefore another (probably similar) tool might actually be more useful to you. Third, new tools are created almost every day, with ever-increasing sets of features, which means that a product that is currently deemed "the best" may be eclipsed by another tool in the future.

We have included tools and products that have proven useful to us, and we suggest that you spend some time learning more about those that might be useful to you. If you are evaluating tools and products for work-related projects, then we suggest that you encourage your coworkers to evaluate the products in this book that interest you, after which you can make a more informed decision. In some cases, it's worthwhile to use several similar tools that have different sets of features. For example, testing tools are often similar, yet they have different strengths and weaknesses, and therefore you can obtain better results by leveraging several testing tools instead of relying on one such tool.

■ WHICH ORGANIZATIONS DO YOU ENDORSE?

We do not endorse any of the organizations and meetups that are listed in this book, and we do not have any type of reciprocation with any of them. We have included them because we believe they are useful. We also attend meetups in the San Francisco Bay Area (because that's where we live), and although similar groups do exist in other cities, San Francisco seems to be a "mecca" for highly active, technically oriented meetups.

You can look for similar groups where you live and also follow the San Francisco-based groups, which include information (videos of presentations, PowerPoint documents, and so forth) that can be useful for people who are unable to attend the events in person.

■ BOOKS AND PROJECTS FROM THE AUTHORS

Oswald Campesato has published several books and has released graphics-based open source projects that are available on Google:

Java Graphics: Concepts to Source Code is available from:
http://search.barnesandnoble.com/Java-Graphics-Programming-Library/Oswald-Campesato/e/9781584500926

Fundamentals of SVG Graphics: Concepts to Source Code is available from:
http://www.amazon.co.uk/Fundamentals-SVG-Programming-Concepts-Paperback/dp/1584502983

Microsoft Silverlight Graphics is available from:
http://www.amazon.com/Microsoft-Silverlight-Graphics-Oswald-Campesato/dp/1598635379

If you are interested in graphics, you can find several open source projects (mainly under the Apache 2.0 license) at:
http://code.google.com/u/ocampesato/

J2ME™ graphics are available as a SourceForge™ open source project at:
http://www.mirrorservice.org/sites/download.sourceforge.net/pub/sourceforge/j/j2/j2me-graphics/

■ WILL THIS BOOK MAKE ME AN EXPERT IN WEB 2.0?

This book will not make you an expert in Web 2.0, and you should be skeptical of any books that make such a claim (as far as we know, there aren't any books that do). Moreover, entire books have been written that cover topics that we discuss in a single chapter (and we mention this fact in several places). On the other hand, many of the chapters are interconnected in the sense that material presented in one chapter can be used in another chapter later in the book. Therefore, this book provides much more than a set of independent chapters, and the material is designed to help you answer the following questions:

- What useful tools are available for a given technology?
- Which tools and products are important for each technology?
- What are the strengths of the tools and products?
- How are the tools and products set up on a user's machine?
- Are additional resources available, and where are they?
- Where are code samples and tutorials for the products/tools in this book?
- How much effort is required to learn the products and tools?

The learning effort clearly depends on your level of knowledge, how much time you can invest, and how quickly you absorb new concepts.

Despite all of the challenges that are involved in learning about Web 2.0, we believe that after you read this book you will have a high level of awareness of the tools and products that are available in many important aspects of Web 2.0 technology.

■ HOW MUCH TIME WILL THIS BOOK SAVE ME?

The answer depends on several factors, but we estimate that it will take approximately 100 hours (and possibly even longer) for many readers to independently learn the material that we present here. Even at the rate of 4 hours a day (and 5 days per week) devoted to your research, you would spend more than an entire month acquiring this knowledge. If you can only commit 10 hours per week to research (which is probably more realistic), then you will need to devote more than 2 months of your time.

Moreover, the preceding time estimate does not take into account other factors, such as knowing which technologies are most relevant to you, knowing which combination of tools/products you need for your development environment, and writing code that uses the tools in this book (and remember that nontrivial code also contains bugs).

On the other hand, both of us have experience with a breadth of Web 2.0 topics, and we also interact with developers from many companies. Because we are in Silicon Valley, we have attended a bevy of conferences, "unconferences," code camps, hackathons, and technical meetups in Silicon Valley over the past 3 years.

All of these factors can influence how much time you will need to learn about Web 2.0, and you can weigh these factors to perform a cost/benefit analysis to determine what works best for you. With all of these points in mind, there's one more question that you probably want to ask us.

■ IS THIS THE ULTIMATE WEB 2.0 BOOK?

Despite the intended levity of this question, there is an important subtext that we want to convey: This book will help you assess Web 2.0 from the standpoint of which of its facets will be beneficial to you. Regardless of whether you are a student, employee, developer, manager, or one of the founding members of a company, this is the message that we wish to convey to you.

## CHAPTER 1

Introduction

In This Chapter:

- Information About This Book
- Web 2.0 in Our Lives
- What is Web 2.0?
- Popular Web 2.0 Products and Tools
- The Current Web 2.0 Landscape
- What About Web 3.0?

This book covers a vast number of topics, tools, and products related to Web 2.0. However, despite the depth and breadth of this book, there are many Web 2.0 topics that are not covered. The reasoning behind the decisions that were made in selecting the content for this book is discussed in the Preface.

The first section of this chapter describes how this book is organized and the rationale for selecting the book chapters. The second section discusses some enabling technologies, such as Wikis and Blogs, that were available during the early stages of Web 2.0 and tools and products that are popular today. The third section covers the major categories of Web 2.0 as of 2009. The last section describes how the "2.0" designation has been adopted in other fields after the emergence of Web 2.0.

Note: Please read the Preface to understand the assumptions that we made for this book.

This chapter gives you a glimpse into some of the important tools, technologies, and facets of the Web 2.0 landscape, while the other chapters focus on content for the chapter-specific topics and bypass virtually all historical information. After you finish this chapter, you will have a high-level understanding of the important aspects of Web 2.0.

■ 1.1 INFORMATION ABOUT THIS BOOK

This section answers some of the questions you may have regarding this book that were not discussed in the preface.

■ 1.1.1 Why Should You Buy This Book?

This book gives you a detailed overview of the important aspects of Web 2.0. It also contains an extensive list of URLs: some are "good to know" and others are technically oriented. Regardless of whether you are a developer or someone with a modest technical background, the less technical URLs can assist you in the following ways:

- you will gain a better understanding of Web 2.0
- you can experiment with popular Web 2.0 products and services
- you might get ideas for developing a new Web 2.0 product

If you live outside of Silicon Valley, you might not know that founders of Web 2.0 start-ups have diverse backgrounds, including development, product development, product management, sales, human resources (HR), and marketing—some are even students who drop out of school to capitalize on their ideas.

Despite the diverse backgrounds of these founders, there is one thing they have in common: they got a great idea and started a Web 2.0 company that people became interested in. Successful Web 2.0 sites are often the result of successfully executing a very simple idea. If you are interested in Web 2.0 because of its potential to make you successful, then your goal should be to remain alert and receptive to opportunities that can lead to a simple yet great idea. Perhaps the information in this book will serve as the spark that ignites the creative fire in you and your own successful Web 2.0 company.

■ 1.1.2 Why Are There Two Social Networking Chapters?

Social networking is a very important aspect of Web 2.0 that shows no sign of slowing in the foreseeable future. As such, we decided to include the two most dominant social networking products and tools: Facebook® and Open-Social™. As you will see, Facebook is both a social networking application and a platform, whereas OpenSocial is a platform only (or more precisely, a consortium of companies).

■ 1.1.3 Why Are There Three Cloud Computing Chapters?

We believe that the three chapters in this book dedicated to cloud computing are important for a large and diverse audience. The first cloud computing chapter discusses large vendors, because they can influence adoption—even if they don't always provide the best services. The second cloud computing chapter discusses a plethora of smaller vendors and alternatives to cloud computing, such as virtualization from VMWare® and distributed caches such as Oracle® Coherence™. The third chapter on cloud computing discusses Java™ and Google App Engine™ (GAE) (announced in April 2009), because the availability of Java on GAE makes GAE attractive to millions of developers in the Java community. In addition, this book is likely to be the first published book that devotes a chapter to Java and GAE.

■ 1.1.4 Why Does This Book Use the Dojo Toolkit and jQuery?

As of 2010, Dojo™ and jQuery™ are two of the most popular, feature-rich, and mature Ajax toolkits, which probably accounts for the fact that they now have a dominant market share among Ajax frameworks. Dojo is a well-designed framework that is supported by a large team of open source developers. Dojo also has many nice enterprise features such as a dependency system that simplifies configuration, good unit test coverage for testing and examples, and good API documentation. Widgets in Dojo, called Dijits, are tested together and released as part of the framework.

At the same time, the set of Ajax frameworks (and their adoption rate) changes from year to year. One significant alternative to Dojo is jQuery, which is rapidly gaining popularity. However, jQuery is less mature and feature rich that Dojo. jQuery UI provides a handful of widgets, but their are far more Dijits available than jQuery UI widgets.

With these points in mind, Dojo is our preferred Ajax framework, but we plan on providing online examples in both Dojo and jQuery, and you are at liberty to convert these code samples into your own Ajax framework.

■ 1.1.5 Versions of Software and Tools in this Book

We made every attempt to ensure that we worked with the most recent versions of every product and tool that we discussed in this book. Even though this book was written in 2009, Web 2.0 continues moving forward with newer versions of existing products and also the new product releases.

Therefore, as this book went to print, we made a final revision to update the book with the latest versions of each product. Moreover, if we find significant new products during which this book goes to print, we will include an online addendum containing any information that we believe will be useful to you.

■ 1.1.6 Appendices with Web 2.0 URLs

Each chapter contains a set of URLs that are related to the chapter material. For your convenience, these links are also included in the appendices, which contain additional Web 2.0-related URLs. The material in these URLs are usually presented as HTML pages (and sometimes as PDF documents), and the material varies in terms of the depth of detail, its complexity, and the volume of information. In some cases, the URLs contain additional URLs that may also be useful for you.

When you look at the URLs in the appendices, keep in mind the following points: First, the usefulness of the material will vary from person to person. Second, the URLs are intended as a starting point for you to learn more about Web 2.0; these links might contain other links that will lead you to additional information. Third, we have found useful material in all of the URLs listed in the appendices, but we do not "endorse" any of them (either directly or indirectly). Fourth, all of the links in the appendices were validated when this book went to press, but it is possible that some of them may no longer be valid. If you find an invalid link, and you are interested in its content, search the Internet to find other URLs with similar material.

■ 1.1.7 Web 2.0 Topics That Are Omitted from This Book

There are many interesting aspects to Web 2.0, but including all of them is beyond the scope and inconsistent with the purpose of this book. Based on the criteria and selection process for the material in this book (see the Preface), we chose to omit the following topics:

- Offline applications
- Really Simple Syndication (RSS)
- Content Management Systems (CMSs)
- Taxonomy/Ontology/Folksonomy
- Microformats
- Tag management
- RESTful services
- Microsoft®-based tools and products
- Scripting languages other than PHP
- Enterprise 2.0
- Government 2.0
- Advertising 2.0
- Search Engine Optimization (SEO)

In some cases, we included URLs that discuss some of the preceding topics; however, if you are interested in more in-depth information about these topics, search the Internet for books and articles about these topics.

■ 1.1.8 The URLs in This Book

The appendices located on the CD-ROM contain many URLs, some of which reference online videos that address topics discussed in this book. Although we tried to only include active URLs, please keep in mind that:

- some URLs may be abandoned by the time this book is published
- some videos may no longer be available after this book is published
- newer videos may become available after this book is published
- the videos vary in their quality and duration
- some videos were made during the "alpha" release of a product

While it's possible to find online videos with detailed information on an individual topic, those resources invariably focus on a single topic, which means that you need to spend time searching for information and culling through URLs to find what's most useful. By contrast, this book provides you with a single resource that addresses many Web 2.0 topics.

Nevertheless, when companies create a product (such as Yahoo® Pipes™) and then provide online resources, we recommend that you view those online resources so that you can learn about the most recent updates on product features and product release dates.

■ 1.1.9 Is This Book Only for Developers?

If you have a strong desire to learn about Web 2.0, and you have a reasonable level of technical skill (even if it is unrelated to Web 2.0), then you will benefit from reading the material in this book. Your technical experience can affect the amount of time and effort it takes for you to grasp the details of the code samples in this book. If you are interested in learning about what Web 2.0 can offer, and not so much about the technical aspects, you can benefit from this book, too.

If you are a manager in a software company, you may be looking for ways to expand your skills to help you sustain or advance your career. As such, consider the value of becoming comfortable with Web 2.0 technologies that your company uses now or is planning to adopt in the future. If your company is assessing the Web 2.0 landscape, then it's advantageous for you to become as knowledgeable about Web 2.0 as possible, because your knowledge could be sufficient to influence the direction of your company.

With these points in mind, you can benefit from this book by reading this chapter and the first half of the remaining chapters (i.e., you can skip the code-specific parts). At a minimum, you will be able to ask project leaders questions, such as "Which Ajax toolkits are we using in our projects and why?" The answers to the questions you ask may help you perform a better gap/risk analysis for your projects.

■ 1.1.10 Do You Discuss the Best Web 2.0 Tools?

The best available tool is the tool that is best suited for your requirements (such as the features of the product you're building) and your constraints (such as time, money, and resources). Also, the tools with the most features might be appealing to you initially, but if they cost more than you are willing to spend, then you probably need to make some compromises. Finally, if you are comparing two or more open source tools, then you need to consider the maturity of the tools, the availability of support for the tools, and the time, money, and effort for making customizations/enhancements to the tools.

For these reasons, we adopted an agnostic approach regarding the tools and products in this book so that we could focus on the "what" (what tools are available) and the "how" (how do the tools work), whereas the "why" (why should anyone use these tools) is a decision best made by you.

■ 1.2 WEB 2.0 IN OUR LIVES

Web 2.0 is becoming inextricably intertwined with our social and professional lives in a way that makes us wonder what exciting new changes Web 2.0 will bring in the near future. Web 2.0 is stimulating, dynamic, and unpredictable, and it will continue to evolve in terms of the ways in which it improve various aspects of our lives.

One important aspect of Web 2.0 is the staggering number of Web 2.0 products and services that you can find on the Internet. Moreover, this number increases daily, which means learning about all of them is virtually impossible, even if you devote all of your available time. However, you can focus on the major categories of Web 2.0, which can be useful if you are interested in writing Web 2.0 applications, or perhaps even starting your own Web 2.0 company.

As you explore the broad spectrum of Web 2.0 services that are available, you will see that those services vary greatly in terms of their sophistication and their usefulness. In fact, some of them might even seem frivolous or even pointless, with virtually no apparent social value or technical sophistication at all. However, end users want services that are fun, and social value (whose definition varies) is a lower priority. End users are rarely concerned with the underlying technical prowess of online services, which is why you should understand the popularity of products and services that are already available. People are interested in entertainment (for example, online games), social interaction (such as Facebook applications), communication tools (such as Twitter™, which in its earlier days was described as "a Web 2.0 application about nothing"), or some other convenience factor (e.g., Yelp℠ reviews for bars and restaurants).

The collaborative nature of the Internet has become widespread in a manner that did not exist before Web 2.0. When people shared movie clips or photographs with friends, it was considered part of the "edutainment" category, which implied an absence of real value, but even companies such as IBM® upload their technical information as YouTube™ videos. University courses can also be taken via a software program that is actually a Facebook application.

Twitter is another example of a tool whose value has been discussed frequently, and there are businesses that rely on Twitter to communicate with their customers.

Although most "tweets" (Twitter posts) are mundane, Twitter does enable people to communicate during emergencies, such as the Minneapolis bridge collapse in 2007 or during forest fires in Southern California. In January 2009, when U.S. Airways Flight 1549 made an emergency landing on the Hudson River, someone posted a picture on Twitter. During the Mumbai tragedy in November 2009, people used Twitter to report on the events. The Southern California fire department maintains a Twitter page, and even newscasters use real-time displays of tweets as news items. Twitter is also making inroads in the judicial system. In March 2009, U.S. District Judge J. Thomas Marten in Wichita, Kansas allowed a reporter to use Twitter in a federal court during a racketeering trial.

Twitter has been used in unexpected and intriguing ways. For instance, in April 2009, Adam Wilson set up a computer to interpret brain waves and send them as tweets, and one month later, astronaut Mike Massimo sent a tweet from the space shuttle Atlantis. (NASA has 36 Twitter accounts.) Then in July 2009, Australian police used Twitter to discourage drunk driving among young people (see the appendices for a link). In August, 2009, IBM filed a patent for a television remote control that sends tweets (and messages to facebook). Twitter was used for visualization during the 2009 MTV Video Music Awards (VMA) (see the appendices for links).

However, there are also risks associated with revealing too much information via tweets. For example, a husband and wife sent numerous tweets while they were on their vacation, and when they returned home, they discovered that many of their belongings had been stolen. Authorities suspect that the burglars were aware of the whereabouts of the couple through the tweets the couple sent while on vacation. A landlord sued one of his tenants because of comments posted on Twitter.

Another significant area of Web 2.0 pertains to social networks, which have already become massive (especially Facebook), because they enable a constant stream of information among people. The information that people share can be textual comments, pictures, videos, and hyperlinks to other sites and events. Social networks have also affected life in unexpected ways, such as when an Australian court ruled in 2008 that foreclosure notifications (for Australian homeowners) sent via Facebook are legally binding.

■ 1.3 WHAT IS WEB 2.0?

Although the first Web 2.0 conference was held in 2004 (and the buzz began in 2005), a consensus about the definition of Web 2.0 is surprisingly elusive. Developers and nontechnical people have different opinions about Web 2.0, and sometimes those opinions differ dramatically, even among the developer community.

Web 2.0 is heavily oriented toward content generation by people who collaborate and share their content and information. Web 2.0 includes blogs, wikis, and Semantic Technology (discussed in Chapter 13). In the Web 2.0 world, the Internet is a dynamic and interactive environment, whereas in Web 1.0 the Internet was viewed more like an online dictionary and repository of static information. Web 2.0 lets people share things, such as photographs, and make them instantly available to friends and other family members. Consider the fact that several hundred million people belong to social networks, and that that number will probably exceed the one billion mark in the near future. Twitter began as a novelty that was used by a small number of people, but now it's commonplace for people to communicate anytime, anywhere, and with anyone who wants to be connected. People use Twitter continuously to send updates to friends and coworkers, whether it's for marketing, reporting, blogging, or simply updating each other about current or upcoming events.

An important part of Web 2.0 involves mash-ups, which can provide convenient and useful services. In the business world, mash-ups and mash-up tools (discussed in Chapter 9) belong to Enterprise 2.0.

■ 1.3.1 Pioneers in Web 2.0

Several companies have influenced the Information Technology (IT) industry by providing free Web 2.0 technology that is available to everyone, and these companies include:

- Yahoo®
- Amazon®
- Google™ (Google Maps™)

Yahoo was created in the mid-1990s as an Internet company that provided a wide array of free services, such as calendars, search capabilities, and developer tools (YUI is a Yahoo Ajax library). In addition, Yahoo was among the first to provide free email to everyone. Internet email providers, such as Yahoo and Microsoft, provided the first four megabytes for free (with a "meter" that showed people how much free space remained in their email account) and charged for larger storage sizes.

In 2003, Google released Gmail™, which was available on an invitation-only basis (people could only get a Gmail account through an invitation from an existing Gmail user). A Gmail account provided one gigabyte of storage for free, which was a gigantic increase for email users. Shortly there-after, Yahoo offered comparable free storage for email, and now Yahoo email users have unlimited storage for free.

Another pioneer in the Internet world is Amazon, which was the first significant Internet company that sold books online. As mundane as this service might seem today, the availability of online books was a radical departure from the brick-and-mortar model for bookstores. Since that time, Amazon has added a number of other products and services, including support for cloud computing (such as EC2). Nowadays, the marketplace is crowded with other companies that either sell books online or provide cloud computing services, but Amazon is a leader in both of these areas.

A third pioneer is Google, whose search engine had a profound impact on the accessibility of information for anyone who had access to a browser. Google is among those companies whose name has entered our daily vocabulary as a verb ("I Googled for the information.").

■ 1.3.2 The Shift from Web 1.0 to Web 2.0

When the Internet became popular during the mid-1990s, people used browsers to navigate to HTML pages. Those HTML pages contained read-only content, regardless of whether the content was static (i.e., a file on the file system of a server) or dynamically generated prior to rendering the content in a browser. The read-only nature of the content meant that people could not modify the content of those HTML pages. Web 2.0 removes the read-only restriction of Web 1.0, thereby enabling people to collaborate by dynamically updating, creating, and sharing content with other users.

Another crucial difference between Web 1.0 and Web 2.0 is the manner in which HTML pages are updated. In Web 1.0, the entire HTML page must be submitted to a server, even if only one field needs to be updated. On the other hand, HTML pages in Web 2.0 can use Ajax to only modify the portions of the HTML page that need to be changed. This so-called "partial page refresh" offers an additional advantage: a faster, more seamless user experience.

Several other trends that began in Web 2.0 are:

- crowdsourcing
- citizen journalism
- viral programming
- viral marketing
- the long tail

These topics are not discussed in this book, but you can find additional information by searching the Internet for articles and books that discuss these topics in detail.

■ 1.3.3   Is Web 2.0 Overrated?

Many technology trends eventually reach saturation, and among some groups, Web 2.0 in 2009 is not nearly as exciting as it was in 2005 and 2006. According to one survey, almost 20% of marketing executives are "tired" of hearing about Web 2.0 (see the appendices for a link).

At the same time, the 2009 global recession adversely affected the availability of venture capital, which in turn affected the creation of new companies and the survival of existing Web 2.0 companies. In late 2008, a *Newsweek* article suggested that "web two dot oh" might turn into "web two dot over" for many Web 2.0 companies. Unlike start-up companies of an earlier era, many Web 2.0 companies have very low start-up costs (and therefore less dependence on venture capitalists) with the goal of being bought by a larger successful company instead of an Initial Public Offering (IPO) strategy. Moreover, in the early stages, such start-ups tend to focus more on their vision and focus less on clearly defined revenue models.

You can find articles on the Internet that describe the ways in which things have gone awry in the past. Keep in mind that learning from these sorts of missteps does not prepare us for new types of pitfalls in the future, or the new ones Web 3.0 might bring us.

The McKinsey report describing the benefits of Web 2.0 can be found here: http://www.mckinseyquarterly.com/Business_Technology/BT_Strategy/ How_companies_are_benefiting_from_Web_20_McKinsey_Global_Survey_ Results_2432.

■ 1.3.4 Advantages/Disadvantages of Web 2.0

Web 2.0 has a technical component, Ajax, and the collaborative nature of its user-generated content that did not exist in Web 1.0. User collaboration lets users provide feedback in many ways (such as responding to blog posts, providing product reviews, sharing movies and pictures, etc.) in a manner that was not possible with Web 1.0.

Here is a partial list of the advantages of Web 2.0:

• a full-page refresh is not required (hence better performance)
• inputted text is saved rather than lost
• page state is maintained

However, the collaborative nature of Web 2.0 also creates more opportunities to "hack" servers, and therefore security is arguably more complex in Web 2.0 than in Web 1.0.

Here is a partial list of the disadvantages of Web 2.0:

• a greater number of security holes
• lack of "bookmarkability"
• cannot track URL history
• harder to code Web 2.0 applications
• potential memory leaks
• lack of support in older browsers
• more testing required (cross-browser support)

One security-related topic is called Cross-Site Scripting (XSS). There are tools available for protecting websites from XSS, such as the free Google tool ratproxy (see the appendices on the CD for a link). Search the Internet for other XSS-related tools so you can determine which tool best fits your requirements.

■ 1.3.5 Early Enabling Technologies of Web 2.0

Web 2.0 began with two important enabling technologies: wikis and blogs. Both of these technologies contributed to the initial momentum behind Web 2.0 because of their collaborative nature, and they have become so popular that they are commonplace even among nontechnical users. The following sections describe these two early enabling technologies in greater detail.

1.3.5.1 *Wikis*

Although wiki-based technology began around the mid-1990s, more wide-spread use of wikis on the Internet probably started around the beginning of 2000. Wikis are powerful and useful because of their collaborative functionality, which gives users a very easy and convenient way of recording ideas, tracking online discussions, and sharing meeting notes.

A wiki often consists of a set of logically related pages that enable collaborative content creation. Users are empowered to create new content and update existing content online, which provides a convenient way to record people's ideas and suggestions. Note that users are not responsible for system administration tasks, such as performing regular backups of their wiki.

Wikis provide a many-to-many functionality in the sense that (unlike blogs) no one is deemed the "owner" of a page; anyone can create a wiki page, and anyone can edit that page (or create new pages). Some distinct advantages to using wikis are:

• good for sharing information
• their informal nature makes it easier for people to contribute
• strong version control
• easy for many people to edit the same page or create new pages

However, there are also some disadvantages to using Wikis, such as:

• not good for project management
• security can become an issue
• inappropriate for sensitive information
• sharing data between different wikis can be difficult

Check the appendices for a link to several open source and commercial wikis, or search the Internet to decide which Wiki best serves the needs of your users.

1.3.5.2 *Blogs*

Blogs first gained traction on the Internet around 2001, and at that time they were called "weblogs." However, that term was soon replaced by "blogs," and the people who wrote blogs became known as "bloggers." Each entry in a user's blog is called a "blog post."

Bloggers often write their comments about topics that interest them, and bloggers can be as factual or as opinionated as anyone else. Bloggers also provide a combination of links to other blog posts or articles, video clips, or images (the specific mix various among bloggers).

You can find bloggers who write commentaries primarily about the daily news, political events, social issues, entertainment, and virtually any other topic. Bloggers have given rise to so-called "citizen journalism," which competes with print media such as newspapers. Today you can find online magazines, or "ezines" that are the digital equivalent of magazines.

The growth of blogs has been explosive: in 2009 the number of blogs (both active and inactive) was approximately 75,000,000, and this figure is increasing every day. Blogs provide a one-to-many technology in the sense that one person creates a blog post and other people can post their feedback in the form of comments.

The quality and popularity of blog posts vary significantly among bloggers. The number of readers of any given blog can vary from a handful of people (e.g., friends and relatives) to hundreds of thousands (or even millions) of people.

There are many, many blogging tools available, and you're virtually guaranteed to find one that fits your specific needs. Two popular blogging tools are Google's Blogger™ and WordPress®. Blogger is an online blogging tool, and you can create an account in a matter of minutes, after which you can immediately create blog posts.

Check the appendices on the CD for a list of other blogging tools and search the Internet with industry-specific keywords to find blogging tools that are specific to your industry.

Several years after blogs became popular, a phenomenon known as *microblogging* appeared and has gained momentum. A *microblog* is a very short and concise blog post that is limited to 140 characters: think of a microblog as a hybrid of a blog post and a tweet (Twitter is discussed in more detail later in this chapter). Microblogging often involves a short comment about a specific event, which might be targeted to an individual or group.

Several microblogging initiatives are available, such as OpenMicro-Blogger®, Jaiku™, and status.net (see the appendices on the CD for links).

■ 1.4 POPULAR WEB 2.0 PRODUCTS AND TOOLS

Whether you're a nontechnical user or a developer, the following Web 2.0 tools are interesting and useful, either in terms of the convenience they offer or the increase in productivity that they provide:

- Flickr®
- YouTube
- Twitter
- Facebook
- Yelp
- De.licio.us™
- SlideShare™

The preceding list is certainly not exhaustive, and you can search the Internet to find a variety of other useful tools. You can perform either a broad search (such as "top 100" lists) or you can perform searches for specific needs (such as blogging tools, real estate tools, etc.) to find useful tools. Sometimes you can find a comparison of the "best" tools, which will undoubtedly help you select the tool that is best for your specific needs.

Note that Twitter is also discussed in Chapter 5 and Facebook is discussed in greater detail in Chapter 7.

■ 1.4.1 Flickr

Flickr is a photo-sharing application that was launched in 2004 and later acquired by Yahoo. Its home page is:
http://www.flickr.com

Flickr provides a set of APIs (including RSS and Atom feeds) to access its contents, and they are often used by mash-ups to render Flickr-based content. By mid-2009, Flickr reported that more than three billion photographs were posted on its website.

While the creators of Flickr undoubtedly had good intentions (i.e., enable people to share photographs with people around the world), there are cultural differences regarding the appropriateness of pictures (such as partially clothed persons). In fact, Flickr implemented a filtering service that helps to address this issue.

In addition, there are privacy issues regarding photographs that are posted without the permission of the person (or people) in those photographs. There can also be religious differences regarding the appropriateness of certain types of photographs.

If you are a developer, Flickr provides licensing terms and support for map-related services for cities.

■ 1.4.2 YouTube

YouTube is a video-sharing application that was launched in 2006 and later acquired by Google. Its home page is:

http://www.youtube.com

YouTube is extremely popular for sharing videos with everyone, be they friends, family, or complete strangers. From a commercial standpoint, YouTube does not appear to be profitable, and ad revenue does not appear to be as lucrative as expected, but end users are generally satisfied with its services. One very interesting fact about YouTube is that large companies, including IBM, have posted training videos that introduce people to IBM's technology (one example is the IBM Mashup Hub, which has been renamed IBM Mashup Center). Thus, YouTube provides a highly useful service to companies and a tremendous number of people.

■ 1.4.3 Twitter

Twitter is a public message-oriented application. Its home page is:

http://twitter.com.home

People post messages called "tweets" containing up to 140 characters on a global queue that is accessible to everyone on Twitter. A person who posts tweets on Twitter is called a "twitterer." One view is that Twitter is about communicating immediate events, and a second view is that Twitter is about improving the speed of communication among people.

Twitter has been described as "aging in reverse," because it was initially popular with older people and then gained popularity with a younger audience. Twitter users include IT industry figures, movie stars, celebrities, and politicians, including the President of the United States.

Tweets are mostly used for casual communication, but they have been used for commercial purposes. For example, tweets can result in better response time regarding product defects if company employees spot such tweets and then initiate a dialogue with the person who posted the tweets. This scenario can be more effective than more traditional email-based support systems.

If you are unfamiliar with Twitter, a good article that will help you familiarize yourself with Twitter terminology is:
http://blogs.techrepublic.com.com/hiner/?p=1715

Twitter can be useful when people need to communicate with each other during emergencies. However, in mid-2009 someone broke into Twitter's system and released several hundred private documents, including internal email messages that discussed confidential details about Twitter. Twitter has recently implemented OAuth (discussed in Chapter 8), which is an open protocol for secure authorization between desktops and web applications.

Although this security breach affected Twitter's staff, recently a variant of the W32.Koobface worm has emerged that specifically targets Twitter by posting a tweet to a website and then posting tweets to the current user's contacts.

Twitter does have potential competitors, including Tumblr® and Yahoo® Meme™, both of which are microblogging tools. Yahoo announced Yahoo Meme in mid-2009, and it is available in English and Spanish. This beta tool has been described as a potentially strong competitor to Twitter, and you can request a Yahoo Meme account here:
http://meme.yahoo.com/home/

1.4.3.1 Some Basic Features of Twitter

Twitter provides a feature called "track" that lets people track specific words, and another feature called "follow" that lets people follow each other. People can follow each other and also block individuals. Twitter makes it very easy to share information with other people, and yet there can be risks involved when people broadcast their location. For example, questions were raised about the security of a U.S. congressman who posted tweets while he was in Iraq (see the appendices).

There are situations in which people will inadvertently find your Twitter ID and decide to follow you, but it might be awkward for you to block them. For example, a customer who has your company email address might use your email prefix to discover your Twitter ID. If that customer decides to follow you on Twitter, your business life may start overlapping with your personal life.

Chapter 5 discusses Twitter in more detail and also provides some Twitter-based tools.

■ 1.4.4 Yelp

Yelp is a free online tool that lets users create public reviews of movies, restaurants, bars, and anything else that people want to review. The Yelp home page is: http://www.yelp.com

Yelp contains many helpful informal reviews that can be particularly useful when you travel to unfamiliar cities. Yelp has a high volume of traffic, with at least twenty million visitors per month.

Yelp also provides APIs (REST and JSON) so that applications (such as mash-ups) can access reviews and ratings on Yelp. In addition, Yelp is a Facebook Beacon partner site (note that there have been privacy issues surrounding Facebook Beacon, which is discussed in Chapter 7).

■ 1.4.5 Del.icio.us

Del.icio.us (now called Delicious) is a free bookmarking site that was created in 2003. Its home page is: http://www.del.icio.us

Delicious lets users associate "tags" with URLs, and then share those tags with other people. A tag can consist of a single word or several words, and the collection of tags that are associated with a URL forms a "tag cloud," which is a visual representation of the relative popularity of specific tags that are associated with the given URL. Currently, Delicious has several million users, along with more than one hundred million bookmarked URLs.

Note that Gnolia is popular and private alternative to Del.icio.us. Its home page is: http://www.gnolia.com

Search the Internet to find more information on Gnolia and other bookmarking sites.

■ 1.4.6 SlideShare

SlideShare is a website devoted to sharing various types of files. Its home page is: http://www.slideshare.net

SlideShare lets you upload and share Adobe® PDF files, Microsoft® PowerPoint™ presentations, and Microsoft® Word™ documents. When you share your documents, you can make them public or private. In addition, SlideShare provides audio support that can be added to documents.

SlideShare has been ranked as a top productivity tool, and SlideShare claims that it is also the largest file-sharing website in the world.

■ 1.5   THE CURRENT WEB 2.0 LANDSCAPE

This book discusses the following commonly used facets and categories of Web 2.0:

- Ajax
- Social networks
- Mash-ups
- Cloud computing
- Java and GAE
- Semantic Technology
- Google Web Toolkit (GWT)
- Comet ("Reverse Ajax")
- Mobile computing

There are several other aspects of Web 2.0 that are not discussed in this book, such as:

- Offline applications
- Microformats
- RESTful services
- Rich Internet Applications (RIAs)
- RSS/ATOM syndication
- Search Engine Optimization (SEO/SEM)

The following subsections provide some high-level information about the major aspects of Web 2.0 that are discussed in more detail in the other chapters of this book.

■ 1.5.1   Ajax (Formerly Called AJAX)

Prior to delving into the details of Ajax, we'll briefly digress to give you some background information on Ajax.

The arrival of Java in the mid-1990s quickly led to Java-based web applications that relied on Java Servlets to generate HTML pages. However, such applications were usually complex and unwieldy in terms of development and maintenance. Around 1998, Java Servlets were supplanted by

Java Server Pages (JSPs), which consisted of scriptlets that were compiled into Java Servlet classes by JSP compilers (and those Java Servlet classes were then compiled into Java byte code).

Around the late 1990s, the open source movement gained significant momentum, and companies began adopting open source projects as part of the "technology stack" for their products. The open source movement led to an environment in which developers created and shared open source tools.

There are several popular repositories for open source projects, such as the Apache Foundation® (http://www.apache.com) and GeekNet™ (http://www.geeknet.com). People often say, "ASF" as the organization, and they often say "Apache" when referring to a license. CodeHaus™ (http://www.codehaus.org) and Freshmeat™ (http://freshmeat.net/) also host open source projects. Note that Apache accepts projects that meet its mission statement, whereas Sourceforge accepts all projects, and also provides a license that can be used in Apache.

By the end of 2004, there were at least fifty Java-based open source User Interface (UI) web frameworks available that facilitated the development of Java-based web applications. Developers were faced with the daunting task of gaining a solid understanding of the benefits and disadvantages of the various frameworks, so they could make better decisions about which UI framework to use for their project.

Then, in 2005, Jesse James Garrett wrote the seminal paper on Ajax, and it captured the imagination of many developers. AJAX was originally an acronym for Asynchronous JavaScript™ and XML. Later, AJAX was replaced by Ajax, which is no longer an acronym.

Although Jesse James Garrett originally thought of Ajax being used in conjunction with technologies such as XSLT, many Web 2.0 applications use JavaScript and an Ajax-based framework on the client and PHP on the server. (Somewhat ironically, many of those who develop Web 2.0 technologies probably have limited knowledge of XSLT.) The popularity of Ajax spread quickly, and before the end of 2005 there was already a wave of Ajax-based web applications. The abundance of Ajax frameworks (described briefly in the next section) requires developers to evaluate those frameworks based on the requirements of their projects (which is the same decision process that occurred years earlier with Java-based UI frameworks).

1.5.1.1 Ajax Toolkits

The top-ten JavaScript-based Ajax libraries of 2009 are:

* Prototype™
* Script.aculo.us™
* Dojo
* YUI™
* jQuery
* MooTools
* Ext-JS™
* GWT™
* SproutCore™

Several of the preceding Ajax libraries are discussed in greater detail in Chapter 3, and the appendices contain additional links. In addition to JavaScript-based Ajax libraries, there are also Ajax tools that are based on other languages, including C++™, Flash™, Java, JavaScript, Lisp™, Perl™, PHP, Python®, Ruby, and Smalltalk™. Details on these Ajax frameworks can be found here:

http://www.ajaxgoals.com/ajax-frameworks.html.

■ 1.5.2 Productivity Tools

Although productivity tools are not specifically associated with Web 2.0 technology, they can help increase your efficiency.

Here is a partial list of productivity tools that are discussed in Chapter 5:

* Yahoo Pipes
* Dapper
* Google Gears™
* Google Native Client™
* Google O3D™

Yahoo Pipes is a free online service that lets you aggregate web content from multiple sources to create a customized view of that content that suits your specific needs. With Yahoo Pipes you can create mash-ups in a visual editor using data represented as JSON, XML, RSS, and ATOM. Yahoo Pipes is based on YUI, and it is conceptually analogous to the Unix "pipe" command in the sense that the output of one or more components becomes the input of another component.

Dapper is another very good (and free) online tool that is similar to Yahoo Pipes. Its home page is: http://www.dapper.net/

Dapper lets you create a "Dapp" by navigating to websites and then selecting the content that you want to include in your Dapp. Dapper lets you select the content (using a virtual browser) that you want to include in a Dapp.

Google Gears is an open source project that enhances your web browser to create more powerful web applications. Google Gears lets you store data in a local database, and improve performance by running JavaScript in the background. In addition, Google Gears will be adding support for HTML5. Google Gears is available on several platforms, including Windows® XP™ and Vista™, MacIntosh®, and Linux® operating systems, and browser support includes Firefox®, Safari®, and Opera®. Although Google has discontinued development on Google Gears, this product will be useful until HTML5 support is available on all (or at least the major) browsers.

Google Native Client lets you invoke 80×86 native code in web applications. Its home page is:

http://code.google.com/p/nativeclient/

Google Native Client gives you the ability to run popular games, such as *Quake* and *XaoS*, in a browser. This early-stage project has several objectives, including portability, security, and browser neutrality, and it is available (along with an SDK) for download for several platforms, including Microsoft Windows, Linux, and MacIntosh.

Google O3D™ is an open source browser plug-in that lets you create and render three-dimensional graphics in a browser. Its home page is:

http://code.google.com/apis/o3d/

Chapter 5 discusses a wide variety of additional tools, including the Semantic Interoperability of Metadata and Information in unLike Environments (SIMILE) project from MIT, testing tools, and automation tools (such as Ant and Maven).

■ 1.5.3 Development Tools and IDEs

Although development tools are not specifically associated with Web 2.0 technology, they can make a significant difference in your productivity and ease of development.

Chapter 6 delves into various development tools and Integrated Development Environments (IDEs) that let you be more productive. The following is a partial list of the IDEs that are discussed in Chapter 6:

- Eclipse™ (open source)
- Flash® Builder™ 4 (Adobe)
- NetBeans™ (open source)
- Oracle® JDeveloper (open source)
- JetBrains® (commercial)

■ 1.5.4 Social Networks

Social networks are groups of people who interact in various ways with other members of the same group. Social networks are similar to clubs and other organizations, but the term "social networks" is frequently associated with an online group, such as Facebook or MySpace® (and many others).

One advantage of online groups is that members can live anywhere in the world, which can be interesting from the standpoint of languages, cultural values and preferences, and other diverse viewpoints about various aspects of life, leisure, and work. Another advantage of social networks is that they let people form groups based on a common theme, such as a foreign language, musical groups, computer software, and outreach groups (such as single or divorced parents). In general, the code of conduct and etiquette for members of these groups is no different from any other group or club.

Social networks can be displayed as a graph in which a node represents a person and an arc between two nodes indicates that there is some type of interaction (for instance, they are on each other's list of friends) between those persons.

Social network analysis refers to the techniques for analyzing the dynamics and interaction among members of a social network. There are various ways to explore the ways in which members interact, such as the number and frequency of messages that people send to each other, the pictures that they post, and who views and adds comments to those pictures.

A social network can also be represented by an XML document (XML is discussed in Chapter 3) for every member of a social network. The root node represents a single member, and the "child nodes" represent the friends of that member.

The social networks that are discussed in this book include Facebook and OpenSocial and they are briefly discussed in the following sections.

1.5.4.1 *The Facebook Platform*

Facebook was created in 2004, and currently there are more than 350 million Facebook users. In early 2007, Facebook released its set of APIs, which let developers create Facebook applications that leveraged the Facebook APIs. Currently, there are thousands of Facebook applications, and Facebook has set up an incubator program to help foster the growth of startups that are based on Facebook.

The availability of the facebook APIs led to the creation of thousands of Facebook applications, and it also caused a radical change in the way developers perceived social networks. The Facebook home page is: http://www.facebook.com

Facebook supports FaceBook Markup Language (FBML), which is similar to JavaScript, and XFBML, and Facebook applications have been written in the following scripting languages:

- PHP
- Python (with GAE)
- Ruby

Facebook has also been used in unexpected ways. For example, a burglar was caught when he forgot to log out of his Facebook account. Facebook conversations have been used as evidence in decisions about cheating during exams. Police who were worried about their reputation checked Facebook and Twitter for criticism (see the appendices for links).

Bebo® is a social network that provides a high degree of compatibility with Facebook at the API level, which greatly reduces the number of code changes needed to port Facebook applications to Bebo.

1.5.4.2 *Zembly*

SUN® Zembly® is a free browser-based tool for building and hosting web applications. Its home page is: http://www.zembly.com*

---

*During the production of this book, Sun suspended Zembly on November 30, 2009. Unfortunately it was too late to remove material referencing the program.

Zembly was created at SUN in 2006, released in 2008 as a private beta, and in 2009 was released in public beta. Zembly addresses the challenge of developing highly scalable and collaborative applications for the Cloud. Zembly provides the following functionality and capabilities:

- create apps for Facebook, Meebo™, OpenSocial, Orkut, and iPhone®
- create and share widgets with other users (Chapter 5)
- integration with Yahoo Pipes (Chapter 5)
- integration with Dapper (Chapter 5)
- integration with Mozilla® Bespin™ (Chapter 11)
- support for Google Orkut

Zembly is a browser-based web-oriented development model that is also a RESTful services integration platform. Chapter 7 discusses the facebook platform (and Zembly) in more detail.

1.5.4.3 *The OpenSocial Platform*

The OpenSocial platform provides a set of open APIs to build social applications. OpenSocial is an open platform that provides standardization in an attempt to overcome the compatibility differences that exist between other social networking sites. Thus, if you write an OpenSocial application, then your application will run unmodified on any OpenSocial-compliant container. OpenSocial focuses on three main areas:

- how to connect people
- how to store data for a profile
- how to work with activities

Compare OpenSocial to other social networking sites, which work in different environments and have different APIs. Although the Facebook and Bebo APIs are very similar, generally this is not the case between any pair of social networking sites outside of OpenSocial.

The following is a list of some of the companies that belong to the OpenSocial consortium:

- Google
- Orkut
- hi5®
- MySpace

Incidentally, if you are ambitious enough, you can read the OpenSocial specifications and create your own OpenSocial container that can interact with other containers in the OpenSocial consortium.

Chapter 8 discusses OpenSocial in more detail, where you will also learn about Apache® Shindig™, which is the reference implementation of OpenSocial.

■ 1.5.5 Mash-Ups

In broad terms, mash-ups are web-based applications that combine or "mash together" information from multiple sources.

Many mash-ups provide convenient services, such as finding restaurants, clubs, and hotels (among other things) in a specific part of a city.

However, there are also enterprise mash-ups, along with tools that enable their creation, which are more business oriented than client-side mash-ups. IBM coined the term "situational applications," which are mash-ups that provide functionality that is intended for a small group of people (typically fewer than twenty).

For example, consider an international company that employs several accountants in different regions or countries in different time zones. A mash-up that meets the specific needs of such a group can be very useful in terms of sharing information in a timely manner, particularly during the busy times of the year. Obviously, a mash-up that provides sensitive details about employees must be made secure, but that is true of other applications as well.

Several downloadable tools are available for creating and managing mash-ups, including the following (some of which will be discussed in greater detail in Chapter 9):

- IBM® Mashup Center™
- Intel® Mash Maker™
- Denodo™
- JackBe™
- Kapow Mashup Server

Search engines are another important aspect of Web 2.0 that is becoming increasingly competitive. Some of the more interesting search engines are:

- Microsoft® Bing™
- Google Caffeine™

- Hakia®
- Kosmix™
- Yebol

Microsoft Bing is a search engine that was released in mid-2009. Its home page is: http://www.bing.com/

Bing (formerly named Kumo) is a replacement for Live Search, and on June 3, 2009, Bing became Microsoft's official search engine. Moreover, Microsoft and Yahoo formed a business partnership in mid-2009, after which Microsoft provided the search technology for Yahoo.

Google Caffeine was announced in mid-2009. Its home page is: http://www2.sandbox.google.com

Google is rewriting some of its infrastructure, and at this point it's not clear if Caffeine will make extensive use of Semantic Technology. Note that in mid-2009 Caffeine did not work on mobile devices, but this might have changed as this book went to print.

A search on Google and a search on Caffeine with the search terms "Caffeine semantic technology" returned slightly different sets of links, but the first two were identical. From a user's perspective the differences might be irrelevant, but from the standpoint of businesses the different rankings can be extremely important because they can affect sales and revenue.

You can get more information about Caffeine here: http://www.mattcutts.com/blog/caffeine-update

Hakia provides a search engine whose home page is: http://www.hakia.com/

In mid-2009, Hakia announced a commercial ontology that is capable of recognizing phrases. Hakia points out that existing tools analyze words individually, and then consecutive words are "combined" to determine additional context, which makes Hakia's tool superior to its competitors.

The Hakia page also contains a link to a website with two HTML frames where you can perform a search and then make a side-by-side comparison between the results returned by Hakia and the results returned by Google.

According to the company founder, Kosmix is an "explore engine" rather than a search engine. Its home page is: http://www.kosmix.com

Despite the inevitable comparisons, the company has stated very clearly that Kosmix is not a competitor to Google. Kosmix is better suited for learning or exploring broad topics rather than searching for specific details about a topic (which search engines can do well). For example, if you want to learn about the important events during an era of a particular country, then Kosmix can assist you in finding relevant information.

Yebol is another search engine whose home page is: http://yebol.com/

Yebol uses patented algorithms to create a directory for queries and users, and also categorizes search terms and websites. According to the company, Yebol has a higher level of abstraction than other search engines. Yebol also uses "multi-dimensional" searches that provide a wider set of related search terms, and Yebol can return more accurate search results compared to other search engines.

Mash-up tools and search engines will be discussed in greater detail in Chapter 9.

■ 1.5.6 Cloud Computing

Cloud Computing has been touted as the "next big thing" because it holds the promise of managing the infrastructure that provides the computing resources for applications, thereby enabling companies to "outsource" many of their IT activities in a reliable and cost-effective manner.

Cloud Computing offers an opportunity to lower the cost of doing business by managing IT infrastructure and hosting applications using a pay-as-you-go model. Cloud Computing aims to provide performance and scalability that is more affordable for individuals and companies with limited budgets.

Prior to the recent interest in Cloud Computing, companies used internal systems to manage their applications and computing resources, sometimes with distributed computing solutions or hosted application solutions.

However, there are Cloud Computing nay-sayers, such as Richard Stallman (the founder of the Free Software Foundation), who describes Cloud Computing in unflattering terms (see the appendices for a link). If you are interested in finding out other opinions about Cloud Computing, the appendices contain the link for an article entitled "Twenty-One Experts Define Cloud Computing."

The major Cloud Computing vendors (and their products), discussed in Chapter 10 are:

• Amazon Elastic Compute Cloud (EC2)™
• IBM® CloudBurst™
• Google App Engine™

- Microsoft® Azure™
- Yahoo

The Cloud Computing products in the preceding list are briefly discussed in the following sections.

1.5.6.1   Amazon EC2

Amazon Web Services (AWS) is generally considered the quintessential Cloud Computing platform. Amazon's EC2 for application development and Simple Storage Service (S3) offers a web interface and lets customers pay for services via credit card.

In August 2008, Amazon enhanced EC2 with Elastic Block Storage™ (EBS), which saves storage after an EC2 instance is terminated. Amazon augmented S3 with SimpleDB™, Simple Queue Service™, Flexible Payments Service™, and Mechanical Turk™, a service now in beta that provides an "on-demand work force."

If you are interested in building Java applications on EC2, you can find more information here: http://www.stax.net

1.5.6.2   IBM Cloud Center

IBM has several Cloud Computing initiatives, one of which is IBM Cloud Labs whose home page is:
http://www.ibm.com/ibm/cloud/labs/

A second IBM initiative, WebSphere CloudBurst Appliance, lets users access virtual software images that can be deployed in a private cloud. A third initiative is IBM Blue Cloud™, which supports a distributed set of computing resources. In 2009, IBM also formed a partnership with Juniper® for the hybrid cloud initiative, with one of the goals being better Service Level Agreement (SLA) support. IBM is also involved in other initiatives, such as launching a public cloud and providing virtualization.

1.5.6.3   GAE

Google released GAE in April 2008, which makes GAE a relatively new entry in the Cloud Computing game (certainly when compared with AWS). GAE is probably best suited for large-scale web applications that need to leverage the capabilities of Google Bigtable™ (which is discussed in more detail in Chapter 10).

From a very high-level perspective, GAE receives HTTP requests and sends HTTP responses. GAE can be used as a highly affordable data repository that can be accessed from applications that are also in GAE or stored elsewhere. People have found interesting ways to use GAE, such as hosting Facebook applications.

The home page for GAE is: http://code.google.com/appengine

Initially, GAE only provided support for Python, but in April 2009 Google announced that GAE would support Java. Keep in mind one important point: GAE supports limited search functionality.

In Chapter 10, you will learn how to create GAE applications by first registering for a free account and then downloading the latest GAE SDK, which is a plug-in for Eclipse that also provides a debugger.

When Google released GAE in 2008, Python was the only supported language; however, in April 2009, Google announced support for Java 5 and Java 6 on GAE, which actually supports a variety of JVM-based languages that are listed here:

http://groups.google.com/group/google-appengine-java/web/will-it-play-in-app-engine?pli=1

Chapter 12 discusses Java and GAE in greater detail.

1.5.6.4 *Microsoft Live Mesh/Azure*

Microsoft Windows Azure is the Cloud Computing product from Microsoft that was released during the Professional Developer Conference (PDC) in November 2009. The Microsoft Windows Azure home page is:

http://www.microsoft.com/azure

The Windows Azure cloud has a *fabric* that is an abstraction layer, which governs many activities in the Azure cloud, such as provisioning hardware, load balancing, failure detection, and so forth.

Chapter 11 discusses smaller vendors and open source alternatives that are available in Cloud Computing.

The following are some smaller vendors that provide Cloud Computing solutions:

- Appistry®
- Engine Yard™
- GoGrid®
- Joyent

- LongJump™
- Rackspace®
- RightScale®

Appistry is a Cloud Computing company that supports Linux and Windows. Its home page is: http://www.appistry.com

Appistry supports Microsoft Windows (32-bit and 64-bit) and several 64-bit versions of Linux, and public cloud support will soon be available for Amazon EC2, GoGrid, and Skytap. The Appistry® CloudIQ™ Platform Community Edition is free, but with a limit of 5 machines and 10 cores.

Engine Yard is one of the few Cloud Computing vendors that provides support for Ruby on Rails™ (RoR), and beta-level support for JRuby™ was released in July 2009. The Engine Yard home page is:
http://www.engineyard.com/

Recall that while GAE also provides support for RoR, any existing Rails applications that use a relational database (such as MySQL®) will not work on GAE because BigTable is nonrelational. Therefore, the underlying database schema needs to be redesigned before the Rails application can be moved to GAE. On the other hand, Engine Yard does not need to redesign the database schema of a Rails application.

GoGrid provides "cloud hosting" services. Its home page is:
http://www.gogrid.com

GoGrid supports Windows and several Linux-based cloud servers with pre-installed software that lets you "get up and running in minutes." GoGrid was the first to provide Windows Server 2003 and 2008 cloud servers, and its parent company ServePath is a Microsoft Gold Certified Partner.

Joyent provides an attractive set of cloud hosting services, along with support for PHP, RoR, and Java. Joyent has formed partnerships with SUN Microsystems and Facebook, and Joyent is also the Cloud Computing provider for SUN. The Joyent home page is:
http://joyent.com/

Joyent provides "accelerators," which is a term that refers to virtualized computing and storage, for USD $45 per month (check the website for pricing updates). Joyent provides free accelerators for Facebook and OpenSocial developers.

LongJump is a multitenant platform that focuses on the Software as a Service (SaaS) layer of the SPI stack. Its home page is:

http://www.longjump.com

LongJump provides an application platform that can be installed behind a firewall, in a private cloud, or it can be made available in LongJump as a PaaS. Moreover, you can install LongJump in an IaaS provider, such as Amazon EC2 or Rackspace Mosso.

Rackspace provides managed hosting, cloud hosting, and online business applications. Its home page is:

http://www.rackspace.com/index.php

Rackspace provides public cloud offering and a private cloud service that is intended for enterprise customers.

RightScale provides a web-based Cloud Computing management platform. Its home page is:

http://www.rightscale.com/

The RightScale cloud management platform lets you select different programming languages and development environments, thereby enabling you to select the cloud provider or IaaS layer that best suits your needs.

Some open source search tools include the following Apache projects:

- Hadoop™
- Hive™
- Thrift™

Hadoop is an Apache open source project for processing large amounts of data. Its home page is:

http://hadoop.apache.org/

Hadoop implements MapReduce, whose name is based on the "map" and "reduce" functions that exist in some programming languages (remember the "map" function in Lisp?). MapReduce™ is a framework created by Google to support distributed computing, especially when large volumes of data are involved.

Hive is a data warehouse infrastructure that is built on top of Hadoop. Its home page is:

http://hadoop.apache.org/hive/

You must first install Java 1.6 and Hadoop (versions 1.7 through 1.9). Hive is not production quality yet (as of this book's writing), and it does not work on Cygwin™, so we will only provide a broad overview of its features.

Thrift is a software framework for scalable cross-language services development. Its home page is:

http://incubator.apache.org/thrift/

Thrift combines a software stack with a code generation engine to build services that work efficiently and seamlessly between C++, Java, Python, PHP, Ruby, Erlang™, Perl, Haskell, C#™, Cocoa®, Smalltalk, and OCaml.

Hadoop is very popular because of its processing power, and it is used by many companies, including Facebook and Yahoo. Hive is an extension of Hadoop, and Thrift was originally developed by Facebook and then donated to the Apache Foundation.

■ 1.5.7   Semantic Technology

Semantic Technology has been a topic of interest for years, and recent developments in this field (circa 2008) make this technology increasingly important and relevant for the near future. Semantic Technology is important for various reasons, as shown here (not necessarily in order of importance):

- improves the relevance of search results
- provides better ad placement in advertising
- discovers "hidden" patterns of behavior
- assists in crime detection
- automatically finds reference papers based on keywords

Semantic Technology discovers relationships that exist among resources and then represents those relationships via some form of metadata. While it's possible for people to manually discover relationships for small systems, the manual approach is impractical whenever a system contains a large number of resources. (Even for small systems, how many people want to spend their time creating metadata?)

Ontologies let us model systems so that we can classify existing resources and add new ones in a reasonably structured and logical manner. An ontology can also help us discover relationships in a system and make inferences that are not apparent without the ontology. People can create private ontologies for their resources (which can be virtually anything) or they can use online systems, such as Freebase™, that have been designed to manage ontologies. Ontologies are normally created for a specific set of resources, such as collections of books, movies, manuals, and so forth. However, Web Ontology Language (OWL) is an ontology specifically designed for Internet resources.

The Semantic Technology product tools that will be discussed in this book include:

- OpenCalais®
- ExpertSystem® Cogito™
- Truevert
- Altova® Semanticworks®
- Franz® Semantic Technologies
- TopBraid

1.5.7.1 OpenCalais

According to the Calais® home page, "Calais is a rapidly growing toolkit of capabilities that allows you to readily incorporate state-of-the-art semantic functionality within your blog, content management system, website, or application."

The list of Calais tools includes:

- Gnosis™ (Firefox plug-in)
- Tagaroo™ (WordPress plug-in)
- Content Feed Explorer™
- Calais Document Viewer™
- Semantic News Search

1.5.7.2 Truevert

Truevert is an interesting Semantic Technology that uses context to deliver relevant search results. Truevert is different from most of its competitors because Truevert does not rely on ontologies or dictionaries. Truevert asserts that its technology works in any language.

1.5.7.3 Altova Semantic Technology

Altova is one vendor that has invested heavily in Semantic Technology. Altova provides a vast array of XML-based products and tools, and its home page is: http://www.altova.com

Altova products include XMLSpy® (an editor for XML documents), MapForce® 2009 (which supports XBRL and HL7), and MissionKit® (for XML and UML), which also won a Jolt Product Excellence and Productivity award. XMLSpy 2009 also provides extension points that lets you use third-party XSLT™ (both 1.0 and 2.0) or XSL-FO™ processors.

Altova also provides tools for creating, editing, and validating XSLT, XSL-FO, XQuery™, XPath™, OOXML, and XML™ schemas. Altova has a set of visual mapping tools that lets you perform mappings for XML, EDI, and flat files.

1.5.7.4   *Franz Semantic Technologies*

Franz Semantic Technologies offer a bundled suite of Semantic Technology products. Its home page is: http://www.franz.com/

Franz provides AllegroGraph™ (described as a Web 3.0 database), AG-WebView™ (an RDF browser), Gruff™ (RDF Browser), TopBraid (Ontology Modeling), and RacePro (OWL Reasoner).

Franz also provides several LISP-based development tools, including Allegro CL™ (Common Lisp), AllegroCache™ (database), Allegro BTrees™(Native BTrees), and Pepito™ (Data Mining).

1.5.7.5   *TopBraid*

TopBraid is a Semantic web application assembly toolkit. Its home page is: http://www.topbraid.com

TopBraid supports TopBraid Composer, which is a tool for modeling and an application development tool for developing and managing ontologies, along with support for RDF, OWL, and SPARQL.

The appendices contain additional links regarding Semantic Technology tools and resources.

Chapter 13 also discusses Semantic Technology in greater detail.

■ 1.5.8   Advanced Project with GWT

GWT lets you write complex Ajax "front-end" in Java. GWT has a very helpful plug-in for Eclipse that can empower developers to write extremely complex applications. The Google Wave™ team stated that Wave would not have been possible without GWT, because the coding would have been too complex. GWT integration is built into GAE, so there will probably be a spike in upcoming GWT applications on the web.

Chapter 14 discusses an advanced example that illustrates many of the technologies that are presented in this book. In brief, the sample application will display (in a slideshow fashion) the members who will be attending an event. This type of code sample can be used as a tool prior to events to help members network with each other. The sample will also display information such as each member's picture, other meetups each user attends, and any comments that users have made prior to the current event.

The example will use a Restful API (provided by meetup.com) to gather JSON-formatted data about the people attending a particular event. GWT will be used to make Ajax calls and update the Document Object Model (DOM) to display information.

■ 1.5.9   Comet: "Reverse Ajax"

Comet, often referred to as "Reverse Ajax," provides web servers with the ability to push data to the browser. Ajax became popular because it allowed browsers to make requests to the server to get additional information for clients. Comet is similar to Ajax, but the server can decide when to push data to the browser.

Chapter 15 covers the basics of Comet, followed by a look at CometD™, which uses the Bayeux™ protocol. We will follow the Java implementation of CometD on the server side and Dojo and jQuery client implementations. After that, Michael Carter (Comet innovator and Orbited™ creator) will explain how to work with Orbited, which is a Python-based solution for Comet. Finally, Michael will give an overview of the current options available for Comet and talk about its future.

■ 1.5.10   Mobile Applications

You have probably noticed the profusion of mobile applications (usually games), especially for the Apple iPhone. Other companies are trying to capture a piece of the market share that is currently dominated by Apple, which has led to the creation of products and tools for creating mobile applications. Currently, there are several mobile-based platforms, including the ones listed here:

- Apple iPhone
- Google Android™
- Palm Pre™
- Samsung®
- Nokia® (Symbian)
- Microsoft® Windows Mobile™
- RIM Blackberry®
- SUN® J2ME™

There are also cross-platform tools, such as Titanium (from Appcelera-tor®), XMLVM™, and Rhomobile™ (based on Rails™), which let you develop a mobile application for one platform and then automatically generate the corresponding code for a different mobile platform. Companies such as Agile Commerce℠, Ansca®, PhoneGap™, and Pivotal Labs® provide interesting services, products, and tools for developing mobile applications.

Chapter 16 and Chapter 17 provide an overview of mobile application development for many platforms, along with code samples (usually created in Eclipse) to help you assess which mobile platforms are most suitable for you.

■ 1.6   WHAT ABOUT WEB 3.0?

This is an interesting question, and the answer can vary because of the fragmented interpretation of what Web 3.0 is, which in turn has produced a number of viewpoints. One side claims that Web 3.0 has already arrived, based on technologies such as HTML5, Comet, and Semantic Technology. Another side asserts that Web 3.0 is still in the future because the underlying technology that is necessary for Web 3.0 does not exist yet. There is also a debate about whether or not Web 3.0 will be the realization of the Semantic Web, as envisioned by Tim Berners–Lee and other industry leaders.

Without delving into a detailed discussion, we have a subjective view of Web 3.0, and in our opinion, an "alpha version" of Web 3.0 will become mainstream within three years, and some of its most significant facets will include the following (not necessarily in order of importance):

• Products and services will leverage Semantic Technology
• Social networks will adopt Semantic Technology
• Mobile computing
• Commoditization of search technology and private search engines
• Cloud computing
• Comet/HTML5
• Offline computing
• Client-side databases

We believe that the state of Web 3.0 in 2009 is roughly comparable to the early state of Web 2.0. While it is true that search-related technology stands to benefit greatly (and perhaps alter dramatically) from the advances in Semantic Technology, there is no so-called "killer app" that will do for Web 3.0 what Ajax has done for Web 2.0.

The transition from Web 2.0 to Web 3.0 will probably be more difficult than the transition from Web 1.0 to Web 2.0, because the former does not have the benefit of a built-in browser object, which enabled Ajax to give significant momentum to Web 2.0. Without a breakthrough technology, superior Web 3.0 tools will be more difficult to develop than their counterparts for Web 2.0. On the other hand, those superior tools may offer us greater sophistication, complexity, and functionality.

If you are interested in Web 3.0, you will probably be interested in Chapter 13 in this book that discusses Semantic Technology and Chapter 18, which explores recent developments that seem destined to occupy important roles as Web 3.0 evolves from its current infancy to greater maturity in the future.

■ 1.7 SUMMARY

This chapter explained the origin of Web 2.0 and how its collaborative nature has changed the way people use the Internet. You learned about the early enabling technologies of Web 2.0 and some of the currently popular Web 2.0 tools. You also learned about the major categories of Web 2.0, along with a brief description of their relevance and role in the Web 2.0 world.

The other chapters in this book will delve into many of these categories in greater detail, and you will see code samples that illustrate how to use them in Web 2.0 applications. This book also has three appendices on the CD-ROM that contain additional links for Web 2.0 sites, books, tools, and products.

Chapter 2 discusses JavaScript, Cascading Style Sheets™ (CSS), browser plug-ins (SVG™, Silverlight™, Flash), JavaScript tools (Caja™, E4X, Raphaël™), HTML5, and HTML5 canvas graphics.

Landscape of the Web

In This Chapter:

- Coding Guidelines
- HTML/JavaScript Examples
- Cascading Style Sheets (CSS)
- HTML and Document Object Model (DOM)
- Browser Plug-Ins
- Assorted JavaScript Technologies and Tools
- HTML5: Browser Support and Code Samples

This chapter discusses various web-related technologies such as HTML, JavaScript, and browser plug-ins. The material in this chapter will help you understand the code samples that are introduced in subsequent chapters (such as Chapter 4). Since HTML5 is a recent development, the HTML-based code samples in this chapter will probably be new to you.

Due to space constraints many concepts pertaining to JavaScript and CSS (among others) were not included in this chapter, which means that you will need to read additional material (available on the Internet) to gain a deeper understanding of the topics that are discussed here. At the same time, if the examples in this chapter are not clear to you, search for online tutorials to help you understand the concepts.

Several JavaScript examples in this chapter highlight several features of JavaScript. We will skip the self-explanatory code constructs and only look at the JavaScript constructs. If you want to see what the JavaScript code actually does, you can launch the code samples in your browser as you follow along with the discussion in the chapter so that you can see the expected results.

Even if you already have some familiarity with JavaScript, it's still worth your while to skim through the material in this chapter so that you can return to it when you encounter examples that refer to the concepts introduced here.

First, we'll look at a quick overview of basic JavaScript functionality, followed by an IFRAME example. Next, we'll discuss HTML and CSS, and look at some examples that illustrate how to use CSS. Then we'll cover client-side management of the DOM that is constructed each time an HTML page is rendered in a browser session.

Then we'll discuss nodes and elements, and show you how to manipulate elements in a DOM. You will see examples of how to manipulate a list of elements in the DOM and how to dynamically update a DOM with new JavaScript elements.

Finally, we'll briefly discuss browser plug-ins, including SVG, Silverlight, and Flash, and then provide some graphics-based examples using the HTML5 `canvas` element. Note that the code samples in this chapter are provided to expose you to the coding syntax and overall style of the code; however, only the key ideas (rather than all the details) of the code samples will be discussed. This (albeit cursory) code overview will let you compare these languages with other languages that you already know.

If you need to become very proficient in JavaScript, search the Internet for links regarding ECMAScript so that you can learn about the new APIs that are available.

■ 2.1 CODING GUIDELINES

There are three important points to remember when coding. The first pertains to manipulating DOM elements directly. In the past (before the existence of Ajax toolkits), it was commonplace for developers to detect browser types and versions programmatically, which involved "if-else" logic. However, new browsers (or newer versions of browsers) sometimes introduced inconsistencies that would break existing code. Thus, direct DOM access is considered "the old way" for some developers, in much the same way that the manual creation of Ajax code is seen as the "the old way." While it's better to avoid direct DOM manipulation, there might be situations in which you will be forced to make manual changes, and the examples in this chapter give you a sense of DOM-related code changes. The key is to leverage robust tools as much as possible to ensure that the code you write is of high quality. In the case of DOM manipulation, you can use a tool such as YUI™, which is in the Yahoo Ajax library.

A second point involves the use of JSLint™ to check for inconsistencies in JavaScript code. JSLint (discussed in Chapter 6) is a very useful tool for JavaScript that contains many options and various levels for checking for errors and warnings.

The third point to remember is that this chapter does not delve into the details of HTML because we assume that you have some experience with HTML. Currently, HTML 4.01 is the latest version of HTML that is available on all modern desktop browsers. If you are interested in HTML5, a working draft is here: http://www.w3.org/TR/html5/

The goal of HTML5 is to provide a set of standard features so that vendors can create tools that conform to it. HTML5 explores how to support both HTML 4.01 and XForms™, and also how to provide new functionality (such as socket support) that does not exist in earlier versions of HTML. Note that Chapter 18 discusses HTML5 in terms of its future implications for the Web.

■ 2.2 HTML/JAVASCRIPT EXAMPLES

This section shows several HTML files that illustrate the basic concepts you need to know about JavaScript. As such, they will be presented without explanation; if you are unfamiliar with these concepts, you can search the Internet for tutorials that will provide additional examples and explain these concepts in more detail.

This chapter provides a rapid overview of the following HTML and JavaScript concepts:

• simple variables and arrays
• loops and conditional logic
• JavaScript functions
• JavaScript objects
• HTML widgets (buttons, input fields, etc.)
• handling mouse events
• HTML window, document, location
• IFRAMEs
• DOM and node management

■ 2.2.1 JavaScript Strings and Arrays

Listing 2.1 displays the HTML page `Basic1.html`, which shows how to perform arithmetic operations, define a loop, and manipulate two-dimensional arrays. Note that some of the Java Script functionality is unavailable with compiled languages such as Java and C#™.

Listing 2.1 Basic1.html

```
<html>
<head></head>

<body>
<script language=javascript>
  var x1 = 5;
  var x2 = 12*x1;

  alert(x1+" feet = "+x2+" inches");

  var sum = 0;
  for(var i=0; i<x1; i++)
  {
     sum += i;
  }

  alert("sum = "+sum);

  var x3 = 7.2;
  alert("Ceiling = "+Math.ceil(x3)+" Floor = "+
        Math.floor(x3)+" Round = "+Math.round(x3));

  var emp = new Array(3);
  emp[0] = "John";
  emp[1] = "Jill";
  emp[2] = "Steve";

  emp[0]    = new Array(3);
  emp[1][0] = "Smith";
  emp[0][1] = "45";
  emp[0][2] = "Single";

  emp[0][0] = "John";
  emp[0][1] = "Smith";
  emp[0][2] = "45";
  emp[0][3] = "Single";

  alert(emp[0][0]+" "+emp[0][1]+" is "+emp[0][2]+" and "+emp[0][3]);
```

```
    var theDate  = new Date();
    var theYear  = theDate.getFullYear();
    var theMonth = theDate.getMonth();
    var theDay   = theDate.getDate();

    alert("Today: "+theDate+" "+"Year: "+theYear+" "+"Day: "+theDay);

    var firstChar = "Hello".charCodeAt(0);

    if (firstChar >= "A" && firstChar <= "Z")
    {
       alert(firstChar+" is an uppercase letter");
    }

    var index = "Hello".indexOf("ell");
    alert("Index of the string 'ell' = "+index);
</script>
</body>
</html>
```

There are several points to note about the code in Listing 2.1. First, a for loop in JavaScript is slightly different from other languages, such as Java, in that the loop variable is defined via var rather than int, as shown here:

```
for(var i=0; i<x1; i++)
{
   sum += i;
}
```

The second thing to note is that JavaScript provides support for built-in objects that contain methods. One example is the JavaScript Date object, shown here:

```
var theDate  = new Date();
var theYear  = theDate.getFullYear();
var theMonth = theDate.getMonth()];
var theDay   = theDate.getDate();
```

JavaScript arrays are declared and initialized as expected, shown here:

```
var emp = new Array();
emp[0] = "John";
emp[1] = "Jill";
emp[2] = "Steve";
```

However, JavaScript arrays differ from Java arrays in that you can initialize multi-dimensional arrays without declaring them as multidimensional arrays first, as shown here:

```
var emp = new Array(3);
emp[0] = "John";
emp[1] = "Jill";
emp[2] = "Steve";

emp[0]      = new Array(3);
emp[1][0] = "Smith";
emp[0][1] = "45";
emp[0][2] = "Single";
```

Notice how JavaScript does not require you to allocate storage for emp[1][0] to assign this element a value, which differs from languages such as Java and C#.

The following code snippet illustrates how to determine whether or not the character at a specific location in a JavaScript string is an uppercase letter:

```
var firstChar = "Hello".charCodeAt(0);

if (firstChar >= "A" && firstChar <= "Z")
{
   alert(firstChar+" is an uppercase letter");
}
```

■ 2.2.2 Handling Mouse Events

Listing 2.2 displays the HTML page BasicFormMouse1.html, which illustrates how to display a message in response to "mouse up" and "mouse down" events that are associated with an HTML button in an HTML page.

Listing 2.2 BasicFormMouse1.html

```
<html>
<head>

<script language="javascript">
  function myButton_onmouseup()
  {
     document.form1.myButton.value = "Mouse Up"
  }
```

```
    function myButton_onmousedown()
    {
        document.form1.myButton.value = "Mouse Down"
    }
</script>
</head>

<body>
  <form name=form1>
    <input type='button' name='myButton' value=' Mouse Up '
           onmouseup="myButton_onmouseup()"
           onmousedown="myButton_onmousedown()">
  </form>
</body>
</html>
```

Listing 2.2 defines an HTML form element that contains an HTML input element as shown here:

```
<input type='button' name='myButton' value=' Mouse Up '
       onmouseup="myButton_onmouseup()"
       onmousedown="myButton_onmousedown()">
```

The input element specifies the JavaScript functions myButton_onmouse-down and myButton_onmouseup, which will be executed whenever users click on the button or release the mouse, respectively. These two JavaScript functions directly update the text displayed on the HTML button as shown here, when users click on the HTML button:

```
document.form1.myButton.value = "Mouse Down"
```

■ 2.2.3 Regular Expressions and String Manipulations

Listing 2.3 displays the HTML page BasicUpperCase1.html, which shows how to capture user input (in this case, the user's name and age) and check to see if the input is text only (i.e., no metacharacters) before displaying a message:

Listing 2.3 BasicUpperCase.html

```
<html>
<head>
<script language="javascript">
```

```
function regExpIs_valid(text)
{
    var myRegExp = /[^a-z¥d ]/i;
    var myRegExp = /^[a-z]$/i;

    return !(myRegExp.test(text));
}

function butCheckForm_onclick()
{
    var myForm = document.form1;
    if (myForm.txtAge.value == "" || myForm.txtName.value == "")
    {
        alert("Please provide values for all input fields");
        if (myForm.txtName.value == "")
        {
            myForm.txtName.focus();
        }
        else
        {
            myForm.txtAge.focus();
        }
    }
    else
    {
        // convert name to uppercase
        var value = myForm.txtName.value;
        myForm.txtName.value = value.toUpperCase();
        alert("Merci " + myForm.txtName.value);
    }
}

function txtAge_onchange()
{
    var txtAge = document.form1.txtAge;
    if (isNaN(txtAge.value) == true)
    {
        alert("A valid age is required");
        txtAge.focus();
        txtAge.select();
    }
}
```

```
function txtName_onchange()
{
   window.status = "Bonjour " + document.form1.txtName.value;
}
</script>
</head>

<body>
<form name=form1>
   Please enter your name and age:
   <br>
   name:
   <input type="text" name="txtName"
          onChange="txtName_onchange()">
   <br>
   age:
   <input type="text" name="txtAge"
          onChange="txtAge_onchange()" size=3 maxlength=3>
   <br>
   <input type="button" name="butCheckForm"
          value="Check Details"
          onclick="butCheckForm_onclick()">
</form>
</body>
</html>
```

Listing 2.3 contains an HTML input field for the user's age that invokes the JavaScript function txtAge_onchange() whenever the user changes this input field, as shown here:

```
<input type="text" name="txtAge"
       onChange="txtAge_onchange()" size=3 maxlength=3>
```

You can also use regular expressions to process user-provided input strings. For example, the JavaScript function regExpIs_valid() checks for a character string using a regular expression, as shown here:

```
function regExpIs_valid(text)
{
   var myRegExp = /[^a-z\d ]/i;
   return !(myRegExp.test(text));
}
```

If you are interested in learning more about regular expressions, there are many books and articles that you can find by searching the Internet.

■ 2.2.4 HTML Frame Elements

Listing 2.4 displays the HTML page BasicFrame1.html, which illustrates how to define an HTML page consisting of two frame elements:

Listing 2.4 BasicFrame1.html

```
<html>
<head></head>

<frameset rows="0,*" border="0">
   <frame src="Basic1.html"          name="basic1">
   <frame src="BasicFormMouse1.html" name="basic2">
</frameset>
</html>
```

The first frame in Listing 2.4 references the HTML page Basic1.html and the second frame references the HTML page BasicFormMouse1.html. You can specify additional frames as needed, and you can also specify nested frames. For example, you might need to display two horizontal frames, where the first frame contains three vertical subframes and the second horizontal frame is subdivided into two horizontal frames. The exact configuration depends on what your needs are, and you can experiment with frames to achieve your desired effect.

■ 2.2.5 HTML IFRAME Elements

The IFRAME element is a so-called "inline frame" that lets you include external objects, including other HTML documents. Although an IFRAME is similar to an OBJECT element, an IFRAME can be a "target" for other links.

Listing 2.5 displays the contents of TwoIFrames.html, which demonstrates how to define two IFRAMEs in one HTML page.

Listing 2.5 TwoIFrames.html

```
<html>
<head>
<title>A Simple IFRAME Example</title>
</head>
```

```
<body>
   <p align="center">
   <iframe id="myIframe1"
           frameborder="1"
           scrolling="yes"
           src="http://www.yahoo.com" width="600" height="400">
   </iframe>
   </p>
   <br>
   <p align="center">
   <iframe id="myIframe2"
           frameborder="10"
           scrolling="yes"
           src="http://www.google.com" width="600" height="400">
   </iframe>
   </p>
</body>
</html>
```

Listing 2.5 defines two IFRAMES whose ID values are myIframe1 and myIframe2, respectively. The first IFRAME is populated with content from http://www.yahoo.com, which is specified in the src attribute, and the second IFRAME is populated with content from http://www.google.com.

Although this HTML page only contains two IFRAMES, you can easily extend this example to include as many IFRAMEs as you need for your website.

2.2.5.1 Inter-IFRAME Communication

From the standpoint of JavaScript, an IFRAME is actually a window, and global variables are only visible inside a window or IFRAME. If you need to communicate between IFRAMEs, you must communicate between a common parent.

For example, Listing 2.5 illustrated how to define an HTML page with two IFRAMEs whose ID values were iframe1 and iframe2. You can get a reference to each IFRAME as shown here:

```
var f1 = top.frame1; (defined inside frame2)
var f2 = top.frame2; (defined inside frame1)
```

If frame1 contains the variable x1 and frame2 contains the variable x2, then you can update the value of x2 in iframe2 from iframe1 as shown here:

```
top.frame2.x2 = 123;
```

We can use a similar syntax to access JavaScript functions. For example, we can invoke the JavaScript function myFunction2() defined in frame2 from frame1 as shown here:

```
top.frame2.myFunction2();
```

We can also access DOM elements that reside in different IFRAMEs. For example, we can access the DOM element mydiv2 that is defined in iframe2 from iframe1 as shown here:

```
var element2 = top.frame2.document.getElementById('mydiv2');
```

Thus, you can communicate between any two IFRAMEs by accessing their common parent element.

■ 2.2.6 Design Patterns and Best Practices

JavaScript design patterns are solutions to well-known problems using the JavaScript programming language. Design patterns can save you time and effort, let you benefit from other people's experience, and help you write better and more consistent code. A set of design patterns can be found here:
http://www.webreference.com/programming/javascript/ncz/column5/

JavaScript best practices consist of JavaScript-specific coding techniques and recommendations, which help you write more consistent code. A collection of best practices can be found here:
http://www.javascripttoolbox.com/bestpractices/

Search the Internet for other lists of design patterns and best practices that you can use to deepen your knowledge of JavaScript.

■ 2.3 CASCADING STYLE SHEETS (CSS)

CSS lets you define "rules" that specify the style or manner in which you want to render elements in an HTML page. CSS helps you modularize your HTML content and because you can place your CSS definitions in a separate file, you can also reuse the same CSS definitions in multiple HTML files.

Moreover, CSS also lets you simplify the updates you need to make to elements in HTML pages. For example, suppose that multiple HTML table elements use a CSS rule that specifies the color red. If you need to change the color to blue later on, you can implement it by simply making one change (i.e., changing red to blue) in one CSS rule.

Without a CSS rule, you would be forced to manually update the color attribute in every HTML table element that is affected, which is error-prone, time-consuming, and extremely inefficient.

The benefits of CSS include (but are not limited to) the following:

• separation of markup and text/data
• performance gains
• easier code maintenance
• code reuse
• consistency between HTML pages

Performance is improved because files containing CSS rules are downloaded once and cached, so there is less code to download whenever you download to different HTML pages that reference the CSS rules in the downloaded files.

Keep in mind though, that CSS definitions can quickly become complex, unwieldy, and difficult to understand in CSS files that contain a lot of rules. Moreover, CSS can adversely affect performance, as discussed here: http://dev.opera.com/articles/view/efficient-javascript/?page=3#reflow

■ 2.3.1 Basic CSS Examples

The examples in this section use HTML <p> elements to illustrate various CSS rules, but you can apply these rules to other HTML elements as well.

Here's an example of a rule that indents every paragraph in an HTML page:

```
p { text-indent: 4em; }
```

There are several ways to apply this formatting rule to every paragraph in an HTML page:

• hard code the definition in each paragraph
• define the rule in a style element
• reference the rule in a CSS file

An example of hard coding the rule in a paragraph element is:

```
<p style="text-indent: 4em;">Here is my paragraph</p>
```

An example of defining the rule in a style element is:

```
<head>
<title></title>
<style type="text/css">
<!--

p { text-indent: 4em; }

--></style>
</head>
<body>
<p>Here is my paragraph</p>
<body>
```

An example of referencing the rule in a CSS file is:

```
<link rel="stylesheet" type="text/css" href="MyCSSDefs.css"
      title="Default">
```

In the preceding code snippet, the CSS file is called `MyCSSDefs.css` and contains the CSS rule for indenting paragraphs.

The next example shows you two CSS rules in which odd-numbered heads are displayed in red and even-numbered heads are displayed in blue:

```
h1, h3, h5 { color: red; }
h2, h4, h5 { color: blue; }
```

You can also define a so-called "selector" to override the behavior of a CSS rule. For example, suppose that you want to render some paragraphs in red instead of indenting them. The CSS rules are:

```
p { text-indent: 4em; }
p.red { color: red; }
```

You can apply the second CSS rule to display a paragraph in red as shown here:

```
<p class="red">
```

This paragraph will be displayed in red without an `indent</p>`.

These simple examples illustrate how you can define CSS rules that specify display properties and then apply those CSS rules to render the content of an HTML page.

However, if you define more than 50 closely related CSS rules, the rendered result becomes more difficult to predict; imagine what would happen if you have hundreds of CSS rules that define the rendering behavior of the various elements in multiple HTML pages.

2.3.1.1 *CSS Class and CSS ID*

Another important point is the difference between class and id in CSS. For example, consider the following CSS rules for an HTML <p> element:

```
p { font-size: 20px }
p.one {font-size:12px}
p.two {color:red}
```

Consider the following HTML fragment:

```
<html>
<body>
<p> this text is 20px size</p>
<p class="one">this text is 12px size</p>
<p class="two">this text is red</p>
</body>
</html>
```

Now let's look at the following CSS rules for an HTML <p> element:

```
p { font-size: 20px }
p#three {font-size:12px}
p#four   {color:red}
```

Consider the following HTML fragment:

```
<html>
<body>
<p> this text is 20px size</p>
<p id="three">this text is 12px size</p>
<p class="four">this text is red</p>
</body>
</html>
```

Since the result is the same as the class-based CSS rules, how do you decide when to use class and when to use id? The following analogy might help you understand the answer to this question. When you take courses at school, each person has a unique "id," and a "class" contains one or more "id" items (one per student). When you are working with CSS, use an id for an item that is unique in an HTML page, and use class for everything else.

You can also define a class and an id without a corresponding HTML element, which means that the following CSS rules are also valid:

```
.one {font-size:12px}
.two {color:red}
#three {font-size:12px}
#four  {color:red}
```

The absence of an HTML element means that (unlike the earlier examples) you can use these CSS rules for other HTML elements and not just the HTML <p> element.

2.3.1.2 CSS Inheritance Rules

Almost all selectors ("margin-top" is one exception) that are nested in other selectors inherit the properties of the "outer" selector.

For example, let's return to the initial set of CSS rules:

```
p { font-size: 20px }
p.one {font-size:12px}
p.two {color:red}
```

In the preceding rules, p.one and p.two inherit from the CSS rule for the <p> element. However, font-size defined in the p.one CSS rule overrides the value of font-size defined in the p CSS rule.

CSS rules provide a rich set of features and tremendous flexibility, however such flexibility can also make it very difficult to maintain a large set of CSS rules. One solution for addressing this complexity is to use Object-Oriented CSS (OOCSS), which is the topic of the next section.

■ 2.3.2 Object-Oriented CSS (OOCSS)

There are at least two open source projects available that support object-oriented-like functionality in CSS: OOCSS by Nicole Sullivan, and Blueprint™, both of which are briefly discussed in the following sub-sections.

2.3.2.1 OOCSS

Nicole Sullivan has written an open source project that is here: http://wiki.github.com/stubbornella/oocss/

Nicole provides code samples and explains how to avoid pitfalls so that you can improve the maintenance, extensibility, and performance of your HTML pages that contain CSS. Download the project and follow the instructions on the website to use this code.

2.3.2.2 Blueprint: Object-Oriented CSS

Blueprint is a CSS tool designed to reduce your development time. Its home page is: http://www.blueprintcss.org/

The Blueprint home page contains a link for downloading the code and a list of companies that are currently using Blueprint.

■ 2.4 HTML AND DOCUMENT OBJECT MODEL (DOM)

Whenever you navigate to a web page, your browser constructs an in-memory DOM representation for that web page. A DOM is a tree-like structure that is associated with an HTML page. The DOM contains a set of elements that "map" to the HTML widgets in the HTML page. You can use JavaScript to find elements in a DOM, similar to how you can use Java to find elements in an XML document.

Early browsers supported DOM Level 0, and the most recent browsers support DOM Level 2, which supports the getElementById functionality that lets you navigate the DOM structure associated with each HTML page.

The DOM in browsers simplifies the following:

• browser type/version detection
• managing DOM elements programmatically
• dynamically creating/updating/inserting DOM elements

However, DOM-related manipulation via JavaScript functions can adversely affect performance. Search the Internet for additional performance-related articles, or start with this useful article that describes the sorts of things to avoid to improve performance:
http://dev.opera.com/articles/view/efficient-javascript/?page=3#reflow

■ 2.4.1 HTML DOM and JavaScript DOM

Browsers add optional HTML tags, even when they're omitted from an HTML page. For example, browsers include an element for an HTML <HEAD> tag, regardless of whether or not it occurs in an HTML page. However, this does not apply to XHTML because tags (such as <HEAD>) that are optional in HTML are not optional in XHTML.

Changes that you make to the DOM via JavaScript are first applied to the DOM, after which those changes are reflected in the HTML page. Unfortunately, if you update an HTML page using something such as innerHTML, then that change is not reflected in the DOM.

■ 2.4.2 Managing Nodes and Elements

There are 11 types of DOM nodes (as described in Chapter 3), and two of the most common are element nodes and text nodes. You will often see an element node referred to as simply an element, and in this book we will follow this same practice. The next several subsections will describe how to do the following:

• find and delete a node
• create a new node
• update a node
• access attributes of a node

2.4.2.1 Finding and Deleting a Node

You can find an element in a DOM tree by using the getElementById method, as shown here:

```
var elem = document.getElementById('myCanvas');
```

This method is very useful when you want to do the following:

• find and delete an element
• find and update an element
• find and replace an element

You can delete the elem note as shown here:

```
elem.parentNode.remove Child (elem);
```

Sometimes you may need to maintain a set of nodes whose values are unique, in which case you first check to make sure that a particular element does not exist, and then you can create a new element and insert that newly created element.

2.4.2.2   *Creating a New Node*

Listing 2.6 displays the HTML page CreateNode1.html, which illustrates how to dynamically create a node and insert it into a DOM.

Listing 2.6 CreateNode1.html

```
<html>
<head></head>

<body>
<script language="javascript">
  var newText;
  var newElem;

  newText = document.createTextNode("NewHeading");
  newElem = document.createElement("h2");
  newElem.setAttribute("align","left");
  alert("alignment = "+newElem.getAttribute("align"));

  newElem.appendChild(newText);
  document.body.appendChild(newElem);

  newText = document.createTextNode("Text in a paragraph");
  newElem = document.createElement("P");

  newElem.setAttribute("align","right");
  alert("alignment = "+newElem.getAttribute("align"));
  newElem.appendChild(newText);
  document.body.appendChild(newElem);

</script>
</body>
</html>
```

The following snippet creates a new element node:

```
var elementNode = document.createElement("newEl");
```

The following snippet creates a new text node:

```
var textNode = document.createTextNode("newText");
```

2.4.2.3 *Updating an Existing Node*

Listing 2.7 displays the HTML page UpdateNode.html, which illustrates how to update the contents of an existing node in a DOM.

Listing 2.7 UpdateNode.html

```
<html>
<head></head>

<body>
  <h2 id="heading1">My Heading</h2>
  <p id="paragraph1">This is a paragraph</p>

  <script language="javascript">
    var htmlElement;
    var headingElement;
    var bodyElement;
    var h2Element;

    htmlElement = document.documentElement;

    headingElement = htmlElement.firstChild;
    alert("heading tag: "+headingElement.tagName);

    if(headingElement.nextSibling.nodeType==3)
    {
        bodyElement = headingElement.nextSibling.nextSibling;
    }
    else
    {
        bodyElement = headingElement.nextSibling;
    }
    alert("body tag: "+bodyElement.tagName);

    if(bodyElement.firstChild.nodeType==3)
    {
        h2Element = bodyElement.firstChild.nextSibling;
    }
    else
    {
        h2Element = bodyElement.firstChild;
    }
    alert("h2 tag: "+h2Element.tagName);

    h2Element.style.fontFamily = "Arial";
  </script>
```

```
</body>
</html>
```

2.4.2.4   *Updating DOM Nodes: Two Techniques*

One technique for updating DOM nodes involves a DOM-based update of the contents of a node. For example, suppose that a DOM contains a node whose ID value is `test` and you need to set the visible text of this node to the string `hello world`. This change can be accomplished with the following code fragment:

```
var testNode = document.findNodeById("test");
var textNode = document.createTextNode("hello world");
testNode.removeFirstChild;
testNode.appendChild(textNode);
```

Another technique uses innerHTML to update the contents of a node. For example, the node whose ID value is `test` can be updated with the text string `hello world` via the following code fragment:

```
var testNode = document.findNodeByName("test");
testNode.innerHtml = "hello world";
```

Although it's easier to update the contents of a node by setting its `innerHtml` attribute, this technique is not portable.

2.4.2.5   *Manipulating Lists of Elements*

Earlier in this chapter, you learned how to find an element based on the value of its ID attribute. You can also process a list of elements that have the same value in their name attribute. For example, the following code snippet illustrates how to retrieve the list of DIV elements whose name attribute is `mytag1`:

```
var allTDs = document.getElementsByTagName("td");
alert("# of table cells: " + allTDs.length);
```

2.4.2.6   *Accessing the Attributes of an Element*

There are three methods for processing the attributes of an element in a DOM via JavaScript: `getAttribute()`, `setAttribute()`, and `removeAttribute()`. These methods can be applied to elements that support attributes.

Suppose that you have an HTML page with an element called myElem that has an attribute called myAttrib. You can find the value of myAttrib1 with:

```
var value = document.getElementById("myElem").
getAttribute("myAttrib");
```

You can set (i.e., update) the value of this attribute with:

```
document.getElementById("myElem").setAttribute("myAttrib",
"newvalue");
```

Finally, you can remove the myAttrib attribute with:

```
document.getElementById("myElem").removeAttribute("myAttrib");
```

Removing attributes can be convenient if attributes contain multiple name/value pairs, such as the style attribute.

■ 2.4.3 Dojo and jQuery Syntax

Although a detailed discussion of Dojo and jQuery toolkits is given in Chapter 4, in this section you will see examples of manipulating DOM elements in Dojo and jQuery. This short introduction will show you the differences in DOM manipulation when you use "pure" JavaScript, Dojo, or jQuery. These brief examples will also give you insight into the syntax of both Dojo and jQuery. The following examples describe how to manipulate the DOM of an HTML page that contains a DIV element whose name is myDiv.

In Dojo, you can update the HTML text of the myDiv node with the following code fragment:

```
dojo.byId("myDiv").innerHTML = "Hello World";
```

In jQuery, the corresponding code fragment is:

```
$("#myDiv").html("Hello World");
```

In Dojo, you can find the DOM element with the ID one as shown here:

```
var elem = dojo.byId("one");
```

In jQuery, the corresponding code fragment is:

```
$("#one");
```

In Dojo, you can remove the `myDiv` node with the following code fragment:

```
dojo.destroy(myDiv);
```

In jQuery, the corresponding code fragment is:

```
$("myDiv").remove();
```

As you can see, both Dojo and jQuery use a shorter syntax to process nodes in a DOM, yet there are important differences between these two Ajax toolkits, which you will learn about in Chapter 4. Since jQuery supports XPath, you will also learn some basic concepts about XPath in Chapter 3.

■ 2.4.4 Distributed DOM

Although this is an advanced topic, several companies have released Web 2.0 collaboration tools that contain code for manipulating and synchronizing information among users via a distributed DOM.

If you have not seen these products, they usually offer dashboard-like functionality that provides audio, video, and chat capability, along with email, RSS feeds, and the ability to share and modify documents in real-time.

If you are interested in this topic, search the Internet for some interesting tools that implement a distributed DOM.

■ 2.5 BROWSER PLUG-INS

Browser plug-ins provide functionality that is not available in browsers. For example, browsers lack native support for Flash, so the Flash plug-in provides that missing functionality.

In the case of SVG, browsers differ in terms of their support for SVG functionality. For example, Firefox provides significant native support for SVG, but with Internet Explorer®, you have to install the Adobe SVG plug-in to get SVG functionality. Check the websites for Firefox, Internet Explorer, and Safari (and other available browsers) to determine which SVG features they support.

Something else to keep in mind is what type of coding is required to communicate between an HTML page and plug-in code. For example, if you embed SVG code in an HTML page and you render that page in Internet Explorer, you need to write additional "glue code" to communicate between the SVG elements and the HTML page, whereas Firefox does not require any additional code.

The following list provides some popular browser plug-ins that will be discussed in the following sections:

- SVG
- Silverlight
- Flash and Flash Lite®

■ 2.5.1 SVG Plug-In

SVG is an open standard (developed by the World Wide Web Consortium [W3C®]) that uses XML to represent two-dimensional geometric objects, such as rectangles, ellipses, polygons, and Bezier curves.

The SVG home page is: http://www.w3.org/Graphics/SVG/

SVG Full is for browsers, whereas SVG Tiny (whose functionality is a subset of SVG Full) is for mobile devices. Native browser support for SVG is available in the following browsers:

- Firefox 2.x/3.x
- Safari
- Opera
- Google Chrome™

Implementations of SVG include:

- Batik™ (Java implementation)
- BitFlash®
- Ikivo®
- Inkscape
- Renesis®

SVG has gained traction in fields where vector graphics, such as rendering maps, are important. In fact, SVG is also used in a White House web page (see the appendices).

SVG support is also available for Internet Explorer, as discussed in the next section.

2.5.1.1 SVG Support: Native Versus Plug-In

The browsers listed in the preceding section provide varying degrees of built-in support for SVG, and you can navigate to their home page to get additional details about the extent of their built-in SVG support.

For all versions of Internet Explorer prior to 7.x, there is no native support for SVG, but you can install the Adobe SVG plug-in in Internet Explorer. Adobe officially ended support for its SVG plug-in on January 1, 2009, but the good news is that Adobe will make this plug-in available in perpetuity, so you can be assured of SVG support in Internet Explorer.

If you intend to render SVG in Internet Explorer, monitor Microsoft's plans regarding what type of native support for SVG in Internet Explorer will be available in the future. Another thing to remember is that communication between HTML and SVG in Internet Explorer requires interdocument communication, which you can learn about here:
http://wiki. svg.org/Inter- Document_ Communication

Google is also involved in SVG, and Brad Neuberg (a Google Developer Advocate in the Open Web Advocacy group) created the SVG Web toolkit with others in the SVG community. SVG Web is a JavaScript library that provides SVG support on a number of browsers, including Internet Explorer, Firefox, and Safari. This library (plus native SVG support) lets you instantly target approximately 95% of the existing installed web base. Additional information and videos introducing the SVG Web toolkit are available here:
http://code.google.com/p/svgweb

2.5.1.2 *Sample SVG Code*

Listing 2.8 displays the contents of MouseRect.svg, which illustrates how to handle mouse events to update the radius of a circle.

Listing 2.8 MouseRect.svg

```
<?xml version="1.0" standalone="no"?>
<!DOCTYPE svg PUBLIC "-//W3C//DTD SVG 1.1//EN"
  "http://www.w3.org/Graphics/SVG/1.1/DTD/svg11.dtd">

<svg width="6cm" height="5cm" viewBox="0 0 600 500"
    xmlns="http://www.w3.org/2000/svg" version="1.1">

  <!-- Change the radius with each click -->
  <script type="text/ecmascript"> <![CDATA[
    function circle_click(evt) {
      var circle = evt.target;
      var currentRadius = circle.getAttribute("r");

      if (currentRadius == 100)
```

```
            circle.setAttribute("r", currentRadius*2);
        else
            circle.setAttribute("r", currentRadius*0.5);
    }
]]> </script>

<!-- Outline the drawing area with a blue line -->
<rect x="1" y="1" width="598" height="498" fill="none"
 stroke="blue"/>

<!-- Act on each click event -->
<circle onclick="circle_click(evt)" cx="300" cy="225" r="100"
        fill="red"/>

<text x="300" y="480"
        font-family="Verdana" font-size="35" text-anchor="middle">
    Click on circle to change its size
    </text>
</svg>
```

The key thing to notice in Listing 2.8 is that you can embed JavaScript code inside a CDATA element. JavaScript code in a CDATA element lets you programmatically manage SVG elements. Moreover, you can bind keyboard events and mouse events to JavaScript functions to process user-initiated events to achieve the desired results.

2.5.1.3 SVG Plug-In for Eclipse

The Spket IDE supports JavaScript and XML development. Its home page is: http://spket.com/

Spket IDE supports code completion, syntax highlighting, and support for XUL/XBL, Yahoo widgets, and SVG. Click the preceding link and select the JAR file for the Spket IDE.

Before you run the JAR file, install Eclipse on your machine (you can follow the instructions in Chapter 6), and then launch the JAR file from the command line as follows:

```
java –jar spket-1.6.17.jar
```

You can install this as a plug-in or as a standalone product, and as you follow the prompts, select the option to install as a plug-in for Eclipse.

Complete the following steps to create an SVG project in Eclipse:

Step 1: Follow the menu path **File > New > Other… > Spket**

Step 2: Select Firefox Extension Project and click the Next button

Step 3: Enter `MySVG1` for the Project name

Step 4: Locate the Firefox directory on your machine and click the Finish button

Eclipse will create an Spket project with the following directory structure:

```
+ MySVG1
+ build.xml
+ chrome.manifest
+ content
  + MySVG1.xul
+ defaults
+ install.rdf
+ locale
+ skin
```

For more information on development with Spket, read the documentation on the Spket home page.

■ 2.5.2 Silverlight Plug-In

Silverlight is a free cross-browser plug-in from Microsoft that uses the .NET framework. Its home page is: http://silverlight.net/

In 2009, Microsoft released Silverlight 4.0 (which is the latest version as of this writing), which is available for Internet Explorer, Firefox, and Safari.

Silverlight uses XML to represent two-dimensional geometric objects, such as those supported by SVG; however, Silverlight and SVG use a slightly different naming convention for XML elements.

Silverlight also supports dynamic scripting languages such as Ruby and Python, which are known as IronRuby and IronPython, respectively, on the Windows platform.

Silverlight documents are XML documents that contain XML namespaces and definitions of geometric objects, similar to those found in SVG documents. Listing 2.9 displays the contents of `Rect1.xml`, which illustrates how to render a rectangle with a linear gradient effect:

Listing 2.9 Rect1.xml

```xml
<Canvas xmlns="http://schemas.microsoft.com/client/2007"
             xmlns:x="http://schemas.microsoft.com/winfx/2006/xml">
   <Rectangle Width="200" Height="100"
             Canvas.Left="50" Canvas.Top="50"
             Stroke="Black" StrokeThickness="4">
     <Rectangle.Fill>
       <LinearGradientBrush StartPoint="0 1"
                            EndPoint="1 1">
         <GradientStop Color="Yellow" Offset="0"/>
         <GradientStop Color="Red"    Offset="0.40"/>
         <GradientStop Color="Blue"   Offset="0.80"/>
       </LinearGradientBrush>
     </Rectangle.Fill>
   </Rectangle>
</Canvas>
```

Listing 2.9 consists of a top-level XML `Canvas` element with two XML namespaces (described in Chapter 3) that contain the XML `Rectangle` element as a child element. The XML `Rectangle` element contains several attributes that specify the dimensions, location, and perimeter color of the rendered rectangle, as shown here:

```xml
<Rectangle Width="200" Height="100"
                      Canvas.Left="50" Canvas.Top="50"
                      Stroke="Black" StrokeThickness="4">
```

Note that the XML `Rectangle` element also contains an XML `Rectangle`. `Fill` element that defines the linear gradient applied to the rendered rectangle.

Visual Studio™ 2008 (and 2010) lets you create Silverlight 4.0 projects that can leverage "code-behind" written in C#. You can also use Microsoft® Blend™ and Microsoft® Expression™, which are visual tools that let you view the rendering of your Silverlight code. In addition, a Silverlight 3.0 plug-in for Eclipse is also available.

■ 2.5.3 Adobe Flash

According to some estimates, Adobe's Flash has upward of 80% market penetration among desktop PCs, and comparable penetration among laptops world wide. Flash has evolved through a number of versions, and you can download Flash 10 (the latest version as of this writing) here: http://www.adobe.com/

Adobe Flash supports ActionScript™, which is a scripting language that resembles JavaScript (and a passing resemblance to C#, which is a programming language from Microsoft).

Listing 2.10 displays the contents of the ActionScript class `ArchRect1.as`, which illustrates how to render a set of rectangles that follow the path of an Archimedean curve.

Listing 2.10 ArchRect1.as

```
package
{
    import flash.display.Sprite;

    public class ArchRect1 extends Sprite
    {
        public function ArchRect1()
        {
            var basePointX:int   = 50;
            var basePointY:int   = 150;
            var currentX:int     = 0;
            var currentY:int     = 0;
            var offsetX:Number   = 0.0;
            var offsetY:Number   = 0.0;
            var radius:Number    = 0.0;
            var Constant:Number  = 0.25;
            var angle:int        = 0;
            var maxAngle:int     = 720;
            var rectWidth:int    = 40;
            var rectHeight:int   = 20;
            var currColor:Number = 0;
            var rect:Sprite      = null;

            for(angle=0; angle<maxAngle; angle++)
            {
                radius   = Constant*angle;
                offsetX  = radius*Math.cos(angle*Math.PI/180);
                offsetY  = radius*Math.sin(angle*Math.PI/180);
                currentX = basePointX+Math.floor(offsetX);
                currentY = basePointY-Math.floor(offsetY);

                if(angle % 2 == 0)
                {
                    currColor = 0xFF0000;
                }
```

```
            else
            {
                currColor = 0x0000FF;
            }

            rect = new Sprite();
            rect.graphics.beginFill(currColor);
            rect.graphics.drawRect(currentX,   currentY,
                                    rectWidth, rectHeight);

            rect.graphics.endFill();
            addChild(rect);
        }
    }
  }
}
```

Listing 2.10 defines an ActionScript class called ArchRect1 that extends the built-in ActionScript Sprite class, which contains a loop that creates a set of rectangles that are appended to an existing DOM structure. The key thing to notice is how a rect object is declared, initialized, and then appended to the existing DOM structure via the addChild() method.

```
public class ArchRect1 extends Sprite
{
    public function ArchRect1()
    {
        // variable initializations (most are omitted)
        var rect:Sprite = null;

        for(angle=0; angle<maxAngle; angle++)
        {
            radius    = Constant*angle;
            . . .
            rect = new Sprite();
            rect.graphics.beginFill(currColor);
            rect.graphics.drawRect(currentX,   currentY,
                                    rectWidth, rectHeight);

            rect.graphics.endFill();
            addChild(rect);
        }
    }
}
```

One point to keep in mind is that ActionScript must be compiled whereas JavaScript is interpreted. (See Chapter 6 for details on creating and launching ActionScript projects in Flash Builder 4.)

In addition, Adobe supports FlashLite (latest version as of this writing is 3.1), which is a technology for mobile devices. One interesting point: earlier versions of Flash Lite were embedded with SVG Tiny, but it seems to have been removed from Flash Lite 3.0 and above. Note that while Flash for the desktop supports ActionScript 3.0, Flash Lite 3.x supports ActionScript 2.0.

You also have the option of using SilverX, which is a free tool that lets you convert Flash into Silverlight.

■ 2.6   ASSORTED JAVASCRIPT TECHNOLOGIES AND TOOLS

This section contains information about Google Caja (safely embedding third-party JavaScript code), ECMAScript for XML (E4X), and the Raphaël JavaScript library that lets you create vector-based graphics and animation effects very quickly with minimal effort.

The last part of this section touches on Block TEA (client-side encryption) and AspectJS (JavaScript method interception), both of which are more advanced tools whose details are outside the scope of this book. Google Closure (not discussed in this chapter) was recently released, and it is a well-tested cross-browser Javascript library that is available from google.

■ 2.6.1   Google Caja

Google Caja ("KA-ha") lets developers embed third-party HTML or JavaScript into their HTML pages in a secure fashion. The Caja home page is: http://code.google.com/p/google-caja/

Adverse side effects (whether they are intentional or not) are always a potential issue whenever you use code that was written by someone else. Mash-ups often use third-party code, which makes Google Caja a good tool to use in your mash-up code. Incidentally, the word Caja means "box" in Spanish, which is an apt description of its purpose.

■ 2.6.2   ECMAScript for XML (E4X)

E4X is an extension of JavaScript with additional support for XML. What is commonly called JavaScript 1.3 is also known as ECMA-262, and E4X is also known as ECMA-357.

The availability of E4X, XML, and JSON means that you need to carefully examine the tradeoffs when you decide which technology to use for your application. Although products such as Zembly (discussed in Chapter 7) provide support for E4X, keep in mind that E4X is not supported by all of the major browsers. This may change in the future, so you need to evaluate the suitability of E4X, XML, and JSON based on your application-specific requirements.

2.6.2.1 Examples of E4X

If you want in-depth knowledge of E4X, you need a basic understanding of HTML, JavaScript, and XML. The E4X examples in this section are very easy, but if you have never dealt with XML, read the XML material in Chapter 3, before reading the examples in this section.

One key concept to remember is that E4X uses "curly brackets" ({}) to access the value of JavaScript variables.

For example, consider the following two statements:

```
var a = 2;
var b = <foo>{a}</foo>
```

The variable b is assigned the XML document <foo>2</foo>.
The next example appends element2 as a child of element1:

```
var element1 = <foo/>;
var element2 = <bar/>;
element1.appendChild(element2);
element1.toXMLString();
```

The structure of element1 is shown here:

```
<foo>
  <bar/>
</foo>
```

E4X lets you create new elements, delete, and update existing elements in an XML document.

■ 2.6.3 Raphael JavaScript Library

The Raphael project is a JavaScript library that lets you render vector-like graphics in an HTML page. It is available for download here:
http://raphaeljs.com/index.html

The home page provides documentation and code fragments, along with a gallery of examples that illustrate how to create animated effects. An open source project containing a variety of graphics code samples for Raphaël can be found here: http://code.google.com/u/ocampesato/

■ 2.7 HTML5: BROWSER SUPPORT AND CODE SAMPLES

HTML5 is the greatest advance in HTML in 10 years (HTML 4.01 was introduced in 1999). You can find the HTML5 draft specifications here: http://www.w3.org/TR/html5/

Although Chapter 17, Mobile Development Part II discusses HTML5 in more detail, this section contains a preview of HTML5 features and the level of HTML5 support in several popular browsers.

Some of the new functionality introduced in HTML5 includes:

• canvas element
• web sockets
• video support
• offline data storage
• cross-document messaging
• access to the back/forward stack

Video support is available via an HTML5 video tag, which lets you play videos without using Flash technology.

The browsers (and their versions) that provide some level of HTML5 are:

• Opera 10.0
• Safari 4
• Google Chrome 3.0
• Firefox 3.5
• Internet Explorer 8

Opera 9.6 (and higher) appears to have the best HTML5 support, followed by Safari 4.0. Both browsers provided some HTML5 support in earlier versions, and both have continued to extend their support for HTML5 features. There is lesser support for HTML5 in Google Chrome 3.0 and Firefox 3.5, and Internet Explorer 8 has the least support.

These browsers can be downloaded here:

• http://www.opera.com/
• http://www.apple.com/safari/

- http://www.google.com/chrome/
- http://www.mozilla.org/
- http://www.microsoft.com/windows/internet-explorer/

Please note that the available versions will probably change by the time this book is printed. For example, Google Chrome 2.0.18 is currently available, but lacks HTML5 support, whereas Google Chrome 3.0 (which does have HTML5 support) has not been released yet.

Check the appendices for articles, demos, and tutorials regarding HTML5, and a comparison of HTML5 support across various browsers.

■ 2.7.1 The HTML5 Canvas Element

This section illustrates how to render 2D and 3D graphics using the HTML5 canvas element. First, make sure that your browser supports the HTML5 canvas element before you attempt to launch the code samples. Note that this example can be viewed in Opera 10.0, and the 3D example in Section 2.7.2.2, 3D Graphics, was written specifically for the 3D support in Opera 10.0.

2.7.1.1 2D Graphics

Listing 2.11 displays the contents of Arch1Rect1.html, which shows how to render a set of rectangles that follow the path of an Archimedean curve.

Listing 2.11 ArchRect1.html

```
<!DOCTYPE html>
<html lang="en">
  <head>
    <meta charset="utf-8">
    <title>Archimedean Spiral</title>
    <script type="text/javascript"><!--
window.addEventListener('load', function () {
  // Get the canvas element in the <body> tag
  var elem = document.getElementById('myCanvas');

  if (!elem || !elem.getContext) {
    return;
  }

  // Get the canvas 2d context
  var context = elem.getContext('2d');
  if (!context) {
```

```
      return;
   }

   var basePointX  = 300;
   var basePointY  = 200;
   var currentX    = 0;
   var currentY    = 0;
   var offsetX     = 0;
   var offsetY     = 0;
   var radius      = 0;
   var spiralCount = 4;
   var Constant    = 0.25;
   var angle       = 0;
   var maxAngle    = 720;
   var rectWidth   = 40;
   var rectHeight  = 20;

   for(angle=0; angle<maxAngle; angle++) {
      radius  = Constant*angle;
      offsetX = radius*Math.cos(angle*Math.PI/180);
      offsetY = radius*Math.sin(angle*Math.PI/180);
      currentX = basePointX+offsetX;
      currentY = basePointY-offsetY;

      // alternate between red and blue
      if(angle % 2 == 0) {
         context.fillStyle = '#f00';
      }
      else {
         context.fillStyle = '#00f';
      }

      // draw the current rectangle
      context.fillRect(currentX, currentY, rectWidth, rectHeight);
   }
}, false);
   // --></script>
  </head>

  <body>
    <canvas id="myCanvas" width="800" height="500">
        Your browser does not support Canvas
    </canvas>
  </body>
</html>
```

Listing 2.11 starts by specifying HTML-related tags, followed by a `<script>` element that defines a function that is executed when the HTML page is loaded into your browser, as shown here:

```
<script type="text/javascript"><!--
window.addEventListener('load', function () {
  // Get the canvas element in the <body> tag
  var elem = document.getElementById('myCanvas');
```

The `elem` variable locates the `myCanvas` tag that is located inside the `<body>` tag included at the end of Listing 2.11. The `elem` variable is a reference to where the graphics will be rendered in the HTML page.

The next line is important because it's the actual context for the rendered graphics:

```
// Get the canvas 2d context
var context = elem.getContext('2d');
```

The next section of Listing 2.11 initializes some JavaScript variables, followed by a loop that creates and appends rectangle elements to the DOM, as shown here:

```
for(angle=0; angle<maxAngle; angle++) {
   radius   = Constant*angle;
   offsetX  = radius*Math.cos(angle*Math.PI/180);
   offsetY  = radius*Math.sin(angle*Math.PI/180);
   . . .
   // draw the current rectangle
   context.fillRect(currentX, currentY, rectWidth, rectHeight);
}
```

The last section of Listing 2.11 contains the `<body>` tag and the closing HTML tags.

If you are interested in learning how to write more graphic-based code using the HTML5 canvas element, an open source project with code samples (including `Arch1Rect1.html`) can be found here: http://code.google.com/p/html5-canvas-graphics/

If you need to render charts and graphs in HTML5 pages, you can use RGraph, which is a canvas library (based on the HTML5 canvas element). Its home page is: http://www.rgraph.net/

2.7.1.2   3D Graphics

An example of 3D graphics animation in HTML5 can be found here:
http://my.opera.com/timjoh/blog/2007/11/13/taking-the-canvas-to-another-dimension

This blog site also contains directions for downloading Opera 10.0 for Windows, Linux, and MacIntosh so that you can view the 3D animation code sample.

■ 2.7.2   Google Chrome

Google Chrome is a free web browser that is built with open source code from Chromium. Its home page is: http://www.google.com/chrome

Google Chrome runs on Windows, MacIntosh, and Linux operating systems.

According to one report, the new Chrome browser will combine Apple Webkit™, Google Gears, and a new JavaScript virtual machine called V8. This combination is supposed to dramatically improve the performance of JavaScript code, particularly the code used in building web applications. The Google Chrome team selected Webkit for the same reason the Android developers did: it's fast, simple, and uses memory efficiently.

Chrome is interesting from the standpoint of its future support for HTML5 features, which will become more significant in version 3.0. Note that while Chrome supports multiple languages (downloadable from the home page), it is currently a Windows-only web browser.

One Chrome feature that is very useful to developers is its resources page, which lets you check load times for the resources and files that are referenced in a website. Simply right-click on a website, click on the Inspect element, and then click on the Resources tab. Check the Chrome home page periodically for information about the release date for Chrome 3.0.

Although Chrome currently has a low percentage of the browser market (Google released Chrome more than a year ago), in 2009 Sony® began selling PCs with Chrome installed. Chrome extensions and hardware support for Google Chrome are also available (see the appendices).

2.7.2.1   Google V8 JavaScript Engine

Google V8™ is an open source JavaScript engine whose home page is: http://code.google.com/p/v8/

V8 implements ECMAScript-262 and is available for Windows, MacIntosh, and Linux Operating System (see the home page for specific details and constraints). V8 is also the JavaScript engine used by the Google Chrome browser.

2.7.2.2   Google Chrome OS

In July 2009, Google announced its intent to release the Google Chrome Operating System in the latter part of 2010. Chrome OS will be an open source operating system that runs on x86 machines and Advanced RISC Machine (ARM) processors, along with a windowing system that runs on a Linux kernel. Although there are few details available at this time, Chrome OS could become a significant platform in 2010 and beyond.

2.7.2.3   Google Chrome Frame

In September 2009, Google released Google Chrome Frame™, which is a free open source plug-in for Internet Explorer. Its home page is:
http://code.google.com/chrome/chromeframe/

This plug-in lets you leverage web technologies, such as the HTML5 canvas tag, in Internet Explorer 6, 7, and 8.

Add the following tag to a web page to use Google Chrome Frame:

```
<meta http-equiv="X-UA-Compatible" content="chrome=1">
```

Google Chrome Frame switches to Google Chrome's WebKit-based rendering engine (which has a better performance) whenever the preceding tag is detected in a web page. Navigate through the various links on the home page to obtain up-to-date information about this plug-in.

A video of Alex Russell (also a contributor in Chapter 18) describing Google Chrome Frame is available here:
http://www.youtube.com/watch?v=sjW0Bchdj-w

■ 2.8   SUMMARY

This chapter started with a rapid overview of how to use JavaScript in HTML pages, such as defining JavaScript variables, JavaScript functions, and how to use regular expressions. Next, you learned about CSS, IFRAMEs, and inter-IFRAME communication. You also learned how to dynamically manage the

DOM of an HTML page, which includes finding, deleting, creating, and updating elements in a DOM.

You also learned about browser plug-ins, including SVG, Silverlight, and Flash. Next, you learned about JavaScript tools such as Google Caja, E4X, and the Raphaël JavaScript library. You also learned about HTML5, including how to create graphics in the HTML5 canvas element. Finally, you learned about additional URLs that provide additional information so that you can learn about many of the topics discussed in this chapter in more detail.

The next chapter discusses XML and JSON, their trade-offs, and various tools for managing XML documents and JSON-based data.

## CHAPTER 3

JSON and XML

In This Chapter:

- Introducing the Concept of JSON and XML
- Working with JSON
- Ajax Libraries Working with JSON
- Advantages and Disadvantages of JSON and XML
- HTML and SGML Versus XML
- VXML and Comma Separated Values (CSV) as Alternatives to JSON and XML
- Advanced Example with Dojo and JSON

JSON, pronounced "Jason," is a lightweight text-based computer interchange format. JSON is often used when serializing data for delivery over a network. Extensible Markup Language (XML) is a specification for creating custom markup languages.

■ 3.1 INTRODUCING THE CONCEPT OF JSON AND XML

JavaScript Object Notation (JSON) was invented by Douglas Crockford as a subset of JavaScript syntax to be a lightweight data format that is easily readable and writable by both humans and machines. In general, JSON is considered terse when compared to other interchange formats. After you become familiar with JSON, you will find it fairly easy to read complex JSON data structures. Even though JSON is based on a subset of the JavaScript programming language, it is considered language independent.

The flexibility of XML has made it increasingly prevalent in programming environments. Unlike the Unix® world, where configuration files are usually text files with either tab-delimited name/value pairs or colon-separated fields, configuration files in the open source world are often XML documents. Most well-known application servers also use XML-based configuration files. The Ant utility relies on XML-based files for defining tasks.

A tremendous amount of data in the business world and scientific community does not use the JSON or XML format. To give you some perspective, roughly 80% to 90% of all software programs were written in either COBOL or Fortran™ in the early 1990s (and NASA scientists were still using Fortran in 2004). Therefore, data integration and migration can be a complex problem. The movement toward XML as a standard for data representation is intended to simplify the problem of exchanging data between systems. You probably already know that XML is ubiquitous in the Java world, yet you might be asking yourself one question: What's all the fuss about XML? In broad terms, XML is to data what relational theory is to databases; both provide a standardized mechanism for representing data.

A nontrivial database schema consists of a set of tables in which there is some type of parent/child (or master/detail) relationship in which data can be viewed hierarchically. An XML document also represents data in a parent/child relationship. One important difference is that database schemas can model many-to-many relationships such as the many-to-many relationships that exists between a student's entity and a class's entity. XML documents are strictly one-to-many, with a single root node. People sometimes make the analogy that XML is to data what Java is to code; both are portable, which means you avoid the problems that are inherent in proprietary systems.

In the database arena, Oracle8i™ lets you store and retrieve documents in a relational table, and Oracle9i has an XML data type. XIndice (ZEEN-dee-chee) is a pure XML-based database that lets you store and retrieve XML documents based on XPath.

In addition, you can use XSL stylesheets to convert XML documents into HTML pages, SVG documents, PDFs, or other XML documents. XSL is a language for extracting information from data arranged in a tree-like fashion. Although its purpose is conceptually straightforward, there is a significant learning curve associated with mastering XSL.

Despite the widespread use of XML, there is still a significant amount of non-XML business data that resides in columns of relational tables or in text files. This chapter provides examples of Perl scripts that can convert text files or database data into XML documents. Once you have created an XML document containing your data, you can avail yourself of the many XML tools that exist today.

XML is a subset of SGML and a successor to EDI and has become ubiquitous in software applications during the past ten years. XML is an open industry standard with a World Wide Web Consortium (W3C®) recommendation that can be found at: http://www.w3.org/TR/REC-xml/

An XML document can be represented in memory as a tree-like structure that consists of a set of nodes whose data values correspond to the data values in the XML document. XML elements can have attributes and contain other XML elements, and the nesting can be arbitrarily deep. When two software applications communicate via XML documents, both applications can use a so-called XML schema to ensure that the input XML document and the output XML document are valid XML and that they conform to the structure that is specified by the XML schema.

In addition to textual data, you can use Base64 encryption to send binary data (but not for security purposes), which means that there is essentially no barrier to sending any type of data that you want in an XML document. Note that Base64 encryption facilitates the transfer of binary data, but its decryption algorithm is universally known, so you need to use another algorithm if you are concerned about encrypting data in an XML document.

XML has spawned many XML schemas for different fields, such as MathML, SportsXML, CML, and so forth. There are also XML technologies for managing XML documents, such as XPath, XQuery, and XSLT. XML has led to the creation of a rich set of tools, including Saxon™ and Xalan™.

When you process XML documents, there are two main techniques: SAX and DOM. SAX is a stream or event-driven way to process one node at a time without maintaining any history. Since SAX does not create an in-memory DOM structure for each XML document, SAX has low memory requirements. However, if you need to perform additional validation (such as enforcing business logic) among nodes, or creating and inserting new nodes in an XML document, then DOM-based processing is an alternative. In contrast with SAX, DOM-based processing creates an in-memory DOM that reflects the structure of the associated XML document.

However, DOM-based processing has higher memory requirements: the in-memory DOM requires four or five times the size of the associated XML document. On the other hand, as hardware prices continue to decrease and processing speed continues to increase, the cost of additional memory and limits on processing speed become less significant factors.

Note that there are tools available that convert between JSON-based data and XML-based data, which means that you can validate JSON-based data by first converting that data into XML, checking that the XML conforms to your XML schema, and then converting the XML back to JSON. Depending on your application requirements, this type of hybrid-like solution may be preferable to working only with JSON or only with XML.

XML is hierarchical, so it's possible to define backward compatible versions of XML documents that require little or no code modification, and it can even reduce the chances of breaking existing code. As a simple example, suppose an XML document requires a first name and a last name, and you create an XML schema to validate XML documents. Then you decide to allow an optional middle name. You can easily modify your existing XML schema to accept both old XML documents and new XML documents so that both are conformant to the new XML schema. Another example involves a five-digit U.S. zip code, that you later modify to accept a nine-digit zip code, and even a six-character Canadian zip code (mixture of digits and uppercase letters). Your existing code does not need to validate this new format because the XML schema handles this validation for you.

Popular open source tools and frameworks also use XML documents to specify configuration-related data. For example, JEE web applications require the XML document web.xml, Struts uses the XML document struts-config .xml, JSF uses jsf-config.xml, Spring™ uses applicationContext.xml, and Google Wave uses the XML document configuration.xml. In addition, many scripting languages support XML, including Perl, PHP, Python, and Ruby. In HTML pages you can use E4X, which is JavaScript support for XML.

XML-based pipelining is also possible when you use XML in conjunction with XML schemas. For example, suppose that an input XML document D1 is transformed into XML document D2, which is then transformed into D3 and finally into D4. Each XML document can conform to different XML schemas, and the validation can be performed before and after each transformation to ensure that the output XML document D4 is both valid XML and conforms to your system requirements. Thus, the tools for managing XML documents can handle massive amounts of data that can be used in transaction-based processing and then stored in relational, native XML, or hybrid datastores (such as Oracle, XIndice, or IBM® DB2® 9 Viper).

Although XML is well-suited for processing documents via software programs, it can be cumbersome to read XML documents, even those that are of moderate size. In addition, XML is verbose and does not provide strong support for enforcing business rules and logic, which is often done programmatically. However, RDF (which is represented via XML) can describe more complex rules and relationships.

■ 3.1.1 XPath, XQuery, XSLT, and XML Documents

This section contains several subsections that provide a conceptual overview of XPath, XQuery, and XSLT, respectively. In brief, XPath is used to navigate the tree-like structure of XML documents. XQuery is a scripting language that uses imperative programming to manage XML documents. XSLT is a scripting language that uses a declarative programming style to perform simple and complex manipulations of XML documents and to apply transforms to create different types of output documents, such as SVG, XHTML, and other XML documents.

3.1.1.1 XPath

XPath is a contraction for XML Path Language, originally defined by the W3C (around 1999), to be used for XSLT and XPointer. As you will see, XPath is well-suited for finding data in XML documents. At the same time, XPath is very interesting in terms of its expressive power; however, this power has two side effects. First, XPath lets you write XPath expressions that are superficially similar, yet they can differ dramatically in terms of performance. Second, it is difficult to grasp the rich variety of data queries that can be devised for retrieving information from tree-like structures of data. When you retrieve data items from linear lists, those items tend to have a "sibling" relationship with each other. On the other hand, the retrieval of data from tree-like structures can necessitate complex search criteria, and it is common to retrieve subtrees of data. In such cases, the traversal of the retrieved data is hierarchical rather than linear in nature. So, while it is relatively easy to learn how to use XPath expressions, developing proficiency in XPath requires a longer learning curve. If you have worked with SQL, you know that it is possible to write SQL queries almost immediately, but expert-level knowledge of SQL query optimization takes much longer. Because XML documents often contain hierarchical data, every element can be reached by a path-like expression. Therefore, XPath is well-suited for traversing XML documents because it has a path-oriented syntax and built-in functions that let you construct XPath expressions for retrieving the node sets that you need. As you will see later, XSL stylesheets are applied to XML documents that contain tree-like data. Therefore, you need to understand how to "navigate around" the nodes of a tree, and that is accomplished with XPath. A keypoint to remember is that every element in an XML document has a corresponding path that describes how to read that element from the root node. This path is called an absolute path. If you randomly select two elements in an XML document, there is always a path from the first element to the second element (and vice versa). If neither element is the root node, then this path is known as a relative path. By way of analogy, suppose you have a set of directories and files under a common directory, such as:

```
abc/
abc/file1.txt
abc/file2.txt
abc/def/file1.txt
abc/ghi/file2.txt
```

The directory abc contains two subdirectories def and ghi. Notice that def contains the file file1.txt and ghi contains the file file4.txt. The top-level directory abc contains two files called file1.txt and file2.txt. The directory abc corresponds to a root node, and it contains two "elements" def and ghi. The elements def and ghi contain two elements as well, which correspond to the files listed earlier. Now let's use this concept to describe the elements in an XML document using XPath notation. Listing 3.1 displays the contents of emp-all.xml, which contains information about a set of employees.

Listing 3.1 emp-all.xml

```
<?xml version="1.0"?>
<employees>
```

```
 <emp id="125">
  <hiredate>10/24/2006</hiredate>
  <firstname>John</firstname>
  <lastname>Smith</lastname>
  <deptno>1000</deptno>
 </emp>
 <emp id="130">
  <hiredate>10/14/2006</hiredate>
  <firstname>Jane</firstname>
  <lastname>Smith</lastname>
  <deptno>2000</deptno>
 </emp>
 <emp id="255">
  <hiredate>12/04/2005</hiredate>
  <firstname>Tom</firstname>
  <lastname>Jones</lastname>
  <deptno>1000</deptno>
 </emp>
 <emp id="290">
  <hiredate>11/04/2005</hiredate>
  <firstname>Tom</firstname>
  <lastname>Edwards</lastname>
  <deptno>3000</deptno>
 </emp>
</employees>
```

Compare the contents of Listing 3.1 with the contents of Listing 3.2, which specifies the complete path from the root node to every element in emp-all.xml.

Listing 3.2

```
/employees/
/employees/emp-125/
/employees/emp-125/firstname
/employees/emp-125/lastname
/employees/emp-125/deptno
/employees/emp-130/
/employees/emp-130/firstname
/employees/emp-130/lastname
/employees/emp-130/deptno
/employees/emp-255/
```

```
/employees/emp-255/firstname
/employees/emp-255/lastname
/employees/emp-255/deptno
/employees/emp-290/
/employees/emp-290/firstname
/employees/emp-290/lastname
/employees/emp-290/deptno
```

Notice that the XML document emp-all.xml does *not* contain elements called emp-125, emp-130, emp-255, and emp-290. The numbers 125, 130, 255, and 290 are added to the string emp- so that we can distinguish between sibling emp elements in emp-all.xml.

■ 3.2 WORKING WITH JSON

JSON is built on two data structures, a collection and a list. Collections in JSON are name/value pairs and they do not maintain any particular order. Collections in JSON are surrounded by curly brackets. An example of a JSON collection is:

```
var person = {
  'firstname': 'Kevin',
  'lastname': 'Nilson',
   'age': 30
}
```

Notice how each key is surrounded by quotes. Each key/value pair is separated by a colon and followed by a comma, except for the final pair. Collections in JSON are similar to Maps in Java. The code creates an object with keys such as firstname, lastname, and age. Using dot notation, you can retrieve the properties of the object. The datatype of the keys and values can be any valid datatype. In the following example, two of the values are strings and the third is a number:

```
alert(person.firstname); //gives Kevin
alert(person.lastname); //gives Nilson
alert(person.age); //returns 30
```

You can also retrieve the properties of an object using bracket notation:

```
alert(person["firstname"]); //gives Kevin
alert(person["lastname"]); //gives Nilson
alert(person["age"]); //gives 30
```

Lists in JSON let you store ordered elements in a particular order. The following is an example of a JSON list:

```
var data = [ 'cat', 'dog', 1, 'mouse' ];
```

Notice how each element is separated by commas. There is a trailing comma after the last element, as with collections. The preceding code creates a list containing four elements: cat, dog, 1, and mouse. You will notice that the datatype of each element in this list is not the same.

The preceding example creates the same Object:

```
var data = new Array( 'cat', 'dog', 1, 'mouse' );
```

Values in a list can be accessed using the list name followed by the index within the bracket:

```
alert(data[0]); //gives cat
alert(data[1]); //gives dog
alert(data[2]); //gives 1
alert(data[3]); //gives mouse
```

Notice that the first index in the list is 0, and the value for that index is cat.

Collections and lists can be used together. Listing 3.3 is an example of JSON with a list and a collection.

Listing 3.3 JSON with a Collection and a List

```
var bookinfo = {
  'authors': [
    {
      'firstname': 'Oswald',
      'lastname': 'Campesato'
    },
    {
      'firstname': 'Kevin',
      'lastname': 'Nilson'
    },
  ],
  'technicaleditor': {
    'firstname': 'Siamak',
    'lastname'; 'Ashrafi'
  }
};
```

JSON is very readable. Even complex JSON with multiple nested collections and lists can be easily read if the JSON is well formatted. JSON uses JavaScript syntax, so JSON definitions can be used inside of JavaScript without any extra parsing steps. Listing 3.3 shows an `bookinfo` object that has a list of authors (`Oswald` and `Kevin`) and a single `technicaleditor` (Ashrafi).

```
alert(bookinfo.authors[1].firstname) //gives Kevin
```

Listing 3.4 shows a simple example of iterating over both collections and lists with a for loop.

Listing 3.4 JSON Used in Javascript

```
<script type="text/javascript">
  var products={
      'fruits' : ['apple','pear','bananna'],
      'vegetables' : ['carrot','corn','potato']
  };

  function showProducts(){
      var msg="";
      for (i in products){
        for (j in products[i]){
          msg = msg + " " + products[i][j];
        }
      }
      alert(msg);
  }
</script>

<button onclick="showProducts()">Show Products</button>
```

■ 3.3 AJAX TOOL KITS WORKING WITH JSON

Ajax Tool Kits have features specially designed for dealing with JSON. Converting JSON from text to string can be very dangerous, because you must `eval` a string to create the object. Eval is a function that takes a string and executes it as JavaScript:

```
var x = eval("1 +2");
alert(x); //gives 3
```

Eval is dangerous because the string could contain malicious code. You must be sure to never directly eval any user-generated content. When using eval to parse JSON into an object, it is recommended by the JSON RFC that you use the following code to prevent unsafe scripts from being run:

```
var my_JSON_object = !(/[^,:{}\[\]0-9.\-+Eaeflnr-u \n\r\t]/.test(
        text.replace(/"(\\.|[^"\\])*"/g, ''))) &&
    eval('(' + text + ')');
```

■ 3.3.1 Dojo and JSON

Many parts of Dojo are designed to work well with JSON. Dojo has support for converting strings to JSON, converting JSON to strings, and using JSON with Ajax calls. Converting an object to a string is very useful. In fact, in some browsers, such as Firefox, you can use the uneval function to convert an object to a string:

```
var myObject = {'favoriteColors': ['Red', 'White', 'Blue']};
var myString = uneval(myObject); // ({favoriteColors:["Red",
"White", "Blue"]});
```

The previous example takes an object that defines your three favorite colors and converts the object to a string using uneval. Dojo also provides a toJson function that converts an object to a JSON string. Dojo's toJson works in all Dojo-supported browsers:

```
var myObject = {'favoriteColors': ['Red', 'White', 'Blue']};
var myString = dojo.toJson(myObject); //({"favoriteColors":["Red",
"White","Blue"]});
```

This previous example also takes an object that defines your three favorite colors and converts the object to a string, but this time using Dojo's toJson function. JavaScript has a very powerful eval function that converts any string and runs it as JavaScript code. Eval can be very useful, but also very dangerous if you are working with user-generated content. One useful way to use eval is to convert strings, in JSON format, into objects.

```
var myString = "{'favoriteColors': ['Red', 'White', 'Blue']}";
var myObject = eval(myString);
```

The preceding example is a string containing JSON that defines your three favorite colors. Eval is used to convert the string to an object. Dojo provides a fromJson function that converts strings, in JSON format, to objects. Dojo prevents any harmful code from being executed:

```
var myString = "{'favoriteColors': ['Red', 'White', 'Blue']}";
var Object = dojo.fromJson(myJsonString);
```

Converting between strings and JSON and between JSON and strings is a very powerful trick that can be used both in code and in debugging. JavaScript provides functions like eval and uneval, and Dojo has great support.

■ 3.3.2 jQuery and JSON

jQuery™ provides functions for making Ajax calls to JSON pages, but jQuery does not provide functions to convert strings to objects. In Chapter 4, Ajax, we will be looking at jQuery support for JSON used in Ajax.

■ 3.3.3 Working with XML

XML lets you provide structure to your data in an accurate, flexible, and meaningful fashion. As such, XML is well-suited for structured information because XML lets you define the format and layout of data according to your specific needs. XML is useful for several reasons, including the fact that XML can help you overcome one of the main limitations of HTML–fixed tags. XML lets you specify the set of tags that you need for your applications.

As you become more involved with XML, you will learn more about the W3C, which is an Internet standards body that (during the late 1990s) created an XML specification designed to overcome the limitations of HTML.

One way to think of XML documents is as a combination of data and so-called mark-up tags, which include everything that is not considered data. Data items in an XML document are marked up or identified in an unambiguous manner so that you can programmatically manipulate the data items. There are some simple rules for XML tags that you must observe when creating a well-formed XML document:

- XML documents must have one top-level node
- tags must close properly
- attribute values must be nonnull and enclosed in quotes
- tags are case sensitive

For example, the following code snippets are syntactically correct XML:

```
<description/>
<city>ca</city>
<emp id="100" firstname="tom" lastname="smith"/>
<i><b>Hello</b></i>
<b><i>Hello</i></b>
```

```
whereas the following snippets are not:
<b><i>Hello</b></i>
<i><b>Hello</i></b>
```

The preceding code snippets illustrate an important distinction between an XML tag and an XML element. For example, `<city>` is an XML tag, whereas `<city>ca</city>` is an XML element. In more formal terms, an XML tag consists of an opening angle bracket, the name of the tag, and the closing angle bracket. On the other hand, an XML element consists of its starting tag, its end tag, and the content in between (if any).

Contrast the preceding rules with HTML, which supports the following:

- tags are not required to close properly
- attribute values do not require quotes
- tags are not case sensitive

3.3.3.1 Document Type Definition (DTD)

DTD is often used to define an XML document. The structure of DTD is to describe the document with a list of legal elements and attributes. DTD is fairly straightforward, so let's jump straight into an example. In this example, we will define a letter in XML. Each letter must contain a to, from, and body:

```
<?xml version="1.0"?>
<!DOCTYPE letter [
<!ELEMENT letter (to,from,body)>
<!ELEMENT to (#PCDATA)>
<!ELEMENT from (#PCDATA)>
<!ELEMENT body (#PCDATA)>
]>
<letter>
  <to>Kevin</to>
  <from>Oswald</from>
  <body></body>
</letter>
```

You can see that this XML document contains an internal DTD. The DOCTYPE is defined as a letter:

```
<!DOCTYPE letter [
```

The letter also contains a to, from, and body, in that exact order:

```
<!ELEMENT letter (to,from,body)>
```

Finally to, from, and body are defined to be of type PCDATA. PCDATA means parsed character data:

```
<!ELEMENT to (#PCDATA)>
<!ELEMENT from (#PCDATA)>
<!ELEMENT body (#PCDATA)>
```

It is very common to place the DTD and XML in separate files. The following is an example of a DTD in a separate file:

```
<!DOCTYPE letter [
<!ELEMENT letter (to,from,body)>
<!ELEMENT to (#PCDATA)>
<!ELEMENT from (#PCDATA)>
<!ELEMENT body (#PCDATA)>
```

You can see here how the XML references the DTD by adding a DOCTYPE:

```
<?xml version="1.0"?>
<!DOCTYPE note SYSTEM "letter.dtd">
<letter>
    <to>Kevin</to>
    <from>Oswald</from>
    <body>Hello</body>
</letter>
```

DTD also has some support for defining multiple elements. + is used to define that an element must occur at least once. * is used to define zero or more occurences. ? is used to define zero or one occurences. | is used to define either/or:

```
<!DOCTYPE letter [
<!ELEMENT letter (to+,from*,body?, (signiture | closing))>
<!ELEMENT to (#PCDATA)>
<!ELEMENT from (#PCDATA)>
```

```
<!ELEMENT body (#PCDATA)>
<!ELEMENT signiture (#PCDATA)>
<!ELEMENT closing (#PCDATA)>
]>
```

The preceding example shows that the letter must be at least one person, but there may be many recipients. It also shows that the message may be from no one, or many people may be listed as from. Next, you can have up to one body, but the body is not requried. Finally, either a signature or a closing must exist.

```
<!ELEMENT letter (to+,from*,body?, (signature | closing))>
```

Now let's look at one possible XML that could be used with this DTD:

```
<?xml version="1.0"?>
<!DOCTYPE note SYSTEM "letter.dtd">
<letter>
  <to>Kevin</to>
  <to>Oswald</to>
  <body>Hello</body>
  <closing>Thanks</closing>
</letter>
```

Notice that two elements are defined for to and no element is defined for from. Also, a closing was used instead of a signature.

Elements can also be defined as EMPTY in the DTD. Examples of this in XHTML are hr and br.

```
<!ELEMENT hr EMPTY>
```

```
<hr />
```

Attributes can also be added to the DTD:

```
<!DOCTYPE letter [
<!ELEMENT letter (to+,from*,body?, (signature | closing))>
<!ELEMENT to (#PCDATA)>
<!ELEMENT from (#PCDATA)>
<!ELEMENT body (#PCDATA)>
<!ELEMENT signature (#PCDATA)>
<!ELEMENT closing (#PCDATA)>
<!ATTLIST letter type CDATA "normal">
]>
```

You can see from the preceding DTD that a `type` attribute can be given to the `letter` element. If the type is not specified, then the default type `normal` is used.

```
<?xml version="1.0"?>
<!DOCTYPE note SYSTEM "letter.dtd">
<letter type="low priority">
  <to>Kevin</to>
  <to>Oswald</to>
  <body>Hello</body>
  <closing>Thanks</closing>
</letter>
```

From the preceding XML, you can see that the `type` of this letter is `low priority`. `#REQUIRED` and `#IMPLIED` can be added to the `ATTLIST` to specify an attribute is required.

```
<!ATTLIST letter type CDATA "normal" #REQUIRED>
```

You can see that the `type` attribute is required for letters.

As you can see, DTDs are very powerful, but they have many limitations. What if you wanted to say that age must be a number between 0 and 130? What if you wanted to limit an element to contain a valid state initial? What if you wanted to allow for an optional middle initial, that must be a letter, and can only be one character long? None of these advanced features are possible with DTD; fortunately XML Schemas, which are discussed in the next section, makes all of that possible.

3.3.3.2 Schemas

Schemas provide the same functionality as DTD, but are a more advanced and more powerful alternative. Schemas are used to define the structure of an XML document. Listing 3.5 shows a basic schema for an order and Listing 3.6 shows the XML for an order.

Listing 3.5 Schema for an Order

```
<?xml version="1.0" encoding="ISO-8859-1" ?>
<xs:schema xmlns:xs="http://www.w3.org/2001/XMLSchema" >
<xs:element name="order">
  <xs:complexType>
    <xs:sequence>
      <xs:element name="salesman" type="xs:string"/>
```

```
        <xs:element name="shipto">
          <xs:complexType>
            <xs:sequence>
              <xs:element name="name" type="xs:string"/>
              <xs:element name="address1" type="xs:string"/>
              <xs:element name="address2" type="xs:string"
minOccurs="0" maxOccurs="1" />
              <xs:element name="city" type="xs:string"/>
              <xs:element name="state" type="xs:string"/>
              <xs:element name="zip" type="xs:integer"/>
            </xs:sequence>
          </xs:complexType>
        </xs:element>
        <xs:element name="item" maxOccurs="unbounded">
          <xs:complexType>
            <xs:sequence>
              <xs:element name="prodid" type="xs:string"/>
              <xs:element name="quantity" type="xs:positiveInteger"/>
              <xs:element name="unitprice" type="xs:decimal"/>
            </xs:sequence>
          </xs:complexType>
        </xs:element>
      </xs:sequence>
      <xs:attribute name="orderid" type="xs:string" use="required"/>
    </xs:complexType>
  </xs:element>
</xs:schema>
```

Listing 3.6 XML for an Order

```
<?xml version="1.0" encoding="ISO-8859-1" ?>
<order  xmlns:xsi="http://www.w3.org/2001/XMLSchema-instance"
  xsi:noNamespaceSchemaLocation="Order.xsd" orderid="ABC123">
  <salesman>Oswald Campesato</salesman>
  <shipto>
    <name>Kevin Nilson</name>
    <address1>123 Some Rd.</address1>
    <city>Mountain View</city>
    <state>CA</state>
    <zip>94043</zip>
  </shipto>
  <item>
    <prodid>123</prodid>
```

```
        <quantity>5</quantity>
        <unitprice>7.95</unitprice>
    </item>
</order>
```

Lets look at the following schema to get an understanding of the syntax of schema.

```
<?xml version="1.0" encoding="ISO-8859-1" ?>
<xs:schema xmlns:xs="http://www.w3.org/2001/XMLSchema" >
```

Here you can see that a schema document is an XML document. You can also see that that namespace xs is defined for schema elements. Namespaces in XML are similar to packages in Java and help to prevent name collisions.

```
<xs:element name="salesman" type="xs:string"/>
```

Simple Elements are XML elements that only contain text. The type attribute defines the datatype of the element. There are several built-in data-types, such as:

- xs:string
- xs:decimal
- xs:integer
- xs:boolean
- xs:date
- xs:time

Sometimes built-in datatypes need further restrictions, which can be added.

```
<xs:element name="address2" type="xs:string" minOccurs="0"
maxOccurs="1"/>
```

You can see that address2 may occur 0 or 1 times. In a more advanced element with restriction's the number of passengers can be limited to the zero to five range, for example.

```
<xs:element name="numpassengers">
  <xs:simpleType>
    <xs:restriction base="xs:integer">
      <xs:minInclusive value="0"/>
      <xs:maxInclusive value="5"/>
    </xs:restriction>
```

```
    </xs:simpleType>
</xs:element>
```

A complex element is an element that contains other elements. `Shipto` is an example of a complex element. You can see from the following XML that `shipto` contains the child elements name, address, city, state, and zip.

```
<shipto>
  <name>Kevin Nilson</name>
  <address1>123 Some Rd.</address1>
  <city>Mountain View</city>
  <state>CA</state>
  <zip>94043</zip>
</shipto>
```

In the following you can see how the `shipto` element is defined as having a nested `complexType` in the schema. Then a sequence element states that the nested elements must occur in the order they are listed (`name`, `address1`, `address2`, `city`, `state`, `zip`).

```
<xs:element name="shipto">
      <xs:complexType>
        <xs:sequence>
          <xs:element name="name" type="xs:string"/>
          <xs:element name="address1" type="xs:string"/>
          <xs:element name="address2" type="xs:string"
              minOccurs="0" maxOccurs="1"/>
          <xs:element name="city" type="xs:string"/>
          <xs:element name="state" type="xs:string"/>
          <xs:element name="zip" type="xs:integer"/>
        </xs:sequence>
      </xs:complexType>.
    </xs:element>
```

Schemas are much more advanced than what can be covered in this book, and this section was intended to provide an introduction to XML Schemas.

3.3.3.3 *Node Types in XML Documents*

Generally speaking, an XML document starts with an XML declaration, followed by a top-level node that can optionally specify one or more namespaces. XML defines 12 types of nodes that can appear in an XML document. These 12 types are defined as numeric constants in the node interface, as shown in Listing 3.7.

Listing 3.7

```
ELEMENT_NODE = 1
ATTRIBUTE_NODE= 2
TEXT_NODE = 3;
CDATA_SECTION_NODE = 4;
ENTITY_REFERENCE_NODE = 5;
ENTITY_NODE = 6;
PROCESSING_INSTRUCTION_NODE = 7;
COMMENT_NODE = 8;
DOCUMENT_NODE = 9;
DOCUMENT_TYPE_NODE = 10;
DOCUMENT_FRAGMENT_NODE = 11;
NOTATION_NODE = 12;
```

Thus, when you need to manipulate a particular node in an XML document, you can programmatically determine the type of that node by comparing its node type with the constants in Listing 3.3. The next several sections will address the following types of nodes in more detail:

• XML declaration statements
• processing instructions
• elements (which can contain attributes)
• comments
• entity references
• CDATA sections (especially in SVG documents)

3.3.3.4 *XML Declaration Statement*

Every XML document in this chapter contains the following XML declaration statement:

```
<?xml version="1.0"?>
```

In general, though, the XML declaration statement will look something like this:

```
<?xml version="1.0" encoding="ISO-8859-1" standalone="no"?>
```

3.3.3.5 *Processing Instructions (PI)*

PI are embedded in an XML document, and they specify one or more name/value pairs that provide information to programs that process the XML document that contains the PI. For example, suppose that an XML document named book.xml contains the following PI:

```
<?xml-stylesheet href="book.xsl" type="text/xsl"?>
```

The preceding PI indicates that the XSL stylesheet book.xsl is associated with the XML document book.xml.

3.3.3.6 *Elements and Attributes*

Elements are very common in XML documents, and every nonempty XML document contains at least one element. An element in XML is code that is delimited with angle brackets "<" and ">," which are the start tag and end tag, respectively, of an element. Elements can contain other elements, and those elements in turn can also contain elements. For all intents and purposes, you can nest elements in other elements to an arbitrary depth, which gives you the ability to represent deeply hierarchical structures in XML. For example, Listing 3.8 contains seven XML elements, some of which are nested. Notice that the firstname and lastname elements in Listing 3.4 contain text, so these elements are nonempty. XML elements can also contain attributes, which are name/value pairs that are "associated" with an XML element, and they are placed inside an XML element after the element name. The following code snippet illustrates the XML element emp, which contains one attribute ID:

```
<emp id="100"> ... </emp>
```

At this point, you might already be wondering whether it's better to use elements or attributes in XML documents, and we'll address this point later in the chapter. Listing 3.8 is a valid XML document in which every XML emp element contains an id attribute.

Listing 3.8

```
<?xml version="1.0"?>
<employees>
<emp id="100">
```

```
  <firstname>John</firstname>
  <lastname>Smith</lastname>
</emp>
<emp id="200">
  <firstname>Edward</firstname>
  <lastname>Jones</lastname>
</emp>
</employees>
```

Note that attribute values must be in quotes, which means that the following XML element is invalid:

```
<emp id=300>
  <firstname>Invalid</firstname>
  <lastname>Attribute</lastname>
</emp>
```

3.3.3.7 Elements Versus Attributes

Listing 3.9 illustrates how to convert the ID attributes in Listing 3.8 into XML elements.

Listing 3.9

```
<?xml version="1.0"?>
<employees>
<emp>
  <id>100</id>
  <firstname>John</firstname>
  <lastname>Smith</lastname>
</emp>
<emp>
  <id>200</id>
  <firstname>Edward</firstname>
  <lastname>Jones</lastname>
</emp>
</employees>
```

Earlier in this chapter we raised the question of whether you should use attributes or elements. Technically speaking, you can use either, and it's common to see XML documents with a mixture of both. However, keep in mind that elements give you greater flexibility because they are "extensible"; i.e., you can add or modify an element so that it contains other elements, whereas attributes do not have this flexibility. Therefore, if there's a chance you will need the flexibility afforded by XML elements, then it's probably better to define a piece of data as an XML element instead of an attribute of an XML element.

3.3.3.8 Comments in XML

Comments in an XML document always begin with `<!--` and end with `-->`. For example, the following code snippet is a valid comment in XML:

```
<!-- this is a comment -->
```

There is no limit to the number of XML comments you can include in an XML document. The only restriction is that XML comments cannot be nested. Therefore, the following snippet is invalid:

```
<!-- this is a comment <!-- nested in another comment --> -->
```

3.3.3.9 Entity References

Because the left angle bracket is used as the start of an element, how would you embed this symbol as part of a text string? The answer is to replace the "<" symbol with &lt. Similarly, you can represent the right angle bracket ">" with > where gt stands for "greater than" (which is also the mathematical meaning of >). The sequence & lets you embed the @ symbol as part of a string of text in an XML document. The sequence " lets you embed a quote as part of a text string in an XML document.

Tip: Think of lt as an acronym for less than which is also the mathematical meaning of the < symbol.

3.3.3.10 CDATA Sections

A CDATA section is ignored by parsers, which means that you can embed code fragments in this type of element. For example, SVG documents often have a CDATA section that contains ECMAScript code that is executed by an SVG renderer that executes the ECMAScript code. SVG renderers can be third-party plug-ins for a browser (such as the Adobe SVG plug-in) or native code that is part of the browser itself (such as Firefox). The Document Object Model (DOM) originated as way of representing the structure of an HTML page in a standardized manner. XML documents also have an associated DOM, which is a tree-like structure that is constructed by DOM parsers. Currently, there are four DOM levels available:

DOM Level 0–unofficial and derived from version 3.x browsers

DOM Level 1–support for nodes, elements, attributes, and navigation

DOM Level 2–added `getElementById` and `event` model and support for namespaces and CSS

DOM Level 3–added XPath, keyboard events, and serialization of documents as XML

You can find more details about DOM support here: http://www.w3.org/DOM. A DOM contains the text of an XML document and additional structure for the DOM itself, which means that a DOM can be several times larger than the XML document. Depending on your system, a large document might be only 100 megabytes in size; for the majority of systems, a file of 100 gigabytes is considered large. One disadvantage of using a DOM pertains to performance-related issues and memory contention for very large documents. One advantage of using a DOM is the ease with which you can traverse the DOM using methods whose names are used consistently in different languages. For example, the method `setAttribute()` is the same in Python, Perl, PHP, ECMAScript, and Java. Moreover, you can read the values of existing nodes, create new nodes, and update or delete the existing nodes of a DOM. However, when performance and memory use are critical, or when read-only access to an XML document is sufficient, SAX might be a better choice, as described in the next section.

■ 3.3.4 Understanding Simple API for XML (SAX)

An alternative to a DOM structure is SAX. SAX was developed for Java, and it is included in the Java 2 SDK (version 1.4). Note that while SAX-based parsing of an XML document consumes less memory, you will need to write additional code for accessing the XML document, and you lose the ability to traverse an in-memory structure that reflects the contents of the XML document (which is what a DOM provides). You will probably find the DOM easier to use, but you may be forced to use SAX when performance and document size preclude the use of DOM. So how does SAX work? By way of analogy, imagine yourself sitting at the side of a highway, where you need to do three things: report the front license plate number of every passing truck, the information written on the side of each truck, and the rear license plate number of each truck using your cell phone. (Most vehicles only have one license plate, so this analogy will be less than perfect.) However, you are not required to keep track of vehicles once they have driven past your location, nor do you need to scan ahead for vehicles that are approaching your location; your reporting responsibility pertains solely to the truck is currently driving past you. In an analogous fashion, SAX-based parsing involves event-based information for the start of an element, the text in an element, and the end of an element. If you want to do something when any of these three events occur, you do so in call-back functions (or methods) that you specify before you start parsing a document. Although there are other events that you can detect during SAX-based parsing, the start/text/end events are sufficient for you to parse an XML document, which will be demonstrated in the next section. Now that you have a basic understanding of well-formed and valid XML documents, DOM, and SAX, let's look at XML namespaces.

3.3.4.1 *XML Namespaces*

XML namespaces are an important part of XML, and they provide a mechanism for creating compound documents, which are XML documents whose elements can belong to different XML vocabularies. The following subsections provide more detailed information about the nature of XML namespaces and their role in processing XML documents. In the XML world, you can think of a namespace as a "tag" that is used as a prefix for XML elements. The tag is defined as a string, and by convention, the string resembles a URL. Keep in mind, though, that such URLs are often meaningless; if you launch a browser and navigate to those URLs, you will get a 404 error message. For example, Listing 3.10 displays the contents of an XML document that contains the namespace http://www/abc/org, which is associated with the prefix abc.

Listing 3.10

```
<?xml version="1.0"?>
<abc:employees xmlns:abc="http://www/abc/org">
...
</abc:employees>
```

The first line is the standard PI that declares the version of XML (in this case, it is 1.0), and the subsequent line defines or associates the tag abc with the string http://www/abc/org. Note that this string is not a valid URL (try it!), and it has no purpose other than to associate the prefix abc with a string that is unique in this XML document.

3.3.4.2 Why Use XML Namespaces?

Namespaces are used to avoid so-called collisions that can occur when two (or more) XML documents use identical tags, but the associated DTDs are different. For example, suppose two companies both have employee information, but they have different formats for the structure of the XML document. You will see an example of how to handle this situation later in this chapter.

3.3.4.3 An XML Document with One Namespace

The XML document in Listing 3.11 illustrates how you can define a namespace and then use that namespace to mark XML elements that belong to the namespace.

Listing 3.11

```
<?xml version="1.0"?>
<abc:employees xmlns:abc="http://www/abc/org">
  <abc:emp id="125">
   <hiredate>10/24/2006</hiredate>
   <firstname>John</firstname>
   <lastname>Smith</lastname>
   <deptno>1000</deptno>
  </abc:emp>
  <abc:emp id="130">
   <hiredate>10/14/2006</hiredate>
   <firstname>Jane</firstname>
   <lastname>Smith</lastname>
   <deptno>2000</deptno>
  </abc:emp>
  <abc:emp id="255">
   <hiredate>12/04/2005</hiredate>
   <firstname>Tom</firstname>
   <lastname>Jones</lastname>
   <deptno>1000</deptno>
  </abc:emp>
  <abc:emp id="290">
```

```
      <hiredate>11/04/2005</hiredate>
      <firstname>Tom</firstname>
      <lastname>Edwards</lastname>
      <deptno>3000</deptno>
    </abc:emp>
</abc:employees>
```

3.3.4.4 An XML Document with Two Namespaces

The XML document in Listing 3.12 illustrates how you can define two
namespaces in the same document, and then associate one XML element
with the first namespace, and the other three XML elements with the second
namespace.

Listing 3.12

```
<?xml version="1.0"?>
<abc:employees xmlns:abc="http://www/abc/org"
               xmlns:def="http://www/def/org">
  <def:emp id="125">
   <hiredate>10/24/2006</hiredate>
   <firstname>John</firstname>
   <lastname>Smith</lastname>
   <deptno>1000</deptno>
  </def:emp>
  <abc:emp id="130">
   <hiredate>10/14/2006</hiredate>
   <firstname>Jane</firstname>
   <lastname>Smith</lastname>
   <deptno>2000</deptno>
  </abc:emp>
  <abc:emp id="255">
   <hiredate>12/04/2005</hiredate>
   <firstname>Tom</firstname>
   <lastname>Jones</lastname>
   <deptno>1000</deptno>
  </abc:emp>
  <abc:emp id="290">
   <hiredate>11/04/2005</hiredate>
   <firstname>Tom</firstname>
   <lastname>Edwards</lastname>
   <deptno>3000</deptno>
  </abc:emp>
</abc:employees>
```

Employee information in company A has the following structure:

```
<!ELEMENT emp (firstname, middlename, lastname)>
```

whereas company B has this structure:

```
<!ELEMENT emp (firstname, lastname)>
```

The XML document in Listing 3.13 illustrates how you can define two namespaces in the same document, and then use one of those namespaces as the default namespace.

Listing 3.13

```
<?xml version="1.0"?>
<abc:employees xmlns:abc="http://www/abc/org"
               xmlns:def="http://www/def/org"
               xmlns="http://www/abc/org">

  <def:emp id="125">
   <hiredate>10/24/2006</hiredate>
   <firstname>John</firstname>
   <lastname>Smith</lastname>
   <deptno>1000</deptno>
  </def:emp>
  <emp id="130">
   <hiredate>10/14/2006</hiredate>
   <firstname>Jane</firstname>
   <lastname>Smith</lastname>
   <deptno>2000</deptno>
  </emp>
  <emp id="255">
   <hiredate>12/04/2005</hiredate>
   <firstname>Tom</firstname>
   <lastname>Jones</lastname>
   <deptno>1000</deptno>
  </emp>
  <emp id="290">
   <hiredate>11/04/2005</hiredate>
   <firstname>Tom</firstname>
   <lastname>Edwards</lastname>
   <deptno>3000</deptno>
  </emp>
</abc:employees>
```

3.3.4.5 XML Support in Browsers

This section will address XML-related support for the following browsers: Internet Explorer 6.x, Firefox 2.x, Opera 9.x, and Safari y.z.

Listing 3.14 displays the contents of the XML document books.xml, which will be used in the Java code samples throughout this chapter. Listing 3.14 displays the contents of SAXReadFile1.java, which shows the contents of books.xml. If necessary, you can download the JAR file xercesImpl.jar and add it to the CLASSPATH environment variable, as shown here (for Windows):

```
SET CLASSPATH=%CLASSPATH%;<full-path-to-location-of-xerces-jar-file>
```

Listing 3.14 books.xml

```xml
<?xml version="1.0"?>
<books>
  <book>
    <author>Oswald Campesato</author>
    <title>SVG Programming</title>
    <desc>A book about SVG Graphics</desc>

    <chapters>
    <chapter id="1">
      <desc>Introduction to SVG</desc>
      <length>24</length>
    </chapter>

      <chapter id="2">
      <desc>SVG and gradients</desc>
      <length>30</length>
    </chapter>
    </chapters>
  </book>

  <book>
    <author>Oswald Campesato</author>
    <title>Silverlight Grahpics</title>
    <desc>A book about Silverlight Graphics</desc>

    <chapters>
    <chapter id="1">
      <desc>Introduction to Silverlight</desc>
      <length>28</length>
    </chapter>
```

```
        <chapter id="2">
        <desc>Colors and Gradients</desc>
        <length>32</length>
        </chapter>
      </chapters>
    </book>
</books>
```

Listing 3.14 contains a top-level XML <books> element, which contains two XML <book> subelements. The first XML <book> element describes the contents of an SVG book and the second XML <book> element describes the contents of a Silverlight book. Listing 3.15 displays the contents of SAXReadFile1.java, which illustrates how to read the contents of an XML document. Note that this Java class will render the contents of the XML document books.xml if no XML filename is specified. Listing 3.16 displays the contents of SAXReadFile1.txt, which is produced when you launch the Java class SAXReadFile1.class from the command line, as described later in this section.

Listing 3.15 SAXReadFile1.java

```java
import java.io.*;

import org.apache.xerces.parsers.SAXParser;
import org.xml.sax.*;
import org.xml.sax.helpers.*;

public class SAXReadFile1 extends DefaultHandler
{
    public void startElement(String namespaceURI,
                             String localName,
                             String qName,
                             Attributes atts)
    {
      System.out.println("startElement: "+qName);
    }

     public static void main(String[] args)
     {
        String xmlFilename = "books.xml";

        SAXReadFile1 sax1 = new SAXReadFile1();
        SAXParser parser  = new SAXParser();
        parser.setContentHandler(sax1);
```

```
     try {
       if(args.length > 0)
       {
    System.out.println("* Parsing file: "+args[0]+"\n");
         parser.parse(args[0]);
       }
       else
       {
    System.out.println("* Parsing file: "+xmlFilename+"\n");
         parser.parse(xmlFilename);
       }
     }
     catch (Exception e) {
       e.printStackTrace();
     }
   }
}
```

Listing 3.16 SAXReadFile1.txt / Parsing file: books.xml

```
startElement: books
startElement: book
startElement: author
startElement: title
startElement: description
startElement: chapters
startElement: chapter
startElement: number
startElement: desc
startElement: length
startElement: chapter
startElement: number
startElement: desc
startElement: length
startElement: book
startElement: author
startElement: title
startElement: description
startElement: chapters
startElement: chapter
startElement: number
startElement: desc
startElement: length
startElement: chapter
```

```
startElement: number
startElement: desc
startElement: length
```

Open a command shell, navigate to the location of the Java class in Listing 3.15, and ensure that the JAR file xercesImpl.jar has been added to the CLASSPATH environment variable. Next, type the following command:

```
java SAXReadFile1.
```

If you inspect the contents of the XML document books.xml, you can confirm that every element in this file has a corresponding line of output in Listing 3.16. The reason for this is simple: each time the SAX parser encounters an element, the name of that element is printed and sent to standard output (which is the command line).

3.3.4.6   What is DOM?

DOM is useful when you need to create, update, or delete elements in an XML document. This is achieved by first creating a DOM, which is an in-memory tree-like representation of an XML document. Next, you can use XPath expressions to navigate to the desired location in the DOM and then perform the desired processing. When your changes are complete, you can save the DOM to an XML document on the file system. The disadvantages of using a DOM structure are the same as the advantages of using SAX: using DOM requires more memory and gives a slower performance.

3.3.4.7   A Simple DOM Example

Listing 3.17 displays the contents of DOMReadFile1.java, which constructs a DOM structure for the contents of the XML document books.xml. This Java class only processes the top-level elements in books.xml, which differs from the output generated by the Java class SAXReadFile1.java. Listing 3.18 displays the contents of DOMReadFile1.txt, which is the output produced by the Java class DOMReadFile1.java.

Listing 3.17 DOMReadFile1.java

```
import javax.xml.parsers.*;
import org.w3c.dom.*;
```

```java
import java.io.*;
public class DOMReadFile1
{
   public static void main(String[] args)
   {
      String fileName = "books.xml";
      File theFile    = new File(fileName);

      int      nodeCount = 0;
      Node     theNode   = null;
      Element rootNode   = null;
      NodeList nodeList  = null;

      Document                   theDocument = null;
      DocumentBuilder            theBuilder  = null;
      DocumentBuilderFactory theFactory      = null;

      if(!theFile.exists())
      {
         System.out.println("Cannot open file "+fileName);
         System.exit(1);
      }

      try {
         theFactory  = DocumentBuilderFactory.newInstance();
         theBuilder  = theFactory.newDocumentBuilder();
         theDocument = theBuilder.parse(theFile);

         rootNode    = theDocument.getDocumentElement();
         nodeList    = rootNode.getChildNodes();
         nodeCount   = nodeList.getLength();

          for(int v=0; v<nodeCount; v++)
         {
            theNode = nodeList.item(v);
            System.out.println("node "+v+" theNode.getNodeName());
         }
      }
      catch(Exception exception) {
         exception.printStackTrace();
      }
   }
}
```

Listing 3.18 DOMReadFile1.txt

```
node 0 = #text
node 1 = book
node 2 = #text
node 3 = book
node 4 = #text
```

Open a command shell, navigate to the location of the Java class in Listing 3.17, and ensure that the JAR file xercesImpl.jar has been added to the CLASSPATH environment variable. Next, type the following command:

```
java DOMReadFile1
```

You will see the following output:

```
node 0 = #text
node 1 = book
node 2 = #text
node 3 = book
node 4 = #text
```

The first part of Listing 3.17 contains a main method that specifies a hard-coded filename and then creates a Java File object, as shown here:

```
String fileName = "books.xml";
File theFile    = new File(fileName);
```

The next part of Listing 3.17 initializes several variables that are needed during the processing of the XML document, as shown here:

```
int      nodeCount    = 0;
Node     theNode      = null;
Element rootNode     = null;
NodeList nodeList = null;
```

The next part of Listing 3.17 initializes three variables that are used for creating a factory object, as shown here:

```
Document                theDocument = null;
DocumentBuilder         theBuilder  = null;
DocumentBuilderFactory theFactory   = null;
```

The next part of Listing 3.17 performs a check to ensure that the hard-coded file actually exists, as shown here:

```
if(!theFile.exists())
    {
        System.out.println("Cannot open file "+fileName);
        System.exit(1);
    }
```

The next part of Listing 3.17 contains a try-catch block that processes the XML document. The first part of the try block initializes the variable theDocument (which is a Document object), as shown here:

```
try {
        theFactory  = DocumentBuilderFactory.newInstance();
        theBuilder  = theFactory.newDocumentBuilder();
        theDocument = theBuilder.parse(theFile);

    }
```

The next part of the try-catch block gets a list of the nodes in the XML document, as shown here:

```
        rootNode    = theDocument.getDocumentElement();
        nodeList    = rootNode.getChildNodes();
        nodeCount   = nodeList.getLength();
```

The next part of the try-catch block iterates through the list of the nodes in the XML document and prints the contents of each node, as shown here:

```
for(int v=0; v<nodeCount; v++)
    {
        theNode = nodeList.item(v);
        System.out.println("node "+v+" theNode.getNodeName());
    }
```

The variable theNode is a reference to the current node in the XML document, and the (text) contents of the node are retrieved with the expression:

```
theNode.getNodeName()
```

The last part of the try-catch block contains the catch block that prints a stack trace in the event of an error, as shown here:

```
catch(Exception exception) {
        exception.printStackTrace();
    }
```

3.3.4.8 XML with Dojo

Dojo provides some basic XML parsing functionality. Dojo can convert XML to a JSON object tree. Dojo can also construct new Doms in a browser-independent way. Listing 3.19 shows how, using Dojo, you can parse a simple XML document representing a person.

To use Dojo to parse XML, you have to start by using `dojo.require` to load the libraries needed for XML parsing:

```
dojo.require("dojox.xml.parser");
```

Listing 3.19 XML Parsing with Dojo

```
<script>
  dojo.require("dojox.xml.parser");

  function parseXML() {
    var xml = "<person>"+
              "<firstname>Kevin</firstname>"+
              "<lastname>Nilson</lastname>"+
              "</person>";
    var dom = dojox.xml.parser.parse(xml);

    var pd = dojo.byId("parsedData");
    var docNode = dom.documentElement;
    pd.appendChild(document.createTextNode("Document contains: " +
docNode.childNodes.length + " elements"));
    pd.appendChild(document.createElement("br"));
    pd.appendChild(document.createElement("br"));
    pd.appendChild(document.createTextNode("firstname = " +
dojox.xml.parser.textContent(docNode.childNodes[0])));
    pd.appendChild(document.createElement("br"));
    pd.appendChild(document.createTextNode("lastname = " +
dojox.xml.parser.textContent(docNode.childNodes[1])));
    pd.appendChild(document.createElement("br"));
    pd.appendChild(document.createElement("br"));
    pd.appendChild(document.createTextNode("Document XML: " +
dojox.xml.parser.innerXML(docNode)));

  }
  dojo.addOnLoad(parseXML);
</script>

<div id="parsedData"></div>
script>
<div id="parsedData"></div>
```

The next step is to tell Dojo to parse the XML into a js object:

```
var xml = "<person><firstname>Kevin</firstname><lastname>Nilson
</lastname></person>";
var dom = dojox.xml.parser.parse(xml);
```

It is very easy to find all of the `childNodes`. This lets you loop over the content of the XML.

```
var docNode = dom.documentElement;
docNode.childNodes.length;
```

You can get the text of the first childNode element element by parsing the `textContent` from the `childNode`.

```
dojox.xml.parser.textContent(docNode.childNodes[0])
```

XML string can easily be re-created from the js object:

```
dojox.xml.parser.innerXML(docNode)
```

3.3.4.9 XML with jQuery

Working with XML in jQuery is very natural. Using jQuery, you can use the Find function to search for XML elements just as you would search for js objects. Listing 3.20 shows XML parsing in jQuery.

Listing 3.20 Sample app.yaml for Google App Engine

```
<script>
$(document).ready(function(){
  var xml=
    "<?xml version=\"1.0\" encoding=\"UTF-8\"?>"+
    "<people>"+
    "<person>"+
    "<firstname>Kevin</firstname>"+
    "<lastname>Nilson</lastname>"+
    "</person>"+
    "<person>"+
    "<firstname>Oswald</firstname>"+
    "<lastname>Campesato</lastname>"+
    "</person>"+
    "<person>"+
    "<firstname>Siamak</firstname>"+
```

```
          "<lastname>Ashrafi</lastname>"+
          "</person>"+
          "</people>";

      $(xml).find('person').each(function(){
        var firstName = $(this).find('firstname').text();
        var lastName = $(this).find('lastname').text();

        $("div#parsedData").append(firstName+' '+lastName+', ');
      });
    });
    </script>
    <div id='parsedData'></div>
```

When the page is fully loaded this function will be executed.

```
$(xml).find('person').each(function(){
```

Search the XML for each person elements

```
var firstName = $(this).find('firstname').text();
var lastName = $(this).find('lastname').text();
$("div#parsedData").append(firstName+' '+lastName+', ');
```

Next, search within the person for the firstname and get the text of the element. Then search within the person for the lastname and get the text of the element. Finally, append the firstname and lastname to the div with the id parsedData. These steps are repeated for every person in the XML.

■ 3.4 ADVANTAGES AND DISADVANTAGES OF JSON AND XML

Over time, XML and JSON have become very popular. XML and JSON have been used as data formats in Web 2.0 and traditional application development. XML and JSON have many advantages, but they also have disadvantages in certain situations.

■ 3.4.1 Advantages and Disadvantages of JSON

Web services use became very popular around 2004–2005. During this period, XML became the standard data transmission format. XML has many advantages over JSON, but XML tends to be more verbose than JSON, so, over time, many XML, based applications have converted to JSON.

The following list contains some of the advantages of JSON:

- flexibility (you can define your own keys)
- little overhead (content is mostly data)
- portable data
- nonproprietary
- common and convenient format for Web services

The following list contains some of the disadvantages of JSON:

- not type safe
- no data validation

JSON has very limited overhead compared to XML.

■ 3.4.2   Advantages and Disadvantages of XML

The following list contains some of the advantages of XML:

- flexibility (you can define your own mark-up tags)
- portable data
- easy-to-describe hierarchical information
- nonproprietary
- common and convenient format for Web services

The following list contains some of the disadvantages of XML:

- verbose

XML creates significant overhead for storing, sending, and receiving XML-based data. If you are new to XML, or skeptical about the advantages of XML, you might ask: What's wrong with using flat files? This is a legitimate and valid question that needs to be addressed. Because flat ASCII files contain text data, you could argue that most of the points regarding XML also apply to text files. While it's possible to work with flat files in many situations, there are some disadvantages to using flat files that can significantly limit your ability to maintain, debug, and enhance your current system. However, XML overcomes those disadvantages, which makes it a superior technology, especially for representing hierarchical data in a straightforward and intuitive manner.

First, it is difficult to modify the structure of flat files without breaking the programs that process them. For example, COBOL programs often rely on a fixed range of columns for extracting information (first name, last name, department, etc.). If you want to insert additional data, you need to find unoccupied columns to insert the new data so that you do not break the logic of existing programs.

Sometimes you can avoid the fixed-length problem by writing programs using Java or C#, or scripting languages such as Perl, Python, and so forth, that use data delimiters (such as a colon or pipe symbol), thereby avoiding the use of hard-coded column ranges. However, programs that read delimited data fields often rely on the sequence or ordering of data items, and therefore rely on the field order to give meaning to the data in a flat file.

For example, suppose a flat file specifies an employee's first name, last name, and department number in the first three (comma-delimited) fields of each line of text in a flat file. These text fields can vary in length to accommodate names of different lengths, unlike many COBOL programs. However, you still cannot insert a new field between the first and second field (or between the second and third field) in the flat file without breaking existing programs. Another inherent problem with flat files pertains to extremely long lines of text that are difficult to read, or worse, cannot be processed due to limitations in record lengths in older programming languages.

Sometimes data spans multiline records, and artificial artifacts (e.g., Boolean flags) are used so that programs can handle such records. Again, such flat files tend to be difficult to read and even more difficult to maintain, debug, and enhance. Another problem with flat files is representing deeply hierarchical data. While it's possible to process one or two levels of data nesting in flat files, it can become extremely tedious to maintain and enhance programs that must process flat files with ten levels of nesting data. Now consider this scenario in flat files with the power of XML, which has a much more intuitive approach for representing deeply nested data. The corresponding programs will increase in complexity, but these programs can be written in a manner that reduces the difficulty of code maintenance.

On the other hand, you can use XML to minimize the previously-mentioned problems with flat files. XML documents can be modified to include new elements whose name reflects their value or purpose without automatically breaking existing programs. Long and multiline records can be represented in a hierarchical manner using XML. There are XML editors (including some that are free) that render XML documents with expandable and collapsible nodes. Please keep in mind that the flexibility of XML is not meant to promote a casual approach to designing XML documents. You can still create XML documents that are poorly designed (from a business requirements perspective) and then create Java or C# programs that can process those XML documents. Then, when you make significant changes to the structure of your XML documents, you will need to modify your Java or C# programs to accommodate the new structure of your XML documents. Always try to structure your data in the best manner possible, given the current constraints that you have, to reduce any future changes you might have to make to the XML structure of your data. If you do a good job of defining the structure of your XML documents to reflect your business requirements, you will not only reduce the number of changes to your XML documents in the future, you will probably also minimize changes to the Java or C# code that processes the XML documents.

■ 3.5   HTML AND SGML VERSUS XML

HTML is extremely popular on the Internet, with literally billions of HTML pages in existence. HTML 1.0 has a very limited number of tags, and with each succeeding release, the number of available tags (and corresponding functionality) has increased. However, the set of available HTML tags is always fixed, regardless of the version of HTML that you use, which means that HTML cannot interpret any of your custom tags. In addition, browsers that can interpret HTML do not strictly adhere to tag rules. For example, you have probably seen HTML pages that have <td> tags without a matching </td> tag. HTML documents can conform to the rules of XML, but they are not required to be a valid XML document. Many HTML browsers can interpret and render HTML pages that are invalid according to XML. (In the next section, you will see an example of an HTML document that is also an XML document.) XML is actually an application profile of the Standard Generalized Markup Language (SGML), which means that SGML systems can manipulate XML documents (but the reverse is probably not true). You can think of XML as a subset SGML in the sense that XML has many (but not all) of the features of SGML. The extensibility of XML makes it much more powerful than HTML (yet less complex than SGML). XHTML is well-formed XML that is also HTML (hence the name, XHTML). XHTML 1.0 and XHTML 1.1 correspond to HTML 4.0 and HTML 4.01, respectively. XHTML pages can be viewed in browsers, and because they are also valid XML, XHTML pages can be manipulated by programs that process XML documents. You can find the entire XHTML specification here: http://www.w3.org/TR/xhtml/1.

■ 3.6   YAML AND COMMA SEPARATED VALUES (CSV) AS ALTERNATIVES TO JSON AND XML

There are many alternatives to JSON and XML. YAML and CSV are two of the most popular, so we will focus on them.

■ 3.6.1   YAML

YAML is a data serialization standard for any programming language. The YAML data structure hierarchy is maintained by outline indentation. Listing 3.21 shows a sample YAML file used to configure the handling of python requests in the Google App Engine (GAE). YAML documents start with an optional --- and end with an optional .... Lists in YAML begin with -. Listing 3.21 shows the list handlers. Lists can also be in the [a, b, c] format. In YAML, hashes are key value pairs. In Listing 3.21 there are many hashes, such as application, version, runtime, and api_version. Notice that keys and strings do not need quotation. YAML ignores all of the leading and trailing whitespace. JSON is a subset of YAML and most JSON files can be parsed by a YAML parser.

Listing 3.21 Sample app.yaml for GAE

```
application: myapp
version: 1
runtime:python
api_version: 1

handlers:
- url: /
  script: home.py

- url: /index\.html
  script: home.py

- url: /stylesheets
  static_dir: stylesheets
```

```
- url: /(.*\.(gif|png|jpg))
  static_files: static/\1
  upload: static/(.*\.(gif|png|jpg))

- url: /admin/.*
  script: admin.py
  login: admin

- url: /.*
  script: not_found.py
```

YAML's popularity seems to be greatest with python developers.

■ 3.6.2 CSV

In CSV, format fields are separated by commas and records are separated by a new line. Listing 3.22 shows a simple CSV file that contains productId, name, and description. The first line of the file is a header, which describes the fields. The header is optional and often not used.

Listing 3.22 CSV File

```
ProductId,Name,Description

1,Cheeseburger,Quarter Pound Patty with Cheese
2,Hamburger,Quarter Pound Patty
3,Fries,French Fries
4,Shake,Vanilla Milkshake
```

CSV was popular as early as the 1960s, but its usage has declined over time.

■ 3.7 ADVANCED EXAMPLE WITH DOJO AND JSON

It is common to use JSON to define what data is on a page, then use JavaScript to build the page. Modern Ajax Frameworks contain feature-rich widgets for displaying JSON data. In this example, we will be showing a Dojo grid, with data loaded from JSON. Figure 3.1 shows the resulting page.

Listing 3.23 shows the JSON file used as the data for the grid. identifier: name is used for this grid. identifier is similar to a primary key in a database. Rows can quickly and easily be looked up by their identifier. The grid contains a list of items. Each item represents a row in the grid.

Fruit	Quantity	Price	
apple	25	$0.65	
banana	42	$0.25	
carrot	33	$0.35	
lemon	13	$0.33	
orange	24	$0.95	
pear	3	$1.15	
watermelon	63	$1.05	

Listing 3.23 JSON for Dojo Grid

```
{
  'identifier': 'name',
  'items':

  [
  {'name': 'apple', 'price': 0.65, 'quantity':25},

  {'name': 'banana', 'price': 0.25, 'quantity':42},

  {'name': 'carrot', 'price': 0.35, 'quantity':33},

  {'name': 'lemon', 'price': 0.33, 'quantity':13},

  {'name': 'orange', 'price': 0.95, 'quantity':24},

  {'name': 'pear', 'price': 1.15, 'quantity':3},

  {'name': 'watermelon', 'price': 1.05, 'quantity':63},

  ]
}
```

Listing 3.24 shows the HTML needed to use the Dojo grid. All that was needed was some script tags and stylesheets, and one div to hold the grid. In this example, the grid ID is grid, but any ID can be used.

Listing 3.24 HTML for the Dojo Grid

```
<html>
<head>
<meta http-equiv="content-type" content="application/xhtml+xml;
charset=UTF-8" />

<script type="text/javascript" src="http://o.aolcdn.com/dojo/1.3.0/
dojo/dojo.xd.js.uncompressed.js"></script>
<script type="text/javascript" src="fruit.js"></script>

<style type="text/css">
@import "http://o.aolcdn.com/dojo/1.3.0/dojox/grid/resources/
Grid.css";
@import "http://o.aolcdn.com/dojo/1.3.0/dojox/grid/resources/
nihiloGrid.css";

.dojoxGrid table {
  margin: 0;
}
</style>
</head>
<body>
<div id='grid'></grid>
</body>
</html>
```

Listing 3.25 shows the JavaScript file used to create the Dojo grid. Notice how little code is needed to provide such great functionality.

Listing 3.25 JavaScript for the Dojo Grid

```
dojo.require("dojo.data.ItemFileReadStore");
dojo.require("dojox.grid.DataGrid");
dojo.require("dojo.currency");

formatCurrency = function(inDatum){
  return isNaN(inDatum) ? '...' : dojo.currency.format(inDatum,
this.constraint);
}

dojo.addOnLoad(function(){
  var jsonStore = new dojo.data.ItemFileReadStore({ url: "fruit.
json" });

  var layout= [
    { field: "name", width: "100px", name: "Fruit" },
```

```
       { field: "quantity", width: "100px", name: "Quantity", styles:
'text-align: right;' },
       { field: "price", width: "100px", name: "Price", formatter:
formatCurrency, constraint: {currency: 'USD'}, widgetClass:
"dijit.form.CurrencyTextBox", styles: 'text-align: right;' }
   ];

   var grid = new dojox.grid.DataGrid({
       id: 'grid',
       query: { name: '*' },
       store: jsonStore,
       structure: layout
   }, 'grid');

   grid.startup();
});
```

The function `formatCurrency` is defined to return ... if the value is invalid, otherwise it returns the formatted USD number.

```
formatCurrency = function(inDatum){
    return isNaN(inDatum) ? '...' : dojo.currency.format(inDatum,
this.constraint);
  }
```

Next, the layout of the grid is defined. Each column is defined in order. The `field` is the key in the JSON data and the `name` is the column header. In the following, you can see how a custom `widgetClass` is used to display the currency for the `price` column.

```
var layout= [
     { field: "name", width: "100px", name: "Fruit" },
     { field: "quantity", width: "100px", name: "Quantity", styles:
'text-align: right;' },
     { field: "price", width: "100px", name: "Price", formatter:
formatCurrency, constraint: {currency: 'USD'}, widgetClass: "dijit
.form.CurrencyTextBox", styles: 'text-align: right;' }
   ];
```

The grid is finally defined by passing a JavaScript object of parameters. The `id` is the `id` of the `div` in the HTML, where the `grid` will be added. The `query` allows for limited sets of JSON to be used. In this example, all of JSON will be used. Next, the `store` and `layout` are defined. Finally, the `startup` function of the grid is called.

```
var grid = new dojox.grid.DataGrid({
    id: 'grid',
    query: { name: '*' },
    store: jsonStore,
    structure: layout
}, 'grid');

grid.startup();
```

JSON can be used in combination with Ajax Frameworks to make eye-catching and feature-rich user interfaces (UI) with limited effort. Dojo also provides Dijit, which ia a great UI widget.

■ 3.8 SUMMARY

JSON and XML have become the standard data format used by all Web 2.0 applications. There are many other data formats in use, but their use seems to be limited to pre-Web 2.0 applications. JSON holds the advantage of being lighter weight than XML, while XML is much more advanced and provides features such as dtd and schema. XML is more mature then JSON and provides greater tooling options. JSON is often used for simple data structures and XML is often used with more advanced data structures.

## CHAPTER 4

Ajax

In This Chapter:

- Introducing the Concept of Ajax
- A Brief History of Ajax
- `XMLHttpRequest`
- Ajax via Ajax Libraries
- Ajax Working with JSON Using Dojo and jQuery
- Limitations of Ajax
- Adoption of Ajax
- Comparison of Existing Ajax Libraries
- Comprehensive Ajax Project
- Advanced Ajax

As you will see in the next section, Ajax has been the main driver in defining Web 2.0. A majority of the most recent improvements to the Web can be credited to Ajax.

■ 4.1 INTRODUCING THE CONCEPT OF AJAX

In the last decade, the Web has come a long way due to advances in JavaScript and the invention of Ajax. Web applications from the late 90s contained mostly static data and limited JavaScript. Early users of the Web found interactive pages that had limited functionality. Over time, Dynamic HTML (DHTML) and Document Object Model (DOM), provided the tools necessary to make web pages more interactive without having to wait for a complete page load. This provided a greater user experience and changed the focus of web design to user interaction.

Ajax originally began as the acronym AJAX for Asynchronous JavaScript and XML. Jesse James Garrett coined the term in February 2005. In Jesse's paper, "Ajax: A NewApproach to Web Applications," he states:

> Ajax isn't a technology. Its really several technologies, each flourishing in its own right, coming together in powerful new ways. Ajax incorporates:
> - standards-based presentation using XHTML and CSS
> - dynamic display and interaction using DOM
> - asynchronous data retrieval using XMLHttpRequest
> - JavaScript to bind everything together

Over time, AJAX evolved to Ajax, because JavaScript and XML are not actually required, nor does the request need to be asynchronous.

Let's start by looking a what Ajax is and why it has become so popular. The basic concept behind Ajax is that, in the background, a web page will use JavaScript to make a request for additional data from the web server. When this request is made, the original page is not reloaded. The data that is returned by the background request can be added to the page using DHTML. In a traditional page, the whole page must be refreshed to receive any information from the server. Ajax provides an easier selection.

Ajax can be easily explained using a web form example that requires users to fill in dropdowns for State, County, and City. The web page can't possibly every city in the country, but it can easily list all of the states. In this example, we'll start with a web page that contains a dropdown listing all of the states (see Figure 4.1). Once the user selects a state, a server request is made to retrieve all of counties for the selected state (see Figure 4.2). Once

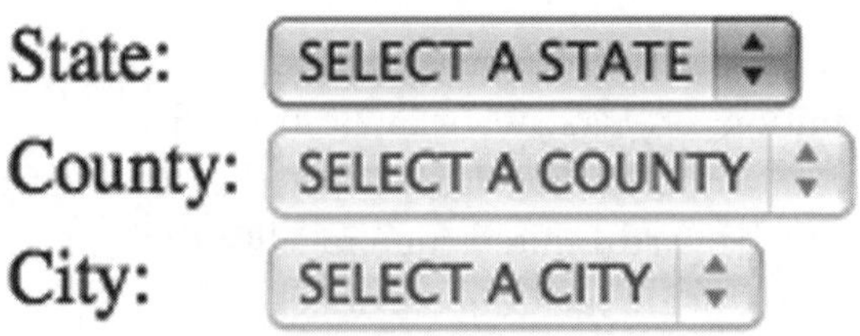

■ **FIGURE 4.1**
Prompt for State

State: SELECT A STATE

County: SELECT A COUNTY

City: SELECT A CITY

FIGURE 4.2
Provide State to
Enable County

State: California
County: SELECT A COUNTY
City: SELECT A CITY

FIGURE 4.3
Provide County to
Enable City

State: California
County: Santa Clara
City: SELECT A CITY

FIGURE 4.4
Provide City

State: California
County: Santa Clara
City: Mountain View

the request is completed, the page is updated using DHTML to populate the County dropdown (see Figure 4.3). Next, the user selects a county and another background request is made to retrieve the cities of the selected county. Finally, using DHTML, the screen displays the cities to the user (see Figure 4.4).

4.2 A BRIEF HISTORY OF AJAX

Ajax evolved from techniques introduced in the mid-1990s by hackers trying to find ways to improve user experience on the Web by asynchronous loading of data. Web pages prior to the Web 2.0 revolution needed an entire page reload to get any new information from the web server. The limitations of the request/response-based Web 1.0 model forced many developers to produce long, static pages. During this time, Internet connection speed also limited user activity on the Web.

■ **FIGURE 4.5**
Ajax Calculator

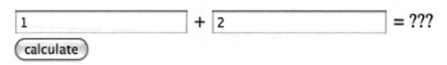

■ 4.2.1   IFrames

In the late 1990s, it became popular to use a hidden IFrame to communicate with the server in the background. To create a GET request, developers would set the src attribute of an IFrame to a web page. The IFrame is invisible to the user of the page, so they don't see the background loading of the page. After the IFrame is loaded, its data can be extracted and parsed with JavaScript and used in the main page. If you want to post data to the server, then DHTML can be used to dyamically create a form inside the IFrame. JavaScript can then be used to submit the form. Figure 4.5 shows an example of a simple online calculator that lets you use an IFrame to make a GET request to add two numbers together and return the result. This example shows how early web pioneers were able to overcome the many limitations of web standards and make improvements.

4.2.1.1 IFrames Using Dojo

Using a hidden IFrame to load pages from a web server is easy. The following code snippet shows a simple web page that accepts two request parameters, first and second. This example uses Dojo to look up DOM elements.

```
String first = request.getParameter("first");
String second = request.getParameter("second");
```

Listing 4.1 shows the server-side code of a JSP page requested by the hidden IFrame.

If first or second is not supplied as a request parameter, then the page will display "???".

```
if(first==null ||second==null){
    out.println("???");
}
```

Listing 4.1 Hidden IFrame written in JSP for Making Server Requests (iframe.jsp)

```
<%
      String first = request.getParameter("first");
      String second = request.getParameter("second");

      if(first==null ||second==null){
           out.println("???");
      }else{
           int result = Integer.parseInt(first) +
           Integer.parseInt(second);
           out. println(result);
      }
%>
```

If both first and second are provided as request parameters, then first and second are converted to integers, added together, and stored in result. Then result is displayed to the page. The only output from this page is result or "???".

```
else{
    int result = Integer.parseInt(first) + Integer.parseInt(second);
    out.println(result);
}
```

Listing 4.2 shows a web page with two input boxes and a button. The user can type a number into each input box and click the button to add them together. At the top of the web page a hidden IFrame loads iframe .jsp with no request parameters. When the IFrame is loaded it will call the JavaScript function showResult().

```
<iframe src='iframe.jsp' id='iframe' onload='showResult()'
style='display: none; visibility: hidden; height: 1px;'></iframe>
```

Clicking the button calls the calculateResult function, which builds a query string from the two input boxes and updates iframe.src to include the query string.

```
function calculateResult(){
    var first = dojo.byId('first').value;
    var second = dojo.byId('second').value;
    var iframe = dojo.byId('iframe');

    iframe.src='iframe.jsp?first='+first+'&second='+second
}
```

When the IFrame is finished loading the remote page it will automatically call showResult, because the onload attribute of the IFrame is configured to call the function. The showResult function will get the content from the IFrame and display it on the page.

Listing 4.2 Calling Hidden IFrame

```
<script type="text/javascript" src="http://o.aolcdn.com/dojo/
            1.3.0/dojo/dojo.xd.js.uncompressed.

<iframe src='iframe.jsp' id='iframe' onload='showResult()'
            style='display: none; visibility: hidden

<input id='first' value='1' onblur="clearResult()"/>
+
<input id='second' value='2' onblur="clearResult()" />
=
<span id='result'></span><br/>
<button onclick="calculateResult()">calculate</button>

<script type="text/javascript">
    function calculateResult(){
        var first = dojo.byId('first').value;
        var second = dojo.byId('second').value;
        var iframe = dojo.byId('iframe');
        iframe.src='iframe.jsp?first='+first+'&second='+second
    }
    function clearResult(){
        result.innerHTML = '';
    }
    function showResult(){
        var iframe = dojo.byId('iframe');
        var result = dojo.byId('result');
        var iframebody = extractIFrameBody(iframe);
        result.innerHTML = iframebody.innerHTML;
    }
    function extractIFrameBody(iFrameEl) {

        var doc = null;
        if (iFrameEl.contentDocument) { // For NS6
            doc = iFrameEl.contentDocument;
        } else if (iFrameEl.contentWindow) { // For IE5.5 and IE6
            doc = iFrameEl.contentWindow.document;
```

```
        } else if (iFrameEl.document) { // For IE5
            doc = iFrameEl.document;
        } else {
        //alert("Error: could not find sumiFrame document");
            return null;
        }
            return doc.body;
        }
</script>

function showResult(){
    var iframe = dojo.byId('iframe');
    var result = dojo.byId('result');
    var iframebody = extractIFrameBody(iframe);
    result.innerHTML = iframebody.innerHTML;
}
```

4.2.1.2   IFrames Using jQuery

Very few changes are needed to replace Dojo with jQuery in the IFrames example. showResult and calculateResult are the only two functions that need to be changed. dojo.byId is replaced by the dollar function in jQuery.

```
function calculateResult(){
    var first = $('#first').val();
    var second = $('#second').val();

    var iframe = $('#iframe')[0];
    iframe.src='iframe.jsp?first='+first+'&second='+second
}

function showResult(){
    var iframe = $('#iframe')[0];
    var result = $('#iframe')[0];
    var iframebody = extractIFrameBody(iframe);

    result.innerHTML = iframebody.innerHTML;
}
```

4.2.1.3   IFrames Example Without an Ajax Library

To run the IFrames example without an Ajax library, you just use document .getElementById to find elements of the page. This will not work as well in older browsers, but it will work in newer ones.

```
function calculateResult(){
    var first = document.getElementById('first').value;
    var second = document.getElementById('second').value;
    var iframe = document.getElementById('iframe');

    iframe.src='iframe.jsp?first='+first+'&second='+second
}

function showResult(){
    var iframe = document.getElementById('iframe');
    var result = document.getElementById('result');
    var iframebody = extractIFrameBody(iframe);

    result.innerHTML = iframebody.innerHTML;
}
```

■ 4.3 XMLHttpRequest (XHR)

XMLHttpRequest (XHR) is a DOM API that can be used to send an HTTP request to a web server from JavaScript. XHR is the most common way to make Ajax calls today. XHR has been the main driver in the adoption of Ajax. XHR allows for both GET and POST requests. Listing 4.3 shows how you can make Ajax calls using XHR. The function ajaxCall is called when the button is clicked. The function starts by checking to see if the window object contains an XMLHttpRequest. If it finds an XMLHttpRequest, then you can create a new XMLHttpRequest.

```
if (window.XMLHttpRequest){
    xmlhttp=new XMLHttpRequest();
```

If the window object doesn't contain an XMLHttpRequest object, then we check to see if the window object contains ActiveXObject. If ActiveXObject is available, then we create a new ActiveXObject.

```
    }else if (window.ActiveXObject){
        xmlhttp=new ActiveXObject("Microsoft.XMLHTTP");
    }
```

Next, we configure xmlhttp so that when the state changes it calls the function state-Change. Then we tell xmlhttp to open the calculator URL.

```
xmlhttp.onreadystatechange=stateChange;
xmlhttp.open("GET",url,true);
xmlhttp.send(null);
```

Listing 4.3 XMLHttpRequest

```
<script type="text/javascript">
var xmlhttp;
function ajaxCall(url){
    xmlhttp=null;
    if (window.XMLHttpRequest){
        xmlhttp=new XMLHttpRequest();
    }else if (window.ActiveXObject){
        xmlhttp=new ActiveXObject("Microsoft.XMLHTTP");
    }
    if (xmlhttp!=null){
        xmlhttp.onreadystatechange=stateChange;
        xmlhttp.open("GET",url,true);
        xmlhttp.send(null);
    }else{
        alert("Your browser does not support XMLHTTP.");
    }
}
function stateChange(){
    if (xmlhttp.readyState==4){// 4 = "loaded"
        if (xmlhttp.status==200){// 200 = "OK"
            document.getElementById('result')
                    .innerHTML=xmlhttp.responseText;
    }else{
            alert(Error:" + xmlhttp.status);
        }
    }
}
</script>
<button onclick="ajaxCall('works.html')">Click</button>
<div id="result"></div>
```

When the state of xmlhttp changes the callback function stateChange. When the ready state becomes 4 and the status becomes 200, the response from the Ajax call is ready.

```
if (xmlhttp.readyState==4){// 4 = "loaded"
    if (xmlhttp.status==200){// 200 = "OK"
        document.getElementById('result').innerHTML=xmlhttp
                .responseText;
```

■ 4.4   AJAX VIA AJAX LIBRARIES

Writing Ajax by hand can be very time consuming and error prone. Ajax Libraries make performing Ajax requests very easy. Libraries add several short-cuts, such as automatically creating a query string from all items in a form.

■ 4.4.1   Ajax via Dojo

In this example, we will look at a very simple Ajax calculator that was written using Dojo. Listing 4.4 shows a simple Ajax-based calculator that demonstrates many of the shortcuts provided by Dojo.

```
dojo.xhrGet({
     form:"calcultorform",
     content: dojo.formToObject("calcultorform"),
```

Listing 4.4 Ajax Using Dojo

```
<script type="text/javascript">
function calculateResult(){
     dojo.xhrGet({
          form:"calcultorform",
          content: dojo.formToObject("calcultorform"),
          load: function(data){
          dojo.byId('result').innerHTML = data;
          },
          error: function(msg){
            clear();
            alert('problem '+msg);
          }
     });
}
function clear(){
     dojo.byId('result').innerHTML='';
}

</script>

<form id="calcultorform" action="/ch4/e1/iframe.jsp">
     <input type="text" name="first" value="1" onblur="clear"/> +
     <input type="text" name="second" value="2" onblur="clear"/> =
     <span id='result'></span><br/>
</form>
<button onclick="calculateResult()">calculate</button>
```

Dojo uses the function `dojo.xhrGet` to perform Ajax calls. `dojo.xhrGet` takes an object as its only parameter. The attributes and functions of the object are used to configure and handle the Ajax call. In Listing 4.4 the `form` attribute is used. The `form` attribute lets you pass in the ID of a form whose action you wish to use as the URL of the Ajax request. Listing 4.4 also used the attribute `content` to specify an object containing the values that will make up the query string. The example in Listing 4.4 also used `dojo.formToObject` to read the `form` with id `calculatorform` and created an object containing the values of the `form`.

```
load: function(data){
      dojo.byId('result').innerHTML = data;
},
error: function(msg){
      clear();
      alert('problem '+msg);
}
```

When the Ajax call is completed, the callback function `load` will be called if there are no errors. If there are errors, then the function `error` will be called.

■ 4.4.2   Ajax via jQuery

In this example, we will show you how to write a simple Ajax calculator using jQuery. you will also learn about the jQuery `serialize` method, which is a shortcut for creating query strings for Ajax requests (see Listing 4.5).

```
var qString = $("#calcultorform").serialize();

$.get("/ch4/e1/iframe.jsp?"+ qString, null, loadResult);
```

As you can see in the preceding code snippet, `calculatorform` is serialized into a query string. Next, `$.get` is used to make an Ajax `get` request, with `loadResult` being called when the call completes.

Listing 4.5 Ajax Using jQuery

```
<script type="text/javascript"src="http://ajax.googleapis.com/ajax/
            libs/jquery/1.3.2/jquery.js"
<script type="text/javascript">
function calculateResult(){
      var qString = $("#calcultorform").serialize();

      $.get("/ch4/e1/iframe.jsp?"+ qString, null, loadResult);
}
```

```
function loadResult(data){
    $('#result')[0].innerHTML = data;
}

function clear(){
    $('result')[0].innerHTML='';

}
</script>
<form id="calcultorform" action="/ch4/e1/iframe.jsp">
    <input type="text" name="first" value="1" onblur="clear"/> +
    <input type="text" name="second" value="2" onblur="clear"/> =
    <span id='result'></span><br/>
</form>
<button onclick="calculateResult()">calculate</button>
```

■ 4.5 AJAX WORKING WITH JSON USING DOJO

As we learned in Chapter 3, JSON is a very powerful and convenient data format. Ajax often uses JSON because of the `json` call. This allows complex datatypes to be returned and easily parsed, with little wire overhead. JSON is often referred to as the X in Ajax, because it is commonly used as the payload when working with Ajax.

Once again we'll use the example of a simple Ajax-based calculator, but this time we will be using JSON for the response returned by the `json` call (see Listing 4.6).

```
dojo.xhrGet({
    form:"calcultorform",
    handleAs: "json",
    content: dojo.formToObject("calcultorform"),
    load: function(data){
        dojo.byId('result').innerHTML = data.result;
    },
```

The function `dojo.xhrGet` makes an Ajax call to the page with id `calculatorform`. The content of `calculatorform` is serialized into an object, which is used as the query string of the XHR request (see Listing 4.7). The result of the page is treated as JSON and the closure defined by `load` is called which pulls the result out of the returned data object and places it in the result span.

Listing 4.6 Ajax Working with JSON Using Dojo

```
<script type="text/javascript">
function calculateResult(){
    dojo.xhrGet({
        form:"calcultorform",
        handleAs: "json",
        content: dojo.formToObject("calcultorform"),
            load: function(data){
                dojo.byId('result').innerHTML = data.result;
        },
        error: function(msg){
            clear();
                alert('problem '+msg);
        }
    });
}

function clear(){
    dojo.byId('result').innerHTML='';
}
</script>
<form id="calcultorform" action="calculatorReturningJSON.jsp">
    <input type="text" name="first" value="1" onblur="clear"/> +
    <input type="text" name="second" value="2" onblur="clear"/> =
    <span id='result'></span><br/>
</form>
<button onclick="calculateResult()">calculate</button>


error: function(msg){
    clear();
    alert('problem '+msg);
}
```

If an error occurs while making the Ajax request, then call the `error` function to call `clear` and `alert` to inform the user of the error.

■ 4.5.1 Ajax Working with JSON in jQuery

Working with JSON in jQuery is very similar to Dojo.

```
var qString = $("#calcultorform").serialize();
$.getJSON("/ch4/e1/iframe.jsp?"+ qString, null, loadResult);
```

Listing 4.7 Ajax Working with JSON in jQuery

```javascript
<script type="text/javascript">
function calculateResult(){
    var qString = $("#calcultorform").serialize();

    $.getJSON("/ch4/e1/iframe.jsp?"+ qString, null, loadResult);
}

function loadResult(data, textStatus){
    if(textStatus == 'success')
        $('#result')[0].innerHTML = data.result;
    else
        alert('error');
}

function clear(){
    $('result')[0].innerHTML='';
}

</script>

<form id="calcultorform" action="/ch4/e1/iframe.jsp">
    <input type="text" name="first" value="1" onblur="clear"/> +
    <input type="text" name="second" value="2" onblur="clear"/> =
    <span id='result'></span><br/>
</form>
<button onclick="calculateResult()">calculate</button>
```

In the preceding code snippet, `calculatorform` is serialized into a query-string format. `getJSON` is then used to make an Ajax request, whose response is parsed as JSON and calls `loadResult`, when the call is completed.

■ 4.6   LIMITATIONS OF AJAX

Ajax requests have many limitations that can make implementation difficult. The first major limitation is that Ajax requests don't add a request to the browser history. If a user clicks the Back button after an Ajax request, he would expect the last action to be undone. Instead, clicking the Back button after an Ajax request often causes the page to revert to the last full page load. Workarounds for dealing with the Back button include using a hidden IFrame to add to the browser's history and changing the anchor of the URL. The anchor of a URL is traditionally used to scroll a user to a specific place on the screen when a page loads. In the URL http://example.com/index.html#myanchor, the anchor is myanchor.

Ajax requests are also limited by origin policy. This limitation is a security restriction that prevents Ajax requests from calling anywhere except from the location of the original request. The host, protocol, and port of all Ajax requests must be exactly the same as the original page. Changing the host, protocol, or port when making an Ajax request causes an error in the browser. Mash-ups attempt to bring together content from all over the Web. Often, mash-ups will proxy their Ajax requests through their originating web server so that the web server requests another domain, not the browser. IFrames are also used to create mash-ups. Each IFrame holds its own origin.

The final major limitation of Ajax is the two HTTP connection limit. This limit is especially restrictive when used with tabs. (The cloud is a combination of all tabs.) The good news is that browsers are starting to adopt higher maximum open request limits. Internet Explorer 8 has bumped the limit from two requests to six. This solves some of the problems, but large portals and mash-ups may still have this limitation.

■ 4.7   ADOPTION OF AJAX

The Ajax boom began soon after the amazing user experience provided by Google Maps. Figure 4.6 shows many of the key features of Google Maps that made it an eye-opening application for web developers. Some of the features include:

- When zooming and moving, the background map tiles load without refreshing the screen

■ **FIGURE 4.6**
Google Maps

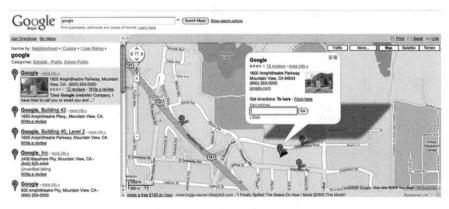

- Searches are done via Ajax calls without refreshing the screen
- You can drilldown into location information via Ajax calls without refreshing the screen

■ 4.7.1 Disadvantages of Ajax

Ajax introduces huge challenges to Search Engine Optimization (SEO). In general terms, SEO is the art of making your site appear as high as possible in search engine results. Search engines often struggle to follow JavaScript and Ajax calls. Ajax pages also have trouble with SEO because much of the indexable content is often no longer part of the original page load. In a Web 2.0 application, content such as help dialogs are often slowly loaded via Ajax. Advertising within your website can also be a huge challenge for Ajax applications. Advertisers often use the first page load to generate ad content. Ajax-based sites also tend to wait much longer before refreshing the page, which means customers will see the same advertisements for a longer period of time.

Bookmarking in Ajax-based pages can be very tricky, because more actions can take place between page loads. A standard bookmark returns you to the state of the original page load—before any user actions took place.

One of the most notable disadvantages of Ajax is that Ajax applications are not accessible to everyone. Older browsers often have limited support for Ajax. Mobile browsers may not correctly display or support XHR. To accommodate as many browsers as possible, you often have to make several forks in your code based on the browser used by the client. Using Ajax libraries can greatly help minimize the "forking" in your code, but they usually only support modern browsers.

■ 4.7.2 Advantages of Ajax

Ajax has many great advantages for web programming. The first major advantage is that Ajax allows for more information on a single page. Features such as full conceptual help, full license agreements, drilldown reporting details, and category breakdown figures can easily be added to a page through Ajax requests. Another great advantage of Ajax applications is that they are often much faster, because the original page load is not burdened with things like contextual help and drilldown information. Often, the Ajax payload is highly optimized in JSON, which leads to a significantly faster-feeling application. Ajax applications also feel more natural to users, because they behave more like desktop applications.

■ 4.8   COMPARISON OF EXISTING AJAX LIBRARIES

The following subsections briefly explain some of the more popular Ajax libraries, such as:

- Dojo
- ExtJS™
- Google Web Toolkit™ (GWT)
- jQuery
- Prototype Script.aculo.us
- SmartClient™
- SproutCore
- TIBCO® General Interface (GI)
- YUI

■ 4.8.1   Dojo

The Dojo toolkit is an Ajax Framework. Dojo offers several well-tested and extensible widgets called Dijits. Dijits are fully localized and available in more than a dozen languages. Dojo is very popular for large enterprise applications. A lot of Java Frameworks are compatible with Dojo, such as JSF, Struts2, and Spring MVC.

■ 4.8.2   ExtJS

ExtJS was originally built as an extension of YUI, but it also works with jQuery and Prototype, or it can be run independently. ExtJS is popular for making desktop-like applications.

■ 4.8.3   GWT

GWT is unique because it lets you write client coding in Java instead of JavaScript. The Java is converted to JavaScript at build time. This lets developers write Ajax applications in Java and use Java Objects in the browser.

■ 4.8.4   jQuery

Many new projects are choosing to use jQuery, whole popularity is growing rapidly. The jQuery user interface provides a few components, but you will need to download third-party components to fill in the gaps. However, the quality of third-party components varies.

■ 4.8.5 Prototype Script.aculo.us

Prototype is a small library that is often combined with Script.aculo.us to build Ajax applications. Rich components are not part of the core library, so you have to download them from third-parties. Use of Protype Script.aculo.us has declined over time.

■ 4.8.6 SmartClient

SmartClient is a very rich, drag-and-drop Ajax library. Several advanced features, such as database tools, require a commercial license. SmartClient can be a bit slow for some applications.

■ 4.8.7 SproutCore

SproutCore applications are designed around the Model-View-Controller (MVC) paradigm. SproutCore focuses on running Business Login in the browser.

■ 4.8.8 Tibco GI

Tibco GI uses a client-side XSL engine that can be really slow to load. You should be careful about where GI is used. GI is recommended for pages that you would traditionally write in Apple or Flash.

■ 4.8.9 YUI

YUI is a general-purpose Ajax library. Its performance and looks are fairly popular. YUI components are well-documented and easy to use.

■ 4.8.10 Understanding the Terms

There are many open source and non-open source projects that are designed to make writing Ajax applications easier. In this book, we generally use the term Ajax Library to talk about the projects. Often you will see JavaScript used instead of Ajax. In other cases you will see toolkit or framework instead of library. In general these terms can be used interchangeably. We prefer to use the term Ajax Library in this book.

■ 4.9 COMPREHENSIVE AJAX PROJECT

The final example in this chapter is a full-featured web applicaiton for taking online orders for cookies. The example will only be covered in Dojo due to spacing issues. The application consists of a tabbed pane with three tabs to divide the functionality. The tab, seen in Figure 4.7, lets users enter their delivery information. The select products tab, seen in Figure 4.8, lets users select the cookies. The order tab, seen in Figure 4.9, lets users submit their order and get an order confirmation.

■ **FIGURE 4.7**
Cookie Order—
Delivery Information

Delivery Information	Select Products	Order

Name:
Address:
City:
State:
Zip Code:
Email Address:

Previous   Next

■ **FIGURE 4.8**
Cookie Order—
Select Cookies

Delivery Information	Select Products	Order

Quantity (0-99)	Name	Price Each	Total Price
0	Chocolate Chip Cookie	$4.00	$0.00
0	Sugar Cookie	$3.70	$0.00
0	Oatmeal Raisin Cookie	$4.50	$0.00
0	Shortbread Cookie	$4.00	$0.00
0	Snickerdoodles	$4.00	$0.00
0	Peanut Butter Cookie	$4.25	$0.00

Previous   Next

■ **FIGURE 4.9**
Cookie Order—
Place Order

Delivery Information	Select Products	Order

To finalize order press "Submit Order"

Submit Order

Previous   Next

Dojo's client-side validation verifies that the data is valid before posting it to the server. It is always preferred to validate on the server side as well, because hackers can easily bypass client-side validation. For simplicity, server-side validation was omitted from this example. The first tab uses several types of validation, such as length, case, numeric, and required. Dijits do much of the heavy lifting when it comes to providing nice looking client-side validation. You can see in Figure 4.10 how Dijits add coloring and labeling to invalid data. The select products tab, as shown in Figure 4.11 also uses the Dijit `NumberSpinner` to collect the quantities of cookies. `NumberSpinner` is one of the UI components provided by Dijits.

■ **FIGURE 4.10**
Cookie Order—Dijit
Validation

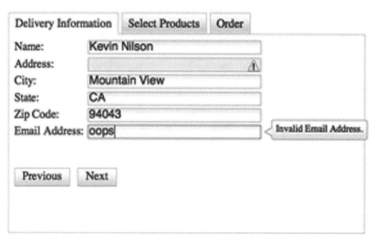

■ **FIGURE 4.11**
Cookie Order—
NumberSpinner

■ **FIGURE 4.12**
Cookie
Order—Order
Confirmation

The order tab can only be reached if all of the data in the previous two tabs is valid. If the user selects the order tab when invalid information exists in one of the first two tabs, then the user will be redirected to the first tab that contains an error. Once the user has correctly filled in all of the data, the third tab can be reached, as shown in Figure 4.9, Figure 4.12 shows the order confirmation for a successful order.

The following example consists of several source files:

- HTML file for UI
- JS for JavaScript client-side logic
- JSON for the configuration of products to sell
- JSP for server-side processing of an order

The HTML file in Listing 4.8 is fairly simple. It consists of a `div` with the ID `mainTabContainer` which holds the entire `TabContainer` for the example. This `div` has the dojoType `dijit.layout.TabContainer`. The `div`s, `Delivery-Info`, `Products`, and `Order` are the body of the three tabs. These `div`s have the dojoType `dijit.layout.ContentPane`.

The code in Listing 4.8 tells `dojo` to convert the `div` with dojoType `dijit.layout.TabContainer` to a tab container. The first key element is `djConfig="parseOneLoad:true"`. The second key element is the `dojo.require` statements that tell `dojo` to include any file needed to create a tab container. The final key element is setting the dojoType tab container to `dijit.layout .TabContainer` and setting each tab's dojoType to `dijit.layout.ContentPane`.

Listing 4.8 HTML for Ajax Order Form

```
<!DOCTYPE Doctype goes here>
<html xmlns="http://www.w3.org/1999/xhtml">
<head>
<meta http-equiv="content-type" content="application/xhtml+xml;
charset=UTF-8" />
<title>Example 5</title>

<script type="text/javascript"
src="http://o.aolcdn.com/dojo/1.3.0/dojo/dojo.xd.js.uncompressed.js"
       djConfig="parseOnLoad: true"></script>
       <script type="text/javascript">

    </script>
<script type="text/javascript" src="ch4e5dojo.js"></script>

<style type="text/css">
    @import
"http://o.aolcdn.com/dojo/1.3.0/dijit/themes/tundra/tundra.css";
    @import
"http://o.aolcdn.com/dojo/1.3.0/dojo/resources/dojo.css"
</style>

</head>
<body class="tundra">
    <div id="mainTabContainer" dojoType="dijit.layout.TabContainer"
        style="width:500px;height:300px">
        <div id="DeliveryInfo" dojoType="dijit.layout.ContentPane"
title="Delivery Information" selected="true">

            <form id="deliveryForm">
                <table>
                    <tr>
                        <td>Name:</td>
                        <td>
                            <input type="text" id="customerName"
name="customerName" value=""

dojoType="dijit.form.ValidationTextBox"
                                    trim="true"
                                    required="true"
                                    invalidMessage="Invalid
Name." />
                        </td>
                    </tr>
```

```
                         <tr>
                              <td>Address:</td>
                              <td>
                                   <input type="text"
id="customerAddress" name="customerAddress" value=""

dojoType="dijit.form.ValidationTextBox"
                                        trim="true"
                                        required="true"
                                        invalidMessage="Invalid
Address." />
                                   </td>
                         </tr>
                         <tr>
                              <td>City:</td>
                              <td>
                                   <input type="text"
id="customerCity" name="customerCity" value=""

dojoType="dijit.form.ValidationTextBox"
                                        trim="true"
                                        required="true"
                                        invalidMessage="Invalid
City." />
                                   </td>
                         </tr>
                         <tr>
                              <td>State:</td>
                              <td>
                                   <input type="text"
id="customerState" name="customerState" value=""

dojoType="dijit.form.ValidationTextBox"
                                        regExp="[A-Z]{2}"
                                        trim="true"
                                        required="true"
                                        uppercase="true"
                                        invalidMessage="Invalid
State." />
                                   </td>
                         </tr>
                         <tr>
                              <td>Zip Code:</td>
                              <td>
```

```
                                        <input type="text"
id="customerZip" name="customerZip" value=""

dojoType="dijit.form.ValidationTextBox"
                                    regExp="\d{5}"
                                    required="true"
                                    invalidMessage="Invalid Zip
Code." />
                    </td>
                </tr>
                <tr>
                    <td>Email Address:</td>
                    <td>
                                <input id="customerEmail"
type="text" id="customerEmail" name="customerEmail"  value=""
dojoType="dijit.form.ValidationTextBox"

regExpGen="dojox.validate.regexp.emailAddress"
                                    trim="true"
                                    required="true"
                                    invalidMessage="Invalid
Email Address." />

                    </td>
                </tr>
            </table>
        </form>

        <br/>
        <button dojoType="dijit.form.Button"
widgetId="deliveryPrevious"  enabled="false">Previous</button>
        <button dojoType="dijit.form.Button"
widgetId="deliveryNext" onclick="forward()" >Next</button>

    </div>
    <div id="Products" dojoType="dijit.layout.ContentPane"
        title="Select Products"  >
        <form id="orderForm">

            <table style="border-collapse:collapse"
border="1" id="tbl">
                <tr>
                    <th>Quantity (0-99)</th>
                    <th>Name</th>
                    <th>Price Each</th>
```

```
                     <th>Total Price</th>
               </tr>
            </table>
        </form>

        <br/>
        <button dojoType="dijit.form.Button"
widgetId="quantityPrevious" onclick="previous()" enabled="false"
>Previous</button>
        <button dojoType="dijit.form.Button"
widgetId="quantityNext" onclick="forward()">Next</button>
     </div>
     <div id="Order" dojoType="dijit.layout.ContentPane"
         title="Order">
        <div id="ordersummary">LOADING</div>
        <br/>
        <br/>

        <button dojoType="dijit.form.Button"
widgetId="orderButton" onclick="sendOrder()">Submit Order</button>
        <br/>
        <br/>
        <button dojoType="dijit.form.Button"
widgetId="orderPrevious" onclick="previous()">Previous</button>
        <button dojoType="dijit.form.Button"
widgetId="orderNext" onclick="forward()">Next</button>

     </div>
  </div>

</body>

</html>

<input type="text" id="customerCity" name="customerCity" value=""
     dojoType="dijit.form.ValidationTextBox" trim="true"
     required="true" invalidMessage="Invalid City." />

...

<input type="text" id="customerState" name="customerState" value=""
     dojoType="dijit.form.ValidationTextBox"
     regExp="[A-Z]{2}" trim="true" required="true"
     uppercase="true" invalidMessage="Invalid State." />

...
```

```
<input type="text" id="customerZip" name="customerZip" value=""
    dojoType="dijit.form.ValidationTextBox" regExp="\d{5}"
    required="true" invalidMessage="Invalid Zip Code." />
```

As you can see in the previous code snippet, Dijit also provides validation textboxes in which you specify fields like `trim` and `required`. Regular expression support is provided by using `regExp`. In this example, we used a regular expression to specify that a state must be two uppercase characters [A–Z] {2}. We also used a regular expression to specify that the zip code must be five digits 5\d{5}.

In the product information tab, JSON is used to configure what products are available for sale. Listing 4.9 shows the JSON coding used in this example. The root object contains one key, `products`, which is the same value of all of the products that are sold. Each product contains the `prodid`, `name`, and `price`. The creating the order page on the second tab is done by loading the products from the JSON file and adding them to the DOM (see Listing 4.10).

Listing 4.9 Product Information in JSON Format

```
{'products':[
    {'prodid':'a001', 'name':'Chocolate Chip Cookie', 'price': 4.00},
    {'prodid':'a002', 'name':'Sugar Cookie', 'price': 3.70},
    {'prodid':'a003', 'name':'Oatmeal Raisin Cookie', 'price': 4.50},
    {'prodid':'a004', 'name':'Shortbread Cookie', 'price': 4.00},
    {'prodid':'a005', 'name':'Snickerdoodles', 'price': 4.00},
    {'prodid':'a006', 'name':'Peanut Butter Cookie', 'price': 4.25},
]}
```

Listing 4.10 JavaScript for Ajax Order Form

```
dojo.require("dijit.form.ValidationTextBox");
    dojo.require("dojo.regexp");
    dojo.require("dojox.validate.regexp");
    dojo.require("dojo.parser");
    dojo.require("dijit.layout.ContentPane");
    dojo.require("dijit.layout.TabContainer");
    dojo.require("dijit.form.Button");
    dojo.require("dijit.form.NumberSpinner");
    dojo.require("dojo.currency");

    function updateQuantity(event){
```

```
        if(event==null)
            return;
        var widgetId = event.currentTarget.id;
        var didgetId = widgetId.substr("widget_".length);
        var spinner = dijit.byId(didgetId);
        if(spinner.isValid()){
            updateTotalPrice(didgetId.substr("quantity".length),
                spinner.value);
        }
}

function updateTotalPrice(prodid, quantity){
    for(i in products){
        if(products[i].prodid==prodid){
            var td = dojo.byId("totalprice"+prodid);
            var totalPrice=(products[i].price * quantity);
                td.innerHTML=dojo.currency.
            format(totalPrice, {currency: "USD"});
        }
    }
}

function configureTabListeners(){
  var tabs = dijit.byId("mainTabContainer");
  dojo.connect(tabs,"_transition", function(newPage, oldPage){
      if(newPage.containerNode.id == 'Order')
          updateOrderSummary();
});

}

function updateOrderSummary(){
  var container = dijit.byId('mainTabContainer');
        if(!deliverFormValid()){
            console.log('Deliver Information Is Not Valid');

            var tab = dijit.byId('DeliveryInfo');

            alert('Deliver Information Invalid');

            setTimeout(dojo.hitch(container,"selectChild",
                tab),0);
            //container.selectChild(tab);
            return;
        }
```

```
            var result = getProductCount();
            var tab = dijit.byId('Products');
            if(result == 'error'){
                    alert('Invalid Product Quantity');
                    setTimeout(dojo.hitch(container,"selectChild",
                        tab),0);
                    return;
            else if(result == 0){
                    alert('No Products Ordered');
                    setTimeout(dojo.hitch(container,"selectChild",
                        tab),0);
                    return;
            }

    }

    function getProductCount(){
      for(i in products){
            var spinner = dijit.byId("quantity"+products[i]
                .prodid);
            spinner.focus();
      }
      var quantity=0;
      for(i in products){
            var spinner = dijit.byId("quantity"+products[i]
                .prodid);
            if(!spinner.validate())
                    return 'error'
            quantity = quantity + spinner.value;
      }
      return quantity;
    }

    function deliverFormValid(){
        var formIds = new Array("customerName","customerAddress",
"customerCity","customerState","customerZip","customerEmail");

        for(i in formIds){
            dijit.byId(formIds[i]).focus();
        }

        for(i in formIds){
                if(!dijit.byId(formIds[i]).validate())
                        return false;
```

```
        }
            return true;
    }
    function sendOrder(){
        var deliveryQuery = dojo.formToQuery('deliveryForm')
        var orderQuery = dojo.formToQuery('orderForm')

            var query = deliveryQuery + orderQuery;
            alert(query)
    }

    function addEvents(){
        dojo.connect(dijit.byId("orderButton"), 'onClick',
            'sendOrder');
        //dojo.connect(dijit.byId("deliveryPrevious"), 'onClick',
            function(evt){back()});
        dojo.connect(dijit.byId("quantityPrevious"), 'onClick',
            function(evt){back()});
        dojo.connect(dijit.byId("orderPrevious"), 'onClick',
            function(evt){back()});

        dojo.connect(dijit.byId("deliveryNext"), 'onClick',
            function(evt){forward()});
        dojo.connect(dijit.byId("quantityNext"), 'onClick',
            function(evt){forward()});
        //dojo.connect(dijit.byId("orderNext"), 'onClick',
            function(evt){forward()});


    }

    function back(){
        dijit.byId('mainTabContainer').back();
    }

    function forward(){
        dijit.byId('mainTabContainer').forward();
    }

    dojo.addOnLoad(addEvents);
    dojo.addOnLoad(loadProducts);
    dojo.addOnLoad(configureTabListeners);

    var products;

    function loadProducts(){
```

```
dojo.xhrGet( {
    url: "products.json",
    handleAs: "json",
    load: function(responseObject, ioArgs) {
        products = responseObject.products;
        var table = dojo.byId('tbl');
        for ( i in products) {
            var tr = document.createElement("TR");
            var td = document.createElement("TD");
            var div = document.createElement("DIV");

            div.setAttribute("id", products[i].prodid);
            td.appendChild(div)
            tr.appendChild(td);

            td = document.createElement("TD");
            var celltext = document.
                    createTextNode(products[i].name);
            td.appendChild(celltext);
            tr.appendChild(td);

            td = document.createElement("TD");
            var celltext = document.createTextNode(dojo
                    .currency.format(products[i].price,
                    {currency: "USD"}));
            td.setAttribute("align", "right");
            td.appendChild(celltext);
            tr.appendChild(td);


            td = document.createElement("TD");
            td.setAttribute("id", "totalprice"+products[i].
                    prodid);
            var celltext = document.createTextNode(dojo
                    .currency.format(0, {currency: "USD"}));

            td.setAttribute("align", "right");
            td.appendChild(celltext);
            tr.appendChild(td);

            table.appendChild(tr);

            var quantitySpinner = new dijit.form.NumberSpin-
                    ner({
                value: 0,
```

```
                              smallDelta: 1,
                              constraints: { min:0, max:99, places:0 },
                              id: "quantity"+products[i].prodid,
                              style: "width:80px"
                        }, products[i].prodid );

                        dojo.connect(quantitySpinner,"onKeyUp",updateQua
                              ntity);

                        dojo.connect(quantitySpinner,"onClick",updateQua
                              ntity);

                        dojo.connect(quantitySpinner,"onBlur",update
                              Quantity);

                  }
            }
      });
}
```

The first step in creating a product page is to make an Ajax call to retrieve the JSON file products.json. The response to this request is handleAs:json, so the result is treated as JSON and parsed to an object. dojo.currency. format is used to format numbers to include a dollar sign and always appear with two decimal places. The spinner in the first column is created by a new calling dijit.form.NumberSpinner.

The following server-side code shown in Listing 4.11, for this example is very simple and is only used to verify the frontend.

Listing 4.11 Order Processing Form

```
name = request.getParameter("customerName");
queryString = request.getQueryString();
out.println("ORDER: "+queryString);

You <%=name%> for your order
```

■ 4.10   ADVANCED AJAX

After writing a few Ajax applications, you may be eager to dive into some more advanced Ajax topics not covered in this book. The following are a few areas we recommend you explore. You can try writing Ajax-enabled rich components. Most programmers only get to slightly modify or enhance existing components. You will learn a lot about browser quirks and usability when you write your own components. You could also write a jQuery plug-in for a jQuery UI library. Accessibility is another area you could explore. Writing games is a very challenging area that could be a lot of fun.

■ 4.11 SUMMARY

Ajax has only been around for less than a decade, but in that short time it has become highly influential in the advances of the Web. Web 2.0 applications are rich in Ajax to focus webpages on user interaction. Ajax makes it possible for a webpage to retrieve additional data from webservers by making requests for more data in the background. Several Ajax Libraries have been developed to simplify writing Ajax applications. As the Web evolves Ajax usage grows at an amazing rate.

CHAPTER 5

Productivity and Testing Tools

In This Chapter:

- Which Tools Are Best?
- Google Wave
- Yahoo Pipes
- Dapper
- Assorted Open Source Tools from Google
- Miscellaneous Productivity Tools
- Twitter
- The MIT SIMILE Project
- Web 2.0 Applications and Product Suites
- Build Automation and Testing Tools
- Benchmarking Tools
- Source Code Management Tools
- Using DTrace for Web 2.0 Applications
- Industry Perspective and Business Focus

In this chapter, we'll look at several "no coding required" tools for improving your productivity, and tools for building frameworks, and that let you write unit tests for testing your code. Although many of these tools are not considered Web 2.0 tools, they're included here because developing Web 2.0 applications often requires using more "traditional" tools to help you share code with other team members (especially if they are located remotely).

Since an in-depth discussion of every tool is beyond the scope of this book, this chapter will take a broad look at several of the more popular tools. This approach has two advantages: First, you will get to know the names of various tools that are available. Second, an overview will help you decide regarding which tools are not suited for your needs. After you decide which tools you want, you can get additional information from their home pages.

The first part of this chapter introduces you to Google Gadgets and Google Wave, and in Chapter 6 you'll learn how to write Google Gadgets for your applications.

Next, we'll discuss productivity ("no coding required") tools, which usually provide a drag-and-drop mechanism for generating content in a web browser. Some of these tools also have program support that lets you invoke your predefined entities from other applications and mash-ups. In particular, Yahoo Pipes provides Yahoo Query Language (YQL) support, which vastly increases the capability of user-defined pipes. In addition, Yahoo Pipes has been integrated with SUN Zembly (discussed in Chapter 7), which is a tool that provides social networking and mash-up capabilities. This type of tool integration lets users create more powerful and richer web applications.

After that we'll discusses Twitter, Twitter plug-ins for Firefox, and examples of how you can use Twitter APIs to retrieve information about a user's tweets.

Finally, we'll discuss open source build framework tools and testing tools that help you compile, test, and deploy your code. These tools perform tasks on your behalf, and they usually provide summary and detail reports so that other developers and managers can see the results of automated tests.

Some of the examples in this chapter require familiarity with XML, and, if necessary, you can read the appropriate sections in Chapter 3. Although many Web 2.0 tools and products work primarily with JSON, keep in mind that the majority of build frameworks and testing tools (and many other tools) use XML-based configuration files, and you might find yourself working with XML more than you anticipated.

■ 5.1   WHICH TOOLS ARE BEST?

The answer depends heavily on your specific requirements. Since Web 2.0 stimulates the development of a lot of new tools, you need an efficient strategy for finding the tools that will be of greatest use to you. Fortunately, several companies maintain websites that list their experimental tools and often provide information about their goals and milestones, and sometimes provide access to the source code for their tools.

The following sites are good places to learn about interesting new tools:

• Mozilla labs: http://labs.mozilla.com/
• Google code: http://code.google.com/
• Adobe labs: http://labs.adobe.com/
• Yahoo labs: http://developer.yahoo.com/
• IBM: http://www.ibm.com/developerworks/

The tools in this chapter are discussed in a broad fashion, so if you're thinking about adopting any of them in job-related tasks, it's important that you read the documentation about these tools to find out more information to help you evaluate these tools. If you are a developer, assess these tools in terms of their support for your "must have" features, their extensibility, and their program support.

In addition, the tools in this chapter have been chosen with the following criteria in mind:

• they provide useful functionality
• their ease of use
• their widespread adoption
• they're growing in popularity

However, there are several points to keep in mind. First, there are many other Web 2.0 tools available that provide a variety of features and functionality, which means that we can only cover a fraction of those tools in this book.

Second, software companies sometimes invest a significant amount of time and effort (and money) to improve existing tools, and other companies will release newer tools (with better functionality) as open source projects.

Third, by the time new tools become available, you might have to update your entire application, not just the part that uses one of these tools.

Fourth, your company might have an investment in a technology stack that precludes replacing individual components, even if those newer components have superior functionality. In other words, even if you find great new tools, you might not be able to use them.

Fifth, some tools, such as the Firefox browser, are available on several major platforms (Windows, MacIntosh, and Linux), whereas others are only supported on one platform (Windows). Sometimes a "great" new tool on one platform might actually have fewer features than a comparable tool that's widely available on a different platform.

Sixth, developers always have their preferred list of tools, and they can be very passionate about them. While other people's opinions can be valuable, it's important for you to get some "hands-on" experience with any tool before you decide whether or not you want to use it. Keep in mind that there are open source tools that have become *de facto* standards, even though they are not necessarily the best tools in their category.

Despite these caveats, investing your time to look at the tools in this chapter is not wasted, because they do provide powerful functionality. Some companies employ people whose job is to learn about and research existing newly released tools just to make recommendations on them.

One advantage to learning about these productivity tools is that many of them can be used by people who do not necessarily have a strong technical background.

■ 5.2 GOOGLE WAVE

Google Wave is a collaboration tool that was announced at the Google I/O conference in San Francisco, in May 2009. The Google Wave home page is: http://wave.google.com

The Google Wave project began in 2007 and was released as an open source tool in late 2009. The Google Wave development team is based in Sydney, Australia, and two of the primary engineers of this product were also involved in the development of Google Maps™.

Google Wave provides a collaborative environment that combines various aspects and elements of email, maps, photos, videos, and voice communication. Users can participate in individual waves and leverage the instant messaging and social networking capabilities of Google Wave. On September 29, 2009, Google released a public version of Google Wave with 100,000 public accounts, along with a set of featured extensions that can be found here: http://wave.google.com/help/wave/extensions.html

A wave starts with a "conversation," which is a lightweight structure and a set of users, and the entire conversation is a shared object (hosted on the server), with all user replies available to all participants. A wave is a hosted conversation that enhances traditional email by providing more functionality.

In fact, a wave is a tree-like structure of messages, and you can restrict access to any subtree in that structure. Google Wave is built entirely on Google Web Toolkit (GWT), which means that developers can write code in Java, either on a desktop or on a mobile device. Google Wave runs in a browser, just as GWT does, with a small amount of extra code required.

Google Wave facilitates both discussion and content collaboration. For example, you can send meeting notes to a list of recipients in a wiki-like fashion on a wave, which lets recipients add comments and updates to the meeting notes. In addition, everyone participating in the wave can see any additions or made modifications to the current wave and respond to them.

One sample application built on the Google App Engine (GAE) is a blogging site that lets you embed waves on a blog. The wave can include both text and images. Instead of going to the blog site, users can respond to a blog entry from their Google Wave client and the response will appear on the blog site.

This functionality is useful for discussion sites and community forums, and for developers, because they can provide useful functionality with very little code.

Moreover, Google Wave can be used in a social networking tool, such as Orkut, to do the following:

• create a Google wave in Orkut
• use contacts other than your Google Wave contacts
• embed a search panel in a Google wave in Orkut

Google Wave support is also available for Android devices. See the appendices for useful links regarding Google Wave, including demos and sample code.

■ 5.2.1 Google Wave Features

Google Wave includes support for the following:

• instant message (IM) – style conversations
• playback functionality
• private reply capability
• creating photo albums
• embedded multimedia

Google Wave is currently only available in English, but there will be support for additional languages in the future. Google Wave provides a set of APIs that lets developers create extensions in a manner that is somewhat analogous to extending Firefox with plug-ins.

Google Wave also supports robots, which are server-side programs that participate in waves. Robots can "watch" what you type and take clusters of words to match against server-side content to make suggestions and corrections to the text. Note that a Google Search extension also lets you perform Google searches inside a Google wave, and there is a robot that provides spellchecking functionality.

You can also embed any OpenSocial gadget (discussed in Chapter 8) in a Google wave, and you can make that gadget live and collaborative. Google Wave has been integrated with Moodle® and Adobe® Flex®, and there is also a jQuery plug-in (called jWave™) available for Google Wave.

See the appendices for numerous links regarding Google Wave. In addition, the Google Wave section in Chapter 12 covers creating a robot in Google Wave.

■ 5.3 YAHOO PIPES

Yahoo Pipes is a free online service that lets you take content from multiple websites and create a customized view of that content that suits your needs. With Yahoo Pipes, you can create mash-ups in a visual editor using JSON, XML, RSS, and ATOM data. Yahoo Pipes is based on YUI (Yahoo's Ajax toolkit), and it is similar to the Unix "pipe" command in the sense that the output of one or more components becomes the input of another component. Thus, a Yahoo pipe consists of dragging and dropping the operations of one or more Yahoo components onto a "canvas," and then linking those components by specifying which component's output is the input for another component.

Yahoo Pipes supports several powerful capabilities. For example, you can manually specify a URL inside any Yahoo Pipes component to retrieve content from the Internet. Another powerful feature is the support for YQL (Yahoo's SQL-like syntax) that can be embedded in any Yahoo Pipes component.

Yahoo Pipes appeals to nontechnical people because of its drag-and-drop style of creating pipes, which doesn't require users to write code. Yahoo Pipes also appeals to developers because you can programmatically invoke a Yahoo pipe from another web page. Thus, Yahoo Pipes leverages its pipe-oriented design in a way that lets you create sophisticated Yahoo pipes quickly and easily.

Some of the advantages of Yahoo Pipes are:

- no coding required (but the optional YQL supports custom code)
- pipes are constructed via simple drag-and-drop operations
- pipes are easy to create and offer powerful and useful functionality
- other applications can access your pipe
- pipes can generate output as XML, JSON, KML, and other formats
- pipes created by others are accessible
- existing pipes are easily cloned

Yahoo Pipes is being used in an increasing number of web sites, and this trend will undoubtedly continue as people discover the capabilities of this tool.

■ 5.3.1 A Simple Yahoo Pipe

The following example illustrates how to create a Yahoo pipe that acts as a simple search engine to find a set of cars within a given radius of a zip code.

Step 1:   Go to http://pipes.yahoo.com/pipes/pipe.edit and click the Create a pipe button

Step 2:   Drag a Google Base widget from the Source to the Canvas

Step 3:   Use your mouse to connect the Google Base widget to the Pipe Output widget

Step 4:   Select Vehicles for the Find input field; Mustang for the With keywords input field; 20 miles for the Within input field; and enter your zip code in the lower-right input field

Step 5:   Click on the Pipe Output widget

The results of this pipe will appear in a scrollable list below the Pipe Output widget. (Note that you might need to change some of the criteria to generate a set of results.) As you scroll through the results list, you can click on each item for more details, including a contact phone number. You can also modify any of the input fields and then click the Refresh button to see the new set of results. If you want to save this Yahoo pipe, simply click the Save button at the top of the page.

■ 5.3.2 Using YQL in Yahoo Pipes

The Yahoo pipe example in the previous section illustrates how easily you can create Yahoo pipes without writing code. You can also embed Yahoo Query Language (YQL) statements in the components of a Yahoo pipe, which is a powerful extension to Yahoo Pipes.

You can find more information on YQL APIs here:
http://developer.yahoo.com/yql/

5.3.2.1 YQL SELECT *Statements and Online Samples*

The following is a simple example of a YQL select statement:

```
select * from html where url=http://finance.yahoo.com/q?s=yhoo"
```

Note how you can query against URLs, which means that a tremendous amount of Internet sites are accessible via YQL.

You can find more YQL statement examples here:
http://developer.yahoo.net/blog/archives/2009/04/yql_execute.html

5.3.2.2 *YQL and Open Data Tables*

A YQL "open data table" is actually an XML file that contains the following information:

- authentication and security options
- a sample query
- a YQL data structure
- pagination options

For example, launch your browser and navigate to the following URL:
http://www.yqlblog.net/samples/helloworld.xml

Here is the XML data that will be rendered in your browser:

```
<?xml version="1.0" encoding="UTF-8"?>
<table xmlns="http://query.yahooapis.com/v1/schema/table.xsd">
<meta>
    <sampleQuery>select * from {table} where a='cat' and b='dog';
    </sampleQuery>
  </meta>
  <bindings>
    <select itemPath="" produces="XML">
```

```
    <urls>
      <url>http://fake.url/{a}</url>
    </urls>
    <inputs>
        <key id='a' type='xs:string' paramType='path'
required="true" />
        <key id='b' type='xs:string' paramType='variable'
required="true" />
    </inputs>
    <execute><![CDATA[
      // Your server-side javascript goes here
      response.object = <item>
        <url>{request.url}</url>
        <a>{a}</a>
        <b>{b}</b>
      </item>;
    ]]></execute>
  </select>
 </bindings>
</table>
```

Note the `execute` element, which defines a CDATA section that contains executable JavaScript code that is executed on the server as E4X. In this example, the terms {a} and {b} are variables that require values before you can execute the code in the CDATA section.

For example, when a and b are assigned the values cat and dog, respectively, the result of executing the code in this CDATA section can be found here:
http://developer.yahoo.com/yql/console/?q=use%20%22http%3A%2F%2Fyqlblog.net%2Fsamples%2Fhelloworld.xml%22%3Bselect%20*%20from%20helloworld%20where%20a%3D%22cat%22%20and%20b%3D%22dog%22%3B%0A

The preceding URL contains buttons to select XML output or JSON output, after which you click on the "test" button in order to see the generated output.

You can find more information about open data tables here:
http://developer.yahoo.com/yql/guide/yql-opentables-chapter.html

5.3.2.3 Yahoo Widgets

The Yahoo Widgets home page is: http://widgets.yahoo.com/tools/

This website provides you with links to download the Software Development Kit (SDK) and create your own Yahoo Widgets. You can also search for pre-defined widgets and download a set of recommended Yahoo Widgets.

5.3.2.4 Combining YQL with Other Tools

You can create some interesting functionality by combining Yahoo Pipes with other tools and the following technologies:

- jQuery and microformats
- HTML5
- GWT (see Chapter 14)

■ 5.4 DAPPER

Dapper is another very good (and free) online tool that is similar to Yahoo Pipes. Its home page is: http://www.dapper.net/

With Dapper, you create a "Dapp" by navigating to web sites and selecting content (using a virtual browser) to include in your Dapp. The input data types for a Dapp include:

- XML
- RSS feeds
- Google Gadgets
- Google Maps
- iCalendar
- Images

The five-step process for creating a Dapp is as follows:

1. the start page
2. collecting sample pages
3. selecting content
4. previewing the feed
5. saving the feed

DapperFox can "RSS-ify any Website," and let you create an RSS feed from sites such as Facebook or YouTube. Dapper also provides rudimentary support for RDF-based web page enhancements, and a link that shows you how to "semantify your website" is here: http://www.dapper.net/semantify

If you are creating a PHP site, follow these two steps for "semantifying" your website:

Step 1: Create Dapps for your site with field names from the supported RDF namespaces

Step 2: Implement a custom code on your PHP site for every Dapp you create.

Now, whenever a search engine robot visits one at your pages with the code, Dapper will send a version of the page with embedded semantics from the Dapp.

■ 5.4.1 Creating a Simple Dapp

The starting page for creating a Dapp can be found here:
http://www.dapper.net/dapp-factory.jsp
You can create a simple Dapp as follows:

Step 1: Specify the input source (URL or RSS feed)

Step 2: Select a data format (such as XML, RSS, Google Gadget, or Google Map)

Step 3: Preview the resulting feed

Step 4: Save your Dapp

For example, create a Dapp with http://www.yahoo.com as the input source and Dapper XML as the data format. Click on Next, and when you arrive at the Yahoo website enter a term in the Search field, and then select that term as a Dapper input variable. After you create a Dapp, you can change the data format (e.g., Google Gadget instead of XML).

■ 5.5 ASSORTED OPEN SOURCE TOOLS FROM GOOGLE

In this section, we'll look at the following Google open source projects:

• Google Gears
• Google Native Client
• Google O3D

Afterward, we'll discuss Google Ajax, Google Playground, and Google Sandbox.

■ 5.5.1 Google Gears

Google Gears is an open source project that enhances your web browser to create more powerful web applications. Google Gears lets you store data in a local database, and improve performance by running JavaScript in the background. Google Gears is available for Windows XP and Windows Vista, MacIntosh, and Linux operating systems, and browser support includes Firefox, Safari, and Opera. You can install Google Gears on any of these systems here:

http://gears.google.com/

After you install Google Gears, you can run sample applications from:
http://code.google.com/apis/gears/sample.html

The applications provide a variety of features. For example, Gearpad is a web-based notepad, and RunningMan is an application that uses Google Gears on Android. Some of these applications require additional software. For example, you need to install a PHP server and MySQL to use Gearpad. Check the appendices for links to a developer tutorial and a summary of the Google Gears APIs.

■ 5.5.2 Google Native Client

Google Native Client lets you invoke 80×86 native code in web applications. Its home page is:

http://code.google.com/p/nativeclient/

Google Native Client gives you the ability to run popular games, such as *Quake* and *XaoS*, in a browser. This early stage project has several objectives, including portability, security, and browser neutrality, and it is available (along with an SDK) for download for several platforms, including Microsoft Windows, Linux, and MacIntosh.

Google recommends Firefox 3.x for running the examples as Native Client modules. If you want to develop your own modules, you will need platform-specific tools, such as XCode for MacIntosh and Visual Studio for Microsoft Windows.

The next two sections show you how to run Native Client applications from the command line and how to install Native Client in Firefox. In both cases, the examples illustrate the commands for Microsoft Windows, which means that you will need to modify these commands for Linux and MacIntosh systems.

5.5.2.1 Launching Google Native Client

You need Python (version 2.5 is recommended) to run the examples on your machine and a local HTTP server.

Complete the following steps to setup Google Native Client:

Step 1: Download the appropriate file from:
http://code.google.com/p/nativeclient/wiki/Downloads

Step 2: Uncompress the Native Client file into a convenient directory

Step 3: Open a command shell and enter the following command in Windows:

```
cd installation_dir\nacl\googleclient\native_client\
tests\earth
```

Step 4: Launch the Google Earth™ client as follows:

```
python run.py
```

If everything is set up correctly, a spinning globe will be rendered in a pop-up window.

Because Native Client code is frequently updated, it's a good idea to choose a directory name that includes the date of the distribution. For example, in Windows, choose a directory such as c:/nacl_windows_0.1_2009_04_23.

5.5.2.2 Installing the Plug-In

Step 1: Download Native Client as described in the previous section and then close all Firefox browser sessions

Step 2: Open a command shell and enter the following two commands in Microsoft Windows:

```
cd installation_dir\nacl\googleclient\native_client
scons.bat –prebuilt firefox_install
```

Make sure you enter "y" when prompted to continue.

Note: if you are using Windows Vista, please see the additional installation instructions at: http://nativeclient.googlecode.com/svn/data/docs_tarball/nacl/googleclient/native_client/documentation/platform-windows.html

Step 3: After the installation is complete, launch a Firefox browser session and go to:

http://nativeclient.googlecode.com/svn/data/docs_tarball/nacl/googleclient/native_client/documentation/getting_started.html#plug-in

Step 4: Start a local HTTP server (if one isn't already running) by opening a command shell and entering the following two commands:

```
cd installation_dir\nacl\googleclient\native_client
python tools\httpd.py
```

Step 5: Navigate to the following HTML page: http://localhost:5103/scons-out/nacl/staging/examples.html/

Click on the bottom-left link to see the Mandelbrot viewer page, which has a Native Client implementation of a Mandelbrot set.

■ 5.5.3 Google O3D

Google O3D is an open source browser plug-in that lets you create and render three-dimensional graphics in a browser. Its home page is:
http://code.google.com/apis/o3d/

Perform the following steps to set up Google O3D:

Step 1: Download the plug-in from:
http://tools.google.com/dlpage/o3d/eula.html/

Step 2: Accept the license agreement

After O3D is installed, experiment with the O3D samples at:
http://code.google.com/apis/o3d/docs/samplesdirectory.html

The appendices contain links for the complete Google O3D source code and information about supported graphics cards.

■ 5.5.4 Google Ajax, Playground, and Sandbox

Google provides a vast assortment of APIs and sample code that you can test and experiment with online.

5.5.4.1 Google Ajax APIs

The Google Ajax APIs for the following Google projects are available here:
http://code.google.com/apis/ajax/

- Google Maps
- Google Ajax Search
- Google Ajax Feed
- Google Visualization
- Google Ajax Language
- Ajax Libraries
- Google Earth

Each of these products contains additional links for developer guides, sample code, FAQs, and products that have been built on top of these products.

The Google playground home page is:
http://code.google.com/apis/ajax/playground/

The parent link for the Google Playground is the Google Ajax APIs link that was discussed previously. However, this website is very useful because it provides a text area where you can edit, run, and debug code for a number of APIs, including the products listed earlier.

The Developer Sandbox at Google I/O is a website built with applications by using Google I/O technologies and products features. The website is:
http://code.google.com/events/io/2009/sandbox.html

■ 5.5.5 Google Innovation

In December 2009, Google held a news conference at the Computer History Museum (located in Mountain View, California) to unveil several interesting products that clearly demonstrated Google's focus on innovation and its emergence as a significant force in the real-time web.

For example, Google Goggles provides object recognition technology that can recognize a wide assortment of objects, such as consumer products, landmarks, artwork, and also plain text. Users can take pictures of objects with their mobile phone and then those pictures scanned for text in order to return search results (based on the text) to the user.

Google Suggest™ provides context-related information that is relevant to the user performing a search. For example, a query with the initial letters "re" returns different results in different cities ("Red Sox" for Boston and "REI" for San Francisco).

Google has voice recognition technology on mobile devices, enabling users to speak entire sentences in English that are then translated almost instantly into Spanish. Voice-based search capability is also available in Mandarin and Japanese, and many other languages will be available in 2010.

Google Local enables users to see local businesses (as well as their ratings) that are in close proximity to a user's physical location.

Google Real Time search provides a list of search results and also a scrollable list of real-time updates, and this functionality is already available on Android and iPhone.

Google has formed partnerships with Twitter, Facebook, and MySpace, which will enable Google to display real-time updates from Twitter, Facebook updates, and MySpace users. Note that users can alter their privacy settings, thereby changing the information that is displayed in Google searches.

■ 5.6 MISCELLANEOUS PRODUCTIVITY TOOLS

This section gives you an overview of some productivity tools, and links to get additional information about the tools that interest you.

Yahoo® Fire Eagle™ is a free online tool that lets you show your location information on your blog (among other things). Its home page is:
http://fireeagle.yahoo.net/

Fire Eagle lets you update your location by various means, such as a web browser or a mobile device. You can also control the degree of information about your location (exact location versus only the city). Fire Eagle uses OAuth protocol (discussed in Chapter 8) for authorizations, and it can interact with other tools, such as Twitter.

Fire Eagle also provides Friends on Fire™, which lets you share your location with your friends on Facebook: http://apps.facebook.com/on-fire/

The home page for the Fireshot plug-in is:
http://screenshot-program.com/fireshot/

The Fireshot plug-in lets you take a partial or full screen capture of any website, save that screen capture, and graphically annotate the saved image with text. Moreover, you can save screen captures, print them, or email them to other people.

Note that the Fireshot plug-in is only available for the Windows platform for Firefox (versions 2.x and 3.x) and Internet Explorer. You can also purchase Fireshot Pro, which provides additional functionality, for USD $34.95 (see their home page for details). You can use Fireshot Pro for a free 30-day trial period, and if you decide not to purchase Fireshot Pro at the end of that period, Fireshot automatically reverts to the free version of Fireshot.

After installing Fireshot and restarting Firefox, you will see the Fireshot icon in the top-right corner of your browser.

Whenever you want to capture a screenshot of a website, simply click on the Fireshot plug-in (if sound is on, you will hear a clicking sound similar to a camera taking a picture). You will see a new browser-sized pop-up window with menu options that let you make annotations directly on your screen capture.

A video that shows you how to capture a page using Fireshot can be found at: http://screenshot-program.com/fireshot/demo.php

Juice™ is a Firefox browser sidebar (developed by Linkool International®): http://juiceapp.com/

Juice 0.1.8 requires Firefox 3.0, and after installing Juice and restarting Firefox, you will see the Juice icon in the top-right corner of your browser.

Whenever you highlight a term, Juice retrieves information from multiple sources (including Google News™, YouTube, and Wikipedia®) and displays a summary of the information that is relevant to the highlighted term. When you navigate to a website, simply click on the Juice icon and you will see additional information about that website.

Juice uses a combination of natural language processing and a dictionary to generate meaningful semantic results. Juice continually updates its own repository of terms with new keywords to improve the relevance and accuracy of its search results. See the Juice home page for additional functionality that may be useful to you.

Other Firefox plug-ins that can produce integrated search results (such as Briteclick and CoolPreviews™) can be found here: https://addons.mozilla.org/

DejaClick™ is a browser plug-in from AlertSite® that lets you manage bookmarks. Its home page is: http://www.dejaclick.com/

DejaClick also lets you record and bookmark your browser activities, after which you can replay the sequence of your activities. Currently, Deja-Click is only available for Firefox.

Adobe® Dreamweaver® is a commercial what-you-see-is-what-you-get (WYSIWYG) editor that provides drag-and-drop functionality to create HTML pages. Its home page is:
http://www.adobe.com/products/dreamweaver

With Dreamweaver, you can alternate between creating content for an HTML page and viewing the output of that HTML page.

The first step is to create a free account (if you do not already have one) so that you can log in and download Dreamweaver. The download file is large (360 MB for Windows and over 600 MB for MacIntosh), so make sure you have enough time to complete the download. You will receive an email notification that contains a link to a video overview of Dreamweaver. Keep in mind that your free trial period ends 30 days after you install Dreamweaver.

More information is available at the Adobe Dreamweaver developer center:

http://www.adobe.com/devnet/dreamweaver/

■ 5.7 TWITTER

Twitter is a free online tool that lets people post text messages (called "tweets") up to 140 characters in length, which is similar to SMS-based text messaging on cell phones. You can create a Twitter account here:

http://www.twitter.com

Currently, there are more than 11 thousand applications based on the Twitter API, and although most of them are primarily for entertainment, there are useful Twitter-based productivity tools and some with potential for monetization.

If you are primarily interested in business use, there are utilities for using Twitter with Microsoft® Outlook™, and for scanning keywords, sharing photos, scheduling tweets, and conducting straw polls. More details about these Twitter utilities can be found here:

http://blogs.techrepublic.com.com/hiner/?p=1697

Twitter recently announced support for Twitter lists, which enable you to group people together in a list. You can create multiple (public or private) lists, and people can subscribe to your Twitter lists.

Although Twitter began as a Ruby-on-Rails (RoR) application, the Twitter development team moved some of the back-end code to Scala (whose roots are in Java) to improve performance and scalability. Specifically, the Ruby-based queueing system for communication has been replaced by a Scala–based system.

Scala provides other advantages to Twitter, such as better support for threads (Ruby only supports green threads), long-lived processes, and the ability to run on multicore servers. An example of a Scala Twitter client can be found here:

http://github.com/dcbriccetti/talking-puffin/tree/master

There are also Java-based tools that can use the Twitter APIs. One such tool is Twitter4J, which you can download (binary and source code) from:

http://yusuke.homeip.net/twitter4j/en/index.html#download

If you are comfortable with the Java programming language, look at the Java class User.java in the Twitter4J library to see how a user in Twitter4J is represented.

See the appendices for additional Twitter tools, including Firefox plugins such as Twitbin, Tweetbar, TwitterNotifier, TwittyTunes, and Twitterbar.

■ 5.7.1 Invoking Twitter APIs

The Twitter APIs are available on the following wiki page:

http://apiwiki.twitter.com/

This website contains links to a number of topics, including FAQs, security, and the REST, and search-related APIs for Twitter.

The documentation for Streaming APIs describes a number of interesting Twitter APIs, many of which are currently under development. The streaming APIs have limited availability, and access to these APIs is granted on a case-by-case basis. Nevertheless, these APIs might provide useful functionality, so it's worth your time to periodically check on their status. In addition, these APIs can be used in conjunction with Twitter4J, which is a Java-based library for Twitter.

5.7.1.1 API for Accessing User Tweets

You can access a user's Twitter timeline with the following API call:

http://twitter.com/statuses/user_timeline/some-user-account-name.xml?count=n

For example, if we replace some-user-account-name.xml with ocampesa2.xml (which is a fictitious Twitter account) and specify a value of 5 for n, we will see an XML document similar to the one in Listing 5.1.

Listing 5.1

```
<?xml version="1.0" encoding="UTF-8" ?>
- <statuses type="array">
- <status>
  <created_at>Sun Sep 06 06:46:47 +0000 2009</created_at>
  <id>3794598334</id>
  <text>74 indispensable qualities of success:
      http://bit.ly/14UI4D</text>
  <source>web</source>
  <truncated>false</truncated>
  <in_reply_to_status_id />
  <in_reply_to_user_id />
  <favorited>false</favorited>
  <in_reply_to_screen_name />
- <user>
  <id>5616702</id>
  <name>Oswald Campesato</name>
  <screen_name>ocampesa2</screen_name>
  <location />
  <description />
  <profile_image_url>http://s.twimg.com/a/1252097501/images/
default_profile_normal.png</profile_image_url>
  <url />
  <protected>false</protected>
  <followers_count>49</followers_count>
  <profile_background_color>9ae4e8</profile_background_color>
  <profile_text_color>000000</profile_text_color>
  <profile_link_color>0000ff</profile_link_color>
  <profile_sidebar_fill_color>e0ff92</profile_sidebar_fill_color>
  <profile_sidebar_border_color>87bc44</profile_sidebar_border_color>
  <friends_count>119</friends_count>
  <created_at>Sun Apr 29 00:06:06 +0000 2007</created_at>
  <favourites_count>1</favourites_count>
  <utc_offset>-28800</utc_offset>
  <time_zone>Pacific Time (US & Canada)</time_zone>
  <profile_background_image_url>http://s.twimg.com/a/1252097501/
images/themes/theme1/bg.gif</profile_background_image_url>
  <profile_background_tile>false</profile_background_tile>
  <statuses_count>86</statuses_count>
  <notifications />
  <verified>false</verified>
  <following />
```

```
    </user>
    </status>
+ <status>
+ <status>
+ <status>
+ <status>
    </statuses>
```

The contents of Listing 5.1 are straightforward, so we don't need a line-by-line discussion of its contents. Suffice it to say that you can determine tweet-specific information that users have posted, along with the people they follow (and who follow them), and other bits of information.

The XML document in Listing 5.1 was generated by manually entering the following string into a browser session:

http://twitter.com/statuses/user_timeline/ocampesa2.xml?count=5

Obviously, you can make such an invocation programmatically from a web application or from a client program that you launch from the command line.

The Twitter timeline API lets you specify other report-related parameters, along with support for XML, JSON, RSS, and Atom. Check the Twitter API documentation for additional information.

■ 5.8   THE MIT SIMILE PROJECT

SIMILE is an acronym for Semantic Interoperability of Metadata and Information in unlike Environments. Its home page is:

http://simile.mit.edu/

The MIT SIMILE project is a collaborative effort involving HP®, the MIT Lab for Computer Science, MIT Libraries, and the W3C. One of the major goals of SIMILE is managing assets and improving interoperability among schemas, digital assets, and services. The SIMILE project leverages the capabilities of the Haystack project (which is not the same as the Facebook Haystack project discussed in Chapter 7). The Haystack Project home page is: http://haystack.lcs.mit.edu

MIT SIMILE is oriented toward the visualization of data (such as photographs) and the ability to search through extremely large sets of digital data. SIMILE projects provide specialized functionality that can be incorporated in mash-ups and combined with the Google Fusion Tables™ database (discussed in Chapter 10), which focuses on collaboration and data visualization. Because of the specialized nature of SIMILE projects, this section provides a condensed summary and links for several of these projects.

The MIT SIMILE project contains the following projects:

- Timeline
- Welkin
- Fresnel
- Timeplot
- Exhibit
- Gadget
- Seek

The SIMILE Timeline project produces interactive timelines for visualizing time-based data. Timeline provides drill down functionality for nodes in the timeline (along with support for mouse-based events). Its home page is: http://www.simile-widgets.org/timeline/

Listing 5.2 shows the contents of `Timeline1.html`, which illustrates how to create a timeline in an HTML page.

Listing 5.2 Timeline1.html

```html
<html>
  <head>
    <script src="http://simile.mit.edu/timeline/api/timeline-api.js"
            type="text/javascript"></script>
    <script>
      var tl;
      function onLoad() {
        var bandInfos = [
          Timeline.createBandInfo({
            width:          "70%",
            intervalUnit:   Timeline.DateTime.MONTH,
            intervalPixels: 100
          }),
          Timeline.createBandInfo({
            width:          "30%",
            intervalUnit:   Timeline.DateTime.YEAR,
            intervalPixels: 200
          })
        ];
        tl = Timeline.create(document.getElementById("timeline1"),
                             bandInfos);
```

```
    }
   </script>
  </head>
  <body onload="onLoad()">
    <div id="timeline1"
          style="height: 250px; border: 1px solid #aaa">
    </div>
  </body>
</html>
```

Listing 5.2 starts by including the Timeline JavaScript library:

```
<script src="http://simile.mit.edu/timeline/api/timeline-api.js"
          type="text/javascript"></script>
```

Next, a JavaScript onLoad() method defines an array consisting of two elements that are created via the Timeline.createBandInfo() method:

```
      Timeline.createBandInfo({
        width:          "70%",
        intervalUnit:   Timeline.DateTime.MONTH,
        intervalPixels: 100
      }),
```

Next, the DIV element, whose id value is timeline1, inserts the array of two timeline elements, as shown here:

```
    tl = Timeline.create(document.getElementById("timeline1"),
                            bandInfos);
```

Finally, the <body> element executes the JavaScript onLoad() when the HTML page is loaded into a browser.

You can find the original (and complete) source code for Listing 5.2 here: http://simile.mit.edu/timeline/docs/create-timelines.html

See the appendices for links to other SIMILE projects.

■ 5.9   WEB 2.0 APPLICATIONS AND PRODUCT SUITES

There are several Web 2.0-based product suites that support tasks that were formerly available only as desktop applications. The two product suites we'll discuss are:

- Google Apps™
- Zoho®

These product suites offer an extensive set of online tools, with both free options and options available for purchase. The correct choice for you depends on your company-specific requirements.

Incidentally, if your needs are relatively simple, another possibility is Gmail, which is not usually described as a "product suite." However, Gmail does provide a set of free online tools (discussed later in this section) that might be adequate for your needs, and you always have the option of switching to a paid option in the future.

■ 5.9.1 Google Apps

Google Apps is an online set of applications. Its home page is:
http://www.google.com/apps/intl/en/business/index.html

Google Apps provides the following set of online applications:

- Calendar
- Documents
- Email and Chat
- Mobile
- Site creation
- Video

In addition, Google Apps provides an administrative control panel, where you can manage (create and delete) users and specify various domain settings. You can also manage the settings for all of the online applications in the preceding list.

For example, if you select the Mobile application, and then choose iPhone (the other choices are Android, Blackberry, and all other devices), you will see a list of Google applications available for mobile devices. Google provides YouTube for your iPhone, so you can watch videos on your phone. In addition, you can browse, bookmark, search, and share videos by sending email links to other people.

Google Apps gives you the option of signing up for a free test account here:
http://www.google.com/a/cpanel/sample/new?hl=en

You can use the free test account for 14 days to explore the features and capabilities of Google Apps.

Another option is the free 30-day trial period that is also available on the Google Apps home page. After the free account expires (or after the 30-day free trial period) you pay US $50 per user per year to use Google

Apps. Google Apps is also available for schools, nonprofit organizations, developers, and resellers.

If you have modest requirements (and you do not want to pay for Google Apps), a third possibility is GMail. Its home page is:
http://www.gmail.com/

GMail provides the following tools for free:

- Email
- Calendar
- Multiple document types
- Management of photos (via Picasa™)
- Text messaging
- Chat capability

Note that unlike Google Apps, Gmail does not provide an administrative control panel, so you will not have system administration functionality.

■ 5.9.2 Zoho

Zoho offers an extensive suite of online tools and applications. Its home page is: http://www.zoho.com/

Zoho provides applications that support the following functionality:

- Email
- Word processing
- Spreadsheets
- Documents
- Wiki
- Chat
- CRM
- Projects
- Meetings
- Invoices
- Office for Microsoft® SharePoint®

If you want to use Zoho for personal use, there is a free option for all of its applications, and a discount for nonprofit organizations. The Zoho pricing model provides many options for businesses, which lets them estimate the expected cost of using Zoho versus the cost of using other alternatives.

5.9.2.1 *Zoho CloudSQL*

One of the more interesting features of Zoho is Zoho® CloudSQL™, which is an extension of the existing Zoho Web API that lets you access data in the cloud via SQL. Its home page is: http://cloudsql.wiki.zoho.com/

Zoho CloudSQL provides support for ODBC and JDBC, and it supports the following SQL dialects:

- ANSI
- Oracle
- SQL Server™
- IBM DB2
- MySQL

See the appendices for more information regarding the Zoho pricing structures, a CloudSQL architectural overview, an API guide, and how to get a Zoho API key.

■ 5.10   BUILD AUTOMATION AND TESTING TOOLS

Build frameworks and testing tools are not specifically Web 2.0 tools, but they are important because they can help you find and fix problems more quickly, and they indirectly help to "enforce" consistent programming styles and practices.

There are numerous open source tools that automate the process of building, testing, and deploying your application. We'll look at a list of build automation tools and testing tools, followed by more detailed information about at least one tool from each list. We'll also provide a list of links for tools not covered in this chapter.

Some of the open source build automation tools that are available are:

- Apache® Ant™
- Maven™
- Apache® Ivy™
- Hudson™
- CruiseControl™

Eclipse and NetBeans are two IDEs (discussed in Chapter 6) that provide support (sometimes through a plug-in) for Apache Ant and Maven.

The following open source testing tools let you submit your code to extensive testing:

- JUnit
- NUnit
- PHPUnit
- XMLUnit
- DBUnit™

There are other tools that are not listed in the preceding lists (such as Anthill, which is a commercial tool), but these tools are widely used by many developers. The next few subsections give you more details regarding Apache Ant, Maven, and JUnit. The other tools will not be discussed in detail.

■ 5.10.1 Apache Ant

Apache Ant is a Java-based build automation tool that lets you define so-called "targets" in an XML-based configuration file to handle the creation/deletion of files and directories, compilation of source code, creation of distribution files, and deployment to various environments (such as test, development, and production environments).

The Apache Ant home page (with downloadable code) can be found here: http://ant.apache.org/

After you download and unzip the Apache Ant distribution, open a Windows command shell (see the online instructions for MacIntosh and Linux) and set the environment variables `ANT_HOME` and `JAVA_HOME` to the appropriate directories. You also need to add the `bin` subdirectory of `ANT_HOME` to the `PATH` environment variable.

The next section discusses a simple Apache Ant "build file" (named `build.xml`) and the various ways that you can use Apache Ant.

■ 5.10.2 A Simple `build.xml` File

Listing 5.3 shows the contents of `build.xml`, which contains three Apache Ant targets.

Listing 5.3 build.xml

```
<?xml version="1.0"?>
<project name="myProject" basedir="." default="compile">
    <property name="src"    value="ant-source"/>
    <property name="output" value="classes"/>

    <target name="compile" depends="create">
```

```
        <javac destdir="bin">
           <src path="${src}"/>
           <classpath refid="jars"/>
        </javac>
    </target>

    <target name="clean">
        <delete dir="${output}"/>
    </target>

    <target name="create" depends="clean">
        <mkdir dir="${output}"/>
    </target>

    <path id="jars">
        <fileset dir="${basedir}/lib">
            <include name="*.jar"/>
        </fileset>
    </path>
</project>
```

Listing 5.3 starts with an XML declaration, followed by the definition of the project:

```
<project name="myProject" basedir="." default="compile">
```

Every Apache Ant-based project has three attributes: name, basedir, and default. These attributes specify the name of the project (myProject in this example), the base directory (the current directory), and the default Apache Ant task (compile in this example), respectively.

Next, Listing 5.3 defines the variables src and output:

```
<property name="src" value="ant-source"/>
    <property name="output" value="bin"/>
```

Next, Listing 5.3 specifies three targets: compile, clean, and create, which will compile code, delete a directory, and create a directory, respectively.

The compile target is shown here:

```
<target name="compile" depends="create">
    <javac destdir="bin">
        <src path="${src}"/>
        <classpath refid="jars"/>
    </javac>
</target>
```

This target compiles the Java source code in the ${src} directory and uses the set of Java jar files that are defined as shown here:

```
<path id="jars">
    <fileset dir="${basedir}/lib">
        <include name="*.jar"/>
    </fileset>
</path>
```

Thus, Apache Ant build files let you define Apache Ant targets that can have multiple dependencies on other Apache Ant targets. Apache Ant also checks for circular dependencies and disallows them to avoid infinite loops. You can also specify variables that "point" to directories containing JAR files without having to explicitly list those JAR files.

One thing to remember is that when a variable has been defined, it is read-only, which means that you cannot redefine its value anywhere else in build.xml.

When you type ant at the command line, the default target in build.xml is executed. If you want to execute the compile target, then type:

```
ant compile
```

If you want to execute the compile target that is defined in build2.xml, then type the following command:

```
ant —f build2.xml compile
```

If you are familiar with the Unix make utility, compare this Apache Ant-based build.xml to a make file in Unix/Linux in terms of which one is more intuitive, and you will understand why Apache Ant has become such a popular and ubiquitous tool for managing build frameworks.

In addition to compiling source code, there are Apache Ant tasks for managing XML documents. For example, an Apache Ant task for generating XML instances of an XML schema can be found here: https://ant-tasks.projects.openhealthtools.org/source/browse/checkout/ant-tasks/trunk/AntTask-GenerateXML/documentation/UserGuide.html

Apache Ant has a rich feature set that is thoroughly documented on the Apache Ant home page. Moreover, you can create custom Java-based extensions of Apache Ant to define customs tasks for handling things that are not available in Apache Ant. Consult the Apache Ant home page for more information regarding custom tasks.

■ 5.10.3   Maven

Maven is a very powerful build framework tool. Its home page is:
http://maven.apache.org

Maven 2 (the latest version) uses a Project Object Model (loosely comparable to an Apache Ant build file) whose default name is `pom.xml` (Maven 1 uses `project.xml`). This XML-based file contains information about each project, including default values for projects such as the build directory, the source directory, and the test source directory.

Maven has several advantages over Apache Ant:

• dependencies become clearer
• the notion that artifacts can be used by other projects
• support for local and remote repositories

Many Apache Ant projects are switching to Maven, and you will see open source projects that provide an Apache Ant build file and a Maven project file.

Listing 5.4 displays the contents of a minimal Maven `pom.xml` file.

Listing 5.4

```
<project>
  <modelVersion>4.0.0</modelVersion>
  <groupId>com.mycompany.app</groupId>
  <artifactId>my-app</artifactId>
  <version>1</version>
</project>
```

Listing 5.4 contains an XML `<project>` element with mandatory child elements. Maven uses `groupId`, `artifactId`, and `version` to create the project's full artifact name:

```
<groupId>:<artifactId>:<version>
```

Thus, the full artifact name for the project in Listing 5.4 is:

```
com.mycompany.app:my-app:1
```

Listing 5.5 shows a "skeleton" of a Maven `pom.xml` file to give you an overview of the types of XML elements that you typically include in a Maven project file.

Listing 5.5

```
<project>
  <repositories>
  ...
  </repositories>
  <plug-inRepositories>
  ...
  </plug-inRepositories>
  <build>
  ...
  </build>
  <reporting>
  ...
  </reporting>

  <profiles>
    <profile>
    ...
    </profile>
  </profiles>
</project>
```

Listing 5.5 gives you a high-level view of the structure of a Maven project file. The file elements are described in detail on the Maven home page.

Maven also provides Eclipse integration, which you can find here: http://m2eclipse.codehaus.org/

You can install Maven from inside Eclipse via the following update site: http://m2eclipse.sonatype.org/update/

■ 5.10.4   Other Build Tools

Apache Ivy is another build tool. Its home page is: http://ant.apache.org/ivy/

Apache Ivy is Apache Ant combined with Maven artifacts, which makes Apache Ivy a "hybrid" alternative to Apache Ant or Maven.

NAnt is a freely available .NET build tool that is the counterpart to Apache Ant. Its home page is: http://nant.sourceforge.net/

Hudson is a more recent build automation tool. Its home page is: https://hudson.dev.java.net/

Note that Hudson is integrated into NetBeans 6.7.1 (and higher).

CruiseControl is a "wrapper" around Apache Ant that is actually a continuous integration tool (with many plug-ins). Its home page is: http://cruisecontrol.sourceforge.net/

Cucumber is a Rails-based build framework. Its home page is: http://wiki.github.com/aslakhellesoy/cucumber

Blue-ridge is a JavaScript testing framework. Its home page is: http://github.com/relevance/blue-ridge/tree/master

■ 5.10.5   JUnit

JUnit is a Java-based tool (created by Kent Beck) that lets you write unit tests for your Java code. The JUnit home page is: http://www.junit.org/

With JUnit, you can create a comprehensive test-based set of Java classes that can be used by the command line via Apache Ant, after which the results can be summarized, placed on a website, and automatically sent to a list of recipients.

5.10.5.1   A Simple JUnit Apache Ant Target

Listing 5.6 displays the contents of a JUnit Apache Ant target that compiles a JUnit Java class.

Listing 5.6

```
<target name="test" depends="compile">
    <junit>
      <classpath refid="jars" />
      <formatter type="brief" usefile="false" />
      <test name="MyFirstJUnitTest" />
    </junit>
  </target>
```

The Apache Ant target in Listing 5.6 uses the JAR files specified in jars (and defined elsewhere) to compile the Java class MyFirstJUnitTest.java (see Listing 5.7).

Note that JUnit report files can be created using different formats (such as HTML and XML). You can also produce reports that summarize multiple "test runs" of the JUnit-based tests for your application.

Listing 5.7 shows the contents of a JUnit class MyFirstJUnitTest.java that is compiled by the Apache Ant target in Listing 5.6.

Listing 5.7 MyFirstJUnitTest.java

```
import junit.framework.*;

public class MyFirstJUnitTest extends TestCase {

    public void test(){
    assertTrue( "MyFirstJUnitTest", true );
  }
}
```

Listing 5.7 starts with an `import` statement that imports the `JUnit` Java class that is contained in the JUnit JAR file, which must be included in the `CLASSPATH` environment variable when you compile these test classes. The remainder of the code in Listing 5.7 defines a single method `test()` in the Java class `MyFirstJUnitTest`, which contains an `assertTrue` statement that will return a value of `true`.

Note that JUnit 4.0 supports the Java annotation `@Test`, which can reduce the number of lines of code in your JUnit test classes.

■ 5.10.6 Other Testing Tools

NUnit and PHPUnit are the JUnit counterparts of .NET and PHP, respectively. NUnit supports all .NET languages. Its home page is: http://www.phpunit.de/

You can learn how to write and run tests in PHPUnit and its home page here: http://www.phpunit.de/

XMLUnit is a test tool for creating unit tests for XML documents .XMLUnit provides both JUnit and NUnit testing for XML. Its home page is: http://xmlunit.sourceforge.net/

DbUnit is a test tool for creating unit tests for datasbase access, and it is an extension of JUnit that is useful for database-driven projects. The DbUnit home page is: http://www.dbunit.org/

■ 5.11 BENCHMARKING TOOLS

You might not think of benchmarking and performance tools as productivity tools, but you should familiarize yourself with this category of tools because they can help you find performance-related issues in your application.

There are numerous open source load testing tools, including Apache® JMeter™, and commercial tools, such as OptimizeIt™ and JProbe®. However, Faban is a powerful tool that lets you set up and run sophisticated simulations and monitor the results.

Ganglia™ is another open source tool (developed at Berkeley) that is a scalable distributed monitoring system for high-performance systems such as clusters and grids. It will be discussed in more detail in Chapter 11.

■ 5.11.1 Faban

Faban is an open source project described as "Next-generation benchmark development/runtime infrastructure." Its home page is:

http://faban.sunsource.net/

Faban has a "Faban Driver Framework," which is a framework that uses a stochastic model to simulate users for your benchmarks. Faban has a "Faban Harness" for programmatically invoking server benchmarks. The Faban Harness also supports external benchmarks, which require you to specify the processes that must be launched to perform those benchmarks.

Tutorials and configuration guides for Faban (including the Faban Driver Framework and the Faban Harness) can be found here:

http://faban.sunsource.net/0.9/docs/toc.html#Tutorials_

■ 5.12 SOURCE CODE MANAGEMENT TOOLS

Source Code Management (SCM) tools offer similar "core" functionality: they let users store different versions of their files (including source code and binary files). However, there are also differences among SCM tools that you should consider when comparing SCM tools.

One point to keep in mind is that companies often choose a particular SCM tool that is the best fit for their needs, and then they decide to migrate to a different SCM tool later on. Sometimes this is because a new SCM tool (or newer version of an existing SCM tool) becomes available that provides some desirable functionality that can improve management tasks and reduce the amount of time (and the learning curve) that developers devote to tasks.

So, if you find two or three SCM tools that closely meet your needs, look for information on the amount of effort it takes to migrate your code between any two of these SCM tools, and whether or not the migration path is automated or manual (or some combination of the two).

If you are unfamiliar with SCM tools, it might be difficult to determine which ones provide the best fit for your requirements. You can ask others for their recommendations, but keep in mind that their development environment could be substantially different from yours. Some of the factors to consider when you are comparing SCM tools are:

• reliability and scalability
• cost (commercial versus open source)
• licensing fees
• ease of use and documentation
• GUI-based management tools
• integration with other tools
• distributed versus centralized repository
• replication support

There are several popular open source SCM tools, including the following:

• Bazaar™
• Git™
• Mercurial
• Subversion®
• Unfuddle™

Bazaar is a distributed source code versioning system. Its home page is: http://bazaar-vcs.org/

You can download Bazaar (along with installation instructions) for Linux, MacIntosh, and Windows from the download link on the home page.

The following website contains links that compare Bazaar with Git, Mercurial, and Subversion: http://bazaar-vcs.org/BzrWhy

Git was designed by Linus Torvalds, the creator of the Linux operating system. Its home page is: http://git-scm.com/

Git is an open source distributed source code versioning system. Git clones do not need a central server because they are a complete repository, including history and revision tracking support.

Mercurial uses a distributed system for source code control. Its home page is: http://mercurial.selenic.com/wiki/

Mercurial is available as a client or as an Eclipse plug-in, which you can install via the following URL (after you have installed Eclipse—see Chapter 6): http://www.vectrace.com/eclipse-update

The Mercurial home page provides tutorials and information for those who are accustomed to other source code control systems, including ClearCase, CVS, Git, Perforce, and Subversion.

Subversion is a very popular SCM. Its home page is: http://subversion.tigris.org/

A detailed comparison of Bazaar, CVS, Git, Mercurial, and Subversion can be found here: http://versioncontrolblog.com/comparison/Bazaar/CVS/Git/Mercurial/Subversion/index.html

An open source Subversion plug-in for Visual Studio (2002 or higher) can be found here: http://ankhsvn.open.collab.net/

Unfuddle is a free hosted source code control system that provides hosting for Git and Subversion. Its home page is: http://unfuddle.com/

The Unfuddle home page contains links with additional information about Unfuddle and details regarding commercial support.

ClearCase is a very good commercial product, but it's also expensive, and you might need a ClearCase administrator to run it.

TortoiseSVN and RapidSVN are two open source GUI-based versions of Subversion and can be found here: http://www.tigris.org/

Some older source code control systems include CVS, PVCS, RCS, and SCCS. Search the Internet if you want more information about these source code control systems.

■ 5.12.1 How to Use Mercurial

This section explains how you can use Mercurial in Eclipse to clone a repository of Noop, which is a JVM-based programming language released in September 2009.

5.12.1.1 Mercurial and Eclipse

First, you need to install Eclipse on your system according to the instructions in Chapter 6, and then install the Mercurial plug-in for Eclipse, which can be found here: http://www.vectrace.com/eclipse-update/

Perform the following steps to install a clone of the Noop source code repository:

Step 1: Launch Eclipse and follow the menu path **File > New > Other…**

Step 2: Select **Mercurial > Clone Repository** and click Next

Step 3: Enter http://code.google.com/p/noop/source/checkout

Step 4: Click the Finish button

5.12.1.2 Mercurial Client

Install Mercurial on your system by downloading a Mercurial client from: http://bitbucket.org/tortoisehg/stable/downloads/

If you have Windows Vista, you can download the Mercurial binary file TortoiseHg-0.8.1–hg-1.3.1.exe (the latest version of Mercurial may be different) and use it to install Mercurial in a directory on your system.

Next, create a clone of the Noop repository by opening a command shell and typing the following command:
hg clone https://noop.googlecode.com/hg/noop

The preceding command will create a noop directory (in the current directory) and place a copy of all the Noop files that are currently in the source code repository into it.

Listing 5.8 shows the contents of HelloWorld.noop.

Listing 5.8 HelloWorld.noop

```
import noop.Application;
import noop.Console;

class HelloWorld(Console console) implements Application {

  Int main(List args) {
    String s = "Hello World!";

    console.println(s);
    return 0;
  }
}
```

■ 5.12.2 Web Containers and Servers

There are several open source application servers and servlet containers available for deploying Java-based web applications:

- JBoss®
- Apache® Geronimo™
- Jetty
- Apache® Tomcat™

JBoss (not to be confused with Yahoo BOSS) and Apache Geronimo are J2EE-compliant application servers, which means that you can deploy Enterprise Application aRchives (EAR) and Web Application aRchives (WAR). In addition, application servers support EJBs (latest version is 3.0 and 3.1 is in development) that are part of EAR files. Apache Geronimo also supports several subprojects, including GBuild, GShell, and XBean.

Java servlet containers, such as Jetty and Apache Tomcat, only support WAR files. Check the appendices for links for JBoss, Apache Geronimo, and Jetty.

5.12.2.1 Download/Install Apache Tomcat 6.x

In Chapter 7 you will use Tomcat 6.x for a NetBeans-based project with Facebook functionality and for the Amazon Toolkit plug-in for Eclipse, which lets you manage Amazon EC2 instances. You can download Apache Tomcat 6.x here: http://jakarta.apache.org/

Uncompress the distribution into a convenient directory, which we will refer to as $TOMCAT_HOME, and then navigate to the `bin` subdirectory of $TOMCAT_HOME and launch Tomcat as follows:

```
catalina.bat run (Windows)
catalina.sh run  (Linux)
```

Next, launch a browser session and navigate to: http://localhost:8080

Note that in Windows, you can also install Tomcat as a service. Read the online Tomcat documentation for more information about Tomcat, including how to install Tomcat as a service on Windows and how to modify the default configuration.

You can also download Jetty and the application servers that were listed at the beginning of this section from the Internet.

The next section discusses the DTrace tracing tool, which can be extremely helpful when debugging applications. Moreover, this tool can be used by people in various roles, such as developers, QA testers, and release engineers. Angelo Rajadurai of SUN Microsystems contributed to the DTrace section, and he encourages you to use the online documentation to create DTrace scripts for debugging applications.

■ 5.13   USING DTRACE FOR WEB 2.0 APPLICATIONS

The deployment stack for a typical Web 2.0 application is becoming increasingly complex, because they rely on multiple technologies. The technology stack includes JavaScript on the browser, multiple layers of APIs (such as OpenSocial), some form of an application server, a web server, a database, native code (such as C/C++), and the operating system.

Thus, a simple click on a web page can result in exercising many layers of the application stack. Performance tuning in these environments often consists of guesswork based on good Google searches. Moreover, we often see that experts of a particular layer tend to lay the blame on the other layers.

Keep in mind that each layer has good debugging tools. DBAs have good GUI and command-line tools to observe every detail of the database. Language debuggers, such as gdb, do a reasonably good job of providing visibility into both scripting and native languages in the stack. Of special note are tools such as JProbe, JMeter, and VisualVM™, which provide insight into Java code. Operating system tools like vmstat, iostat, mpstat, and truss provide insight at the operating system level.

While these tools are important for performance tuning and understanding each layer in isolation, they not provide any insight into the entire system or the interaction between different layers. For example, these tools can't find SQLs executed by clicking a JavaScript button on a browser. In addition, some of these tools are not usable in production. The truss utility can slow down your application to the point where it becomes unusable in production.

Typically, developers have resorted to using custom debugging code to address this issue. This is often seen in debug-enabled versions of applications. These debug-enabled versions need special flags, which reduces the performance of the applications, which is why they're not normally used in production.

So, how do we address this issue? Sun's solution to this problem is dynamic instrumentation. Just imagine utopia for a minute: What if you could dynamically insert code into a live, running application and collect data at the point of instrumentation? What if you could turn these instrumentations on and off dynamically? What if you could use the same instrumentation at every layer of your application? What if this instrumentation supported popular languages like C, C++, Java, PHP, Python, Ruby, JavaScript?

This is exactly what DTrace does for you, because it lets you look at every layer of your application infrastructure. DTrace lets you collect data for a few seconds (just incurring a performance penalty for those few seconds) and then disable the data collection dynamically without restarting any applications. DTrace doesn't need any new code from the developer. DTrace can fully observe performance-tuned code (no -g flag is needed).

■ 5.13.1 DTrace Fundamentals

Now that we understand the purpose and benefits of DTrace, let's take a quick look at its fundamentals. DTrace works on an event/callback model whereby you register for an event and implement a callback, which is executed when that event occurs.

For example, the execution of a function, accessing a file, the execution of a SQL statement, and garbage collection in Java are all examples of events. You typically collect data such as function arguments, the time taken to execute a function, and SQL statements in the callback. In DTrace, these event definitions are called probes; the callback is called an action; and the occurrence of the event is called a probe firing. DTrace lets you limit the probe firings by using predicates, which are Boolean statements that need to evaluate to true before the action is executed.

A typical D-script looks like this:

```
probe
/predicate/
{
  action
}
```

5.13.1.1 Probe Definitions

A probe consists of four colon-separated fields *provider:module:function:name*. The *provider* specifies the layer that is used. The *module* and *function* specify the module and function that are used. The *name* represents the location in the function. For example, use entry as the name when you enter the function.

The following string is an example of a probe:

```
pid1234:libc:malloc:entry
```

This probe definition indicates that the probe is fired when the process, whose ID is 1234, enters the malloc function in the libc library.

You can also use wild cards in any of these probes, as shown here:

```
pid1234:*:*open*:entry
```

This probe is fired when any function with open in its name is called from any library for process ID 1234.

For simplicity, the absence of a field is taken as a wild card:

```
pid1234:::entry
```

This probe is fired when any function in any library is called for process ID 1234.

5.13.1.2 Predicates

You can construct predicates by using the built-in variables and arguments that are passed to a function. Two examples are shown here:

execname == "mysql"—will return true if the probe is fired by the mysql process

uid == 123—will return true if the probe is fired by a process owned by userid 123

5.13.1.3 Sample Scripts

The following example demonstrates how scripts can be very simple:

```
proc:::execute-success
{
  trace(execname)
}
```

The preceding script will print all of the commands and processes that are started in the system.

A slightly more complicated example is shown here:

```
syscall::open:entry
{
  printf("%s opened %s¥n",execname,copyinstr(arg0))
}
```

The preceding script will show you all of the files that are opened in the system.

In addition, D-scripts can span multiple layers. Listing 5.9 shows the contents of a script that reports how much time you are spending on the different layers of an Apache MySQL PHP (AMP) stack. You get the percentage of time spent in Apache, Java, MySQL, the browser, and the operating system. This functionality is similar to AMP-top.

Listing 5.9

```
#!/usr/sbin/dtrace -qs

BEGIN
{
  total=mysqlcnt=httpcnt=phpcnt=javacnt=ffxcnt=othercnt=0;
  printf("%10s %10s %10s %10s %10s %10s¥n","% MYSQL","% APACHE","%
FIREFOX","% PHP","% Java","% OTHER");
}

php*:::request-startup
{
  inphp[pid,tid]=1;
}

php*:::request-shutdown
{
  inphp[pid,tid]=0;
}

profile-1001
{
  total++;
  (execname=="mysqld")?mysqlcnt++:¥
      (execname=="httpd")?(inphp[pid,tid]==1?phpcnt++:httpcnt++):¥
      (execname=="java")?javacnt++:¥
      (execname=="firefox-bin")?ffxcnt++:othercnt++;
}
```

```
tick-30s
{
  printf("%10s %10s %10s %10s %10s %10s¥n","% MYSQL","% APACHE","%
FIREFOX","% PHP","% Java","% OTHER");
}

tick-2s
{
  printf("%10d %10d %10d %10d %10d %10d¥n",mysqlcnt*100/total,¥
           httpcnt*100/total,ffxcnt*100/total, phpcnt*100/total,¥
           javacnt*100/total,othercnt*100/total);
  total=mysqlcnt=httpcnt=phpcnt=ffxcnt=javacnt=othercnt=0;
}
```

5.13.1.4 Resources

The following are a few additional resources that you may find useful.

DTraceToolkit is a collection of over 200 scripts, which you can find here: http://opensolaris.org/os/community/dtrace/dtracetoolkit/

A DTrace hands-on lab (a step-by-step guide to learning DTrace) can be found at:
http://developers.sun.com/learning/javaoneonline/j1lab.jsp?lab=LAB-9400&yr=2008

A DTrace community page for all things DTrace is located at:
http://opensolaris.org/os/community/dtrace/

Additional information regarding DTrace is available at:
http://www.sun.com/bigadmin/content/dtrace/index.jsp

■ 5.14 INDUSTRY PERSPECTIVE AND BUSINESS FOCUS

Tom Crouch is a Technical Evangelist at Yahoo and he has provided his insight into Web 2.0 and the use of Yahoo Pipes in the IT industry.

Some find the term "Web 2.0" difficult, partly because the Web isn't like traditional software. The idea of version numbers makes sense for traditional software that must be deployed to each computer individually. Each version is a discrete entity different from the versions before and after it and you can simply ask which version a user is running.

The Web isn't like that, and for several reasons. First, unlike traditional software, the Web is the intersection of the technology on the page and in the browser. Users' experience is constrained by the version of the browser they are running and how it can interact with the web page they are viewing. Consequently, the Web is constantly evolving in little jumps. A standards body, such as the W3C, will define a number of possible features, only some of which will be implemented by browser manufacturers. These features are then implemented by some web sites, at which point they become exposed to users, and more browser manufacturers may start to add them to their software. In addition, browser manufacturers add their own nonstandards to this "mixture," and later on the more popular features often get copied by other manufacturers and become ad hoc standards.

What we consider Web 2.0 was the intersection of a number of ad hoc standards, a clever implementation by Jesse James Garrett, and a general culture shift in the use of the web. Jesse James Garrett realized that the XML HTTP request or XHR feature of Microsoft's Internet Explorer would allow him to do what he coined "Asynchronous JavaScript And XML," or AJAX. Essentially, what Jesse James Garrett figured out was that the browsers contained the ad hoc standards that would let him update web pages without loading a whole new page. This brought in a new wave of improved user experience that birthed what we think of as "web apps." While this technology shift doesn't define Web 2.0, this shift was essential for Web 2.0 to exist. However, the real shift which lets us look back and place a marker where the Web had changed, was the advent of user contributions to web pages.

With Jesse James Garrett's new AJAX concept as a new model for interaction on the Web, people quickly built sites that gave users a much greater ability to contribute to the content of the site itself. As the Web became increasingly mainstream, the focus shifted from sites that were informational (which was "Web 1.0") to sites that made user contributions the primary content. Sites such as Flickr, YouTube, WordPress, and others are powered primarily by users of those sites rather than teams of programmers and editors. This is an important distinction in Web 2.0, because we have made the publication and creation of sites democratic, rather than something restricted to the "Technorati."

So, what does this say about "Web 3.0"? Well, I believe that, like Web 2.0, we'll only be able to look back and spot the trend after it happened because of the gradual change that's the nature of the Web. However, data management may be the next big thing. Currently, users of Web 2.0 expose increasing amounts of data through their social networks and their devices (iPhones, Blackberries, etc). It's becoming increasingly difficult for users to control, manage, and understand the data that they own and expose and in turn use and are exposed to. There is a trend of users with a better understanding of the rights to data they share, with licenses such as Creative Commons, and the access controls they provide to that data. Services such as Yahoo!'s Fire Eagle are specifically designed to let users control and manage the access to sensitive information, such as their location. While Fire Eagle targets one specific kind of information, this level of control will become increasingly important as more of the technology in our lives is enabled to share data on the Web. People are starting to "share by default" with services like Twitter and facebook, but this often has repercussions and tools to manage this problem are sure to emerge.

■ 5.14.1   How Will Yahoo Pipes Evolve During the Next Several Years?

One of the tools from Yahoo that helps people manage and manipulate data is Yahoo Pipes. This tool provides a data manipulation layer for common data, such as RSS and other feeds. It's very visual and uses lots of AJAX to help you manage data, so perhaps that puts this tool somewhere on the edge of Web 3.0. However, feeds are pretty open, which means that manipulating them is pretty easy.

Something that's a little harder involves getting data from web services. The reason is simple: all of those web services are different. We've recently put a lot of work into Pipes 2.0, which we call the "Yahoo Query Language." This language works a lot like SQL, which is a staple for programmers everywhere to access information from databases.

The reason this is so important to the Web and to Pipes is because it easily unlocks all of the data that is available via web services. No longer do developers have to learn how to do SOAP and XML–RPC and REST to get data from the most popular sites. This means search data for a term is as easy as *select * from search.web where query = "term."* This functionality is dramatically easier than the previous methods.

Because web services allow for authentication, they can provide much richer data about a user's personal preferences. This means that the kind of data that YQL can help you access tends to be more personal and richer than those exposed to Pipes. This can become something that people increasingly rely upon. Since YQL can be embedded in Pipes, it's possible to achieve a hybrid model where the complex personal data is managed in a very visual way.

The key to success in Web 2.0 applications is to understand how users interact with data. Data is at the center of your application, not the technology or the marketing. You should focus both your product and technology decisions around how users will want to interact with the data that your application provides. This will probably take the form of an API to syndicate content, but also some default views allowing user interaction. By understanding the data that your users will want to create and manage, you can provide the best experience for them whether they interact with that data on your site or via an API. Your application will quickly become the center of their focus for that data because you've put a focus on how they want to use it, rather than on how you want to build a site. From this standpoint, you can merge your business objectives with the needs of the user to find a place of shared value.

When you create a start-up, you are trying to be innovative in a particular area. It's important to take advantage of existing software or services that can let you focus on that mission. For example, while you could spend six months tuning your database, people aren't looking at you for your database expertise, they are looking at you for your innovation. Using existing services or open source software to implement the common tasks is important. Rather than building your own infrastructure, leveraging cloud hosting lets you concentrate on the part of your business that is new and different from your competitors. Services such as YQL or EC2 should be your building blocks to quickly test ideas without getting bogged down in the details of technology that isn't the core of your business. If someone can supply you with what you need at a reasonable cost, it makes much more sense to build on top of previous work and focus your energy on the creation of something new, rather than the repetition of existing work.

■ 5.15 SUMMARY

This chapter discussed several useful productivity tools that support drag-and-drop functionality for creating things that can be used manually or programmatically. For example, a tool such as Yahoo Pipes provides drag-and-drop functionality that lets you define very powerful pipes. You can also create mash-ups or web applications that use your pipes and combine the results with data from other web services.

Next, you learned about build framework tools such as Apache Ant, along with an example of a build file that contains "targets" that specify the tasks that you want to perform (e.g., compile, test, deploy, and so forth) on the code base of your application.

The next chapter discusses developer tools, including browser plug-ins (such as Firebug®) and JavaScript tools (such as Venkman™) that are useful for debugging web applications.

## CHAPTER 6

Debugging Tools

In This Chapter:

- Introducing the Concept of Debugging
- Integrated Development Environments (IDEs)
- Rich Internet Applications (RIAs)
- Firebug®
- Firebug Lite®
- Venkman™
- Firefox Web Developer Add-On
- JSLint
- JsUnit™
- Selenium™
- WireShark®
- Google Gadgets™
- Google Wave

Debugging code is one of the biggest challenges for developers. Many tools have been developed to help ease the pains of debugging and empower the developer with knowledge. In this chapter we will explore modern debugging tools.

■ 6.1 INTRODUCING THE CONCEPT OF DEBUGGING

Debugging is one of the first things a programmer learns as they gain experience programming. Even the simplest programs often contain bugs, so good debugging tools and techniques are essential in order to become effective software engineer. In this chapter, we will focus on the tools that make debugging easier and developing bug-free code possible. There are a lot of tools available, and covering them all is beyond the scope of this book. Instead, we tried to focus on some of the more popular and most powerful ones. We will only scrape the surface of many of these tools, because they are too complex to cover in one chapter. Hopefully, you can use the information in this chapter to decide what tools work best for you. None of these tools are required for web development, but they often make doing it easier.

■ 6.2 INTEGRATED DEVELOPMENT ENVIRONMENTS (IDES)

This section covers developer tools, such as IDEs, which let teams of developers work on different modules of the same project in an organized manner. We'll look at three open source IDEs: Eclipse, SUN NetBeans, and Oracle JDeveloper. There are a lot of plug-ins available for Eclipse, including the Amazon® Toolkit™ (discussed in Chapter 10), which let you deploy AWS applications.

SUN NetBeans is a Java IDE that also supports Java ME™, C/C++, and scripting languages such as PHP, Python, and Ruby. Oracle 11G JDeveloper is heavily oriented toward the Application Developer Framework (ADF). Both JDeveloper and NetBeans support JSF-based project development. If you are interested in developing JavaFX™ applications, you can use a number of tools, including Eclipse (with a JavaFX plug-in), NetBeans, Exadel™ JavaFX™ Studio (also an Eclipse plug-in), or JBoss® Seam™.

If you plan to work with C# or Silverlight™, you can use Microsoft Visual Studio, which has a free trial download. You can also search the Internet for other open source and commercial IDEs, such as JetBrains from IntelliJ®. Note that Visual Studio and IntelliJ are not discussed in this chapter.

If any of the previously mentioned IDEs appeal to you, it's a good idea to download them and experiment with their features so that you can make an informed choice. Deciding which IDE to use depends on several factors, including the type of applications that you want to develop, the tools that your team members use, the plug-ins that you need, and the amount of money that you (or your company) are willing to spend.

IDEs can increase your productivity when you learn to leverage their features. IDEs make refactoring code easier, simplify management of project-related files, and enable you to track third-party artifacts (such as JAR files) for your project. While it's possible to write code in text editors, this approach tends to work best for projects involving a small number of files (i.e., fewer than 20 files). However, modern projects often involve teams of developers working on different modules of the same project. IDEs are sophisticated tools and they can help you manage hundreds or thousands of project-related files.

There are a lot of IDEs available, some of which are commercial products and others are open source products. Here is a partial list of IDEs:

- Eclipse (open source)
- Flash Builder 4 (Adobe)
- NetBeans (open source)
- JDeveloper (open source)
- JetBrains (commercial)
- Visual Studio (commercial)

We'll look at Eclipse and NetBeans in this chapter, and you can search the Internet for more information about the other IDEs in the preceeding list.

■ 6.2.1 Eclipse

Eclipse is an open source IDE that was developed by IBM, who later donated the Eclipse project to the open source community. The Eclipse home page is: http://www.eclipse.org

Eclipse was designed to support plug-in architecture, which means that you can install third-party extensions to Eclipse that provide functionality that is unavailable in Eclipse itself.

6.2.1.1 Installing an Eclipse Plug-In

To install the Amazon web services plug-in for Eclipse version 3.4, launch Eclipse and complete the following steps:

Step 1: Follow the menu path **Help > Software Updates**

Step 2: Select the Available Software tab

Step 3: Select the Add Site dialog box

Step 4: Enter http://aws.amazon.com/eclipse/

Step 5: Click the OK button

Step 6: Select all components of the archive

Step 7: Click on the Install button

Eclipse will guide you through a few more self-explanatory steps, such as clicking on the checkbox to accept the terms of the license agreement. After completing the installation (typically within a few minutes), you will be prompted to restart Eclipse. Note that the only difference in installing other Eclipse plug-ins is the URL you must specify in step 4. A list of Eclipse plug-ins is here:

http://www.eclipseplugincentral.com/

■ 6.2.2   Adobe Flash Builder 4

Adobe Flash Builder 4, formerly called FlexBuilder, lets you create Action-Script applications (among other things). Flash Builder 4 is available in several languages for Windows and MacIntosh. You can find a free 30-day trial download of Adobe Flash Builder 4 here:

http://labs.adobe.com/downloads

Since FlexBuilder is based on Eclipse, you can use your knowledge of Eclipse to create ActionScript-based projects. In Chapter 2, Landscape of the Web, you saw an example of an ActionScript class called `ArchRect1.as`, which renders a set of rectangles that follow the path of an Archimedean curve. We'll create an ActionScript project with this same code sample. After you install Flash Builder, open a command shell in Windows and navigate to the installation directory and launch `Gumbo.exe`. After a minute or so the main screen for FlexBuilder will appear. You can create the `Arch1Rect1` project by following the **File > New > ActionScript Project > Next** menu path, entering the name `ArchRect1` in the Project Name: input box, and then clicking the Finish button. Flash Builder 4 will create the ActionScript class `ArchRect1.as` with the following skeleton code:

```
package
{
    import flash.display.Sprite;
    public class ArchRect1 extends Sprite
            {
                            public function ArchRect1()
                                            {
    // insert your code here
                                            }
                }
    }
```

You can manually enter the `ArchRect1.as` code from Chapter 2 into this class, or you can find the source code in an open source project here: http://code.google.com/p/actionscript3-graphics/

This open source project is available with an Apache 2.0 license, and it contains other examples of graphics-based code samples that were developed in Flash Builder 4.

■ 6.2.3   SUN NetBeans

NetBeans is an open source IDE that was developed by SUN and later donated to the open source community. The NetBeans home page is: http://www.netbeans.com

NetBeans also supports a plug-in architecture. A list of NetBeans plug-ins is here: http://plugins.netbeans.org/PluginPortal/

■ 6.2.4   Oracle JDeveloper

Oracle JDeveloper is an IDE that was developed by Oracle, which later donated released JDeveloper as an open source project. JDeveloper also supports a plug-in architecture, which means that you can install third-party extensions to JDeveloper that provide functionality that is unavailable in JDeveloper. In spite of being very powerful, JDeveloper never gained great much popularity. JDeveloper is designed to simplify the development of Java SOA applications and user interfaces. Using JDeveloper is one of the fastest and easiest ways to developer Web Services Clients. JDeveloper has support for the full development lifecycle. The JDeveloper homepage is: http://www.oracle.com/technology/products/jdev/index.html

■ 6.2.5   IntelliJ IDEA

IntelliJ IDEA has been considered by many Java developers to be the best Java IDE on the market. IntelliJ IDEA has a lot of great wizards and advanced features that you would traditionally find in a product like Visual Studio. IntelliJ IDEA has been a commercial IDE costing $599 for a commercial license, $249 for a personal license, and $99 for an academic license. Starting with version 9, IntelliJ IDEA will offer a free Community Edition, with limited features, and an Ultimate Edition, which is fully loaded. JetBrains, the company behind IntelliJ IDEA, has alway been a huge supporter of the open source community and offers a free open source license for open source development. IntelliJ IDEA use seems to be on the decline due to advances in Eclipse, the availability of good Eclipse plug-ins, and advances in NetBeans.

■ 6.2.6 Aptana Studio

Aptana™ Studio is a free open source IDE for web developers. Aptana Studio is an authoring tools for HTML, CSS, and JavaScript. Aptana also supports a plug-in architecture, which means that you can install third-party extensions to Aptana that provide functionality that is unavailable in Aptana. Aptana Studio comes in a stand-alone version and as an Eclipse plugin. The Aptana Studio home page is here: http://www.aptana.org/

Aptana RadRails is a free open source IDE built on top of Aptana Studio. RadRails provides tight integration with Aptana Cloud serices. The Aptana RadRails home page is here: http://aptana.com/

■ 6.3 RICH INTERNET APPLICATIONS (RIA)

■ 6.3.1 Adobe AIR

One of the better known RIAs is Adobe® AIR™, which enables you to create applications using Flex and ActionScript. The Adobe AIR runtime lets you build Rich Internet Applications that run outside the browser. Adobe AIR runs on multiple operating systems. The Adobe AIR homepage is here: http://www.adobe.com/products/air/

■ 6.3.2 SUN JavaFX

A more recent RIA is SUN JavaFX 1.2, which provides a scripting language and support for mobile devices. You can develop JavaFX 1.2 applications with NetBeans 6.5.1 or by installing a JavaFX plug-in for Eclipse 3.4.x. In the latter case, you can get the complete instructions for installing the JavaFX 1.2 plug-in here: http://javafx.com/docs/gettingstarted/eclipse-plugin/

If you are comfortable installing Eclipse plug-ins, you can install the JavaFX plug-in from: http://javafx.com/downloads/eclipse-plugin/

Next, create a new JavaFX project, either in NetBeans in Eclipse 3.4.x, with the preceeding JavaFX plug-in Listing 6.1 shows the contents of the ArchRect1.fx file, which renders a set of rectangles that follow the path of an Archimedean curve.

Listing 6.1 Main.fx

```
import javafx.scene.Group;
import javafx.scene.Scene;
import javafx.stage.Stage;
import javafx.scene.paint.Color;
import javafx.scene.shape.*;
import java.lang.Math;

var basePointX = 300;
var basePointY = 200;
var currentX   = 0;
var currentY   = 0;
var offsetX    = 0.0;
var offsetY    = 0.0;
var radius     = 0.0;
var Constant   = 0.25;
var angle      = 0;
var maxAngle   = 720;
var rectWidth  = 80;
var rectHeight = 40;
var shapes     = Group{};
var newShape  : Rectangle;
var currColor : Color;

 for(angle in [0..maxAngle]) {
  radius   = Constant*angle;
  offsetX  = radius*Math.cos(angle*Math.PI/180);
 offsetY  = radius*Math.sin(angle*Math.PI/180);
  currentX = basePointX+Math.floor(offsetX);
  currentY = basePointY-Math.floor(offsetY);

  // alternate between red and blue
  if(angle mod 2 == 0) {
    currColor = Color.RED;
  }
  else {
    currColor = Color.BLUE;
  }

  // draw the current shape
  newShape = Rectangle {
    x:          currentX,
    y:          currentY,
```

```
        width:        rectWidth,
        height:       rectHeight,
        arcWidth:     3*rectWidth/4,
        arcHeight:    3*rectHeight/4,
        fill:         currColor,
        strokeWidth: 1
    };

    insert newShape into shapes.content;
}
Stage {
  title : "Sample Graphics"
  scene: Scene {
        width:    800
        height:   500
        content: shapes
  }
}
```

Listing 6.1 starts with several import statements that import existing JavaFX classes (which are referenced later in the code), followed by a set of variables that are declared and initialized. The for loop construct resembles Python more than Java: for(angle in [0..maxAngle]). Parameters are assigned values via a ":" in a JSON™-like manner, as shown here:

```
newShape = Rectangle {
    x:            currentX,
    y:            currentY,
    width:        rectWidth,
    height:       rectHeight,
    arcWidth:     3*rectWidth/4,
    arcHeight:    3*rectHeight/4,
    fill:         currColor,
    strokeWidth: 1
};
```

Each newly initialized object is inserted rather than appended to a DOM–like structure: insert newShape into shapes.content;

Finally, a Stage element is constructed and populated with the set of previously created Rectangle elements, as shown here:

```
Stage {
  title : "Sample Graphics"
  scene: Scene {
          width:   800
          height:  500
          content: shapes
  }
}
```

Thus, JavaFX is a scripting language that resembles a mixture of Java, Python, JSON, and declarative-style programming. You can find the source code for various graphics-based JavaFX 1.2 code samples (including `Main .fx` in Listing 6.3) in an open source project that is available under an Apache 2.0 license here:

http://code.google.com/p/javafx12-graphics/

■ 6.4 FIREBUG

Firebug® is considered a must-use tool for web developers. Firebug is a Firefox extension that is free and open source. Firebug lets developers inspect and edit HTML, modify CSS, monitor network activity, debug and profile JavaScript, find errors, explore the DOM, execute JavaScript on the fly, and log on from JavaScript. You can find installation instructions the latest information about FireBug here: http://getfirebug.com

Getting started with Firebug is very easy. After Firebug is installed, start it by clicking the small Firebug icon at the bottom right of your browser. Firebug can also be opened by following the **Tools > Firebug > Open Firebug** or **Tools > Firebug > Open Firebug in New Window** menu path.

■ 6.4.1 Inspect and Edit HTML and CSS

Firebug lets you view the current state of the HTML—even if the page has been modified with JavaScript. Firebug lets you use the mouse to select an element on the page, which will highlight the HTML associated with that element. To enable the Inspect functionality, follow the **Tools > Firebug > Inspect** element menu path or click on the Inspect icon at the top-left of the Firebug window. Figure 6.1 shows how you can view the HTML and CSS of the button by hovering over it with the mouse.

■ **FIGURE 6.1**
Inspect HTML with
Firebug

■ **FIGURE 6.2**
Modify CSS with
Firebug

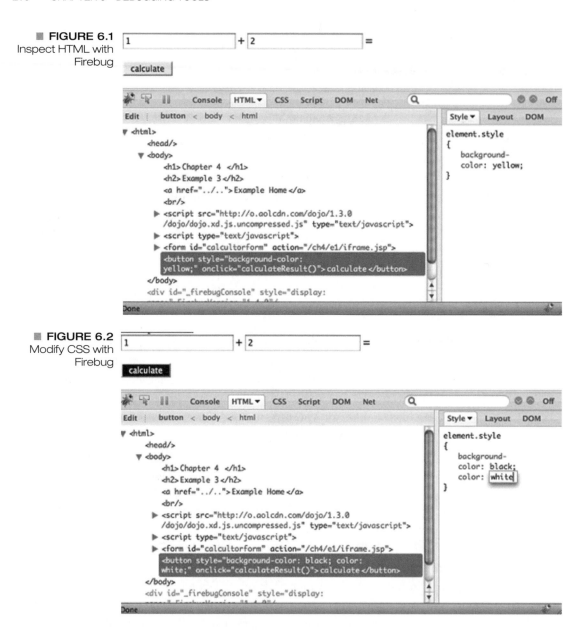

Figure 6.2 shows how, using Firebug, we changed the style of the button to black with white letters. This feature is very useful when a developer is trying to determine the best styling of an element. Firebug lets you try multiple combinations of styling on several elements without ever refreshing the page. Once you get the look you want, update your CSS and refresh the

page. Remember, changes to the CSS via Firebug will be lost if the page is refreshed or the browser is closed.

■ 6.4.2 Monitor Network Activity

Firebug provides great information about a network. This can be useful, because you can see if JavaScript files are returning 404 rather than the actual script. Often, this will explain why a page is broken and can be fixed by updating the JavaScript reference. You can also see what data was sent in an Ajax call. Firebug can show you details about the request order and how long each request took. Starting at the left in Figure 6.3, you can see each requested item on the web page. Notice that all requests are GET. Next, you can see that some of the response codes were 200, while other items were cached and used response code 304. Next is the domain that the resource came from followed by the size of the download to get the resource. Finally, there is a timeline showing how long each resource took to load. This is very useful in helping to find out why pages are loading slow.

Often, if parts of a page are not working it is because the wrong URL was used and response 404 is given. Be aware that some web pages give friendly 404 pages that return 200, so sometimes you have to drill down by clicking the arrow on the far left to see what was returned in the response. Figure 6.4 shows a drill down into the request for home3.html. Firebug has three very useful tabs: Headers, Response, and HTML. Headers shows the request and response headers. You can find useful information, such as cookies, in that tab. The Response tab shows the data passed in the request and

■ FIGURE 6.3
Firebug
Networking

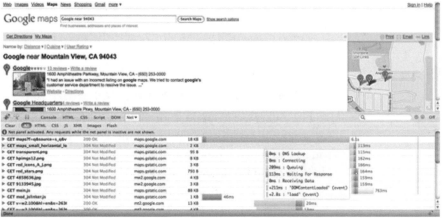

■ **FIGURE 6.4**
Firebug Request
Response Drill-
Down

■ **FIGURE 6.5**
Firebug Debugging
JavaScript

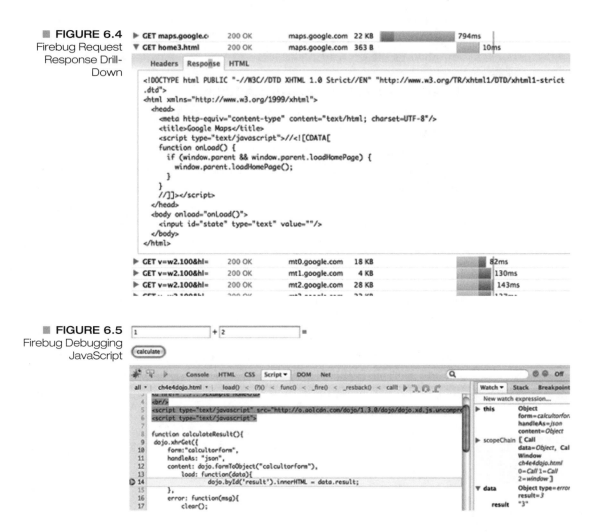

the HTML tab shows a preview of what the HTML would look like in a browser.

■ 6.4.3   Debug and Profile JavaScript

Firebug offers great support for debugging JavaScript. Figure 6.5 shows Firebug stopping at a breakpoint so we can see the JSON returned by the Ajax call. You can start debugging your JavaScript by selecting the Script tag at the top. Then, in the drop down on the left of the next line, select the file you want to debug. Using the buttons at the top right corner, you can continue, step into, step over, and step return. In the Watch window, you can see and inspect all of the variables. You can see that `data.result` is 3. You can modify any variable in the Watch window, which is often useful in debugging edge conditions.

Firebug has a nice profiler that lets you see what functions are called, how many times they are called, their average time to execute, min. and max. time, and what JavaScript file the method exists in. You can turn the profiler on by selecting the console, then clicking the Profile button. Figure 6.6 shows a profile for Google Maps. This profile information could be very useful in helping you find at why a page is running slow.

■ 6.4.4 Find Errors

Firebug is a nice tool for helping you find errors. Figure 6.7 shows how Firebug lists the number of JavaScript errors for a page in the bottom right corner. If you click on the error count, Firebug will show you the line number and JavaScript file for each error. You can also click on the error to go directly to the code where the error occurred.

■ **FIGURE 6.6**
Google Maps
Profile

Function	Calls	Percent	Own Time	Time	Avg	Min	Max	File
aa()	1	35.5%	107.096ms	236.531ms	236.531ms	236.531ms	236.531ms	main.js (line 2)
insertTiles	1	3.6%	10.854ms	11.162ms	11.162ms	11.162ms	11.162ms	maps.google.com (line 11)
resizeApp	4	3.05%	9.192ms	24.855ms	6.214ms	0.683ms	13.882ms	maps.google.com (line 8)
getWindowHeight	4	3.04%	9.16ms	9.16ms	2.29ms	0.056ms	8.981ms	maps.google.com (line 8)
xt	1	2.12%	6.389ms	7.575ms	7.575ms	7.575ms	7.575ms	main.js (line 1396)
calculateOffsetTop	12	1.99%	6.002ms	6.002ms	0.5ms	0.041ms	5.02ms	maps.google.com (line 8)
a	1	1.8%	5.443ms	5.443ms	5.443ms	5.443ms	5.443ms	main.js (line 1415)
Bh	4	1.72%	5.199ms	5.218ms	1.305ms	0.029ms	5.039ms	main.js (line 55)
Cl	17	1.51%	4.545ms	13.722ms	0.807ms	0.741ms	1.277ms	main.js (line 528)

■ **FIGURE 6.7**
Firebug Profile
JavaScript

Firebug also has a great feature called Break on All Errors. Break on Errors stops the debugger when an error occurs. Figure 6.8 shows how you can turn Break on All Errors on.

■ **FIGURE 6.8**
Enable Firebug
Break on All Errors

As you can see in Figure 6.9, you can inspect all of the variables and see exactly why the error occurred. This is very useful debugging errors that are hard to reproduce and seldom occur. It is recommended to leave Break on All Error enabled during development, so if unusual errors occur you can debug them.

■ **FIGURE 6.9**
Firebug Break on
All Errors

■ 6.4.5 Exploring the DOM

Firebug contains a DOM tab that lets you inspect the DOM of a page and make edits that will be immediately seen on the page. Figure 6.10 shows the DOM tab. Note how you can drill down into objects to get access to additional attributes.

■ 6.4.6 Execute JavaScript on the Fly

As Figure 6.11 shows, by using the Firebug console, you can execute any JavaScript you wish.

■ **FIGURE 6.10**
Firebug DOM

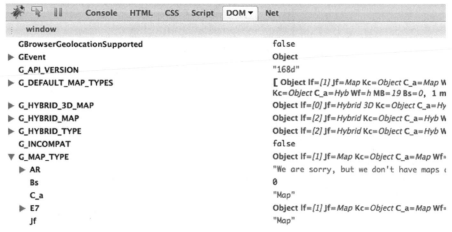

■ 6.4.7 Log from JavaScript

As you can see in Figure 6.11, you can log on from JavaScript using `console.log`. Firebug also supports `console.debug`, `console.info`, `console.warn`, and `console.error`, which are all logged with different colors.

■ **FIGURE 6.11**
Logging on From
JavaScript

■ 6.5 FIREBUG LITE

Firebug is a great developer tool, but it is only available as a Firefox plug-in. Firebug Lite contains a subset of the functionality of Firebug and runs in Internet Explorer, Opera, and Safari. You can add Firebug Lite to any page by adding the following line of JavaScript:

```
<script type='text/javascript'

        src='http://getfirebug.com/releases/lite/1.2/firebug-lite-
compressed.js'></script>
```

Often, it may be hard to add the script tag to a page, so a simpler option is to add the bookmarklet found here: http://getfirebug.com/lite.html

A bookmarklet is basically a bookmark that contains JavaScript. You can drag your bookmarklet onto you bookmark bar with your mouse. Figure 6.12 shows a screenshot of Firebug Lite. Note that Firebug Lite which is very similar to Firebug, so we will not cover it in detail.

FIGURE 6.12
Firebug Lite HTML Inspect

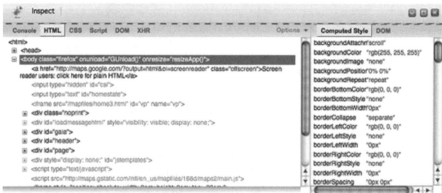

■ 6.6   VENKMAN

Venkman is Mozilla's JavaScript debugger. Venkman is basically the same product as Firebug, but Venkman has the advantage that it can be used with certain versions of Firefox, Netscape®, and Mozilla SeaMonkey. In the past Venkman was once very popular, but over time Firebug has become the de-facto standard for JavaScript Debugging. Due to it's limited use and declining usage, we will skip the details of Venkman.

■ 6.7   FIREFOX WEB DEVELOPER ADD-ON

The Firefox Web Developer Add-on is a must-have tool for web developers. Web Developer adds a menu and toolbar with various web developer tool.

The first menu lets you disable several browser features. The Disable menu lets you disable features such as caching, Java, and JavaScript. Disabling caching can be useful if you are having trouble getting the browser to use your latest JavaScript file when you refresh a page during development. The Cookies menu lets you disable cookies, see cookies, reset cookies, and modify cookies. The CSS menu lets you disable CSS, view CSS used on a page, dynamically add a CSS from your file system to the current page, and edit the CSS on a page (see Figure 6.13).

■ **FIGURE 6.13**
Showing Styles in
the Firefox Web
Developer Add-on

The Images menu provides the following functionalities: disable all images, display image information (alt attributes, dimensions, file size, etc.), find broken images, outline images, and show a page with information about all images on a given page. The Information menu gives access to tons of information on the page, such as displaying IDs and class information, displaying title information, displaying JavaScript, and displaying color. Figure 6.15 shows the many options of the Information menu.

One of the most useful features is View color information. Figure 6.16 shows how View color information shows the colors and their codes for all colors on a page. This can be very useful when making CSS files.

The Miscellaneous menu provides the following functionalities: clearing private data, showing page comments, showing hidden elements, editing HTML, making frames resizable, and small screen rendering. The Outline menu lets you outline various elements, such as frames, headings, links, and tables. The Resize menu lets you resize the browser. This is useful for testing what your page will look like when rendered under different page sizes. You should always test for 1024 × 768 and 800 × 600. The Tools menu has tools that let you: validate HTML, validate CSS, show the error console, show the

■ **FIGURE 6.14**
CSS of Page

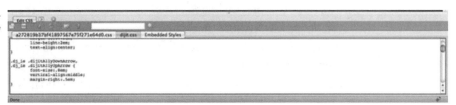

■ **FIGURE 6.15**
Information
Menu

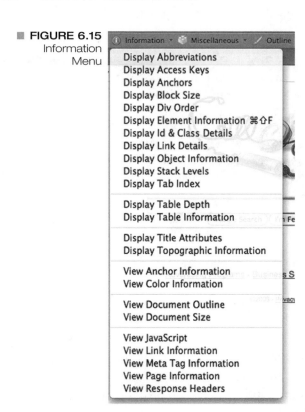

■ **FIGURE 6.16**
Colors of the Page

Java console, and many other tools. The View source menu lets you view the source of the original page download and download the generated source at the current time. The generated source is different from the original source, because JavaScript can modify the elements of a page at any time. The last menu item, Options, lets you configure the Web Developer plug-in. The right side of the menu bar shows if the page is standards compliant, has CSS errors, or has JavaScript errors.

■ 6.8 JSLINT

JSLint was created by Douglas Crockford, creator of JSON. It is a free, open source, static analysis tool that can be used to find bugs in your JavaScript code. JSLint checks for issues, such as making sure you are not using variables before declaring them and JSLint helps you improve the quality of your code. JSLint is very easy to use–all you need to do is paste your JavaScript into a web page.

■ 6.9 JSUNIT

JsUnit is a unit testing framework for JavaScript and a free open source tool. JsUnit is inspired by JUnit, a great unit testing framework for Java. To use JsUnit, start by writing an HTML file that contains various unit tests. This file is called a test script. The test script must include jsUnitCore.js. All functions in the test script that begin with "test" are unit tests. The following is a simple unit test that contains two asserts. `assertEquals` takes three arguments: error message, expected value, and actual value.

```
function testWithValidArgs() {
    assertEquals("2 times 3 plus 5 is 11", 11, multiplyAndAddFive(2,
3));
    assertEquals("Should work with negative numbers", -15, multiply
AndAddFive(-4, 5));
}
```

In this example, `multiplyAndAddFive(2,3)` should return 11, but if it doesn't the error message `2 times 3 plus 5 is 11` appears.

After you write your test script launch `testRunner.html` in your browser. Then input the URL of the test file and run the script. A green bar means success and red bar means failure. Clicking on show selected or Show all allows you to see any error details by. `testRunner.html` can also be run off-line, but it is recommended to run it online, due to security restrictions of Ajax calls.

JsUnit also lets you write test suites. A test suite is a combination of multiple test scripts. Test suites can also contain other test suites. Test suites help you modularize your tests scripts.

JsUnit also contains a server component for automating unit tests in a build environment, but we feel that it is beyond the scope of this book.

Unit testing is a very important tool for helping you reduce the number of bugs in your code. Unit testing also helps you write better, more modular code. Unit testing makes it very easy to test edge conditions that may be difficult to produce in a real environment.

■ 6.10 SELENIUM

The Selenium IDE is a free open source Firefox add-on that lets you easily create integration tests in Firefox. Integration tests test the functionality of a web page, not the fine-grained methods. In a web environment, integration tests often work by clicking on buttons and verifying that the appropriate actions took place on the web page. The Selenium IDE lets you record test steps by clicking within the web page. To get started with Selenium IDE, install the Firefox Selenium IDE add-on. Next, navigate to the web page you want to visit. Open the Selenium IDE by selecting Selenium IDE under the Tools menu. Selenium IDE is already recoding when it is opened. Next, click on buttons and fill in forms until you want to verify a value. To verify a value, highlight the text you want to verify, then right-click and select Verify Text Present. Notice that, in the Selenium IDE, all of the steps you took were added to a table with the columns command, target, and value. You can manually modify or add steps by clicking in the Selenium IDE. At the very top of the Selenium IDE is the Base URL. URLs used in the test steps will be relative to the Base URL. At the top-right there is a Stop button that stops the recording. On the top-left is a test cases and test suites button.

Test-driven development has proven to be very effective in improving coding quality. If you find a bug in your software it is, recommended that you start by writing a test and watching it fail. This will verify that you are testing it correctly. Next, fix the bug and verify the test passes. Now you can add your test to the suite of tests for the application and guarantee that the bug won't come back without you knowing—if you run your tests.

■ 6.11 WIRESHARK

Wireshark® is a free, open source network protocol analyzer. Wireshark is often the tool of choice for network engineers to inspect network traffic for various devices, such as email, printers, web servers, VOIP phones, etc. Wireshark is very advanced and complicated to use, but in cases where you have to hire a network engineer to solve your problems, you may need to use Wireshark. Wireshark was originally named Ethereal and renamed to Wireshark in 2006. Many engineers will only recognize it by its original name. Wireshark can be used to capture traffic, and then save it to a libpcap-formatted file. Then you can email the file to someone who can open the file in Wireshark. This makes Wireshark very useful for working with vendors.

■ 6.12 GOOGLE GADGETS

Google Gadgets are embeddable HTML/JavaScript applications that you can include in iGoogle, Google Maps, and Google Wave. Google Gadgets contain a CDATA section, which can be a mixture of JavaScript code, HTML, and plain text. SVG uses CDATA sections for the same purpose (see Chapter 2). Google Gadgets are also used in OpenSocial applications (discussed in Chapter 8), where they are referred to as OpenSocial Gadgets. The documentation for Google Gadgets can be found here:
http://code.google.com/apis/gadgets/docs/fundamentals.html

Let's look at two examples of Google Gadgets, starting with a very simple `hello, world` Google Gadget. Listing 6.4 shows the contents of `helloworld.xml`, which is a Google `hello, world` Gadget.

Listing 6.4 helloworld.xml

```
<?xml version="1.0" encoding="UTF-8" ?>
<Module>
  <ModulePrefs title="hello world example" />
  <Content type="html">
    <![CDATA[
      Hello, world!
    ]]>
  </Content>
</Module>
```

Listing 6.4 starts with an XML declaration, followed by three lines that define this XML document as a Google gadget. The next section is a CDATA section that displays the `Hello, world` message as shown here:

```
<![CDATA[
     Hello, world
]]>
```

As you can see, a basic Google Gadget can be created with just a few lines of simple code. The second example shows you how to create a Google Gadget that contains an HTML5 canvas element with graphics-based code. Listing 6.5 show the contents of the Google Gadget ArchRect1.xml, which renders a set of rectangles that follow the path of an Archimedean curve.

Listing 6.5 ArchRect1.xml

```
<?xml version="1.0" encoding="UTF-8" ?>
<Module>
<ModulePrefs title="Archimedean Spiral" width="800" height="500" />
<Content type="html">
  <![CDATA[
<html lang="en">
  <head>
    <meta charset="utf-8">
    <title>Archimedean Spiral</title>
    <script type="text/javascript"><!--
window.addEventListener('load', function () {
  // Get the canvas element in the <body> tag
  var elem = document.getElementById('myCanvas');

  if (!elem || !elem.getContext) {
    return;
  }

  // Get the canvas 2d context
  var context = elem.getContext('2d');
  if (!context) {
    return;
  }

  var basePointX  = 300;
  var basePointY  = 200;
  var currentX    = 0;
  var currentY    = 0;
  var offsetX     = 0;
  var offsetY     = 0;
  var radius      = 0;
  var spiralCount = 4;
```

```
var Constant   = 0.25;
var angle      = 0;
var maxAngle   = 720;
var rectWidth  = 40;
var rectHeight = 20;

for(angle=0; angle<maxAngle; angle++) {
   radius  = Constant*angle;
   offsetX = radius*Math.cos(angle*Math.PI/180);
   offsetY = radius*Math.sin(angle*Math.PI/180);
   currentX = basePointX+offsetX;
   currentY = basePointY-offsetY;

   // alternate between red and blue
   if(angle % 2 == 0) {
      context.fillStyle = '#f00';
   }
   else {
      context.fillStyle = '#00f';
   }

   // draw the current rectangle
   context.fillRect(currentX, currentY, rectWidth, rectHeight);
}
}, false);
   // --></script>
 </head>

 <body>
   <canvas id="myCanvas" width="800" height="500">
       Your browser does not support Canvas
   </canvas>
 </body>
</html>
 ]]>
</Content>
</Module>
```

Look carefully at the code in Listing 6.5 and you will see that the code consists of three sections, where the middle section is identical to the HTML5 file ArchRect1.html that you saw in Chapter 2. The first section consists of five lines (shown in Listing 6.6) that identify this file as an XML document and a Google Gadget.

Thus, a graphics-based Google Gadget can be easily created from an existing HTML5 page that contains an HTML5 canvas element with graphics-based code. You can find the source code for various graphics-based Google Gadgets (including ArchRect1.xml) in an open source project that is available under an Apache 2.0 license here:
http://code.google.com/p/html5-canvas-gadgets/

Note that you cannot use <html>, <head>, or <body> tags for Google Gadgets because Google Gadgets generate their own tags, so you only include the content that appears in the <body> tag. Even so, if you include any of the preceeding tags (as is the case in Listing 6.5) the Google Gadget renders correctly, but when you write your own Google Gadgets you should heed this restriction.

Listing 6.6

```
<?xml version="1.0" encoding="UTF-8" ?>
<Module>
<ModulePrefs title="Archimedean Spiral" width="800" height="500" />
<Content type="html">
  <![CDATA[
The last three lines contain the closing tags for the Google
gadget, as shown here:
  ]]>
</Content>
</Module>
```

Listing 6.7 ArchRect1.xml

```
<?xml version="1.0" encoding="UTF-8" ?>
  <Module>
  <ModulePrefs title="State Example" height="120">
  <Require feature="wave-preview" />
  </ModulePrefs>
    <Content type="html">
<![CDATA[

<div id="content_div" style="height: 50px;"></div>

  <script type="text/javascript">

var div = document.getElementById('content_div');

function buttonClicked() {
```

```
    var value = parseInt(wave.getState().get('count', '0'));
    wave.getState().submitDelta({'count': value + 1});
}

// Reset value of "count" to 0
function resetCounter(){
    wave.getState().submitDelta({'count': '0'});
}

function stateUpdated() {
    if(!wave.getState().get('count')) {
        div.innerHTML = "The count is 0."
}
else {
    div.innerHTML = "The count is " + wave.getState().get('count');
    }
}

function init() {
    if (wave && wave.isInWaveContainer()) {
        wave.setStateCallback(stateUpdated);
    }
}
gadgets.util.registerOnLoadHandler(init);

</script>
    <input type=button value="Click Me!" id="butCount" onClick=
"buttonClicked()">
    <input type=button value="Reset" id="butReset" onClick=
"resetCounter()">
]]>
</Content>
</Module>
```

Any OpenSocial gadget can be embedded in a Google wave, and you can also make your gadget live and collaborative. OpenSocial gadgets are discussed in more detail in chapter eight. Listing 6.6 displays the contents of a Google Wave Gadget.

The code in Listing 6.7 is available online here: http://gadget-doc-examples.googlecode.com/svn/trunk/wave/button-counter.xml

The JavaScript code in listing 6.7 ought to be very familiar, and you can leverage your knowledge of JavaScript to write Google Gadgets. The "wave" variable is provided by the Google Gadget container that executes the code in of gadget. Consult the online documentation for information about the various plates of a Google Wave.

■ 6.13 SUMMARY

Writing and debugging Web 2.0 Applications can be very difficult. Thankfully developers have great debugging tools that help developers figure out how to fix unexpected behaviors, or bugs. Many IDEs help to improve developer productivity and simplify viewing code by color coding, highlighting and formatting code. Many of these tools feature profiling tools that will help you solve performance problems. Firebug has become one of the main tools used by most developers in their daily work, but their are many other tools that provide functionality not found in Firebug. As the web applications you write become more complex, the use of debugging tools will become more valuable.

## CHAPTER 7

The Facebook Platform

In This Chapter:

- Social Networking
- Facebook
- SUN Zembly
- Bebo
- Identity Management for Web 2.0 Applications

The goal of this chapter is to help you get started with the Facebook platform in conjunction with some third-party tools and products (such as Zembly and NetBeans) that you can leverage when you create Facebook applications.

First, we'll discuss various aspects of Facebook, including its core components FBML, XFBML, FQL™, and FBJS™, and Facebook Connect™. We'll show you now to register Facebook applications, and discuss several open source projects donated by Facebook. We'll also look at some examples of Facebook integration with other tools and technologies.

One point to note is that Facebook discontinued its support for its Java-based client in 2008, which might make you wonder why we included a discontinued project. The answer to this is two-fold. First, a discontinued tool does not mean that that tool lacks value; second, our goal is to provide you with information regarding available tools that can assist you in making a more informed decision about the components of the technology stack that you select for your tasks.

This chapter also covers SUN Zembly, which is a free online tool that lets you create applications for Facebook, Meebo, OpenSocial, and iPhone, all of which are hosted in the SUN computing cloud. SUN Zembly also provides strong support for creating mash-ups (described in more detail in Chapter 9), integration with Yahoo Pipes (discussed in Chapter 5), and Yahoo Bespin ("BEE spin") (discussed in Chapter 11).

Next, we'll look at the Bebo social network, where you can create Bebo social networking applications, and how you can convert Facebook applications to Bebo applications.

Finally, we'll discuss Identity Management, which is an increasingly important topic for the Facebook and OpenSocial platforms.

■ 7.1 SOCIAL NETWORKING

Social networking increased dramatically over the last decade. A social networking site is an online community that lets people meet, interact, and collaborate in various ways, such as sharing information and photos, and exchanging ideas. Social networks are free to join and try to attain "viral growth" to increase their user base.

Social networks let members create groups based on common interests, such as hobbies, politics, sports, religion, and food. Social networks let people communicate with their friends, family members (local and distant), coworkers, current friends, long-lost childhood friends, former spouses, and so forth. Members log into their accounts and check email messages for news, status updates from their friends, and invitations to upcoming events.

Social networking sites appeal to different audiences, and each site has its own demographics. For example, MySpace encourages self-expression and lets users create customized HTML pages. MySpace is popular among people who like to spend time creating their own websites. By contrast, Facebook is more popular among college-age students who are more interested in the activities of their friends.

The popularity of social networks also varies worldwide. For example, Bebo is very popular in the UK, Orkut (which was acquired by Google) is popular in South America, Facebook and MySpace are popular in the United States, and Mixi® is popular in Asia.

As you will see in Chapter 8, the OpenSocial platform is a consortium of companies with social networking sites (Google Orkut, MySpace, Hi5,

LinkedIn®, and others) that can develop OpenSocial "containers" whose functionality is defined in an OpenSocial specification.

As this book went to print, Microsoft announced Microsoft® Vine™, which is a product in private beta that focuses on helping people in a group share important information.

■ 7.2 FACEBOOK

In 2009, Facebook exceeded 350 million users worldwide to become the largest social networking site in the world. Its home page is:
http://www.facebook./com

In early 2007, Facebook made its internal APIs available to the developer community, which enabled people outside of Facebook to develop a variety of Facebook applications. Other social networks (such as Bebo) made a concerted effort to make their APIs compatible with the Facebook APIs. Thus, Facebook sparked the creation of a social networking "ecosystem" in which Facebook is the dominant component.

On May 22, 2007, Facebook made its developer platform available for free. This bold strategy spurred the development of thousands of Facebook applications, because developers around the world were able to use Facebook APIs within their code (which is stored on an application service provider or on their own machine).

Shortly thereafter, other companies (including Bebo and SUN Zembly) adopted a similar strategy, while others (Google, MySpace, and hi5) formed a consortium, which is discussed in the next chapter.

When Twitter was released in 2006, its functionality consisted of a single global "stream" in which everyone's comments were immediately displayed to everyone. Other applications have incorporated similar functionality, including Meetup.com and Facebook, whereby users can see a stream of status updates from other people. The Facebook News Feed is arguably the central part of the experience for Facebook users.

Facebook recently added several new features, including support for real-time searches, which is similar to Twitter's real-time search.

Another recent feature is support for @ tagging when users update their status on Facebook. Recently, there have been comparisons made between the "@" functionality available on Facebook and Twitter. When Facebook users include the @ symbol, a drop-down list containing events, friends, and groups appears. Users then make their selection from the drop-down list, and when the status update is published, the @ symbol is not displayed.

A third feature is Facebook Event, which creates automatic guest lists using previous events. Users can create new invitation lists based on the people who were invited to the five most recent events, and they can be invited individually or collectively.

A fourth important change occurred in August 2009 with the release of Facebook Lite, which is a "slimmed down" version that supports core features, such as status updates and access to profile information.

■ 7.2.1 Facebook Features and Services

Facebook provides services or "modules" to improve the end user's experience when they are using Facebook. This section describes some of the major features that have made Facebook such a popular platform for people throughout the world.

7.2.1.1 Facebook Photos

One of the most popular Facebook applications is Facebook photos, which can be found here:

http://www.facebook.com/video/video.php?v=151887435468&ref=nf

Facebook Photos is the largest photo site in the world, surpassing sites such as Flickr and Photobucket®. Facebook handles over 15 billion images, and each image is actually stored in four sizes, for a total of more than than 60 billion files.

Each week, Facebook processes more than 25 terabytes of photos, and currently stores more than 50 petabytes of data. At peak capacity, Facebook serves more than 500,000 images per second.

Users can manage their photos by using photo albums, which can hold a maximum of 200 photos (there is no limit to the number of albums). Users can add captions and "tag" people in the photos.

7.2.1.2 Facebook Connect

Facebook Connect may have been an important factor in Facebook surpassing MySpace as the largest social networking site in the world. Its home page is:

http://developers.facebook.com/connect.php

Facebook Connect lets users connect their Facebook account and information to your website and find any existing friends who are also using your site. Facebook Connect provides your website with several advantages, including Facebook functionality, the authenticated identities of 350,000,000 potential users, and the Facebook distribution channels.

When users publish a story on their Facebook page, Facebook Connect lets them continue that conversation on their own website. Users can also invite their Facebook friends to join their website, and they can even find relationships among new Facebook visitors because Facebook Connect provides a social graph containing those existing relationships.

Facebook Connect was designed to be scalable and highly performant by reducing latency and server-side calls. Facebook Connect also focuses on ease of use and deployment, and with no modifications to the server-side programming model.

On the server, the major components of Facebook Connect are the application server and the Facebook server, while the client-side involves a combination of HTML and FBML. The underlying data layer attempts to optimize data access, partly through embedding Facebook data on websites.

7.2.1.2.1 FACEBOOK CONNECT AND THIRD-PARTY INTEGRATION

Facebook Connect can be integrated with third-party products and tools, such as ASP.NET. In addition, you can integrate Facebook Connect with Microsoft Windows Azure (discussed in Chapter 10) and Microsoft Silverlight. Check the appendices on the CD for links that contain more information. In 2010 you may also see MySpace providing integration with Facebook Connect, and Yahoo has already announced its support for Facebook Connect.

7.2.1.3 Facebook Pages

Facebook Pages lets users create a "presence" on Facebook that resembles a user profile, which can be used to communicate with other audiences (such as customers). Its home page is:

http://www.facebook.com/advertising/?pages

Perform the following steps to create a Facebook Page:

Step 1: Navigate to the home page and click on the Create a Page button

Step 2: Select a category (Local, Brand, or Artist)

Step 3: Enter a name in the Name of Consumer Product input field

Step 4: Check the authorization box and add your signature

Step 5: Click the Create Page button

Step 6: Publish the Page

After a few moments, Facebook will create your new Facebook page, and you can click on Become a fan to add yourself to your page.

For example, we created a Facebook page for this book by selecting Products and specifying Web 2.0 book as the name of the product.

7.2.1.4   *Facebook Pages and Twitter*

If you want to send Facebook Page updates to Twitter, click on the Click here link and perform the following steps:

Step 1: Click on the Link a Page to Twitter button

Step 2: Click on the Link to Twitter button

Step 3: Click on the Allow button to allow access to your Facebook account

You can manage the Facebook pages linked to your Twitter account from: http://www.facebook.com/twitter/

7.2.1.5   *fbFund*

Facebook created fbFund, which provides money to companies creating Facebook applications. Its home page is:
http://developers.facebook.com/fbFund.php

Facebook administrates the fbFund, and Accel Partners and The Founders Fund provide the funding. Facebook provides a set of criteria for the fbFund selection process, and users can submit multiple Facebook applications.

Facebook provides funding (from US $25,000 to US $100,000) and mentoring to assist companies in becoming successful with their Facebook applications. Check the Facebook home page for more details and recent updates.

■ 7.2.2   **Facebook Applications**

This section describes the main features of Facebook, and how you can create a Facebook application. We'll also look at some additional features of the Facebook platform that can help you create more sophisticated Facebook applications.

Facebook users have a social graph that charts their relationships with other users and applications. Each user has a profile that contains his or her public and private information.

Facebook applications support PHP and Python, and client libraries written in PHP 5 and JavaScript. Facebook previously supported Java-based clients, but that was discontinued in May 2008.

You can find client library downloads and detailed information here: http://wiki.developers.facebook.com/index.php/Client_Libraries

The Facebook platform developer community also maintains an extensive set of client libraries, but Facebook does not provide official support. Languages for the client libraries include ActionScript, C++, C#, Erlang, and Perl.

You can find links with additional details regarding these client libraries here: http://wiki.developers.facebook.com/index.php/Client_Libraries

Now let's take a closer look at Facebook applications.

7.2.2.1 Scripting Support in Facebook Applications

HTML pages typically involve a combination of HTML tags, JavaScript, and Cascading Style Sheets (CSS). If you have ever written JavaServer Pages (JSPs), you have undoubtedly used JSP tags, which provide support for loops and conditional logic so you can include scriptlets in an HTML page.

When you create Facebook applications, not only can you use HTML, but also PHP, CSS, and other tag libraries. In particular, you can use FaceBook Markup Language (FBML) and XFMBL, which is an extension of FBML that lets you write FBML in IFRAME applications.

Instead of using "pure" JavaScript in Facebook applications, you will use FaceBook JavaScript (FBJS), and instead of SQL, Facebook supports Facebook Query Language (FQL), which lets you retrieve details about Facebook users. Finally, Facebook applications use a set of Facebook APIs that are geared toward social applications.

Facebook handles the authentication for applications, and when Facebook APIs are used, a POST request is sent to the Facebook server, which returns a response that can be either XML or JSON-formatted data.

Facebook applications consist of various components that can be accessed programmatically, including the Application canvas, profile box, and directory. In addition, Facebook applications can programmatically send alerts, notifications, and message attachments.

7.2.2.2 *How to Create Facebook Applications*

First, create a free Facebook user account, and then find a free hosting service provider where you can store your application code.

Perform the following steps to create a Facebook application:

Step 1: Navigate to the Facebook developer page here:
http://developers.facebook.com/

Step 2: Click on the Start Now button

Step 3: Click on the Allow button in the dialog box

Step 4: Click on Set up New Application

Step 5: Enter MyFirst1 as the application name

Step 6: Click on the Agree button and then the Save Changes button

Select the Developer Mode checkbox to ensure that your application is not publicly available before you have completed your development.

Facebook will create a new application called MyFirst1, and after a few moments you will see the following information:

```
Application ID 136670004801
API Key  39a5cc8c59bf72349a1d531dcf2a629b
Secret b5aacd2393cf31904e5ff9192f3ee3e0
```

The `Application ID` is an identifier for this application. The `API Key` is an authentication token that is submitted every time your application makes an API call. The `Secret` key is used by Facebook to authenticate the API requests of your application.

Next, provide your email address for the input fields Developer Contact Email and User Support Address, and then click the Save Changes button.

Facebook saves the values you provide, and then you will see a screen that contains links for additional downloads, including the Client Library, Platform Documentation, Code Samples, and Unofficial Client Libraries.

One very useful link is the Test Console link, which contains tabs that let you test the results of the PHP code that makes API calls and the output from the FBML code in your application.

Note that you can use a Callback URL and a Base URL on your system if you do not want to use a third-party hosting service. For example, if you want to use http://my.local.machine/FacebookCallback for the Callback URL and http://my.local.machine/ for the Base URL, update the host file on your system as follows:

127.0.0.1 my.local.machine

Verify that your update is valid by launching your browser and navigating to: http://my.local.machine/

If you made a correct entry in the host file, you will see the following text in your browser:

It works!

7.2.2.3   A Simple Facebook Connect Application

You can create "external" Facebook applications that have the same type of functionality as Facebook ones, such as accessing FBML, invoking Facebook APIs, submitting news feed items, finding friends, sending invites (the same as what's available on Facebook now).

First, you must be a Facebook developer.

Perform the following steps to create a Facebook Connect application (jot down the API key created in Step 1 to use in Step 5):

Step 1: Navigate to:
http://www.facebook.com/developers/createapp.php

Step 2: Specify a name for your application

Step 3: Accept the Developer Terms of Service and save the changes

Step 4: Use the default values on the Basic tab

Step 5: On the Connect tab, set the Connect URL to the root directory of where you will implement Facebook Connect, which might look like this: http://www.mysite.com/

Step 6: Add an image file by clicking on Change your Facebook Connect logo

Step 7: Specify a value for Base Domain if you intend to use Facebook Connect for multiple subdomains

Step 8: Click on Save Changes to save everything

■ 7.2.3 Facebook Core Components

This section provides a quick overview of the five major Facebook components, which are listed here:

- the Facebook API
- FBML
- XFBML
- FQL
- FBJS

In addition, the following subsections contain links to Facebook websites and sample code fragments that illustrate the type of functionality that you can use in Facebook applications.

7.2.3.1 Facebook API

The Facebook website contains information about the Facebook APIs here: http://wiki.developers.facebook.com/index.php/API

The Facebook API uses a Representational State Transfer (REST)-like interface, which is a topic not covered in this book. You can find more information about REST by searching the Internet, and an overview of REST (with additional links) is also available here: http://en.wikipedia.org/wiki/Representational_State_Transfer

7.2.3.2 Facebook FBML

FBML is an XML-based markup language containing entities (XML elements) that are derived from HTML. An example of an FBML tag is:

```
<fb:name uid="444444">is a friend of mine</fb:name>
```

Note that the preceding code snippet contains an fb prefix, which is a Facebook namespace that appears in FBML elements. The definition of the Facebook fb namespace is here: http://apps.facebook.com/ns/1.0

The Facebook wiki, with details about FBML, can be found here: http://wiki.developers.facebook.com/index.php/FBML

7.2.3.3 Facebook XFBML

Facebook provides XFBML as a mechanism for embedding FBML in HTML pages. Currently, Facebook provides support for a number of tags, such as fb:comments, fb:eventlink, fb:loginbutton, fb:name, and fb:photo, which have intuitive names that correspond to their functionality.

You can indicate that an HTML page is actually an XHTML page by including the following code fragment at the beginning of an HTML page:

```
<!DOCTYPE html PUBLIC "-//W3C//DTD XHTML 1.0 Strict//EN"
"http://www.w3.org/TR/xhtml1/DTD/xhtml1-strict.dtd">
```

```
<html xmlns="http://www.w3.org/1999/xhtml"
xmlns:fb="http://www.facebook.com/2008/fbml">
```

This code fragment will ensure that your HTML pages are rendered properly in other browsers.

The following URL lets you test XFBML code:

http://www.somethingtoputhere.com/demo/xfbml_console/index.html

Copy a block of XFBML code in the text area and then click the Render XFBML button to see the results.

Additional information about XFBML is here:

http://wiki.developers.facebook.com/index.php/XFBML

7.2.3.4 Facebook FQL

FQL is a SQL-like query language that lets you extract data from Facebook tables. If you are unfamiliar with SQL, there are many online tutorials that will help you gain a rudimentary understanding of SQL statements. Unlike standard SQL, Facebook FQL provides support for both XML and JSON responses.

Facebook applications use FQL statements so you can manage the data that is stored in Facebook tables. Facebook provides an extensive set of tables, including album, comment, cookies, connection, event, friend, friend_request, friendlist, group, page_fan, photo, profile, status, and user.

As a simple example, the following FQL query returns the value of uid from the user table when the value of name equals 'John Smith':

```
SELECT uid FROM user WHERE name = 'John Smith'
```

The following FQL query returns the value of uid from the user table when the value of name equals 'John Smith':

```
SELECT uid FROM user WHERE name = 'John Smith' AND uid IN (SELECT
uid2 FROM friend WHERE uid1 = 1001)
```

In PHP, an FQL query would be handled as follows:

```
$query = "REPLACE THIS WITH AN FBL QUERY";
$result = $facebook->api_client->fql_query($query);
```

7.2.3.5 *Facebook FBJS*

FBJS lets you write Facebook applications that use JavaScript code. More-over, FBJS lets you manage Document Object Model (DOM) objects, process events, and make Ajax invocations. However, whenever a Facebook application invokes a Facebook API, Facebook will parse and modify HTML pages belonging to Facebook applications as follows:

Step 1: Unsupported JavaScript constructs are removed

Step 2: The application ID is prepended to JavaScript functions and variables

For example, suppose that your Facebook application ID is 55555 and your Facebook application contains the JavaScript function in Listing 7.1.

Listing 7.1

```
function hello(name) {
  var msg = "hello, "+name:
  return msg;
}
```

Facebook will modify the contents of Listing 7.1 and generate the code in Listing 7.2.

Listing 7.2

```
function 55555_hello(55555_name) {
  var 55555_msg = "hello, "+55555_name:
  return 55555_msg;
}
```

7.2.3.5.1 FBJS DOM Objects

FBJS DOM objects implement many of the methods that are available in JavaScript DOM objects, including appendChild, insertBefore, removeChild, and cloneNode.

However, properties such as `parentNode` and `nextSibling` are modified by prepending the string `get`, and using Camel-case notation for the new method name.

For example, the method `parentNode()` in JavaScript is called `getParentNode()` in FBJS (note that the FBJS method name is not `getparentNode()`), and the JavaScript method `nextSibling()` becomes `getNextSibling()` in FBJS.

Some FBJS properties have both a "setter" method and a "getter" method. For example, the JavaScript property `src` has the FBJS getter method `getSrc()` and the FBJS setter method `setSrc()`.

An extensive list of JavaScript method names and their corresponding FBJS method names can be found here:
http://wiki.developers.facebook.com/index.php/FBJS

7.2.3.5.2 FBJS AJAX

FBJS provides Ajax objects for developers that you can use by simply instantiating a new Ajax class as shown here:

```
var myAjax = new Ajax();
```

Note that Facebook proxies Ajax requests and may perform additional processing on the returned data set. The Ajax class supports the following standard events:

- Abort()
- ondone(data)
- onerror
- post(url,query)

The Ajax class also supports the following properties:

- Ajax.FBML
- Ajax.RAW
- Ajax.JSON
- responseType

The variable responseType can be Ajax.FBML, Ajax.JSON, or Ajax.RAW, which corresponds to FBML content, JSON content, and original content, respectively.

A detailed explanation of the FBJS Ajax properties can be found here:
http://wiki.developers.facebook.com/index.php/FBJS

A detailed example of using the Ajax class (along with PHP code) is here:
http://wiki.developers.facebook.com/index.php/FBJS/Examples/Ajax

7.2.3.6 Facebook Haystack

Facebook processes an enormous volume of data on a daily basis, so managing that data effectively is an extremely important priority. Facebook Haystack is the technology that enables Facebook to effectively manage photo storage based on three criteria: performance, scalability, and cost-effectiveness.

An interesting look at how Haystack stores billions of pages can be found here: http://blog.admon.org/2009/09/haystack-new-storage-solution-for-billions-of-photos/

7.2.3.7 Facebook Open Source Projects

A list of Facebook open source projects is available here:
http://developers.facebook.com/opensource.php

The Facebook open source projects include: Thrift, Scribe, memcached, Cassandra™, PHPEmbed, and Facebook Mirror™.

■ 7.2.4 Facebook Integration with Other Products

Earlier in this chapter, you learned how to link Facebook Pages and post updates in your Facebook page to your Twitter account. In addition to integration with Twitter, Facebook also provides integration with other tools and products, including SalesForce and Adobe Flex.

7.2.4.1 Facebook Tornado

In September 2009, Facebook released project Tornado, which is an open source Python-based web server that supports Friendfeed:
http://github.com/facebook/tornado

Download and uncompress Tornado in a convenient directory and then run the following command:

```
python setup.py build
```

The demo subdirectory contains various examples of how to use Facebook Tornado, including Google App Engine (GAE), which is the topic of the next section.

7.2.4.1.1 FACEBOOK TORNADO AND GAE

This section is optional because it requires some knowledge of Python, which is not covered in this book, and some understanding of GAE, which is discussed in Chapter 10 and Chapter 12.

The set-up steps are here:

Step 1: Download and install Python (2.5 or higher)

Step 2: Download and install the GAE SDK for Python from: http://code.google.com/appengine/downloads.html#Google_ App_Engine_SDK_for_Python

Step 3: Move into the demo/appengine subdirectory of Facebook Tornado

Step 4: Launch the GAE server:

$GAE_HOME/dev_appserver.py

Step 5: Launch your browser and navigate to: http://localhost:8080

Step 6: Enter your email address and click the Login button

If everything is working correctly, you will see a top-level banner with the (left-justified) text Tornado Blog, and a New post link and a Sign out link, both of which are on the right side of the banner.

Enter some text in the text area and then click the Publish post button at the bottom of the page. Your text will be published as a blog entry.

After you have finished working with this GAE demo, read the source code or experiment with the other demos that are available in Facebook Tornado.

7.2.4.2 FaceConnector

Clara Shih created FaceConnector™ (formerly called Faceforce), which is the first business application that integrates Facebook with SalesForce.

Clara Shih provides some tips for small businesses here: http://www.facebook.com/note.php?note_id=66332094821

FaceConnector can be found here: http://salesbookapp.com/faceconnector/

7.2.4.3 Adobe Flex Integration

Note: the information in this section was obtained from the following website: http://www.adobe.com/devnet/facebook/articles/build_your_first_facebook_air_app.html

The prerequisites for integrating Adobe AIR with Facebook are:

- a Facebook account
- Adobe Flex Builder 3
- ActionScript 3.0 Client Library for the Facebook Platform
- Adobe® AIR™

You can download Flex Builder 3 from:
https://www.adobe.com/cfusion/tdrc/index.cfm?product=flex

You can download the ActionScript 3.0 Client Library for the Facebook Platform from:
http://code.google.com/p/facebook-actionscript-api/

You can download Adobe AIR from: http://get.adobe.com/air/

Because you might not have access to all of the prerequisites, the following steps provide a high-level description of what is required to integrate Facebook and Adobe AIR:

Step 1: Create a Facebook account

Step 2: Add the Developer application to your Facebook account

Step 3: Register a Facebook application to obtain an application API key

Step 4: Create an Adobe AIR application that communicates with Facebook

Step 5: Deploy the Adobe AIR application

See the Appendix for additional links regarding Facebook and Adobe Flex integration.

7.2.4.4 Adobe Flash Integration

An example of Facebook and Adobe Flash integration can be found here: http://www.adobe.com/devnet/facebook/

Steven Shongrunden wrote the code for Listing 7.3, which is available here: http://www.adobe.com/devnet/facebook/samples/index.html

Listing 7.3 shows the contents of Steven's sample code, which illustrates how to integrate Facebook with Adobe Flash:

Listing 7.3

```
<?xml version="1.0" encoding="utf-8"?>
<mx:Application xmlns:mx="http://www.adobe.com/2006/mxml"
                layout="vertical" applicationComplete="init();"
                backgroundColor="0xFFFFFF" backgroundImage="">
  <mx:Script>
    <![CDATA[
        import com.facebook.Facebook;
        import com.facebook.events.FacebookEvent;
        import com.facebook.net.FacebookCall;
        import com.facebook.data.users.FacebookUser;
        import com.facebook.data.users.GetInfoData;
        import com.facebook.commands.users.GetInfo;
        import com.facebook.utils.FacebookSessionUtil;

        private var fbook:Facebook;
        private var session:FacebookSessionUtil;

        private var API_KEY:String = "xxxx";
        private var SECRET_KEY:String = "xxxx";

        private function init():void {
            session=new FacebookSessionUtil(API_KEY, SECRET_KEY,
                                            loaderInfo);
            session.addEventListener(FacebookEvent.CONNECT,
                                     onConnect);
            fbook=session.facebook;
        }

        private function onConnect(e:FacebookEvent):void {
            status.text = "Facebook API Ready";
        }

        private function doneLoggingIn():void {
            session.validateLogin();
        }

        private function sayHello():void {
            var call:FacebookCall = fbook.post
                                    (new GetInfo([fbook.uid],
                                                 ['first_name',
                                                  'last_name']));

            call.addEventListener(FacebookEvent.COMPLETE,
                                  handleGetInfoResponse);
        }
```

```
            private function handleGetInfoResponse
                    (e:FacebookEvent):void {
                var responseData:GetInfoData = e.data as GetInfoData;

                if (!responseData || e.error){ // an error occurred
                    status.text = "Error";
                    return;
                }

                var firstName:String =
                            responseData.userCollection.getItemAt(0)
                                                    .first_name;
                var lastName:String =
                            responseData.userCollection.getItemAt(0)
                                                    .last_name;

                output.text = "Hello " + firstName + " " + lastName;
            }
        ]]>
    </mx:Script>

    <mx:Button label="1. Login to Facebook" click="session.login();" />
    <mx:Button label="2. Done logging in" click="doneLoggingIn()" />
    <mx:Button label="3. Say Hello" click="sayHello()" />

    <mx:Label id="status" text="Please log in" />
    <mx:Label id="output" text="Hello" />
</mx:Application>
```

Listing 7.3 is an XML document whose root element Application contains a namespace prefix mx, which is used to include different elements in the same mx namespace.

Listing 7.3 also contains the XML <mx:Script> element, which in turn contains a CDATA section that starts with various Facebook import statements, as shown here:

```
        import com.facebook.Facebook;
        import com.facebook.events.FacebookEvent;
        import com.facebook.net.FacebookCall;
        import com.facebook.data.users.FacebookUser;
        import com.facebook.data.users.GetInfoData;
        import com.facebook.commands.users.GetInfo;
        import com.facebook.utils.FacebookSessionUtil;
```

These import statements are similar to the import statements in Java classes, and they let you instantiate classes that are required later in the code.

Listing 7.3 contains two variables whose current values must be replaced by Facebook application keys:

```
private var API_KEY:String = "xxxx";
private var SECRET_KEY:String = "xxxx";
```

Listing 7.3 also contains a set of methods to access the Facebook server and retrieve data.

The last part of Listing 7.3, after the closing <mx:Script> tag, contains the definitions of three Button elements and two Label elements, as shown here:

```
<mx:Button label="1. Login to Facebook" click="session.login();" />
<mx:Button label="2. Done logging in" click="doneLoggingIn()" />
<mx:Button label="3. Say Hello" click="sayHello()" />

<mx:Label id="status" text="Please log in" />
<mx:Label id="output" text="Hello" />
```

The Button elements specify the methods to use when users click on each of the buttons. When users click on the first button, the login() method of the session object is executed. Note that when users click on the second and third buttons, the code invokes the two methods, doneLoggingIn() and say-Hello(), that are defined in the CDATA section in Listing 7.3.

7.2.4.5 *Facebook Applications and Alfresco*

Next, we'll look at how to create a Facebook application that is integrated into Alfresco™, which is an open source Content Management System (CMS). The Alfresco home page is: http://www.alfresco.com/

The following website describes Facebook integration with Alfresco: http://wiki.alfresco.com/wiki/Facebook

After you add the Facebook Developer application (if you have not already done so), complete the following steps:

Step 1: Create a Facebook application called Alfresco1

Step 2: Log into the Alfresco web client

Step 3: Navigate to the Web Scripts subdirectory of Data Dictionary

Step 4: Create the subdirectory com/facebook/_apps, and add the file in Step 5

Step 5: Create a file app.<API-KEY>.js with the text from Listing 7.4

Step 6: Create the subdirectory com/alfresco/facebook under Web Scripts

Step 7: Add the file in Step 8 to the subdirectory in Step 6

Step 8: Create a file hellofriends.post.desc.xml with the text from Listing 7.5

Step 9: Add the file in Step 10 to the org/alfresco/facebook subdirectory

Step 10: Create the file hellofriends.post.fbml.ftl with the text from Listing 7.6

The template in Listing 7.5 iterates through your Facebook friends and displays their names.

Listing 7.4

```
app.id="<Application id>";
app.secret="<Secret>";
```

Listing 7.5

```
<webscript>
 <shortname>Hello Friends</shortname>
 <url>/facebook/Alfresco1/</url>
 <format default="fbml"/>
 <authentication>user</authentication>
</webscript>
```

Listing 7.6

```
Hello from
<#list facebook.friends as friend>
 <fb:name uid="${friend}"/><#if friend_has_next>, </#if>
</#list>
```

7.2.4.6 *Facebook and JSPs*

In this section, we'll create a NetBeans project with JSPs that use Facebook APIs to get a list of Facebook friends.

In high-level terms, a JSP page is a JavaServer page that contains a mixture of HTML and scriptlets, which consist of Java-like code. JSP pages are dynamically compiled into Java servlets. If you want to learn more about JSPs, search the Internet for tutorials that provide detailed information about JSPs.

We need to do two things before we can create the NetBeans project in this section: install the Tomcat servlet container (see Chapter 5 for instructions) and then install NetBeans (see Chapter 6 for instructions). After creating the NetBeans project, register it with Facebook to get API keys.

Complete the following steps to create a project in NetBeans (6.5 or higher):

Step 1: Follow the menu path **File > New Project**

Step 2: Select Java Web under Categories

Step 3: Select Web Application under Project

Step 4: Enter `Facebook1` in the Project Name field

Step 5: Select Tomcat and Java EE 5 (or Glassfish if it's installed)

Step 6: Click through the remaining options

NetBeans will create a project and display the contents of the JSP page index.jsp.

Next, perform the following steps to add a Facebook service to this project:

Step 1: Click on the Facebook1 project in the Projects panel

Step 2: Click on the Services tab

Step 3: Expand the nodes **Web Services > Facebook > Social Networking Service**

Step 4: Expand the [restserver.php] node and select friends_get

Step 5: Click on friends_get and drag it into the body of index.jsp

A pop-up window will appear, and after accepting the default values you will see the following message:

"Generating code for GET SaaS Service…"

NetBeans will take at least one minute (or longer) to generate the required code and insert that code into the JSP page `index.jsp`.

Listing 7.7 shows the contents of the JSP page index.jsp, which also contains the generated Facebook code.

Listing 7.7

```jsp
<%@page contentType="text/html" pageEncoding="UTF-8"%>
<!DOCTYPE HTML PUBLIC "-//W3C//DTD HTML 4.01 Transitional//EN"
    "http://www.w3.org/TR/html4/loose.dtd">
<html>
    <head>
        <meta http-equiv="Content-Type" content="text/html;
charset=UTF-8">
        <title>JSP Page</title>
    </head>

    <body>
        <%@ page import="org.netbeans.saas.*, org.netbeans.saas
.facebook.*" %>

        <%
          try {
              String format = null;
              String flid = null;

        RestResponse result = FacebookSocialNetworkingService
.friendsGet(request, response, format, flid);
            if(result.getDataAsObject(facebook.socialnetworkingservice
.facebookresponse.FriendsGetResponse.class) instanceof
            facebook.socialnetworkingservice.facebookresponse
.FriendsGetResponse)
                {
facebook.socialnetworkingservice.facebookresponse.FriendsGetResponse
resultObj =
            result.getDataAsObject(facebook.socialnetworkingservice
.facebookresponse.FriendsGetResponse.class);
                }
                else
                {
            if(result.getDataAsObject(facebook.socialnetworkingservice
.facebookresponse.ErrorResponse.class) instanceof
            facebook.socialnetworkingservice.facebookresponse
.ErrorResponse)
                    {
```

```
facebook.socialnetworkingservice.facebookresponse.ErrorResponse
resultObj =
      result.getDataAsObject(facebook.socialnetworkingservice
.facebookresponse.ErrorResponse.class);
```
```
// Uncomment the print Statement below to print result.
//out.println("The SaasService returned: "+result
    .getDataAsString());
                  }
              }
            catch (Exception ex) {
              ex.printStackTrace();
            }
          }
        %>
        <h1>Hello World!</h1>
      </body>
</html>
```

Listing 7.7 contains a mixture of HTML and JSP code. The first line of code identifies the code as a JSP page, as shown here:

```
<%@page contentType="text/html" pageEncoding="UTF-8"%>
```

The next section of Listing 7.7 contains HTML tags, and then the BODY tag references Facebook classes, as shown here:

```
<%@ page import="org.netbeans.saas.*,
              org.netbeans.saas.facebook.*" %>
```

The preceding code snippet imports the required classes that are in the org.netbeans.saas package and the org.netbeans.saas.facebook pages.

The next section in Listing 7.7 contains a try/catch block that uses the friendsGet method of the FacebookSocialNetworkingService class (which is a Java servlet that was generated during the creation of this NetBeans project), as shown here:

```
RestResponse result = FacebookSocialNetworkingService
        .friendsGet(request, response, format, flid);
```

The next section of Listing 7.7 contains some conditional logic, and you can see the results of the initial invocation of the friendsGet() method here:

```
out.println("The SaasService returned:
        "+result.getDataAsString());
```

If you're interested, Listing 7.8 shows the structure of the Java-related portion of the Facebook1 project.

Listing 7.8

```
+ src
  + conf
    + MANIFEST.MF
  + java
    + org
      + netbeans
        + saas
          + RestConnection.java
          + RestResponse.java
          + Facebook
            + FacebookSocialNetworkingService.java
            + FacebookSocialNetworkingServiceAuthenticator.java
            + Facebooksocialnetworkingserviceauthenticator
              .properties
            + FacebookSocialNetworkingServiceCallback.java
            + FacebookSocialNetworkingServiceLogin.java
```

Listing 7.8 contains two Java classes, FacebookSocialNetworkingService Callback.java and FacebookSocialNetworkingServiceLogin.java, both of which are Java servlets that are used in the JSP page in Listing 7.7. The other two Java classes are Plain Old Java Objects (POJOs) that are used by the other Java servlets.

Listing 7.9 shows the steps that NetBeans performs during the compilation of the code in the Facebook1 project.

Listing 7.9

```
Created dir: C:/Users/Owner/.netbeans/6.7/config/WebServices/Social-
NetworkingService/catalog/FacebookResponse-jaxb/build

Created dir: C:/Users/Owner/.netbeans/6.7/config/WebServices/Social-
NetworkingService/catalog/FacebookResponse-jaxb/src

Consider using <depends>/<produces> so that XJC won't do unnecessary
compilation

Compiling file:/C:/Users/Owner/.netbeans/6.7/config/WebServices/
SocialNetworkingService/catalog/FacebookResponse.xsd
```

```
Writing output to C:/Users/Owner/.netbeans/6.7/config/WebServices/
SocialNetworkingService/catalog/FacebookResponse-jaxb/src

Deleting directory C:/Users/Owner/.netbeans/6.7/config/WebServices/
SocialNetworkingService/catalog/FacebookResponse-jaxb/build

Created dir: C:/Users/Owner/.netbeans/6.7/config/WebServices/
SocialNetworkingService/catalog/FacebookResponse-jaxb/build

Compiling 155 source files to C:/Users/Owner/.netbeans/6.7/config/
WebServices/SocialNetworkingService/catalog/FacebookResponse-jaxb/
build

Building jar: C:/Users/Owner/.netbeans/6.7/config/WebServices/
SocialNetworkingService/catalog/FacebookResponse-jaxb/Facebook-
Response-src.jar

Building jar: C:/Users/Owner/.netbeans/6.7/config/WebServices/Social-
NetworkingService/catalog/FacebookResponse-jaxb/FacebookResponse.jar

Deleting directory C:/Users/Owner/.netbeans/6.7/config/WebServices/
SocialNetworkingService/catalog/FacebookResponse-jaxb/build

Deleting directory C:/Users/Owner/.netbeans/6.7/config/WebServices/
SocialNetworkingService/catalog/FacebookResponse-jaxb/src

xjc-jar:
BUILD SUCCESSFUL (total time: 1 minute 18 seconds)
```

Listing 7.9 is interesting because it clearly shows that the NetBeans Facebook1 project uses XML schemas (discussed in Chapter 3) and JAXB, which is a Java-XML binding technology that generates Java classes from XML elements in an XML schema. You will learn more about JAXB in Chapter 12, XML, Java, and GAE.

Next, register the Facebook1 application in Facebook and copy the two generated keys into the following NetBeans project file:

```
org.netbeans.saas.facebook
    .facebooksocialnetworkingserviceauthenticator.properties.
```

Now run the Facebook1 project by clicking F6 (or select Run from the navigation bar), after which NetBeans will generate more code, launch a browser session, and render the JSP page index.jsp.

Listing 7.10 shows the output generated during the execution of this project.

Listing 7.10

```
init:
deps-module-jar:
deps-ear-jar:
deps-jar:
Created dir: C:/Users/Owner/Documents/NetBeansProjects/Facebook1/
build/web/WEB-INF/classes
Created dir: C:/Users/Owner/Documents/NetBeansProjects/Facebook1/
build/web/META-INF
Copying 1 file to C:/Users/Owner/Documents/NetBeansProjects/
Facebook1/build/web/META-INF
Copying 3 files to C:/Users/Owner/Documents/NetBeansProjects/
Facebook1/build/web
library-inclusion-in-archive:
Copying 1 file to C:/Users/Owner/Documents/NetBeansProjects/
Facebook1/build/web/WEB-INF/lib
library-inclusion-in-manifest:
Created dir: C:/Users/Owner/Documents/NetBeansProjects/Facebook1/
build/empty
Copying 1 file to C:/Users/Owner/Documents/NetBeansProjects/
Facebook1/build/web/WEB-INF/classes
compile:
compile-jsps:
In-place deployment at C:/Users/Owner/Documents/NetBeansProjects/
Facebook1/build/web
Deployment is in progress...
deploy?config=file%3A%2FC%3A%2FUsers%2FOwner%2FAppData%2FLocal%2FTem
p%2Fcontext445103841295028826.xml&path=/Facebook1
OK - Deployed application at context path /Facebook1
start?path=/Facebook1
Start is in progress...
OK - Started application at context path /Facebook1
run-deploy:
Browsing: http://localhost:8080/Facebook1/
run-display-browser:
```

```
run:
BUILD SUCCESSFUL (total time: 2 seconds)
```

Listing 7.10 contains compilation steps (including the compilation of JSP pages), followed by the deployment step, where NetBeans will launch a browser session and render the following link:

http://localhost:8080/Facebook1/FacebookSocialNetworkingServiceLogin/

7.2.4.7 *Developing Java Applications in Facebook*

The open source project Facebook-Java-API is a Java-based Facebook API client that is based on the original Facebook client that was discontinued in May 2008. Facebook-Java-API is the most active and mature library for Java. Its home page is:

http://code.google.com/p/facebook-java-api/

Java-based Facebook applications involve hosting them directly from your web server in an IFrame. This approach eliminates all cross-domain issues and the need to proxy calls through other servers, thereby simplifying the Ajax calls to your web server.

Facebook loads the IFrame and parses a token in the query string. Next, the Facebook-Java-API adds a filter to add Facebook user information to the session, which gives you access to user information via Java servlets. You can retrieve user-related information (such as a user's Facebook friends) via HTTP requests from your web server to Facebook.

This technique (i.e., your web server acting as a proxy for accessing Facebook) appears to increase the complexity of application development (and the burden on your web server) when compared to the OpenSocial model. Note that OpenSocial applications proxy through the OpenSocial server, which then calls your web server. The Facebook model also requires your server to perform additional session management tasks, and it also eliminates the caching of service calls, which is available in the OpenSocial model.

Several other Facebook-Java libraries can be found here:

http://wiki.developers.Facebook.com/index.php/Java/

You can also develop Facebook applications using SUN® Glassfish™, which is an open source application server. Its home page is:

https://glassfish.dev.java.net/

Additional information about creating Facebook applications in Glassfish can be found here:

http://blogs.sun.com/sduv/entry/write_facebook_applications_using_java

This concludes our discussion of Facebook in this chapter. Go to the Facebook home page to find other useful how-to links, recent updates, and other relevant information. The next section discusses SUN Zembly, which is an interesting multi-faceted social networking tool from SUN.

■ 7.3 SUN ZEMBLY

Zembly* is a free browser-based product from SUN for building and hosting web applications. Its home page is: http://www.zembly.com

Zembly was created at SUN in 2006, released in 2008 as private beta, and then released as public beta in 2009. Zembly provides an integrated environment that lets users quickly create widgets and social applications for Facebook, iPhone, Meebo, and Orkut. Zembly is based on a browser-based web-oriented development model that is also a RESTful services integration platform.

You can register for a free Zembly account at: https://zembly.com/ui/signup

Zembly provides both drag-and-drop functionality and a set of APIs that developers can leverage in their web applications. Zembly consists of four major components:

- a browser-based IDE
- an application repository (and hosting)
- application platform support
- a Web API Gateway (WAG)

The browser-based IDE supports syntax highlighting and code completion, along with an advanced code editor. Zembly is an application repository that implements metadata-based models whereby metadata is stored with applications that users develop in Zembly. The Zembly hosting feature eliminates the need to manage external servers for hosting and scaling Zembly-based applications. The application platform support in Zembly means that users can write Facebook applications that leverage the full functionality of FBML and FBJS. In addition, Zembly provides wizard support that lets users easily manage tasks, such as publishing their applications to various social networking platforms.

---

*During the production of this book, SUN suspended Zembly on November 30, 2009. Unfortunately it was too late to remove the material referencing the program.

The Zembly WAG vastly reduces the amount of code that is typically required to make web API invocations in an application. Moreover, the web API Gateway lets developers use client libraries in various languages, including FX, Java, and JavaScript, and upcoming support for PHP.

■ 7.3.1 Zembly Features

Zembly provides the following functionality and capabilities:

• create apps for Facebook, Meebo, OpenSocial, Orkut, and iPhone
• create and share widgets with other users (see Chapter 5)
• integration with Yahoo Pipes (see Chapter 5)
• integration with Dapper (see Chapter 5)
• integration with Yahoo Bespin (see Chapter 9)

The public beta release of SUN Zembly includes other capabilities, such as support for private source code, templates, Ajax libraries, and the availability of SUN Zembly APIs that let you call Zembly from external applications. Currently, Zembly does not support PHP or Ruby, but there are plans for providing such support in the future.

The next section describes the steps you must follow to create a simple Zembly application, which will help you in creating your own Zembly applications.

■ 7.3.2 Zembly Applications and Tools

In Chapter 5, you learned how to use Zembly to create mash-ups. Zembly also lets you to create widgets and applications. For example, check out the Zembly "hello world" widget here:
http://zembly.com/things/5805412d9c2e49de8ddd577b20683636

Click on the Edit this widget button to view the HTML, CSS, and JavaScript files.

In addition to mash-ups and widgets, you can use Zembly to create Orkut applications. First, register for a free Orkut account here:
http://www.orkut.com/Main#Home

Now register for a free developer sandbox account here:
http://sandbox.orkut.com

Next, navigate to the Zembly home page and follow the instructions for creating a Zembly Orkut application that are listed here:
http://wiki.zembly.com/wiki/Creating_a_simple_Orkut_application

Another tool is the Zembly Client Library (ZCL), which provides easy access to data services in Zembly. The ZCL home page is: http://kenai.com/projects/zcl/pages/Home

You can download ZCL for Java (ZCL4J) to review code samples that show you how to write applications in Java, JavaFX, and PHP in ZCL. Note that ZCL uses OAuth for authentication with Zembly.

■ 7.3.3 Zembly Web Gateway API

Zembly lets developers use data services from many vendors (such as Amazon, Twitter, and Yahoo), and provides two ways for you to access those vendors' APIs. The Zembly WAG is an open source project that is available on the SUN Project Kenai home page: http://kenai.com/

In the following sections, you will learn two methods for using Zembly WAG. The first method involves installing the Zembly WAG in NetBeans, and the second is to access the APIs from a browser. There is also a detailed example of how to execute a Facebook FQL query.

7.3.3.1 Installing Web Gateway API in NetBeans

SUN WAG is already included in NetBeans 6.8 (see Chapter 6 for installation instructions). However, you can also install SUN WAG in earlier versions of NetBeans by following the menu path **Tools > Plug-ins**, typing Zembly in the Search text field, and then selecting Zembly WAG and clicking the Install button.

Instead of exploring Zembly WAG in NetBeans, the next section will show you how to access the SUN WAG from a browser, followed by an example of executing a Facebook FQL query.

7.3.3.2 Adding Web Gateway APIs to a Domain

The functionality that is available with the WAG plug-in for NetBeans is also available from a browser session here: https://zembly.com/ui/apiBrowser

Locate the API key and the secret password, which were generated when you created a Facebook application earlier in this chapter, and then complete the following steps:

Step 1: Select the All domains category (if you have not defined any domains)

Step 2: Click on the Facebook.com domain in the right panel

Step 3: Click on the fql API

Step 4: Click on the query Data services

Step 5: Click on the Call it now button

Step 6: Enter the following expression in the query input field:

```
SELECT uid FROM user WHERE name = 'John Smith'
```

Step 7: Click on Keys for Facebook and specify your API key and secret password

Step 8: Click on the Test button

Listing 7.11 shows the results that are displayed in the right-side panel after you complete Step 8.

Listing 7.11

```
[
 -{
    uid: 520415291
  }
]
```

If you change the default format from JSON to XML, the result will be an XML-formated response, as illustrated in Listing 7.12.

Listing 7.12

```
<fql_query_response
        xmlns=http://api.facebook.com/1.0/
        xmlns:xsi=http://www.w3.org/2001/XMLSchema-instance
        list="true">
  <user>
   <uid>520415291</uid>
  </user>
</fql_query_response>
```

The bottom panel on this website (under the Log label) displays detailed information about the request and response parameters. Listing 7.13 shows the request parameters and their values, which were sent when you made the initial request.

Listing 7.13

```
=== REQUEST === :
POST : http://api.facebook.com/restserver.php
KeySet : [{"key":"********"},{"secret":"********"}]
Request Body : {"v":"1.0","query":"SELECT uid FROM user WHERE name =
'John Smith'","api_key":"********","method":"facebook.fql
.query","format":"JSON","call_id":"1253841776633","sig":
"ea9250b3fa8d83005b569422726f8707"}
Content-type : application/x-www-form-urlencoded; charset=UTF-8
```

Listing 7.13 contains information about the POST request, which displays the masked values of the Facebook API keys in KeySet. Listing 7.13 also contains the contents of the Request Body, which includes the complete FQL statement that was specified earlier.

Finally, Listing 7.14 shows the RESPONSE parameters and the values that were returned after you made the initial request.

Listing 7.14

```
=== RESPONSE === :

StatusCode : 200
Transfer-Encoding : chunked
Date : Fri, 25 Sep 2009 01:22:55 GMT
P3P : CP="DSP LAW"
Expires : Mon, 26 Jul 1997 05:00:00 GMT

Set-Cookie : datr=
1253841775-0e6146fbdf1bfa2fd37ad6856749ed8bd71eb889c6a98719471af;
expires=Sun, 25-Sep-2011 01:22:55 GMT; path=/; domain=.facebook.com

X-Cnection : close
Content-Type : application/json
Server : Apache/1.3.41.fb1
Pragma : no-cache
Cache-Control : private, no-store, no-cache, must-revalidate,
post-check=0, pre-check=0
Response Body Size : 0
Response Body : [{"uid":520415290}]
```

Listing 7.14 contains the values for various headers, particularly the Response Body, which contains the value of uid, as shown here:

```
Response Body : [{"uid":520415290}]
```

Note that FQL query statements must contain indexable columns in the WHERE clause. You can find a list of FQL tables and their indexable columns (which are marked with an *) here: http://wiki.developers.facebook.com/index.php/FQL_Tables

■ 7.4 BEBO

Bebo is social networking product that lets users create social network applications. Its home page is: http://www.bebo.com

From your Bebo account, you can access email from AOL, Yahoo, or Gmail, and manage/edit RSS feeds. Bebo supports most of the Facebook APIs, and you can "port" a Facebook application to Bebo quite easily.

Before you create a Bebo application, perform the following:

Step 1: Make sure that you have access to a server that you can store your application code on, such as the server where you store your Facebook-related code

Step 2: Create a free Bebo account on the Bebo home page

Step 3: Navigate to the Bebo developer quick-start page here: http://developer.bebo.com/

Click on the link under the arrow marked "1" to download an API library (Java, PHP, or Ruby)

Step 4: Click on the link under the arrow marked "2" to install the Developer application

After you complete the set-up steps, create a Bebo application here: http://apps.bebo.com/developerapp/create

The Bebo APIs are highly compatible with the set of Facebook APIs, and their names are often the same. Bebo made a concerted effort to ensure a high degree of compatibility, which simplifies the process of porting applications between Facebook and Bebo. In fact, Blake Comagere published instructions for porting applications from Facebook to Bebo, and you can find them here: http://dev.aol.com/ondemandvideo/bebo-dev-nite-commagere

In the next section, Jennifer Glore of Sun Microsystems has provided some useful information on Identity Management. Please check the appendices for additional links regarding Identity Management.

■ 7.5 IDENTITY MANAGEMENT FOR WEB 2.0 APPLICATIONS

Identity management is a critical infrastructure component for any application today. Identity management is quite diverse and covers such topics as:

- The entire lifecycle of identities within a system, which includes identity creation, maintenance, and deletion
- Access control—authentication and authorization
- Provisioning users
- Single Sign-On (SSO) capabilities
- Providing a secure environment where privacy is maintained and identity theft is not a concern
- Compliance with legal regulations and auditing

When it comes to Web 2.0 applications, end users demand a certain functionality that raises a variety of identity management concerns. Today, end users use a diverse set of applications to accomplish a variety of tasks. Users expect these applications to integrate seamlessly (i.e., share personal information) without the need to provide identity credentials multiple times. An application developer must figure out how to accomplish this task in the most user-friendly way while still maintaining privacy and enforcing security. There are a variety of technologies that address this sector of identity management that are discussed in the next section.

■ 7.5.1 Key Technologies

The currently available technologies that address identity management are listed here:

- Security Assertion Markup Language (SAML)
- OpenSAML
- Shibboleth®
- OpenSSO
- OpenID™
- OAuth

The following subsections provide information about these technologies, along with their limitations.

7.5.1.1 SAML

SAML is an XML-based standard that is developed and maintained by OASIS for the consistent and secure exchange of identity information (authentication and authorization) between organizations. Within the standard, the three key components are the user, the identity provider, and the service providers. Identity providers maintain and authenticate users while service providers provide a service to the users. Service providers create and maintain the application, but delegate identity management to the identity provider.

The most common case where SAML is used is in web SSO. A user is given access to multiple services, which could be provided by multiple service providers, by logging in only once. Authentication and authorization is delegated to the identity provider by the various service providers. This is called federated SSO.

SAML 2.0 is the latest version and can be found here: http://www.oasis-open.org/specs/#samlv2.0.

Typically, most applications that want to use SAML use third-party software toolkits or platforms that provide SAML support. They then integrate with these software components to provide SAML support in their application. All parties involved in federated SSO must implement SAML for everything to function properly.

OpenSAML is an open source toolkit that contains C++ and Java libraries that provide SAML support. Its home page is here: https://spaces.internet2.edu/display/OpenSAML/Home/

OpenSAML lets developers provide SAML support in their applications while also allowing for extensibility. OpenSAML is maintained as part of the Shibboleth project.

The current version is OpenSAML 2, which provides support for SAML 1.0, 1.1, and 2.0.

7.5.1.2 Shibboleth

Shibboleth is an open source software implementation that provides a federated SSO framework via SAML. It is popular in the research and education communities. It also provides additional privacy functionality that lets users and their home site control which attributes are released to each of the applications. Details regarding Shibboleth can be found here: http://shibboleth.internet2.edu/

7.5.1.3 OpenSSO

OpenSSO is an open source project sponsored by Sun Microsystems. Its home page is: https://opensso.dev.java.net/

This project was founded in 2005, and it provides core identity services, such as security for web applications, SSO, and federation. OpenSSO is downloaded roughly 1500 times per month and about 60 new members join every month. The latest release of OpenSSO can be downloaded at: https://opensso.dev.java.net/public/use/index.html

More information about federating Google Apps with OpenSSO is available here:

https://www.sun.com/offers/details/google_apps_opensso.xml?intcmp=2974

7.5.1.4 OpenID

OpenID is a decentralized authentication protocol that provides access control for applications. Its home page is here: http://openid.net/

Users who access an application that uses OpenID will need OpenID credentials with the OpenID authentication provider that the application uses. Users can then log in with their credentials and gain access to other services from different providers without having to log in again. The services that users can access with one set of credentials are those that use the same authentication source. OpenID authentication is now provided by several large websites, such as AOL, Google, PayPal®, VeriSign®, and Yahoo.

Users are required to sign up for an OpenID username and password with the authentication provider prior to using an application that supports OpenID. This gives users the choice of which authentication providers they choose to sign up with, while still allowing them the SSO experience.

Website applications that want users to authenticate with OpenID can get more information here: http://openid.net/add-openid/add-getting-started/

There are many libraries available (Java, Perl, PHP, Python, Ruby, C++, etc.) that allow applications to add OpenID support to a website. In addition, there are a lot of plug-ins available for applications built on popular content management systems, such as blogs, wikis, etc.

There have been concerns about OpenID and phishing attacks. You can find more information here:

http://wiki.openid.net/OpenID_Phishing_Brainstorm

7.5.1.5 OAuth

OAuth was designed with the user experience in mind. Its home page is: http://oauth.net

Today, users do not rely on just one website or application for all of their needs. Instead, they use multiple websites (i.e., social networks, photo sharing sites, etc.) and expect a seamless and secure integration between all of their sites so that their information can be shared. OAuth is an open protocol that provides the mechanism for services to accomplish this secure integration. OAuth developers looked at several proprietary mechanisms and found a common way that this functionality could be provided. Services that use OAuth can securely share user information (i.e., contact lists, photos, etc.) without requiring users to expose their username and password. All of this is done behind the scenes without knowledge of the user.

OAuth Core 1.0 is the current version, and libraries for PHP, Rails, Python, C, .NET, and Perl are available here: http://oauth.net/code

Some popular websites such as Twitter provide OAuth support, and a Twitter OAuth FAQ is available here: http://apiwiki.twitter.com/OAuth-FAQ

For more information on OAuth, look at the OAuth home page at: http://oauth.net/ and review the Beginner's Guide to OAuth here: http://hueniverse.com/2007/10/beginners-guide-to-oauth-part-i-overview/

■ 7.5.2 Conclusions

Regardless of the application, developers must think about identity management. In Web 2.0, developers should really concern themselves with how to make SSO easy for their users and how they can provide users with the ability to share information with other applications. Examine the available technologies to determine which one provides the best solution for your requirements.

■ 7.6 SUMMARY

This chapter introduced you to the Facebook platform and its major components, including Facebook Connect. You learned how to create a simple Facebook application. You also learned about other products and tools that integrate with Facebook.

Next, you learned about SUN Zembly and its ability to create social applications for Facebook, Meebo, OpenSocial, and iPhone. You learned how to create a simple Facebook application in Zembly. You also learned about the Bebo social network and its high degree of API compatibility with Facebook APIs. Finally, you learned about identity management, the issues that are involved, and some of the available technologies that provide solutions.

The next chapter covers the OpenSocial platform and the major social networks that support OpenSocial.

## CHAPTER 8

The OpenSocial Platform

In This Chapter:

- The OpenSocial Landscape
- OpenSocial Markup Language (OSML)
- OpenSocial Gadgets
- The OpenSocial Technology Stack
- OpenSocial Applications in Eclipse
- OpenSocial and Major Vendors
- Google Friend Connect (GFC)
- Apache Shindig
- Integrated OpenSocial Sample Application

In this chapter, we'll discuss the OpenSocial platform and some of the companies that belong to the OpenSocial consortium. We'll also look at examples of how to create OpenSocial applications for the companies in the consortium.

First, we'll look at a brief description of the OpenSocial platform, which is similar to Facebook (i.e., both are social networks) and discuss some of the important differences between the two. You will also learn about the OpenSocial markup language, which includes tags and templates, followed by OpenSocial Gadgets, and the OpenSocial technology stack.

Next, you will learn how to create OpenSocial applications for major vendors, including Yahoo, Google Orkut, and MySpace. After that, we'll discuss Apache Shindig, which is the reference implementation of the OpenSocial specification, along with code samples that you can run from the command line. The final section contains an integrated sample application.

■ 8.1   THE OPENSOCIAL LANDSCAPE

Google announced the OpenSocial platform in August 2007. The home page for the OpenSocial Foundation is:

http://www.opensocial.org

OpenSocial is not just for social network sites, but for creating personal dashboards, corporate environments, and professional organizations. Open-Social is a community of companies (including Google) that are collaborating to improve the OpenSocial specification, which defines the architecture of an OpenSocial container. This specification is open to the public, which means that any company (or any individual) can create an OpenSocial container simply by implementing the specification.

Any application that is written for one OpenSocial container will run on all of the other OpenSocial containers that conform to the specification. Note that anyone who writes an OpenSocial container can include features that are beyond the functionality specified in the OpenSocial specification. However, the inclusion of additional features in an OpenSocial container does not guarantee portability among all of the other OpenSocial containers.

OpenSocial provides a common set of Application Performance Indicators (APIs) for social networks, and its initial release was in November 2007. One important benefit of writing social networking applications based on OpenSocial is that those applications will work on other social networks (including Hi5, MySpace, Ning®, Orkut, and Yahoo) without any code modifications.

Based on all of the OpenSocial containers (there are at least 30) that are available throughout the world, OpenSocial has a reach of more than 600,000,000 users, and more than 300,000,000 application installations. Visit the OpenSocial home page to get the latest status of OpenSocial.

OpenSocial applications involve client-side and server-side processing, and applications communicate with an OpenSocial server via REST calls that can return data in JSON or XML. Apache Shindig (discussed later in this chapter) is the reference implementation of the OpenSocial specification. If you create OpenSocial applications using the plug-in for Eclipse, you can launch your applications in Eclipse using either Apache Shindig or Jetty.

You can find mash-ups (which are discussed in Chapter 9) involving OpenSocial and a website with a description of OpenSocial Best Practices in the appendices.

■ 8.2 OPENSOCIAL MARKUP LANGUAGE (OSML)

As you saw in Chapter 7, Facebook has FaceBook Markup Language (FBML), and the corresponding markup language in OpenSocial is OSML. The main aspects of OSML are OpenSocial tags and OpenSocial templates, which provide functionality that simplify the use of OpenSocial tags.

■ 8.2.1 OpenSocial Tags

This section highlights the various tags that are supported in OSML 0.9. Some of the more common tags are:

- `<Require feature="..."/>`
- `<os:Name>`
- `<os:PeopleSelector>`
- `<os:Badge>`
- `<os:Get>`

The `<Require feature="..."/>` tag is required to use OSML tags in HTML pages. Here is an example:

```
<Require feature="osml">
```

Since OSML tags are a subset of OpenSocial templating, and you can use the latter tags in the earlier list by including the following code snippet:

```
<Require feature="opensocial-templates">
```

The `<os:Name>` tag lets you identify a particular person, as shown here:

```
How are you <os:Name person="${Viewer}"/>?
```

The `<os:PeopleSelector>` tag lets you display a list of persons, as shown here:

```
<form action="/friend_list.php" method="POST">
  A list of friends:
  <os:PeopleSelector group="${ListOfFriends}"
                     multiple="true" max="20"
                     inputName="friendlist"/>
</form>
```

The `<os:Badge>` tag lets you show information about a person, as shown here:

```
<os:Badge repeat="${ListOfFriends}" person="${currperson}"/>
```

The `<os:Get>` tag lets you insert HTML content into the Document Object Model (DOM) of the current page, as shown here:

```
Information about ${Viewer.Name}:
<os:Get href="http://www.acme.com/UserInfo.html?userId=${user.Id}"/>
```

In addition to tag support, OSML also supports expressions, for example:

```
${Users.info[0].LastName}
```

The OSML tags in this section also support various attributes, which can be found here:
http://sites.google.com/site/opensocialdraft/Home/osml-tags

■ 8.2.2 OpenSocial Templates

OpenSocial templates provide a mechanism, similar in spirit to the Model-View-Controller (MVC) pattern, which lets you separate markup from coding logic. This separation simplifies code maintenance and readability (among other things).

If you have ever worked with tag libraries (such as JavaServer Pages (JSP) tags), then you will be very comfortable with the OpenSocial template support for loops and conditional logic.

Before we loot at an example, note that there are three techniques for rendering data in an HTML page in an OpenSocial application:

Method 1: create an innerHTML string

Method 2: dynamically update the DOM

Method 3: use an OpenSocial template

The first method is nonportable (and may be disallowed in the future). The second method is often used, but as you learned in Chapter 2, a better coding practice involves using toolkits and libraries that handle any type of direct DOM manipulation. Thus, the third method is the recommended solution.

Listing 8.1 shows the contents of a data element, and Listing 8.2 displays the contents of a `<script>` element that renders the data in Listing 8.1.

Listing 8.1

```
var song = {
  title:      'Heaven Can Wait For You',
  url:        'http://www.acme.com/johndoe/greatesthits/song1.mp3',
  artist:     'John Doe',
  album:      'Greatest Hits',
  albumImage: 'http://www.acme.com/johndoe/greatesthits.jpg'
}
```

Listing 8.1 defines a variable `song` containing JSON-formatted data used in the script tag defined in Listing 8.2.

Listing 8.2

```
<script type="text/os-template">
  <a href="${url}">
  <img src="${albumImage}"/>
  ${title} BY ${artist} FROM ${album}
  </a>
</script>
```

Listing 8.2 defines a template containing a `<script>` element whose type is `text/os-template`, along with the tags `url` and `albumImage` that reference text in Listing 8.1.

As you can see, Listing 8.1 contains the specific data values, and the template in Listing 8.2 manipulates that data with variables. This separation is recommended not only for OpenSocial applications, but for web development in general.

■ 8.3 OPENSOCIAL GADGETS

This section focuses on OpenSocial gadgets (including how you can create them), and contains an overview of the OpenSocial Gadgets APIs.

OpenSocial Gadgets are a combination of HTML, Cascading Style Sheets (CSS), and JavaScript. Gadgets are defined using XML-based syntax, and they are embedded in gadget containers. Although we will not get into discuss the details, you can read all about OpenSocial Gadgets here: http://code.google.com/apis/gadgets/docs/spec.html

Note that Google Gadgets API extensions include the following types:

- Ads
- Calendar
- Finance APIs
- Maps
- OpenSocial
- Spreadsheets

Thus, OpenSocial Gadgets comprise one type (and the only type) of Google Gadgets discussed in this chapter. You can find additional information about the other Google Gadget API extensions here:
http://code.google.com/apis/gadgets/docs/overview.html

■ 8.3.1 Creating and Submitting OpenSocial Gadgets

Listing 8.3 lists the contents of a "hello world" OpenSocial Gadget.

Listing 8.3

```
<?xml version="1.0" encoding="UTF-8" ?>
<Module>
  <ModulePrefs title="hello world example" />
  <Content type="html">
    <![CDATA[
      Hello, world!
    ]]>
  </Content>
</Module>
```

Listing 8.3 defines an XML <Module> element that contains two child elements. The first child element is the XML ModulePrefs element that specifies the title of the gadget via the title attribute. The second child element is the XML <Content> element, which contains a CDATA section with the text Hello, world!, which is rendered in an HTML page that contains this embedded gadget.

The list of required and recommended fields for submitting an OpenSocial Gadget can be found here:
http://www.google.com/ig/submit

Next, follow the instructions in the Gadget preparation section here:
http://code.google.com/apis/gadgets/docs/publish.html#Submitting

■ 8.3.2 Google Gadgets and Other Tools

This section lists some of the tools that can be combined with Google Gadgets.

Here is a link for using Google Gadgets in OpenSocial applications: http://zhenhua-guo.blogspot.com/2008/07/google-gadget-and-opensocial .html

A Java™-based code sample of GWT, Google Gadgets, and OpenSocial is here: http://www.pathf.com/blogs/2008/10/gwt-gadgets-and-opensocial/ #more-1219

You can also combine Google Web Toolkit (GWT), Google Gadgets, and iGoogle. The tools that you need to create Google Gadgets with GWT for iGoogle are:

- GWT
- GWT Google Gadget API
- an iGoogle account
- access to the iGoogle Sandbox
- storage area to serve Gadgets to iGoogle

Additional details regarding GWT, Google Gadgets, and iGoogle are available here: http://www.pathf.com/blogs/tag/opensocial/

Another important tool is the Google Gadgets Editor (GGE), which can be found here: http://code.google.com/apis/gadgets/docs/legacy/gs.html#GGE

In addition to testing custom-written Google Gadgets, GGE provides you with a file menu with commands for creating, saving, renaming, uploading, deleting, and publishing gadgets.

■ 8.4 THE OPENSOCIAL TECHNOLOGY STACK

The OpenSocial technology stack is made up of four components: the Gadget Container (JavaScript), the Gadget Server, the OpenSocial Container (JavaScript), and the OpenSocial Gateway Server.

The Gadget Container manages communication, the OpenSocial API, and security. The Gadget Server handles the rendering of the contents of a gadget in HTML pages. The OpenSocial Container is a layer above the

Gadget Container, and it manages the functionality specific to OpenSocial. Finally, the OpenSocial Gateway handles the communication between the container and the server.

The OpenSocial platform is based on an open specification that can be found here:

http://code.google.com/apis/opensocial/docs/0.8/spec.html

In addition, OpenSocial supports various programming languages, including Java, PHP, Python, and Ruby, and you can also integrate Flash into OpenSocial applications.

As you would expect, OpenSocial also provides a set of APIs that let you perform a variety of tasks. For example, you can make a person request with a JSON request parameter object, as shown here:

```
osapi.people.getViewer({fields: ['name', 'birthday']})
    .execute(function(result) {
  alert('Your name is ' + result.name + '!');
  alert('Your birthday is ' + result.birthday + '!');
});
```

A complete list of live OpenSocial containers can be found here: http://wiki.opensocial.org/index.php?title=Main_Page#Container_ Information

If you decide to write your own OpenSocial container, there are tests available to ensure that your container complies with the OpenSocial specification. A suite of tests for an OpenSocial container can be found here: http://code.google.com/p/opensocial-resources/wiki/ComplianceTests

The next section describes the steps that you must take to create an OpenSocial application. The simple application that you will create will help you understand the steps involved in creating your own OpenSocial applications.

■ 8.5 OPENSOCIAL APPLICATIONS IN ECLIPSE

The OpenSocial Development Environment (OSDE) is a plug-in for Eclipse that lets you develop OpenSocial applications. Its home page is: http://code.google.com/p/opensocial-development-environment/

First, install Eclipse (as described in Chapter 6) and then install the OpenSocial plug-in for Eclipse from: http://opensocial-development-environment.googlecode.com/svn/update-site/site.xml

■ 8.5.1 A Basic OSDE Application

After you install Eclipse and the OSDE plug-in for Eclipse, perform the following steps:

Step 1: Follow the menu path **File > New > Other...**

Step 2: Click on OSDE, click OpenSocial Project, and click Next

Step 3: Enter MyOS1 in the input field next to Project name: and click Next

Step 4: Enter MyOS1 for the title and provide an email address, then click Next

Step 5: Click the radio button next to Type HTML

Step 6: Click the checkbox next to Generate a set of sample code

Step 7: Click the three checkboxes for Fetching/Posting/Sharing

Step 8: Click the Finish button

Eclipse will generate an OpenSocial project containing two XML files and a project file with the following directory structure:

```
+ MyOS1
+ target
  + gadget.xml
+ .project
+ gadget.xml
```

Double-click on the XML files to render them in the middle screen.

Launch the MyOS1 OpenSocial application from the navigation bar as follows: **OSDE > Launch Apache Shindig**

If you are working on Windows and you experience difficulties, read the instructions found here:

http://rlabs.wordpress.com/2009/03/30/setting-up-osde-on-windows-with-eclipse-342-and-java-16/

■ 8.6 OPENSOCIAL AND MAJOR VENDORS

This section provides information about OpenSocial applications for various social networks, including Yahoo and Google Orkut.

■ 8.6.1 Yahoo Application Platform (YAP) and OpenSocial

YAP is a platform that lets users create OpenSocial applications using tools provided by Yahoo. The developer site is located here:
http://developer.yahoo.com/yap/

The home page contains an extensive set of links that provide Best Pratices, prerequisites, and information for creating, registering, and submitting your applications.

8.6.1.1 Yahoo Markup Language (YML)

YML is an XML-based mark-up language whose tags can be included in the HTML pages of OpenSocial applications, where YAP converts the YML tags into HTML (at runtime).

YML tags simplify application development because they simplify the code required to access user-specific information. YML tags also provide User Interface (UI) widgets and data encapsulation, and confidential data is only displayed to those who have the appropriate permission to view that data.

YML Lite is a strict subset of YML, and some of the intuitively named tags are shown here:

- `yml:a`
- `yml:form`
- `yml:name`
- `yml:user-badge`

8.6.1.2 Yahoo Social API SDKs

Yahoo provides several SDKs that allow access to the Yahoo Social APIs. Currently, Yahoo provides SDKs for the following programming languages:

- PHP
- Flash
- Objective-C Cocoa

You can download the Yahoo Social PHP SDK distribution from:
http://developer.yahoo.com/social/sdk/php/

Uncompress the distribution and follow the installation steps in the INSTALL.txt file, which include the following:

- a server with PHP installed to run the sample code
- a web-based application ID for Yahoo
- an OAuth consumer key

The sample subdirectory contains the following files:

```
delicious.php
popupmanager.js
sampleapp.php
```

The PHP-based sample application will help you get started with writing your own PHP-based Yahoo applications.

■ 8.6.2 Google Orkut

Google Orkut is an OpenSocial container that supports social applications that conform to the OpenSocial specification. Its home page is:
http://www.Orkut.com.

Register for a free Orkut account on the home page and then sign up for the development sandbox here:
http://sandbox.orkut.com/SandboxSignup.aspx

The preceding website has an extensive set of links that provides documentation, tutorials, reference material, and sample code to assist you in creating an Orkut application.

After you complete your Orkut application, go to the following URL to submit your application:
http://www.orkut.com/Main#AppDirectorySubmit.aspx

Check the appendices for additional links.

■ 8.7   GOOGLE FRIEND CONNECT (GFC)

GFC is an OpenSocial application that lets Internet users connect with their friends. Its home page is:
http://www.google.com/friendconnect/

GFC uses a combination of various standards, such as OpenID, OAuth, and OpenSocial.

GFC uses a Google `Conversation` element that is part of Google Web Elements, which lets you embed Google products in HTML pages with simple code snippets. The Google Web Elements home page is:
http://www.google.com/webelements/

Google Web Elements let you choose from the following products: Calendar, Conversation, Custom Search, Maps, News, Spreadsheets, and YouTube News.

Note that GFC leverages the Google `Conversation` element to let visitors add their comments to any website that contains the Google `Conversation` element. In addition, visitors can join conversations on GFC, and their comments can be automatically translated into different languages. The Google `Conversation` element can be found here:

http://www.google.com/webelements/social/conversation

Listing 8.4 shows the contents of a code snippet for the Google `Conversation` element that you can paste directly into an HTML page.

Listing 8.4

```
<!-- Google Conversation Element Code -->
<iframe frameborder="0" marginwidth="0" marginheight="0"
        border="0" style="border:0;margin:0;width:250px;height:440px;"
        src="http://www.google.com/friendconnect/discuss?scope=site"
        scrolling="no" allowtransparency="true">
</iframe>
```

Listing 8.4 contains a simple XML `iframe` element with various attributes specifing the dimensions of the `iframe`, and a URL, whose contents will be rendered in the `iframe`.

After you embed the Google `Conversation` element in an HTML page, visitors can sign in using AOL®, Google, OpenID, and Yahoo. When visitors add comments, their photograph is displayed next to their comments.

In addition, the comments gadget lets visitors translate comments into different languages via the Translate link. Simply click on the link and select one of the languages in the pop-up list to translate the text.

■ 8.7.1   GFC APIs

GFC supports a set of APIs that let you access people and activities. Some of the more common APIs are listed here:

- OWNER
- OWNER FRIENDS
- VIEWER
- VIEWER FRIENDS
- ADMINS

OWNER returns the profile information of a site, for example:

```
req.newFetchPersonRequest('OWNER')
```

OWNER FRIENDS returns the members of a site, for example:

```
req.newFetchPeopleRequest(new opensocial.IdSpec({'userId' : 'OWNER',
'groupId' : 'FRIENDS'}))
```

VIEWER returns the logged-in user, for example:

```
req.newFetchPersonRequest('VIEWER')
```

VIEWER FRIENDS returns the members of a site who are also the friends of a user, for example:

```
req.newFetchPeopleRequest(new opensocial.IdSpec({'userId' : 'VIEWER',
'groupId' : 'FRIENDS'}))
```

ADMINS returns the profile information for the administrators of a site, for example:

```
opensocial.DataRequest.newFetchPeopleRequest(new
opensocial.IdSpec({'userId' : 'OWNER', 'groupId' : 'ADMINS'}))
```

Additional details about the GFC APIs is here:
http://code.google.com/apis/friendconnect/
You can also find GFC code samples here:
http://code.google.com/apis/friendconnect/code.html

■ 8.7.2 GFC Gadgets

GFC Gadgets support OpenSocial Specification 0.9, which contains several new features (including OSML and data pipelining) that can improve both the development and performance of gadgets.

The following link contains an example of GFC buttons:
http://www.ossamples.com/da_apisamples/button_examples.html

Listing 8.5 displays a portion of the code from the preceding link.

Listing 8.5

```
<!DOCTYPE html PUBLIC "-//W3C//DTD HTML 4.01//EN">
<html>
  <head>
  <style type="text/css">
```

```
          #example6 a   {font-size: 20px;  font-family: courier; }
          #example7 .gfc-icon { font-size: 10px; }
        </style>
        <link href="http://code.google.com/css/codesite.pack.01312008.css"
            type="text/css" rel="stylesheet"/>

          <script type="text/javascript" src="http://www.google.com/jsapi">
          </script>
          <script type="text/javascript">google.load('friendconnect', '0.8');
          </script>

          <script type="text/javascript">
            var SITE_ID = '05406184314992429615';
            // location of rpc_relay.html and canvas.html
            google.friendconnect.container.setParentUrl('/da_apisamples/');
            google.friendconnect.container.loadOpenSocialApi({
                  site: SITE_ID,
                  onload: function() { renderButtons(); }});
          </script>
        </head>
        <body>
         <div >
           <h2> Google Friend Connect Branded Button/Link Examples</h2>
           <!-- Portions of the HTML table are omitted -->
           <table>
             <tr>
               <td>
                 <code>
&lt;style type=&quot;text/css&quot;&gt;<br/>
       #example6 a   {font-size: 23px; font-family: courier; }<br/>
       ...<br/>
google.friendconnect.renderSignInButton({ &apos;id&apos;: &apos;
example6&apos;,&apos;style&apos;:&apos;text&apos;,&apos;text&apos;:
&apos;This link text is styled.&apos;});</code>
               </td>
               <td><div id="example6"></div></td>
             </tr>
           </table>

          <script type="text/javascript">
            function renderButtons() {
              google.friendconnect.renderSignInButton({'id':'example3',
              'text':'Click here to join','style':'standard'});
              google.friendconnect.renderSignInButton({'id':'example5',
```

```
        'text':'Click here to sign in:','style':'text'});
        google.friendconnect.renderSignInButton({ 'id': 'example6',
        'text': 'This link text is styled.', 'style': 'text' });
      };
    </script>
    </body>
</html>
```

The entire listing is available here:
http://www.ossamples.com/da_apisamples/button_examples.html

As you can see, the part of code in Listing 8.5 that is enclosed by the `<code>` tags is rendered as text, and the result of executing each code invocation is a rendered button.

You can find a list of GFC gadgets here:
http://www.google.com/friendconnect/directory/request?id=01526777257828458339&hl=en

Check the Appendix for information on creating and submitting your own GFC gadgets, and for more details about GFC plug-ins for WordPress, Drupal, and PHPBB.

■ 8.8 APACHE SHINDIG

Apache Shindig is an open source project that is also the reference implementation of the OpenSocial specification. The Apache Shindig home page is: http://incubator.apache.org/shindig/

The main components of Apache Shindig are the following:

• Gadget Container JavaScript
• GadgetServer
• OpenSocial Container JavaScript
• OpenSocial Data Server

Each of these components was briefly discussed earlier in this chapter.

■ 8.8.1 Building Apache Shindig

As of February 2009, Apache Shindig could not download an automatic build of a project. However, you can download the source code from the Shindig repository here:
http://incubator.apache.org/shindig/#tab-building

The instructions in this section for the Java-based setup of Shindig were taken from the preceding URL.

The software prerequisites for building Shindig for Java are the following:

• Java (JDK/JRE) 1.5 or later
• a Subversion client
• Apache Maven

The following list describes the steps for building and launching Shindig with Java from the command line:

• download the Shindig code
• build Shindig with Maven (version 2.x)
• launch Shindig

Make sure you have installed an application server or a web container on your system so that you can deploy (copy) the Web Archive (WAR) file to your server or container.

For example, you can follow the steps in Chapter 6 for downloading and installing Tomcat 6.x on your system. Note that the instructions in Listing 8.7 specify a `Jetty` container (go to the Jetty homepage and follow the set-up instructions for Jetty).

8.8.1.1 Downloading the Shindig Code

Create a subdirectory and download the Shindig code, as shown here:

```
mkdir /home/smith/src/shindig
cd /home/smith/src/shindig
svn co http://svn.apache.org/repos/asf/incubator/shindig/trunk/
```

8.8.1.2 The Shindig README file

Listing 8.6 shows the contents of the README file, which contains instructions for building Shindig with Java.

Listing 8.6 README

```
Welcome to Apache Shindig!

* Read java/README for instructions on using the java gadget servers.
* To build and run the Java server see BUILD-JAVA
* Read php/README for instructions on how to run a php gadget server
  instead of a java gadget server.
```

```
* Read javascript/README for instructions for using the Shindig
  Gadget Container JavaScript to enable your page to render Gadgets
  using gmodules.com or a server started up as described above.
```

For more information, see http://incubator.apache.org/shindig

8.8.1.3 *The Shindig* BUILD-JAVA *file*

Listing 8.7 contains the first portion of the BUILD-JAVA file, which tells you how to build Shindig using Java.

Listing 8.7 BUILD-JAVA

```
Installing and running the various java servers
========================================================

1) Install Maven 2.0.8 or higher (see http://maven.apache.org)

2) Make sure the JAVA_HOME environment variable is set to the location
   of your JDK/JRE, and that the maven executable is in your PATH.

3) From the base source directory ( eg cd .. )
   * mvn - Cleans the source tree and then builds all the java
     classes, packages them into jars and installs them in your local
     repository also adds source jars ( by default ~/.m2/repository
     on Unix/OSX)
   * mvn install - does the above but does not clean first
   * mvn -Psocial - builds only the social parts
   * mvn -Pgadgets - builds only the gadget parts

   You must perform at least a "mvn" to place build all the artifacts
   and place them in you local maven repository.

4) To Run, using a embedded Jetty Webapp container, in the base
   project directory (eg cd .. )
   * First do a full build as in step 3
   * mvn -Prun - to run Jetty with both social and gadgets
   * mvn -Prun -DrunType=gadgets - to run Jetty with only the
     gadgets server
   * mvn -Prun -DrunType=social - to run Jetty with only the social
     server

5) To Run with a different port
   * cd java/server
   * mvn clean install jetty:run -DrunType=<full|gadgets|social>
                                 -Djetty.port=<port>
```

6) Once running, you can test the gadget rendering server by hitting this url:
http://localhost:8080/gadgets/ifr?url=http://www.labpixies.com/campaigns/todo/todo.xml

Or you can take a look at the sample container here:
http://localhost:8080/gadgets/files/samplecontainer/samplecontainer.html

The following sections provide more detailed information for Steps 3, 4, and 6 of the BUILD-JAVA file in Listing 8.7.

8.8.1.4   Building and Running the Shindig Code with Maven

The following steps show you how to build a WAR file for the Gadget server:

```
cd /home/smith/src/shindig
mvn
```

Copy the generated WAR file into the appropriate directory of your application server or web container.

Start a Jetty server on port 8080 of your system:

```
mvn —Prun
```

Test the Gadget code by launching your browser and navigating to the following URL:
http://localhost:<port>/gadgets/ifr?url=http://www.labpixies.com/campaigns/todo/todo.xml

8.8.1.5   Building Shindig as an Eclipse Project

Follow the instructions in Chapter 6 for installing Eclipse on your system and then install the Maven plug-in for Eclipse from:
http://m2eclipse.sonatype.org/update/

Select the Maven Integration checkbox.

Next, create a new Eclipse project for Shindig by completing the following steps:

Step 1: Follow the menu path **File > New > Java Project** and specify the name Shindig1

Step 2: Select Create project from existing source

Step 3: Navigate to the Java subdirectory of the downloaded Shindig source code

Step 4: Click the Finish button

After Eclipse has finished creating the new project, perform the following steps:

Step 5: Right-click on the project `Shindig1`

Step 6: Select Maven : Enable Dependency Management

Step 7: Right-click on the project `Shindig1`

Step 8: Select Maven : Update Source Folders

Step 9: Right-click on the project `Shindig1`

Step 10: Select Maven : Download Sources

■ 8.8.2 OpenSocial Java Client

If Java is your preferred language, you can experiment with an existing Java-based OpenSocial client available here:

http://code.google.com/p/opensocial-java-client/

Download either the JAR file `opensocial-java-client-20081218.jar` (which contains the OpenSocial library with support for REST and SOAP) or the zip file `opensocial-java-client-20081218.zip` (which contains documentation, dependencies, sample code, and source code) into a convenient directory and, in the latter case, expand the zip file.

The URL for Getting Started with the Java Client Library is:

http://code.google.com/p/opensocial-java-client/wiki/GettingStarted

You can find sample Java code here:

http://code.google.com/p/opensocial-java-client/source/browse/#svn/trunk/java/samples

The next section displays the contents of the file `README-samples.txt`, which tells you how to run the Java client classes, followed by the Java class `DisplayFriends.java`, which you can compile and run from the command line.

■ 8.8.3 Display Friends in Shindig

Listing 8.8 shows the contents of `README-samples.txt`, which tells you how to run the sample Java classes from the command line.

Listing 8.8 README-samples.txt

This folder contains a number of simple Java samples that use the accompanying library to retrieve information from various OpenSocial containers.

```
TO RUN:
-------
1. Generate a Java archive of the library and compile the samples:
open a terminal window, navigate to trunk/java, and execute the
"compile-samples" Ant target (requires Ant, which you can download
from http://ant.apache.org/):

ant compile-samples

2. Navigate to trunk/java/samples/bin (the location of the compiled
samples) and set your class path:

2a) UNIX (bash):
export CLASSPATH=../../dist/opensocial.jar:../../lib/*:.
-- OR, if that doesn't work, try: --
export CLASSPATH=../../dist/opensocial.jar:../../lib/commons-codec-
1.3.jar:../../lib/oauth-20081115.jar:../../lib/httpclient-4.0-beta2
.jar:../../lib/httpcore-4.0-beta3.jar:../../lib/commons-logging-
1.1.1.jar:.

2b) Windows:
set CLASSPATH=..\..\dist\opensocial.jar;..\..\lib\*;.

3. Execute the sample by typing "java" followed by the name of the
class without the .class extension:

java DisplayFriends
```

Listing 8.9 displays the contents of `DisplayFriends.java`, which illustrates a Java client that retrieves and displays a user's friends. Note that `DisplayFriends.java` has been reformatted to fit these pages, and the unmodified code is available here:
http://code.google.com/p/opensocial-java-client/source/browse/trunk/java/samples/DisplayFriends.java

Listing 8.9 DisplayFriends.java

```
/* Copyright (c) 2008 Google Inc.
*
* Licensed under the Apache License, Version 2.0 (the "License");
* you may not use this file except in compliance with the License.
```

```
* You may obtain a copy of the License at
*
* http://www.apache.org/licenses/LICENSE-2.0
*
* Unless required by applicable law or agreed to in writing, software
* distributed under the License is distributed on an "AS IS" BASIS,
* WITHOUT WARRANTIES OR CONDITIONS OF ANY KIND, either express or
  implied.
* See the License for the specific language governing permissions and
* limitations under the License.
*/

import org.opensocial.data.OpenSocialPerson;
import org.opensocial.client.OpenSocialClient;

import java.util.Collection;

public class DisplayFriends
{
    public static void main(String[] args)
    {
        OpenSocialClient c = new OpenSocialClient("orkut.com");

        // orkut supports both the REST and RPC protocols; RPC is
            preferred
        // because RPC supports batch requests
        c.setProperty(OpenSocialClient.Properties.RPC_ENDPOINT,
        "http://sandbox.orkut.com/social/rpc");

        // Credentials provided here are associated with the gadget
            located at
        // http://opensocial-resources.googlecode.com/svn/samples/
            rest_rpc/sample.xml;
        // If you install this gadget, you can substitute your own
            OpenSocial ID
        // for the one used below and fetch your profile data and
            friends
        c.setProperty(OpenSocialClient.Properties.CONSUMER_SECRET,
        "uynAeXiWTisflWX99KU1D2q5");

        c.setProperty(OpenSocialClient.Properties.CONSUMER_KEY,
        "orkut.com:623061448914");

        c.setProperty(OpenSocialClient.Properties.VIEWER_ID,
        "03067092798963641994");
```

```
      try {
          // Retrieve the friends of the specified user using the
          // OpenSocialClient method fetchFriends
          Collection<OpenSocialPerson> friends =
          c.fetchFriends("03067092798963641994");

          System.out.println("----------");

          // The fetchFriends method returns a typical Java
             Collection object
          // with all of the methods you're already accustomed to
             like size()
          System.out.println(friends.size() + " friends:");

          // Iterate through the Collection
          for (OpenSocialPerson friend : friends)
          {
              // Output the name of the current friend
              System.out.println("- " + friend.getDisplayName());
          }

          System.out.println("----------");
      } catch (Exception e) {
          System.out.println("Request failed:" );
          e.printStackTrace();
      }
   }
}
```

Listing 8.9 contains a main method that instantiates an OpenSocialClient object and performs some initialization, followed by a try/catch block that retrieves a collection of friends, as shown here:

```
Collection<OpenSocialPerson> friends = c.fetchFriends
                                 ("03067092798963641994");
```

The next section of code contains a loop that iterates through the collection and prints information about each element (which is a friend of the current user):

```
      for (OpenSocialPerson friend : friends)
      {
          // Output the name of the current friend
          System.out.println("- " + friend.getDisplayName());
      }
```

The catch portion of Listing 8.9 reports errors that occur during the try portion of the code block.

■ 8.8.4 Compiling the Sample Shindig Code

Open a command shell and navigate to the Java subdirectory of the unpacked OpenSocial Java client code and compile the sample code with the following ant command:

```
ant compile-samples
```

Note that during the compilation of the sample code, the JAR file opensocial.jar is created and placed in the dist subdirectory.

Next, launch the DisplayFriends Java class:

```
java DisplayFriends
```

You will see the following output:

```
----------
6 friends:
- Arne Roomann-Kurrik
- Dan Holevoet
- Jeremy Joslin
- John Nolan
- Manoj Koushik
- ryan boyd
----------
```

Next, launch the BatchRequests Java class:

```
java BatchRequests
```

You will see the following output:

```
----------
Info. for API DWH
ID: 03067092798963641994
Thumbnail URL: http://www.orkut.com/img/i_nophoto64.gif
Friends:
- Arne Roomann-Kurrik
- Dan Holevoet
- Jeremy Joslin
- John Nolan
- Manoj Koushik
- ryan boyd
----------
```

Next, launch the `DisplayProfileData` Java class:

```
java DisplayProfileData
```

You will see the following output:

```
----------
Info. for API DWH
ID: 03067092798963641994
Thumbnail URL: http://www.orkut.com/img/i_nophoto64.gif
----------
```

If you receive error messages about missing Java classes, look in the `java/lib` subdirectory and try adding the appropriate JAR files to the `CLASSPATH` environment variable.

If you are working on a Linux system and you need to find out which JAR file contains a given Java class, you can use the following code from the command line:

```
jar tvf sample.jar |grep JavaSample
```

■ 8.9   INTEGRATED OPENSOCIAL SAMPLE APPLICATION

This section will walk you through writing a simple OpenSocial application using Java App Engine, Dojo, and JSON. The purpose of this application is to allow readers to share comments about this book with each other. To keep the example simple, we did not expend any effort on UI design (see Figure 8.1).

■ **FIGURE 8.1**
Comment Sharing

Social Example

Location:	
Message:	
Submit Reset	

Date	Name	Source	Location	Message
1254347040427	Kevin Nilson	opensocial	Chapter 4	Great Example
1254187534753	Ashrafi Siamak	web	Chapter 11	I didn't realize how many options are available.
1254187416798	Oswald Campesato	web	Chapter 5	I can't believe how much I learned

Note that we will only discuss the front-end code in this application, which is where the OpenSocial code resides. If you are interested in the details of the back-end code, look at the integrated application in Chapter 12, which contains the same back-end code as this application.

You can find a link to a running copy of this application in Orkut and MySpace by visiting the book's website here:
http://web2-book.com

Listing 8.10 shows the contents of the HTML page for this integrated application.

Listing 8.10

```
<!DOCTYPE HTML PUBLIC "-//W3C//DTD HTML 4.01 Transitional//EN">
<html>
    <head>
        <meta http-equiv="content-type" content="text/html;
                charset=UTF-8">
        <link type="text/css" rel="stylesheet"
              href="http://socialexample.appspot.com/
                        SocialNetworking.css">
        <title>Social Example</title>

        <link rel="stylesheet" type="text/css"
href="http://ajax.googleapis.com/ajax/libs/dojo/1.3/dijit/themes/
            tundra/tundra.css">
        <style type="text/css">
            body, html { font-family:helvetica,arial,sans-serif;
                    font-size:90%; }
        </style>

        <script type="text/javascript"
                src="http://ajax.googleapis.com/ajax/libs/dojo/1.3/
                        dojo/dojo.xd.js"
        djConfig="parseOnLoad: true"></script>

        <style type="text/css">
            @import "http://ajax.googleapis.com/ajax/libs/dojo/1.3/
                        dojox/grid/resources/Grid.css";
            @import "http://ajax.googleapis.com/ajax/libs/dojo/1.3/
                        dojox/grid/resources/tundraGrid.css";
            .dojoxGrid table
            { margin: 0; } html, body { width: 100%; height: 100%;
              margin: 0; }
```

```
        </style>
    </head>

    <body>
        <h1>Social Example</h1>

    <body class="tundra ">
        <div dojoType="dijit.form.Form" id="myForm" jsId="myForm"
            encType="multipart/form-data" action="" method="">
            <table style="border: 1px solid #9f9f9f;"
            cellspacing="10">
            <tr>
                <td>
                    <label for="location">
                        Location:
                </td>
                <td>
                    <input type="text" name="location"
                                    required="true"
                        dojoType="dijit.form.ValidationTextBox"/>
                </td>
            </tr>
            <tr>
                <td valign="top">
                    <label for="message">
                        Message:
                </td>
                <td>
                    <textarea id="message" name="message"
                            dojoType="dijit.form.Textarea"
                            style="width:200px;"></textarea>
                </td>
            </tr>
            <tr colspan="2" align="center">
                <td>
                    <button dojoType="dijit.form.Button"
                            type="submit"
                            name="submitButtonTwo"
                            value="Submit">
                            Submit
                    </button>
                    <button dojoType="dijit.form.Button"
                            type="reset">
```

```
                            Reset
                        </button>
                    </td>
                </tr>
            </table>

            <input type="hidden" name="bookId" value="1"/>
            <!-- OS -->
            <input type="hidden" name="name" id="name" value=""/>
            <input type="hidden" name="account" id="account"
                value=""/>
            <input type="hidden" name="source" value="opensocial"/>
        </div>
        <div id="gridholder"></div>
    </body>
</html>
```

Note that Listing 8.10 uses Dojo, and that the form in this example does
not have an action, because we will send the data to the server using Ajax.

The first portion of Listing 8.10 contains a simple data entry form that
takes the location and message the user wishes to add. Next, a grid is provided
that displays any data that may have been entered during previous sessions.

The JavaScript in this example is reproduced here:

```
var store;
var grid;

dojo.require("dijit.form.Form");
dojo.require("dijit.form.Button");
dojo.require("dijit.form.ValidationTextBox");
dojo.require("dijit.form.Textarea");
dojo.require("dojox.grid.DataGrid");
dojo.require("dojo.data.ItemFileWriteStore");

function listbookscallback(data){
    grid.setStore(new dojo.data.ItemFileWriteStore({
        data: data.data
        }));
}

function reloadGrid(x){
    var params = {};
    params[gadgets.io.RequestParameters.CONTENT_TYPE] =
        gadgets.io.ContentType.JSON;
```

```
        params[gadgets.io.RequestParameters.REFRESH_INTERVAL] = 0;

        gadgets.io.makeRequest("http://socialexample
        .appspot.com/listbookmessages?t="+new Date().getTime(),
        listbookscallback, params);
}

function addBookMessage(){
        var query = dojo.formToQuery("myForm");
        query=query+'&t='+new Date().getTime();

        var params = {};
        params[gadgets.io.RequestParameters.CONTENT_TYPE] =
gadgets.io.ContentType.TEXT;
        params[gadgets.io.RequestParameters.REFRESH_INTERVAL] = 0;
        gadgets.io.makeRequest("http://socialexample.appspot.com/
                    addbookmessage?"+query, reloadGrid, params);

}
function loadNameAndAccount(){
        var req = opensocial.newDataRequest();
        req.add(req.newFetchPersonRequest(opensocial.IdSpec.PersonId.
OWNER), 'owner');
        req.send(response);
}

function response(data) {
        dojo.byId('name').value=data.get("owner").getData()
            .getDisplayName();
        dojo.byId('account').value=data.get("owner").getData().getId();
};

dojo.addOnLoad(function() {
        store = new dojo.data.ItemFileWriteStore({
            data:{
                "identifier":"date",
                "label":"date",
                "items":[]
            }
            });

        loadNameAndAccount();
        reloadGrid();

        var myForm = dijit.byId("myForm");
        dojo.connect(myForm, "onSubmit", function(e) {
```

```
        e.preventDefault();
        if (myForm.isValid()) {

            if(dojo.trim(dojo.byId("message").value)==""){
                alert("Please add a message");
            }else{

                addBookMessage();

            }
        }else{
            alert("Form not Valid");
        }
});

dojo.byId("name").focus();

// set the layout structure:
var layout = [{
    field: 'date',
    name: 'Date',
    width: 'auto'
},
{
    field: 'name',
    name: 'Name',
    width: 'auto'
},
{
    field: 'source',
    name: 'Source',
    width: 'auto'
},
{
    field: 'location',
    name: 'Location',
    width: 'auto'
},
{
    field: 'message',
    name: 'Message',
    width: 'auto'
}];
```

```
    // create a new grid:
    grid = new dojox.grid.DataGrid({
        query: {
            date: '*'
        },
        store: store,
        clientSort: true,
        rowSelector: '20px',
        structure: layout
    },dojo.byId("gridholder"));

    grid.startup();
});
```

The JavaScript in this example is straightforward. It starts with several dojo.require statements for loading the required JavaScript, followed by the functionality that is used during the onLoad event. The store for the grid is defined to start with an empty data JSON object.

Next, we call the JavaScript method loadNameAndAccount(), which in turn calls the JavaScript method opensocial.newDataRequest() to look up the owner, or user, of the page.

When the Ajax calls to get user information (on the server), the callback response is issued. The response function sets the account and name in hidden form variables. Then the reloadGrid method is called, which makes an Ajax call to retrieve the grid information.

Note that Ajax calls in OpenSocial must proxy through the OpenSocial server, which is often convenient, because the OpenSocial server often caches the calls. However, in this example, we do not want any caching; therefore, we set the value of the parameter gadgets.io.RequestParameters .REFRESH_INTERVAL to 0 and we added the timestamp to the query string. Setting the query string to the timestamp makes each request unique, so caching will not occur.

The data returned by the Ajax call is JSON-formatted data, as shown here:

```
{"identifier":"date","label":"date",

"items":[{"name":"Ashrafi Siamak","location":"Chapter 11","message":
"I didn't realize how many options are available.","id":7003,"date":
1254187534753,"source":"web","bookId":1,"account":""},
```

```
{"name":"Oswald Campesato","location":"Chapter 5","message":"I can't
believe how much I learned","id":7002,"date":1254187416798,"source":
"web","bookId":1,"account":""},

{"name":"Kevin Nilson","location":"Chapter 1","message":"What a
Great Chapter","id":7001,"date":1254187371336,"source":"web","book-
Id":1,"account":""}]}
```

In the next section of the JavaScript code, we configure the `Form` submit button so that the JavaScript method `addBookMessage` is executed whenever users click on the submit button.

Note that the `addBookMessage` method must proxy through the OpenSocial server, and that it uses cache prevention techniques. If the form is invalid, the user will be alerted to fix the form. Finally, the layout of the grid is defined, and for simplicity, each `col width` is set to `auto`.

■ 8.9.1 Working with OpenSocial: Our Findings

Based on the preceding sample application, developing OpenSocial applications can be very challenging work. OpenSocial servers always attempt to cache data because of the high volume of concurrent users.

In the sample application, it was necessary to set the value of the parameter `gadgets.io.RequestParameters.REFRESH_INTERVAL` to 0 whenever we made Ajax requests, and we also added a timestamp to the query string to prevent caching of Ajax calls. If your calls cannot be cached, then you shouldn't use these techniques on any OpenSocial server.

In addition, debugging OpenSocial pages can be challenging, because the gadget you are working on is loaded into an IFrame. When debugging in Firebug, it is difficult to see and debug Ajax calls. In Firefox you can show the IFrame content as a stand alone web page by right clicking on the IFrame and selecting. In Orkut, the request for the main iframe will end in `ifr=`. Once your open social application is running stand alone (not the iFrame), you can easily isolate your Ajax calls and debug with Firebug. In Orkut, requests will end with `makerequest` and in MySpace the request will end with `relay`. Inspecting the request and response of Ajax calls is one of the easiest and powerful tools to use in OpenSocial.

Orkut has a few distinctions when compared with other OpenSocial servers. When working with Orkut, the gadget XML of your application is cached. You can add the query string `bpc=1` to request that the OpenSocial server get a new copy of your gadget XML from your server. When working with Orkut, you need a fast way to make updates on a publicly accessible web server. For some services, working with vi is the only way to make quick updates, which is a very challenging developer environment. If you are using GAE you can quickly deploy applications, but you are limited to 100 uploads a day. MySpace lets you modify the HTML inside you gadget XML using a text area on their developer site. The biggest problem with working in MySpace is that you have to pull your updates out of the MySpace text area and put them back into your IDE to save in SVN. If you have dynamic code in your gadget file, then you must carefully merge your changes back in if you're using the MySpace text area.

In general, OpenSocial development is very challenging. OpenSocial servers have disabled alerts and the console.log. It is nearly impossible to use the Firebug console, because the page you are trying to write is embedded in an iFrame.

Hopefully, you'll find this section helpful, but surely there is a better solution to developing OpenSocial applications. Developing OpenSocial applications as if they were regular applications can greatly increase your productivity. In most cases, only minor JavaScript changes are needed to let you run the HTML in your gadget as a regular HTML file. You first need to isolate the XML from the gadget, so you can load the HTML in web mode.

Listing 8.11 shows the contents of OpenSocial.jsp, which illustrates how to isolate the XML data from a gadget.

Listing 8.11 OpenSocial.jsp

```
<%
request.setAttribute("type", "opensocial");
%><?xml version="1.0" encoding="UTF-8" ?>
 <Module>
   <ModulePrefs title="Social Example">
     <Require feature="opensocial-0.8" />
   </ModulePrefs>
   <Content type="html">
     <![CDATA[
       <jsp:include page="/WEB-INF/Main.jsp"/>
     ]]>
   </Content>
 </Module>
```

If you want to see this page in web mode, then load the JSP page Web. jsp in Listing 8.12.

Listing 8.12 Web.jsp

```
<%
request.setAttribute("type", "web");
%>
<jsp:include page="/WEB-INF/Main.jsp"/>
```

Next, partition the JavaScript into three nonoverlapping sections: common, web, and OpenSocial. Common is the JavaScript code that can work in both deployments. Web contains versions of the Ajax calls that directly call the server. The OpenSocial contains different versions of OpenSocial code that will proxy Ajax calls through the OpenSocial server, as shown in Listing 8.13.

Listing 8.13

```
<% if("web".equals(request.getAttribute("type"))){ %>
function addBookMessage(){
    var xhrArgs = {
        url: "addbookmessage",
        form: "myForm",
        handleAs: "text",
        load: function(data){
            reloadGrid();
        },
        error: function(error){
            alert("error");
        }
    }

    var deferred = dojo.xhrPost(xhrArgs);
}

<% }else if("opensocial".equals(request.getAttribute("type"))){ %>

function addBookMessage(){
    var query = dojo.formToQuery("myForm");
    query=query+'&t='+new Date().getTime();

    var params = {};
    params[gadgets.io.RequestParameters.CONTENT_TYPE] =
        gadgets.io.ContentType.TEXT;
```

```
        params[gadgets.io.RequestParameters.REFRESH_INTERVAL] = 0;
        gadgets.io.makeRequest("http://socialexample.appspot.com/" +
        "addbookmessage?"+query, reloadGrid, params);
}
<%}%>
```

Note that if you load the page Web.jsp, then the type variable is set to web and the JavaScript method addBookMessage uses dojo.xhrPost to send the data to the server. If you load the JSP page OpenSocial.jsp, then the type variable is set to opensocial and the JavaScript method gadgets.io.makeRequest will be used to proxy requests through the OpenSocial server, and then send data to the server. Both versions will call the JavaScript method reloadGrid when they are complete.

You should increase your productivity by using the following method. Once you get things going in MySpace, switch to the web version to do the majority of your work. Setting your project up in this fashion also makes it easy to plug in mock versions of your service calls. This lets you work on the front-end while your backend is still under development. A simple example is a version of reloadGrid that uses hardcoded JSON. This mock version could be used until you have time to create your datastore and write code to convert datastore objects into JSON. We highly encourage you to experiment with developing OpenSocial applications by working outside the OpenSocial environment.

■ 8.10 SUMMARY

In this chapter, we introduced you to the OpenSocial consortium and some of the companies that belong to it. Next, we discussed OpenSocial Markup Language, including tags and templates, followed by OpenSocial Gadgets and the OpenSocial technology stack. We also looked at OpenSocial applications for Yahoo (which supports a markup language called YML) and Google Orkut.

We also discussed Shindig, which is the Apache open source reference implementation for OpenSocial, and you learned how to run Java-based code samples from the command line.

The next chapter discusses mash-up tools, various products and companies that are involved in search technology, and how to combine mash-ups with search technology.

## CHAPTER 9

Mash-Ups and Search Technology

In This Chapter:

- Mash-Ups
- Mash-Up Tools and Products
- Search Technology
- Search-related Engines
- Industry Perspective and Business Focus

This chapter covers mash-ups and search technology, which are important aspects of Web 2.0. Mash-ups have had a significant impact on the advancement of Web 2.0 (especially in the early stages), and you would probably be hard-pressed to find Internet users who have not seen a mash-up on the Web. Search technology is becoming more diverse in terms of the open source tools that are available, which are part of the underlying technology for mash-ups.

We'll start this chapter by exploring mash-ups and the various ways in which mash-ups are used, and also look at the mash-up tools that are available. The mash-up tools discussed in this chapter include IBM Mash-up Center, Intel Mash Maker, Denodo, and JackBe. We'll also discuss mash-ups that are created with programming languages such as Java, Python, and Ruby.

Next, we'll look at search-related tools, including Yahoo® Build Your Own Search Service™ (BOSS), Google Squared, and Google CSE, and open source search tools.

There are many good tools and products available for mash-ups and for performing web-based searches, and the tools we'll discuss in this chapter were chosen based on the following factors:

- useful functionality
- easy to use
- ability to be invoked programmatically
- the maturity/longevity

Keep in mind that mash-up tools continue to evolve and improve in various ways, such as in their feature set or the ease with which they can be created (which is also true of Ajax toolkits). Thus, you might need to periodically "upgrade" your knowledge of the newer versions of tools described in this chapter.

■ 9.1 MASH-UPS

The following high-level overview describes several technologies that predate mash-ups, starting with Common Object Request Broker Architecture (CORBA®), then Java Enterprise JavaBeans™ (EJBs), followed by Enterprise Application Integration (EAI) and Enterprise Information Integration (EII), and then Simple Object Access Protocol (SOAP) and Web Services. Since entire books have been written on each of these topics, the overview focuses on the problems that each technology did and did not solve.

During the 1990s, CORBA enabled communication between software programs running on heterogeneous environments (i.e., remote machines with different operating systems). CORBA is a comprehensive system consisting of 15 major components, and although CORBA is still used for messaging purposes (and mainly as an underlying "invisible" technology), it is considered a legacy technology.

In the late 1990s, after the availability of Java, a group proposed an alternative system based on Java EJBs, which is simpler than CORBA because of one very important simplification: all of the software programs were written in Java.

Meanwhile, desktop browsers appeared in the early 1990s, starting with Mosaic™, Netscape®, and Internet Explorer. Browsers supported JavaScript, which many people erroneously thought was similar to Java (perhaps because of the similarity in names). DOM support in browsers began with DOM Level 0 in 1996, and continued with DOM Level 2 in 1998/2000, and DOM Level 3 in 2004. DOM Level 2 introduced the method `getEle-mentById()`.

Prior to DOM Level 2, JavaScript code was often used to validate the content of input fields, such as ensuring that text strings were not null and only contained alphanumeric characters, and validating formats for input fields, such as zip codes. However, DOM Level 2 let programmers write client-side JavaScript code to manage the DOM of an HTML page.

In February 2005, Jesse James Garrett published his seminal paper on Ajax, which is based on `XMLHttpRequest`, which has been available in Internet Explorer since the late 1990s. Ajax, and its support for partial page refresh, let programmers write JavaScript code that combined Ajax and DOM Level 2 features. Consumer mash-ups soon became popular and ubiquitous, but they were still based on handwritten code, which was error-prone and difficult to maintain. This led to a proliferation of Ajax toolkits whose popularity still varies from year to year (and sometimes from month to month).

Enterprise software systems did not "need" mash-ups; they favored portals instead, which provide a simultaneous view of data from a number of sources that was assembled on a server and then delivered to a browser, rather than the ad hoc manner of consumer mash-ups. Enterprise systems focused on EAI and EII.

EAI involves overcoming communication barriers between software applications due to various factors, such as incompatible software languages, different hardware platforms, and security issues. On the other hand, EII focuses on integration at the data level rather than the software application level.

Service Oriented Architecture (SOA) became popular because of one particular design principle: "endpoints" provided a well-known, specific service. These services were loosely coupled, so programmers could combine them to suit their business needs. Moreover, endpoints provided data in a manner that shielded the outside world from the internal workings of the systems that produced the data. Note that SOA is an architecture that is often implemented via web services (using SOAP), but the two terms are not interchangeable.

SOAP became a popular mechanism for providing XML-based data at endpoints. In addition, an endpoint provided an XML-based Web Services

Descriptor Language (WSDL) file that clearly defined the structure of that XML-based data. However, the complexity of WSDL files and SOAP-based calls led to the creation of REpresentational State Transfer (REST) as a simpler alternative to SOAP. As a simple example, the following REST call returns the `Del.icio.us` tags starting from 1 and ending with 3 for the user `ocampesato`:

```
http://del.icio.us/api/ocampesato/tags/example?start=1&end=3
```

In a similar manner, the verboseness of XML led to the popularity of JSON™ (discussed in Chapter 3, JSON and XML), which is a structurally simpler alternative.

Mash-ups frequently use web services (which often support both SOAP and REST) that deliver data in various formats, including XML (RSS/Atom are very popular) and JSON. Consumer mash-ups aggregate data from multiple disparate sources (as few as two but sometimes dozens) and then present the data in a manner that is useful to end users.

Although mash-ups are primarily associated with consumer mash-ups (for entertainment and convenience) and to a lesser extent, enterprise mash-ups, another significant beneficiary of mash-ups (and other facets of Web 2.0) is the U.S. military. In 2009, the U.S. Defense Information Systems Agency (DISA) deployed a JackBe Presto enterprise mash-up server, and DISA uses mash-ups to address various types of disasters (both natural and man-made).

Moreover, you can even create mash-ups that combine data from Software as a Service (SaaS)-based applications (for example, from SalesForce .com®), and applications that reside on Google App Engine (GAE), Amazon, or some other cloud computing provider. Thus, you can think of a mash-up not only as a specific application, but also as a "logical container" that can retrieve information from virtually anywhere on the Internet.

■ 9.1.1 Consumer and Enterprise Mash-Ups

Mash-ups provide value by combining ("mashing together") data from two or more data sources. Early mash-ups were something of a novelty because they combined data in ways that hadn't been seen in other software applications. One common mash-up involved overlaying restaurant locations on a Google Map of a specific region (e.g., based on zip codes) that also highlighted details about each restaurant.

You can create mash-ups in various programming languages, including Groovy, Java, Python, and Ruby, and the appendices contain links to articles that explain how to use these languages to create mash-ups.

In the following subsections, we'll look at two categories of mash-ups: consumer mash-ups and enterprise mash-ups.

9.1.1.1 Consumer Mash-Ups

Consumer mash-ups combine data to provide simple yet useful online services, such as the previous example of the restaurants displayed on a map. These mash-ups initially had a nice-to-have quality about them, and as people became increasingly reliant on the convenience they offer, these mash-ups became must-haves and they can quickly became part of our daily tool set because of their usefulness and convenience.

Mash-ups can be created by combining information from well-known sites, such as the following:

- Flickr and YouTube
- Amazon and eBay®
- Facebook and Bebo
- Facebook and Twitter
- Facebook and Salesforce

Consumer mash-ups provide useful information such as weather updates, maps, directions, and product price information. The following is a short list of popular consumer mash-ups:

- Walk Score™
- Housingmaps
- DriveScore™
- Google Maps and Craigslist®
- Every Block™

There are hundreds (perhaps thousands) of mash-ups available, some of which combine multiple web services to create a single mash-up. Before you create a mash-up, search the Internet to see if a mash-up with comparable functionality already exists.

9.1.1.2 Enterprise Mash-Ups

Enterprise mash-ups are sometimes called "server-side mash-ups" or "proxy-style mash-ups," because a component in the server acts as a proxy to the (usually composite) service that delivers data to a client. Mash-up tools that create enterprise data mash-ups tend to focus on helping you to create composite services quickly and easily.

Although enterprise mash-up tools vary in terms of the input data sources that they support for creating mash-ups, they tend to support the following types of input data sources:

- database data
- web services
- XML or JSON data
- applications
- websites
- email
- spreadsheets
- text files

Adoption of enterprise mash-ups has been slower than consumer mash-ups, but enterprise mash-up tools are becoming increasingly popular with businesses. For example, Denodo Technologies (which is discussed later in this chapter) has a product that it calls an "enterprise data mash-up" tool for creating composite services. This tool simplifies the process by creating and deploying a web service whose input data can be extracted from a relational database, an XML document, and an existing third-party web service.

■ 9.1.2 Design Patterns and Best Practices

Mash-up design patterns are solutions to categories of mash-ups, and they can save you time and effort, and let you benefit from other people's experience. Mash-up Best Practices are recommendations about things to do and things to avoid when creating mash-ups.

Michael Ogrinz is the author of the book *Mash-up Patterns* (and a contributor to this chapter) which contains an analysis of 34 mash-up patterns in 5 main categories. His book is highly recommended because of its detailed description of the advantages and disadvantages of different types of mash-ups. It can help you decide on the type of mash-ups that are best suited for your specific requirements.

■ 9.2 MASH-UP TOOLS AND PRODUCTS

Mash-up tools can be web-based, downloadable, or hosted. For example, Yahoo Pipes is a web-based tool (discussed in Chapter 5) that lets you create and store definitions of pipes online. On the other hand, OpenKapow is a downloadable mash-up tool that you install and configure on your system, whereas the IBM Mash-up Center is a hosted mash-up tool. Thus, the purpose of your mash-ups lets you reduce the list of potential mash-up tools that you need to evaluate for your mash-ups.

Now let's discuss some of the powerful mash-up tools that are available from the following vendors:

- IBM Mash-up Center
- WSO2 Mash-up Server
- Intel Mash Maker
- Denodo
- JackBe Presto

■ 9.2.1 IBM Mash-Up Center

The IBM Mash-up Center is a tool that lets you create, store, and share widgets and mash-ups. It is made up of Lotus Mash-ups® and the InfoSphere Mash-up Hub™, and its home page is:
http://www-01.ibm.com/software/info/mash-up-center/

The IBM Mash-up Center has a widget creation environment that enables the code-less creation of widgets that retrieve information from both internal enterprise sources and external sources. Users can share widgets with team members by storing them in a common area, which means that users can search for existing widgets and use them to quickly create mash-ups with them.

9.2.1.1 Set-up Procedure for the IBM Mash-Up Center

The set-up steps for the IBM Mash-up Center are:

Step 1: Download the IBM Mash-up Center from:
http://www.ibm.com/developerworks/downloads/ls/lsmash-up-center/index.html

Step 2: Uncompress the distribution in a convenient directory

Step 3: Navigate to the launchpad subdirectory

Step 4: Run the file `launchpad.exe` for Windows or the launchpad shell script for Linux

Step 5: Select your preferred language from the pop-up window

The left-side panel of the pop-up window provides the following options:

- First Steps Welcome
- Work with Mash-up Center
- Administrative Tasks
- Information Resources
- Exit

You are now ready to create an IBM mash-up, and you can find detailed instructions in the PDF guide located here:
http://www-10.lotus.com/ldd/mash-upswiki.nsf/dx/mash_tut_English
.pdf/$file/mash_tut_English.pdf

■ 9.2.2 WSO2

WSO2™ is actually an open source SOA company that provides a middle-ware tool based on SOA. In 2009, WSO2 won the InfoWorld Best-of award for WSO2 Carbon. The WSO2 home page is:
http://wso2.com/

WSO2 lets you not only use languages such as Java, C, or PHP to easily create services, but existing input sources as well. In either case, the services you create can be used to create mash-ups. WSO2 supports the following list of products, which shows that WSO2 is more than just a mash-up product:

- Web services application server
- Web services framework
- Data services server
- Enterprise Service Bus (ESB)
- Business process server
- Mash-up Server

One point to note is that while many of the other enterprise mash-up tools focus on creating consumable input sources for widgets and mash-ups, WSO2 focuses on how to leverage the architectural nature of SOA to produce services, which includes creating mash-ups with the WSO2 Mash-up server. Despite the differences in philosophy, these two approaches produce the same result: easy-to-create mash-ups that are powerful and deliver the desired functionality.

The current release of the WSO2 Mash-up Server contains 220 JAR files from numerals open source projects. Some of the open source projects include Axis2™, Batik, Geronimo, JAXB™, Shindig™, Xalan, and Xerces™.

WSO2 also supports widgets, and Jonathan Marsh created a detailed blog post that describes how to create widgets for the WSO2 Server: http://jonathanmarsh.net/category/wso2-mash-up-server/

In addition, various embeddable widgets for the WSO2 Identity Server are available here:

http://www.ohloh.net/p/identityserver/widgets

9.2.2.1 *Set-up Steps for the WSO2 Mashup Server*

The setup steps for the WSO2 Mashup Server are:

Step 1: Download the WSO2 Mash-up Server from:
http://wso2.com/products/compose/wso2-mash-up-server/

Step 2: Expand the ZIP file into a directory, which we will call `WSO2MASH-UP_HOME`

Step 3: Open a command shell and navigate to `WSO2MASH-UP_HOME/bin`

Step 4: Launch the following file:

```
startup.bat (Windows)
startup.sh (Linux)
```

Note that the current release of WSO2 Mash-up Server has not been fully tested on JDK1.6.

9.2.2.2 *WSO2 Sample Code*

The WSO2 Server provides sample JavaScript code in the `scripts/samples` subdirectory of `WSO2MASH-UP_HOME`, which includes the following:

```
exchangeRate.js
formulaFlicks.js
RESTSample.js
sudoku.js
tomatoTube.js
TwitterMap.js
yahooGeoCode.js
```

■ 9.2.3 Intel Mash Maker

Intel Mash Maker is a browser plug-in for Firefox and Internet Explorer that lets you create mash-ups. Its home page is:
http://mashmaker.intel.com/web/

One goal of Mash Maker is to let non-technical end users enhance existing websites with customized functionality tailored to their needs. Mash Maker lets users enhance websites through a collection of widgets, each of which can enhance the functionality or meaning of a given website. Thus, Mash Maker provides mash-up functionality, but unlike other mash-up tools, it does not let users combine stand-alone services.

Intel's Mash Maker supports Microsoft Windows XP and Vista, Linux, and Apple MAC (Leopard and Tiger®) running Mozilla Firefox. Browser support includes Microsoft Internet Explorer 7.x (or higher) and Mozilla Firefox 1.x (or higher). Intel's Mash Maker also supports mobile devices (check the Mash Maker home page for the most up-to-date information).

Intel's Mash Maker is based on iFrames as described here:
http://mashmaker.intel.com/web/techinfo/widgetapi.html

A component in a Mash Maker mash-up is called a widget, which is represented by an XML `<widget>` element. Intel's Mash Maker also supports Google Gadgets (discussed in Chapter 5), and according to Intel, Google Gadgets are not as powerful as Mash Maker Widgets.

9.2.3.1 Download and Installation

Complete the following steps to install Intel Mash Maker:

Step 1: Download the Intel Mash Maker from:
http://mashmaker.intel.com/web/download.html

Step 2: Select a browser (Firefox or Internet Explorer) and provide your name and email address

Step 3: Click on the download link to install the plug-in

Step 4: Restart your browser

9.2.3.2 A Simple Mash Maker Example

After you complete the installation steps for Mash Maker, look for three adjacent icons below the toolbar that resemble the letter M, a grid, and a star (use your mouse to hover over icons until you find them).

The left-most icon enables/disables Mash Maker, the middle icon opens a vertical sidebar that displays a set of Mash Maker options, and the right-most icon lets you save your work.

Click on the Widgets tab and you will see a list of widgets, such as Google Maps, Calendar, and a Photo Tile. Next, navigate to a website and double-click on any of your widgets to add them to the website.

Note that the Intel Mash Maker download page also contains a link to a how-to video that provides further details for using Mash Maker.

9.2.3.3 *iFrames and Widgets*

Mash Maker widgets are defined in XML-based code snippets in an XML `<widget>` element. Listing 9.1 shows a simple example of the contents of a Mash Maker widget.

Listing 9.1

```
<widget title="MyWidget"
 description="this widget does nothing special"
 author="John Smith"
 author_email=jsmith@yahoo.com

 icon=http://mashmaker.intel.com/icons/mycar.png
 version="1"
 >
<settings
 href="http://mashmaker.intel.com/widgets/car_settings.html"/>
<content hidden="true"
 href="http://mashmaker.intel.com/widgets/mywidget.html"/>
</widget>
```

Listing 9.1 consists of the XML `widget` element, which contains `title`, `icon`, and `version` attributers that let you specify the widget's name, an icon for the widget, and the version of the widget API, respectively.

Check the appendices for Mash Maker links that contain additional information.

■ 9.2.4 Denodo Technologies

Denodo provides an enterprise data mash-up product that can combine structured and unstructured data and then publish the combined data as a service in multiple formats, such as XML and JSON. Denodo also won the Infoworld 2009 Technology of the Year Award. The Denodo Technology home page is:

http://www.denodo.com/english/index.html

The input data for a Denodo mash-up can be from a variety of sources, including:

- a database
- web services
- applications
- websites
- email

An online video describing Denodo 4.1 (in English) can be found here: http://www.denodo.com/english/products.html

■ 9.2.5 JackBe

JackBe offers free trial downloads of its enterprise mash-up software platform, called Presto™, on its home page:

http://www.jackbe.com/

JackBe Presto runs as a web application in a servlet container, such as Apache Tomcat (typically 5.x or higher). After you install Presto, you can access the administrative URL for both Apache Tomcat and JackBe Presto.

JackBe Presto provides three important components. The first component is the Presto Enterprise Mash-Up Server that lets you manage your mash-ups. The second component is the Presto Wires Visual Composer™, which lets you create mash-ups in a browser. The third component is the Presto Mash-Up Connector, which is a two-way connector for connecting Presto with other systems, such as Oracle Fusion™, ESBs, and Microsoft® Excel™. JackBe also lets you create enterprise mash-ups with Microsoft SharePoint. Additional information about JackBe Presto products can be found here:

http://www.jackbe.com/products/

According to the JackBe website, you can set up JackBe Presto "in 3 minutes," and the JackBe Presto installation process in the next section required less than 10 minutes (so the claim is realistic). The installation procedure is straightforward, so even if you are unfamiliar with Apache Tomcat, you should be able to complete the installation quickly.

JackBe Presto uses "mashlets" (which are portal widgets), and its Mashlet wizard simplifies the process of creating template-based mashlets. JackBe Presto mash-ups leverage the Ext JS Ajax toolkit, so you have an advantage if you are already familiar with this toolkit. Two other interesting aspects about JackBe mashlets is that they can be published as standard JSR-168 portlets, and they can also run on an iPhone.

9.2.5.1 *JackBe Registration, Download, and Installation*

Complete the following steps to install JackBe Presto:

Step 1: Create a free JackBe account here:
http://www.jackbe.com/enterprise-mash-up/

You will receive an email message containing the activation key you need the first time you start Presto.

Step 2: Download the Presto Developer Edition (116MB zip file) from:
http://www.jackbe.com/enterprise-mash-up/

Step 3: Open a command shell and uncompress the Presto distribution into a convenient directory.

Step 4: Navigate to the directory in Step 3 and type the following:

```
setup.bat (Windows)
setup.sh (Linux)
```

The installer will prompt you for information (accept the default values when possible) and the installation will be completed in a few minutes.

Step 5: Start the Presto repository by navigating to the prestorepository/hsqldb subdirectory and typing the following command:

```
server.bat (Windows)
server.bat (Linux)
```

Step 6: Start the Presto server by navigating to the mash-up server subdirectory and typing the following command:

```
startPresto.bat (Windows)
startPresto.sh (Linux)
```

Step 7: Launch your browser and navigate to the following URL (replace port 8080 with the port you selected during the installation):
http://localhost:8080/presto

Step 8: Click on the Upgrade button and then copy and paste the activation key

Step 9: Navigate to the URL in Step 7 and log in as admin/adminadmin

Note that Presto installs the Apache Tomcat servlet container (the default port is 8080) and you can confirm that the installation completed successfully by launching your browser and navigating to the following URL (change port 8080 to the number that you chose during the installation): http://localhost:8080/adminserver

You can see additional JackBe mash-up samples here: http://localhost:8080/mash-upsamples/

9.2.5.2 A Simple JackBe Mash-Up

JackBe provides Mash-up Studio, which is an Eclipse-based IDE that you can download after you complete the free user registration here: http://www.jackbe.com/enterprise-mash-up/content/download-presto-developer-edition

Download the Mash-up Studio zip file (its name is similar to presto-dev-install-2_6_1.zip) and unzip it into a convenient directory.

In addition, JackBe lets you create advanced mashlets as described here: http://www.jackbe.com/prestodocs/v2.5/prestolibrary/wwhelp/wwhimpl/js/html/wwhelp.htm?context=prestolibrary&topic=mash-upDev

9.2.5.3 Creating a Mash-Up with the JackBe Eclipse Plug-In

This section describes the steps for creating a mash-up using the JackBe Presto plug-in for Eclipse.

Follow the instructions in Chapter 6, Debugging Tools, for downloading and installing Eclipse 3.4 (or higher), and then complete the following steps:

Step 1: Install the JackBe plug-in for Eclipse using the following URL: http://www.jackbe.com/downloads/presto/mash-upstudio

Step 2: Follow the **File > New > Other > Mash-up > Mash-up Project** menu path and click Next

Step 3: Specify the name Mash-up1 and click Finish

Check the document InstallationGuide.pdf (located in JackBe Presto's top-level directory) for step-by-step instructions on installing other JackBe products, and for deploying Presto to other application servers.

■ 9.2.6   Yahoo BOSS Mash-Up Framework

The Yahoos BOSS mash-up framework is an experimental Python library you can download from:

http://developer.yahoo.com/search/boss/mash-up.html

This framework lets you mash up data from Yahoo BOSS with third-party data using a SQL-like syntax.

9.2.6.1   A Simple BOSS Mash-Up Example

Listing 9.2 contains the contents of a code sample from the BOSS mash-up framework home page.

Listing 9.2

```
from templates import publisher
from util import text, console
from yos.boss.ysearch import search
from yos.yql import db, udfs

dl = db.select(name="dl", udf=udfs.unnest_value,
 url="http://feeds.delicious.com/rss/popular/iphone")
yn = db.create(name="yn", data=search("iphone", vertical="news",
 count=50))

def overlap_predicate(r1, r2):
 return text.overlap(r1["title"], r2["title"]) > 1

tb = db.join(overlap_predicate, [dl, yn])
tb = db.group(by=["yn\$title"], key=None, reducer=lambda x,y: None,
            as=None, table=tb, norm=text.norm)

serp = publisher.Serp(template_dir="templates/california",
      title="boss 'iphone'", endpoint="http://yahoo/search")

for row in tb.rows:
 serp.add(url=row["dl\$link"], title=row["yn\$title"],
 abstract=row["yn\$abstract"], dispurl=row["yn\$sourceurl"],
 source=row["dl\$creator"])

serp.dump("iphone.html")
```

Listing 9.2 is a very compact Python script that searches for the string iphone in Yahoo News, performs a second search from del.icio.us, and mashes up the results in an HTML page.

9.2.6.2 Yahoo Search BOSS

Vik Singh (the architect of BOSS) created an interesting project that is a Python-based integration of Yahoo BOSS and GAE (including the source code). This project lets you make unlimited queries, and you have unrestricted use of the results. In addition, various companies currently use Yahoo Search BOSS, including Hakia, OneRiot, Dayl.com, and Cluuz™. The distribution for this project can be found here: http://zooie.wordpress.com/2008/08/04/yahoo-boss-google-app-engine-integrated/

Complete the installation steps in Chapter 10, to install GAE on your system (if you don't have it already), then complete the following steps:

Step 1: Download the distribution qa.zip

Step 2: Uncompress it in your GAE directory

Step 3: Go to the qa directory

Step 4: Specify your BOSS ID in the appid entry in the config file

Step 5: Change the application name to your GAE name in the app.yaml file

■ 9.2.7 Consumer Mash-Ups and Online Tools

You already know that you can create consumer mash-ups that combine data from web services (SOAP or REST) and return XML (such as RSS) and then combine that data with Google Maps. In addition, you can create mash-ups that use a Yahoo pipe or Dapper dapp (see Chapter 5). The following sections discuss several online tools that let you create mash-ups: Google Web Elements, Google Maps, and KML.

9.2.7.1 Google Web Elements

Google Web Elements provides a simple way to insert "elements" (also called Google Widgets) into your website. Its home page is: http://www.google.com/webelements/

Currently, there are eight Google Web Elements that you can embed in an HTML page via a simple copy-and-paste process. Google Web Elements is a painless mechanism for adding maps, news, and search capability to a website. You can also embed Google documents, presentations, and spreadsheets into your website with equal ease.

When you look at the website for Google Web Elements, it is more like a portal than a mash-up, with no coding required. However, widgets are becoming increasingly commonplace, and more powerful and sophisticated, so keep this in mind when you are trying to design a website that has relatively simple requirements. Another point to remember is that embedding widgets (versus creating a mash-up) in a website via copy and paste can make a website easier to maintain. These are useful points to keep in mind when you are developing mash-ups.

9.2.7.2 Google Maps

Google Maps is a freely available tool from Google. Its home page is:
http://maps.google.com/

If you intend to use the Google Maps API in your website, register for a free Google Maps API key here:
http://code.google.com/apis/maps/signup.html

The preceding website also provides a list of features and restrictions for the Google Maps API key.

The Google Maps API is based on Ajax (discussed in Chapter 4) and the API uses the latitude and longitude of a site to display that site on a map, which in turn can be embedded in different websites.

You can also combine the data returned by the Google Maps API with data from other sources to create mash-ups.

9.2.7.3 KML

KML is an XML-based format for specifying and displaying geographic data in maps in mobile-based and desktop browsers. KML also has an XML-schema (see the link in the next section) that specifies mandatory and optional elements. You can use KML-based data as part of a mash-up or to "tag" the location of a picture that has been uploaded to a website. For example, suppose you belong to a travel club in which members upload pictures they take during their trips. If those pictures have geographic data, you can take a "virtual trip" of someone's actual trip, or select the locations of a subset of those pictures that you can include as part of your own itinerary.

An especially interesting website is the KML Interactive Sampler, which lets you add visual content (such as lines, polygons, and balloons) simply by clicking on links, after which you can see the visual results on a map and the corresponding XML-based elements inside a KML document.

The KML Interactive Sample (see the appendices for the link) is a good way to learn about KML. An example of a simple KML document is shown in the next section.

9.2.7.3.1 A Simple Example of KML Document

Listing 9.3 shows the contents of a simple KML document that contains nothing more than an XML Document element. This is the KML document on the KML Interactive Sample website.

Listing 9.3

```
<?xml version="1.0" encoding="UTF-8"?>
<kml xmlns="http://www.opengis.net/kml/2.2">
 <Document>

 </Document>
</kml>
```

Now look at Listing 9.4, which contains the contents of a KML document that is generated after clicking on the Linear Ring link in the Lines and Paths folder on the KML Interactive Sample website.

Listing 9.4

```
<?xml version="1.0" encoding="UTF-8"?>
<kml xmlns="http://www.opengis.net/kml/2.2">
  <Document>
    <name>KmlFile</name>
    <Style id="thickBlackLine">
      <LineStyle>
        <color>87000000</color>
        <width>10</width>
      </LineStyle>
    </Style>
    <Placemark>
      <name>Relative</name>
      <visibility>1</visibility>
```

```
        <description>Black line (10 pixels wide), height tracks
terrain</description>
        <styleUrl>#thickBlackLine</styleUrl>
        <LineString>
          <tessellate>1</tessellate>
          <altitudeMode>relativeToGround</altitudeMode>
          <coordinates>
            -112.2532845153347,36.09886943729116,645
            -112.2540466121145,36.09919570465255,645
            -112.254734666947,36.09984998366178,645
            -112.255493345654,36.10051310621746,645
            -112.2563157098468,36.10108441943419,645
            -112.2568033076439,36.10159722088088,645
            -112.257494011321,36.10204323542867,645
            -112.2584106072308,36.10229131995655,645
            -112.2596588987972,36.10240001286358,645
            -112.2610581199487,36.10213176873407,645
            -112.2626285262793,36.10157011437219,645
          </coordinates>
        </LineString>
      </Placemark>
    </Document>
</kml>
```

Listing 9.4 contains an XML coordinates element that lists the data points that correspond to a triangle-like object that is rendered on top of a map. Note that the points in Listing 9.4 consist of a set of line segments that form the outline of a triangle when they are placed on a map. (A triangle in the Euclidean plane is defined by three vertices, and not in terms of eleven points, such as the points in Listing 9.4.)

This concludes our discussion of mash-ups and mash-up tools. The next section discusses search technology and search engine tools.

■ 9.3 SEARCH TECHNOLOGY

The search technology facet of Web 2.0 is both interesting and challenging, and the subject of considerable ongoing research. In this section we'll discuss open source and free search tools, including Google Custom Search Engine™ (CSE), Google Site Search™ (GSS), Google Squared, and Yahoo BOSS. We'll also look at search engines, including Microsoft® Bing®, Google Caffeine™, Hakia, Kosmix, and Yebol.

The Real-Time Web has been under discussion since early 2008, and it continues to gather momentum. The Real-Time Web refers to the ability to search and receive information in real time via tools such as Twitter. Although Real-Time Search is part of the Real-Time Web, some people make a distinction to emphasize the search-specific component of the Real-Time Web.

Twitter (and Twitter-like tools such as Jaiku) excel in Real-Time Search, whereas more traditional search engines are designed to find "historical" information by crawling the Internet and indexing websites. However, you can expect to see some of the well-established search engines offering some type of Real-Time Search functionality in the near future.

Currently, there are at least 10 search engines that provide Real-Time Search, including Topsy® whose home page is: http://www.topsy.com and Scoopler® whose home page is: http://www.scoopler.com/

One interesting fact is that all startups that have Real-Time Search products perform searches on Twitter, which may have prompted the observation that Real-Time Search is the combination of Twitter (discussed in Chapter 5) and Yahoo BOSS.

■ 9.3.1 Google Search Tools

Google also provides a set of search-related tools, some of which will be discussed in the following sections.

9.3.1.1 Google Custom Search Engine (CSE)

The Google CSE home page is:

http://www.google.com/coop/cse/

The Google CSE lets users create a customized search engine that can search one or more websites, and add the search box (and the results) on users' websites.

In addition, users can embed custom search elements to their websites, as described here:

http://www.google.com/webelements/customsearch/

An example of a custom search element (listed on the preceding website) is shown here:

```
<div id="cse" style="width:100%;">Loading</div>
```

```
<script src="http://www.google.com/jsapi" type="text/javascript">
</script>
<script type="text/javascript">
 google.load('search', '1');
 google.setOnLoadCallback(function(){
   new google.search.CustomSearchControl().draw('cse');
 }, true);
</script>
```

9.3.1.1.1 A SIMPLE GOOGLE CSE

When you create a Google CSE, you need to specify the name, description, language, and the list (or type) of sites that the CSE will search.

Complete the following steps to create an English-based CSE called MySearch1 that searches http://www.yahoo.com and http://www.newyorker .com/.

Step 1: Enter the two websites in the Sites to Search text area (you can modify this list later if you wish)

Step 2: Click the Terms of Service checkbox

Step 3: Click the Next button

Google will create your CSE and send you a confirmation email message. Finally, click on the Finish button and Google will display a website that lets you manage all of the CSEs that you have created.

You can get the CSE HTML code fragment by clicking on Control panel and then clicking on the code link in the left-hand column.

For example, the CSE code fragment for the CSE MySearch1 that we just created is:

```
<form action="http://www.google.com/cse" id="cse-search-box">
 <div>
 <input type="hidden" name="cx" value="016927582394720466362:_
-gmkbfhnbs" />
 <input type="hidden" name="ie" value="UTF-8" />
 <input type="text" name="q" size="31" />
 <input type="submit" name="sa" value="Search" />
 </div>
</form>
```

```
<script type="text/javascript" src="http://www.google.com/coop/cse/
brand?form=cse-search-box&lang=en"></script>
```

Now you can copy and paste the preceding code fragment into any website that you want to have search engine functionality.

9.3.1.2 Google Site Search (GSS)

GSS is a commercial tool (a minimum of USD $100 per year) and its home page is:

http://www.google.com/sitesearch/index.html

GSS uses Google's search technology to provide search results that are tailored to your website. The home page contains links for additional information, such as pricing, testimonials, features, and a demo of this tool. Click on the Product Tour link to watch a video that explains how to set up GSS for a website.

9.3.1.3 Google Squared

Google Squared is an interesting tool from Google that is available here:

http://www.google.com/squared

Unlike other tools that provide results as a list of links to websites, Google Squared presents search results in a grid called a "square." Users can modify the columns in the square, and an Add button lets users add new items. Users must first sign in before they can save their edited results. Google Squared is designed to provide a more interactive experience for users, and it differs from Wolfram Alpha, which is defined as a "knowledge computation engine."

As a simple example, a Google Squared search with the terms "google squared competitors" returned the following response:

```
"Google Squared couldn't automatically build a Square about google
squared competitors"
```

Another search on Google Squared with the terms "google squared competitors" returned a rectangular array consisting of two rows, where each row provided information about a website. The columns in the array were labeled Item Name, Image, Description, and so forth.

Google Squared appears to work considerably better for short queries about popular topics and not as well for longer queries.

Google uses the term Rich Snippets to describe the new types of information that it will provide in search results. Rich Snippets are capable of processing both RDFa and microformats, which lets Google provide richer search results.

■ 9.3.2 Yahoo Search Tools

Yahoo offers a set of interesting search-related tools, including Yahoo BOSS and Search Monkey. Note that this section only discusses Yahoo BOSS. You can search the Internet for details regarding Yahoo Search Monkey.

9.3.2.1 Yahoo BOSS

The Yahoo BOSS home page is:
http://developer.yahoo.com/search/boss
 Yahoo BOSS is currently a free tool for developers, but at some point Yahoo will introduce a pricing structure. Yahoo will continue providing free API access below a certain threshold level, so check the home page periodically for pricing-related updates.
 Companies that use products and tools based on BOSS include Cluuz, Hakia, InsiderFood, OneRiot, and PostRank™. The BOSS home page contains a video by Vik Singh (the architect of BOSS) describing Yahoo's rationale for creating the BOSS open search engine and how to use it.

9.3.2.1.1 A SIMPLE YAHOO BOSS EXAMPLE

If you do not already have a free Yahoo application ID, you can obtain one here:
https://developer.apps.yahoo.com/wsregapp/
 After you complete the registration, replace MY-APPID with your application ID in Listing 9.5, which displays a PHP code block that illustrates how to use Yahoo BOSS in an HTML page.

Listing 9.5

```
define ('APP_ID', 'MY-APPID');
$query = $_GET ['q'] . '+site:mydomain.org';
$API = 'http://boss.yahooapis.com/ysearch/web/v1/';
$request = $API . $query .'?format=xml&appid='. APP_ID;
```

```
$x = curl_init($request);
curl_setopt($x, CURLOPT_RETURNTRANSFER, 1);
curl_setopt($x, CURLOPT_HEADER, 0);
$xml = simplexml_load_string (curl_e xec($x));

foreach ($xml->resultset_web->result as $result) {
 print '<a href="'.$result->clickurl.'">'.$result->title.'</a><br
/>';
}
```

In the second line of Listing 9.5, you need to replace `mydomain.org` with your own domain:

```
$query = $_GET ['q'] . '+site:mydomain.org';
```

The third line in Listing 9.5 contains the reference to the Yahoo BOSS API:

```
$API = 'http://boss.yahooapis.com/ysearch/web/v1/';
```

The fourth line in Listing 9.5 specifies XML-formatted data:

```
$request = $API . $query .'?format=xml&appid='. APP_ID;
```

Navigate to the Yahoo BOSS website for additional information on the BOSS APIs.

■ 9.3.3 Open Source Search Tools

This section covers the following search tools and applications:

- Apache® Lucene™ (text search)
- Apache® Solr™ (built on top of Lucene, with additional features)
- Sphinx (SQL full-text search engine)
- Katta (distributed Lucene index)

9.3.3.1 Apache Lucene

Apache Lucene is an open source project that provides text searches. Its home page is:

http://lucene.apache.org/

Apache Lucene is a Java-based text search engine that creates search indexes. With Lucene you can index any text-based information and then search specific criteria to find text. Note that there are Lucene extensions that provide indexes for other types of documents, such as PDFs, HTML pages, Microsoft Word documents, and XML (search the Internet for additional Lucene extensions).

9.3.3.1.1 SETTING UP LUCENE WITH TOMCAT

You can set up Lucene to work with Tomcat™ by completing the following steps.

Step 1: Download Tomcat (if you have not already done so) from: http://tomcat.apache.org/

Step 2: Uncompress the Tomcat distribution and install it. If you downloaded a zip file, you can simply unzip that file into a convenient directory and start Tomcat from the command line with $TOMCAT_HOME/bin, using either catalina.bat for Windows or catalina.sh for Linux

Step 3: Download Lucene from: http://www.apache.org/dyn/closer.cgi/lucene/java/

Step 4: Uncompress the Lucene distribution into a convenient directory

Step 5: Copy luceneweb.war into $TOMCAT_HOME/webapps

Step 6: Start Tomcat

Step 7: Navigate to the following URL and replace the default port with the port number you specified during the Tomcat installation process: http://localhost:8080/luceneweb

You are now ready to use Lucene. Please read the Lucene documentation here:
http://lucene.apache.org/java/2_4_1/
If you downloaded a different version of Lucene, go to the Lucene home page to navigate to the documentation link that corresponds to your version of Lucene.

9.3.3.1.2 LUCENE SUBPROJECTS

Lucene also has the following subprojects (which are not discussed in this chapter):

• Droids
• Lucene.Net

- Lucy (C port)
- Mahout
- Nutch
- PyLucene (Python port)
- Tika

9.3.3.2 Apache Solr

Apache Solr enhances Apache Lucene with additional search functionality. Its home page is:

http://lucene.apache.org/solr/

Solr can be installed as a stand-alone scalable search server that manages a set of documents. You can insert documents into Solr via XML over HTTP and retrieve them via HTTP GET.

Solr provides query functionality that supports multiple response formats (including XML and JSON), sorting, and a query parser to return high-relevancy responses.

Solr handles high-volume traffic because it provides scalability through replication with other Solr servers, and an extensible plug-in-based architecture that you can customize to meet your application-specific needs.

In addition, Solr also provides a configurable caching mechanism, an administrative page, and extensive statistics regarding queries, updates, and caching-related details. According to recent reports, Solr provides the majority of the features of its commercial competitors (see the appendices for links).

9.3.3.2.1 SETTING UP SOLR WITH TOMCAT

You can set up Solr to work with Tomcat by completing the following steps.

Step 1: Download Tomcat (if you have not already done so) from:
http://tomcat.apache.org/

Step 2: Uncompress the Tomcat distribution and install it. If you downloaded a zip file, simply unzip it into a convenient directory and start Tomcat from the command line with $TOMCAT_HOME/bin, using either `catalina.bat` for Windows or `catalina.sh` for Linux

Step 3: Download Solr from:
http://www.apache.org/dyn/closer.cgi/lucene/solr/

Step 4: Uncompress the downloaded file and in the distribution subdirectory you will find a WAR file. The latest version of Solr is 1.3.0, and for this distribution the WAR file is called `apache-solr-1.3.0.war`

Step 5: Copy the Solr WAR file into $TOMCAT_HOME/webapps

Step 6: Create the subdirectory $TOMCAT_HOME/bin/solr/conf

Step 7: Copy the files from $SOLR_HOME/example/solr/conf into the subdirectory you created in Step 6

Step 8: Start Tomcat

Step 9: Navigate to the following URL and replace the default port with the port number you specified during the Tomcat installation process:
http://localhost:8080/apache-solr-1.3.0

Step 10: Click on the Solar Admin link on the website in Step 9

You are now ready to perform Solr administrative tasks.

Note that Step 6 and Step 7 are "workarounds," so that you can immediately configure Solr to work with Tomcat.

Please read the Solr documentation to set up Solr properly and to learn how to perform the Solr administrative tasks.

9.3.3.3 *Sphinx*

Sphinx is a SQL full-text search engine. Its home page is:
http://www.sphinxsearch.com/

Sphinx provides a SQL syntax for performing searches on database content. In addition, Sphinx lets you perform searches on plain text and HTML. Several well-known sites use Sphinx, including Craigslist and Daily Motion™. You can download Sphinx from:
http://www.sphinxsearch.com/downloads.html

Uncompress the distribution in a convenient location and then navigate to the API subdirectory, which contains several PHP and Python sample scripts.

Listing 9.6 shows the contents of the Python script `test2.py` (reformatted slightly for improved legibility), which illustrates how to perform a text search in Sphinx.

Listing 9.6 test2.pg

```
#
# $Id: test2.py 489 2006-11-22 22:00:40Z shodan $
#
from sphinxapi import *
import sys

docs = ['this is my test text to be highlighted',
 'this is another test text to be highlighted']
words = 'test text'
index = 'test1'

opts = {'before_match':'<b>', 'after_match':'</b>',
 'chunk_separator':' ... ', 'limit':400, 'around':15}

cl = SphinxClient()
res = cl.BuildExcerpts(docs, index, words, opts)

if not res:
 print 'ERROR:', cl.GetLastError()
else:
 n = 0
 for entry in res:
 n += 1
 print 'n=%d, res=%s' % (n, entry)
```

Listing 9.6 initializes some variables and then performs a very simple Sphinx-based search with the following code:

```
cl = SphinxClient()
res = cl.BuildExcerpts(docs, index, words, opts)
```

If the response res is nonnull, its contents are printed via the following code:

```
 for entry in res:
 n += 1
 print 'n=%d, res=%s' % (n, entry)
```

Note that a comparison of Solr and Sphinx can be found at: http://finance.yahoo.com/banking-budgeting/article/107638/fabulous-freebies-2009.html?mod=banking-budgeting

9.3.3.4 Katta

Katta is an open source project that implements a distributed Lucene index. Its home page is:

http://katta.sourceforge.net/

Katta is designed to efficiently handle very large volumes of data, which is accomplished (in part) because Katta replicates shards on multiple servers. Katta also works well with Hadoop clusters.

You can download the latest version of Katta here:

http://sourceforge.net/projects/katta/files/

Uncompress the distribution in a convenient directory and navigate to the bin/build subdirectory, which contains the following shell scripts for managing a Katta cluster:

```
katta-config.sh
katta-daemon.sh
katta-daemons.sh
nodes.sh
start-all.sh
stop-all.sh
```

The bin/build/ant subdirectory contains an Ant-based build file that you can use as follows:

```
ant -f common-build.xml <specify-a-target>
```

■ 9.4 SEARCH-RELATED ENGINES

This section covers search-related engines, some of their features, and examples of emerging search-related tools such as the following:

- Microsoft Bing
- Google Caffeine
- Hakia
- Kosmix
- Yebol

■ 9.4.1 Microsoft Bing

Microsoft Bing is a search engine that was released in mid-2009. Its home page is:

http://www.bing.com/

Microsoft launched Bing with a significant marketing campaign (supposedly at a cost of more than USD $50,000,000). Bing (formerly named Kumo) was designed as a replacement for Live Search, and on June 3, 2009, Bing became Microsoft's official search engine. Moreover, Microsoft and Yahoo formed a business partnership in mid-2009, after which Microsoft provided the search technology to Yahoo.

Microsoft refers to Bing as a "decision engine" rather than a "search engine," and although Bing and Google are superficially different, they differ very little in terms of searching for terms. Mary-Jo Foley suggests that "decision engine" is a euphemism for "shopping engine" in one of her blog posts: http://blogs.zdnet.com/microsoft/?p=3801

Bing offers a variety of features, including travel-related functionality and a cashback program. In addition, BingTweets combines Bing-based searches with Twitter tweets, and can be found here:
http://bingtweets.com/

An earlier study (with a very small number of participants) found that one out of three users preferred Bing over Google. However, in the most important category—search results—most users felt that neither was superior to the other.

Bing is attempting to improve search results for shopping and travel, both of which are currently listed on Bing's home page. While it may be possible for Bing to excel in these (and other) areas, analysts have concluded that Bing is unlikely to unseat Google from its dominant position.

According to the following article, there are "notable similarities" between Bing's travel page and the website Kayak.com™:
http://topnews.us/content/25827-travel-web-site-kayak-says-microsoft-s-bing-travel-similar-its-own-website

The following website provides both Bing and Google-based search results:
http://www.bingandgoogle.com/

9.4.1.1 Bing API 2.0 SDK

The Bing APIs are part of Microsoft's Project Silk Road™, which consists of tools and services designed to increase traffic for online publishers.

Bing API 2.0 provides support for JSON, XML, and SOAP, various source types, and unlimited use of the APIs.

You can download the Bing API 2.0 SDK from:
http://www.microsoft.com/downloads/details.aspx?FamilyId=0F513086-078B-47A8-A889-842DC93A69AB&displaylang=en

Complete the following steps to add a Bing service to a WCF application:

Step 1: Apply for a new AppID here:
http://www.bing.com/developers/createapp.aspx

An example of an AppID is here:
D2DE7616CE361017DE925AF1F55B6B61E107C123

Step 2: Create a Visual Studio WCF application

Step 3: Right-click on the project and select Add Service Reference

Step 4: Enter the following URLs in the input field under the label Address:
http://api.bing.net/search.wsdl?AppID=YourAppId&Version=2.2
http://api.bing.net/search.wsdl?AppID=D2DE7616CE361017D
E925AF1F55B6B61E107CE55&Version=2.2

You can also access Bing APIs from your browser by issuing a request with your AppID. Launch your browser and enter the following URL, which will return an XML-based response:
http://api.search.live.net/xml.aspx?Appid=YOUR-APPID&query=beer&sources=web

If you want a JSON-based response, use the following URL:
http://api.search.live.net/json.aspx?Appid=YOUR-APPID&query=beer&sources=web

An example of using the Bing 2.0 APIs with RSS can be found here:
http://api.search.live.com/rss.aspx?source=web&query=beer+chicago

You can also use the Bing 2.0 APIs with JavaScript, PHP, and Silverlight™. Check the documentation for code samples and additional details.

Note that Microsoft released the Bing APIs with no usage quotas (as of mid-2009), and you can find detailed information about Bing APIs here:
http://www.bing.com/developers

■ 9.4.2 Google Caffeine

Google Caffeine was announced in mid-2009, and its home page is:
http://www2.sandbox.google.com

Google is rewriting some of its infrastructure, and at this point it's not clear if Caffeine will make extensive use of Semantic Technology. Note that as of mid-2009, Caffeine did not work on mobile devices.

A search on Google and a search on Caffeine with the search terms "Caffeine Semantic Technology" returned slightly different sets of links, but the first two links were identical. From a user's perspective the differences might be irrelevant, but for businesses the different rankings can be extremely important because they can affect sales and revenue.

You can find more information about Caffeine here:
http://www.mattcutts.com/blog/caffeine-update

■ 9.4.3   Hakia

Hakia provides a semantic search engine. Its home page is:
http://www.hakia.com/

In mid-2009, Hakia announced a commercial ontology that is capable of recognizing phrases. Hakia points out that existing tools analyze words individually, and then consecutive words are "combined" to determine additional context, which makes Hakia's tool superior to its competitors.

The Hakia home page also contains a link to a website with two HTML frames, so you can perform a search and then make a side-by-side comparison between the results returned by Hakia and the results returned by Google.

Hakia also has a website for health-specific searches, but it's not always apparent which search engine provides a better set of results. The same search on Hakia and Google can display similar links that are ordered differently on the page. An interesting point of comparison is to contrast the links that Hakia and Google provide when you search for something that does not exist (such as a cure for cancer). For example, if you search Google for "cure for cancer," the first link in the result set is an article from CNN ("Where's the cure for cancer?"), whereas Hakia returns the link "Cancer Cure?" in the list of sponsored links in the frame on the right side of the page.

Another point to note is that Hakia does not use indexes (or the "inverted index" method) for page analysis. Hakia analyzes web pages in their entirety via Query Detection and Extraction (QDEX), which lets Hakia extract more semantically meaningful information.

■ 9.4.4 Kosmix

According to the company founder, Kosmix is an "explore engine" rather than a search engine. Its home page is:
http://www.kosmix.com

Despite the inevitable comparisons, the company has stated very clearly that Kosmix is not a competitor to Google. Kosmix is better suited for learning or exploring broad topics rather than searching for specific details about a topic (which search engines can do well). For example, if you want to learn about the important events during an era of a particular country, then Kosmix can assist you in finding relevant information.

As an example, if you enter the keywords "the roman empire" in the search box, Kosmix returns a web page that contains the following results and categories:

- An "at a glance" paragraph
- Roman emperors
- Crisis of the Third Century
- Several videos
- A set of images
- Comments in blog entries
- News and blogs
- Twitter tweets
- References
- Reviews and guides

Kosmix provides significantly more contextual information than a list of links based on keywords.

■ 9.4.5 Yebol

Yebol is a semantic search engine whose home page is:
http://yebol.com/

Yebol uses patented algorithms to create a directory for queries and users, and also categorizes search terms and websites. According to the company, Yebol has a higher level of abstraction than other search engines. Yebol uses "multi-dimensional" searches that provide a wider set of related search terms, and Yebol can return more accurate search results compared to other search engines.

Yebol uses Amazon cloud computing services for its knowledge base, which contains more than 10 million concepts and more than 1 billion websites, which Yebol claims is scalable to 100 million concepts and more than 10 billion websites for the next phase of its product.

A side-by-side comparison of the search terms "Yebol Semantic Technology" yielded a comparable number of links in both Google and Yebol. The first link for both search engines was the same, and there were other identical links (in a different order) in the two result sets. Yebol and Bing were both announced in mid-2009, and at this point it's still too early to predict which will capture a larger market share.

■ 9.5 INDUSTRY PERSPECTIVE AND BUSINESS FOCUS

Michael Ogrinz (author of *Mash-up Patterns*) has provided his insight on mash-ups and their role in the IT industry, and about mash-ups from the standpoint of IT managers and software managers who want to integrate mash-ups into their infrastructure and future products.

■ 9.5.1 Background

As the Web and its underlying infrastructure evolved in scope, speed, and capability, a desire arose to codify these advancements. The term "Web 2.0" quickly gained popularity, which conveyed a new level of features or functionality, and opinions vary about its origin. Some people believe that Web 2.0 arose from Rich Internet Applications (RIAs) based on technologies like Flash or AJAX, and others saw Web 2.0 arising from "the Web as a platform" (based on open APIs). Another factor may be the explosion of social networking and collaboration sites, whose members think of Web 2.0 as a massively complex living organism whose intrinsic value far exceeded the sum of its constituent parts. However, we must be careful to draw some boundaries around our definition of Web 2.0, which help us differentiate Web 2.0 from Web 3.0.

Web 2.0 is fundamentally about the shift from a transaction-based to an interaction-based experience. Before Web 2.0, publishers created content that was passively consumed by audiences, which is similar to the traditional publishing experience except the barriers to entry had become much lower. Even online transactions were not much different than a traditional brick-and-mortar experience; the primary difference was one of convenience.

The increase in vendors selling products online also created a greater need for differentiation, and better-funded firms spent considerable time and money to create a more pleasing environment for their customers. This "battle-for-eyeballs" stimulated the development of richer interfaces and the tools to create them. Companies knew the effectiveness of word-of-mouth for increasing sales, so they integrated this communication into the sales and marketing experience via online forums. Similarly, content creators also enabled user feedback, story ratings, and most importantly, data via open APIs.

Web 2.0 probably arrived when people recognized the Web as a new and unique platform and began to *intentionally* exploit these differences, which is the key point that will help us determine when we have reached Web *3.0*. With Web 2.0, we *purposely* took advantage of the Web to provide new services, whereas with Web 3.0, this will no longer be a voluntary process.[1] The act of generating online material will be inseparable from making these resources openly accessible for others to use in their own new creations.

■ 9.5.2 Mash-Ups, Web 2.0, and Beyond

Web 3.0 will probably evolve gradually, but mash-ups signal its emergence. Mash-ups are composite applications whose elemental parts can come from multiple disparate web resources. For example, combine census statistics, restaurant reviews, and a Google map and you have a visual representation of where you can enjoy a fine meal. You could also extract comments from sites such as Twitter, scan for product keywords, and mix in some sentiment-analysis software, and derive great market research about particular items. Mash-ups serve to create new products from ex-

---

1. Some people use Web 3.0 synonymously with the term "the Semantic Web," which refers to a web that can be parsed and understood by computers as easily as humans. Sir Tim Berners-Lee, creator of the World Wide Web, described this concept in the May 2001 issue of *Scientific American*.

isting raw materials, and they often use open APIs that are created for consumption of data.

Such APIs are an integral part of Web 3.0, and their absence indicates we have not reached Web 3.0. However, a new class of mash-up tools brings us closer to Web 3.0. For instance, products such as Kapow and Convertigo[2] let users impose their own APIs on sites that don't already offer an interface, which is an important step forward. Although the process isn't automatic, people now have programmatic access to information without the involvement of the content's owner. In short, once material is published to the Web, it's fair game.[3]

This is one of the reasons Gartner Research has predicted that by 2010, 80% of new enterprise applications will be based on mash-ups.[4] According to Gartner Fellow David Cearley, "Because mash-ups can be created quickly and easily, they create possibilities for a new class of short-term or disposable applications that would not normally attract development dollars."[5]

Within the corporate enterprise the potential for mash-ups is enormous. Firms collectively spend billions of dollars each year collecting data and developing applications to manage it. These highly specialized products are a veritable treasure chest of resources that can be combined and remixed to provide new solutions without having to start from scratch.

Virtually every market benefits from this technology. In the book, *Mash-up Patterns*, we are presented with 34 high-level generic problems that enterprise mash-ups address across 5 major categories: Harvest, Enhance, Manage, Assemble, and Test. The accompanying examples cover industries including finance, pharmaceutical, entertainment, construction, and retail.

However, there are several challenges to reaping this value.

---

2. A short, impartial, and certainly *not* comprehensive list.

3. Of course, this raises numerous concerns about copyright and intellectual property, which the legal system must address.

4. Gartner Identifies the Top Ten Disruptive Technologies for 2008 to 2012 (Press Release) http://www.gartner.com/it/page.jsp?id=681107

5. Gartner Press Release (ibid)

First, there is the matter of taking stock of a firm's potentially mash-able internal resources, and because a key goal is reuse, such resources could include databases, web services or SOA architectures, and web and desktop applications. The mash-up products a firm chooses are largely dependent on the resources a firm already possesses.

Second, a company needs to decide *how* it will use mash-up technology. Will it be another arrow for the IT department's quiver, or will end-users receive equal access to the technology to create their own solutions?

Finally, security and governance must be considered. Whatever mash-ups infrastructure a firm decides upon it must make sure that existing requirements for information privacy and security remain in full effect.

Cost is an important issue, and most vendors are extremely flexible regarding cost, so don't let this deter you from any initial exploration of this technology. Remember: "no one pays list price anymore." More-over, Return-on-Investment (ROI) is always an important consideration. Mash-ups are a powerful technology, but unless they are attached to a specific business case where the benefits can be easily quantified, it will be hard to measure their value. Select your initial projects carefully so that you can incrementally demonstrate how mash-ups surpass more traditional development approaches.

■ 9.5.3 Products and Resources

Commercially,[6] mash-up products fall broadly into two categories: mash-up enablers and mash-up platforms.[7] Enablers such as Kapow, Convertigo, Connotate, OpenSpan, and Lansa (to name few) "crack" open closed environments and interfaces to create the standards-based APIs that platforms like JackBe's Presto and IBM Mash-up Center allow to be visually linked to create new solutions. Unfortunately, in this

---

6. Sadly, there are no open source mash-up tools that offer a fraction of their commercial counterparts at this time.

7. Reference Architecture for Enterprise Mash-ups, Gartner Research:
   http://www.gartner.com/DisplayDocument?doc_cd=151491

nascent state of enterprise mash-up development, *all* of these products have very distinct and unique capabilities that make comparative analysis all but impossible. This is actually a good thing as it forces you to focus on the actual problems you want mash-ups for as opposed to which tool looks the best on paper.

Most firms will do well to choose both a mash-up enabler and a mash-up platform even though some specific products have a slight overlap in each category. If your firm already has a vast repository of available databases and services, then you may be able to get by with a platform alone.

The beauty of mash-up enabling tools is that they aren't dependent on the skill-set used to create the applications from which they will harvest data. As long as the system exposes an interface with which the tool can interact, the only requirements involve an understanding of what data you want to extract, and familiarity with the mash-up enabling tool. For example, if you want to create an API on a web application using Kapow, you only need to understand Kapow and not whether or not the application was built using Java, .NET, or PHP. Whether it was built by in-house staff that have since been reassigned, or purchased from a commercial vendor, it's the *web interface* that the mash-up enabler goes after, not the implementation technology. The same rule applies if you are creating an API around a database. The fact that it's Oracle, Sybase, Microsoft, or IBM is irrelevant. Mash-up enablers just need to point-and-click to make sure they extract the right data from the schema. They don't need to understand the nuances between Transact-SQL and PL/SQL. At first there may be a scarcity of developers comfortable with the tooling around mash-ups, but because the products are generally technology agnostic, companies can leverage a potential abundance of resources. As we will discover in the next section, mash-up platforms have even lower barriers to entry.

■ 9.5.4 Implementation

It is recommended that companies view mash-up technology as a chance to realign aspects of the function of IT. Instead of dedicated teams of developers and analysts creating case-specific applications and functionality, assess your existing applications and resources. Deploy a small swat-team of developers with mash-up enabling tools to build open APIs against these products, which can work in parallel with the original development teams with minimal disruption.

Next, make sure that each API is vetted for appropriate security and access control restrictions. If the source system requires a username and password, then the API should, too. Ultimately, these requirements must reach the end user (via the mash-up platform) so that information remains appropriately protected.

The new APIs could be used as part of a traditional development project, so by this stage we have already achieved a measure of value. However, the real jump comes by deploying a mash-up platform. If you choose to focus strictly on IT, then you are giving them a tool to easily combine the APIs to create solutions more quickly and easily.

Should you decide to deploy the technology to everyone, you will empower every employee in your company to potentially address their own issues without directly involving IT. This is possible because of an important point about mash-up platforms: they are extremely easy to use. It's not like giving users a set of development tools for Java or .NET; these products hide all of the underlying complexity via very intuitive interfaces. Creating a new mash-up-powered solution can be as simple as drag-and-drop and connecting boxes via lines to indicate the relationships between them. The "boxes" are abstractions around the APIs created by the mash-up enabler team.

Mash-ups have potential drawbacks, so it's important for firms to consider the reasons it may be wise *not* to empower its users, at least during the initial exploration of mash-up technology.

As people spend more time experimenting, productivity in other areas can suffer.

Poor coordination across groups can lead to a duplication of efforts and repeated mistakes.

A constant stream of new products may confuse the organization and its employees. Previously, IT was the de facto source of new applications internally.

End users are unfamiliar with the Best Practices IT has refined through years of professional development activities. This can lead to the creation of brittle, unstable, or nonscalable products.

There can be remediation challenges when multiple systems are combined because a singular failure can cascade across numerous solutions.

Most of these challenges can be addressed by making sure there is a central place for both IT and end users to communicate. If a company already has an established collaboration or social networking product, then it can be leveraged for this purpose. Alternatively, many mash-up platforms contain tools to foster a community for sharing, rating, and discussing mash-ups.

■ 9.5.5 Conclusions

The evolution of the Web has not just occurred within the lifeless servers, routers, and desktops that comprise it. It has occurred in *us* as well. We are no longer content to accept technology on its own terms: we listen to the music we choose, where we choose; we read the stories and articles that we find interesting; we praise the products we like, and decry the ones we don't—and we force the market to move and react to our uproar. We have achieved new expectations for participation that don't vanish when we cross the threshold of work to sit down at our desks.

If your IT department still views its users as a captive audience, then it's overlooking this fundamental shift and ignoring vast possibilities for reducing costs while fostering innovation. Mash-ups unleash the information locked in a company's systems and the creativity trapped within its employees to allow anyone to quickly meet specific business challenges. The question to be asked is not, "Why should I look at mash-ups in my enterprise," but "Why haven't I considered mash-ups sooner?"

■ 9.6 SUMMARY

This chapter introduced you to mash-ups and showed you how to create them using tools from several companies, including Denodo, IBM, Serena, Intel, and JackBe. You also learned about the availability of mash-ups in other programming languages, such as Java, Python, and Ruby.

We also discussed search technology and showed you how to create your own search functionality using Yahoo BOSS. You also learned how to create a search application using Yahoo SearchMonkey.

We looked at GSS, along with an example of how you can leverage this technology.

The next chapter discusses cloud computing and shows you how to create applications with Amazon® Web Services™, GAE, IBM® Cloud Labs™, and Microsoft Windows Azure.

## CHAPTER 10

Cloud Computing Part I

In This Chapter:

- What is Cloud Computing?
- Amazon Web Services (AWS)
- IBM Cloud Labs
- Google App Engine (GAE)
- Microsoft Windows Azure
- Yahoo Cloud Computing
- Other Cloud Computing Initiatives
- Industry Perspective

Although cloud computing is hardly a new concept, it has gained a lot of visibility in the IT industry recently. A top-100 list of cloud computing companies was published in 2008, and in 2009 cloud computing gained additional
momentum, despite some of its critics, such as Richard Stallman. Larry Ellison
(CEO of Oracle) also dismissed the importance of cloud computing in 2008,
but a year later he changed his position, which may have been influenced by
Oracle's acquisition of SUN (which also has a cloud computing platform).

While cloud computing appears poised to exert a far-reaching impact
on the IT industry, cloud computing still represents different things to different people, which probably makes confusion both inevitable and unavoidable. The competitive cloud computing market means vendors have to offer
increasingly attractive features, which makes it difficult to stay current on the
differences between cloud computing vendors.

For example, the pay-as-you-go model is often based on hourly
consumption of resources, but at least one vendor calculates cost by CPU

consumption. For small companies, the difference in cost between these two pricing structures may be comparable, but if a company is using a lot of high-volume applications, the cost differential could be significant.

This chapter begins with an overview of cloud computing and the current landscape. This is followed by the three types of cloud computing models, issues surrounding cloud computing services, and questions that you need to ask cloud computing vendors.

Next is a discussion of Amazon EC2 (and the Amazon® Cloudfront™ offering), along with information and links regarding scalability, reliability, and cost. After that, we'll look at IBM Cloud Labs, which is a cloud computing service.

We'll also discuss GAE in terms of its usefulness, its advantages, and the languages it currently supports: Python and Java. You will learn how to create an account and how to get a free API key so that you can see an example of a simple GAE application.

Finally, we'll discuss Microsoft Windows Azure. You'll learn how it works, the rationale for its architecture, and the languages it currently supports. You will also learn the sequence of steps for creating a simple Microsoft Azure application.

The vendors discussed in this chapter and the next were chosen based on the product features they provide at the time this book was written and we recommend that you visit the respective home page to check the latest status of these product features.

■ 10.1   WHAT IS CLOUD COMPUTING?

Cloud computing refers to a set of services that are available to users in a transparent manner; i.e., users are unaware of the location, nature, or details of those services. Cloud computing services handle all of the details for storing and managing information on the Internet, which means that users are shielded from all of the details. Cloud computing services provide information just like any other data source, therefore, cloud computing services are transparent.

Please note that our definition does not require automatic scaling and self-curing. However, as more companies offer cloud computing services, competition also increases, and the expectations for services will change over time. Therefore, as cloud computing matures, nice-to-have features may become must-have features; in particular, we believe that automatic scaling and self-healing will become mandatory features in the near future. In addition consolidation among cloud computing companies can influence which products become more attractive in terms of price and features.

A recent initiative involves Business Intelligence (BI) in the cloud, and RightScale® (discussed in Chapter 11) is one of the cloud computing companies that wants to provide BI-based tools.

Another recent initiative comes from the U.S. Government and its involvement with cloud computing. In September 2009, the Federal CIO Vivek Kundra provided a brief overview of the government's plans regarding cloud computing, which can be found here:
http://apps.gov

In contrast to Service-Oriented Architecture (SOA), which is an architectural style that forms the basis for recent software development, cloud computing is described by the SPI model, which is discussed later in this section. Some of the advantages of cloud computing services include:

- a pay-as-you-go model
- almost no initial costs
- scalability
- resources are allocated on an as-needed basis
- reduced cost and complexity for IT departments

The pay-as-you-go model means that users only pay for what they use, and so they do not incur costs for hardware idle time. In addition, cloud computing services handle hardware and IT-related tasks, so you do not need to buy, configure, and maintain hardware. For new start-ups with a handful of people, these two aspects of cloud computing provide an affordable way to deliver a web-based product.

However, there are other issues that need to be considered. First, how does cloud computing address security and data privacy? During the HotCloud 2009 conference, a paper was presented ("The Case for Enterprise-Ready Virtual Private Clouds") that suggested creating private virtual clouds to handle security issues. This paper, along with two other proposed solutions called trusted cloud computing platforms and private virtual infrastructure, offered methods for protecting your data.

Second, who is accountable if any of your transactional data is lost? If your company uses cloud computing services to conduct business transactions in countries with different currencies, who calculates and keeps track of any associated taxes?

Other questions pertain to the nebulous nature of cloud computing services, which is perhaps no different from other computing services. For instance, is anything that delivers information via the Internet a cloud computing service? If you launch your browser and you navigate to a website, are you "consuming" a cloud computing service? What about service providers that charge a small fee (or none at all) for users to access their personal data on a remote server?

Although there are many cloud computing vendors, the current major ones are:

- Amazon EC2
- IBM Cloud Labs
- Google App Engine (GAE)
- Microsoft Azure
- Force.com™

This chapter covers the first four vendors in the preceding list, whereas Force.com is discussed in Chapter 11.

■ 10.1.1 Public, Private, and Hybrid Clouds

There are three broad categories of clouds: public, private, and hybrid. Public clouds are good if you need lots of scaling and if you are not concerned with security in the cloud. Public clouds provide standardized services on the providers' cloud and access is by subscription. The public cloud adopts a "buy none and rent all" hardware model. Amazon and GAE are two well-known examples of public clouds.

Private clouds provide the same services as public clouds, but (as you would expect from their name) they are behind a firewall. Private clouds are good if you want to own everything and you do not need to scale (with a relatively fixed number of machines), but they are also the least flexible and have higher operating costs. Your company can own and manage a private cloud or you can use a services provider to manage it. Note that private clouds can also rent servers on an as-needed basis. The private cloud adopts a "buy all and rent none" hardware model. IBM Cloud Burst is an example of a private cloud.

Hybrid clouds are private clouds that can also access resources outside the firewall during periods of peak demand. Hybrid clouds maintain some data storage "in-house" and rent bandwidth with a pay-as-you-go model, and high-frequency application data is maintained in a memory cache. Thus, the hybrid cloud avoids migrating from a private cloud to a public cloud and follows a "buy some and rent some" hardware model. Large corporations are drawn to hybrid clouds because they can lower their hardware costs, avoid the complexity of migrating data to a public cloud, and avoid exposing sensitive data in a public cloud.

Now that you know some of the differences between the clouds, you need to think about when it's a good idea to store data and applications in the cloud, and whether to put them in public, private, or hybrid clouds.

If you need to store large amounts of data that is also projected to increase regularly over time, then you can obviously benefit from storing that data in the cloud, and the type of cloud is dependent on the sensitivity of the data involved. Second, consider using a cloud computing vendor for applications that tend to run in "bursty mode," which require a lot of resources when they launch. Third, applications that are used by employees worldwide (or by employees who are geographically dispersed) can benefit from the consolidation that occurs when applications are deployed to the cloud. In addition to the benefits of deploying applications to the cloud, your company can also benefit from having data back-ups made by cloud computing vendors.

On the other hand, you should probably avoid deploying applications to the cloud when those applications involve sensitive data, mandatory compliance requirements such as Sarbanes-Oxley (SOX), high-performance requirements, or extremely large data systems (petabytes of data).

As you have probably surmised, the primary beneficiaries of cloud computing are young start-ups that are trying to develop a successful web-based application. These start-ups (especially the smaller ones) have no "legacy code" (sometimes they have almost no code at all) to constrain them, and their disk space and performance requirements are usually modest. Thus, they are virtually unencumbered in terms of selecting a cloud computing vendor, and they can choose the vendor that gives them the best deal.

One other point to keep in mind pertains to application performance, and using the cloud primarily as a hosting service. If you have applications that perform poorly because of their architecture, you may obtain some initial benefits by deploying those applications to the cloud, but you might be simply postponing the need to redesign those applications. If an application is fundamentally flawed in its architecture, think carefully before deploying that application to the cloud. While the distributed nature of the cloud can provide important advantages (parallel processing becomes much more affordable), remember that there is also a learning curve associated with writing applications based on a distributed model.

■ 10.1.2 Questions to Ask Cloud Computing Vendors

While one benefit of cloud computing is that it's cheap, it is also efficient and economical (pay-as-you-go). Cloud computing can be a benefit to different application domains, including financial, medical, and scientific.

In general, end users and small companies are interested in ways to leverage public clouds, whereas larger corporations typically have more demanding requirements, such as using a private cloud (or a hybrid cloud) that is managed internally or by a cloud computing provider.

The following are some useful criteria for comparing different vendors to determine which one provides the most beneficial solution for your needs:

- pricing structure
- performance and availability
- autoscaling and self-healing
- Service Level Agreement (SLA)
- vendor lock-in, migration, ease of deployment
- flexibility and customization
- security and data privacy
- development/testing/debugging tools/APIs
- Business Intelligence (BI)/analytics
- cost of migrating applications

Keep in mind that the preceding list is not exhaustive, and that the priority of these items depends on your specific needs. Start by reordering the list so that it reflects your needs and priorities as closely as possible, and then use it as a guide when comparing cloud computing vendors. You might find yourself in a situation where vendor A provides some key features and vendor B provides another set of key features, but neither one provides all of your must-have features. Sometimes vendor consolidation will solve this problem for you, but more often than not you will have to make a detailed comparison to determine which vendor provides the best fit for your needs.

If you are involved in the development of your company, and you have existing applications, the last bullet item is particularly important in your decision-making process. Pay close attention to cloud computing vendors that provide features (such as automatic load balancing) that do not require a significant level of developer resources. Developers want to spend their time in development, and they will resist administrative-like tasks.

Read the SLAs of different vendors to assess which companies provide the level of support that best fits your current and projected needs. Vendor lock-in can affect some companies differently than others, but there are general things to look for, including:

• Will you need to rewrite parts of your application?
• Will your IT staff requite additional training?
• What is the cost of moving your data between vendors?
• Does the vendor have a proprietary system?

Other factors to consider involve the bandwidth between you and the computing vendor, and how much data you need to upload to the cloud. If your company has experienced costly mistakes in the past, make sure that you have the level of support that minimizes the chances of repeating those mistakes with a cloud computing vendor.

■ 10.1.3 The Software Platform Infrastructure (SPI) Model for Cloud Computing

Purists assert that a cloud computing service or product must provide automatic scaling (cloud resources scale up or down depending on current computing needs) and self-healing (problem detection and correction); otherwise that service product is utility computing. Since very few companies meet both these criteria, the majority of so-called cloud computing providers provide utility computing services.

In this book, we use a less stringent "definition" for cloud computing services. In our view, a cloud computing company is a company that provides a service or product that belongs to the SPI model of cloud computing:

• Software as a Service (SaaS)
• Platform as a Service (PaaS)
• Infrastructure as a Service (IaaS)

Two other terms that you may have seen are Database as a Service (DaaS) and Hardware as a Service (HaaS), but they are not part of the SPI model, and they will not be discussed in this chapter.

In general, cloud computing vendors provide greater flexibility and a finer-grained level of control (IaaS), or they emphasize simplicity (PaaS). The following sections briefly describe the three levels of the SPI model.

10.1.3.1   SaaS

SaaS (such as SalesForce.com) involves web-based access to applications that run outside of your company. Thus, you do not need to manage software-related details (such as upgrades and testing new releases) or hardware-related details (such as configurations, machine failures, and so forth).

SaaS companies handle the storage space for hardware and the IT staff. In addition, you do not need to deal with leasing hardware equipment or amortization of company-owned hardware. SaaS typically involves a reasonable monthly fee that can be significantly more economical than an in-house system, but not quite as good as a pay-as-you-go model.

SaaS also embraces the concept of *multitenancy,* which means that different companies run on the same set of computers and share the same resources.

However, some countries have blacklisted vendors that are part of an SaaS product, and this might pose a reliability problem (see the appendices for a related link).

Another possibility is *application hosting,* where a service provider hosts your application, and tends to include database hosting and backup/recovery of database data. Application hosting does resemble SaaS, but it generally does not provide customized support for different customers to the extent of SaaS.

If you are a small start-up, or your requirements are modest, then the small fee makes application hosting quite affordable. For example, FatCow is a service provider that provides eight terabytes of disk space for free. However, if you have significant computing requirements, application hosting might not be robust enough for your needs.

10.1.3.2   PaaS

The PaaS hosting model in cloud computing provides the following features:

- scaling is on a language rather than the instances
- you must code in a specific language, such as Python or AppForce™
- faster to deploy, but there is vendor "lock-in"
- virtualized Operations System (OS) handles the scaling
- you can choose the OS for deploying instances

A good example of PaaS is GAE, which provides a high degree of scalability and simplicity in several ways. First, GAE only supports Python and Java. Second, GAE provides a layer of abstraction that shields users from the details of the infrastructure. However, since GAE is nonrelational, applications that use an RDBMS (such as MySQL) cannot directly migrate those applications to GAE.

Thus, PaaS can be more complicated (and therefore less attractive) as a solution for large-scale existing applications, especially if they use relational databases.

10.1.3.3 IaaS

The IaaS hosting model in cloud computing provides the following features:

- you can start new instances without knowing where those new instances will actually reside
- instances span multiple boxes transparently
- significant cost savings
- more successful because there are no constraints

A good example of IaaS is AWS, which lets users deploy applications on a variety of technology stacks, and then launch those applications on an as-needed basis. Thus, AWS provides flexibility and control: users have access to an AWS environment that is comparable to their local one, which means that applications can behave in a similar manner. Although this flexibility lets users test the performance of applications with different configurations, users need to be more involved in the details of managing their AWS environment.

Recently, another type of cloud computing service has appeared whereby users are given dedicated servers rather than a set of virtual instances that are located on shared servers.

NewServers™ claims to be the only company that offers this type of cloud computing service. Its home page is:
http://newservers.com/

NewServers provides pay-as-you-go services and also claims that its dedicated servers offer better performance than virtual instances, because performance can be adversely affected when different companies are running virtual instances on the same server.

■ 10.2 AMAZON WEB SERVICES (AWS)

AWS was launched in 2002. Its home page is:
http://aws.amazon.com/

Since its initial launch, Amazon has released a suite of products and services under the AWS umbrella, many of which are available as web services:

- Amazon Elastic Compute Cloud (EC2)
- Amazon Simple Storage Service™ (S3)
- Amazon SimpleDB™
- Amazon Simple Queue Service™ (SQS)
- Amazon CloudFront™
- Alexa Web Information Services™ (AWIS)

Amazon provides a suite of products that are designed for scalability and a pay-as-you-go cost model. In early 2009, Amazon charged for CPU usage based on an hourly rate, whereas GAE charged only for CPU cycles. In some cases it's possible that this finer level of granularity could become substantial. Check both sites for details regarding their most recent definition of pay-as-you-go service.

AWS provides a web interface for managing virtual machines, creating your own Amazon Machine Images (AMIs), managing Elastic Block Storage (EBS) volumes and Elastic IPs, and configuring firewall settings and security groups.

Another point to keep in mind is that although Amazon is among the early cloud computing vendors, its deployment process requires more manual steps than other vendors. However, Amazon is attempting to revamp and streamline its deployment process so that it will be more automated.

Recently, Amazon formed a partnership with IBM to provide support for IBM products in the Amazon cloud (discussed later in this chapter) and for the open source project Hadoop (discussed in Chapter 11). Amazon also announced that it will provide an autoscaling solution; check the Amazon home page for updates regarding the availability of this feature.

Amazon also introduced several new features recently. The first is the Amazon Virtual Private Cloud™ (VPC), which lets users use Virtual Private Network™ (VPN) to connect to isolated AWS computing resources. Amazon VPC currently integrates with EC2, and other AWS services may be supported in the future. Amazon provides access to Amazon VPC (which is a limited beta program) here:

http://aws.amazon.com/vpc/

Another recent feature is the Amazon Multi-Factor Authentication™ (MFA). Its home page is:

http://aws.amazon.com/mfa/

Amazon MFA provides a six-digit single-use authentication code, and MFA continually generates new random codes that are dedicated to individual users of this service.

Finally, the Amazon Management Console™ has added support for Amazon CloudWatch, which lets users monitor their EC2 instances using a point-and-click web interface.

If you have not done so already, visit the Amazon home page and create a free account.

■ 10.2.1 Amazon EC2

Amazon EC2 provides a cloud computing environment in which you can deploy and launch your applications and "scale up" when an increase in the number of users accessing your applications necessitates more resources. Conversely, you can "scale down" when there is a reduction in the demand for resources.

With Amazon EC2, you must first create an AMI–which is described in more detail in the next section–that contains all of your application-specific files. From a high-level perspective, you can use Amazon EC2 by performing the following steps:

Step 1: Create an AMI

Step 2: Upload the AMI into Amazon S3

Step 3: Configure security and network access

Step 4: Select instance types and OSes

Step 5: Start an AMI instance (as many as you need)

Step 6: Manage the AMIs (start, stop, or terminate)

The next section describes AMIs in more detail so you can better understand the process of creating and uploading your application-specific AMIs to Amazon EC2.

10.2.1.1 AMIs

An AMI contains your application-specific files. You can create an AMI for different OSes, including Windows, Linux, and MacIntosh. AMIs can also be shared, which is very convenient, but it's important to be cautious with respect to public AMIs. Although it's unlikely, it's possible that a public AMI can contain some type of malware (you can be certain about the content of your own AMI but not the AMI of someone else). Check the appendices regarding existing Amazon AMIs for additional information.

■ 10.2.2 Amazon S3

Amazon S3 is a key-based object store, and users can assign a unique key (which is a string) to data so that they can retrieve the data when they need it. Users can make their data public or private, and they can access their data via Representation State Transfer (REST) and Single Object Access Protocol (SOAP) web services. Public data can be accessed via BitTorrent by appending the ?torrent parameter to GET requests in REST invocations.

Amazon S3 provides scalable storage that lets developers leverage the scalability of Amazon S3 with minimal cost and investment. Data stored in Amazon S3 is secure, highly available (99.99%), accessible anywhere on the Web, and can be accessed quickly.

When users create an Amazon S3 bucket, Amazon lets them specify where they want to store their data, the U.S.A. or Europe. However users from all over the world can use Amazon S3 to store almost any type of data. A single object can be as large as five gigabytes, and users can store an unlimited number of objects in Amazon S3.

Amazon S3 provides a pay-as-you-go model, which involves a multitiered system that starts from USD $0.15 per gigabyte for 55 terabytes, and decreases for larger volumes of data. Storage costs differ slightly, but prices are comparable, and you can find more pricing information for Amazon S3 in the appendices.

In addition, there are various third-party tools that work with Amazon S3. For example, the Amazon S3 Firefox Organizer™ is a Firefox plug-in for Amazon S3 that lets you manage files and folders via drag-and-drop operations. This plug-in works with Firefox versions 1.5 through 3.1 and on Windows, Mac, and Linux.

There is an Ant task (discussed in Chapter 5) available for uploading files and directories to an S3 bucket. An open source library written in Groovy for AWS is also available. A code sample that combines S3, EC2, SQS, Lucene, and Ruby for crawling websites is also available, and you can find the relevant links in the appendices.

You can get a free Amazon S3 account by clicking on the Sign up for This Web Service button here: http://aws.amazon.com/s3/

10.2.2.1 Cloudberry Lab

Cloudberry Lab provides a set of freeware and commercial tools for managing cloud-based resources for Amazon and SUN. Its home page is: http://cloudberrylab.com/

Cloudberry S3 Explorer (freeware) for Amazon S3 provides a user interface for managing Amazon accounts, buckets, and files that are stored in Amazon S3. It is available for Windows XP/2003/Vista, and requires Microsoft .NET Framework 2.0 and an Amazon S3 account. Cloudberry Explorer lets users view the contents of S3 buckets, copy files between local computers and Amazon S3, and copy files between two Amazon S3 accounts.

Cloudberry S3 Explorer for SUN is also available for Windows XP/2003/Vista, with features similar to the freeware version; however, the system requirements include Microsoft .NET Framework 2.0 and a Sun Cloud Storage Service account.

Cloudberry S3 Explorer for Amazon S3 mobile provides a user interface for managing Amazon resources on Windows Mobile devices.

The Cloudberry Lab home page contains many useful links, such as a link for a Firefox plug-in for Amazon, links for viewing product videos, and download links for its set of products.

■ 10.2.3 Amazon SimpleDB

In December 2007, Amazon announced unlimited beta for Amazon SimpleDB, which is a database that is accessible via a web service.

SimpleDB (which is built on the Erlang programming language) works with Amazon EC2 and Amazon S3. Amazon SimpleDB automatically indexes data and provides simple APIs for uploading and downloading data. Amazon SimpleDB provides the following advantages:

- no installation required
- no license required
- no monthly minimum fee
- scalability without tuning

Users can create multiple domains, each with one or more records, and each record consisting of items and attributes. SimpleDB does have have any schemas or one-to-many relationships, and everything is treated as a string. Note that SimpleDB does have APIs that support comparisons of dates and numbers.

SimpleDB provides a ScratchPad, which is a simple and intuitive HTML page that lets users manage their domains. This code-less interface provides a drop-down list of actions (such as list, create, update, or delete) that are executed via a corresponding SimpleDB API. Each user-initiated action generates an HTTP request, which returns an XML-based response that displays the results of each request. In addition, queries are limited to a maximum of five seconds of execution time.

The ScratchPad lets users create new domains and then add new content to them. Users can insert a row in a domain by adding a new item and any number of attributes, where an attribute is a name/value pair. An attribute can have a maximum length of one kilobyte.

The ScratchPad provides query-based functionality (such as retrieving records whose attribute name matches a user-provided value) to issue queries against a specific domain, but the syntax for queries is not based on SQL.

Users can also set up their applications to execute Amazon SimpleDB queries whose syntax is very similar to standard SQL syntax. For example, a SimpleDB `select` statement has the following syntax:

```
select output_list
from domain_name
[where expression]
[sort_instructions]
[limit limit]
```

The cost of Amazon SimpleDB is USD $1.50 per gigabyte per month for storage, USD $0.14 per CPU hour, and upload costs are USD $0.10 per gigabyte.

■ 10.2.4 Amazon CloudFront

Amazon CloudFront provides a pay-as-you-go web service for delivering content that also works with Amazon S3. Its home page is: http://aws.amazon.com/cloudfront/

Amazon CloudFront lets users access files that they have already stored in an Amazon S3 bucket by "registering" the bucket in a CloudFront distribution. Users call the `CreateDistribution` API to retrieve the domain name of a distribution. Users use the domain name of the distribution in their applications, which ensures that requests for data are routed appropriately by Amazon CloudFront, which determines the optimal edge location. Amazon CloudFront uses edge locations in three continents: North America (eight cities), Europe (four cities), and Asia (two cities).

Amazon CloudFront also maintains access logs that display detailed information regarding requests for content. Users are allowed a maximum transfer speed of 1,000MB per second and a maximum request rate of 1,000 requests per second (users can request a higher limit from Amazon).

As mentioned in the beginning of this section, users can use Amazon CloudFront with Amazon S3. When Amazon CloudFront needs an object that is not already in an edge location, it issues a request to Amazon S3 to access that object. Copies of frequently accessed objects are cached in multiple edge locations, thereby providing faster access to content (and also reducing costs). When space is limited at an edge location, Amazon uses a Least Frequently Used (LFU) algorithm for removing objects from an edge location.

Amazon CloudFront is useful for hosting frequently accessed files for websites and distributing applications to users, and it offers lower costs for transferring media files (such as audio and video). Note that monthly Amazon bills differentiate costs incurred from using Amazon S3 versus costs associated with using Amazon CloudFront.

You can create a free Amazon CloudFront by going to its home page and clicking on the Sign Up For Amazon CloudFront button.

After you create your Amazon CloudFront account, you have to perform the following steps to use it:

Step 1: Prepare an origin server

Step 2: Create a distribution

Step 3: Confirm that the distribution is ready

Step 4: Link to your object

Detailed instructions for the preceding steps can be found here: http://docs.amazonwebservices.com/AmazonCloudFront/latest/Getting-StartedGuide/

■ 10.2.5 Amazon SQS

Amazon SQS is a hosted service that supports the creation of queues (in the U.S. and Europe) for managing messages. Its home page is: http://aws.amazon.com/sqs/

Amazon SQS lets users manage their queues with a set of APIs, such as `CreateQueue`, `DeleteQueue`, and `SendMessage`, which let users create a queue, delete a queue, and send a message, respectively.

Amazon SQS lets users create an unlimited number of queues with no restriction on the number of messages, which can be managed via a web service that interacts with Amazon's messaging infrastructure. Amazon SQS also lets users create workflows that can interact with Amazon EC2 and other Amazon web services.

Messages contain arbitrary text (with an 8KB restriction in length), and they can be stored for a maximum of four days in queues. Amazon SQS uses a locking mechanism for processing messages, and the timeout period can be modified programmatically. Amazon SQS queues can also be shared with other users, and restrictions can be imposed based on time and IP addresses. Visit the Amazon SQS home page to sign up for Amazon SQS and to learn other useful information, such as the Amazon SQS life cycle and the pricing structure for this service.

■ 10.2.6 Alexa Web Information Service (AWIS)

The AWIS home page is: http://aws.amazon.com/awis/

AWIS lets users retrieve information about websites that Alexa has gathered through its internal web crawling and analysis techniques. The type of information available is similar to the Alexa website, which includes site usage, popularity, contact information, and supported character sets. AWIS also provides historical information (within the past year) regarding websites. AWIS lets users retrieve information about websites and subcategories of categories, which is filtered through Alexa traffic data and ranked according to popularity.

■ 10.2.7 Amazon Elastic MapReduce

Google introduced a framework called MapReduce™ that uses a divide-and-conquer strategy for processing large data sets on clusters of computers. In July 2009, Amazon Elastic MapReduce™ was introduced as a beta-level web service. Its home page is:

http://aws.amazon.com/elasticmapreduce/

Amazon Elastic MapReduce™ is a pay-as-you-go web service for processing large amounts of data (in the petabyte range) on clusters of machines, and it uses a Hadoop-based framework (discussed in Chapter 11) that runs on the Amazon EC2 and Amazon S3 infrastructure.

Amazon Elastic MapReduce enables the provisioning of resources on an as-needed basis to perform data-intensive tasks, which eliminates the need for configuration, tuning, and managing capacity requirements.

Amazon Elastic MapReduce also allows you to implement data processing applications in several languages, including Java, Perl, Ruby, Python, PHP, R, and C++. You can test these applications on different instance types and job flow sizes to pick the best settings for your specific case.

There are two methods for starting an Amazon MapReduce job flow. One method involves logging into the AWS Management Console, selecting the required number of Amazon EC2 instances, selecting an application on Amazon S3, and then launching an Amazon MapReduce job flow. The other method involves a command-line tool.

The Amazon Elastic MapReduce web service provides the following services:

- create job flow requests
- status of job flows
- add new steps to running job flow
- terminate running job flow

You can get a free Amazon Elastic MapReduce account by going to its home page and clicking on the Sign Up For Elastic MapReduce button. Check the appendices for a link to the pricing structure for Amazon Elastic MapReduce.

■ 10.2.8 Creating Amazon EC2 Applications

On March 25, 2009, Amazon announced the availability of its free AWS tool-kit for Eclipse (which requires Java 1.4 or higher), which can be found here: http://aws.amazon.com/eclipse/

This toolkit is designed to facilitate the deployment of Java-based projects to the Amazon cloud. Make sure that you register for a free Amazon account and that you install Eclipse (the instructions are in Chapter 6) on your system.

Complete the following steps to create an Amazon EC2 application in Eclipse:

Step 1: Install the AWS toolkit for Eclipse using the following URL: http://aws.amazon.com/eclipse/

Step 2: Specify an AWS instance in Eclipse as follows:

1. Follow the menu path **Window > Show View > Other**

2. Select Amazon EC2

3. Select EC2 Instances

4. Click the OK button

Note that in Step 2 you will see four entries:

1. EC2 AMIs

2. EC2 Elastic Block Storage

3. EC2 Instance

4. EC2 Security Groups

You can experiment with the other three entries, but they are outside the scope of this book.

Step 3: After completing the previous step, you will probably see AWS account not configured correctly displayed as a hyperlinked message. If so, click on it and supply the correct account-related information.

Step 4: Now you can configure an AWS instance in Eclipse as follows:

1. Follow the menu path **Window > Show View > Server > Servers**

2. Right-click and navigate to **New > Server**

3. Select Tomcat 6.x and follow the prompts to complete the configuration

Note that the exact prompts in the installation steps might differ slightly due to different versions of software.

Next, complete the installation steps for Tomcat (described in Chapter 5), and configure a Tomcat instance for Amazon EC2 as follows:

Step 1: On the Amazon splash page, click on Create an Amazon EC2 Tomcat Cluster

Step 2: Click on Tomcat v6.0 Server and click the Next button

Step 3: Click the browse button and navigate to a Tomcat installation

Step 4: Click the Finish button

Note that the Amazon toolkit for Eclipse also provides an option for SimpleDB management. The Amazon view in Eclipse contains four tabs labeled EC2 Instances, EC2 AMIs, EC2 Elastic Block Storage, and EC2 Security Groups. Click on the appropriate tab to view the status and other details of the current Amazon resources displayed in each tab.

This concludes our discussion of Amazon-related cloud computing services. The next section discusses IBM and cloud computing, along with the recent partnership between IBM and Amazon.

■ 10.3 IBM CLOUD LABS

IBM has several cloud computing initiatives, one of which is IBM Cloud Labs. Its home page is: http://www.ibm.com/ibm/cloud/labs/

A second IBM initiative, WebSphere CloudBurst appliance, lets users access virtual images that can be deployed in a private cloud. According to IBM, this appliance is the first of its kind, and facilitates the develop-test-deploy cycle for applications, after which resources are automatically deallocated and become available in a shared resource pool. WebSphere CloudBurst offers advantages to customers who want to manage SOA in the cloud.

A third initiative is IBM Blue Cloud, which supports a distributed set of computing resources. In 2009, IBM also formed a partnership with Juniper for the hybrid cloud initiative, with one of the goals being better

SLA support. IBM is involved in other initiatives, such as launching a public cloud and providing virtualization.

■ 10.3.1 IBM and Amazon Partnership

IBM has formed a partnership with Amazon to provide users with access to both development and production AMIs. Thus, users can run various IBM products and software on Amazon EC2 (check the appendices for additional platform-specific details), including the IBM products listed here:

- IBM DB2 Express-C
- IBM Mashup Center
- IBM WebSphere sMash
- IBM WebSphere Application Server
- IBM WebSphere Portal Server
- IBM Informix Dynamic Server

IBM development AMIs are available free of charge, but users will incur EC2-based costs. IBM provides documentation and guides to assist developers in using the IBM development AMIs, which can be downloaded from several websites (see the appendices for links), including the IBM section of the AWS featured partners site.

IBM production AMIs include IBM software, Linux Suse™, and Amazon EC2 service for a one-hour charge (check the Amazon website for pricing and availability). The production AMIs will initially be available as a beta service, with premium support to come. Note that IBM production AMIs are unavailable for download.

If you use PHP, you might be interested in a PHP cloud API from an initiative involving IBM, Microsoft, and Zend®, which is available here: http://searchcloudcomputing.techtarget.com/news/article/0,289142, sid201_ gci1369993,00.html?track=NL-1329&ad=728878&asrc=EM_NLN_9436840 &uid=2443175

■ 10.4 GOOGLE APP ENGINE (GAE)

GAE provides a PaaS-based model of cloud computing that was released in early 2007 with support for Python. Its home page is: http://code.google.com/appengine.

In early 2009, GAE announced support for Java (see Chapter 12 for more details). Support for Java and other JVM-based languages clearly makes GAE more attractive to the global community of Java developers. GAE also provides support for frameworks such as Django®, which is a Content Management System (CMS).

In December 2009, Google released version 1.2.8 of GAE for Java developers and Python developers. This version contain numerous bug fixes and new tool support for managing tasks and queues. This version also provided better Java support for JPA and JDO, along with Support for JAXB (discussed in Chapter 12).

The following is a partial list of GAE features:

• automatic scaling
• load balancing
• user authentication (APIs)
• support for Python and Java
• support for XML, XQuery, and XSLT
• support for JDO and JPA
• an API for XMPP
• support for scheduled tasks (e.g., Cron)

GAE also supports a local development environment so that developers can simulate a GAE environment on their own system.

The administrator's console provides a view into your data. Currently, there are no open source GAE browsers available, but users are developing their own tools that provide a GUI-based view of their data that is stored in GAE.

■ 10.4.1 Assessing GAE for your Company

There are several points to consider before you choose GAE. The first is that GAE only supports: Python and JVM-based languages such as Java. A second point to keep in mind is the perception of vendor lock-in and a closed environment regarding GAE. Your decision-making process will have to take into account factors such as company policy regarding new technologies, your technology stack, and the skill set of your developers.

The third point is Bigtable, whose denormalized structure is fundamentally different from the currently popular RDBMSes, which are founded on relational theory. Fortunately, GAE supports both JDO and JPA (discussed briefly in Chapter 12), which will simplify your migration to GAE.

Currently, Google offers a free quota of 5 million page uses per month. Google states that Google crawlers find GAE apps in the same fashion as any other site; i.e., no special treatment is given to GAE applications.

You can find more information about language support for GAE here: http://groups.google.com/group/google-appengine-java/web/will-it-play-in-app-engine

If you want to learn more about the underlying principles of Bigtable, you can read more details here: http://labs.google.com/papers/Bigtable.html

■ 10.4.2 Upcoming GAE Features and Pricing Structure

The following is a list of GAE features that Google planned to release in 2009:

• billing (storage, bandwidth, and email)
• more modules for importing files
• design for a queue to support background tasks
• more detailed usage reporting for handlers

After billing is released, many other (nonpurchasable) quotas will be set to very high values (a total of 20 quotas are available). Google is also trying to improve both the portability of GAE to other hosting services and the performance of the SDK. Check the documentation page for Google's GAE roadmap for more information.

The pricing structure for GAE is available here: http://googleappengine.blogspot.com/2009/02/new-grow-your-app-beyond-free-quotas.html

Check this website periodically to find the most current pricing information.

■ 10.4.3 Google Bigtable

Google Bigtable is a distributed datastore that supports queries and transactions via GQL, which is a language similar to SQL. Bigtable consists of entities and properties, which are similar to rows and columns (attributes) in a table in an RDBMS. Each property of an entity can contain almost anything: text, binary code, images, byte code, and so forth. Thus, each property is essentially a small BLOB; however, the content of each property cannot exceed 1MB. When you access data in Bigtable, keep in mind that the current limit for transactions is 30 seconds.

Additional the user-accessible services include:

- scalable datastore (Bigtable)
- Google accounts
- memcache
- image manipulation

With the exception of indexes, Bigtable does not store any metadata, which differs markedly from RDBMSes. Data conversion occurs at runtime by the Python code that retrieves entities and properties. The Python methods cast the data in a property to the desired type (e.g., date).

For example, you can define a Python-based datastore model class to access Bigtable data as shown here:

```
class ContactPeople(db.Model):
    message = db.StringProperty(required=True)
    who     = db.StringProperty()
    ...
```

In the preceding code fragment, both the message variable and the who variable are String properties.

Google provides a query language called GQL, which is similar to SQL. A sample GQL query is shown here:

```
db.GqlQuery("SELECT * FROM ContactPeople "
            "WHERE who = 'Dave' "
            "ORDER BY when DESC").fetch(100)
```

As you may expect, a property in the ORDER clause of a GQL query must contain data that can be indexed (i.e., it cannot be pure binary data); if not, GAE returns an error message.

Although GQL statements resemble SQL statements, there are important differences between the two. For example, GQL does not support join statements, which means that GQL statements can only execute against a single table. However, you can use ReferenceProperty to handle one-to-many and many-to-many relationships. In addition, the WHERE clause of SELECT statements only supports inequalities (>, >=, <, and <=) on a single column. Since GQL statements return a maximum of 1,000 rows per call, additional application-based logic is required if more than 1,000 rows are in the result set.

Therefore, differences between GQL and SQL may necessitate rewriting SQL statements in existing applications to migrate them to GAE.

■ 10.4.4 Installing the GAE SDK for Python

The GAE SDK is available for Windows, MacIntosh, and Linux. The following steps explain where you can download the SDK with Step 3 being Windows-specific:

Step 1: Sign up for a free GAE account here:
http://code.google.com/appengine/

Provide the mandatory information to create an account

Step 2: Download the GAE SDK from:
http://code.google.com/appengine/downloads.html

Step 3: Launch the installer (the version number may vary):
GoogleAppEngine_1.2.3.msi

After the installer completes the installation, you create a simple GAE application, as described in the next section.

■ 10.4.5 A "Hello, World" Example in Python

This section describes the steps to create and launch a very simple Python-based "Hello, World" GAE application.

Step 1: Create a helloworld directory with the file helloworld.py with the following:

```
print 'Content-Type: text/plain'
print ''
print 'Hello, world!'
```

Step 2: Create a configuration file called app.yaml in the helloworld sub-directory with the following lines:

```
application: helloworld
version: 1
runtime: python
api_version: 1

handlers:
- url: /.*
  script: helloworld.py
```

Step 3: Open a command shell and go to the directory where you installed the GAE SDK and launch the GAE server as follows:

```
dev_appserver.py helloworld/
```

In the preceding command, the Python script `dev_appserver.py` and the subdirectory `helloworld` are in the same directory (you need to specify the relative path to the `helloworld` subdirectory if your configuration is different).

Step 4: Launch your browser and navigate to the following URL:
http://localhost:8080/

If everything was performed correctly, you should see the string "Hello, world!" in your browser.

You can find additional information and other useful links here:
http://code.google.com/appengine/docs/python/gettingstarted/helloworld.html

■ 10.4.6   Uploading Applications to GAE

After you create a GAE application, complete the following steps to upload your application to Google:

Step 1: Create your application here: http://appengine.google.com

Step 2: Verify that the application identifier in your `appengine-web.xml` file matches the one you chose in Step 1

Step 3: Run `appcfg` to upload your application and deploy it to Google's servers by navigating to the `appengine-java-sdk` directory and typing the following command (adjust the syntax as required for Linux and MacIntosh):

```
bin\appcfg.cmd update <your web application>
```

Step 4: Test your application at (replace `app-id` with your application id):
http://<app-id>.appspot.com

■ 10.4.7   "Fusion Tables" Database

In June 2009, Google announced the availability of its online Fusion Tables™ database for managing, merging, and visualizing data from multiple sources. The announcement regarding Fusion Tables can be found here:
http://googleresearch.blogspot.com/2009/06/google-fusion-tables.html

Fusion Tables has the following restrictions and features:

- maximum of 100MB per table
- maximum of 250MB per user
- upload data from spreadsheets or CSV files
- export data as CSV files
- data visualization via charts or maps
- tools for finer-grained data visualization

Although this experimental database has SQL-like support, its primary purpose is for merging data from multiple sources, graphically oriented data visualization, and real-time collaboration and data manipulation for groups of users.

A "tour" of Fusion Tables features can be found here: http://tables.googlelabs.com/public/tour/tour1.html

A comparison of Linked Open Data (a W3C initiative) and Fusion Tables can be found here: http://go-to-hellman.blogspot.com/2009/06/linked-data-vs-google-fusion-tables.html

■ 10.5 MICROSOFT WINDOWS AZURE

Microsoft Windows Azure is a cloud computing product from Microsoft that was during the Professional Developer Conference (PDC) in November 2009. The Microsoft Windows Azure home page is: http://www.microsoft.com/azure

The Windows Azure cloud has a *fabric,* which is an abstraction layer that governs many activities in the Azure cloud, such as provisioning hardware, load balancing, failure detection, and so forth. The fabric contains many virtualized instances of Windows, and when necessary, the fabric can replace failed instances with new instances transparently. The fabric also provides fault-tolerant storage services in the Azure cloud, and those services are scalable and accessible to applications.

Users deploy their applications to the Azure cloud with metadata that indicates the number of instances that are required and the roles associated with those instances. The fabric will provision those roles onto the instances, provide load balancing, and then monitor those roles.

Windows Azure provides scalability (up or down), so you can increase or decrease the number of active instances associated with an application that is running in the Azure cloud.

Users can obtain a local developer fabric with storage services that emulate the Azure cloud to test their applications locally, after which those applications can be deployed to the Azure cloud.

Since Windows Azure supports a PaaS model, Microsoft may be competing with GAE more than with Amazon EC2. Microsoft plans to support Java, Python, and Ruby in Windows Azure, and GAE already supports Java and Python.

A blog post from September 2009 that makes a comparison between GAE and Windows Azure is here:

http://blogs.claritycon.com/blogs/kevin_marshall/archive/2009/09/09/building-cloud-applications-windows-azure-vs-google-app-engine.aspx

Although the pricing structure for Windows Azure and GAE is comparable, GAE offers a slightly better pricing model, as shown here:

http://oakleafblog.blogspot.com/2009/07/comparison-of-azure-and-google-app.html

Microsoft will provide both pay-as-you-go and a discounted rate if you agree to a six-month commitment. Since prices are subject to change, check the Microsoft Azure website periodically the most current pricing information. Check the appendices for links about pricing model information for Windows Azure.

Users who switch to Windows Azure can run some native code in the Azure cloud, leverage their existing knowledge of SQL server, and benefit from Visual Studio integration. Note that Microsoft Azure will provide a fully relational cloud database service, which differs from the other major cloud computing vendors.

In addition to Windows Azure, Microsoft is involved in virtualization solutions, such as Hyper-V, and application virtualization. Search the Internet for more information about Microsoft and virtualization, and see Chapter 11 for more information about virtualization solutions using VMWare software.

■ 10.5.1 Windows Azure Features and .NET Services

The following is partial list of Windows Azure features:

• applications can be ASP.NET or WCF apps

- support for any .NET language
- REST support
- BLOB storage support
- message queues
- SQL Azure database
- high scalability (petabyte range and beyond)
- LiveID and ActiveDirectory integration
- works with Java clients

Microsoft Azure also provides the following .NET services:

- Access control
- Service Bus
- Workflow (early stage)

Microsoft .NET services provide the "glue" that lets Azure applications and SQL Azure databases work with existing software applications. The .NET Access control service provides authorization services that developers can leverage when they develop Windows Azure applications. The .NET Service Bus provides an infrastructure that developers can use to enable communication between applications that reside in different systems.

Windows Azure also provides a management tool for managing storage accounts. You can get additional information about this tool here:
http://code.msdn.microsoft.com/windowsazuremmc

■ 10.5.2 SQL Azure

SQL Azure is combination of SQL Services and SQL Data Services. Its home page is:
http://www.microsoft.com/azure/sql.mspx

SQL Azure is an extension (that will evolve over time) of SQL Server that includes cloud-based functionality. However, the previous data model, Authority, Container, Entity (ACE) will be replaced by Transact-SQL (TSQL).

The SQL Azure database service provides the following features:

- scalability
- backup and recovery
- table storage (nonrelational)
- relational database service

The nonrelational table storage facility in Windows Azure lets users process and analyze both structured and partially structured data. In addition, the relational database service in Windows Azure supports TSQL over Tabular Data Stream (TDS).

10.5.2.1 Using SQL Azure

Sign up for a free SQL Azure account to receive an email notification that contains a SQL Azure invitation code. Next, complete the following steps:

Step 1: Navigate to the following URL:
https://sql.azure.com

Step 2: Log into your email account

Step 3: Enter the invitation code that was sent to you. It will look something like this:

XXXXXF93-428A-42AB-945C-45D6C24C7ZZZ

Step 4: Create a server by specifying an administrator username and password

After you complete Step 4, you will see a web page with the following links at the top of the page:

• Azure Services
• Windows Azure
• SQL Azure
• .NET Services
• Live Services

Create a SQL Azure database by performing the following steps:

Step 1: Log into your Azure account

Step 2: Click on the Manage link

Step 3: Click on the Create Database button

Step 4: Specify a database name and click Create

Repeat the preceding steps each time you want to create a new database, and click the Delete button whenever you want to delete one of them.

On the same screen, you can reset your password and view the connection strings for a database. The following is an example of connection strings for a database:

```
ADO.NET:
Server=tcp:xxxxxdyk2d.ctp.database.windows.net;Database=master;User
ID=your-userid-is-here;Password=myPassword;Trusted_Connection=False;
```

```
ODBC:
Driver={SQL Server};Server=tcp:xxxxxdyk2d.ctp.database.windows.
net;Database=master;Uid=your-userid-is-here;Pwd=myPassword;
```

```
OLE DB:
Provider=SQLNCLI10;Server=tcp:xxxxxdyk2d.ctp.database.windows.
net;Database=master;Uid=your-userid-is-here;Pwd=myPassword;
```

■ 10.5.3   Windows Azure Development

There are software prerequisites you need to install on your system to create Windows Azure applications. You also need to register for an account, after which you can download the Windows Azure SDK and the associated tools for Visual Studio.

The software prerequisites are:

- Windows Vista or Windows 2008 (with latest service packs)
- Internet Explorer 7.0 with ASP.NET or WCF HTTP activation
- Visual Web Develop Express or Visual Studio 2008
- .NET 3.5 SP1
- SQL Server 2005 Express or SQL Server 2008 Express

After you download and install the prerequisite software, perform the following steps:

Step 1: Register for a Community Technology Preview (CTP) of Windows Azure here:
http://www.microsoft.com/azure/register.mspx

Step 2: After Microsoft sends you an email notification containing your invitation code, navigate to the Azure Services Developer portal here:
https://lx.azure.microsoft.com/Cloud/Provisioning/Default.aspx

When you navigate to the preceding URL, you will need to sign in with a Windows Live ID, which can also be used for accessing Hotmail and Messenger

Step 3: Go to the following URL:
http://www.microsoft.com
and click the Try it Now link

Step 4: Click the first pair of links to download Windows Azure SDK and Windows Azure Tools for Visual Studio

After you complete the set-up and installation steps, you can create Windows Azure applications in Visual Studio and simulate Windows Azure locally. When you are finished developing and debugging your application, you can deploy your application on Windows Azure.

■ 10.6 YAHOO CLOUD COMPUTING

Yahoo has three different cloud-related products:

• MObStor
• Sherpa
• Apache Hadoop

This section discusses MObStor and Sherpa, and Apache Hadoop will be discussed in Chapter 11.

Currently, Yahoo does not provide direct public access to Sherpa or MObStor, so check Yahoo periodically for more information regarding their availability in the future. Despite the current unavailability of Sherpa, and MObStor, Yahoo has released a number of tools and products that are widely used by developers, so it's worth keeping track of these two services so that you can compare their benefits with similar services from other vendors.

■ 10.6.1 Yahoo MObStor

In mid-2009, Yahoo announced MObStor, which is an unstructured storage cloud that started as Yahoo's initial photo storage system. Yahoo incorporated Best Practices to develop MObStor into a cloud that is the basis for Yahoo's unstructured storage requirements.

MObStor is a reliable and secure data storage system that is accessible through a RESTful API. Yahoo is improving MObStor by working on the following areas:

• better performance
• lower cost

- high availability
- speed of data access
- consistency

MObStor consists of three layers. The top layer is the Global Object Management Layer, which provides the RESTful APIs that let you access the data in MObStor. The middle layer is the Local Object Management Layer, which manages metadata and handles access control. The third layer is the Object Store Layer, which handles the physical storage of data.

Note that MObStor provides storage needs for a myriad of unstructured data types, whereas Facebook Haystack (discussed in Chapter 7) supports the storage of any homogeneous data type (such as photos).

■ 10.6.2 Yahoo Sherpa

While MObStor focuses on handling unstructured data, Sherpa (also announced in mid-2009) is a service for managing structured data. The Sherpa data model involves a key-value storage system with data stored as JSON BLOBS in tables that have primary keys. Sherpa can handle Yahoo's requirement for scaling horizontally geographically. Sherpa is actually a sharded datastore that uses an enhanced sharding algorithm, a high-performance message bus, and small units of data storage. One interesting aspect of Sherpa is that several Yahoo services, including Y!OS and YQL, use Sherpa for data storage.

■ 10.7 OTHER CLOUD COMPUTING INITIATIVES

At least two other large vendors may become involved in cloud computing, but at this point it's too early to determine the extent of their involvement.

Apple is building a massive data center whose sheer size suggests that Apple will provide cloud computing, and HP is involved in cloud computing services and research.

Apple has been constructing a billion-dollar data center that will occupy 500,000 square feet, which is larger than the data centers of Google, Microsoft, or IBM. The development of this data center does not necessarily mean that Apple will become involved in cloud computing, but its size encourages this sort of speculation.

In 2007 there was speculation that Apple would form a partnership with Google, but in 2009 there were articles suggesting that Apple and Google would be competitors. More recent articles (late in 2009) put forth various other possibilities, such as competition between Apple and Microsoft and also a partnership between Apple and Adobe (or perhaps that Apple would buy Adobe).

HP is another company involved in cloud computing. HP offers the following services:

- CloudPrint™
- Gabble™
- Magcloud™
- Snapfish™

The HP cloud computing research can be found here:
http://www.hpl.hp.com/research/cloud.html

Another HP website with information about its cloud computing initiative is:
http://h20338.www2.hp.com/enterprise/us/en/technologies/cloud-computing.html

■ 10.8 INDUSTRY PERSPECTIVE

Marina Fisher at Sun Microsystems has contributed material a for cloud computing industry perspective.

■ 10.8.1 Economy of the Cloud and How to Get Started

Cloud computing is the next big buzz in the industry. It is referred to as a massive computer and storage infrastructure that can be provisioned on-demand with a corresponding pay-per-use model. A cloud economy brings new opportunities for start-up, midsize, and large companies. Start-ups leverage cloud services from Amazon, GAE, Joyent, and others to deploy their applications in a scalable environment in just a matter of minutes. Cloud computing lets developers focus on their core IP and application features. Thus, it helps to minimize time spent on server and infrastructure management.

However, does cloud computing fit everyone's need? Definitely not. There are a number of companies that find it more economical to own their servers and storage instead of deploying on the cloud. The economy of in-house deployment versus running applications on the cloud really depends on a multitude of criteria. For example, how large your user base is and how frequently your application data is being accessed. A higher volume of calls to the cloud APIs results in a higher cost. Also, if portability of your data is critical, a cloud may not be an optimal solution. You need to answer many other questions as well, such as what are the ways you plan to manage your application; how do you address disaster recovery, high availability, security, and other constraints critical to your application.

With these points in mind, many of the today's Web 2.0 applications, such as social networking and social media, are deployed on a cloud. The reason is that it's easy and inexpensive to get started, you pay per use, can scale up and down the underlying resources, and it's quite reliable (Amazon EC2 still goes down occasionally as do other clouds, so don't expect 99.999% uptime).

The following are the three main services of cloud computing:

1. SaaS, with applications like salesforce.com, Oracle on Demand, Apps .Gov, and Google docs

2. PaaS which is targeted for developers such as GAE, Force.com, and Microsoft Azure

3. IaaS, which comprises basic storage and compute, capabilities offered by Amazon EC2 and S3, Windows Azure BLOBS, Rackspace Cloud Files, Nirvanix Storage Delivery Network, AT&T, Verizon, Nebula from NASA, and VMWare vCloud Express.

Sun Microsystems works with cloud service providers and enterprises to build private, public, and hybrid clouds. Today's cloud offerings leverage Sun technologies such as MySQL, Solaris and OpenSolaris, ZFS filesystem, Open Storage, and CMT systems (see Figure 10.1).

Sun Microsystems has also been building the Sun Open Cloud platform since December 2008. The platform is both a computer and

■ **FIGURE 10.1**

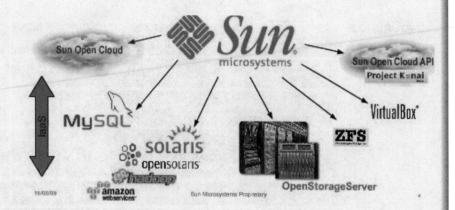

storage cloud that utilizes core Sun technologies including systems, storage, virtualization, and tools.

The Sun Open Cloud platform has multiple layers. The bottom layer contains physical resources like servers, storage, and networking, which are managed by the data center management layer. The Virtualization layer is based on Sun's OpenSolaris and Xen. The Data Center Abstraction Layer (DAL) and the Virtual Data Center Layer (VDC) are part of the cloud layer, which includes computer and storage service, data center management control, and cloud-specific features like accounting, billing, and metering. Finally, cloud APIs, which are REST-style web services and WebDAVs for file storage, and the GUI make up the top layer. Both APIs and the GUI let users configure the cloud environment.

The Sun Open Cloud platform is shown in Figure 10.2.

The key differentiators in Sun's cloud effort is the ability to manage virtual environments from a portal with VDC and a commitment to open source, standard-based, interoperable cloud APIs. A copy of the cloud APIs can be previewed here:

http://kenai.com/projects/suncloudapis

Sun's VDC which represents a collection of virtual machines, storage, and networks, is accessible via a GUI tool. The GUI lets users configure their environments by dragging and dropping individual components of their multitiered environment, such as virtual subnets, storage, and virtual

■ FIGURE 10.2

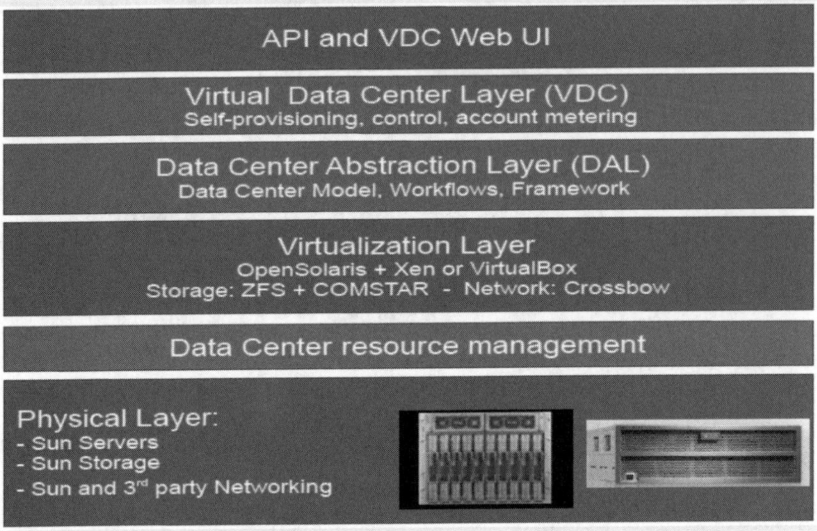

machines. Users can then copy or clone existing environments. These centralized GUI-based management capabilities are not a typical component of public cloud offerings like Amazon, Rack Space, or GoGrid. Thus, developers utilize third-party providers' solutions, such as RightScale, to manage their virtual environment.

Today's cloud providers offer either a generic set of computer services or a specific development platform. For example, Joyent offers accelerators for facebook, OpenSocial, and Bebo applications on a secure and reliable OpenSolaris environment. Developers can also deploy an application of their choice, such as Java or C/C++, on Joyent's accelerator. Engine Yard offers a dedicated platform for Ruby on Rails (RoR) developers. Amazon EC2 lets you pick a flavor of Linux and select components of your Linux, Apache, MySQL, PHP, Perl (LAMP) stack to build an AMI.

To connect to your virtual environment, cloud providers like Amazon or Joyent issue a root access to 'ssh' to your environment. For example, with Amazon EC2, to access your Unix/Linux environment, you use the ssh command with your private key:

```
ssh -i id_rsa-gsg-keypair root@ec2-67-202-51-223.compute-1
.amazonaws.com
```

To access your instance programmatically, cloud providers offer REST- style web services that are often supported in PHP, Java, and more. GoGrid, for example, supports Java, Perl, PHP, Python, Ruby, and C# clients that can send HTTP GET or POST requests to the cloud web services.

To standardize access to the cloud, a few industry consortia have been created recently. The Open Cloud Consortium is an organization that works on developing standards for cloud computing. These standards include interoperable frameworks, cloud computing benchmarks, and reference implementations. The consortium's home page is: http://www. pencloudconsortium.org

Rackspace, Microsoft, GoGrid, Nirvanix, and others teamed up to create an open source Simple Cloud API that can be found here: .http://www.simplecloud.org/

These will allow developers to utilize a consistent set of interfaces to access cloud file storage, queue services, and document databases from various cloud providers. So far, however, there hasn't been a consistent set of APIs.

IDEs are also adding support for deploying applications on the cloud. Some of the IDEs that support this feature include Aptana, WaveMaker Cloud Edition, NetBeans, and Zend.

Finally, different cloud providers implement their SLAs accordingly by offering encryption, firewalls, static IPs, and more. Depending on your application needs, you should pick providers that offer HIPPA or PCI regulatory compliance.

■ 10.9 SUMMARY

In this chapter, we introduced you to various aspects of cloud computing, such as the SPI model. We also discussed the multitude of cloud computing services from Amazon, and how to use the Amazon toolkit for Eclipse. Next, we covered IBM cloud computing services, and addressed hybrid and private clouds.

We explained GAE and Bigtable, and then installed the GAE plug-in for Eclipse to create a simple GAE application. Next, we discussed Microsoft Windows Azure, and created a simple Microsoft Windows Azure application. Finally, we covered the Yahoo-based cloud computing services, such as Yahoo MObStor and Yahoo Sherpa.

The next chapter discusses additional cloud computing offerings, including open source cloud computing tools such as Hadoop and Hive, and alternatives such as Terracotta and the Oracle Coherence product that is a grid-based enabling technology for cloud computing.

CHAPTER 11

Cloud Computing Part II

In This Chapter:

- Midsize Cloud Computing Vendors
- Sun Cloud
- Cloud Computing Integrated Applications
- Cloud Computing and Open Source
- Alternatives to Cloud Computing
- Business Focus

In the previous chapter, we discussed the cloud computing features of several major vendors. This chapter focuses on the feature sets of several smaller cloud computing vendors, various open source products for cloud computing, and grid-based alternatives to cloud computing products.

We'll start by looking at a variety of cloud computing products, each with a short description and a URL where you can find additional details.

Next, we'll discuss the Apache Hadoop open source project, which can handle very large volumes of data and supports parallel processing. We'll also discuss Hive, which is an open source project (donated by Facebook) that is built on top of Hadoop.

After that, we'll look at some open source initiatives in cloud computing, including free tools, the scientific community and cloud computing, organizations, and consortia.

Finally, we'll examine Oracle Coherence and Terracotta, which are two grid-based alternatives to cloud computing.

■ 11.1 MIDSIZE CLOUD COMPUTING VENDORS

This section discusses start-ups and midsize vendors that provide competitive cloud computing solutions. Although these vendors offer similar functionality, there are also notable differences. For example, companies such as Akamai® provide inexpensive scalability for static content, while others (such as RightScale) provide an "interface-like" functionality between your company and the major vendors (some of which were discussed in Chapter 10.

The plethora of cloud computing vendors means that there are many choices available, and competition tends to lower prices and improve feature sets, all of which are good for customers. Moreover, monopolistic practices are less likely to succeed, which is an additional benefit to customers.

However, greater competition also means that some companies might not survive in the "long term" (five or more years), or they might abandon their cloud computing platform. When you consider cloud computing companies (big or small), you should consider this disaster-recovery scenario: if a company goes out of business, how much will it cost to migrate your data and applications to another cloud computing vendor? Regardless of whether you look at large or small vendors, you should compare each of them to select the vendor that best suits your needs.

■ 11.1.1 Appistry

Appistry is a cloud computing company that supports Linux and Windows. Its home page is: http://www.appistry.com

Appistry supports Microsoft Windows (32-bit and 64-bit) and several 64-bit versions of Linux, and public cloud support will soon be available for Amazon EC2, GoGrid, and Skytap. The Appistry CloudIQ Platform Community Edition is free, but with a limit of 5 machines and 10 cores.

The CloudIQ platform consists of a CloudIQ Manager, which provides a single point of management for cloud environments and applications, and a CloudIQ Engine that is a run-time container for application code that can be written in Java, C/C++, or .NET. The CloudIQ Engine has a distributed and fault-tolerant memory cache, support for load balancing, and a hierarchical security model.

The CloudIQ platform also lets you manage applications and services, and the CloudIQ Manager console provides information about multiple fabrics simultaneously. You can also specify dependencies between services and applications and track them with the CloudIQ Manager.

Appistry uses the notion of Fabric Archives (FAR), which can be shared libraries, services, and applications. FARs are deployed to a so-called fabric, and you can monitor that fabric via the CloudIQ Manager or you can interact with it programmatically via a set of Representational State Transfer (REST) APIs. In addition, the CloudIQ Manager monitors dependencies and also ensures that everything is maintained in a synchronized state.

You can download all-in-one installers that install the Appistry run-time, administrative tools, and the SDK from:

http://www.appistry.com/community/content/downloads/download

■ 11.1.2 Engine Yard

Engine Yard is one of the few cloud computing vendors that provides support for Ruby on Rails™ (RoR), and beta-level support for JRuby was released in July 2009. The Engine Yard home page is:

http://www.engineyard.com/

Recall that while Google App Engine (GAE) also provides support for RoR, any existing Rails applications that use a relational database (such as MySQL) will not work on GAE because BigTable is nonrelational. Therefore, the underlying database schema needs to be redesigned before the Rails application can be moved to GAE. On the other hand, Engine Yard does not need the database schema of a Rails application redesigned.

Engine Yard is also a contributor to both Ruby and Rails, and also maintains Ruby version 1.8.6. Engine Yard also deploys very large Rails sites as evidence of its extensive in-house Ruby expertise.

Engine Yard provides a Solo plan (with a maximum of three servers) that lets you manage RoR applications in the cloud. According to Engine Yard, Solo lets you deploy your Rails application to Amazon EC2 in 10 minutes. When you navigate to the Solo website, you deploy applications by providing values for required input fields, and optionally search and upload Ruby gems with your application. The Engine Yard Solo plan supports the following:

• Engine Yard technology stack
• Database backup
• Background job management

- Resource monitoring
- Web firewall
- Environment cloning

The Engine Yard beta plan allows for a maximum of twenty servers, all of the features as the Solo plan, and the following additional features:

- autoscaling
- database failover
- dedicated database
- load balancing
- self-healing

Engine Yard provides a pricing estimator so you can estimate your monthly cost based on the number of servers you need and your bandwidth, which is further sub-divided into selectable values for daily page views, average page size, total number of backups, and backup frequency. Engine Yard is "fully metered" beyond a minimum of USD $25 per month, which will cost a maximum of USD $115 per month if you use an instance full-time.

■ 11.1.3 GoGrid

GoGrid provides "cloud hosting" services. Its home page is:
http://www.gogrid.com

GoGrid supports Windows and several flavors of Linux-based cloud servers with pre-installed software that lets you "get up and running in minutes." GoGrid was the first to provide Windows Server 2003 and 2008 cloud servers, and its parent company, ServePath, is a Microsoft Gold Certified Partner.

GoGrid has formed a partnership with AppZero®, whose product lets you migrate Windows-based web applications over to GoGrid. According to GoGrid, AppZero provides the only mechanism for application migration without violating Microsoft's licensing terms.

GoGrid also makes several assertions about its product and services. First, GoGrid claims to have the best Service Level Agreement (SLA) in the industry, whose terms are publicly available, along with a guarantee of 100% uptime, and 24/7 premium support. Second, GoGrid states that it offers support for Windows 2008, free load balancing, and free 24/7 support, none of which is offered by Amazon EC2.

In May 2009, GoGrid released its .NET SDK, which lets you build services around the GoGrid computing infrastructure.

■ 11.1.4 Joyent

Joyent provides an attractive set of cloud hosting services, along with support for PHP, RoR, and Java. Joyent has formed partnerships with SUN Microsystems and Facebook, and Joyent is also the cloud computing provider for SUN. The Joyent home page is:

http://joyent.com/

Joyent provides "accelerators," which is a term that refers to virtualized computing and storage, for US $45 per month (check the website for pricing updates). Joyent provides free accelerators for Facebook and OpenSocial developers.

Joyent also provides a "connector," which is a web-based suite of tools that includes email, calendar, and contacts (among others). A free version of the Joyent connector is available, and for a small fee you can add other services (such as web hosting).

In September 2009, Joyent also announced a private cloud offering, which you can get more details on from the Joyent home page.

■ 11.1.5 LongJump

LongJump is a multitenant platform that focuses on the Software as a Service (SaaS) layer of the SPI stack. Its home page is:

http://www.longjump.com

LongJump provides an application platform that can be installed behind a firewall, in a private cloud, or it can be made available at LongJump as a Platform as a Service (PaaS). In addition, you can install LongJump in an Infrastructure as a Service (IaaS) provider such as Amazon EC2 or Rackspace Mosso.

LongJump focuses on reducing the time-to-market for new applications and developing composite Service-Oriented Architecture (SOA) applications. LongJump also provides web-based information regarding security, data visualization, and process automation.

LongJump has positioned itself as a competitor of SalesForce.com with its CRM-based solution that provides applications for sales force automation, email marketing, and collaboration. In addition, LongJump provides a free 15-day trial of its CRM Gold Edition.

■ 11.1.6 Rackspace

Rackspace provides managed hosting, public and private cloud hosting, and online business applications. Its home page is:
http://www.rackspace.com/index.php

The managed hosting service provides an extensive set of products and services, such as backups, managed storage, reporting, professional services, and security. Rackspace also emphasizes its commitment to providing robust support-related services.

The Rackspace cloud suite consists of three hosting services: cloud sites, cloud servers, and cloud files. The cost of these services starts at USD $100 per month, USD $0.015 per hour, and USD $0.15 per gigabyte, respectively.

The Rackspace private cloud service for eight virtual servers starts at USD $6,000 per month, or USD $54,000 per year. However, a comparable VMWare license would cost significantly less, so you need to carefully weigh the features and trade-offs of these (and other) solutions.

Rackspace released a set of REST-based APIs for its cloud server products in July 2009, and the source code for the APIs should be made available later in the year. One month earlier (June 2009) there was speculation about Amazon releasing its Amazon Web Services (AWS) APIs, so this might foreshadow the beginning of a trend among cloud computing vendors trying to become more competitive with Amazon.

Rackspace provides an open community store and cloud servers that are available for a free 30-day trial period. Check the appendices for links to additional information.

■ 11.1.7 RightScale

RightScale provides a web-based cloud computing management platform. Its home page is: http://www.rightscale.com/

The RightScale cloud management platform lets you select different programming languages and development environments, thereby enabling you to select the cloud provider or IaaS layer that best fits your needs. Another interesting aspect of RightScale is its support for deployment across public or private clouds, along with performance, scalability, and security. RightScale asserts that its platform uses open standards, which gives you high portability and also avoids vendor lock-in.

RightScale offers several plans (ranging from free to a monthly cost of US $5,000) as shown here:

- Developer Edition
- Website Edition
- Grid Edition
- Premium Edition
- Enterprise Edition

The RightScale home page provides links with detailed information regarding each of the plans in the preceding list.

The Developer Edition (which is free) lets you configure your own applications, or you can select a preconfigured deployment (including a LAMP application and a Rails application). You have the choice of using either an AWS account or a RightScale trial account, but you will not be able to save anything in the RightScale account.

RightScale also offers a range of services depending on the plan that you choose, including those shown here:

- Management Dashboard
- Server templates
- Multiserver deployments
- Automation Engine
- Multicloud Engine
- MySQL™ manager
- Auditing
- Support
- Professional services

RightScale uses an extensive set of scripts but does not require any new languages or programming paradigms. In addition, RightScale provides a deployment process whereby customers can transition to RightScale products, starting from a deployment sheet, followed by the creation of backups, and the installation of software. In August 2009, RightScale collaborated with other cloud computing vendors to provide Business Intelligence (BI) support. Check the RightScale home page to get details on pricing information, free trial downloads, and the availability of demos.

■ 11.1.8   GridGain

GridGain™ is a free Java-based cloud computing solution. Its home page is: http://www.gridgain.com/

GridGain began as a grid computing framework that evolved into an open cloud platform that leverages Java-based features, such as annotations, along with support for AOP and integration with the Spring framework.

GridGain can be downloaded for free for Unix, MacIntosh, and Windows. You can also download online documentation, such as Javadoc APIs and a user's guide, along with demos and a user's forum. GridGain is dual licensed under both LGPL and Apache 2.0. GridGain is available for download here: http://www.gridgain.com/downloads.html

■ 11.1.9   iCloud

iCloud® is an online product that provides cloud computing services in 15 languages. Its home page is: http://www.icloud.com/

iCloud uses an XML Virtual Machine, and some of the XML-based technologies required by iCloud are not fully supported by all browsers. Currently, iCloud works best in Internet Explorer, while support for Firefox is still in beta as of mid-2009 (check the website for the latest information).

The iCloud platform is available in three versions: Standard (which is free), Premium, and CafeSpace. The pricing for the latter two versions will be announced in the near future.

The iCloud platform lets you store, share, and manage any type of file in a folder-based hierarchical structure. File types include pictures, music, videos, and documents. iCloud also provides a document editor that is compatible with Microsoft Word.

Some of the iCloud tools and applications include the following:

• an IDE
• Balanced Scorecard
• calendar, calculator, and contacts
• email
• instant messaging
• Notepad
• XML editor

You can start working in iCloud by navigating to the following link and entering a username and password:
http://os.icloud.com/ff.html

After you log into iCloud, you will see an integrated environment that resembles a dashboard, with access to email, a chat program, a calendar, widgets, and other iCloud tools. At the bottom of the screen is a set of icons, one of which is a console that provides command-shell access using DOS-like commands (but no support for Linux commands) so you can navigate around your home directory.

The left-side of the screen provides a vertically oriented set of "buttons," such as viewing all of the iCloud applications that are available (there are many of them), search capabilities (for files and users), support from iCloud, and a log-off button.

Other cloud-related initiatives include Java Composite Application Platform Suite (CAPS) and Sun xVM VirtualBox™ (discussed later in this chapter).

■ 11.2 CLOUD COMPUTING INTEGRATED APPLICATIONS

Several vendors offer a "suite" of products that are available online, usually on a subscription basis (similar to the SaaS model). This section will give you an overview of the following products:

- NetSuite®
- SalesForce
- webappvm™

Google Apps is another integrated product suite that was discussed in Chapter 5.

■ 11.2.1 NetSuite

NetSuite is a web-based suite of tools. Its home page is:
http://www.netsuite.com/portal/home.shtml

NetSuite is in the CRM arena (and a direct competitor of SalesForce), so it offers CRM-based tools, such as dashboards and inventory management. The eCommerce set of products includes pricing and billing, web analytics, and reporting. NetSuite also provides an extensive set of additional products, including ERP financial modules, inventory, order fulfillment, and purchasing.

NetSuite supports SuiteApps, which is the term that NetSuite uses for applications that extend the core functionality of NetSuite. SuiteApps are available for a number of different industries including manufacturing, retail, and nonprofit industries. NetSuite provides a third-party developer program whose members develop new applications for SuiteApps. NetSuite offers a free trial version of its software services.

■ 11.2.2 SalesForce

SalesForce is a highly successful SaaS-based company that was established 10 years ago. Its home page is:
http://www.salesforce.com/

SalesForce offers a free 30-day trial of its software products, which includes both a cloud platform and a cloud infrastructure for CRM-based products. Some of the sales-related applications include accounts and contacts, marketing and leads, opportunities, analytics and forecasting, and approvals and workflow.

The Force.com platform lets developers write custom cloud applications using the SalesForce interface and an editor that has drag-and-drop functionality, which facilitates rapid development. This platform provides preexisting components that can be combined quickly and integrated in a straightforward manner. Alternatively, developers can develop their own interfaces using a combination of Cascading Style Sheets (CSS), Flash, HTML, and JavaScript, along with support for Ajax functionality.

Force.com provides access to a database and easy-to-use tools that let users create their own objects via a custom object wizard to manage the data that is stored in their database. Force.com also provides an Eclipse plug-in (for Eclipse 3.3.x) that you can install from:
http://www.adnsandbox.com/tools/ide/install/

In addition, SalesForce AppExchange™ is an online store containing several hundred cloud computing applications that are already integrated with SalesForce CRM (and also available for a free trial period and for purchase).

SalesForce has a proprietary programming language called Apex, which resembles Java. Listing 11.1 displays a very simple Apex interface Purchase-Order that contains one method called discount(), followed by an Apex implementation class called CustomPurchaseOrder that implements the method discount() by returning a static constant.

Listing 11.1

```
public interface PurchaseOrder {
  Double discount();
}

public class CustomPurchaseOrder implements PurchaseOrder {
  static final Integer DEFAULT_DISCOUNT = .05;

  public Double discount() {
    return DEFAULT_DISCOUNT;
  }
}
```

Apex supports a lot of data types, including Blob, Boolean, Date, Decimal, Integer, Collections, Enumerations, and user-defined classes.

Force.com also has a code share website with projects that are written in Apex that can access other websites and products, such as Amazon AWS, Facebook, Google App Engine (GAE), and Twitter.

■ 11.3 CLOUD COMPUTING AND OPEN SOURCE

In addition to the commercial cloud computing vendors that we've looked at so far in this chapter and the previous one, there are also open source initiatives and organizations that are developing cloud computing tools and products. These open source projects are available through different organizations, such as the Apache Foundation, UCB, and the scientific community. In addition, there are several open source databases that provide cloud-related functionality, and they will be discussed later in this section.

■ 11.3.1 Apache Open Source Projects

This section discusses the following Apache open source projects:

• Hadoop
• Hive
• Thrift

Hadoop is very popular because of its processing power. It is used by many companies, including Facebook and Yahoo. Hive is an extension of Hadoop, and Thrift was originally developed by Facebook and then donated to the Apache Foundation.

11.3.1.1 Apache Hadoop

Hadoop provides a platform for processing large amounts of data. Its home page is:

http://hadoop.apache.org/

Hadoop implements MapReduce, whose name is based on the "map" and "reduce" functions that exist in some programming languages (perhaps you remember the "map" function in the Lisp programming language). MapReduce is a framework created by Google to support distributed computing, especially when large volumes of data are involved.

MapReduce is similar to a divide-and-conquer strategy: an initial task is repeatedly divided into a number of smaller tasks to create a tree-like structure of tasks. Workers are assigned to complete the subtasks, after which the results are returned to the parent task. The top-level, or master node, that is responsible for the initial task then merges the results of the subtasks into a solution to the original task. MapReduce excels because it leverages distributed processing to "parallelize" operations whenever it is possible to do so.

Hadoop also uses the Hadoop Distributed File System (HDFS), which achieves high reliability by replicating small blocks of data for a degree of co-location with subtasks, thereby increasing performance.

11.3.1.1.1 SETTING UP HADOOP AS A SINGLE-NODE INSTALLATION

Before you set up Hadoop, download and install the required software:

Step 1: Download Java 1.6 from:
http://java.sun.com/

Step 2: Download Cygwin from:
http://www.cygwin.com/

Step 3: Download ssh from:
http://www.ssh.com/

Step 4: Navigate to the following URL and download the latest version of Hadoop:
http://www.apache.org/dyn/closer.cgi/hadoop/core/

Note that the Hadoop sample code in this chapter is based on version 0.19.0 (see the Appendices for more details).

Information about setting up Hadoop for distributed operations is available here:

http://hadoop.apache.org/core/docs/current/quickstart.html

11.3.1.1.2 HADOOP SUBPROJECTS

Hadoop also provides the following subprojects:

- Hadoop core
- HBase
- Pig
- ZooKeeper
- Hive

These projects will not be discussed in this chapter, but if you want more information, so navigate to the Hadoop home page where you can find links for all of these sub-projects.

11.3.1.2 Apache Hive

Apache Hive is a data warehouse infrastructure that is built on top of Hadoop. Its home page is:

http://hadoop.apache.org/hive/

You must first install Java 1.6 and Hadoop (versions 1.7 through 1.9), both of which are described in the previous section. Hive is not production quality yet (as of this book's writing), and it does not work on Cygwin, so this section will only give you a high-level view of its features.

Facebook created Hive to process very large amounts of data, which started from the gigabyte range in 2006 and then increased to terabytes of data in 2007. Hive provides log processing, text mining, document indexing, and predictive modeling,

Hive provides the following five major components:

- a shell (similar to MySQL)
- a driver (the core of the engine that manages the Hive life cycle)
- a compiler (parses an HQL query, creates a query plan, and searches for an optimal path)
- an execution engine (a directed acyclic graph for mapreduce passes)
- a metastore (stores the schema and the location of tables in HTFS).

Hive uses a table-driven model that supports partitions and buckets, and Hive even allows you to load JSON and YAML data into Hive tables. In addition to processing large volumes of data, Hive can make unstructured data look like tables regardless of the format of the unstructured data.

Hive provides a command-line interface (CLI) that resembles the CLI of other databases (such as Oracle and MySQL). This CLI lets you perform SQL operations to manage tables and load datasets into tables.

11.3.1.3 *Apache Thrift*

Facebook originally created Thrift (and Hive), and in 2007 Thrift was released as an open source project (and an Apache open source project since 2008). Its home page is:

http://incubator.apache.org/thrift/

Thrift is a software framework for scalable cross-language service development that combines a software stack with a code generation engine to build services that work efficiently and seamlessly between C++, Java, Python, PHP, Ruby, Erlang, Perl, Haskell, C#, Cocoa, Smalltalk, and OCaml.

Thrift lets you define data types and interfaces in a file, which the compiler uses to generate code. The following is an example of a user-defined Thrift file:

```
struct UserProfile {
  1: i32 uid,
  2: string name,
  3: string blurb
}
service UserStorage {
  void store(1: UserProfile user),
  UserProfile retrieve(1: i32 uid)
}
```

The preceding code sample specifies a service for storing user objects, and the Thrift-generated code handles the serialization of objects and the use of remote methods.

Thrift is available as a direct download from:

http://gitweb.thrift-rpc.org/?p=thrift.git;a=tree

■ 11.3.2   Sector/Sphere

Sector/Sphere is distributed storage and computing infrastructure (written in C++) that only runs on Linux. Its home page is:
http://sector.sourceforge.net/

Sector/Sphere is a parallel processing engine with straightforward interfaces, and this project is comparable to Google's GFS/MapReduce. Sector/Sphere is designed for high scalability, reliability, and performance. For example, Sector/Sphere uses a PUSH model that outperforms the PULL model of MapReduce. According to the website, a 128-node system with 512 cores performed two to four times faster than Hadoop in various applications.

Note that Sector/Sphere is a network filesystem rather than a generic filesystem. By contrast, other filesystems (including Lustre and PVFS) achieve high performance via expensive hardware.

The online user's guide tell you how to perform the installation and configuration steps. For example, configuration of the security server involves the file `master_acl.conf`, whose contents will look something like this:

```
#list of IP addresses or ranges from which a slave can join the system
#by default the system is open: i.e., any node can become a slave node
#you should change this for a production system
#E.g., 192.168.0.0/24 allows all IPs within 192.168.0.0-255 to join

0.0.0.0/0
```

The client configuration file will look something like this:

```
#Master address
MASTER_ADDRESS
    ncdm161.lac.uic.edu:6000

#user's name
USERNAME
    text

#password
PASSWORD
    xxx

#master's certificate file
CERTIFICATE
    /home/gu/master_node.cert
```

Check the online documentation for details regarding what tools and classes are available for Sector/Sphere.

■ 11.3.3 UCB Elastic Utility Computing Architecture for Linking Your Programs To Useful Systems (EUCALYPTUS)

EUCALYPTUS is an open source IaaS-based cloud computing offering that is used by NASA. Eucalyptus (note the mixed-case name instead of the acronym) was developed at the University of California at Berkeley. Its home page is:

http://eucalyptus.cs.ucsb.edu/

One important advantage of Eucalyptus is its API-compatibility with Amazon AWS, and that AWS-compatible tools will work on Eucalyptus with little or no customization.

Another advantage of Eucalyptus is its use of on-site hardware infrastructure to implement private and hybrid clouds. Eucalyptus supports self-service and legacy application support, which can assist you in reducing IT costs.

Eucalyptus Systems (accessible from the ENTERPRISE link at the top of the home page) provides an "enterprise solution," which is a fee-based customized consulting solution for customers.

Eucalyptus is available in multiple file formats for Linux, and the Eucalyptus source code. Check the Appendices for the Eucalyptus download link and detailed information regarding Eucalyptus installation.

■ 11.3.4 Cloud Computing in the Scientific Community

This section describes Nimbus and CluE, which are two cloud computing initiatives for the scientific community, followed by GEON, which is a project for Earth Sciences.

11.3.4.1 Nimbus

Nimbus is an open source IaaS-based cloud computing tool. Its home page is: http://workspace.globus.org/

Nimbus is based on the Xen hypervisor, and it lets you convert your cluster into a cloud and provides support for Amazon EC2 Web Service Descriptor Languages (WSDLs), which are XML-based documents that describe Simple Object Access Protocol (SOAP)–based web services.

Nimbus lets you launch self-configuring virtual clusters, and the Nimbus architecture is extensible, which means you can add customizations.

The Nimbus architecture is implemented via a number of lightweight components, including a site manager, a cloud client, a context broker, and an EC2 backend.

Note that the Nimbus dependencies include Java (1.5 or higher) and bash for service nodes; Python (2.3 or higher), bash, ebtables, DHPCd, and Xen on the hypervisor nodes. The dependencies can be installed by a script-based installer.

11.3.4.2   CluE (Cluster Exploratory)

CluE is a joint initiative between IBM and Google that was launched in 2007. Its home page is:

http://www.nsf.gov/pubs/2008/nsf08560/nsf08560.htm

The purpose of CluE is to provide a research environment for exploring new ways of performing highly intensive computing. CluE is an environment for data analysis and visualization, and a mechanism for managing data-intensive systems.

The Google–IBM cluster is massive: more than 1,000 processors, terabytes of memory, and hundreds of terabytes of storage. The cluster will comprise 1,600 processors and configured with open source software such as Linux and Apache Hadoop, and it will also use MapReduce and the Google File System (GFS). Management and monitoring will be handled by IBM's Tivoli™.

The San Diego SuperComputer Center (SDSC) joined the IBM–Google partnership, and researchers from the SDSC received a two-year NSF grant that will let them conduct research using the CluE cluster. The SDSC home page is:

http://www.sdsc.edu/

■ 11.3.5   Other Cloud Computing Initiatives

In addition to commercial and open source products for deploying applications to the cloud, there are initiatives and tools underway in other areas, including:

• Databases
• IDEs
• Linux® Ubuntu™

Many of the databases that are discussed in this section are in alpha or in beta, and in some cases, you must build the distribution from the downloaded source code. These databases are clearly oriented toward developers, but since they have the potential to become very powerful systems, it's worth your while to learn about them and watch their progress in the near future.

The IDEs are geared toward developers as well, and this is an area where you might see competition from numerous vendors. Linux Ubuntu is a Linux-based operating system that has become extremely popular, especially in Asia.

■ 11.3.6 Cloud Computing and Databases

The following databases support cloud computing functionality:

- MySQL
- Hypertable
- Bigdata
- Drizzle
- MongoDB
- Apache CouchDB™

11.3.6.1 MySQL

MySQL provides several cloud-based services and support for Amazon EC2. Its home page is:

http://www.mysql.com/products/enterprise/cloud.html

MySQL Enterprise is a subscription-based model that provides monthly updates and service packs with the most recent bug fixes on a quarterly basis. MySQL Product Support provides 24/7 priority support for issues regarding MySQL applications. MySQL Professional Services provides a range of fee-based consulting services, including application design and development, and MySQL-specific services.

11.3.6.2 Hypertable

Hypertable is an open source scalable database (currently in alpha). You can download the source code from:

http://www.hypertable.org/download.html

Hypertable is intended for large and highly dynamic data sets and applications that manage those data sets. Hypertable can run on filesystems such as GlusterFS, Hadoop DFS, or Kosmos.

The design of Hypertable is influenced by Google Bigtable, with the goal of handling petabytes of data in a database. Hypertable focuses on scalability (as does Bigtable) instead of transactions, and Hypertable sorts tables via one primary key. Hypertable provides HQL (similar to SQL) for managing tables.

Hypertable integrates with ActiveRecord (the ORM for Ruby on Rails), provides support for Thrift (discussed earlier in this chapter), and lets Thrift clients access Hypertable via Ruby. Hypertable is written primarily in C++ to optimize performance, which differs from other initiatives such as HBase, and it is available for MacIntosh and various flavors of Linux.

11.3.6.3   *Bigdata*

Bigdata is an open source project that focuses on high concurrency. You can download it from:

http://sourceforge.net/projects/bigdata

Bigdata has a distributed architecture that supports high I/O rates for clusters ranging from one hundred to several thousand machines. Although Bigdata is similar to Google Bigtable, Bigdata also provides support for workflows, an RDF store (RDF is discussed in Chapter 13, Semantic Technology), and OWL Lite. In addition, Bigdata supports the Sesame 2 API, which provides programmatic support for querying RDF data.

Bigdata is highly flexible (there are 70 configurable options), and there are pre-written configuration files for supporting various modes, including Full Feature, Fast Load, and RDF-Only. Currently, Bigdata uses ZooKeeper, and in the future there might be additional integration with Hadoop.

Bigdata is actually an Eclipse project, which you can install in Eclipse via the Bigdata trunk in the subversion repository found here:

https://bigdata.svn.sourceforge.net/svnroot/bigdata/trunk

For illustrative purposes (but without details), Listing 11.2 displays a code block from SampleCode.java that is located here:

http://bigdata-sails/src/samples/com/bigdata/samples

Listing 11.2

```
// use one of our pre-configured option-sets or "modes"
Properties properties =
    sampleCode.loadProperties("fullfeature.properties");

// create a backing file for the database
File journal = File.createTempFile("bigdata", ".jnl");
```

```
properties.setProperty(
    BigdataSail.Options.FILE,
    journal.getAbsolutePath()
    );
// instantiate a sail and a Sesame repository
BigdataSail sail = new BigdataSail(properties);
Repository repo = new BigdataSailRepository(sail);
repo.initialize();
```

Check the online documentation for additional information and complete code samples.

11.3.6.4 *Drizzle*

Drizzle is a lightweight scalable database (written in C++) that uses InnoDB to provide an ACID-compliant engine. Its home page is:
https://launchpad.net/drizzle

The Drizzle database is based on a fork of the MySQL codebase, and its goals are to provide a reliable, scalable, easy-to-use database. Drizzle has a client/server architecture, with support for SQL, and is designed to run concurrently on multi-CPU systems and to optimize both cloud-based and .Net Applications. By way of comparison, the website describes Drizzle as "somewhere between SQLite and MySQL."

The design goals for Drizzle include a microkernel architecture, additional "pluggable" interfaces, and fewer data types. In addition, plans are underway to remove additional features, including prepared statements, stored procedures, and triggers (among others).

Drizzle supports various field types, including `blob`, `datetime`, `enum`, `decimal`, `double`, `varbinary`, and `varchar`. Note that Drizzle has been assigned port 4427, whereas MySQL uses port 3306.

Drizzle is available for various platforms, including Linux, Mac, and Solaris®, but not Microsoft Windows (but this could change in the future). Drizzle is available for download at:
https://code.launchpad.net/drizzle/trunk

11.3.6.5 *MongoDB*

MongoDB is an open source document-oriented database (written in C++). Its home page is:
http://www.mongodb.org/display/DOCS/Home

Part of the design philosophy of MongoDB is to "bridge the gap" that exists between key/value stores and RDBMSes. MongoDB provides support for various types of data, including binary, JSON, and object-based data. MongoDB also provides indexing, profiling, replication, and fail-over support. In addition, there is early support for auto-sharding to provide cloud-level scalability.

MongoDB uses collections and supports indexes, but keep in mind that MongoDB is designed for problems that do not have heavy transactional requirements, and are not easily solved by traditional RDBMSes. MongoDB documents have a JSON-like structure that supports nested objects and provides extensions to JSON (such as a Date data type). However, MongoDB stores data in a binary format, which differs from JSON.

In addition, the Babble project (which is an application server) uses Mongo. The Babble home page is:
http://www.babbleapp.org/db

For illustration, Listing 11.3 contains a code portion from the Java class QuickTour.java.

Listing 11.3 QuickTour.java

```java
import com.mongodb.Mongo;
import com.mongodb.DBCollection;
import com.mongodb.BasicDBObject;
import com.mongodb.DBObject;
import com.mongodb.DBCursor;
import com.mongodb.MongoAdmin;

import java.util.Set;
import java.util.List;

public class QuickTour {
    public static void main(String[] args) throws Exception {
        // connect to the local database server for the 'mydb'
database
        Mongo db = new Mongo("127.0.0.1", "mydb");

        // get a list of the collections in this database and print
them
        Set<String> colls = db.getCollectionNames();

        for (String s : colls) {
            System.out.println(s);
        }
```

```
    // create a document and insert it
    BasicDBObject doc = new BasicDBObject();

    doc.put("name", "MongoDB");
    doc.put("type", "database");
    doc.put("count", 1);

    BasicDBObject info = new BasicDBObject();
    info.put("x", 203);
    info.put("y", 102);
    doc.put("info", info);
    coll.insert(doc);

    // get the current document
    DBObject myDoc = coll.findOne();
    System.out.println(myDoc);

    DBCursor cur = coll.find();

    while(cur.hasNext()) {
        System.out.println(cur.next());
    }
  }
}
```

Listing 11.3 contains several import statements and then defines the Java class QuickTour, which contains a static main method that instantiates a Mongo object from the Mongo class (which is the first import statement).

The next part of Listing 11.3 retrieves the existing collections (if any that are already stored in Mongo and then prints their contents. The next part instantiates two BasicDBObject objects doc and info and populates them with data, and then inserts the doc object into the current Mongo instance, as shown here:

```
    // create a document and insert strings
    BasicDBObject doc = new BasicDBObject();

    doc.put("name", "MongoDB");
    doc.put("type", "database");
    doc.put("count", 1);
    doc.put("count", 1);

    BasicDBObject info = new BasicDBObject();
    info.put("x", 203);
    info.put("y", 102);
    doc.put("info", info);
    coll.insert(doc);
```

The last part of Listing 11.3 retrieves the populated object and then prints its contents. Although this example is slightly artificial, the code gives you an understanding of the type of Java code that is required to perform various operations.

The original code sample for Listing 11.3 can be found here: http://github.com/mongodb/mongo-java-driver/blob/2cb7e43599354bff 6ecba523dc02817816796981/examples/QuickTour.java

11.3.6.6 Apache CouchDB

Apache CouchDB is another document-oriented database (written in Erlang). Its home page is:
http://couchdb.apache.org/

Documents are stored in CouchDB with a unique identifier that can be used to access (via REST calls) individual documents. CouchDB provides support for JavaScript-based queries that are similar to MapReduce, along with a RESTful JSON API. CouchDB accesses the underlying database using HTTP requests, and you can find third-party client libraries that let you make requests to CouchDB.

Note that CouchDB is not a relational or object-oriented database, nor is it intended to replace a traditional RDMS. Although CouchDB and MongoDB have similarities, you can find a comparison between them here: http://www.mongodb.org/display/DOCS/Comparing+Mongo+DB+ and+Couch+DB

■ 11.3.7 Cloud Computing Editors and IDEs

There are several cloud computing editors and IDEs available:

- iCloud IDE
- Mozilla Bespin
- WaveMaker™

This section only discusses Mozilla Bespin and WaveMaker. The iCloud IDE is part of the iCloud offering that was discussed earlier in this chapter. In Chapter 10 you learned that Amazon released a toolkit for Eclipse that provides support for SimpleDB. Amazon will probably release more cloud computing IDEs, and some additional plug-ins for cloud computing in "traditional" IDEs such as NetBeans and Eclipse.

11.3.7.1 Mozilla Bespin: An Editor/IDE

Bespin is a Mozilla code editor (currently, version 0.5) that provides a web-based programming environment that leverages desktop-based development in conjunction with cloud computing. This product is currently a prototype. Its home page is:

http://labs.mozilla.com/projects/bespin/

Bespin promotes open standards, and it uses the HTML5 `Canvas` tag to implement things such as scroll bars and dashboards.

Bespin is an extensible and self-hosted framework whose goals include: location-independent access, an integrated command-line, and real-time code collaboration. Bespin supports syntax highlighting and flexibility for indentation.

Bespin has been integrated with various other tools. For example, Bespin on Rails is a plug-in that lets you embed the Bespin editor component into Rails views. Bespin integration with Helma, which is a JavaScript runtime based on Rhino provides a server-side library. Bespin has also been integrated with XWiki.

11.3.7.2 WaveMaker: Cloud-Based IDE

WaveMaker is a free cloud-based IDE. Its home page is:

http://www.wavemaker.com/cloud/

WaveMaker Cloud Edition is an open source IDE for cloud computing that is a hosted version of WaveMaker Enterprise Edition 4.0. WaveMaker lets you deploy to your Amazon EC2 account.

In addition, you can obtain a free desktop version of WaveMaker for Linux, MacIntosh, and Windows.

WaveMaker provides support for major databases, and it also provides a visual builder tool with drag-and-drop functionality to develop web applications that use Ajax widgets (based on Dojo) and web services. Web applications are based on Spring and Hibernate, which makes those applications scalable.

WaveMaker provides a Cloud Edition tutorial that explains how to create an application and then add a customer detail tab, an orders tab, and a web service. The tutorial is available here:

http://dev.wavemaker.com/wiki/bin/view/Documentation/CloudTutorial

■ 11.3.8 Ubuntu and Cloud Computing

Ubuntu is a Linux-based operating system that supports cloud-based services. Its home page is:

http://www.ubuntu.com/

According to its website, Ubuntu is currently the only Linux-based operating system that is a cloud operating system. The goal of Ubuntu is to provide open source software systems that are based on de facto standards (such as Amazon EC2, the Amazon S3 API, and Eucalyptus) and the best available components. In addition, Ubuntu plans to provide an infrastructure layer that will let users deploy private and public clouds.

Canonical (the provider of Ubuntu) supports three options for Ubuntu-based cloud computing services. One option is the Ubuntu Server Edition that is available for Amazon EC2 as a public cloud, which is an IaaS-based solution. The Server Edition also provides integration with other systems (such as Dell™ OpenManage™, HP OpenView™, and IBM Tivoli), with support for deploying proprietary software, and Ubuntu's enhanced security. In addition, the Server Edition provides administrative tools for system management and a web-based interface for cloud configuration.

The second option is the Ubuntu Enterprise Cloud (UEC) that is powered by Eucalyptus (discussed earlier in this chapter). This option is also an IaaS-based solution. The UEC is set up as a private cloud (with features similar to Amazon EC2) inside an organization. The UEC also leverages a set of tools called Euca2ools that are based on several open source Python libraries. You can find more details about these tools here:

http://open.eucalyptus.com/wiki/Euca2oolsGuide/

The third option is Ubuntu One, which is a SaaS-based solution that lets users synchronize their files on Ubuntu computers and share documents. You must download and install Ubuntu software on your system, which requires you to create an account and get an Ubuntu subscription. Ubuntu One is in public beta and currently only runs on Ubuntu 9.04, however improved functionality is expected when Ubuntu 9.10 is released.

Note that no licensing is required because of the open source technology stack, and fee-based support contracts are available from Canonical®.

■ 11.3.9 Cloud Organizations and Cloud Manifesto

Currently, there are two cloud computing organizations:

- Open Cloud Consortium (OCC)
- Cloud Computing Interoperability Forum (CCIF)

The following sections provide information about these organizations, including their background. The Open Cloud Computing Manifesto (OCCM), which was started by a consortium, is covered after the OCC and CCIF sections.

11.3.9.1 OCC

The home page for OCC is:

http://www.opencloudconsortium.org/

The OCC is managed by the Center for Computational Science Research, Inc. (CCSR) and develops benchmarks, standards, frameworks, and interoperability between clouds. The OCC also focuses on developing metrics and methodologies for the cloud computing industry.

The various OCC initiatives are managed by several working groups, including the standards and interoperability group, the standard cloud performance measurement group, the information sharing, security, and clouds group, and the open cloud testbed group. Current OCC members include Aerospace, Cisco®, MIT Lincoln Labs, and Yahoo.

OCC uses the following tools (which were discussed earlier in this chapter):

- Eucalyptus
- Hadoop
- Sector/Sphere
- Thrift

According to the OCC home page, the OCC does not have any affiliation with Eucalyptus, Hadoop, or Thrift.

11.3.9.2 CCIF

The home page for CCIF is:

http://groups.google.com/group/cloudforum

The CCIF is exploring interoperability among cloud computing platforms, and one of its goals is establishing a global cloud computing community.

Members of the CCIF are exploring aspects of cloud computing, such as taxonomy, governance, and security. Although all of these topics (and there are many others) are important, perhaps taxonomy is of the most immediate relevance because it addresses classification-related details, such as the differences between cloud computing, virtualization, and grid-based technology.

11.3.9.3 OCCM

The OCCM is here:

http://opencloudmanifesto.org/

The OCCM provides a set of guidelines that establish and promote open standards for cloud computing. The OCCM does intend to establish another standards-based organization for cloud computing, with no membership, dues, or fees involved. The OCCM was started by a relatively small group that is trying to get as many cloud computing vendors as possible to embrace the OCCM, which is published under the Creative Commons Attribution Share Alike License 3.0.

As of early 2009, there were 150 organizations that have joined this initiative; however, Amazon, Google, Microsoft, and SalesForce have not. Check the Appendices for additional links.

■ 11.3.10 Monitoring Tools

Ganglia is an open source project (downloadable from Sourceforge.com) that is also a scalable distributed monitoring system for high-performance computing systems. Its home page is:

http://ganglia.info/

Ganglia is an outgrowth of the Millennium Project at the University of California at Berkeley, and it links clusters in universities throughout the world. Ganglia has a hierarchical design that is scalable up to 2,000-node clusters with high concurrency. Ganglia uses XML-based technologies for managing and transporting data, and it has been ported to numerous operating systems (a lot of Linux versions, but not Windows) and processors.

Ganglia can also be used to monitor Hadoop systems to generate run-time metrics for Hadoop systems. In addition, users can monitor their cloud instances (such as Amazon instances) using the following format:

http://<your-instance-name-here>.amazonaws.com/ganglia/

Check the Ganglia home page for additional details, downloads, and documentation (and for backward compatibility of different versions of Ganglia).

Hyperic™ is another monitoring tool (now part of SpringSource®, which, in turn, was acquired by VMWare®) for monitoring and managing large-scale systems. Its home page is:

http://www.hyperic.com/

Hyperic HQ is available as an open source edition and an enterprise edition, which is available as a free 30-day trial download and on a commercial basis. The Hyperic home page contains links for both version of Hyperic HQ.

Puppet is a Ruby-based open source automation tool that can be used for automation of the cloud (used by Stanford, Google, and others). Its home page is:

http://reductivelabs.com/trac/puppet

Instead of specifying configuration details in configuration files, Puppet lets each client specify the services that it needs and then communicates that information to a server. Puppet has "inverted" (loosely speaking) the typical configuration-based model that is prevalent among other configuration tools.

Various organizations use Puppet, including Slide™, Google, Stanford University, Harvard Law School, 24/7 Real Media®, and Alfresco. Puppet supports multiple flavors of Linux, Solaris, and MacIntosh.

■ 11.4 ALTERNATIVES TO CLOUD COMPUTING

Some alternatives to cloud computing include Oracle Coherence, Terracotta, and virtualization solutions. Oracle Coherence is a commercial product and Terracotta is an open source product, both of which provide an in-memory distributed caching mechanism. Another option is Scaleout Software®, which provides a distributed cache for grids and server farms (this product is not discussed in this chapter).

Recently, virtualization-based solutions have become very popular, and VMWare has virtualization products that target both large-scale scenarios and end users. Note that SUN VirtualBox and Microsoft Virtual PC™ also provide virtualization, and while these two tools can run in the cloud, they are not intended to "replace" the cloud.

■ 11.4.1 Oracle Coherence

Oracle Coherence provides a clustered caching technology that is scalable and reliable. Coherence is available for download from:

http://www.oracle.com/technology/products/coherence/index.html

Oracle Coherence provides many cache-related features, along with the ability to manage your Coherence grid. Coherence supports .NET connectivity and integration with open source frameworks (including Spring and Hibernate).

Check the online documentation for additional information regarding Oracle Coherence. In addition to powerful functionality, Oracle Coherence makes it very easy to create and manage the contents of a Coherence cache, as discussed in the next section.

11.4.1.1 *Creating Oracle Coherence Caches*

This section explains how to create a Coherence cache, populate the cache with data, and then retrieve that data from the cache.

Step 1: Download the Oracle Coherence distribution for Java from: http://www.oracle.com/technology/software/products/ias/ht-docs/coherence.html

Step 2: Expand the distribution into a convenient directory

Step 3: Open a command shell, and in $COHERENCE_TOP/bin launch the server:

```
cache-server.cmd (Windows)

cache-server.sh  (Linux)
```

Step 4: Open another command shell, and in $COHERENCE_TOP/bin launch a client:

```
coherence.cmd (Windows)

coherence.sh (Linux)
```

The command shell launches the `cache-server.cmd` script and displays information about the Coherence services, and the second command shell displays output messages as well (and also updates the messages in the first command shell).

After a few moments, the second command shell will display the following prompt:

```
Map (?):
```

Now create a cache called `oswald1` with the following command:

```
cache oswald1
```

Coherence will create a new cache and then display the following output:

```
2009-09-11 16:06:52.688/214.707 Oracle Coherence GE 3.5.1/461
<Info> (thread=main, member=2): Loaded cache configuration from
"jar:file:/C:/downloads/coherence-
v3.5.1/coherence/lib/coherence.jar!/coherence-cache-config.xml"
```

```
2009-09-11 16:06:53.267/215.286 Oracle Coherence GE 3.5.1/461 <D5>
(thread=DistributedCache, member=2): Service DistributedCache joined
the cluster with senior service member 1
```

```
2009-09-11 16:06:53.435/215.454 Oracle Coherence GE 3.5.1/461 <D5>
(thread=DistributedCache, member=2): Service DistributedCache: re-
ceived ServiceConfigSync containing 258 entries
```

```xml
<distributed-scheme>
  <!--
  To use POF serialization for this partitioned service,
  uncomment the following section
  <serializer>
  <class-
  name>com.tangosol.io.pof.ConfigurablePofContext</class-
  name>
  </serializer>
  -->
  <scheme-name>example-distributed</scheme-name>
  <service-name>DistributedCache</service-name>
  <backing-map-scheme>
    <local-scheme>
      <scheme-ref>example-binary-backing-map</scheme-ref>
    </local-scheme>
  </backing-map-scheme>
  <autostart>true</autostart>
</distributed-scheme>
```

Create a new entry in the cache oswald1 as follows:

```
put food pizza
```

Retrieve the value of the name/value pair with this command:

```
get food
```

and you will see the expected output:

```
pizza
```

11.4.1.2 Oracle Coherence Sample Code

Listing 11.4 displays the contents of the Java class `MyFirstSample.java`, which illustrates how to create a cache, populate it with a string, and then display the contents of that entry. Note that this sample was created and compiled in Oracle JDeveloper 11.1.1 after appending the `CLASSPATH` variable with the appropriate JAR files.

Listing 11.4 MyFirstSample.java

```java
package com.oracle.coherence.handson;

import com.tangosol.net.CacheFactory;
import com.tangosol.net.NamedCache;

public class MyFirstSample
{
    public MyFirstSample() {}

    public static void main(String[] args)
    {
        // ensure we are in a cluster
        CacheFactory.ensureCluster();

        // create or get a named cache called mycache
        NamedCache myCache = CacheFactory.getCache("abc");

        // put key, value pair into the cache.
        myCache.put("hello", "world");
        System.out.println("Value in cache is "+myCache
                .get("hello"));
    }
}
```

Listing 11.4 defines the Java class `MyFirstExample` with an empty constructor and a `main` method that calls a `static` method in the `CacheFactory` class to establish a cluster, and then retrieves an existing cache called abc. The next part of Listing 11.4 shows you how to populate the cache with the key/value pair `hello`/`world`, and then retrieve and print the value of the key `hello` (which is `world`), as shown here:

```java
CacheFactory.ensureCluster();
NamedCache myCache = CacheFactory.getCache("abc");
myCache.put("hello", "world");
System.out.println("Value in cache is "+myCache
        .get("hello"));
```

Listing 11.4 is an extremely simple Java class that illustrates the ease with which you can programmatically manage a Coherence cache from Java code.

■ 11.4.2   Terracotta

Terracotta is an open source project that is available here:
http://www.terracotta.org/

You can register for a free Terracotta account on this website. After you receive an email message with an account activation link, you can then download Terracotta to your system.

Terracotta provides a distributed caching mechanism with shared memory that can be accessed via an Least Recently Used (LRU) algorithm. Terracotta provides a console for monitoring cache performance and managing the contents of the cache.

In August 2009, Terracotta acquired Ehcache™, which is a widely used Java caching solution that has been deployed to enterprise systems and ships as part of Java products, such as Hibernate and Spring.

One area where Terracotta excels in is its ability to correctly replicate cache entries, which is of paramount importance for application integrity. Keep in mind that although Terracotta's coherent replication is safe, it is based on distributed shared memory, and therefore there are trade-offs involved.

Terracotta's strong points include:

• high performance and availability
• in-memory speed
• cache visibility
• coherence

The challenge involved in improving and sustaining performance is latency, which can occur in three places: in an application, in the Terracotta cache, and in the database. The cache latency depends on the type of data (read-only versus read-write) in the cache and the size of the data (kilobytes versus gigabytes) in the cache. Terracotta focuses on reducing the cache latency, which occurs at the expense of the garbage collector. Terracotta provides predictable latency because Terracotta scales the number of JVMs to reduce latency.

Terracotta also provides a product called Examinator that lets you monitor Terracotta clusters. This product has an object browser that provides detailed diagnostics and the structure or topology of individual clusters.

Terracotta claims to have the fastest coherence engine available. Terracotta can be combined with an ORM such as Hibernate, but you need to determine the trade-off between additional complexity and additional performance.

Distributed caches act as a layer between applications and databases, and although they can improve application performance, they can also be complex and costly. Caches can be classified in terms of their "coherency," which refers to how well the information about updates to cache entries (or the insertion of new entries) is made available to the entire set of application servers.

By contrast, Memcached is a tool that resembles a sharded-like repository rather than a distributed cache. Memcached focuses on predictable latency rather than fixed latency. However, Memcached does not let you lock the cache, and Memcached has coherence issues (as does Ehcache) and is not thread-safe.

Terracotta is a hybrid memory solution that does not lose data when you restart it. Currently, you cannot use Terracotta with Hibernate search (which uses a Lucene index). Future Terracotta functionality will include platform independence, cache events, transactions, distributed query, and wide area networks.

Terracotta Examinator is a "reference implementation" of the Terracotta Distributed Cache. Its home page is:

http://www.terracotta.org

11.4.2.1 Terracotta Plug-In for Eclipse

Follow the instructions in Chapter 6, Debugging Tools, for installing Eclipse, and then install the Terracotta plug-in for Eclipse, which you can find here: http://download.terracotta.org/eclipse/update/

11.4.2.2 Launching Terracotta and the Terracotta Console

You can launch the Terracotta Developer Console as follows:

```
%TERRACOTTA_HOME%\bin\dev-console.bat (Windows)
${TERRACOTTA_HOME}/bin/dev-console.sh& (Linux)
```

You can launch Terracotta from the command line as follows:

```
%TERRACOTTA_HOME%\bin\admin.bat (Windows)
$TERRACOTTA_HOME/bin/admin.sh (Linux)
```

11.4.2.3 *Terracotta Integration with Other Software*

Terracotta can integrate with the following list of servers and frameworks:

- Apache® Struts™
- BEA WebLogic™
- CGLIB™
- Collections™ (Apache® Commons™)
- EhCache™
- Geronimo
- Glassbox
- Glassfish
- Hibernate
- iBatis™
- IBM JDK®
- IBM WebSphere
- IBM WebSphere CE
- JBOSS Application Server
- JBOSS Cache
- Jetty
- Lucene™
- Maven (Terracotta plug-in)
- Quartz™
- Rife
- Spring
- SUN® Hotspot™
- Tree Map™ Cache
- Tomcat
- Wicket™

Details about TerraCotta integration with other software can be found here: http://www.terracotta.org/web/display/orgsite/Spring+Integration

Oracle Coherence and Terracotta are both viable options, as they provide many robust features. One obvious difference is that Terracotta is an open source project, which makes Terracotta a very attractive product.

However, you should make a detailed comparison of these products to determine whether or not you need a commercial product to meet your specific needs.

■ 11.4.3 Virtualization Software

Virtualization refers to the technique whereby one operating system can run inside another. This section describes the following three virtualization tools:

• VMWare
• SUN VirtualBox
• Microsoft Virtual PC

VMWare is emerging as a leader in the virtualization field, with a set of enterprise-level products and solutions. VirtualBox and Virtual PC provide services for end users, and VirtualBox is required for PalmPre™ mobile application development. Thus, these three virtualization tools provide solutions for different types of virtualization needs.

11.4.3.1 VMWare

VMWare provides virtualization tools that have become increasing popular since 2005. Its home page is:
http://www.vmware.com/

In August 2009, VMWare acquired SpringSource, which is a PaaS-based cloud computing company, and may make VMWare more competitive with IBM in the cloud computing arena. VMware provides a product called Lab Manager (for creating test images), and the combination of Lab Manager with the SpringSource technology stack might be a viable alternative to IBM's Cloudburst. VMWare also provides automation services (check the Appendices for related links).

11.4.3.2 SUN VirtualBox

The home page for SUN VirtualBox is:
http://www.virtualbox.org/

VirtualBox is an x86 virtualization product that is also an open source product under the GPL license. VirtualBox runs on Linux, MacIntosh, OpenSolaris, and Windows, and it supports many guest operating systems, including most flavors of Windows.

VirtualBox provides a well-modularized design that lets you start a virtual machine from a GUI and manage that virtual machine from the command line. The settings for virtual machines are specified in XML-based configuration files, so you can use the definitions on different computers.

VirtualBox provides software to improve performance and to enable more seamless integration. VirtualBox lets you define certain directories as shared folders, which can be accessed from virtual machines and shared among users. In addition, VirtualBox lets you connect any USB device seamlessly to virtual machines. The Remote Desktop Protocol (RDP) and USB over RDP support enables virtual machines to act as servers that can virtualize other clients.

Note that the PalmPre plug-in for Eclipse uses the SUN VirtualBox for running the Palm emulator (discussed in Chapter 16).

11.4.3.3 Microsoft Virtual PC

Microsoft provides a virtualization tool called Virtual PC. Its home page is: http://www.microsoft.com/windows/virtual-pc/

Virtual PC lets you run Windows XP applications on Windows 7, and it also provides USB support. Note that there are some configuration requirements for setting up Virtual PC (check the Appendices for links that contain additional information).

■ 11.5 BUSINESS FOCUS

Andrew Dong of VMWare has provided us with his perspective on cloud computing.

■ 11.5.1 What are the major benefits of cloud computing?

The first benefit is cost savings: cloud computing is a cost-effective way to acquire and use IT, and in particular, it greatly reduces the up-front investment and reliance on scarce IT/data center administration expertise.

Another benefit involves flexibility, scalability, and agility: cloud computing makes companies more flexible and scalable, and more agile in adapting to changing business needs by virtue of allowing them to quickly scale up or down capacities without much penalty.

A third one is business continuity/disaster recovery: implementing a business continuity/disaster recovery solution tends to be cost prohibitive, and cloud infrastructure, which is externally managed, remotely accessible, location independent, and typically virtualized, makes it feasible.

■ 11.5.2 What are the major downsides of cloud computing?

One area of concern is vendor lock-in, which is especially true of PaaS vendors. A second concern is the reduced level of control, which can be a serious concern for some customers. A third area involves security and compliance challenges, especially with regard to confidential data. A fourth area pertains to potentially poor application performance due to increased network latency. A fifth area involves increased bandwidth consumption that could negate potential cost savings in some cases.

■ 11.5.3 Which companies/verticals benefit the most from cloud computing?

Virtually all companies can benefit from cloud computing, but start-ups and SMBs with low or no legacy (investment in a data center and so forth) fall into the "sweet spot" of cloud computing. Applications that are good candidates for cloud computing include those with significant variance in usage patterns: variance between peak load and average load, variance between average load and low load, and so forth. In addition, leveraging cloud computing for cyclical businesses and one-off events is particularly compelling.

■ 11.5.4 What are the major use cases for cloud computing?

There are at least five major uses cases for cloud computing:

- Web application hosting
- Disaster recovery/remote storage
- Test, development, and application release
- Content Delivery Network (CDN)
- Scientific computation

■ 11.5.5 What is the state of the adoption of cloud computing today?

Cloud computing has obviously reached buzzword status in recent years, and due to its compelling value proposition, cloud computing is expected to gain widespread adoption in the foreseeable future.

On the other hand, cloud computing is at the early stage of the adoption curve, with lots of hype. Start-ups are embracing it in earnest, but enterprise adoption is very limited. Many companies are interested, but adoption in enterprises has been largely limited to small scale, and adoption has been "bottom-up" rather than from a strategic angle.

■ 11.5.6 What are the issues that prevent widespread adoption of cloud computing?

The following technical issues prevent the widespread adoption of cloud computing:

- Compliance/privacy issues
- Licensing
- Security
- Vendor lock-in

However, major deterrents for adopting cloud computing are more of a nontechnical nature, such as: trust/comfort, maturity/reliability of services/vendors yet to be proven, budget tied to servers (Capital Expenditure), and heavy investment in data center/IT infrastructure in large enterprises.

■ 11.5.7 What are the technical challenges in developing/deploying apps in the cloud?

A major challenge is the design of applications for an inherently clustered environment in which individual servers can be unreliable. Applications need to be as stateless as possible.

Security is another big area because companies need to completely rethink their security considerations, which involve data security, network security, security testing, and privacy design. In addition, persistent data management, including database backup and clustering, is also a major challenge.

■ 11.5.8   How will cloud computing evolve in the next few years?

We should see the development of more specialized cloud services, and cloud services that are built on top of other cloud services. We will also see greater federation of cloud services and seamless integration of private clouds and public clouds, enabled by standardizations around cloud portability and virtualization technologies.

■ 11.5.9   How would you compare virtualization and cloud computing?

Virtualization is a logical choice for enabling the platform for cloud computing, and cloud computing is a natural extension of virtualization technologies. For example, the arguably best-known IaaS cloud service, Amazon EC2, is based on a custom version of the Xen virtualization platform. And this is also demonstrated in the recent surge of interest and adoption of private/internal clouds, which are built on top of virtualization platforms.

■ 11.5.10   What will be VMware's strategy on cloud computing in the next few years?

VMware is highly motivated and uniquely positioned to become a top provider of enabling technologies for cloud computing by leveraging its dominance in virtualization. To serve customers building private clouds, VMware will continue to enhance its virtualization platform, management infrastructure, and solutions, and roll out solutions and services on top of them to make it as easy as possible to build private clouds on VMware's technology stack. At the same time, VMware will roll out solutions and services to cloud service providers so they can provide public cloud services based on the same VMware virtualization infrastructure. VMware will also push for seamless federation of private and public clouds via partnering and push for standardization. In addition, VMware will build more and more application awareness into its virtualization infrastructure and solutions so it can provide compelling products for customers to build PaaS cloud services.

424 CHAPTER 11 CLOUD COMPUTING PART II

■ 11.6 SUMMARY

This chapter discussed a number of midrange cloud computing vendors and described some important differences in their features. You read about integrated applications suites from companies such as Apple, NetSuite, and SalesForce. You also learned about open source projects such as Apache Hadoop, Apache Hive, and Scribe. Next, you learned about cloud computing initiatives in the scientific community, such as Eucalyptus and CluE. Finally, you learned about some alternatives to cloud computing, such as Oracle Coherence and Terracotta, along with virtualization products, such as VMWare.

The next chapter discusses Java-related products and tools, such as JAXB and Castor (for creating Java–XML bindings) and also provides an overview of Java for GAE, along with a sample project.

## CHAPTER 12

XML, Java, and GAE

In This Chapter:

- Java–XML Binding Tools
- Java and Google App Engine (GAE)
- Java and GAE Code Samples
- Java/GAE Clouds and Alternatives
- A Java AppEngine Integrated Example

This chapter focuses on the tools and technologies that can assist you in managing XML-based documents in Java and in Google App Engine (GAE). Fortunately, GAE provides support for XML processing that includes Document Object Model (DOM), SAX, and XSLT. Although it is conceptually simple to manage the DOM of an XML document, your application-specific requirements may involve complex manipulation of XML documents, so it is important to learn about the tools that exist, the XML-related processing capabilities that they possess, and the level of effort that is needed to use them.

Some Java knowledge is required for Chapter 7, Chapter 13, and Chapter 14, in addition to this one. This chapter requires a basic knowledge of XML, Java classes, Java servlets, and Java Server Pages (JSPs). If you are unfamiliar with any of these concepts, and you cannot find the appropriate material in the book, check the appendices for relevant links or search the Internet for free tutorials.

First, will look at Java–XML binding tools that generate Java classes, which can be used to manage XML documents. Since you can use Java to manipulate XML documents, you can avoid the direct manipulation of a DOM structure that is associated with an XML document (which is a very good thing). JAXB and Castor are two Java-based open source tools that provide Java–XML binding support. Note that this section leverages the material in Chapter 3, which discusses how to use Java-based programs for managing the DOM structure of XML documents.

Since GAE supports Java Data Objects (JDO), the next part of the chapter explores Object Relational Mapping (ORM) tools and technologies that let you map XML documents to a datastore. Castor JDO was released in 2009, which means that Castor provides JDO support in addition to Java–XML binding support.

Next, we'll discuss the high-level features of Java on GAE, and the required software, where to download that software, and how to create an account so that you can upload your Java code to GAE.

The next part of the chapter contains a Java "Hello, world" example, a Java servlet example, and a Java Enterprise Edition™ (JEE) web application. The final section provides a comprehensive project that illustrates how to combine Java App Engine with Dojo, JSON, the App Engine datastore, and JDO.

■ 12.1 JAVA–XML BINDING TOOLS

As you learned in Chapter 10, Google App Engine announced support for JAXB (in December, 2009), and this section provides information about it.

In Chapter 3, you learned about Java technologies and tools that let you validate XML documents against an XML schema and how to generate Java–XML bindings to manipulate XML documents from Java methods. However, before you can generate the Java–XML bindings, you need an XML schema that describes the structure of conformant XML documents. So, if you want to use these tools for manipulating the contents of the XML document books.xml, whose contents are displayed in Listing 3.10, you must first create an XML schema.

In this section, you will learn about two tools that generate Java–XML bindings. You will also see code samples that illustrate how to manipulate XML documents through methods in Java code so that you can avoid "walking the DOM," which is the technique used in the Java class `DOMReadFile1` `.java` in Chapter 3.

■ 12.1.1   JAXB: Java–XML Bindings

JAXB is an open source project that provides Java–XML bindings. You can download the reference implementation from:

https://jaxb.dev.java.net

JAXB generates Java–XML bindings, which means that JAXB generates Java classes (called "bindings") that correspond to elements defined in an XML schema. These Java classes provide you with a layer of abstraction so you can avoid direct manipulation of the DOM of an XML document.

Note that versions 2.0 and higher of JAXB (2.2 is the latest version) use Java annotations, which means that you need Java 5 or higher to generate the Java–XML bindings from an XML schema.

After you generate the Java–XML bindings, you write application-specific Java classes that are "on top of" the JAXB Java–XML bindings. Now you can manage XML documents indirectly by calling Java methods in Java classes, which tends to be much simpler and much less error-prone than directly manipulating the DOM structure of XML documents.

Keep in mind that whenever your XML schema changes, you need to regenerate the Java–XML binding classes, and the necessary changes to your custom Java code depend on the extent and nature of the structural changes to the XML schema. However, updating your custom Java code is almost always easier than updating DOM-specific code, which means that JAXB simplifies code maintenance and code development.

The following are the high-level sequence of steps for generating JAXB-based Java classes from an XML schema:

Step 1: Create an XML schema

Step 2: Specify the required schema elements

Step 3: Generate the Java classes (the Java–XML bindings)

Step 4: Write custom Java code "on top of" the Java–XML bindings

Custom Java code that uses JAXB-based Java code involves instantiating suitable Java objects that represent the structure and the data in an XML document. Whenever you instantiate such a Java class, you usually verify whether or not an XML document conforms to your XML schema (and generates appropriate error messages when the XML document is not conformant).

12.1.1.1 A Simple JAXB Example

This section provides you with an example of generating Java-based bindings from an XML schema to describe the structure of conformant XML documents.

The files in this section are the XML schema books.xsd and the JAXB binding file books.xjc.

Listing 12.1 shows the contents of the XML schema books.xsd, which is the schema that defines the structure of conformant XML documents (such as books.xml in Listing 3.10).

Listing 12.1 books.xsd

```
<xsd:schema elementFormDefault="qualified"
            targetNamespace="http://xmlns.oac.org/book"
            xmlns:xsd="http://www.w3.org/2001/XMLSchema"
            xmlns:xs="http://www.w3.org/2001/XMLSchema"
            xmlns:book="http://xmlns.oac.org/book">

 <!-- This XML Schema defines the structure of a set of books -->
 <xs:element name="Books" type="book:BooksType"/>

 <xs:complexType name="BooksType">
  <xs:sequence>
   <xs:element ref="book:BookType"
       minOccurs="0" maxOccurs="unbounded"/>
  </xs:sequence>
 </xs:complexType>

 <xs:complexType name="BookType">
  <xs:sequence>
   <xs:element ref="book:AuthorType"
       minOccurs="1" maxOccurs="1"/>
   <xs:element ref="book:TitleType"
       minOccurs="1" maxOccurs="1"/>
   <xs:element ref="book:ChaptersType"
       minOccurs="1" maxOccurs="1"/>
```

```
    </xs:sequence>
   </xs:complexType>

  <xs:element name="AuthorType">
   <xs:complexType>
    <xs:sequence>
     <xs:element name="author" type="xs:string"/>
    </xs:sequence>
   </xs:complexType>
  </xs:element>

  <xs:element name="TitleType">
   <xs:complexType>
    <xs:sequence>
     <xs:element name="title" type="xs:string"/>
    </xs:sequence>
   </xs:complexType>
  </xs:element>

  <xs:element name="ChaptersType">
   <xs:complexType>
    <xs:sequence>
     <xs:element ref="book:chapter"
         minOccurs="0" maxOccurs="unbounded"/>
    </xs:sequence>
   </xs:complexType>
  </xs:element>

  <xs:element name="chapter">
   <xs:complexType>
    <xs:sequence>
     <xs:element name="number" type="xs:string"/>
     <xs:element name="desc"   type="xs:string"/>
     <xs:element name="length" type="xs:string"/>
    </xs:sequence>
   </xs:complexType>
  </xs:element>
</xsd:schema>
```

Listing 12.2 displays the contents of the JAXB binding file books.xjb, which specifies the elements in the XML schema for which you want to generate Java binding classes.

Listing 12.2 books.xjb

```xml
<?xml version="1.0" encoding="UTF-8"?>
<jaxb:bindings xmlns:jaxb="http://java.sun.com/xml/ns/jaxb"
               xmlns:xsd="http://www.w3.org/2001/XMLSchema"
               version="1.0">

  <jaxb:bindings schemaLocation="xsd/books.xsd" node="/xsd:schema">
    <jaxb:schemaBindings>
      <jaxb:package name="org.oac.book"/>
    </jaxb:schemaBindings>
  </jaxb:bindings>
</jaxb:bindings>
```

In Listing 12.2, the entire XML schema is specified, which means that every element in the XML schema will be "mapped" to a corresponding Java–XML binding class.

Listing 12.3 contains an Ant `target` in a `build.xml` file that generates the Java–XML binding classes via JAXB.

Listing 12.3 Ant target

```xml
<target name="compile-jaxb" depends="init"
        description="Compile all Java source files">
  <echo message="Compiling the book schema..." />

  <xjc schema="xsd/books.xsd" package="org.oac.book"/>

  <echo message="Compiling the JAXB Java book source files..." />
  <javac destdir="jaxb-classes" debug="on" fork="true"
         memoryInitialSize="100m" memoryMaximumSize="1000m">
    <src path="org" />
    <classpath refid="classpath" />
  </javac>
</target>
```

Another way of generating the Java binding classes is by specifying an appropriate goal in a Maven `pom.xml` file. A third way is to do so directly from the command line after you have add the JAXB-related JAR files to the `CLASSPATH` environment variable. However, the first two methods are preferred because they can be included in a larger build framework that handles many of these low-level tasks in an automated, reliable, and consistent manner.

12.1.1.2 JAXB Plug-in for Eclipse

The JAXB plug-in for Eclipse is available here:
https://jaxb-workshop.dev.java.net/plug-ins/eclipse/xjc-plug-in.html

This website also provides a JAXB 2.0 plug-in for IntelliJ IDEA® (5.1 or higher). You can use the instructions in Chapter 6, Productivity and Testing Tools, for installing an Eclipse plug-in in order to install the JAXB plug-in.

■ 12.1.2 Castor: Java–XML Binding Support

Castor is an open source project that lets you generate not only Java–XML bindings (which is what JAXB does), but also provides datastore persistence through its JDO support in version 2.3. The Castor home page is:
http://www.castor.org/

Castor provides three ways to generate Java–XML bindings:

• Introspection mode
• Mapping mode
• Descriptor mode

Castor works in conjunction with XML schemas.

A simple and straightforward example of the Introspection mode is shown here:

```
// Create a new Person
Person person = new Person("John Smith");
person.setDateOfBirth(new Date(1985, 12, 25));

// Create a File to marshal the Person data
writer = new FileWriter("test.xml");

// Marshal the person object
Marshaller.marshal(person, writer);
```

Read the Castor documentation to find examples for using the mapping and the descriptor mode for generating Java–XML bindings.

Castor also has the following tool for generating an XML schema from an XML document:

```
org.exolab.castor.xml.schema.util.XMLInstance2Schema
```

Although this tool does not provide a 100% success rate, according to the Castor website it "does a reasonable job." You might find this tool helpful for XML documents that are moderately complex in terms of the hierarchical structure of the elements.

You can quickly generate Java–XML bindings whenever the structure of an XML document is essentially "flat"; i.e., the data in the XML document is nothing more than a set of name/value pairs. Because this type of XML document has a very simple structure, it is very easy to generate an XML schema for it.

12.1.2.1 Castor Plug-in for Eclipse

The instructions for installing the Castor plug-in for Eclipse is here:
http://www.castor.org/how-to-setup-castor-project-in-eclipse.html

Please use these instructions (and you can also refer to the installation-related instructions for Eclipse plug-ins in Chapter 5) to install the Castor plug-in for Eclipse.

12.1.2.2 Castor: ORM and JDO Support

In May 2009, Castor JDO was released, which is a Java-based tool that provides ORM support. You need to learn about ORMs if you plan to use the GAE support for JDO (which is an ORM). Castor JDO was released in 2009, which means that Castor provides JDO support in addition to Java–XML binding support.

12.1.2.3 JAXB Versus Castor

JAXB is very powerful because it can generate Java–XML bindings for an arbitrarily complex XML schema. Use JAXB if you have an existing XML schema that defines the structure of XML documents that are large, complex, and difficult to validate manually. For example, if you have a web application involving financial transactions that also manages user input as XML documents, it's vitally important that you validate all XML documents after input and after they have been modified programmatically. However, JAXB does not provide ORM support.

On the other hand, if you have simple XML documents, and an XML schema is unnecessary, then you can use Castor to generate Java–XML bindings. If you need ORM support, then you can use Castor (but not JAXB).

■ 12.1.3 Other Java–XML Binding Tools

Some of the open source tools that have Java–XML binding capabilities are:

- XMLBeans™
- XStream
- Nux
- JiBX

You can search the Internet to find these tools and their home pages, which include download links, documentation, and code samples. Since these tools have different strengths and weaknesses, you can either read their documentation or find comparison reviews on the Internet. After you have evaluated all of these Java–XML binding tools based on your application-specific needs, you will be in a better position to select the tool that is most appropriate. One such comparison is here:
http://db.apache.org/jdo/jdo_v_jpa.html

■ 12.2 JAVA AND GOOGLE APP ENGINE (GAE)

In April 2009, Google announced Java 5 and Java 6 support for GAE, and despite the rumors and speculation regarding Java support for several months prior, the formal announcement generated considerable excitement in the Java community throughout the world. Now that GAE supports Java, you can create standard Java-based web applications and deploy them on GAE, which lets you leverage GAE's scalability. In addition, developers can create applications that are written in several JVM-based languages and application frameworks.

The GAE Java environment provides support for Java servlets, JDO 2.3, JavaMail™, JCache™, and JPA 1.0. Java servlets are very useful in terms of providing custom functionality for Java-based web applications, and servlets are commonly used in Model-View-Controller (MVC)-based frameworks.

JDO uses Plain Old Java Objects (POJOs) to access data in databases. The JDO adopts the approach known as a "separation of concerns," whereby Java objects perform the data manipulation and JDO interface methods handle the database manipulation. This approach leads to a highly independent Java view of the data when compared to the database view of the data.

Java Persistence Architecture (JPA) is the most recent Java specification that manages data between Java objects and relational databases. Note that Hibernate and TopLink™ are two other ORMs that provide similar functionality.

Open source projects are available for both JDO™ and JPA. The home page of the Apache JDO project is: http://db.apache.org/jdo/index.html

The Apache OpenJPA™ home page (which contains a download link for OpenJPA) is: http://openjpa.apache.org/

A comparison of the functionality and features of JDO, JPA, and EJB™ 2.0 is here:

http://techno-drifter.blogspot.com/2009/04/java-persistence-jdo-jpa-hibernate-ejb.html

Note that DataNucleus Access Platform is an open source implementation of JDO and JPA, and GAE Memcache provides a distributed caching mechanism for caching query results. User authentication can be managed via Google Accounts, and the Images services can manage image data in multiple formats (and perform computationally intensive image processing).

The Java SDK for GAE includes tools for testing and uploading applications, and an Ant™-based build file. The Google plug-in for Eclipse simplifies the process of creating GAE applications. The development server (which simulates the GAE environment) runs locally so that you test your applications during the development cycle. One important command-line tool is `AppCfg`, which assists you in managing your application, includes uploading applications to GAE. In addition, you can manage datastore indexes and download log data from the command line.

GAE also provides support for "cron" jobs, which are tasks that are scheduled for execution based on user-provided criteria. In addition, GAE provides a Secure Data Connector (SDC), which lets you connect to servers inside of Google. SDC is secure and open, does not require changes to network settings, and data is encrypted with SSL.

Remember, GAE is a nonrelational store (as shown in Chapter 10, Cloud Computing Part I), and therefore migrating applications that store data in a relational database involves denormalizing the database schema and writing application code to handle the functionality (such as referential integrity) that is currently performed by relational databases. Migration-related details of existing applications are beyond the scope of this book, and depending on the complexity of your application, you might need a Database Administrator (DBA) to assist you in the migration process.

Check the appendices for links regarding additional information about quotas, pricing information, and the GAE roadmap.

■ 12.2.1 Language and Framework Support

The features and restrictions listed in this section are subject to change, so it is important to check Google's website for the most up-to-date information regarding GAE.

In addition to the GAE quotas, Java-based applications are currently restricted to 30 seconds of execution time for each request, and 10 MB for requests and responses. Moreover, GAE applications cannot do any of the following:

• write to the filesystem
• open sockets
• spawn subprocesses or threads
• call other system calls

12.2.1.1 Languages Supported by GAE

Some JVM-based languages will work "out of the box," whereas others will work after applying specific patches, or only for certain versions. The JVM-based languages that are supported by GAE (specific versions of those languages are provided in parentheses) include the following:

• JRuby
• Groovy (1.6.1)
• Scala
• Jython (2.2 and 2.5)

JEE support in GAE includes the following:

• Servlets (version 2.4 and also HTTPS)
• JSPs (including JSTL)
• Java Persistence API (JPA)
• JavaMail (some restrictions)
• JavaBeans™ Activation Framework (JAF)
• XML Processing (including DOM, SAX, and XSLT APIs)
• JSF 1.1

Since Java GAE supports XML processing, you can leverage your existing knowledge of DOM, XPath™, XQuery™, and XSLT™ (introduced in Chapter 3), and determine which features of these tools that will be useful while developing web applications in GAE.

GAE also added support for Representational State Transfer (REST) web services, and if you decide to make RESTful calls in an application, then you must add the JAR file `org.restlet.gae.jar` to the directory `/war/WEB-INF/lib` and to the project build path. You can find more information here: http://wiki.restlet.org/docs_1.2/13-restlet/275-restlet/252-restlet.html

If you are unfamiliar with RESTlets, you can find additional information here:
http://www.restlet.org/documentation/2.0/

12.2.1.2 Library and Frameworks Supported by GAE

GAE does support the following libraries and frameworks:

- Spring
- Spring-ORM (2.5.6)
- Hibernate (via JPA)
- Struts™ 2
- Sitemesh (2.4.2)
- Restlet®
- Jersey
- Wicket™
- Sinatra
- Helma NG™
- Modjy
- Compass™
- VRaptor
- Seam
- Apache Commons™ FileUpload
- log4j™
- Direct Web Remoting (DWR)
- Tiles™
- Grails™
- WebORB
- Tapestry™

Check the following website for the most recent and up-to-date information regarding GAE support for languages, tools, and frameworks: http://groups.google.com/group/google-appengine-java/web/will-it-play-in-app-engine?pli=1

12.2.1.3   Technologies and Features Not Supported By GAE

GAE does not support JDBC because the GAE datastore is not a relational datastore. In addition, GAE does not provide support for any of the following:

- JAX-RPC or JAX-WS
- JMX
- JCA
- JNDI
- JMS
- EJB
- RMI

The following features are not supported in Java GAE:

- JNDI environment variables (`<env-entry>`)
- EJB resources (`<resource-ref>`)
- `<distributable>` element
- servlet scheduling with `<run-at>`

12.2.1.4   GAE Plug-ins for Eclipse and NetBeans

GAE has a plug-in for Eclipse for developing and deploying Java applications to GAE. The GAE plug-in supports as-you-type validation to ensure that your code is compatible with GAE. This Eclipse plug-in lets you develop Google Web Toolkit (GWT)-based applications, GAE applications, or both. In addition, the GAE plug-in can also run the server in the Eclipse debugger.

GAE provides plug-ins for Eclipse and NetBeans for developing GAE applications (see the appendices for links), and you can follow the instructions in Chapter 5 to install either of them.

12.2.1.5   JSR Support in GAE

GAE provides support for the following JSRs:

- JSR-154 (Java Servlet)
- JSR-220 (JDO &JPA)

- JSR-243 (JDO & JPA)
- JSR-919 (Mail)
- JSR-107 (Memcache)

The appendices do not contain links for these JSRs, so you can search the Internet to find the details about these specifications.

■ 12.2.2 Java Applications for GAE in Eclipse

This section describes the software you need to download and the sequence of steps you must follow to create Java applications for GAE in Eclipse and deploy them to GAE:

Step 1: Download/install Java 6

Step 2: Install Eclipse 3.3 or higher

Step 3: Install the GAE plug-in for Eclipse

Step 4: Install the GAE SDK for Java

Step 5: Create a Java GAE application

Step 6: Deploy the Java GAE application to GAE

The first step is to download and install Java 6, which can be found here: http://java.sun.com/javase/downloads/index.jsp

The second step is to download Eclipse 3.3 or higher, which can be found here:
http://www.eclipse.org/downloads/

Note that Chapter 5 also describes how to download and install Eclipse on your system.

The following sections provide a detailed explanation of the learning steps so that you can create GAE web applications in Eclipse.

12.2.2.1 Install the GAE Plug-in for Eclipse

Please follow the instructions described in Chapter 6 to download and install Eclipse (3.3 or higher) and the GAE plug-in for Eclipse.

Create your first GAE application in Eclipse, as shown here:
http://code.google.com/eclipse/docs/getting_started.html#installing

12.2.2.2 Install the GAE SDK for Java

The following steps explain where you can download the SDK, followed by the installation step for a Windows system:

Step 1: Sign up for a free GAE account here:
http://code.google.com/appengine/

Provide the required information and then submit the form. You will soon receive a notification that confirms your new account.

Step 2: Download the GAE SDK from:
http://code.google.com/appengine/downloads.html

Step 3: Uncompress the distribution `appengine-jav-sdk-1.2.2.zip` (the version might be slightly different) in a convenient directory

The installer will complete the installation in a few minutes. You are now ready to create a simple GAE application, as described in the next section.

12.2.2.3 A Java Application for GAE in Eclipse

This section shows you how to create a Java application in GAE using Eclipse 3.4. Please keep in mind that the menu paths may be different in Eclipse 3.3 and Eclipse 3.5.

Complete the following steps to create a Java-based application in GAE:

Step 1: Install the GAE plug-in for Eclipse (described earlier in this chapter)

Step 2: Create a new web application project in Eclipse 3.4 by following the menu path: **File > New > Other > Google > Web Application Project**

Step 3: Name the project HelloWorld and specify `oac.hello` as the package name

Step 4: Select Use App Engine and deselect GWT

Step 5: Click Finish

Eclipse will create the Eclipse `AppEngine1` project. Listing 12.4 shows the files and directory structure of this project.

Listing 12.4

```
+ AppEngine1
  + .classpath
  + .project
  + .settings
    + com.google.appengine.eclipse.core.prefs
  + src
```

```
      +log4j.properties
 + src
   + META-INF
     + jdoconfig.xml
 + src
   + oac
     + appengine
       + AppEngine1Servlet.java
 + war
   + index.html
   + WEB-INF
   + appengine-web.xml
     + logging.properties
     + web.xml
     + classes+log4j.properties
     + classes
       + META-INF
         + jdoconfig.xml
     + classes
       + oac
         + appengine
           + AppEngine1Servlet.class
     + lib
       + appengine-api-1.0-sdk-1.2.2.jar
       + datanucleus-appengine-1.0.2.final.jar
       + datanucleus-core-1.1.4-gae.jar
       + datanucleus-jpa-1.1.4.jar
       + geronimo-jpa_3.0_spec-1.1.1.jar
       + geronimo-jta_1.1_spec-1.1.1.jar
       + jdo2-api-2.3-ea.jar
```

12.2.2.4 *Deploying Files to GAE from Eclipse*

Perform the following steps to deploy files to GAE from Eclipse:

Step 1: Click the GAE Deploy button on the toolbar

Step 2: Enter your Google account username (your email address) and password

Step 3: Click the Upload button

Eclipse retrieves the application ID and version information from the appengine-web.xml configuration file and then uploads the contents of the war directory.

■ 12.2.3   The Structure of GAE Java Applications

If you have worked with Java WAR files, then you already understand their structure, so you feel free to skim through this section and focus on the GAE-specific information (such as configuration files).

Web applications for GAE have the following structure:

* `WEB-INF/web.xml`
* `WEB-INF/appengine-web.xml`
* `WEB-INF/datastore-indexes.xml` (optional)
* `WEB-INF/lib/appengine-api.jar`

An application can contain one or more of the following:

* `WEB-INF/classes/` directory structure
* `WEB-INF/lib/*.jar`
* `WEB-INF/lib/*.zip`
* static resources

The `WEB-INF/web.xml` file contains information about your Java GAE application, such as its Java servlets and the conditions under which each servlet is called. The latter is defined by a "servlet mapping," which is a path-like expression that you associate with a servlet.

Listing 12.5 shows the contents of a `web.xml` configuration file that specifies a servlet and a servlet mapping.

Listing 12.5 web.xml

```
<web-app xmlns="http://java.sun.com/xml/ns/javaee" version="2.5">
    ...
    <servlet>
        <servlet-name>login</servlet-name>
        <servlet-class>oac.MyLoginServlet</servlet-class>
    </servlet>
    <servlet-mapping>
        <servlet-name>login</servlet-name>
        <url-pattern>/login</url-pattern>
    </servlet-mapping>
    ...
</web-app>
```

Listing 12.5 contains an XML `<servlet>` element that defines the servlet `MyLoginServlet` in the package `oac`. This Java servlet is identified by the name `login`, and can be referenced elsewhere in the `web.xml` file.

Listing 12.5 also contains the XML `<servlet-mapping>` element that associates a path-like expression with the Java servlet. In this example, whenever users enter a URL that contains the expression /`login`, then the Java servlet `login` (in other words, `MyLoginServlet`) is executed.

The `WEB-INF/appengine-web.xml` file is a GAE-specific configuration file that contains information about your application.

Listing 12.6 displays the contents of a sample `appengine-web.xml` file.

Listing 12.6 appengine-web.xml

```
<appengine-web-app xmlns="http://appengine.google.com/ns/1.0">
    <application>myfirstapp</application>
    <version>1</version>
</appengine-web-app>
```

Listing 12.6 contains an XML `<application>` element that contains the string `myfirstapp`, and an XML `<version>` element that contains the number 1.

The optional `WEB-INF/datastore-indexes.xml` file contains the indexes that GAE will use for the queries that are called by your application.

The JAR file `WEB-INF/lib/appengine-api.jar` is mandatory, and it contains various Java classes that are required for every Java GAE application.

■ 12.2.4 Creating a Google Wave Robot in Eclipse

Prior to creating a robot in Eclipse, make sure that Java 6 is installed on your system, and then download the four JAR files (they are required for Step 5 in the instructions) here:

http://code.google.com/p/google-wave-resources/source/browse/trunk/samples/extensions/robots/java/tweety/#tweety/war/WEB-INF/lib

Complete the following steps to create a Google Wave robot in GAE:

Step 1: Register with GAE here:
https://appengine.google.com

Step 2: Install the Google plug-in for Eclipse

Step 3: Install the GAE SDK

Step 4: Create a new web application (follow the steps in the previous section)

Step 5: Copy the four JAR files that you downloaded into `war/WEB-INF/lib`, and add them to the build path for your application

Step 6: Create the event handler servlet that extends `AbstractRobotServlet`

Step 7: Fill in the code for the `processEvents()` method

Step 8: Create the servlet mapping by editing `war/WEB-INF/web.xml`

Step 9: Create a configuration file `in_wave/capabilities.xml`

Step 10: Add the profile servlet with an icon

Step 11: Add an application ID to `war/WEB-INF/appengine-web.xml` and then deploy it to GAE

Step 12: Test your robot and add it to the wave Participant ID here: yourappengineid@appspot.com

Steps 6, 7, 8, 10, and 11 are the locations you need to insert your robot-specific code. You can also share your robot with other people by nominating it for the samples gallery here:
http://wave-samples-gallery.appspot.com

An online tutorial for creating robots (contains code) can be found here:
http://code.google.com/apis/wave/extensions/robots/java-tutorial.html

The Java classes for a robot that creates a wave can be found here:
http://google-wave-resources.googlecode.com/svn/trunk/samples/extensions/robots/java/blogbot/src/com/google/wave/extensions/blogbot/BlogbotServlet.java
Or can be found here:
http://google-wave-resources.googlecode.com/svn/trunk/samples/extensions/robots/java/polly/src/com/google/wave/extensions/polly/AdminWavelet.java

■ 12.2.5 Starting the GAE Server

As you learned earlier in this chapter, the GAE server can run locally so that you can test your application during the development cycle. You can start the GAE server by opening a command shell and entering the following commands:

```
cd $APPENGINE_HOME/bin
dev_appserver.cmd (Windows)
dev_appserver.sh (Linux)
```

Launch your browser and go to: http://localhost:8080

There are additional options available, such as starting the GAE server on a different port. You can see the various options by entering the following command:

```
dev_appserver.cmd —help
```

You will see the following:

```
Usage: <dev-appserver> [options] <war directory>
Options:
  --help, -h                 Show this help message and exit.
  --server=SERVER            The server to use to determine the latest
   -s SERVER                   SDK version.
  --address=ADDRESS          The address of the interface on the local
   -a ADDRESS                  machine to bind to (or 0.0.0.0 for all
                               interfaces).
  --port=PORT                The port number to bind to on the local
                             machine.
   -p PORT
  --sdk_root=root            Overrides where the SDK is located.
  --disable_update_check     Disable the check for newer SDK versions.
```

■ 12.3 JAVA AND GAE CODE SAMPLES

This section provides you with some simple Java-based code samples and some more complex Java code samples that you can use with GAE. Check the appendices for links to code samples for other GAE services, such as JCache and JavaMail/User Services. In addition, you can use unmodified JSP pages (if they do not contain Google login-related functionality) in GAE.

■ 12.3.1 A JSP Example

Listing 12.7 contains the contents of the JSP file guestbook.jsp, which illustrates how to call GAE from a JSP page.

Listing 12.7 guestbook.jsp

```
<%@ page contentType="text/html;charset=UTF-8" language="java" %>
<%@ page import="com.google.appengine.api.users.User" %>
<%@ page import="com.google.appengine.api.users.UserService" %>
<%@ page import="com.google.appengine.api.users.UserServiceFactory"
%>
```

```
<html>
  <body>
<%
    UserService userService = UserServiceFactory.getUserService();
    User user = userService.getCurrentUser();
    if (user != null) {
%>
<p>Hello, <%= user.getNickname() %>! (You can
<a href="<%= userService.createLogoutURL(request.getRequestURI())
%>">sign out</a>.)</p>
<%
    } else {
%>
<p>Hello!
<a href="<%= userService.createLoginURL(request.getRequestURI())
%>">Sign in</a>
to include your name with greetings you post.</p>
<%
    }
%>
  </body>
</html>
```

Listing 12.7 is a simple JSP page whose GAE-specific code starts with three import statements, as shown here:

```
<%@ page import="com.google.appengine.api.users.User" %>
<%@ page import="com.google.appengine.api.users.UserService" %>
<%@ page import="com.google.appengine.api.users.UserServiceFactory" %>
```

In fact, you will see these same three import statements in all of the GAE-based Java code samples in this chapter, because they are necessary to instantiate a GAE User object.

The next section of GAE code instantiates a User object, as shown here:

```
<%
    UserService userService = UserServiceFactory.getUserService();
    User user = userService.getCurrentUser();
    if (user != null) {
%>
```

If the User object is not null, a greeting is displayed, after which the user is given the option to sign out from here:

```
<a href="<%= userService.createLogoutURL(request.getRequestURI())
%>">sign out</a>.
```

However, if the User object is null, then the user is directed to a sign-in page, as shown here:

```
<a href="<%= userService.createLoginURL(request.getRequestURI())
%>">Sign
```

The next section shows a Java servlet that is similar in functionality to the JSP page guestbook.jsp in Listing 12.7.

■ 12.3.2   A Java Servlet Example

Listing 12.8 shows the contents of the Java servlet SignGuestbookServlet .java, which illustrates how to call GAE from a Java servlet. Listing 12.9 displays the contents of the XML configuration file web.xml, which references the Java servlet in Listing 12.8.

Listing 12.8 SignGuestbookServlet.java

```
package guestbook;

import java.io.IOException;
import java.util.logging.Logger;
import javax.servlet.http.*;
import com.google.appengine.api.users.User;
import com.google.appengine.api.users.UserService;
import com.google.appengine.api.users.UserServiceFactory;

public class SignGuestbookServlet extends HttpServlet {
    private static final Logger log =
            Logger.getLogger(SignGuestbookServlet.class.getName());

    public void doPost(HttpServletRequest req, HttpServletResponse
                    resp)
            throws IOException {
        UserService userService = UserServiceFactory.getUserService();
        User user = userService.getCurrentUser();

        String content = req.getParameter("content");
        if (content == null) {
```

```
        content = "(No greeting)";
    }
    if (user != null) {
        log.info("Greeting posted by user " +
                        user.getNickname() + ": " + content);
    } else {
        log.info("Greeting posted anonymously: " + content);
    }
    resp.sendRedirect("/guestbook.jsp");
    }
}
```

The Java servlet in Listing 12.8 contains a doPost() method that determines who called the servlet and logs the user-specific information, along with the posted message, in a log file. The Java code in Listing 12.8 is standard Java code, so we'll only examine the GAE-specific code, which starts with the three GAE-specific import statements, as shown here:

```
import com.google.appengine.api.users.User;
import com.google.appengine.api.users.UserService;
import com.google.appengine.api.users.UserServiceFactory;
```

The imported GAE Java classes are used to instantiate a GAE-specific User object, as shown here:

```
    UserService userService = UserServiceFactory.getUserService();
    User user = userService.getCurrentUser();
```

The last portion of doPost() re-directs to the JSP file guestbook.jsp, which is located in the top-level directory of the current web application.

Listing 12.9 displays a portion of the configuration file web.xml, which illustrates how to reference the Java servlet SignGuestbookServlet.java from Listing 12.8.

Listing 12.9 web.xml

```
<web-app xmlns="http://java.sun.com/xml/ns/javaee" version="2.5">
    ...
    <servlet>
        <servlet-name>sign</servlet-name>
        <servlet-class>guestbook.SignGuestbookServlet</servlet-
class>
    </servlet>
```

```
<servlet-mapping>
    <servlet-name>sign</servlet-name>
    <url-pattern>/sign</url-pattern>
</servlet-mapping>
...
</web-app>
```

Listing 12.9 contains a fragment of the web.xml file with information that is specific to the Java servlet in Listing 12.8. The first thing to notice is that the XML <servlet> element contains two child elements that specify a servlet named sign and a servlet class guestbook.SignGuestbookServlet. Next, the XML <servlet-mapping> element contains two child elements that specify the servlet named sign (which is the servlet that is defined in the earlier XML <servlet> element) and the URL pattern /sign, which means that the Java servlet SignGuestbookServlet will be executed whenever a URL contains the pattern /sign.

■ 12.3.3 Google Wave, GAE, and Twitter

Marcel Prasetya of Google wrote a Java-based open source project illustrating how to communicate between Twitter and Google Wave using GAE. The home page for this project (which includes the source code for the Tweety client) is:

http://code.google.com/p/google-wave-resources/source/browse/trunk/samples/extensions/robots/java/tweety/

Listing 12.10 contains the method appendTweet() of the Java servlet TweetyServlet.java, which illustrates how to append a set of Twitter tweets to a Google Wave blip.

Listing 12.10

```
/**
 * Appends a tweet as a blip to the the given {@link Wavelet}.
 *
 * @param wavelet The {@link Wavelet} to append the tweet to.
 * @param tweet The tweet to be appended.
 */
private void appendTweet(Wavelet wavelet, Tweet tweet) {
    // metadata: author, creation time, and tweet id annotation.
    TextView textView = wavelet.appendBlip().getDocument();
```

```
textView.setAuthor(tweet.getAuthor() + "@" + getRobotAddress());
textView.setCreationTime(tweet.getTime());
textView.setAnnotation(TWEET_ID_ANNOTATION_KEY, tweet.getId());

// Remove @user, in the case of @reply tweet.
String content = tweet.getText().replaceFirst(AT_REPLY_REGEX, "");
textView.insert(0, content);

// Linkify the content.
Matcher matcher = Pattern.compile(URL_REGEX).matcher(content);
while (matcher.find()) {
  textView.setAnnotation(new Range(matcher.start(),matcher.end()),
      LINK_ANNOTATION_KEY, matcher.group());
  }
}
```

Listing 12.10 defines the `appendTweet()` Java method that takes a wave and a tweet as parameters. This method appends the tweet to the wave by retrieving the text from the wave, setting various attributes (such as author and creation time), and then appending the content of the tweet to the wave.

If you are unfamiliar with Google Wave, please read the sections in Chapters 5 and 6, that provide information about Google Wave concepts.

Marcel Prasetya's presentation during the Google Wave hackathon at Google is here:

http://docs.google.com/present/view?id=ajfcq4h4mvxw_ 0f9xph2cg

■ 12.3.4 Create an Eclipse Project

You can create a Java-based Eclipse project that uses Tweety by adding four JAR files to your project, all of which are available here:

http://code.google.com/p/google-wave-resources/source/browse/trunk/
samples/extensions/robots/java/tweety/#tweety/war/WEB-INF/lib

Note that you already downloaded these JAR files in a previous section in this chapter.

■ 12.3.5 GAE JDO

This section shows you how to create an Eclipse-based web application that uses JDO. If you did not already know, the Google plug-in for Eclipse supports development of web applications that also use JDO to access the datastore. We recommend Eclipse-based development of GAE applications because manual tasks are performed automatically, which helps reduce the amount of time required for debugging your web applications.

In addition to the project files generated by Eclipse, the JDO web application also requires the following three files:

- `PMF.java`
- `SignGuestbookServlet.java`
- `guestbook.jsp`

However, before we discuss the Java class and JSP page, let's consider some of the tasks that the Google plug-in automatically performs for GAE web applications:

- includes the required JAR files in WEB-INF/lib
- includes a `jdoconfig.xml` file in the META-INF directory
- performs a post-compilation step on data classes

For example, Eclipse automatically places the following JAR files in the `WEB-INF/lib` directory of a project (note that JAR file version numbers might be different for your configuration):

```
appengine-api-1.0-sdk-1.2.0.jar
datanucleus-appengine-1.0.0.final.jar
datanucleus-core-1.1.0.jar
datanucleus-jpa-1.1.0.jar
geronimo-jpa_3.0_spec-1.1.1.jar
geronimo-jta_1.1_spec-1.1.1.jar
jdo-api-2.3-SNAPSHOT.jar
```

The preceding list of JAR files lets you write web applications that use JDO or JPA.

If you decide to not use Eclipse to create a JDO-based application, then you must manually copy these JAR files from $APPENGINE_SDK/lib/user/orm into the WEB-INF/lib subdirectory of your application.

In addition to placing the required JAR files in the correct subdirectory, Eclipse also creates a `jdoconfig.xml` configuration file in the META-INF directory. Listing 12.11 displays the contents of `jdoconfig.xml`, which displays the JDO-related configuration details.

Listing 12.11 jdoconfig.xml

```
<?xml version="1.0" encoding="utf-8"?>
<jdoconfig xmlns="http://java.sun.com/xml/ns/jdo/jdoconfig"
    xmlns:xsi="http://www.w3.org/2001/XMLSchema-instance"
    xsi:noNamespaceSchemaLocation="http://java.sun.com/xml/ns/jdo/
jdoconfig">

    <persistence-manager-factory name="transactions-optional">
        <property name="javax.jdo.PersistenceManagerFactoryClass"
            value="org.datanucleus.store.appengine.jdo.Datastore-
JDOPersistenceManagerFactory"/>
        <property name="javax.jdo.option.ConnectionURL"
value="appengine"/>
        <property name="javax.jdo.option.NontransactionalRead"
value="true"/>
        <property name="javax.jdo.option.NontransactionalWrite"
value="true"/>
        <property name="javax.jdo.option.RetainValues"
value="true"/>
        <property name="datanucleus.appengine.autoCreateDatastoreTxns"
value="true"/>
    </persistence-manager-factory>
</jdoconfig>
```

Listing 12.11 starts with an XML declaration, followed by the XML
<jdoconfig> element that contains definitions for XML namespaces. The
XML <persistence-manage-factory> element contains a set of child elements that are essentially name/value pairs for various properties of the JDO
manager.

Now let's return to the additional Java classes and the JSP page that we
discussed earlier in this section. Listing 12.12 displays the contents of the Java
class PMF.java, which illustrates how to use the PersistenceManagerFactory
Java class in GAE.

Listing 12.12 PMF.java

```
package guestbook;

import javax.jdo.JDOHelper;
import javax.jdo.PersistenceManagerFactory;

public final class PMF {
  private static final PersistenceManagerFactory pmfInstance =
```

```
       JDOHelper.getPersistenceManagerFactory("transactions-optional");

  private PMF() {}

  public static PersistenceManagerFactory get() {
    return pmfInstance;
  }
}
```

Listing 12.12 contains two JDO-specific import statements that are used in the instantiation of a static PersistenceManagerFactory instance in the PMF Java class. As you can see, this Java class contains an empty constructor and a static get() method that returns the PersistenceManagerFactory object.

Listing 12.13 displays the contents of the Java servlet SignGuestbook-Servlet.java, which is also part of the GAE web application.

Listing 12.13 SignGuestbookServlet.java

```
package guestbook;

import java.io.IOException;
import java.util.Date;
import java.util.logging.Logger;
import javax.jdo.PersistenceManager;
import javax.servlet.http.*;
import com.google.appengine.api.users.User;
import com.google.appengine.api.users.UserService;
import com.google.appengine.api.users.UserServiceFactory;

import guestbook.Greeting;
import guestbook.PMF;

public class SignGuestbookServlet extends HttpServlet {
  private static final Logger log = Logger.
getLogger(SignGuestbookServlet.class.getName());

  public void doPost(HttpServletRequest req, HttpServletResponse resp)
               throws IOException {
      UserService userService = UserServiceFactory.getUserService();
      User user = userService.getCurrentUser();

      String content = req.getParameter("content");
      Date date = new Date();
      Greeting greeting = new Greeting(user, content, date);

      PersistenceManager pm = PMF.get().getPersistenceManager();
```

```
        try {
            pm.makePersistent(greeting);
        } finally {
            pm.close();
        }

        resp.sendRedirect("/guestbook.jsp");
    }
}
```

Listing 12.13 contains a JDO-specific `import` statement and two custom-written Java files, as shown here:

```
import javax.jdo.PersistenceManager;
import guestbook.Greeting;
import guestbook.PMF;
```

The other thing to notice is how you need to modify the `doPost()` method so that the JDO-specific functionality is used, as shown here:

```
        Greeting greeting = new Greeting(user, content, date);

        PersistenceManager pm = PMF.get().getPersistenceManager();
        try {
            pm.makePersistent(greeting);
        } finally {
            pm.close();
        }
```

Now let's take a look at Listing 12.14, which displays the contents of the JSP page `greeting.jsp`, which you have to include in the AppEngine web application.

Listing 12.14 greeting.jsp

```
<%@ page contentType="text/html;charset=UTF-8" language="java" %>
<%@ page import="java.util.List" %>
<%@ page import="javax.jdo.PersistenceManager" %>
<%@ page import="com.google.appengine.api.users.User" %>
<%@ page import="com.google.appengine.api.users.UserService" %>
<%@ page import="com.google.appengine.api.users.UserServiceFactory"
%>
<%@ page import="guestbook.Greeting" %>
<%@ page import="guestbook.PMF" %>
```

```
<html>
  <body>

<%
    UserService userService = UserServiceFactory.getUserService();
    User user = userService.getCurrentUser();
    if (user != null) {
%>
<p>Hello, <%= user.getNickname() %>! (You can
<a href="<%= userService.createLogoutURL(request.getRequestURI())
%>">sign out</a>.)</p>
<%
    } else {
%>
<p>Hello!
<a href="<%= userService.createLoginURL(request.getRequestURI())
%>">Sign in</a>
to include your name with greetings you post.</p>
<%
    }
%>

<%
    PersistenceManager pm = PMF.get().getPersistenceManager();
    String query = "select from " + Greeting.class.getName();
    List<Greeting> greetings = (List<Greeting>) pm.newQuery(query)
.execute();
    if (greetings.isEmpty()) {
%>
<p>The guestbook has no messages.</p>
<%
    } else {
        for (Greeting g : greetings) {
            if (g.getAuthor() == null) {
%>
<p>An anonymous person wrote:</p>
<%
            } else {
%>
<p><b><%= g.getAuthor().getNickname() %></b> wrote:</p>
<%
            }
%>
<blockquote><%= g.getContent() %></blockquote>
```

```
<%
        }
    }
    pm.close();
%>
```

```
    <form action="/sign" method="post">
      <div><textarea name="content" rows="3" cols="60"></textarea></
div>
      <div><input type="submit" value="Post Greeting" /></div>
    </form>
  </body>
</html>
```

Listing 12.14 contains a JDO-specific import statement and two import statements for the custom Java classes, as shown here:

```
<%@ page import="javax.jdo.PersistenceManager" %>
<%@ page import="guestbook.Greeting" %>
<%@ page import="guestbook.PMF" %>
```

Listing 12.14 contains a JSP scriptlet for calling the JDO-related functionality, which is shown here:

```
<%
    PersistenceManager pm = PMF.get().getPersistenceManager();
    String query = "select from " + Greeting.class.getName();
    List<Greeting> greetings = (List<Greeting>) pm.newQuery(query).
    execute();
%>
```

The remainder of Listing 12.14 contains conditional logic that determines the string that will be persisted, followed by a statement that releases the JDO manager:

```
    pm.close();
```

Now that you have the necessary Java classes, let's create a GAE application that uses JDO.

12.3.5.1 A JDO Eclipse Project

Create a new GAE project in Eclipse by following the menu path: **New > Other > Google > Web Application Project > Next**

Enter a name in the Project name input field and a package name in the Package input field, and click the Finish button. Let's use JDOSample1 for the project name and Greeting for the package name.

Launch your application by clicking on Run in Eclipse and then go to: http://localhost:8080

You will see the following output:

```
Hello App Engine!
Available Servlets:
JDOSample1
```

Click on the JDOSample1 link and you will see the following output:

```
Hello, world
```

Now that you have a deployable AppEngine application, add the three custom classes from the previous section to your project, and, if everything was done correctly, you can launch your JDO-based web application.

This concludes our discussion of JDO in GAE applications. Another important feature of GAE is its support for JPA, which is described in the next section.

■ 12.3.6   GAE JPA

This section shows you how to create an Eclipse-based web application that uses JPA. In addition to the project files that are generated by Eclipse, the JPA web application also requires the following two files:

• PMF.java
• Employee.java

The Java class PMF.java encapsulates the JPA-related functionality, and the Java class Employee.java is simply an example of a class that you want to keep using JPA.

Listing 12.15 displays the contents of EMF.java, which contains JPA-specific code that you will use in the GAE plug-in that you will create in the next section.

Listing 12.15 EMF.java

```
import javax.persistence.EntityManagerFactory;
import javax.persistence.Persistence;
```

```
public final class EMF {
    private static final EntityManagerFactory emfInstance =
        Persistence.createEntityManagerFactory("transactions-optional");

    private EMF() {}

    public static EntityManagerFactory get() {
        return emfInstance;
    }
}
```

Listing 12.15 contains two persistence-specific import statements that are used in the instantiation of a static EntityManagerFactory instance in the EMF Java class. As you can see, this Java class contains an empty constructor and a static get() method that returns the EntityManagerFactory object.

Listing 12.16 displays the contents of Employee.java, which uses JPA-based functionality.

Listing 12.16 Employee.java

```
import javax.persistence.Entity;

@Entity
public class Employee {
    private empName = "";

    public Employee(String empName)
    {
        this.empName = empName;
    }

    public void setEmpName(String empName);
    {
        this.empName = empName;
    }

    public String getEmpName();
    {
        return(this.empName);
    }
}
```

Listing 12.16 defines an Employee class that (for simplicity) only specifies an employee name. Note the use of the @Entity annotation, which is required for JPA-based persistence.

There is one more file that we need to discuss before creating the JPA web application—the XML-based configuration file `persistence.xml`, for JPA. This file is automatically generated for you by Eclipse, and its contents can be seen in Listing 12.17.

Listing 12.17 persistence.xml

```
<?xml version="1.0" encoding="UTF-8" ?>
<persistence xmlns="http://java.sun.com/xml/ns/persistence"
  xmlns:xsi="http://www.w3.org/2001/XMLSchema-instance"
  xsi:schemaLocation="http://java.sun.com/xml/ns/persistence
     http://java.sun.com/xml/ns/persistence/persistence_1_0.xsd"
version="1.0">

  <persistence-unit name="transactions-optional">
<provider>org.datanucleus.store.appengine.jpa.DatastorePersistence-
          Provider</provider>
    <properties>
      <property name="datanucleus.NontransactionalRead"
                      value="true"/>
      <property name="datanucleus.NontransactionalWrite"
                      value="true"/>
      <property name="datanucleus.ConnectionURL" value="appengine"/>
    </properties>
  </persistence-unit>

</persistence>
```

Listing 12.17 starts with an XML declaration, followed by the XML `<persistence>` element that contains definitions for XML namespaces. In addition, there is an XML `<persistence-unit>` element, an XML `<provider>` element, and an XML `<properties>` element with several child elements that are essentially name/value pairs for various properties.

Now that you have the necessary Java classes, let's create a GAE application that uses JPA.

12.3.6.1 A JPA Eclipse Project

Create a new GAE project in Eclipse, just as you've created other projects, and specify JPASample1 as the project's name. Next, add the Java classes EMF `.java` and `Employee.java` to this newly created project, and then run it to see the output displayed on the screen.

■ 12.4   JAVA/GAE CLOUDS AND ALTERNATIVES

Despite the benefits and advantages of using Java on GAE, there are alternatives available, including Stax, GigaSpaces®, and jClouds. This section provides details about Stax, along with cursory-level information about GigaSpaces and jClouds.

■ 12.4.1   Stax

Stax is an alternative to GAE that provides Java support in the cloud. Its home page is: http://www.stax.net

Stax is an open platform that supports Flex®, GWT, Hibernate, Spring, Struts, and Wicket (among others), along with scripting languages, such as ColdFusion®, JRuby, JSPs, Jython, and Scala.

Go to the Stax registration page to request a beta account. After you have received your email confirmation, log on to Stax with your username and password.

Details about Stax can be found here: http://www.stax.net/product

Note that Stax provides the Java Platform as a Service (PaaS), but as of yet it does not provide a plug-in for Eclipse.

12.4.1.1   *Create a Stax Application*

Download the Stax SDK for Windows or Linux using the `curl` command, as shown here:

```
curl -L http://stax-downloads.s3.amazonaws.com/sdk/stax-sdk-0.3.6-
dist.zip > stax-sdk.zip
```

Next, open a command shell and navigate to the `STAX_HOME` directory and make sure you set the `STAX_HOME` environment variable to the `STAX_HOME` directory.

For example, in Windows you would type something like this:

```
SET STAX_HOME=c:\stax-0.3.6
```

Next, create a new application called `MyFirstAPP` in the `\tmp` directory, which is a basic J2EE web application:

```
stax create -a MyApp --template basic \tmp
```

Options for creating Stax-based applications include `basic` (creates a WAR file), `gwt` (for GAE), `simple` (creates an EAR file), `struts` (Apache Struts), `wicket` (Apache Wicket), and `coldfusion` (Adobe Coldfusion 8).

The MyApp Stax application contains a WAR file called `webapp.war` in the MyApp/build subdirectory. The contents of the WAR file are shown here:

```
WEB-INF/classes/
WEB-INF/classes/example/
WEB-INF/lib/
WEB-INF/classes/example/HelloServlet.class
WEB-INF/lib/jstl-1.2.jar
WEB-INF/stax-web.xml
WEB-INF/web.xml
index.jsp
```

This application contains five files. First, there is a Java servlet called `HelloServlet.class` in the `WEB-INF/classes/examples` subdirectory. Next, there is a `jstl` JAR file in the `WEB-INF/lib` subdirectory. Third, there is a standard `web.xml` file, and then a Stax-specific file called `stax-web.xml` in the `WEB-INF` subdirectory. Finally, there is a JSP file `index.jsp` in the top-level directory.

Launch a local version of your application on port 8080:

```
staxd run –port 8080
```

Open a browser and navigate to the following URL:

```
http://localhost:8080
```

You will see the text string "This application is still under development." Click on the following link:

```
Click here to see a Servlet
```

You will see the following message:

```
"Hello Servlet World!"
```

12.4.1.2 *Deploy a Stax Application to the Stax Cloud*

In the previous section, you created a Stax application called MyApp in the $STAX_HOME/MyApp subdirectory. You can deploy this application to the Stax cloud by opening a command shell, ensuring that STAX_HOME is set correctly, and then typing the following two commands (for Windows):

```
cd $STAX_HOME/MyApp
stax deploy -a MyApp -m "first deploy"
```

The output will look similar to Listing 12.18.

Listing 12.18

```
running: C:\stax-sdk-0.3.6\scripts\deploy.groovy
init:
    [mkdir] Created dir: C:\downloads\stax-sdk-0.3.6\MyApp\webapp\
WEB-INF\classes
compile:
    [javac] Compiling 1 source file to C:\downloads\stax-sdk-0.3.6\
MyApp\webapp\WEB-INF\classes
dist:
    [mkdir] Created dir: C:\downloads\stax-sdk-0.3.6\MyApp\build
      [war] Building war: C:\downloads\stax-sdk-0.3.6\MyApp\build\
webapp.war
      [zip] Building zip: C:\downloads\stax-sdk-0.3.6\MyApp\build\
webapp-src.zip
stax-classpath:
    [echo] stax home: c:\downloads\stax-sdk-0.3.6
deploy:
    [input] skipping input as property stax.username has already
been set.
    [input] skipping input as property stax.password has already
been set.
uploading application to: http://api.stax.net/api
    [deploy] Deploying application: ocampesato/MyApp (environment: )
API call: http://api.stax.net/api/application.deployArchive
.......................uploaded 25%
.......................uploaded 50%
.......................uploaded 75%
.......................upload completed
deploying application to server(s)...
Aug 8, 2009 8:44:07 PM org.apache.commons.httpclient.HttpMethodBase
getResponseBody
WARNING: Going to buffer response body of large or unknown size.
Using getResponseBodyAsStream instead is recommended.
Aug 8, 2009 8:44:08 PM net.stax.api.StaxClientBase executeUpload
```

```
INFO: upload complete, response=<?xml version="1.0"
encoding="UTF-8"?>
<ApplicationDeployArchiveResponse>
  <id>ocampesato/myapp</id>
  <url>http://myapp.ocampesato.staxapps.net</url>
</ApplicationDeployArchiveResponse>
```

12.4.1.3 Monitoring Stax Applications

Every Stax application has an operations page in the AppConsole that displays information about the application. This information includes charts about memory use, such as peak memory and total memory consumption. In addition, the heap-related information can reveal the existence of potential memory leaks in an application.

■ 12.4.2 GigaSpaces

GigaSpaces is an alternative to GAE that provides Java support in the cloud. Its home page is: http://www.gigaspaces.com/mycloud

GigaSpaces provides a cloud computing framework called eXtreme Application Platform (XAP), where you can run production-level applications. GigaSpaces claims that it provides linear scalability of applications through the virtualized middleware layer of XAP.

You can create a free GigaSpaces account here:
http://www.gigaspaces.com/user/register

Next, download the latest version of XAP (currently, version 7.0) for Windows (32 -bit and 64 -bit), Linux, or Java 5 (or higher) from:
http://www.gigaspaces.com/LatestProductVersion

Uncompress the distribution in a convenient directory, and in the `bin` subdirectory you will find Windows BAT files and Linux shell scripts for managing a GigaSpaces instance, as shown here:

```
startJiniLUS.bat
startJiniLUS.sh
startJiniTX_Mahalo.bat
startJiniTX_Mahalo.sh
```

You can learn how to create a GigaSpaces cloud application here:
http://www.gigaspaces.com/wiki/display/XAP7/Step+Two+-+Creating
+the+Hello+World+Application

■ 12.4.3   jClouds

jClouds is a Java-based open source project that provides web-based interface to other cloud computing providers, including Amazon and RackSpace. Its home page is: http://code.google.com/p/jclouds/

jClouds products are compatible with GAE, and there are plans for developing new Java-based products that will provide access to Azure blobs and Rackspace cloud servers.

You can find sample Java source code that uses servlets, Guice™, and GAE here:

http://jclouds.googlecode.com/svn/trunk/aws/s3/samples/googleappengine/

■ 12.5   A JAVA APPENGINE INTEGRATED EXAMPLE

This section discusses an example of an application that combines the functionality of Java AppEngine, Dojo, JSON, GAE datastore, and JDO.

For this example, we chose to use JDO rather than JPA. JPA and JDO both simplify reading and writing to databases by letting you work with objects directly.

In general, JPA is the *de facto* standard for working in Java. JPA is much newer than JDO, but JDO never acquired a substantial following in Java. When working with the GAE datastore, there are many limitations. Due to these limitations JDO is well suited for GAE applications. At the time of this writing, JPA also had better documentation than JDO. In general, JPA is favored over JDO when working with the GAE datastore, and for regular J2EE development.

The purpose of this application is to let readers share comments about this book with each other. Since this example is for illustrative purposes, we spent minimal time on the User Interface (UI) design (see Figure 12.1). This example discusses both the front-end and the back-end code, whereas the example in

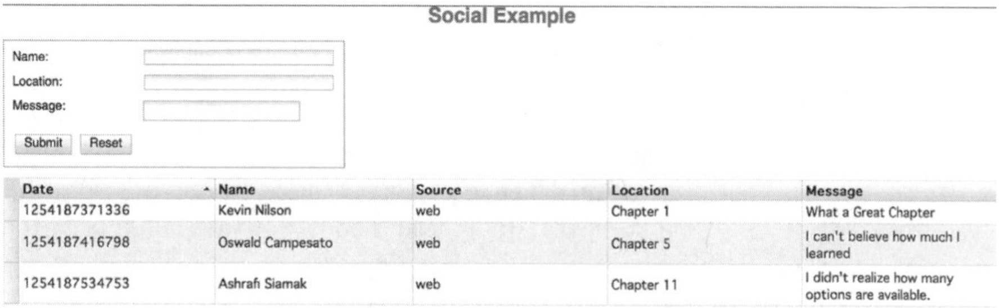

■ **FIGURE 12.1**
User Interface
Design

Date	Name	Source	Location	Message
1254187371336	Kevin Nilson	web	Chapter 1	What a Great Chapter
1254187416798	Oswald Campesato	web	Chapter 5	I can't believe how much I learned
1254187534753	Ashrafi Siamak	web	Chapter 11	I didn't realize how many options are available.

Chapter 8, only discussed the front-end code. We encourage you to add your comments about this book and see a working version of this example here: http://socialexample.appspot.com/

The first point to keep in mind is that OpenSocial Ajax requests must be proxied through the OpenSocial Server. In this example, which is a stand-alone web application, you can call your web server directly from Ajax.

Listing 12.19 shows the contents of the HTML page for this code sample:

Listing 12.19

```
<!DOCTYPE HTML PUBLIC "-//W3C//DTD HTML 4.01 Transitional//EN">
<html>
  <head>
    <meta http-equiv="content-type" content="text/html;
charset=UTF-8">
    <link type="text/css" rel="stylesheet" href="SocialNetworking
.css">
    <title>Social Example</title>
        <link rel="stylesheet" type="text/css"
href="http://ajax.googleapis.com/ajax/libs/dojo/1.3/dijit/themes/
tundra/tundra.css">
        <style type="text/css">
            body, html { font-family:helvetica,arial,sans-serif;
font-size:90%; }
        </style>
        <script type="text/javascript"
                src="http://ajax.googleapis.com/ajax/libs/dojo/1.3/
dojo/dojo.xd.js"
                djConfig="parseOnLoad: true"></script>

        <script type="text/javascript" src="socialnetworkingexample
.js"></script>

    <style type="text/css">
    @import "http://ajax.googleapis.com/ajax/libs/dojo/1.3/dojox/
grid/resources/Grid.css";
    @import "http://ajax.googleapis.com/ajax/libs/dojo/1.3/dojox/
grid/resources/tundraGrid.css";
    .dojoxGrid table
        { margin: 0; } html, body { width: 100%; height: 100%;margin:
0; }
</style>
```

```
    </head>
      <body>
        <h1>Social Example</h1>

        <body class="tundra ">
            <div dojoType="dijit.form.Form" id="myForm"
                jsId="myForm" encType="multipart/form-data" action=""
                method="">
              <table style="border: 1px solid #9f9f9f;" cellspacing="10">
                <tr>
                    <td>
                        <label for="name">
                            Name:
                    </td>
                    <td>
                        <input type="text" id="name" name="name"
                         required="true"
                                dojoType="dijit.form
                                .ValidationTextBox"
                        />
                    </td>
                </tr>
                <tr>
                    <td>
                        <label for="location">
                            Location:
                    </td>
                    <td>
                        <input type="text" name="location"
                         required="true"
                                dojoType="dijit.form
                                .ValidationTextBox"
                        />
                    </td>
                </tr>
                <tr>
                    <td valign="top">
                        <label for="message">
                            Message:
                    </td>
                    <td>
                            <textarea id="message" name="message"
                                    dojoType="dijit.form.Textarea"
style="width:200px;">
```

```
                                </textarea>
                </td>
                        </tr>
                        <tr colspan="2" align="center">
                                <td>
                                        <button dojoType="dijit.form.Button"
type="submit"
                                                name="submitButtonTwo"
value="Submit">
                                                Submit
                                        </button>
                        <button dojoType="dijit.form.Button" type="reset">
                                Reset
                        </button>
                                        </td>
                        </tr>
                </table>
        <input type="hidden" name="bookId" value="1"/>
        <input type="hidden" name="account" value=""/>
        <input type="hidden" name="source" value="web"/>
        </div>
        <div id="gridholder"></div>
    </body>
</html>
```

The first part of Listing 12.19 contains a simple data entry form with input fields for the name, location, and message that users want to insert into the back-end database. Next, a grid is provided that displays the data (if any) that has been entered during previous sessions.

Note that this example uses the Dojo toolkit, and that the data entry form does not specify an action because we will send data to the server using Ajax.

The section in Listing 12.19 containing JavaScript code is shown here:

```
var store;
var grid;
dojo.require("dijit.form.Form");
dojo.require("dijit.form.Button");
dojo.require("dijit.form.ValidationTextBox");
dojo.require("dijit.form.Textarea");
dojo.require("dojox.grid.DataGrid");
dojo.require("dojo.data.ItemFileWriteStore");
```

```
function reloadGrid(){
    grid.setStore(new dojo.data.ItemFileWriteStore({
        url: 'listbookmessages'
    }));
}

function addBookMessage(){
    var xhrArgs = {
        url: "addbookmessage",
        form: "myForm",
        handleAs: "text",
        load: function(data){

            reloadGrid();

        },
        error: function(error){
            alert("error");
        }
    }

    var deferred = dojo.xhrPost(xhrArgs);
}

dojo.addOnLoad(function() {

    store = new dojo.data.ItemFileWriteStore({
        url: 'listbookmessages'
    });

    var myForm = dijit.byId("myForm");
    dojo.connect(myForm, "onSubmit", function(e) {
        e.preventDefault();
        if (myForm.isValid()) {

            if(dojo.trim(dojo.byId("message").value)==""){
                alert("Please add a message");
            }else{

                addBookMessage();

            }
        }else{
            alert("Form not Valid");
        }
    );
```

```
            dojo.byId("name").focus();

            // set the layout structure:
            // omitted for brevity
            }];

            // create a new grid:
            grid = new dojox.grid.DataGrid({
                query: {
                    date: '*'
                },
                store: store,
                clientSort: true,
                rowSelector: '20px',
                structure: layout
            },dojo.byId("gridholder"));

            grid.startup();
});
```

The JavaScript in this example is straightforward, which starts with several dojo.require statements for loading the required JavaScript, followed by the functionality that is called during the onLoad event.

The store for the grid is defined to use the URL listbookmessages to receive its data in the grid. Next, we configure the form Submit button to call addBookMessage when users click on it. If the form is invalid, users will be alerted to update the input fields in the form.

Next, the layout of the grid is defined, and for simplicity, each col uses auto for the width. Finally, the JavaScript creates the grid and calls grid startup.

The format of the JSON used by the grid is reproduced here:

```
{"identifier":"date","label":"date",

"items":[{"name":"Ashrafi Siamak","location":"Chapter
11","message":"I didn't realize how many options are available.","id
":7003,"date":1254187534753,"source":"web","bookId":1,"account":""},

{"name":"Oswald Campesato","location":"Chapter 5","message":"I can't
believe how much I learned","id":7002,"date":1254187416798,"source":
"web","bookId":1,"account":""},

{"name":"Kevin Nilson","location":"Chapter 1","message":"What a
Great Chapter","id":7001,"date":1254187371336,"source":"web","bookId
":1,"account":""}]]}
```

The identifier is similar to a primary key and it is used to look up rows; in this example, the items are the rows of the table.

Listing 12.20 displays a portion of the XML-based configuration file web.xml, which contains the definitions of two Java servlets (and their associated mappings) used in this application.

Listing 12.20

```
<?xml version="1.0" encoding="UTF-8"?>
<!DOCTYPE web-app
    PUBLIC "-//Sun Microsystems, Inc.//DTD Web Application 2.3//EN"
    "http://java.sun.com/dtd/web-app_2_3.dtd">

<web-app>
  <servlet>
    <servlet-name>dataservlet</servlet-name>
    <servlet-class>
      com.javaclimber.socialnetworking.server.AddBookMessageServlet
    </servlet-class>
  </servlet>

  <servlet>
    <servlet-name>listbookmessagesservlet</servlet-name>
    <servlet-class>
      com.javaclimber.socialnetworking.server.ListBookMessagesServlet
    </servlet-class>
  </servlet>

  <servlet-mapping>
    <servlet-name>dataservlet</servlet-name>
    <url-pattern>/addbookmessage</url-pattern>
  </servlet-mapping>

  <servlet-mapping>
    <servlet-name>listbookmessagesservlet</servlet-name>
    <url-pattern>/listbookmessages</url-pattern>
  </servlet-mapping>

  <welcome-file-list>
    <welcome-file>Web.jsp</welcome-file>
  </welcome-file-list>
</web-app>
```

This application also contains a mandatory configuration file jdoconfig .xml that is located in the war/WEB-INF/classes/META-INF/ subdirectory.

You can check the contents of jdoconfkoolk here:
http://code.google.com/appengine/docs/java/datastore/usingjdo.html

Google suggests making a singleton class for EntityManagerFactory, because you can save time by reusing the same instance.

Listing 12.21 displays the contents of the Java class EMF.java, which uses the singleton pattern to return an instance of an Entity Manager.

Listing 12.21 EMF.java

```java
package com.javaclimber.socialnetworking.server;

import javax.persistence.EntityManagerFactory;
import javax.persistence.Persistence;

public final class EMF {
    private static final EntityManagerFactory emfInstance =
        Persistence.createEntityManagerFactory("transactions-optional");

    private EMF() {}

    public static EntityManagerFactory get() {
        return emfInstance;
    }
}
```

Listing 12.22 shows the contents of the Java class BookMessage.java, which lets you store data in the datastore.

Listing 12.22 BookMessage.java

```java
package com.javaclimber.socialnetworking.server;

import java.io.Serializable;
import java.util.Date;

import javax.persistence.Basic;
import javax.persistence.Entity;
import javax.persistence.GeneratedValue;
import javax.persistence.GenerationType;
import javax.persistence.Id;

@Entity
public class BookMessage implements Serializable {

    @Id
    @GeneratedValue(strategy = GenerationType.IDENTITY)
    private Long id;
```

```java
@Basic
private long bookId;

@Basic
private Date date;

@Basic
private String name;

@Basic
private String source;

@Basic
private String account;

@Basic
private String location;

@Basic
private String message;

public Long getId() {
   return id;
}

public void setId(Long id) {
   this.id = id;
}

public long getBookId() {
   return bookId;
}

public void setBookId(long bookId) {
   this.bookId = bookId;
}

public Date getDate() {
   return date;
}

public void setDate(Date date) {
   this.date = date;
}

public String getLocation() {
   return location;
}
```

```java
    public void setLocation(String location) {
        this.location = location;
    }

    public String getMessage() {
        return message;
    }

    public void setMessage(String message) {
        this.message = message;
    }

    public String getName() {
        return name;
    }

    public void setName(String name) {
        this.name = name;
    }

    public String getSource() {
        return source;
    }

    public void setSource(String source) {
        this.source = source;
    }

    public String getAccount() {
        return account;
    }

    public void setAccount(String account) {
        this.account = account;
    }
}
```

In Listing 12.22, the Java class BookMessage implements the interface Serializable so that instances of this class can be persisted. The id is marked as an identity. In addition, the class is marked with the annotation Entity and all fields, except the id, are marked with the annotation Basic.

Earlier in this section, you saw the contents of the configuration file web.xml, which contains two Java servlets called AddBookMessageServlet and ListBookMessagesServlet.

Listing 12.23 shows the contents of the Java servlet AddbookMessage-Servet, which illustrates how to store messages in the datastore.

Listing 12.23 AddBookMessageServlet.java

```
package com.javaclimber.socialnetworking.server;

import java.io.IOException;
import java.io.PrintWriter;
import java.io.StringWriter;
import java.util.Date;
import java.util.List;

import javax.persistence.EntityManager;
import javax.servlet.ServletException;
import javax.servlet.http.HttpServlet;
import javax.servlet.http.HttpServletRequest;
import javax.servlet.http.HttpServletResponse;

public class AddBookMessageServlet extends HttpServlet {
    @Override
    protected void doPost(HttpServletRequest req, HttpServlet
                          Response resp)
        throws ServletException, IOException {
            EntityManager em = null;
    try {
    em = EMF.get().createEntityManager();

        BookMessage bm = new BookMessage();
        bm.setDate(new Date());
        String bid=req.getParameter("bookId");
        if(bid!=null)
            bm.setBookId(Integer.parseInt(bid));
        bm.setName(req.getParameter("name"));
        bm.setLocation(req.getParameter("location"));
        bm.setMessage(req.getParameter("message"));
        bm.setSource(req.getParameter("source"));
        bm.setAccount(req.getParameter("account"));

        em.persist(bm);

    } finally {
        if (em != null)
            em.close();
    }
```

```
        }

        @Override
        protected void doGet(HttpServletRequest req, HttpServlet-
                             Response resp)
            throws ServletException, IOException {
          doPost(req, resp);
        }
}
```

The code in Listing 12.23 for the Java servlet AddBookMessageServlet is straightforward: first we get an EntityManager, then we fill the BookMessage POJO, and then we persist the BookMessage.

Next, Listing 12.24 displays the contents of the Java servlet ListBookMessagesServlet, which illustrates how to return JSON data (containing the message in the datastore) used to populate the grid.

Listing 12.24 ListBookMessagesServlet.java

```java
package com.javaclimber.socialnetworking.server;

import java.io.IOException;
import java.io.PrintWriter;
import java.io.StringWriter;
import java.util.ArrayList;
import java.util.Collection;
import java.util.Collections;
import java.util.List;

import javax.persistence.EntityManager;
import javax.servlet.ServletException;
import javax.servlet.http.HttpServlet;
import javax.servlet.http.HttpServletRequest;
import javax.servlet.http.HttpServletResponse;

import org.codehaus.jackson.map.ObjectMapper;

public class ListBookMessagesServlet extends HttpServlet {
    @Override
    protected void doGet(HttpServletRequest req, HttpServlet-
                         Response resp)
        throws ServletException, IOException {

      EntityManager em = null;
```

```
        PrintWriter out = resp.getWriter();

        try {
            em = EMF.get().createEntityManager();

            List<BookMessage> messageList = em.createQuery(
                "SELECT bm FROM BookMessage bm").getResultList();
            List<BookMessage> copy=new ArrayList<BookMessage>();
            copy.addAll(messageList);
            Collections.reverse(copy);

            Store store=new Store();
            store.setIdentifier("date");
            store.setLabel("date");
            store.setItems(copy);

            ObjectMapper mapper = new ObjectMapper();
            StringWriter w=new StringWriter();
            mapper.writeValue(w, store);
            out.println(w.getBuffer().toString());
        } finally {
            if (em != null)
                em.close();

            if (out != null)
                out.close();
        }
    }
}
```

The code in Listing 12.24 for the Java servlet ListBookMessagesServlet
is also straightforward: first we instantiate an EntityManager and then we
query for the BookMessages in the datastore.

Next, we convert the POJO data to JSON data and print it. In addition,
note that the EntityManager is closed in a finally block, which guarantees
that close will be called, even if an exception is thrown.

■ **12.6 SUMMARY**

This chapter introduced you to Java–XML binding tools, which generate
Java classes that provide a layer of abstraction on top of XML documents,
thereby simplifying XML document management. You also learned about

Java and GAE, and how to write a simple "Hello, World" Java program and deploy it to GAE. Next, you learned how to write a JEE web application using Java servlets on GAE. Finally, you saw a comprehensive project that illustrated how to combine Java AppEngine with Dojo, JSON, the GAE datastore, and JDO.

The next chapter discusses various aspects of Semantic Technology, including open source and commercial tools, and companies that have created products for Semantic Technology.

## CHAPTER 13

Semantic Technology

In This Chapter:

- The Semantic Web and Semantic Technology
- OpenCalais
- Expert System
- Truevert
- Semantic Technology from Commercial Vendors
- Other Projects, Tools, and Products
- Comments about Web 3.0
- Industry Perspective

This chapter discusses various aspects of Semantic Technology, which has become increasingly important in many vertical markets. The combination of Web 2.0 and Semantic Technology will undoubtedly spur the development of increasingly sophisticated products that will provide meaningful and useful information. In fact, some browser plug-ins (such as Juice™) and search engines (such as Swoogle) have already incorporated some of features of Semantic Technology.

In this chapter, we'll start with a short introduction to the Semantic Web, followed by a discussion of Resource Description Framework (RDF), RDFS, and Web Ontology Language (OWL). Next, we'll discuss open source RDF tools, such as Jena and Sesame.

Then we'll look at OpenCalais, which is a Semantic Technology product that can be combined with other tools, such as the Yahoo BOSS search tool. After that, we'll go over some Semantic Technology tools that are available from other companies, including Cogito from ExpertSystem and Truevert.

Next, we'll examine some of the Semantic Technology products and services from major vendors, including IBM, Oracle, Yahoo, and Microsoft. Finally, we'll touch on Web 3.0 and some of the tools that claim to provide Web 3.0 functionality.

■ 13.1 THE SEMANTIC WEB AND SEMANTIC TECHNOLOGY

The Web is a phenomenal place to find documents and information, but the lack of semantics also increases the time and effort to retrieve meaningful information quickly and easily. In general, you get information by performing a search in a search engine, scanning through the links in the result set, and then navigating to the links that appear to be useful.

Although there are many queries that return links that are exactly what you need, there are also many queries that don't. In the latter case, you have several alternatives: change your query terms and hope that you will find more relevant links, perform the same search in a different search engine, or use a "brute force" approach whereby you navigate to various links in the hope that you will find something useful. This last approach is clearly time-consuming and tedious, which has motivated people to create repositories where people can contribute domain-specific documents, thereby promoting document reuse and enabling people to find useful documents quickly.

According to Tim Berners-Lee, who is credited with inventing the Internet, the Semantic Web is actually quite simple, because it's just about relationships among entities. In an article that appeared in *Scientific American* in 2001, Tim Berners-Lee describes how a "semantic web agent" searches the Internet to find a medical specialist to treat the mother of an imaginary girl. This view of Web 3.0 is reactive: a problem or task arises, and an agent finds one or more solutions to the problem.

Tim Berners-Lee believes that the mechanics of a Semantic Web agent require a reannotation of the Web in which suitable metadata is added to web pages. Proponents of RDF believe that RDF and OWL will provide the mechanism by which web pages can be annotated with the necessary metadata for the Semantic Web.

In simplified terms, Semantic Technology attempts to make inferences about blocks of text in a manner that is meaningful and useful. In other words, Semantic Technology tries to make the same sort of inferences that you make when you read a text-based document. Semantic Technology is relevant for processing large quantities of text, which suggests that Semantic Technology will become ubiquitous in our lifetime.

However, please remember that Semantic Technology is very complex. Therefore, this chapter only provides an overview of some of the products and tools that are available, many of which require a significant level of technical expertise and knowledge to use effectively.

When you have finished reading this chapter, you will be in a better position to make an informed decision about what you want to learn. Then, you can decide for yourself how to devise a realistic plan to achieve your learning objectives.

■ 13.1.1 The Semantic Technology Landscape

In general terms, semantics involve the study and interpretation of a body of text (or speech) to determine its meaning. Artificial Intelligence (AI) and computational linguistics are two disciplines that began in the mid-twentieth century that address facets of semantics.

A simple and convenient "definition" of AI is based on Alan Turing's test for sentience: if a human who is interacting with a system cannot determine if the response is from a software program or from a human, then that software program qualifies as AI.

AI gained popularity around the middle of the twentieth century and has been mythologized by movies about talking computers or androids that are capable of superior reasoning, astonishing calculations, and typically lack human emotions.

One branch of AI is Knowledge Representation (KR), which pertains to the nature of knowledge and systems that contain facts about the world. In general, KR systems also provide some type of semantics that support deductive reasoning. Various types of KR-related systems were devised, including expert systems and neural networks that could "learn" from the addition of new facts.

During the 1970s and 1980s, Prolog® and KL-ONE became popular programming languages for expert systems, and during the 1990s the Dublin Core® (from which we get the XML namespace prefix dc) was established. Dublin Core deals with semantics and metadata, which are core aspects of Semantic Technology.

Computational linguistics originally dealt with the translation of text between different languages based on a grammar for each language. Human languages involve syntax (correct sentence structure), vocabulary, and word forms, and grammars for languages tend to be very sophisticated and can easily involve thousands of rules for determining the meaning of a sentence.

Two subfields of computational linguistics address speech recognition and speech synthesis by means of software. Both of these fields have made significant strides over the past decade, and we encounter them almost every day. For example, automated telephone support systems for providing information and routing are commonplace, and in the next several years vehicles equipped with speech recognition will become commonplace. The accuracy of speech recognition systems continues to improve and the cost continues to decrease, which suggests that such systems will become commonplace in many aspects of our daily lives.

Semantic Technology infers meaning from a corpus and uses metadata to represent the derived meaning. By contrast, Information Technology (IT) relies on "hard-wired" meaning, and therefore does not attempt to derive meaning. Thus, Semantic Technology addresses complex problems that are outside the realm of traditional IT.

Recently, there has been discussion about cloud computing and the Semantic Web, and one discussion is here:
http://cloudofdata.com/2009/05/the-semantic-web-gang-live-in-san-jose/

Semantic Technology tools and products use different strategies and techniques, some of which are listed here:

- RDF-based tools
- dictionaries/thesauri
- rules-based engines
- probability/statistics
- microformats
- bottom-up versus top-down

Some Semantic Technology tools use a combination of these techniques. For example, Calais uses RDF in conjunction with a dictionary or a thesaurus. Calais also uses a rules engine that contains thousands of rules for parsing sentences. Truevert differs from most other companies because Truevert uses a statistical approach to perform an analysis of documents and then makes semantic inferences about their content.

Microformats are simple systems for representing information. For example, RDFa is a microformat that uses HTML tags to embed metadata in web pages; hCard provides information; hCalendar provides information about events. Microformats are used by many companies and mash-up tools, such as the IBM Mashup Center (discussed in Chapter 9).

The "bottom-up" approach typically uses RDF-based technology to annotate the content of websites, whereas the "top-down" approach uses existing information to infer meaning.

Another area of development pertains to Semantic Web Services (SWS), which are web services that provide semantic information. SWSs involve a Web Service Modeling Ontology (WSMO), and you can find more information about its current status here:

http://cms-wg.sti2.org/home/

■ 13.1.2 Taxonomies, Ontologies, and Folksonomies

Classification systems have been available for centuries, because they let people manage information more efficiently. Whenever we organize entities (such as physical objects or ideas) or analyze events (such as natural events), we invariably define some type of structure that helps us discern meaning about those entities and events. In some cases, we create models that help us explain and predict what will happen (and also when and why things happen). Thus, structure is a key aspect of classification because structure provides some degree of order, harmony, and consistency to events that might otherwise seem random (or even chaotic).

One very simple example of a structured system is the system for classifying books in a public library. This system lets you search among a vast number of books so that you can locate the specific book you want. An even simpler example of a classification system is the alphabetized list of names in a phone book.

In general terms, classification systems are either top-down in design (usually by a set of domain experts) or they are bottom-up (and they might also have a collaborative design). However, the type of classification system that is most useful depends on the characteristics of the "problem domain" that you are trying to classify. For example, public libraries obviously use a different classification system from websites that let people create tags for topics and events that are discussed on a website.

A *taxonomy* is a hierarchical system for defining entities ("things") and the relationships among those entities. For example, the Dewey Decimal System for classifying books in public libraries is a taxonomy. In general, taxonomies tend to change slowly over time, and usually there are "domain experts" who decide when and how changes will be made to the existing taxonomy.

An informal definition of an *ontology* is a representation of the entities, and the relationships between those entities, of a system or problem domain. An ontology can be created for virtually any problem domain, and some tools (such as Freebase™) give people the freedom to define an ontology for almost anything.

An informal definition of a *folksonomy* is an ontology whose structure can be edited by end users. Consider the set of tags and categories for a website: a site administrator might create an initial set that can be modified by users who add their own tags and categories to the website. Unlike a taxonomy, a folksonomy is often available in an environment in which end users are empowered to make changes whenever it's appropriate to do so.

In general, products and tools that are based on Semantic Technology are concerned with the following three operations:

• storing information (facts) about entities
• retrieving information about entities ("show me the authors of this book")
• making inferences or drawing conclusions based on the stored facts

The ability to make correct inferences about a set of facts is vitally important, especially when the data sets are so large that it is impractical to check them manually. Many fields can benefit from tools and products that leverage semantic technology, including:

• Advertising (analysis of user behavior)
• Financial (XBRL-based reporting)
• Government (intelligence operations)
• Health care
• Social networks
• Governance and compliance
• Life sciences research

13.1.2.1 *Sample Ontologies and Design Patterns*

Now that you have a rudimentary understanding of ontologies, the next step is to design an ontology that models your problem domain. Fortunately,

there are online repositories of ontologies that can provide you with ideas for your own ontology. You can find one of them here:
http://protege.cim3.net/cgi-bin/wiki.pl?ProtegeOntologiesLibrary

If you are interested in learning about the various types of ontology patterns, you can download a set of ontology design patterns from:
http://sourceforge.net/projects/odps/

You can check the appendices and search the Internet for additional links regarding ontologies and other ontology design patterns.

■ 13.1.3   RDF, RDFS, OWL, DARPA Agent Markup Language (DAML), and SPARQL

Earlier in this chapter, we covered some of the classification systems that are available for categorizing entities. In this section, you will learn about some of the technologies that are available for representing and managing semantic information.

Many Semantic Technology products (including OpenCalais) make extensive use of RDF, so a solid understanding of RDF will help you in understanding RDF-based technologies. Incidentally, OpenCalais can generate response data using JSON and RDF, which means that you can use Open-Calais without extensive knowledge of RDF.

The Semantic Web shifts away from a human- and document-oriented viewpoint toward a machine- and semantic-oriented view of the Web. The Semantic Web also contains metadata about entities (such as documents) so that logically related entities can be grouped together and located quickly and easily.

Another point to keep in mind is that RDF-based technologies use various XML-based namespaces (which were discussed briefly in Chapter 3, JSON and XML). The use of namespaces is important because they let processors interpret the content of RDF/XML documents in an unambiguous manner.

Finally, keep in mind that XML is a useful technology for Semantic Technology because XML is very good for storing data. However, XML does not provide semantics about the data, which led to the creation of XML-based vocabularies, such as RDF, that can represent semantics.

13.1.3.1 RDF

RDF is a World Wide Web Consortium (W3C) recommendation that is part of the Semantic Web activity of the W3C. RDF-based information is represented via XML, and it is designed to be processed by computers rather than people. RDF is based on the notion that entities and resources have properties that can be expressed via statements, and a statement can be represented using a "triple" of information that specifies a subject, a predicate, and an object.

An RDF triple is often called an RDF triplet or an RDF statement. Note that a resource can be a person, a property, or an abstract entity, so virtually anything can be expressed using RDF-based syntax. RDF is well-suited for expressing statements about resources, and RDF-based statements that describe resources can also be represented by a directed and labeled graph of nodes.

RDF is expressed via an XML-based syntax that involves namespaces (XML and namespaces were discussed in Chapter 3), which is called RDF/XML. An RDF document contains RDF triplets that represent information about entities and the relationship between those entities.

The purpose of a Uniform Resource Identifier (URI) is to uniquely identify an entity or a concept, which is why URIs are used in RDF triplets. The Semantic Web consists of many triplets, and because the subject of one triplet is the object of another triplet, the Semantic Web can be represented as a gigantic graph. The nodes in this graph are the triplets, and the line or arc between any pair of nodes indicates that the two nodes are related in some manner. Since each URI uniquely identifies one node, we can specify a relationship between two nodes by referring to their corresponding URIs.

Some commonly used RDF attributes are: `rdf:RDF`, `rdf:about`, `rdf:description`, `rdf:resource`, `rdf:datatype`, and `rdf:ID`. Note that `rdf:RDF` and `rdf:description` are bona fide XML elements in RDF/XML documents.

When you want to represent a resource as an RDF triplet in an RDF/XML document, the `rdf:RDF` attribute is the root element of the RDF/XML document. The `rdf:about` attribute specifies the resource you want to define. The rdf:description attribute (which is also an XML element) "encapsulates" the properties of a specific resource. In addition, the rdf:about attribute is also an attribute of rdf:description.

The `rdf:resource` attribute defines a resource that identifies a property in an RDF triplet. Finally, the `rdf:datatype` and `rdf:ID` attributes are used for defining the datatype and the ID of a resource. Although there are other RDF-based attributes, these are probably the most frequently used.

13.1.3.1.1 EARLY PREDECESSORS OF RDF

The LISt Processing (LISP) language was created during the 1950s and was well-suited for representing a collection of facts about resources. Such collections were early forms of "expert systems," which consisted of a set of facts and a set of rules that could be used for making inferences.

Two useful techniques for making inferences are called "forward chaining" and "backward chaining." These techniques are used in LISP (and other languages) and RDF-based systems that provide rule engines. For example, Jena (described later in this chapter) is a Java-based open source RDF tool that provides a rule engine that supports both forward-chaining and backward-chaining.

The Prolog language is a rule-based language that gained popularity in the 1980s and was the language that formed the foundation for the Fifth Generation project in Japan. Prolog provides a set of built-in functions that makes it easier to write compact code for making inferences from a set of facts.

Although LISP and Prolog are still in use, you can use RDF to store information about resources via RDF-based triplets that are defined in an XML/RDF document, which can be stored on a filesystem or in a database. There are also many RDF-based open source tools (and commercial tools) available for retrieving information and making inferences.

13.1.3.1.2 USING PLAIN XML TO REPRESENT STATEMENTS

As a simple example, look at the following four statements about this book:

1) "**This Web 2.0 book** has an **author** whose name is **Oswald**."
2) "**This Web 2.0 book** has an **author** whose name is **Kevin**."
3) "The number of **chapters** in **this Web 2.0 book** is **18**."
4) "The **page count** for **this Web 2.0 book** is **400**."

Listing 13.1 contains one XML representation of preceding the statements.

Listing 13.1 authors.xml

```
<xml version="1.0">
<web20book>
<authors>
  <author>Oswald</author>
```

```
<author>Kevin</author>
</authors>
<chapters>17</chapter>
<pagecount>400</pagecount>
</web20book>
```

The structure of `authors.xml` in Listing 13.1 is clear, and it captures the essence of the statements in the list. Although you can also use JSON to represent the statements in the list, a JSON-based representation will not help us make the transition from "just XML" to RDF.

You already have an intuitive understanding of the type of information you expect to find in `authors.xml`, such as more details about the individual chapters, their title, their content, and so forth.

However, suppose you are given the following statements:

5) "**Kevin** has a **son** whose name is **Andy**."

6) "**Oswald studies Japanese** at school."

Although both of these statements are factual, neither of them is directly related to the information you would expect to find in the XML document `authors.xml`. In fact, statements 5 and 6 are "orthogonal" to the data and metadata about `authors.xml` in the sense that the personal information about Kevin and Oswald is not related to the book-specific information that is specified in `authors.xml`.

Although you can use plain XML to represent the information in Listing 13.1, there are limitations to this approach that are intrinsic to XML. For example, there is no provision in XML to perform any sort of validation between two XML elements that are collocated in the same XML document.

Schematron is an open source project that provides an enhancement to XSL stylesheets to provide validation between elements. Schematron is an ISO standard that supports XSLT 1.0 and 2.0. Its home page is:

http://www.schematron.com/

However, Schematron is designed for adding business-related logic to an XSL stylesheet so that you can enforce constraints between elements in an XML document. Schematron does not support functionality that lets you traverse the contents of an RDF/XML document to make inferences about the entities in it. Thus, Schematron is a very useful tool, but it does not overcome the inherent limitations of plain XML.

13.1.3.1.3 USING RDBMS TABLES TO REPRESENT STATEMENTS

How would you represent the information in `authors.xml` and statements 5 and 6 in a meaningful fashion in the RDBMS world? One solution is to create two tables: a `WEB20BOOK` table containing the information in `authors.xml`, and a `AUTHOR_DETAILS` table contains the personal information about the authors. You would also specify the foreign key that links these two tables together.

Now consider what happens if we add the following additional facts:

7) "**Oswald likes** to eat **pizza**."
8) "**Kevin likes** to eat **dessert**."

Once again, we can create a third RDBMS table and specify the appropriate foreign keys so that the information in statements 7 and 8 can be included in an RDBMS schema.

However, you can see the limitations of using a relational-based approach for representing information about entities: the database schema must be continually updated to accommodate new facts, which quickly becomes cumbersome and complex.

Consider what would happen if you attempted to represent all of the objects in your house, and all the interrelationships that exist between any pair of objects. If you are undaunted, consider the scenario where you want to model everything that is available on the Web using an RDBMS schema. Clearly, this task is extremely complex, especially when you limit yourself to the traditional functionality that is provided by relational databases (if you think this is an easy task, create an RDBMS-based solution for this task).

RDF provides an alternative to RDBMS and "pure" XML that lets you represent entities (and their properties) and the relationships between entities. RDF represents information in a manner that is meaningful, manageable, and flexible so that it can support the information in authors.xml and other "orthogonal" information. Now that you understand the rationale for using RDF, let's take a look at how to represent statements via RDF, which is the topic of the next section.

13.1.3.1.4 HOW TO WRITE VALID RDF TRIPLETS

Earlier in this chapter, you learned that an RDF triplet specifies three things: a subject, a predicate, and an object. Each RDF triplet is represented as an XML element in an RDF/XML document. The confusing aspect about

RDF statements is that a URI is used to uniquely identify a resource, which is expressed as an XML element in an XML/RDF document. The XML-based representation of a resource also contains child XML elements that represent properties and associated property values (essentially name/value pairs) about that resource.

Consider the first statement in the list from earlier, which is reproduced here:

"**This Web 2.0 book** has an **author** whose name is **Oswald**."

An XML element that represents the information in this statement is shown here:

```
<rdf>
  <Description about="web20book">
    <author>Oswald</author>
  </Description>
</rdf>
```

As you can see, the preceding XML element contains the information that is described in the original statement. We can make this XML element a valid RDF triplet by adding namespaces and qualifying the elements with the appropriate namespaces, as shown in Listing 13.2.

Listing 13.2

```
<rdf:RDF
    xmlns:rdf="http://www.w3.org/1999/02/22-rdf-syntax-ns#"
    xmlns:auth="http://purl.org/author/1.0">
  <rdf:Description rdf:about="web20book">
    <auth:author>Oswald</auth:author>
  </rdf:Description>
</rdf:RDF>
```

You can verify that the RDF triplet in Listing 13.2 is a valid RDF triplet by pasting the contents of Listing 13.2 to:

http://www.xul.fr/en-xml-rdf.html

The other three statements from the list can be expressed as RDF triplets in a similar fashion.

13.1.3.1.5 SQL Versus RDF

Here are two questions to consider: How does RDF compare to other systems that store information, such as traditional database systems?

How do you decide when to use a relational database versus an RDF-based system (and vice versa)?

By way of illustration, suppose you want to describe the skills, experience, and tasks of all of the employees at a large company. Generally, this information is stored in an RDBMS, which consists of a set of tables that hold employee data, personal data, and Human Resources (HR)-sensitive data. RDBMSes support SQL, which can be used to generate a variety of reports that contain employee-specific information.

However, traditional RDBMSes do not provide built-in support for making inferences about the data. If you use SQL-based queries to make deductive-like inferences, those SQL queries can quickly become complex and difficult to enhance. For example, suppose you wanted to find the employees (if any exist) who have worked on at least three different projects over the past five years, where each project lasted at least three months and was completed on time.

Assuming that the relevant information is stored in the appropriate tables, imagine the effort involved in writing a SQL-based report to extract that information. Before you write such a report, consider the following:

- How many SQL statements are required?
- How do you verify that the results are correct?

The solution for this task is both nontrivial and far from obvious, even for people who have extensive experience in writing complex SQL statements. Don't forget that you also need to know the structure of the tables that store the data, and the relationships between the tables (such as the foreign keys). Moreover, when you consider that it's quite easy to devise other scenarios that are even more complex than the first query, you might want to consider using an RDF-based system. Note that some RDBMSes (such as Oracle) provides some RDF-based support, so it is worth your while to assess whether or not these systems have sufficient support for RDF to meet your requirements.

Although the underlying concept for RDF is straightforward, the use of RDF triples in an XML document can be confusing if you are unaccustomed to this style of representing information about resources, so it's a good idea to look at a lot of examples of RDF triplets to become more comfortable with RDF-based representation.

13.1.3.1.6   A Sample RDF Document

Listing 13.3 displays the contents of rdf1.xml, which is an example of a simple RDF document.

Listing 13.3 rdf1.xml

```
<?xml version="1.0"?>

<rdf:RDF
xmlns:rdf="http://www.w3.org/1999/02/22-rdf-syntax-ns#"
xmlns:book="http://www.oac.books/book#">

<rdf:Description
rdf:about="http://www.oac.books/book/Java
Graphics">
<book:author>Oswald Campesato</book:author> <book:publisher>Charles
River Media</book:publisher> <book:year>2002</book:year>
</rdf:Description>

<rdf:Description
rdf:about="http://www.oac.books/book/SVG
Graphics">
<book:author>Oswald Campesato</book:author> <book:publisher>Charles
River Media</book:publisher> <book:year>2003</book:year>
</rdf:Description>
.
.
.

</rdf:RDF>
```

Listing 13.3 contains two xml namespaces (which are discussed in Chapter 3), followed by two XML <description> elements that belong to the rdf namespace. Notice that both XML <description> elements contain a set of XML elements (in the book namespace) that are essentially name/value pairs.

As you know, there are tools that can verify whether or not XML documents are valid and well-formed (and also conformant to an XML schema). Similarly, and in an analogous manner, there are RDF validators that can verify whether or not an RDF document is well-formed. You can find one RDF validator here:
http://www.w3.org/RDF/Validator/

As you experiment with RDF, use this validator as often as necessary, especially if you are unfamiliar (or uncomfortable) with RDF-based documents. Since this validator lets you validate every RDF triplet that you create, it is a valuable learning tool that will help you with the mechanics of working with RDF.

13.1.3.1.7 ALTERNATIVES TO RDF

Notation3 (also referred to as N3) is under development by Tim Berners-Lee and others in the Semantic Web community. Its home page is:
http://www.notation3.com/

N3 differs from RDF in two significant areas: N3 is not based on XML and N3 is designed for human readability. N3 is a Context Free Grammar (CFG) that is consistent and relatively simple, and yet N3 tries to provide support for RDF expressions and rules.

You can see the difference between N3 and RDF by examining this RDF triplet:

```
<rdf:RDF
    xmlns:rdf="http://www.w3.org/1999/02/22-rdf-syntax-ns#"
    xmlns:dc="http://purl.org/dc/elements/1.1/">
  <rdf:Description rdf:about="http://en.acme.org/TBL">
    <dc:title>TBL</dc:title>
    <dc:publisher>Internet</dc:publisher>
  </rdf:Description>
</rdf:RDF>
```

Compare the preceding RDF triplet with its N3 counterpart here:

```
@prefix dc: <http://purl.org/dc/elements/1.1/>.
<http://en.acme.org/TBL>
  dc:title "TBL";
  dc:publisher "Internet".
```

Clearly, the N3 representation is more compact (and also non-XML) compared to RDF. In terms of compactness, N3 compares to RDF as JSON compares to XML, because both N3 and JSON clearly eschew the verbose type of syntax that is embraced by RDF and XML.

13.1.3.2 RDFS

RDFS extends RDF and lets you specify additional constraints and properties regarding RDF triplets. RDFS allows you to define groups of entities, relationships between entities, and attributes or properties of those entities.

In particular, RDFS provides a class element that is written as `rdfs:Class`. The `rdf` and the `rdfs` namespaces are different, and they are shown here along with several other commonly used namespaces so that you can make an easy side-by-side comparison of them:

```
xmlns:dc="http://purl.org/dc/elements/1.1/"
xmlns:owl ="http://www.w3.org/2002/07/owl#"
xmlns:rdf ="http://www.w3.org/1999/02/22-rdf-syntax-ns#"
xmlns:rdfs="http://www.w3.org/2000/01/rdf-schema#"
xmlns:xsd ="http://www.w3.org/2001/XMLSchema#">
```

In addition to the RDF and RDFS namespaces, RDF/XML documents can contain other namespaces that are unrelated to either RDF or RDFS. For example, you might need a `food` namespace that pertains to food and a `book` namespace that contains book-related information. Two possible definitions for these namespaces are shown here:

```
xmlns:food="http://www.acme.food/food#">
xmlns:book="http://www.acme.book/book#">
```

You can define as many additional namespaces as you need, but too many namespaces can make RDF/XML documents difficult to read.

RDFS also has a property element, which can be expressed by `rdfs:type` and `rdfs:subClassOf`. Because an RDFS property is a class that can also have a subproperty, RDFS lets you define relationships among entities in a hierarchically-oriented manner. If you are familiar with object-oriented programming languages, it will help you as you work with RDFS.

13.1.3.3 OWL

The OWL home page is:

http://www.w3.org/2004/OWL/

OWL is designed for processing-oriented applications rather than visual representations of information. OWL also enables better interoperability than what can be achieved using only XML, RDF, or RDF Schema. OWL has three sublanguages: OWL Lite, OWL DL, and OWL Full, with OWL Full being the most powerful of the three.

OWL documents use RDF, RDFS, and XML schema namespaces (which are listed in the previous section). The OWL namespace is:

```
xmlns:owl ="http://www.w3.org/2002/07/owl#"
```

OWL extends the functionality of RDFS by letting you differentiate between an entity and a class, determining when two entities in different domains are identical, and constructing a subclass of an existing class. OWL focuses on processing information rather than visually displaying a set of entities and their relationships. Thus, OWL is designed for managing ontologies.

OWL introduces a Class (which is a collection) and a Thing (which is an individual), and OWL supports the intersection and union of classes, and the complement of a class, in much the same manner as set theory supports these same operations. OWL is designed to support the architecture of the Web, which differs from earlier languages that were developed for specific communities.

OWL is a layer of abstraction above RDF that leverages RDF (and also RDF schema) to enhance ontologies so that they become more scalable, distributed, and extensible with respect to the Web. OWL provides a facility for richer property and class descriptions, and lets you specify relations between classes, the cardinality of a class, and so forth.

An example of an OWL document is here:
http://publib.boulder.ibm.com/infocenter/sr/v6r0/index.jsp?topic=/com
.ibm.sr.doc/cwsr_configrn_classifications06.html

The preceding OWL document contains a set of ENTITY definitions, XML namespaces, and a set of elements. The first portion of the document is reproduced here:

```
<!DOCTYPE rdf:RDF [
  <!ENTITY xsd "http://www.w3.org/2001/XMLSchema#">
  <!ENTITY rdf "http://www.w3.org/1999/02/22-rdf-syntax-ns#">
  <!ENTITY rdfs "http://www.w3.org/2000/01/rdf-schema#">
  <!ENTITY owl "http://www.w3.org/2002/07/owl#">
  <!ENTITY ns_transport "file://www.ibm.com/WSRR/Transport#">
]>
```

```
<rdf:RDF
  xmlns:xsd="&xsd;"
  xmlns:rdf="&rdf;"
  xmlns:rdfs="&rdfs;"
  xmlns:owl="&owl;"
  xmlns:ns_transport="&ns_transport;"
>

  <owl:Ontology rdf:about="&ns_transport;TransportOntology">
    <rdfs:label>A transport classification system.</rdfs:label>
    <rdfs:comment>Cars and buses and some superclasses.</
rdfs:comment>
  </owl:Ontology>
```

13.1.3.4 OWL Validators and Tools

A useful OWL validator can be found here:
http://www.mygrid.org.uk/OWL/Validator

Copy and paste an RDF/XML document into the website, or enter the URL of an OWL-RDF ontology, and this website will validate the ontology. This tool can also provide the classes and properties that are defined in the ontology using the OWL Abstract Syntax. Note that the author of this website does not provide guarantees regarding the correctness of the results that are returned by this tool.

Another useful OWL validator that can validate OWL 2 (DL, EL, QL, and RL) and provide output as DL syntax or functional syntax is here: http://owl.cs.manchester.ac.uk/validator/

Swoogle is a search engine for finding OWL ontologies. Its home page is: http://swoogle.umbc.edu/

13.1.3.5 DAML and Ontology Inference Layer (OIL)

The DAML home page is: http://www.daml.org/

DAML is based on XML and RDF, which means that DAML is more expressive than XML for describing entities and the relationships between them. OIL is an ontology infrastructure for the Semantic Web.

We will not provide any additional details about DAML and OIL because they have been superseded by DAML+OIL, which in turn was superseded by OWL.

13.1.3.6   *SPARQL*

SPARQL is the query language for RDF that lets you write queries for retrieving data from data sources that provide RDF-based information, which can be in the form of result sets for RDF graphs. Although SPARQL and SQL both use some of the same keywords (such as SELECT, FROM, and WHERE), RDF data is heavily graph-oriented, whereas SQL data often involves sets of row-based data.

SPARQL queries usually contain a set of triple patterns (called a *basic graph pattern*) that resemble RDF triples, except that the subject, predicate and object may all be variables.

13.1.3.6.1   A SIMPLE SPARQL QUERY

Information regarding basic RDF can be found here:
http://www.w3.org/TR/rdf-sparql-query/#basicpatterns
Consider the following simple SQL query:

```
SELECT title
FROM  books;
```

The preceding clause returns the title of each book that is stored in the books table.

A SPARQL query would be as follows:

```
SELECT ?title
WHERE
{
  <http://example.org/book/book1> <http://purl.org/dc/elements/1.1/
title> ?title.
}
```

The data for the SPARQL query can be found here:
```
<http://example.org/book/book1><http://purl.org/dc/elements/1.1/title>
"SPARQL Tutorial"
```
The result of the SPARQL query is:

```
Title
SPARQL Query
```

One difference between SQL and SPARQL is that variables in SPARQL are always preceded by a question mark. The SELECT clause in both queries specifies the variables in the query results, but the SQL query contains a `FROM` clause whereas the SPARQL query does not.

Unlike the preceding query (which is very simple), SPARQL queries can become very complex, so if you intend to become proficient in SPARQL, be prepared for a significant learning curve.

13.1.3.6.2 ALTERNATIVES TO SPARQL

Although SPARQL is the most popular language for managing RDF-based information, there are alternatives available, such as:

- RDQL
- RQL
- Versa
- XUL

RDQL is a SQL-like predecessor to SPARQL. You can find W3C links that provide tutorials, use cases, and examples for using RDQL. Jena (discussed later in this chapter) also provides a tutorial for RDQL and an RDF Backus–Naur Form (BNF) article.

RQL is a declarative query language for RDF and RDF schemas (implemented in RDFSuite) that lets you query RDF schemas and resource descriptions.

Versa is a query language that is implemented in Python by 4Suite. Versa is influenced by XPath (discussed in Chapter 12) rather than SQL, and Versa expressions are processed by a Versa query processor.

XUL (pronounced "zool") is an XML-based UI language (developed by Mozilla) that provides a template element to specify rules for matching data in RDF.

XUL consists of several components, including RDF, eXtensible Binding Language (XBL), and eXtensible Tag Framework (XTF). The RDF component of XUL is used for writing XML files that lets you define a structured list from an RDF file.

■ 13.1.4 Semantic Technology Tools

This section discusses some of the RDF tools that are available, such as Jena and Sesame, both of which are popular open source RDF tools. The functionality of RDF tools depends on their specific purpose, which can include programming tools for RDF-based repositories, managing the contents of an RDF repository, and graphically displaying the data and objects of an RDF repository. The appendices contain additional links where you can learn more about the tools.

13.1.4.1 *Programming Tools and Environments for RDF*

RDF-based programming tools vary in terms of their support for programming languages, which often means Java and C. The Redland tool also provides interfaces for PHP, Perl, Tcl, and Prolog.

Some of the tools that provide programming environments for RDF include:

- Jena™
- RDFLib
- Redland

13.1.4.1.1 JENA

Jena is an open source Java-based framework for creating semantic applications. Its home page is: http://jena.sourceforge.net/

Jena has evolved in conjunction with the HP Labs Semantic Web Programme, which is here: http://www.hpl.hp.com/semweb/

Jena provides support (and in some cases, APIs) for RDF, RDFS, OWL, and SPARQL. Jena also includes code from various open source projects from the Apache Software Foundation, including Xerces, JUnit, Jakarta ORO, and ICU4J.

Version 2.6 of Jena (currently, the latest release) requires Java 5 or higher, and some JAR file dependencies that were required for earlier versions of Jena (such as the ANTLR JAR file) have been removed.

Jena also includes a general-purpose rule engine that supports rule-base inference on RDF graphs. In fact, Jena actually has two internal rule engines: one engine supports backward chaining and the other is a RETE-based engine that supports forward chaining.

Jena has a rule-based reasoner (which runs in either forward chaining mode or backward chaining mode), where a rule is defined by means of a Java Rule object (which is a Java-based class provided by Jena).

Jena also includes a SPARQL query engine and provides support for in-memory and persistent storage.

13.1.4.1.2   Download/Install Jena

You can download Jena from:

http://jena.sourceforge.net/downloads.html

Download the Jena distribution and unpack it in a convenient directory.

Jena contains JAR files from numerous open source projects and technologies, some of which are listed here (and some are discussed in other chapters):

- JSON (discussed in Chapter 3)
- JUnit (a testing tool for Java code created by Kent Beck)
- Lucene (discussed in Chapter 9)
- Stax™
- Xerces (Apache project and a Java-based DOM parser)

13.1.4.1.3   A DOM-to-Jena Java Example

Listing 13.4 shows the contents of the Java file `DOM2Jena.java`, located in the doc/ARP subdirectory of the Jena distribution, which illustrates how to process the contents of the RDF file `testing/wg/Manifest.rdf`.

Listing 13.4 DOM2Jena.java

```
import javax.xml.transform.*;
import javax.xml.transform.dom.*;
import javax.xml.transform.sax.*;
import org.xml.sax.*;
import org.w3c.dom.*;
import javax.xml.parsers.*;
import java.io.*;
import com.hp.hpl.jena.rdf.arp.*;
import com.hp.hpl.jena.rdf.model.*;

/**
 * @author Jeremy J. Carroll
 *
 */
public class DOM2Jena
{
    public static void main(String args[]) throws Exception
    {
        // Create DOM:
        DocumentBuilderFactory factory = DocumentBuilderFactory.newIn-
stance();
```

```
    // DOM must have namespace information inside it!
    factory.setNamespaceAware(true);
    DocumentBuilder domParser = factory.newDocumentBuilder();
    Document document = domParser.parse(
                        new File("../../testing/wg/Manifest
.rdf"));

    // Make DOM into transformer input
    Source input = new DOMSource(document);

    // Make SAX2Model SAX event handler
    Model m = ModelFactory.createDefaultModel();
    SAX2Model handler = SAX2Model.create(
        "http://www.w3.org/2000/10/rdf-tests/rdfcore/Manifest
.rdf", m);

    // Make a SAXResult object using this handler
    SAXResult output = new SAXResult(handler);
    output.setLexicalHandler(handler);

    // Run transform
    TransformerFactory xformFactory = TransformerFactory.newIn-
stance();
    Transformer idTransform = xformFactory.newTransformer();
    idTransform.transform(input, output);

    // Use Model
    m.write(System.out, "N-TRIPLE");
  }
}
```

Listing 13.4 starts with various import statements that import Java
classes included in the JAR files that are part of the Jena distribution. After
some initialization steps, an XML document is created from the RDF file
Manifest.rdf (located in the appropriate subdirectory) via this statement:

```
    Document document = domParser.parse(
                        new File("testing/wg/Manifest.rdf"));
```

The next section creates an input source for the transformer (defined
later in the code) as shown here:

```
    // Make DOM into transformer input
    Source input = new DOMSource(document);
```

Next, a `Model` object and a `SAX2Model` object are created to define a `SAXResult` object for the transformer, as shown here:

```
// Make a SAXResult object using this handler
SAXResult output = new SAXResult(handler);
```

The next section creates the `Transformation` object, as shown here:

```
// Run transform
TransformerFactory xformFactory = TransformerFactory.newIn-
stance();
Transformer idTransform = xformFactory.newTransformer();
idTransform.transform(input, output);
```

Finally, the output is generated via the following code line:

```
// Use Model
m.write(System.out, "N-TRIPLE");
```

Before you can compile this Java class from the command line, append the JAR files in `$JENA_HOME/lib` to the `CLASSPATH` environment variable, and then navigate to the directory `$JENA_HOME/doc/ARP` and type the following command:

```
javac DOM2Jena.java
```

Launch the Java class `DOM2Jena` as follows:

```
java DOM2Jena
```

Since the output is very large, redirect the output to a file that you can view in a text editor.

Listing 13.4 provides a simple example of managing RDF documents using the Jena framework. Another RDF tool that might be of interest to you is Sesame, which is discussed in the next section.

13.1.4.2 *Sesame: a Triple-Based Database System for RDF*

As you saw earlier, one important aspect of RDF-based data is its ability to store RDF data in a repository (the others include retrieving and making inferences).

Sesame is an Aduna® open source framework for RDF. The Sesame home page is: http://www.openrdf.org/

Sesame has introduced Sesame RDF Query Language (SeRQL) pronounced "circle," which combines features of RQL, RDQL, N-Triples, and N3, and also adds some of its own features.

Sesame 2.2.4 contains more than 70 JAR files, some of which are from open source projects, as shown here:

```
activation-1.1.jar
aopalliance-1.0.jar
cglib-2.1_3.jar
commons-httpclient-3.1.jar
jstl-1.1.2.jar
spring-aop-2.5.1.jar
spring-core-2.5.1.jar
spring-webmvc-2.5.1.jar
```

13.1.4.2.1 DOWNLOAD/INSTALL SESAME

This section shows you how to deploy the two Sesame WAR files that are provided in the Sesame distribution (in the $SESAME_HOME/war directory):

```
openrdf-sesame.war (Sesame server)
openrdf-workbench.war (Sesame workbench)
```

Perform the following steps to download Sesame and deploy the two Sesame WAR files to Tomcat:

Step 1: Download the latest version of Sesame from:
 http://www.openrdf.org/download.jsp

Step 2: Download the ZIP file and uncompress it in a convenient directory

Step 3: Copy the preceding WAR files into $TOMCAT_HOME/webapps

Step 4: Start Tomcat

Step 5: Go to the Sesame server here:
 http://localhost:8080/openrdf-sesame

Step 6: Go to the Sesame workbench here:
 http://localhost:8080/openrdf-workbench

The Sesame workbench lets you manage Sesame repositories, which means that you can create, delete, and update Sesame repositories.

Other tools are available, including Mulgara™ and Tucana, and you can compare their features to Sesame to determine which tool is best suited for your requirements.

13.1.4.3 Rhodonite: a Graphical Editor for RDF

Graphical editors for RDF are extremely useful because they provide a graphically oriented representation of RDF-based repositories. These editors let you create, update, and manage the structure of repositories. Graphical editors display the set of defined classes, their properties, and a graph that shows how classes are related to each other.

Rhodonite is a RDF editor and browser. Its home page is:
http://rhodonite.angelite.nl/

Rhodonite provides drag-and-drop functionality, import/export, and multilingual support, and the ability to work in multiple windows with different RDF repositories.

A free download is available (you must provide your name and email address) from a link on the home page. After you receive an email notification from Rhodonite, click on the enclosed link to download the Rhodonite distribution.

Other well-known graphical editors for RDF (which are not discussed in this book) include the following:

- IsaViz
- Orient
- Protégé
- SWOOP

Check the appendices (or search the Internet) for links for more information about these editors.

The next section describes several significant Semantic Technology tools that are based on RDF, starting with the OpenCalais.

■ 13.2 OPENCALAIS

Calais is a subsidiary of Thomson Reuters® that has been involved in Semantic Technology for many years. Calais created the OpenCalais product. Its home page is:
http://www.opencalais.com

The following description comes from the OpenCalais home page (reprinted with permission from Calais): "The Calais web service automatically creates rich semantic metadata for the content you submit—in well under a second. Using natural language processing, machine learning, and other methods, Calais analyzes your document and finds the entities within it. But, Calais goes well beyond classic entity identification and returns the facts and events hidden within your text as well."

Regarding the "Open" in Calais, the website states: "The Calais web service is free for commercial and noncommercial use. We've sized the initial release to handle millions of requests per day and will scale it as necessary to support our users."

Calais provides users with the following:

- an automatic semantic metadata generation service for commercial and noncommercial use
- the ability to extract entities, facts, and events from unstructured text, and return metadata in open, interoperable, and portable formats
- a web service and open API supported by a growing toolkit of developer frameworks, plug-ins, and applications

Some of the viable OpenCalais use-cases (and there are many of them) are listed here:

- automatically tag archived assets for improved search and navigation
- detect and alert on significant events in content
- drive statistical analysis of document semantics
- create topic hubs and microsites
- create richer customer profiles in the advertising space

■ 13.2.1 The Calais Viewer

The Calais Viewer is here: http://viewer.opencalais.com/

Navigate to this web site and copy and paste the text in Listing 13.5 into the text area of the Calais Viewer.

Listing 13.5

```
The web service is free for commercial and noncommercial use. We've
sized the initial release to handle millions of requests per day and
will scale it as necessary to support our users.
```

Next, click on the Submit button in the lower-right corner of the screen. After a few moments you will see the output in Listing 13.6.

Listing 13.6

```
Date
2009-05-20
Body
```

The web service is free for commercial and noncommercial use. We've sized the initial release to handle millions of requests per day and will scale it as necessary to support our users.

Now click on the Show RDF button and you will see the RDF output, a portion of which is shown in Listing 13.7 (reformatted for easier viewing).

Listing 13.7

```
<rdf:RDF xmlns:rdf="http://www.w3.org/1999/02/22-rdf-syntax-ns#"
         xmlns:c="http://s.opencalais.com/1/pred/">
<rdf:Description c:allowDistribution="true" c:allowSearch="true"
c:calaisRequestID="fc9ff6d5-8ae2-4de2-9dd6-3edd2b9fb055"
c:docRDFaccessible="true" c:externalID="calaisbridge"
c:id="http://id.opencalais.com/182HLz4Z-IOpEY-Hg*N6vw"
rdf:about="http://d.opencalais.com/dochash-1/18b5216e-14e1-3ae9-9841-
e481ecf1ec87">
<rdf:type rdf:resource="http://s.opencalais.com/1/type/sys/DocInfo"/>

<c:document>
<![CDATA[<Document><Date>2009-05-20</Date><Body>The web service is
free for commercial and non-commercial use. We've sized the initial
release to handle millions of requests per day and will scale it as
necessary to support our users.</Body></Document>]]> </c:document>

<c:docTitle/>
<c:docDate>2009-05-20 00:00:00</c:docDate>
<c:externalMetadata c:caller="calaisbridge"/>
<c:submitter>calaisbridge</c:submitter>
</rdf:Description>
....
</rdf:RDF>
```

■ 13.2.2   A Simple OpenCalais Example

Before you use OpenCalais, create a free OpenCalais account and request an API key, both of which can be found on the following site: http://www.opencalais.com/apps/register

Calais will send you an email message containing a Service Key (consisting of 26 characters and digits).

Call an OpenCalais web service by completing these four steps:

Step 1: Launch the OpenCalais test page FORM1.htm (see Listing 13.8) from your browser

Step 2: Enter your Service Key in the LicenseID input field

Step 3: Enter a document in the Content text area field

Step 4: Click on the Submit Query button

Shortly after you click the Submit Query button, OpenCalais will return the response in an RDF-based XML document in your browser.

Listing 13.8 displays the contents of FORM1.htm, which lets you enter a text string in an HTML <textarea> input field, and then send that text string to an OpenCalais web service.

Listing 13.8 HTMLForm.htm

```
<html>
<head>
  <title>Calais test page</title>
</head>
<body>
<form action="http://api.opencalais.com/enlighten/rest/"
      method="post" accept-charset="utf-8">
   licenseID: <input type="text" name="licenseID" />
   <input type="submit" /><br />
   content: <br />
   <textarea rows="15" cols="80" name="content" ></textarea><br />
   paramsXML: <br />

   <textarea rows="15" cols="80" name="paramsXML" /></textarea><br />
</form>
</body>
</html>
```

Listing 13.8 starts with an HTML <head> tag with a title string. The second portion contains an opening HTML <body> tag that is followed by an HTML <form> tag, as shown here:

```
<form action="http://api.opencalais.com/enlighten/rest/"
      method="post" accept-charset="utf-8">
```

The `<action>` tag specifies the REST-based OpenCalais URL that will service this HTML page when you click the `<submit>` button.

The next portion of Listing 13.8 is an HTML `text` field for the license key you obtained in the previous section:

```
licenseID: <input type="text" name="licenseID" />
```

Next is an HTML `textarea` field where you will enter the text you want to send to the OpenCalais web service:

```
<textarea rows="15" cols="80" name="content" ></textarea><br />
```

Next is an HTML `textarea` field where you can enter any additional parameters you want to send to the OpenCalais web service:

```
<textarea rows="15" cols="80" name="paramsXML" /></textarea><br />
```

The final portion of Listing 13.8 contains the closing HTML `<body>` and `<html>` tags.

■ 13.2.3 OpenCalais Code Samples

OpenCalais code samples are available in several languages, including C# and PHP, using RESTful services. Please read the following article, which tells you how to enable the OpenCalais PHP and JSON code samples in Safari and Firefox: http://opencalais.com/node/3237

The following subsections provide examples of how to use OpenCalais with PHP, JSON, C#, and REST.

13.2.3.1 OpenCalais Code Samples

Listing 13.9 displays the contents of a portion of `CalaisManualPostExamples.cs`, which is a C# program that illustrates how to call an OpenCalais web service using REST.

Listing 13.9

```
static void Main(string[] args)
{
    string response = null;

    m_CParams = m_ParamsRDF; //or your custom params
    m_Content = m_Content;   //or  your custom content
    m_Licence = m_Licence;   // your key
```

```
        //add proxy if needed: new WebProxy("some uri : some port");
        WebProxy proxy = null;

        if (proxy != null)
        {
            proxy.Credentials =
                new NetworkCredential("userName", "password", "domain");
        }
        //MANUL POST/GET
        response = ProccessText(
                        "http://api.opencalais.com/enlighten/rest/",
                        eMethod.POST,
                        "application/x-www-form-urlencoded",
                        CreatePostParams(),
                        proxy);

    //Calais Client POST
    //response = PostWithCalaisClient(proxy);

    Console.WriteLine(response);
    Console.Read();
}
```

Listing 13.9 starts with a static `Main` method that initializes some class methods (defined elsewhere), which require a free license key that you can get from Calais.

The next part of Listing 13.9 initializes a WebProxy instance variable with your credentials. The actual call to Calais is shown here:

```
        response = ProccessText(
                        "http://api.opencalais.com/enlighten/
                            rest/",
                        eMethod.POST,
                        "application/x-www-form-urlencoded",
                        CreatePostParams(),
                        proxy);
```

If you are familiar with C#, the code in Listing 13.9 for calling Open-Calais is fairly straightforward. The complete source code for `CalaisManual-PostExamples.cs` is available here: http://www.opencalais.com/REST

Check the appendices for links to code samples that illustrate how to use OpenCalais with PHP and JSON.

13.2.3.2   *OpenCalais Featured Applications*

OpenCalais provides additional featured applications here: http://www.opencalais.com/showcase

The preceding web page contains the following applications:

- Calais Module for Drupal
- Tagaroo
- SemanticProxy
- Gnosis

The descriptions of the preceding applications are as follows:

The Calais Modules for Drupal were created by Phase2 to integrate the powers of the Calais web service with Drupal, which integrates semantic metatagging of content through the Calais engine.

Tagaroo provides automated tag generation and image location for WordPress® bloggers.

SemanticProxy, created by the Calais team, makes it easy to generate rich semantic metadata for individual web pages. Simply paste the page's URL into the tool. Programmatic use of SemanticProxy requires a Calais API key (your current Calais key will work).

Gnosis is a FireFox or Internet Explorer plug-in that automatically identifies people, company, places, etc., on web pages as you browse, and lets you launch various searches based on the type of entity identified (a location, a company, a person, etc.).

■ 13.2.4   **OpenCalais Tools**

A list of OpenCalais tools is available from: http://www.opencalais.com/tools

This list of tools includes the following:

- Calais Web Service
- Calais Marmoset
- Calais Yahoo Pipes
- Calais Tagaroo
- Gnosis
- MOSS 2007 OpenCalais Integration
- Calais Popfly Block
- Calais Submission Tool
- Calais Logos

More information about several of the OpenCalais tools in the preceding list is provided in the following sections.

13.2.4.1 *OpenCalais and Other Tools*

OpenCalais also provides support for Yahoo Pipes, which can be done in two ways:

Method 1: Install and configure the Pipes Service on your own server

Method 2: Copy the Web Service Pipe template from Yahoo! Pipes and paste it to the following link. Replace [Your Calais API Key] with a valid Calais API key (be sure to remove the square brackets).

If you decide to use the first option (i.e., install and configure the Pipes Service on your own server), you can find more detailed documentation here: http://www.opencalais.com/CalaisPipes-Server

If you decide to use the second option, then here is the format of the HTTP request:

http://pipes.opencalais.com/CalaisPipes/CalaisPipes?licenseID=[Your Calais API Key]&richLinks=true

OpenCalais has been combined ("mashed up") with other unrelated tools to create some interesting combinations, such as OpenCalais with Yahoo BOSS and with Twitter.

■ 13.3 EXPERT SYSTEM

Expert System has a tool called Cogito, which is based on Semantic Technology. Its home page is: http://www.expertsystem.net/

Expert System Cogito can analyze websites and documents containing unstructured text and then discern relationships in that text. Cogito uses Semantic Technology to determine which words are meaningful, which Expert System claims is superior to traditional search engines because Cogito can "automatically understand the true meaning of words." Expert System is also involved in providing solutions for advertising and mobile devices.

Expert System provides the following set of products:

• Cogito Semantic Search
• Cogito Categorizer

- Cogito Discover
- Cogito Monitor
- Cogito Focus
- Cogito Semantic Advertiser
- Cogito Answers
- Cogito Intelligence Platform

Cogito analyzes documents to find entities and relationships between them that are semantically meaningful and useful. Cogito performs full-sentence analysis and disambiguation based on a repository of 350,000 concepts and 2.8 million relationships, and Expert System claims that Cogito has better precision for entities than the other systems discussed in this chapter.

■ 13.4 TRUEVERT

Truevert is a "green"-oriented search technology that uses Semantic Technology. As of early 2009, Truevert is a free beta product. The Truevert home page is: http://www.truevert.com

Unlike other Semantic Technologies (including OpenCalais), Truevert does not use dictionaries or thesauri. Truvert's technology leverages statistical techniques as it performs a comparison of similar documents to make semantic inferences about the content of a given document.

■ 13.5 SEMANTIC TECHNOLOGY FROM COMMERCIAL VENDORS

Several large vendors have invested heavily in Semantic Technology, including IBM, Oracle, Microsoft, and Altova. This section provides an overview of the Semantic Technology tools that these companies have created.

■ 13.5.1 Oracle Semantic Technology

During the 1990s Oracle provided technology for storing XML documents that can be stored as CLOBs or by a technique known as "sharding," which involves registering an XML schema to create a set of tables and indexes "behind the scenes" where XML documents are stored. Oracle also lets you manage XML documents via PLSQL (for CLOB-based storage), XQuery™, and XSLT. Oracle also supports RDF-based technology in the Oracle Spatial

11g database, which supports an RDF management platform that enables the development of semantically enriched applications in a number of vertical markets, including defense, life sciences, and CRM/ERP systems.

Oracle Spatial 11g supports applications that use RDF and OWL, OWL-based inferences, and user-defined rules. RDF/OWL models are stored as directed graphs in Oracle Spatial 11g, and a native inference engine provides inference support. RDF-based data stored in Oracle Spatial 11g can be queried via SQL statements that have additional embedded semantic capabilities.

Oracle also supports Jena, Sesame, an RDF plug-in for Protégé, and a loader for N-Triple files.

Oracle Semantic Technology code is here:
http://www.oracle.com/technology/tech/semantic_technologies/sample_code/index.html

■ 13.5.2 IBM Semantic Technology

IBM has several projects and initiatives pertaining to Semantic Technology, and this section provides an overview of some of them.

Swoop is an OWL ontology editor. Its home page is:
http://semanticweb.org/wiki/Swoop

Swoop is a collaborative project by IBM, Clark & Parsia, and the University of Manchester.

Download the Swoop distribution from its home page, uncompress it into a convenient directory, and launch Swoop from a command shell with the following command:

```
runme.bat (Windows)
runme.sh (Linux)
```

When the Swoop editor is visible, follow the **File > Load > Ontology** menu path and either specify an OWL document or use the OWL document from: http://publib.boulder.ibm.com/infocenter/sr/v6r0/index.jsp? topic=/com.ibm.sr.doc/cwsr_configrn_classifications06.html

Swoop will parse the OWL document and render a tree-based graphical display of its contents, and when you click on a node, Swoop will display detailed information about that node.

Boca is an RDF repository component whose home page is:
http://ibm-slrp.sourceforge.net/2006/11/20/boca-the-rdf-repository-component-of-the-ibm-semantic-layered-research-platform/

A Boca server can manage millions of RDF triples stored in an IBM DB2 database, and Boca clients can either process RDF-based data through the Boca server or RDF data that is colocated with the client. Note that Boca provides partial compatibility with Jena APIs.

The IBM Semantic Layered Research Platform contains links to additional tools. Its home page is:

http://ibm-slrp.sourceforge.net/

■ 13.5.3 Microsoft Semantic Technology

Microsoft conducts research in Semantic Technology, and this section briefly discusses some of the tools that are available from Microsoft and third-party developers.

Microsoft Bing (discussed in Chapter 9) was announced in mid-2009, and generated plenty of speculation regarding the extent to which Bing would use Semantic Technology.

Zentity provides a research-oriented set of tools that lets companies maintain their digital library. Its home page is:

http://research.microsoft.com/en-us/projects/zentity/

Zentity provides a model that contains a core set of entities, including File, Lecture, Paper, Publication, and so forth, along with support for creating and designing custom entities and data models. Zentity provides a search API, support for authentication, and extensive documentation.

SemWeb is a Semantic Web RDF library written in C# for either Mono or .NET 1.1/2.0. Its home page is:

http://razor.occams.info/code/semweb/

SemWeb lets you manage RDF data, provides support for SPARQL, and supports the ability to persist data to a datastore. SemWeb also provides partial support for inferences and RDFS.

An article that makes the interesting assertion that Microsoft is "filling the gap between CouchDB and Semantic Web" is available here:

http://www.sitepoint.com/blogs/2008/03/26/microsoft-set-to-launch-semantic-web-light/

■ 13.5.4 Altova Semantic Technology

Altova provides a vast array of XML-based products and tools. Its home page is: http://www.altova.com

Altova products include XMLSpy (an editor for XML documents), MapForce 2009 (which supports XBRL and HL7), and MissionKit (for XML and UML), which also won a Jolt Product Excellence and Productivity award. XMLSpy 2009 also provides extension points that let you use third-party XSLT (both 1.0 and 2.0) or XSLFO processors.

Altova also provides tools for creating, editing, and validating XSLT, XSLFO, XQuery, XPath, OOXM L, and XML schemas. Altova has a set of visual mapping tools that let you perform mappings for XML, EDI, and flat files.

In addition, Altova provides SemanticWorks 2009, which is a visually oriented editor for managing RDF, RDFS, and OWL (which includes Lite, Full, and DL). SemanticWorks 2009 also lets you convert between RDF/XML and N-Triples, and perform semantics checking for ontologies.

Altova provides freely downloadable products, including Authentic 2009, which is a content editor for XML documents. Authentic 2009 supports multiple formats, including XML, DITA, DocBook, and NewsML.

Another free product is AltovaXML 2009, which is a tool that consists of an XML validating parser, an XSLT 1.0 engine, a schema-aware XSLT 2.0 engine, and a schema-aware XQuery 1.0 engine.

You can download a free 30-day trial of SemanticWorks 2009 from the Altova home page.

Eclipse integration and Visual Studio integration is available for several Altova products, including XMLSpy 2009, MapForce 2009, Stylevision 2009, UModel 2009, and Authentic 2009. Additional Altova tools are here:

http://www.altova.com/solutions/semantic-web-tools.html

■ 13.5.5 Franz Semantic Technologies

Franz Semantic Technologies offers a bundled suite of Semantic Technology products. Its home page is: http://www.franz.com/

Franz provides AllegroGraph™ (described as a Web 3.0 database), AG-WebView™ (an RDF browser), Gruff™ (RDF browser), TopBraid™ (ontology modeling), and RacePro (OWL reasoner).

Franz also provides several LISP-based development tools, including Allegro Common Lisp™ (CL), AllegroCache™ (database), Allegro BTrees™ (Native BTrees), and Pepito™ (Data Mining).

AllegroGraph 3.2 supports various tools and languages, including RDF, RDFS, SPARQL, Prolog, Python-based clients, Jena, Sesame, and TopBraid Composer.

Download the free version of AllegroGraph from the Franz website into a convenient directory, and if you have a Windows platform, launch the binary installer and follow the prompts to complete the installation. Navigate to the `bin` subdirectory you installed Allegro in to start the Allegro server. The `doc` subdirectory contains a set of HTML files with additional instructions and details that explain how to use AllegroGraph.

■ 13.5.6 TopBraid

TopBraid is a Semantic Web application assembly toolkit that supports three main tools: RDF, OWL, and SQARQL. Its home page is:
http://www.topbraid.com

In mid-2009, NASA chose TopBraid for its Semantic Technology platform in the NASA Constellation Program (see the appendices for the related link).

TopBraid Composer is a tool for modeling an application development tool for developing and managing ontologies, and a support for RDF, OWL, and SPARQL.

TopBraid Composer is an Eclipse plug-in that is available in three versions. The Free edition supports RDF, OWL, and SPARQL, but there is no support from TopBraid. The Standard edition supports multiple databases (such as Oracle 11g and Sesame) and supports inference engines, such as Jena rules, SWRL, OWLIM, and Pelle. The Maestro edition provides an internal web server so that you can test applications during the development cycle. The TopBraid home page contains a link where you can find additional information, including a matrix that lists the set of features that are supported by the three editions of TopBraid Composer.

TopBraid Ensemble is a web-based toolkit for creating applications, including RIAs (which are based on Adobe Flex), mash-ups, and wikis. Ensemble also supports an RQL queries constructor and support for SPARQLMotion scripts.

TopBraid Live is an application platform that is integrated with Composer and Ensemble, and provides support for single-click deployment of ontology models and applications.

TopBraid also supports over 100 services for SPARLMotion, and a Java-based server that supports two network protocols.

■ 13.6 OTHER PROJECTS, TOOLS, AND PRODUCTS

The following sections provide short descriptions of several Semantic Technology projects and tools that might be of interest to you. In addition, this section provides short descriptions of several other semantic tools that are currently available, including Mozilla Ubiquity.

■ 13.6.1 Open Source RDF-based Projects

This section provides an overview of several open source projects, including DBpedia, Linked Data, and Common Tag. These RDF-based projects provide repositories of rich content, and, in some cases, public APIs are available that let you to programmatically query and retrieve structured data that you can use for your own purposes.

13.6.1.1 DBpedia

The DBpedia project extracts structured data from Wikipedia. Its home page is:

http://dbpedia.org/About

DBpedia is an RDF-based knowledge base that contains approximately 300,000,000 RDF triples and information about 3 million entities (people, places, companies, and so forth). DBpedia provides multilingual support (currently, 30 languages), links to images, and links to other datasets.

DBpedia has two other important features: the ability to execute queries against Wikipedia and the ability to link other datasets to DBpedia. The latter is particularly important because of the vast number of heterogeneous systems that would otherwise be cumbersome to link together.

DBPedia provides various types of ontologies that are available online. You can use the existing ontologies or modify them to fit your needs.

An interesting diagram of DBpedia and links to other data sets can be found here:

http://esw.w3.org/topic/SweoIG/TaskForces/CommunityProjects/Linking OpenData

13.6.1.2   *Other Useful Projects*

The Linked Data project lets to link datasets together (or facilitate the process of doing so) using RDF and URIs. Its home page is:
http://linkeddata.org/

The Common Tag project is an RDFa-based open tagging format for connecting content (such as concepts in a document). Its home page is:
http://www.commontag.org/Home

The Firefox Operator plug-in leverages HTML pages that use microformats, such as RDFa, that can provide some additional semantic meaning about a specific HTML page. The Firefox Operator plug-in is here:
https://addons.mozilla.org/en-US/firefox/addon/4106

Mozilla Ubiquity is a research project that is exploring how to use an interface that leverages natural language. Its home page is:
http://labs.mozilla.com/projects/ubiquity/

To give you an idea of how to use Ubiquity in HTML pages, Listing 13.10 shows an example of an HTML page with an embedded Google map.

Listing 13.10

```
<html xmlns="http://www.w3.org/1999/xhtml"
     xmlns:xf="http://www.w3.org/2002/xforms">
<script
 src=http://ubiquity-xforms.googlecode.com/svn/tags/0.7.1/build/
dist/src/ubiquity-loader.js
 type="text/javascript">/**/</script>
<script src="http://maps.google.com/maps?file=api&amp;v=2&amp;sensor
=false&amp;key=MAPS- API-KEY"
type="text/javascript">/**/</script>
 <body>
   <xf:output value="'4 Pear Tree Court, London, EC1R ODS'"
class="geolocation" />
 </body>
</html>
```

■ 13.7   COMMENTS ABOUT WEB 3.0

When you consider that there are still differing opinions about Web 2.0, attempts to define Web 3.0 are probably fraught with peril. Nevertheless, this section provides some insight into what Web 3.0 might actually be.

The first view is the simplest to describe: Web 3.0 is the same as the Semantic Web. So, if you define one you immediately have the definition of the other. A second view of Web 3.0 is its ability to create intelligent software agents that will search the Internet for topics, events, and people (among other things) that might interest you. In theory, such agents will be able to make inferences about things that interest you based on the information in your profile and anticipate areas that are unrelated ("orthogonal") to your current profile. While the first scenario is plausible (even today), the second is a formidable challenge.

For example, suppose you attend an event where you meet someone who invites you to a Japanese anime movie, and even though you've never had any interest in anime, you spontaneously decide to see it.

In addition, suppose that your profile does not contain anything related to Japanese anime (e.g., the Japanese language, manga, etc.). In this scenario, an intelligent agent working on your behalf would be hard-pressed to deduce that you would ever be interested in watching a Japanese anime movie.

One variant of the second scenario that becomes more plausible: suppose that your intelligent agent had access to another person's profile that is similar to yours (for this scenario, let's ignore how your intelligent agent would have access to such a profile). In this case, your intelligent agent could construct a new list of interests for you by calculating the "difference" between the two profiles. Thus, you would be exposed to interests that might otherwise appear "orthogonal" from your perspective.

Remember, we can be impulsive and sometimes even unpredictable, which makes it very difficult for us to anticipate the sorts of things that will interest us next year (or perhaps even next week!). Random events can play a significant role in determining our interests.

A third scenario involves software agents that can "mine" repositories and silos of data to extract meaningful and relevant information. Regardless of the definition of Web 3.0, it's likely to be fascinating, stimulating, and probably addictive in ways that we have yet to experience in Web 2.0. The last chapter of this book contains the viewpoints of several well-known industry leaders regarding the future of the Web, which includes the realization of Web 3.0.

■ 13.8 INDUSTRY PERSPECTIVE

Tom Tague of Calais has provided his insight into Semantic Technology and its role in the IT industry.

■ 13.8.1 What is your "definition" of Web 2.0? Web 3.0?

There are a number of ways this question has been answered, and I'm not sure any of them help the layman all that much. From our content-centric point-of-view, during Web 2.0, content was atomized. It flew off the page via RSS feeds, APIs, and widgets on social networks. Meanwhile, audiences were disaggregated. People turned to social media services where their friends helped filter the news. Instead of programmed portals or newspaper sites, they started their day with Digg, Technorati, Facebook, or (more recently) Twitter.

However, this constituted a fragmented media marketplace, and we continued to suffer from information overload. Although it became much easier to know what your friends were reading, that did not simplify the task of finding the precise information you needed when you needed it.

Therefore, Web 3.0 is about rectifying the problems that were created in Web 2.0. This means that Web 3.0 is about adding intelligence to the network and structure to the content to support advanced filtering for targeted and timely delivery and more sophisticated browser-based meta-navigation search paradigms with the power to bring the right information to the right person at the right time.

From the content producer point-of-view, Web 3.0 is also about automating time-consuming content operations, bringing new efficiencies to the publishing process, and making it easy to enhance content with open data assets. Today, that helps everyone from the independent blogger to the multinational media conglomerate.

■ 13.8.2 How will Semantic Technology evolve during the next several years?

We will continue to see new developer tools and infrastructure services that make it easier to leverage the core capabilities of Semantic Ttechnology, examples of which include Yahoo SearchMonkey and Google Rich Snippets. These new capabilities will be brought to bear in solving some truly difficult problems: the challenges we still face as a global community, as students, as researchers, and as entrepreneurs.

As a result, we expect that, in the longer term, we will see a creative explosion around both professional and consumer end user applications. We are already starting to see them pop up across a number of verticals, and the entrepreneurs are starting to poke around.

Perhaps the most exciting work in this arena will focus on the browsers and deliver new paradigms for navigation, such as UIs that support real-time mash-ups, customization and enhancement of data, content, and services. You already see this sort of initiative from folks like Edwin Khodabakchian of Feedly.

Our point of inflection in the Semantic Web lies at the point of consumption. So our task is to simultaneously refine and enrich our digital experience from content and community to commerce.

■ 13.8.3 How will OpenCalais influence Semantic Technology?

Our impact will be threefold:

1) We will continue to support the free generation of semantic metadata. This will let folks everywhere contribute to the underlying semantic "content" of the Data Web, while gaining new efficiencies in their operations and putting linked data assets to work to provide users with a better experience.

2) We will help fuel a wave of creativity—inspiring innovators to find new ways to leverage metadata, linked data, and the rapidly emerging ecosystem of linked content.

3) At Thomson Reuters, we will develop new semantically enabled services that extend the value and utility of our high-value content for professionals worldwide and consumers on the Web.

■ 13.8.4   What are the important differences (and similarities) between OpenCalais and other Semantic Technology products?

OpenCalais is free, extremely robust, and almost infinitely scalable. To be clear, we want to provide the semantic plumbing for all, the Web's content and become the de facto standard for the creation of semantic metadata.

■ 13.8.5   Where are the opportunities for creating successful Semantic Technology applications?

It's hard to think of a single industry or area of life wherein we as humans can't do a better job, making it easier for people to be productive, creative, and successful in their work and in their lives. Semantic Technologies can help most with processes that benefit from greater automation, seamless integration of data and information sources, and improved personalization.

■ 13.8.6   What advice do you have for developers who want to create successful Semantic Technology applications? What technical and nontechnical skills do they need to acquire?

1) Get started today and start simple. Don't try to boil the ocean, but rather tackle one small project or one small task, like tagging some content.

2) Find a partner on the business-end of your field with a strong knowledge of your customer's challenges and the problems they face everyday.

3) Don't go it alone. Leverage the emerging community of se-mantic experts. The community is lively and dynamic today, so jump in and connect. There are a lot of people offering tools, resources, advice, and ideas free of charge.

■ 13.8.7 What advice do you have for people who want to create start-ups?

Find a good problem to solve, whereby normal human behavior—the way we would all prefer to transact and interact—is thwarted by clumsy or overly complex technology.

And then tear it up. Do the work on the back-end to make it easy for the human being on the front end.

■ 13.9 SUMMARY

This chapter introduced you to some important technologies of Semantic Technology, such as RDF, OWL, and SPARQL, and open source Java-based tools, such as Jena and Sesame.

Next, you learned about OpenCalais, which is a Semantic Technology free beta product that can be combined with a search technology, such as Yahoo BOSS. You also learned about products such as Truevert, and Cogito from ExpertSystem. Finally, you learned about some of the Semantic Technology tools for commercial vendors, including Oracle, IBM, Microsoft, and Altova.

The next chapter discusses Google Web Toolkit (GWT) and provides examples of writing applications that leverage Google App Engine (GAE).

## CHAPTER 14

Web 2.0 Comprehensive Project

In This Chapter:

- Google Web Toolkit (GWT)
- Meetup Networking Code
- JFXtras JavaFX Raffle Tool Background
- JFXtras JavaFX Raffle Tool Code

Web 2.0 applications can be difficult to understand because a variety of technologies are often used. The examples in this book so far are fairly basic and focused on a few key topics. This chapter will walk you through a moderately complex Web 2.0 application.

■ 14.1 CHAPTER OVERVIEW

The purpose of this chapter is to go through the steps for building a moderately complex Web 2.0 application. Web 2.0 applications can be very complex because server-side and client-side code are often written in different languages; client-side JavaScript is single threaded, which forces asynchronous calls and you are often calling external APIs that you don't control. This chapter will help you understand and overcome these complexities when writing applications.

■ 14.1.1 Project Overview

One of the co-authors of this book organizes three users groups in Silicon Valley—the Silicon Valley Web Developer Java User Group, the Silicon Valley

Google Technology User Group, and the Silicon Valley JavaScript Meetup. Before most meetings there is a networking hour for members to meet each other. However, members of each group tend to sit in their chairs and eat pizza instead of socializing and networking with one another.

Several attempts have been made to get the user groups to become more of a community, such as: giving quick talks during the networking hour, using round tables instead of stadium-style seating, and having people explain problems they are having to get help from the others. None were successful in building a community out of the user groups. The combined efforts of all of the attempts have made some impact, but not a lot.

The objective of this project is to encourage user group attendees to meet one another. We will make the first attempt at using software to solve this problem. The application is a Web 2.0 application that shows information about the users in the user groups. This application can run like a slideshow during the networking hour. The application will show information about the members attending the event, such as a picture of attendees, their biography, and any comments they made when registering for the event.

You could run the group on your own website, but it is tons of work. Before each meeting you have to email the members twice (one week before and one day before the event), update the home page with the next event, and update the calendar to show the event. Before long you'd start thinking about automating some of these tasks, perhaps with Meetup.com (see Figure 14.1). Moving to Meetup.com would be a great improvement, and all three groups are using Meetup.com as their website. One really great feature of Meetup.com is that it offers APIs to access information about your meetup. You can find a description of the Meetup.com APIs here: http://www.meetup.com/meetup_api

■ **FIGURE 14.1**
Meetup
Networking Tool

FIGURE 14.2
JavaFX Raffle
Spinner

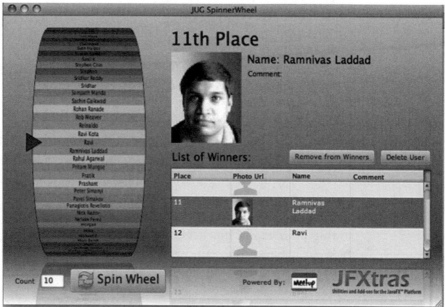

■ 14.2 GOOGLE WEB TOOLKIT (GWT)

This project uses GWT as its Ajax framework. You are probably asking your-self, "Why did we choose GWT for this project?" One of the main reasons was that the use of GWT is expected to grow rapidly. GWT is different than traditional Ajax frameworks because you write your client-side logic in Java instead of JavaScript.

Some of the main advantages of GWT are:

- There are no JavaScript syntax errors (Java is mostly typed in)
- There is great IDE support (Java IDE support is far better that JavaScript IDE support)
- You can call remote methods like regular methods
- The server side model can be used directly on a client
- It is supported by Google, and there is little chance of Google disappearing
- There is an advanced build system, so users only download files needed in their browser
- Java is compiled into optimized JavaScript

Another reason for GWT is that our project will be hosted on Google App Engine (GAE). GAE has a nice Eclipse plug-in for development that creates a simple web application starter project with GWT preconfigured. Since GAE provides free hosting for small and mid-load application hosting, it is a great place to host your application. Many start-ups move their existing code to GAE and start new projects on GAE with great success. Rather than explaining GWT in detail, let's walk you through this application to see how GWT works.

The previously mentioned project uses GWT 1.7 because the example was finished before GWT 2.0 was released. GWT 2.0 was released in December of 2009 and provides some great advantages. GWT 2.0 was released with a new profiling tool called Speed Tracer™. Speed Tracer only runs on Google Chrome, built on top of HTML5, and helps developers find performance problems in the browser. Speed Tracer is similar to Fire-Bug profiler, but much more powerful because of the additional hook to WebKit, which is the underlying engine of Google Chrome. GWT 2.0 also adds code splitting, which decreases the download time of JavaScript when the application loads. Code splitting works by allowing coders to separate off parts of their code that are not needed when an application loads. For example, you may want to load the JavaScript of your help menu on an "as needed" basis, since most users will not use the help system. Finally, GWT 2.0 provides a UIBinder that allows designers to lay out components along with the HTML, similar to using JSP tags.

■ 14.3   MEETUP NETWORKING CODE

The code in this project is open sourced as a Google code project here: http://code.google.com/p/meetup-networking/

This book focuses on a simple and easy-to-understand version of this project. We intend to polish the code and also enhance its functionality. You can download the latest code from the Google code project. We will only be looking at the main parts of the code in this chapter, because the source files are too large in their entirety to show in a single page of a book. Load the project into your IDE from the code provided on the CD or from the Google code project. To check out the code from SVN use the following command:

```
svn checkout http://meetup-networking.googlecode.com/svn/trunk/
meetup-networking-read-only
```

Let's start by looking at the Meetup.com APIs. The APIs are designed for mash-ups. To make a request, you call a simple URL and use the query string to specify what type of data you want to return and in what format. The URL we will be using for this example is:

```
"http://api.meetup.com/rsvps.json/?event_id="+ eventId + "&key=" +
apiKey
```

This URL returns JSON code that is shown in Listing 14.1.

Listing 14.1 JSON of RSVPs From Meetup.com API

```
{"results":[
    {"zip":"94709","lon":"-122.26000213623047","link":
            "http://www.meetup.com/members/123",
    "guests":"0","answers":[],"state":"CA","city":"Berkeley",
            "country":"us",
    "coord":"37.880001068115234","response":"maybe","updated":
            "Mon Jun 15 19:23:28 EDT 2009",
    "created":"Mon Jun 15 19:23:28 EDT 2009","name":"Alice",
            "comment":""
},
    {"zip":"94043","lon":"-122.08000183105469","link":
            "http://www.meetup.com/members/456",
    "guests":"0","answers":[],"state":"CA","city":"Mountain
            View","country":"us",
    "coord":"37.40999984741211","response":"yes","updated":"Mon Jun
            15 15:39:58 EDT 2009",
    "created":"Mon Jun 15 15:39:58 EDT
            2009","name":"Bob","comment":""
},
    {"zip":"94301","lon":"-122.1500015258789","link":
            "http://www.meetup.com/members/789",
    "guests":"0","answers":[],"state":"CA","city":"Palo
            Alto","country":"us",
    "coord":"37.439998626708984","response":"yes","updated":
            "Fri Jun 12 19:04:31 EDT 2009",
    "created":"Fri Jun 12 19:04:31 EDT 2009","name":"Fred","comment":
""},
],
"meta":{"lon":"","count":169,"next":"","link":
        "http://api.meetup.com/rsvps/","total_count":3,
"url":"http://api.meetup.com/rsvps/?order=name&key=123&event_id=123&
        page=200&resource=%2Frsvps.json%2F&format=json&offset=0",
```

```
"id":"","title":"Rsvps for meetups","updated":"2009-06-16 19:36:35
    EDT",
"description":"API method for accessing meetup rsvps","method":
    "Rsvps","lat":""}
}
```

This JSON code has two main parts: results and meta. meta provides information about the request. results is important because it contains information about who is attending the meetup.

Calling the API from the client is difficult because Ajax has a same-origin policy that prohibits you from making Ajax calls to domains that are not the same as your current domain. JSONP lets you to get around this restriction, but GWT does not support JSONP. Another technique that is popular in mash-ups is to proxy Ajax requests through your server. Figure 14.3 is a sequence diagram that shows how we will proxy Meetup.com calls through our web server. Don't worry about the Plain Old Java Objects (POJO), which we will cover that soon.

Listing 14.2 shows a portion of the server-side code for calling Meetup .com.

Listing 14.2 Java Server-Side Code to Capture "Content of" Page

```java
private String callPage(String urlStr) throws IOException {
  URL url = new URL(urlStr);
  BufferedReader reader = null;
  StringBuilder result = new StringBuilder();

  try {
    reader = new BufferedReader(new InputStreamReader
            (url.openStream()));

    String line;
    while ((line = reader.readLine()) != null) {
      result.append(line);
    }
  } finally {
    if (reader != null)
      reader.close();
  }

  return result.toString();
}
```

FIGURE 14.3
Ajax Proxy
Sequence Diagram

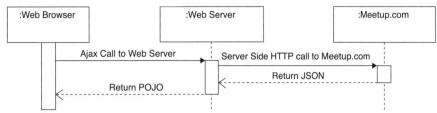

JSON is very easy to use in JavaScript, but not in Java. Remember, we are using GWT, so if we can convert the JSON to POJO, then we can use the POJOs on the client side and server side. Let's first write POJOs to hold the data in JSON. Our first POJO is called `MeetupResponse` and Listing 14.3 displays the Java code.

Listing 14.3 Meetup Response POJO

```java
package com.javaclimber.web20fundamentals.meetup.client;

import java.io.Serializable;

public class MeetupResponse implements Serializable{
    private Result[] results;
    private Meta meta;

    private String details;
    private String problem;

    public void setProblem(String problem) {
        this.problem = problem;
    }

    public String getProblem() {
        return problem;
    }

    public void setDetails(String details) {
        this.details = details;
    }

    public String getDetails() {
        return details;
    }

    public Meta getMeta() {
        return meta;
    }
```

```
    public void setMeta(Meta meta) {
        this.meta = meta;
    }

    public Result[] getResults() {
        return results;
    }

    public void setResults(Result[] results) {
        this.results = results;
    }
}
```

Note that `MeetupResponse` holds an array of `results` and `meta`, as expected. It also holds `details` and `problem`. These fields are only returned if you have done something wrong in your request, such as not passing an API key, or passing an invalid API key. Now let's look at Listing 14.4, which shows the Java code for the Meta POJO.

Listing 14.4 Meta.java

```
package com.javaclimber.web20fundamentals.meetup.client;

import java.io.Serializable;

public class Meta implements Serializable {
    private String lon;
    private int count;
    private String next;
    private String link;
    private int total_count;
    private String url;
    private String id;
    private String title;
    private String updated;
    private String description;
    private String lat;
    private String method;

    public String getLon() {
        return lon;
    }

    public void setLon(String lon) {
        this.lon = lon;
    }
```

```java
public int getCount() {
   return count;
}

public void setCount(int count) {
   this.count = count;
}

public String getNext() {
   return next;
}

public void setNext(String next) {
   this.next = next;
}

public String getLink() {
   return link;
}

public void setLink(String link) {
   this.link = link;
}

public int getTotal_count() {
   return total_count;
}

public void setTotal_count(int total_count) {
   this.total_count = total_count;
}

public String getUrl() {
   return url;
}

public void setUrl(String url) {
   this.url = url;
}

public String getId() {
   return id;
}

public void setId(String id) {
   this.id = id;
}
```

```
      public String getTitle() {
         return title;
      }

      public void setTitle(String title) {
         this.title = title;
      }

      public String getUpdated() {
         return updated;
      }

      public void setUpdated(String updated) {
         this.updated = updated;
      }

      public String getDescription() {
         return description;
      }

      public void setDescription(String description) {
         this.description = description;
      }

      public String getLat() {
         return lat;
      }

      public void setLat(String lat) {
         this.lat = lat;
      }

      public String getMethod() {
         return method;
      }

      public void setMethod(String method) {
         this.method = method;
      }
   }
}
```

Finally, let's look at the result POJO in Listing 14.5, which is the most complex and holds all of the data we will be using in our application.

Listing 14.5 Result.java

```java
package com.javaclimber.web20fundamentals.meetup.client;

import java.io.Serializable;

public class Result implements Serializable {
    private String zip;
    private float lon;
    private String link;
    private int guests;
    private String[] answers;
    private String state;
    private String city;
    private String country;
    private float coord;
    private String response;
    private String updated;
    private String created;
    private String name;
    private String comment;

    public String getZip() {
        return zip;
    }

    public void setZip(String zip) {
        this.zip = zip;
    }

    public float getLon() {
        return lon;
    }

    public void setLon(float lon) {
        this.lon = lon;
    }

    public String getLink() {
        return link;
    }

    public void setLink(String link) {
        this.link = link;
    }
```

```
public int getGuests() {
    return guests;
}

public void setGuests(int guests) {
    this.guests = guests;
}

public String[] getAnswers() {
    return answers;
}

public void setAnswers(String[] answers) {
    this.answers = answers;
}

public String getState() {
    return state;
}

public void setState(String state) {
    this.state = state;
}

public String getCity() {
    return city;
}

public void setCity(String city) {
    this.city = city;
}

public String getCountry() {
    return country;
}

public void setCountry(String country) {
    this.country = country;
}

public float getCoord() {
    return coord;
}

public void setCoord(float coord) {
    this.coord = coord;
}
```

```java
   public String getResponse() {
      return response;
   }

   public void setResponse(String response) {
      this.response = response;
   }

   public String getUpdated() {
      return updated;
   }

   public void setUpdated(String updated) {
      this.updated = updated;
   }

   public String getCreated() {
      return created;
   }

   public void setCreated(String created) {
      this.created = created;
   }

   public String getName() {
      return name;
   }

   public void setName(String name) {
      this.name = name;
   }

   public String getComment() {
      return comment;
   }

   public void setComment(String comment) {
      this.comment = comment;
   }
}
```

The next step is to convert the JSON returned from Meetup.com to POJOs. There are over a dozen JSON to POJO conversion libraries listed here: http://json.org/

Although the `json.org` and `json.lib` libraries or both easy to use and efficient, we ever, we will be using the Jackson JSON processor, because of its high performance. You can learn more about Jackson here: http://jackson.codehaus.org/

Working with Jackson is very easy. The following code shows how to convert a JSON string to a `MeetupResponse` POJO. Just so our client is not aware of the various Jackson exceptions, let's convert all exceptions thrown by the parser to a `MeetupNetworkingException`. This also makes it easy to swap out JSON libraries without changing client code.

Listing 14.6 Method to Convert JSON to MeetupResponse POJO

```
private MeetupResponse parseJSON(String json)
    throws MeetupNetworkingException {
  ObjectMapper mapper = new ObjectMapper();

  MeetupResponse eventData = null;
  try {
    eventData = (MeetupResponse) mapper.readValue(json,
      MeetupResponse.class);
  } catch (JsonParseException e) {
    e.printStackTrace();
    throw new MeetupNetworkingException(e);
  } catch (JsonMappingException e) {
    e.printStackTrace();
    throw new MeetupNetworkingException(e);
  } catch (IOException e) {
    e.printStackTrace();
    throw new MeetupNetworkingException(e);
  }
  return eventData;
}
```

Now let's look at how Ajax calls can be made to pass the `MeetupResponse` POJO to the client. Listing 14.7 shows a portion of `web.xml` with servlet-related meta-data to handle the request.

Listing 14.7 Defining MeetupServlet in web.xml

```
<?xml version="1.0" encoding="UTF-8"?>
<!DOCTYPE web-app
    PUBLIC "-//Sun Microsystems, Inc.//DTD Web Application 2.3//EN"
    "http://java.sun.com/dtd/web-app_2_3.dtd">
```

```
<web-app>
  <servlet>
    <servlet-name>meetupServlet</servlet-name>
    <servlet-class>
        com.javaclimber.web20fundamentals.meetup.server
            .MeetupServiceImpl
    </servlet-class>
  </servlet>
  <servlet-mapping>
    <servlet-name>meetupServlet</servlet-name>
    <url-pattern>/meetupnetworking/meetup</url-pattern>
  </servlet-mapping>
  <welcome-file-list>
    <welcome-file>MeetupNetworking.html</welcome-file>
  </welcome-file-list>
</web-app>
```

The next step is to define the client stub for making remote calls. Right now we only need the lookupMeetupInfo method, but later the lookupProfile method will be useful. This client stub acts as an interface for remote methods that can be called. In GWT, making remote calls is just like making local calls, but passing a callback.

Listing 14.8 and Listing 14.9 are two Java interfaces that specify the Java methods that we will implement in Java classes later in this section.

Listing 14.8 Meetup Service Interface

```
package com.javaclimber.web20fundamentals.meetup.client;

import com.google.gwt.user.client.rpc.RemoteService;
import com.google.gwt.user.client.rpc.RemoteServiceRelativePath;

/**
 * The client side stub for the RPC service.
 */
@RemoteServiceRelativePath("meetup")
public interface MeetupService extends RemoteService {

  MeetupResponse lookupMeetupInfo(String apiKey, String eventId)
      throws MeetupNetworkingException;

  Profile lookupProfile(String urlLink) throws MeetupNetworking-
      Exception;
}
```

Listing 14.9 defines the `async` counterpart to the `MeetupService`. The `MeetupServiceAsync` is called by you when you write your client code. GWT provides the implementation for `MeetupServiceAsync`, so you do not need to write an implementation.

Listing 14.9 Meetup Service Async Interface

```
package com.javaclimber.web20fundamentals.meetup.client;

import com.google.gwt.user.client.rpc.AsyncCallback;

/**
 * The async counterpart of <code>MeetupService</code>.
 */
public interface MeetupServiceAsync {

  void lookupMeetupInfo(String apiKey, String eventId,
      AsyncCallback<MeetupResponse> callback);

  void lookupProfile(String urlLink, AsyncCallback<Profile>callback) ;
}
```

Listing 14.10 shows the Java implementation class for the Java interface in Listing 14.8.

Listing 14.10 Meetup Service Server–Side Implementation

```
package com.javaclimber.web20fundamentals.meetup.server;
/**
 * The server side implementation of the RPC service.
 */
@SuppressWarnings("serial")
public class MeetupServiceImpl extends RemoteServiceServlet implements
    MeetupService {

  public MeetupResponse lookupMeetupInfo(String apiKey, String
                                                      eventId)
      throws MeetupNetworkingException {
    String json = "";

    try {
      json = callPage("http://api.meetup.com/rsvps.json/?event_id="
          + eventId + "&key=" + apiKey);
    } catch (IOException e) {
      e.printStackTrace();
      throw new MeetupNetworkingException(e);
    }
```

```
      MeetupResponse eventData = parseJSON(json);

      removeNoRSVP(eventData);
      return eventData;

   }

   private void removeNoRSVP(MeetupResponse eventData) {
      Result[] results = eventData.getResults();
      if (results == null)
         results = new Result[0];
      List<Result> yesList = new ArrayList<Result>();
      for (int i = 0; i < results.length; i++) {
         if ("yes".equals(results[i].getResponse()))
            yesList.add(results[i]);
      }
      eventData.setResults(yesList.toArray
      (new Result[yesList.size()]));
   }

   private MeetupResponse parseJSON(String json)
         throws MeetupNetworkingException {
      //CODE REMOVED, ALREADY COVERED
   }

   private String callPage(String urlStr) throws IOException {
      URL url = new URL(urlStr);
      BufferedReader reader = null;
      StringBuilder result = new StringBuilder();

      try {
         reader = new BufferedReader(new InputStreamReader
         (url.openStream()));

         String line;
         while ((line = reader.readLine()) != null) {
            result.append(line);
         }
      } finally {
         if (reader != null)
            reader.close();
      }

      return result.toString();
   }
```

```
public Profile lookupProfile(String urlLink)
    throws MeetupNetworkingException {
  //CODE REMOVED WILL EXPLAIN CODE LATER
}

private Profile parseProfileData(String pageData) {
  //CODE REMOVED WILL EXPLAIN CODE LATER
}

}
```

The Java method `lookupMeetupInfo` in Listing 14.10 takes the `apiKey` and `eventId` and creates a URL for getting information about the people who attended a Meetup.com event. Next, the `callPage` function is called, which returns the JSON containing the attendee information. Next, we call `parseJSON`, which converts JSON to POJOs using Jackson. Our last step is to remove anyone who didn't RSVP "yes" to the event, which is easy, because we are now working with POJOs.

Now let's change gears and look at the client side of things. We will start with a normal HTML page (Listing 14.11) with regular tags and then we will define an `EntryPoint` class that will add functionality to the page using GWT.

Listing 14.11 Meetup Networking HTML Code

```
<!DOCTYPE HTML PUBLIC "-//W3C//DTD HTML 4.01 Transitional//EN">
<html>
<head>
<meta http-equiv="content-type" content="text/html; charset=UTF-8">
<link type="text/css" rel="stylesheet" href="MeetupNetworking.css">
<title>Meetup Networking</title>

<script type="text/javascript" language="javascript"
  src="meetupnetworking/meetupnetworking.nocache.js"></script>
  </head>
<body>
<iframe src="javascript:''" id="__gwt_historyFrame" tabIndex='-1'
  style="position: absolute; width: 0; height: 0; border: 0">
</iframe>
<div id="menuContainer" style="position: absolute; top: 0px; left:
    0px; width: 100%" ></div>
<h1>Meetup Networking</h1>

<div id="home" class="display">
  <table align="center" id="homet1">
    <tr>
```

```
          <td colspan="3" style="font-weight: bold;"
              align="center">Take Me To:</td>
        </tr>
        <tr>
          <td id="networkingButtonContainer"></td>
          <td width="30px"> </td>
          <td id="spinnerButtonContainer"></td>
        </tr>
      </table>
      <br />
      <br />
      <table align="center" id="homet2" class="hidden">
        <tr>
          <td colspan="3" style="font-weight: bold;" align="center">
            Change EventId or API Key:
          </td>
        </tr>
        <tr>
          <td align="center" id="changeEventButtonContainer"></td>
        </tr>
      </table>
  </div>

<div id="networking" class="noDisplay">
</div>

</body>
</html>
```

The HTML page in Listing 14.11 contains two main div elements. The first div is id home, and that is what you see when you are on the home page. The second div is id networking, and that is where the meetup attendee information is shown. The second div is not visible. Now let's look at how JavaScript is added to the page with GWT. The first thing we will do (see Listing 14.12) is add a menu bar to the top of the page.

Listing 14.12 Using GWT to Build the Page

```
private void addMenu(final Button networkingButton, Timer timer) {
    final Timer fTimer = timer;

    MenuBar homeMenu = new MenuBar(true);
    homeMenu.addItem("Home", new Command() {
        public void execute() {
```

```
        fTimer.cancel();
        RootPanel.get("home").setStyleName("display");
        RootPanel.get("networking").setStyleName("NoDisplay");
      }
    });

    MenuBar networkingMenu = new MenuBar(true);
    networkingMenu.addItem("Launch", new Command() {
      public void execute() {
        networkingButton.click();
      }
    });
    networkingMenu.addItem("About", cmd);
    networkingMenu.addItem("Google Code Project", new Command() {
      public void execute() {
        Window.open("http://code.google.com/p/meetup-networking/",
            "_blank", "");
      }
    });

//REMOVED CODE

    MenuBar menu = new MenuBar();
    menu.addItem("Home", homeMenu);
    menu.addItem("Networking", networkingMenu);
    menu.addItem("SpinnerWheel", spinnerMenu);
    menu.addItem("Web 2.0 Fundamentals Book", bookMenu);

    // Add it to the root panel.
    RootPanel.get("menuContainer").add(menu);
}
```

You can see how easy it is to create a menu with GWT. GWT uses the command pattern to handle events in the menu. Note that the homeMenu has a command that stops a timer, then shows the home div and hides the networking div. You can see how the About menu will open a web page. The most important menu is the networkingMenu, which is used to start the slideshow that shows meetup members. Let's look at Listing 14.13, which shows you how the networkingButton is created and added to the form. networkingButton is used to start the slideshow. Much of the code has been removed to highlight networkingButton. The full code can be seen here: http://code.google.com/p/meetup-networking/

Listing 14.13 Adding the Networking Button

```
public void onModuleLoad() {
  final Button networkingButton = new Button("Networking");

  RootPanel.get("networkingButtonContainer").add(networkingButton);

  final DialogBox dialogBox = new DialogBox();
  dialogBox.setText("Meetup Id");
  dialogBox.setAnimationEnabled(true);
  final Button submitButton = new Button("Submit");
  submitButton.getElement().setId("submitButton");
  VerticalPanel dialogVPanel = new VerticalPanel();
  dialogVPanel.addStyleName("dialogVPanel");
  dialogVPanel.add(new HTML("<b>Event Id:</b><br/>"));
  dialogVPanel.add(eventIdField);
  dialogVPanel.add(new HTML("<br/><b>API Key:</b><br/>"));
  dialogVPanel.add(apiKeyField);
  dialogVPanel.add(new HTML("<br/>"));
  dialogVPanel.setHorizontalAlignment(VerticalPanel.ALIGN_CENTER);
  dialogVPanel.add(submitButton);
  dialogBox.setWidget(dialogVPanel);

  final MyHandler handler = new MyHandler(eventIdField, apiKeyField,
      dialogBox, meetupService);

  submitButton.addClickHandler(new ClickHandler() {
    public void onClick(ClickEvent event) {
      String eventId = eventIdField.getText().trim();
      String apiKey = apiKeyField.getText().trim();

      RootPanel.get("homet2").setStyleName("visible");
      if ("".equals(eventId) || "".equals(apiKey)) {
        if (dialogBox.isShowing()) {
          Window
              .alert("You must supply both an Event Id and API
              Key.");
          dialogBox.hide();
          return;
        }
      }

      dialogBox.hide();
      handler.showMeetupUsers();
    }
```

```
    });

    addMenu(networkingButton, timer);

    networkingButton.addClickHandler(handler);
}
```

The code in Listing 14.13 creates and adds a button to networkingButtonContainer. Next, the code defines a dialog that can be used to collect your eventId and apiKey, which are used by the Meetup.com APIs. Next, a handler is defined that handles users clicking on the button. Before looking into the details of the handler, let's look at the dialog's submit button ClickHandler. When a user clicks the networkingButton, the dialog is shown to collect the eventId and apiKey. When the submit button is clicked, the user wishes to close/hide the dialog. The handler will check to see if values are provided and alert the user if values were not submitted. If input verification succeeds, then the networkingButton's handler's showMeetupUsers method is called. Now let's look into the click handler code (see Listing 14.14) for the networkingButton.

Listing 14.14 Networking Button Click Handler

```
public MyHandler(TextBox eventIdField, TextBox apiKeyField,
        DialogBox dialogBox, MeetupServiceAsync meetupService) {

//CODE REMOVED

    public void onClick(ClickEvent event) {
        showMeetupUsers();
    }

//CODE REMOVED

    public void showMeetupUsers() {
        String eventId = eventIdField.getText().trim();
        String apiKey = apiKeyField.getText().trim();

        if ("".equals(eventId) || "".equals(apiKey)) {
            dialogBox.show();
            dialogBox.center();
            eventIdField.setFocus(true);
            eventIdField.selectAll();

            return;
        }
```

```java
RootPanel.get("home").setStyleName("noDisplay");

final HTML loadingHTML = new HTML(
    "<font color='red'><b>Loading...</b></font>");
RootPanel.get("networking").clear();
RootPanel.get("networking").add(loadingHTML);
RootPanel.get("networking").setStyleName("display");

final int[] count = { 0 };
final int[] callsFinished = { 0 };

meetupService.lookupMeetupInfo(apiKey, eventId,
    new AsyncCallback<MeetupResponse>() {
        public void onFailure(Throwable caught) {
          Window.alert("ERROR: " + caught.getMessage());
        }

        public void onSuccess(MeetupResponse response) {
          final Result[] results = response.getResults();

          for (int i = 0; i < results.length; i++) {
            final Result result = results[i];

            meetupService.lookupProfile(results[i].getLink(),
                new AsyncCallback<Profile>() {
                    public void onFailure(Throwable caught) {
                    callsFinished[0]++;
                      if (callsFinished[0] == results.length) {
                        startSlideShow();
                      }
                    };

                    public void onSuccess(Profile profile) {

                      if (profile != null) {
                        String user = "";
                        user += "<div class='display'
                        id='user"
                            + count[0] + "'>";

                        count[0]++;
                        user += "<table><tr><td
                        valign='top'>";
                        user += "<img src='"
                            + profile.getImage()
                            + "'/>";
```

```
                                user += "</td><td width='20px'><td
                                valign='top'>"
                                        + "<h2>"
                                        + result.getName()
                                        + "</h2>"
                                        + "<b>BIO:</b><br/>";
                                user += profile.getBio();
                                user += "<br/><br/><b>COMENTS:
                                </b><br/>";
                                user += result.getComment();
                                user += "<br/></td></tr></table>"
                                        + "</div>\n";

                                HTML html = new HTML(user);

                                RootPanel.get("networking")
                                        .add(html);
                            }
                            callsFinished[0]++;
                            if (callsFinished[0] == results.length) {
                                startSlideShow();
                            } else {
                                loadingHTML
                                        .setHTML("<font color='red'>
                                        <b>Loading...</b>"
                                                + callsFinished[0]
                                                + " of "
                                                + results.length
                                                + " completed</font>");
                            }
                        }
                    };
                });
            }
        }
    });
}
```

Listing 14.14 contains an onLoad method that calls the method showMeetupUsers, which makes a remote call for each person to look up additional information on a person's profile page. When each remote call returns, we will create a div containing the users information and add that div to the main networking div. When all Ajax calls are completed, startSlideShow (see Listing 14.15) is called.

Listing 14.15 Method to Run Slide Show

```
private void startSlideShow() {
  RootPanel.get("networking").remove(
  loadingHTML);

  HTML memberView = new HTML(
    "<table width='100%'><tr><td width='50%' id='first'
    valign='top'> </td><td width='50%' id='second'
    valign='top'> </td></tr></table>");
  RootPanel.get("networking").add(
    memberView);

  HTML mcount = new HTML(
    "<div class='noDisplay' id='numMembers'>"
    + count[0]
    + "</div>");
  RootPanel.get("networking").add(mcount);

  hideAll();
  show2Members();
  timer.scheduleRepeating(10000);
}

public void hideAll() {
  for (int i = 0; i < count[0]; i++) {
    DOM.getElementById("user" + i).setClassName("noDisplay");
  }
}

public void show2Members() {

  int numMembers = Integer.parseInt(DOM.getElementById("numMembers")
      .getInnerHTML().trim());

  int first = Random.nextInt(numMembers);
  int second = Random.nextInt(numMembers);

  if (first == second)
    second = Random.nextInt(numMembers);

  DOM.getElementById("first").setInnerHTML(
      DOM.getElementById("user" + first).getInnerHTML());

  DOM.getElementById("second").setInnerHTML(
      DOM.getElementById("user" + second).getInnerHTML());
}
```

The `startSlideShow` method starts by removing the `loading div`, then a HTML table with two cells is added to the `networking div`. This table will be used to show information about two attendees at a time. Next, a hidden div keeps count of how many members are available for the slideshow. The next step is to hide all of the attendees' profiles. Call the method `show2Members`, which randomly selects two users and shows them in the display table. Finally, the timer is started to show different members every 10 seconds. The code for creating a timer in `entryPoint` is shown here:

```
timer = new Timer() {
  @Override
  public void run() {
    handler.show2Members();
  }
};
```

■ 14.4 JFXTRAS JAVAFX RAFFLE TOOL BACKGROUND

After working on the slideshow example using Meetup.com APIs, we realized that Jim Weaver's JavaFX-based raffle tool was due for a rewrite and was a perfect fit. In January of 2008, Jim Weaver wrote a JavaFX based raffle tool based on early builds of JavaFX that Sun was releasing to the community. Jim wrote the raffle tool as an example project for his blog: http://learnjavafx.typepad.com.

The code used in original spinner wheel was incompatible with the released version of JavaFX. To remedy this, Steven Chin has completely rewritten with many nice enhancements the JavaFX Spinner Wheel to run with the released version of JavaFX. The next section walks you through some of the key features of the JavaFX SpinnerWheel code. You can learn more about Steve on his blog here: http://steveonjava.com

■ 14.5 JFXTRAS JAVAFX RAFFLE TOOL CODE

The following section on JavaFX was kindly contributed by Stephen Chin.

JavaFX is a new RIA technology developed by Sun that runs on the Java platform and brings together graphics, animation, media, and cross-device support. One of the early adopters of JavaFX was Jim Weaver, who wrote the first book on the interpreted version of JavaFX, and developed some community tools, such as the JUG SpinnerWheel application. The JavaFX platform has come a long way since the first version of the JUG SpinnerWheel was written, and it seemed like a good opportunity to do a complete rewrite that also demonstrated some of the new capabilities of JavaFX. In this section, we will demonstrate a new version of the JUG SpinnerWheel that demonstrates the following capabilities of the JavaFX platform:

- Scenegraph Composition and Animation—Similar to 3D applications, JavaFX has a scene graph that can be used to compose graphic elements for display. It also comes with built-in syntax for doing complex animations, which we will use to animate the SpinnerWheel.
- Advanced Graphics Effects—The SpinnerWheel will be rendered in pseudo-3D using a `PerspectiveTransform` effect, and a `ReflectionEffect` will give it a glass-like appearance.
- Web Service Integration—JavaFX makes it easy to call Web Services and process the responses in either JSON or XML format. We will also use a third-party library called JFXtras to do object marshalling.

Figure 14.4 shows the completed JUG SpinnerWheel application with a very large wheel containing all of the participants for the next Silicon Valley Web JUG meeting.

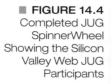

■ FIGURE 14.4
Completed JUG
SpinnerWheel
Showing the Silicon
Valley Web JUG
Participants

■ 14.5.1 Building the JUG Spinner UI

Everything in JavaFX starts with a Stage. The JavaFX Stage maps to different containers based on the deployment medium of your application. If you choose to deploy as a Web Start application, the stage maps to a JFrame; in a browser, it maps to the Applet frame; and on a mobile device, it maps to the entire device display. The Stage is also where you can declare information about the application, including its title, width and height, icons, and scene contents, as shown in Listing 14.16.

Listing 14.16 JavaFX Stage Declaration for the JUGSpinnerWheel

```
Stage {
    title: "JUG SpinnerWheel"
    icons: [
        Image {
            url: "{__DIR__}java-duke-guitar_mini.png"
        }
        Image {
            url: "{__DIR__}java-duke-guitar_normal.png"
        }
    ]
    width: 750
    height: 500
    scene: ResizableScene {
        content: JUGSpinnerUI {}
    }
}
```

While JavaFX is compiled into Java byte codes that are run by the JVM, the language itself is tailored for User Interface (UI) development. One of the features of JavaFX is the declarative coding style that lets you construct nested objects in hierarchical declarations. While this is a very simple code example, it contains several fundamental JavaFX coding constructs, including:

- Object instantiation—In JavaFX, a class name followed by curly brackets constructs a new instance of an object.
- String literals—Text surrounded by single or double quotes is turned into a string literal in JavaFX. Listing 14.16 demonstrates variable expansion within a string by surrounding a variable (in this case, the built-in __DIR__ constant) with curly brackets.

• Sequence construction—JavaFX has a built-in datatype, called a sequence, that takes the place of arrays and lists in Java. To construct a new sequence, enclose a list of elements in square brackets, such as the icons sequence shown in Listing 14.17. The bulk of the JUG SpinnerWheel UI is created in the JUGSpinnerUI class, which is of type ResizableCustomNode. The key portions of the JUGSpinnerUI code are shown in Listing 14.17, with ellipses used to indicate where additional code has been omitted.

Listing 14.17 JUG SpinnerUI Custom Node Definition to Layout the Main UI

```
public class JUGSpinnerUI extends ResizableCustomNode {
    def backgroundGradient = ResizableRectangle {
        cache: true
        fill: LinearGradient {
            endX: 0
            stops: [
                Stop {color: Color.LIGHTBLUE, offset: 0}
                Stop {color: ColorUtil.darker(Color.LIGHTBLUE, .5),
                offset: .8}
                Stop {color: Color.WHITE, offset: 1}
            ]
        }
    }

    def controls = ResizableHBox {spacing: 10, content: [
        Label {text: "Count"},
        TextBox {text: "1", columns: 3, action: spin},
        Button {
            text: "Spin Wheel"
            font: Font {size: 20}
            action: spin
            ...
        }
    ]}

    def meetupLink = Hyperlink { ... }
    def jfxtrasLink = Hyperlink { ... }
    def logos = ResizableHBox {
        spacing: 10
        content: [
            Spacer {}
            Label {text: "Powered By:"}
```

```
                Hyperlink { ... },
                Hyperlink { ... }
            ]
        }

    override function create() {
        Deck {
            content: [
                backgroundGradient,
                Grid {
                    border: 20
                    hgap: 10
                    vgap: 20
                    rows: [
                        row([
                            JUGSpinnerModel.jugSpinnerWheel,
                            JUGSpinnerModel.winnerDisplay
                        ]),
                        row([controls, logos])
                    ]
                }
            ]
        }
    }
}
```

The only function you need to implement a `CustomNode` is the `create()` function, which returns a JavaFX node. In this example, we are using a few layout classes from the JFXtras project, including `Deck` and `Grid`, which let you easily build resizable interfaces. The `Grid` class takes a sequence of rows, each of which can have multiple cells in a nested sequence. This is used to divide the UI into four sections that resize to fit their contents, as shown in Figure 14.5.

Both the Controls and Logos sections are created using a simple `ResizableHBox`, which is filled with built-in JavaFX controls for the buttons and links. The Spinner Wheel and Winner Display are both nested JavaFX custom nodes that have additional logic to work with the nested controls. The full source code for both classes are available for download from the book's website, but Listing 14.18 has the full source code from the `JUGSpinnerWheel` class, which shows how to create animation in JavaFX.

FIGURE 14.5
SpinnerWheel UI
Broken Down by
Grid Sections

Listing 14.18 JUG SpinnerWheel Class Demonstrating Animation in JavaFX

```
public class JUGSpinnerWheel extends ResizableCustomNode {
    var winners = bind JUGSpinnerModel.winners with inverse;
    var members = bind JUGSpinnerModel.members with inverse;

    public-read var spinning = false;

    var spinner:SpinnerWheel;

    public function spin(countParam:Integer) {
        if (sizeof winners == sizeof members) {
            Alert.inform("Congratulations!", "No need to spin the
            wheel, all "
                            "of your members are winners already!");
            return;
        }
        def count = Math.min(countParam, sizeof members - sizeof
        winners);
        spinning = true;
```

```
            var oldCentered = spinner.centered;
            var prospectiveWinners:Member[];
            Timeline {
                keyFrames: for (i in [1..count]) {
                    def random = Math.random() * sizeof members;
                    def upALittle = oldCentered - 3;
                    var newCentered = oldCentered = Math.
                    round(oldCentered +
                        Math.max(70, sizeof members) + random);
                    def newWinner = bind newCentered mod sizeof members
                    as Integer;
                    while (Sequences.indexOf([winners, prospectiveWin-
                    ners],
                            members[newWinner]) != -1) newCentered++;
                    insert members[newWinner] into prospectiveWinners;
                    [
                        KeyFrame {
                            time: i * (7s / count) - (6s / count)
                            values: spinner.centered => upALittle
                                    tween Interpolator.EASEOUT
                        },
                        KeyFrame {
                            time: i * (7s / count)
                            values: spinner.centered => newCentered
                                    tween Interpolator.SPLINE(.2, .8,
                                    .6, 1.0)
                            action: function() {
                                JUGSpinnerModel.pickWinner(newWinner);
                                if (i == count) {
                                    spinning = false;
                                }
                            }
                        }
                    ]
                }
            }.play();
        }

        override function create() {
            spinner = SpinnerWheel {
                effect: Reflection {topOffset: 10, fraction: .25}
```

```
            entries: bind for (member in members) member.name
            layoutInfo: GridLayoutInfo {
                width: 250, minWidth: 200, hgrow: NEVER, fill:
                VERTICAL
            }
        }
    }
}
```

Animation in JavaFX is based on key frames that can be interpolated to create smooth animation. To create a new animation, you start with the Time-frame class, and pass in a sequence of KeyFrame objects. In the case of the JUG SpinnerWheel, all of the complicated perspective transforms to animate the wheel are taken care of by the SpinnerWheel control whenever the centered variable is updated. To update spinner.centered, two KeyFrames are used in sequence. One to raise the wheel slightly (just like a person is stretching before the swing), and a second to rotate the wheel downward to match the location of the new winner. They both use the tween keyword with an Interpolator to provide smooth animation; the former using the built-in EASEOUT interpolator for a slight deceleration, and the latter using a custom SPLINE interpolator to ease the wheel to a smooth stop. The final touch is a Reflection effect applied to the SpinnerWheel that gives the bottom of the UI a glassy, transparent look. There is a wide variety of JavaFX effects from drop shadows to 3D lighting that can be applied with a single-line instantiation and assignment just like this.

■ 14.5.2 Calling Web Services from JavaFX

JavaFX provides built-in capabilities for making asynchronous web requests to services on the Internet. It also has both a JSON and XML parser built-in that lets you pull information out of the web request to populate your backend model and update the UI. In addition to the built-in capabilities, we will also be using the object marshalling capability of the JFXtras add-on project to simplify the creation of Plain-Old JavaFX Objects (POJFXO)automatically, based on the server response. Similar to the earlier examples in the chapter, we will also be using the Meetup.com API to populate the member information for the SpinnerWheel. In this instance, we will be using the event API to fetch a list of users that have RSVP'ed for the event. The basic Representational State Transfer (REST) call is: http://api.meetup.com/rsvps.json/event_id=eventId key=apiKey

The Event ID is pulled out of other web service calls to meetup.com, which retrieves the most recent event for the group—you should provide your own API key for making the request. In this case, we have chosen to get responses in JSON format, although JavaFX can handle XML just as well. Once successfully parameterized, Meetup.com will return a response in the following format:

```
{ "results": [
  {
    "zip":"94044",
    "lon":"-122.48999786376953",
    "photo_url":"http:\/\/photos1.meetupstatic.com\/photos\/
                member\/1\/4\/b\/a\/member_5333306.jpeg",
    "response":"no",
    "name":"Andres Almiray",
    "comment":"Can't make it :-("
  },
  ...
]}
```

As you can see in the response object, the rest of the results are omitted, but the result would contain one record for each of the attendees of the event. Making REST calls and processing the response using the JFXtras JSONHandler is as easy as 1, 2, 3:

1. **Create your POJFXO**—In this instance, the fields that we care about from the response are photoUrl, name, response, and comment:

   ```
   public class Member extends JFXObject  public var place:Integer;
   public var photoUrl:String;
   public var name:String;
   public var response:String;
   public var comment:String;
   ```

2. **Create a JSONHandler to parse the response**—The JSONHandler needs two arguments, the fully qualified class name of the data type, and an

onDone callback that will be used to pass back the response after parsing is complete. Here is the full implementation:

```
var memberParser:JSONHandler = JSONHandler {
   rootClass: "org.jfxtras.jugspinner.data.MemberSearch"
   onDone: function(obj, isSequence): Void {
      members = (obj as MemberSearch).results;
}}
```

The MemberSearch class is simply a class wrapper around a sequence of Member objects:

```
public class MemberSearch {
   public var results:Member[];
}
```

3. **Make the HttpRequest to the server**—The last step is to call the built-in HttpRequest class to make the asynchronous web request for the data. The minimal implementation requires a URL to call (which is the same Meetup.com call shown earlier), and an onDone callback that will call the memberParser:

```
HttpRequest {
   location: rsvpQuery
   onInput: function(is: java.io.InputStream) {
      memberParser.parse(is);
}}.start();
```

The start method on HttpRequest will fire the web service call asynchronously, which will populate the members of the model object, and trickle through to the UI automatically via the JavaFX bind facility. Integrating your back-end web applications with client technologies has never been this easy! You can check out the full-featured version of the JUG Spinner on the JFXtras community website here: http://jfxtras.org/

This is also a great resource to learn more about the JavaFX language with the largest independent collection of samples and resources for learning JavaFX on the Web.

■ 14.6 SUMMARY

In this chapter we worked with Meetup.com APIs to develop two applications that can be used to assist in running user groups. The first application is written as a traditional Web 2.0 browser application using GWT with the purpose of helping user group members network with on another. The second application is written in JavaFX as a RIA that helps you raffle of prizes at a user group. Both of these applications can be used to help you understand a full featured simple applicaiton that integrates with third party APIs. Both applications are open source and are great examples of using modern new Web 2.0 technologies.

## CHAPTER 15

Comet

In This Chapter:

- Introducing the Concept of Comet
- CometD
- Orbited
- Industry Perspective

Comet gives web servers the ability to push information to the browser as needed. In this chapter, we will explore methods of pushing data using Comet.

■ 15.1 INTRODUCING THE CONCEPT OF COMET

Comet is a very powerful feature that has yet to reach mass adoption. Over time, Ajax became very popular because it lets developers make remote web requests with JavaScript to get additional information from web servers. When developers get the additional information, a web page can be updated without refreshing the entire page. Comet is similar to Ajax, and often called Reverse Ajax, because Comet lets the server push data to the client. There are currently two techniques that are considered Comet—long polling and streaming. Long polling is a technique for simulating Comet, but it is not considered Comet.

HTTP Protocol is a connectionless protocol, which means once a browser gets its data it closes its socket connection to the web server. This makes sending data from the server to the client at random intervals very challenging. Another limitation is that most browsers have a two concurrent-requests-per-domain limit. Any additional requests that are made (while there are two pending requests) are placed in a queue. When one of the original requests finishes, the first request on the queue will be made. The browser handles this queueing without your knowing or being notified in any way. As a simple example is if a web page has 100 images, only 2 images will load at a time. Once an image finishes loading, then another image will begin to load. At most two images will load concurrently. Several Open-Source frameworks, such as CometD, Orbited, Grizzly™, and Kaazing™ have been created to help simplify writing Comet applications. Next, we will discuss the current various strategies for Comet applications.

■ 15.1.1 Polling

Polling is technically not considered Comet, but it has been used for many years to simulate the same functionality as Comet. Polling works by making repeated Ajax calls on a fixed interval. If data is available, the call will return the data and possibly stop polling. If data is not available, it will continue polling while waiting for data. Figure 15.1 shows how polling works. There are two major disadvantages to polling. The first is that many wasted requests will be made. For example, if your poll interval is 1 second and your query completes in 9.2 seconds, then 9 wasted requests are made. Imagine how large this overhead would be for a chat application if everyone in the chat left for lunch. Polling leads to a very large overhead of unnecessary requests. The second disadvantage is that data is, on average, half of a poll interval old when it is delivered. In the previous example, the query will be complete in 9.2 seconds, but the data will not be delivered until 10 seconds has passed.

Implementing code for polling is very easy. The basic idea is to make an Ajax call to check for data, and check to see if the data is available. If data is available, then you can use the data and you are finished, but if the data is not available you must use setTimeout to re-execute the Ajax request for the data. Listing 15.1 shows the code for polling. For this example we'll simulate a long-running sql call that is running in the background and to know when it is finished.

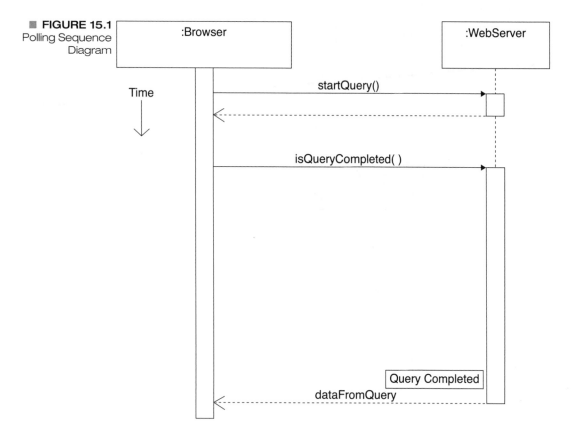

■ FIGURE 15.1
Polling Sequence
Diagram

The query begins when the Start Query button is clicked, which calls
startQuery( ), as shown here.

```
<div id="result">Status Here</div>
<button onclick="startQuery()">Start Query</button>
```

Listing 15.1 Client-Side Polling Code

```
<script type="text/javascript">
 function startQuery(){
 dojo.byId('result').innerHTML = 'running'
  dojo.xhrGet({
      url:"longQuery.jsp?type=start",
      handleAs: "text",
```

```
      load: function(data){
        pollForResult()
      },
      error: function(msg){
      alert('problem '+msg);
      }
  });
}

function pollForResult(){
  dojo.xhrGet({
      url:"longQuery.jsp",
      handleAs: "text",
      load: function(result){
        dojo.byId('result').innerHTML=dojo.byId('result').innerHTML
        + "*";
        if(result == 'not complete'){
          setTimeout('pollForResult()', 1000);
        }else{
          showResult(result);
        }
      },
      error: function(msg){
      alert('problem '+msg);

      }
  });
}

function showResult(result){
  dojo.byId('result').innerHTML = result;
}
</script>

<div id="result">Status Here</div>
<button onclick="startQuery()">Start Query</button>
```

Listing 15.1 contains the function `startQuery` makes an Ajax request to `longQuery.jsp` and passes it a parameter of `type=start` to record the start time of the simulated 10 second background query. When the Ajax call completes the query, we need to call `pollForResults( )` to get the results, as shown here.

```
function startQuery(){
  dojo.byId('result').innerHTML = 'running'
```

```
dojo.xhrGet({
    url:"longQuery.jsp?type=start",
    handleAs: "text",
    load: function(data){
      pollForResult()
    },
    error: function(msg){
    alert('problem '+msg);
    }
  });
}
```

The function `pollForResults` is repeatedly called in a recursive fashion until the query completes. The function makes an Ajax call to `longQuery.jsp` to see if the query completed. The call to `longQuery.jsp` will return not complete if the 10 seconds has not elapsed since starting the query. The call will return query data if the query has finished. In the first case, when not complete is returned, then after a one second delay the function `pollForResult` will recall itself to see if the query has completed. This repeated calling to `pollForResult` will continue until the query has completed. Once the query is completed, then `showResult` is called and the UI is updated.

```
function pollForResult(){
  dojo.xhrGet({
      url:"longQuery.jsp",
      handleAs: "text",
      load: function(result){
        dojo.byId('result').innerHTML=dojo.byId('result').innerHTML
+ "*";
          if(result == 'not complete'){
            setTimeout('pollForResult()', 1000);
          }else{
            showResult(result);
          }
      },
      error: function(msg){
      alert('problem '+msg);

      }
  });
}
```

Listing 15.2 Server Side Polling Code

```
<%
if("start".equals(request.getParameter("type"))){
  session.setAttribute("queryStart", new Long(System.currentTimeMil-
  lis()));
}else{
  Long start = (Long)session.getAttribute("queryStart");

  if(start == null){
    start = new Long(System.currentTimeMillis());
    session.setAttribute("queryStart", start);
  }

  if(start + 10000 < System.currentTimeMillis()){
    out.print("query data");
  } else{
    out.print("not complete");
  }
}%>
```

The server side code is just a simulation of a long-running query (see Listing 15.2). The code checks if this is a call to a new query by comparing the request parameter type start.

If it is a new query, then the time of the query is recorded, as shown here.

```
if("start".equals(request.getParameter("type"))){
  session.setAttribute("queryStart", new Long(System.
  currentTimeMillis()));
}
```

When future polling requests are made, they will not set the type to start in the request parameter. These polling requests will start when the query starts. If we don't know when the query starts, we will start a new query and store the starting time. Then we check if the query has been running for 10 seconds; if so, then we return query data, otherwise we return not complete as shown here.

```
}else{
  Long start = (Long)session.getAttribute("queryStart");

  if(start == null){
    start = new Long(System.currentTimeMillis());
    session.setAttribute("queryStart", start);
```

```
    }

    if(start + 10000 < System.currentTimeMillis()){
      out.print("query data");
    } else{
      out.print("not complete");
    }
}
```

For some applications, polling is a great option, but you must keep in mind the disadvantages, which include delayed results and unnecessary requests. The biggest advantage of polling is that it is very easy to use and all that is needed is simple Ajax and JavaScript coding.

■ 15.1.2 Long Polling

Long polling is very similar to polling, but consists of a server-side sleep rather than a client-side poll interval. The technique of long polling is considered Comet. Long-polling applications start by making an Ajax call to get data from the server. Then the server thread sleeps until data is available. When data is available, the thread will be woken up and return the data. In many cases, only one request is needed to get data.

Figure 15.2 shows a sequence diagram of a long-poll request.

Note that in Figure 15.2 only one request was required to get the data. If the query runs for a long time, it is recommended to complete the request without the data and make another long-poll request. Requests will eventually time out and throw exceptions if they are open too long. Server-side sleep should be interrupted after a minute or two so you can avoid errors.

Implementing code for long polling is a bit more complicated on the server side because it requires some advanced threading code. Since advanced threading is beyond the scope of this book, our server side will just sleep for a fixed amount of time. The client side of long polling is almost exactly the same as polling (see Listing 15.3). The only difference is replacing the setTimeout polling call with an immediate call.

The query is started by someone clicking Start Query, which calls the startQuery method, as shown here.

```
<div id="result">Status Here</div>
<button onclick="startQuery()">Start Query</button>
```

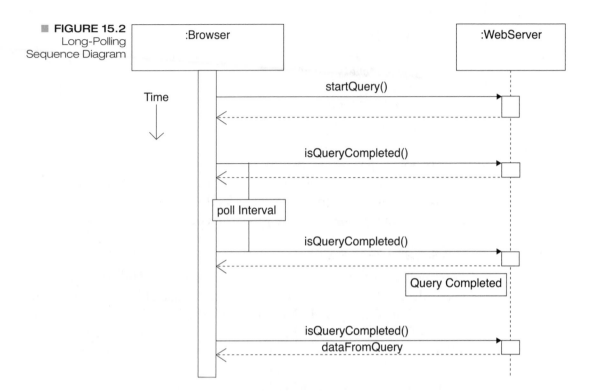

Listing 15.3 Client Side LongPolling Code

```javascript
<script type="text/javascript">
function startQuery(){
 dojo.byId('result').innerHTML = 'running'
 dojo.xhrGet({
    url:"longQuery.jsp?type=start",
    handleAs: "text",
    load: function(data){
      pollForResult()
    },
    error: function(msg){
    alert('problem '+msg);
    }
  });
}
function pollForResult(){
  dojo.xhrGet({
```

```
      url:"longQuery.jsp",
      handleAs: "text",
      load: function(result){
        dojo.byId('result').innerHTML=dojo.byId('result').innerHTML
+ "*";
        console.log(result);
        if(result == 'not complete'){
          pollForResult();
        }else{
          showResult(result);
        }
    },
      error: function(msg){
      alert('problem '+msg);
      }
  });
}
function showResult(result){
 dojo.byId('result').innerHTML = result;
}
</script>
<div id="result">Status Here</div>
<button onclick="startQuery()">Start Query</button>
```

The startQuery function in Listing 15.3 is exactly the same as in the polling example. It starts by updating the UI to running, then makes an Ajax request to longQuery.jsp with the parameter of type equals start. After the query is started, it calls the pollForResult function.

```
function startQuery(){
  dojo.byId('result').innerHTML = 'running'
  dojo.xhrGet({
    url:"longQuery.jsp?type=start",
    handleAs: "text",
    load: function(data){
      pollForResult()
    },
    error: function(msg){
    alert('problem '+msg);
    }
  });
}
```

The function `pollForResults` is almost the same as it was in the polling example. The only difference is that the recursive call to the function `pollForResult` happens immediately instead of waiting for a `poll` interval before making a recursive call, as shown here.

```
function pollForResult(){
  dojo.xhrGet({
      url:"longQuery.jsp",
      handleAs: "text",
      load: function(result){
          dojo.byId('result').innerHTML=dojo.byId('result').innerHTML
+ "*";
          console.log(result);
          if(result == 'not complete'){
            pollForResult();
          }else{
           showResult(result);
          }
      },
      error: function(msg){
      alert('problem '+msg);
      }
  });
}
```

On the server side if it is a new query, then we store the start time and exit. If it is not, then we sleep for 10 seconds. If the query began more than 10 seconds ago, then we return the data without sleeping (see Listing 15.4).

Listing 15.4 Server-Side Long Polling Code

```
<%
if("start".equals(request.getParameter("type"))){
      session.setAttribute("queryStart", new Long(System.current-
TimeMillis()));
}else{
      Long start = (Long)session.getAttribute("queryStart");

      if(start == null){
              start = new Long(System.currentTimeMillis());
              session.setAttribute("queryStart", start);
      }
```

```
        if(start + 10000 < System.currentTimeMillis()){
                out.print("query data");
        } else{
                try{
    Thread.sleep(10000 - (System.currentTimeMillis() - start));
                }catch(InterruptedException e){
                }
                out.print("query data");
        }
}%>

if("start".equals(request.getParameter("type"))){
        session.setAttribute("queryStart", new Long(System.current-
        TimeMillis()));
}else{
        Long start = (Long)session.getAttribute("queryStart");
        if(start == null){
                start = new Long(System.currentTimeMillis());
                session.setAttribute("queryStart", start);
        }
        if(start + 10000 < System.currentTimeMillis()){
                out.print("query data");
        } else{
                out.print("not complete");
        }
}
```

■ 15.1.3 Streaming

Streaming is the most advanced form of Comet. Streaming lets you send multiple chunks of data to the client with varying amounts of time between each transmission. Streaming lets you open one connection and push data whenever needed. Figure 15.3 shows a sequence diagram that explains streaming.

Note in Figure 15.3 that once a connection is open the server can push data as many times needed and at any time. This is achieved because neither the client nor server never closes the HTTP connection. Implementing streaming without a framework is beyond the scope of this chapter, so a coding example will not be included. Streaming over HTTP also has problems in many network proxy servers. Some proxy servers will wait until the connection is closed before passing on the packets to the next network node, which stops the data you are trying to push.

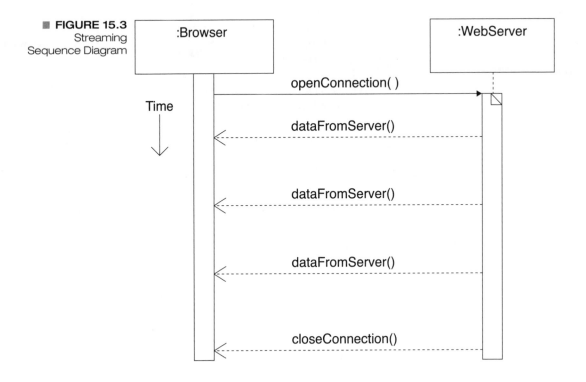

■ 15.1.4 Server-Side Threading Concerns

Traditional web servers, such as Apache, have a one-thread per request limitation. This is a problem for Comet applications, because in many cases a request will be sleeping on the server.

Thread management overhead often becomes a problem after thread counts exceed 300. In addition, large thread counts consume large amounts of memory. Version 3 of the Java Servlet specification adds asynchronous support to servlets, which eliminates the one thread per request limit.

A thread can start a request, so then if the request decides to sleep, the thread can be used by other requests. Once the request is ready to proceed a new thread is assigned to the request. The asynchronous additions to the version 3 of the Java Servlet specification remove what was previously a big problem when implementing Comet applications.

■ 15.2 COMETD

CometD is a Dojo Foundation project that is heavily influenced by Webtide®, the company behind Jetty. CometD implements the Bayeux™ protocol in several languages. Bayeux is a protocol for transporting asyncronous messages primarily over HTTP. The main purpose of Bayeux is to allow real-time two-way communication between browsers and web servers via Ajax. CometD is a really nice framework for doing Comet, because it abstracts away the complex details related to server-side sleep. CometD is based on long polling. In the examples in this chapter we will use Dojo and jQuery for the client side and Jetty (Java) on the server side.

■ 15.2.1　CometD and JavaScript

CometD is the main object that is used in JavaScript to provide Comet functionality. You can access CometD with Dojo as follows:

```
var cometd = dojox.cometd;
```

You can access CometD with jQuery as follows:

```
var cometd = $.cometd;
```

The next step is to pass the URL of your Bayeux server to CometD for Dojo or jQuery, as shown here:

```
cometd.configure('http://localhost:8080/cometd');
```

The preceding code is shorthand to set the URL. The other option is to pass an object of parameters. The possible parameters are URL, logLevel, maxConnection, backoffIncrement, maxBackoff, reverseIncomingExtensions, jsonpFailureDelay, and requestHeaders. The code to pass parameters is:

```
cometd.configure({url: 'http://localhost:8080/cometd'});
```

After you configure CometD call handshake to connect to the Bayeux server:

```
cometd.handshake();
```

CometD also has a shortcut method called init that configures and calls handshake:

```
cometd.init('http://localhost:8080/cometd');
```

■ 15.2.2　Publish and Subscribe from JavaScript

Once you are connected to the Bayeux server you can publish messages:

```
cometd.publish('/somechannel', {firstName: 'Kevin', lastName:
          'Nilson'});
```

In the preceding message, an object containing firstName=Kevin and lastName=Nilson is broadcast to anyone subscribing to the channel somechannel.

Channels are part of the Bayeux specification and they are similar to topics in JMS. Just like with traditional television, when a broadcaster broadcasts a show on channel 9, then everyone whose TV is turned to channel 9 will receive the broadcast. Channels can be segmented by using a /. Bayeux contains three types of channels: metachannels, service, and normal channels. Metachannels are created by the Bayeux server. Metachannels give information about events, such as handshake errors, connection, disconnection, and reconnection. You must listen to metachannels rather than subscribing to them. You can get events out of metachannels using the following code:

```
var _connected = false;
cometd.addListener('/meta/connect', function(message) {
  var wasConnected = _connected;
  _connected = message.successful;
  if (!wasConnected && _connected) {
    // Reconnected
  }
  else if (wasConnected && !_connected) {
    // Disconnected
  }
});
```

Service channels are used for nonbroadcast or request/response style of communication.

Service channels should be used when you want to send a message to a single client.

Subscribing to a channel is very easy:

```
var subscription = cometd.subscribe('/somechannel', function() { ...
});
cometd.unsubscribe(subscription);
```

■ 15.2.3 Publish and Subscribe from Java

You must extend Bayeux service to write Java server-side Bayeux code. Each Bayeux service can publish messages and subscribe to channels. Bayeux service is considered a normal client, just like a browser. The easiest way to publish data in Java is to send the data as a Map with a String key and a Object value.

After creating a `Map` containing the data you want to publish, you must look up the channel you wish to publish to, then publish the data. The following is Java code that can be used to publish data:

```
Map<String, Object> data = new HashMap <String, Object> ( );
data.put(firstName, Kevin);
data.put(lastName, Nilson);
data.put(age, 30);

Channel c = getBayeux( ).getChannel( ''/test,false );
c.publish( getClient( ), data, null);
```

Subscribing to channels in Java is easy. You begin by looking up the channel the same way you would to publish. Finally, you subscribe to the channel and pass a string that represents a callback function. When messages are published, the callback function will be called.

```
Channel c = getBayeux( ).getChannel( "/test",false );
subscribe(channel, "testMessage");
c.unsubscribe(getClient( ));
public void testMessage(Client from, String channel, Map<String,
Object> data, String id) {
    //GOT MESSAGE
}
```

■ 15.2.4 HTTPServletRequest

For tasks such as authentication and authorization or to look something up from the `HTTPSession`, it is easy to access the `HTTPServletRequest`. CometD makes the request available by adding it to a `ThreadLocal` variable. The following code can be used within a callback to get the request:

```
Request AbstractBayeux b = (AbstractBayeux) getBayeux();
if (b.isRequestAvailable())
  HttpServletRequest request = b.getCurrentRequest();
```

The request is only added to the `ThreadLocal` if the CometD servlet has an `init-param` configured to set `requestAvaliable` to true in the XML file `web.xml`.

```
<init-param>
  <param-name>requestAvailable</param-name>
  <param-value>true</param-value>
</init-param>
```

■ 15.2.5   Security Policy

Bayeux provides a pluggable security policy that lets you add restrictions, such as preventing a certain user from publishing. One thing to keep in mind when writing a security policy is that everyone is a client, including the server. Another thing to keep in mind is that any client can publish any message on any channel, unless you prohibit them in the security policy.

The following are the methods you must implement in your security policy:

```
//Test if a message should be allowed to create a new Channel
boolean canCreate(Client client, java.lang.String channel, Message
message)
```

```
//Test if a handshake message should be accepted.
boolean canHandshake(Message message)
```

```
//Test if a client can publish a message to a channel
boolean canPublish(Client client, java.lang.String channel, Message
messsage)
```

```
//Test if a client is allowed to subscribe to a channel
boolean canSubscribe(Client client, java.lang.String channel, Mes-
sage messsage)
```

■ 15.2.6   Channel, Queue, and Client Listeners

CometD has several listeners that let you observe events on the server. Webtide was very interested in feedback on, and very eager to enhance CometD.

One of the most common cases for using Comet is to listen to events on JMS and broadcast the events to all of the users subscribed to the event. In this case, you would create a channel to represent the event. You would need to know when a channel is created, so you can subscribe in JMS. You also need to know when a channel is removed, so you can unsubscribe from JMS. Adding channelAdded and channelRemoved can be done as shown in the following code:

```
getBayeux().addListener( new BayeuxChannelListener(){
   public void channelAdded(Channel channel){
       //new channel
   }
```

```
    public void channelRemoved(Channel channel) {
        //no more subscribers to channel
    }
});
```

Another listener notifies you when a client is disconnected. This gives you the ability to unsubscribe a client from all JMS topics he is subscribed to. When a client disconnects, you and the client are notified if the disconnect was due to timeout or if the client specifically called for a disconnect.

```
client.addListener(new RemoveListener(){
    public void removed(String clientId, boolean timeout){
        System.err.println("Client "+clientId+timeout?" timedout":"
        disconnected");
    }
});
```

CometD follows a classic producer-consumer model. When messages are produced they are added to the client's queue by the producer.

The consumer is the Jetty thread pool delivering the messages. The producer and consumer operate on different threads. A single user's queue could grow very large and you would never be notified, which would make it possible for malicious code to fill someone's queue until the server is out of memory. You can to configure the size the queue can reach before you are notified. The following is the API to notify you of queue growth. You first set the max queue size for a client and if the queue grows beyond that size, you are notified by a call to the QueueListeners queueMaxed method.

```
client.setMaxQueue(int max);

client.addListener(new QueueListener(){

    public boolean queueMaxed(Client from, Client to, Message message){
        //return true is you should allow to add to queue
        //you may want to disconnect the client
        return true;
    }
});
```

The final listener we will discuss is DeliverListener, which notifies you that Jetty is about to deliver all of the messages in your queue. The

`DeliverListener` works by calling `deliver` just before delivering the messages in your queue to the browser as shown here.

```
client.addListener(new DeliverListener() {
  public void deliver(Client arg0, Queue<Message> queue) {
    //Deduplicate here if queue size is large
  }
});
```

■ 15.2.7 Conclusion

CometD is very easy to use. Simple applications, such as chat applications, can be done without adding a single line of server code. CometD provides easy options for both broadcast and single receiver messaging. The CometD servers are just some of the many server implementers of the Bayeux protocol. Weblogic and Websphere have both implemented the Bayeux protocol. Over time, Bayeux has grown to be a standard well-adopted protocol. Comet and the CometD implementation have become the standard open source implementation of Bayeux.

■ 15.3 ORBITED

The following section was contributed by Michael Carter, creator of Orbited.

If browsers had a TCP socket there would be no need for Comet-style communication. In JavaScript, you could open a socket directly in an existing chat server and create a rich, JavaScript/Document Object Model (DOM)-based GUI. This would be the easiest possible way to create a chat application — install an IRC server, connect from the browser, make a GUI, and you're done. This is what Orbited does; it puts a TCPsocket in the browser.

Now let's look at Listing 15.5, which shows you how to log into an IRC server.

Listing 15.5 Logging Into an IRC server

```
<script src="Orbited.js"></script>
<script>
sock = new Orbited.TCPSocket();
Orbited.getLogger('Orbited.TCPSocket').enabled=true;
sock.onopen = function() {
  sock.send('NICK testuser\r\n');
```

```
    sock.send('USER test 8 * :Test User\r\n')
    sock.send('JOIN #orbited\r\n');
}
sock.open('irc.freenode.org', 6667);
</script>
```

This script in Listing 15.5 opens a socket to an IRC server, sends the appropriate IRC frames to log in with the nickname `testuser`, and then joins the channel `#orbited`.

■ 15.3.1 Integration

The most frequent problem for developers using existing Comet libraries is integrating them into their own system. The result is a large-scale fragmentation of Comet library implementations. The OpenSource community is filled with abandoned, half-finished Comet implementations that only work with specific languages and frameworks. This is a problem that web servers don't have, thanks to CGI, FASTCGI, SCGI, and `mod` language interfaces. Python, PHP, Perl, C, C++, and Java programmers can use Apache as a web server, and still write their application with their own custom libraries. This is what Orbited does for the Comet world.

Orbited uses raw TCP as the interface to the back-end system. Orbited can integrate with any system that uses a TCP socket.

■ 15.3.2 Architecture

Orbited is a proxy, pure and simple. It speaks in Ajax and Comet to the browser, and TCP to the back-end. When a browser opens an Orbited.TCP socket to a back-end server, conceptually it is opening a socket directly to that server. In reality, Orbited uses Comet and Ajax to make a request for Orbited to open a TCP connection to the TCP server on behalf of the browser. Orbited will open that socket and proxy data between the two endpoints.

■ 15.3.3 Details

When you call `Orbited.TCPSocket.open(www.example.org", 6667)`, the browser makes an Ajax request to Orbited to open a socket connection to `www.example.org:6667`. Orbited replies with a socket session key.

The browser then opens a Comet channel to Orbited, identified by the socket session key. When the back-end server sends data back over TCP,

Orbited sends that data to the browser over the Comet channel. This triggers a call to `Orbited.TCPSocket.onread(data);`

When you call `Orbited.TCPSocket.send("some data")`, the browser makes an Ajax request to Orbited and includes "some data" and the socket session. Orbited sends "some data" to the back-end server, and then replies to the Ajax request with `OK`.

As you can see, the actual method Orbited uses is straightforward.

■ 15.3.4 Orbited is Not a Message Queue

Many looking for a Comet library want to use a publish and subscribe API, but Orbited is not built as a publish/subscribe system. Instead, you can choose a message queue of your choice to use in conjunction with Orbited. A few of the popular choices are MorbidQ, RabbitMQ, and ActiveMQ. The reason these three are particularly popular is that Orbited ships with a Stomp client, so the JavaScript code can easily connect to any of these message queues as shown in Listing 15.6:

Listing 15.6 Connecting to STOMP Server

```
<script src="/static/Orbited.js"></script>
<script>TCPSocket = Orbited.TCPSocket</script>
<script src="/static/protocols/stomp/stomp.js"></script>

stomp = new STOMPClient();
stomp.onconnectedframe = function() {
    stomp.subscribe("/foo/bar");
    stomp.send("hello world", "/foo/bar");
};
stomp.onmessageframe = function(frame) {
    console.log('received message body:', frame.body, 'headers:',
                frame.headers);
};
stomp.connect('messagequeue.example.com', 61613);
```

Note that this API looks a lot like CometD/Bayeux, where you have a basic mechanism for subscribing/publishing to channels. Orbited's solution to the problem is to decouple the Comet implementation from the message queue, so that each project can concentrate on a particular problem and solve it. This lets you choose the message queue that has the best performance characteristics for your particular application.

■ 15.3.5 Goals and Strengths of the Orbited Project

The purpose of Orbited is to solve problems associated with Comet and solve them efficiently. We want to avoid other problems, such as implementing distributed message queues and scalable chat servers. With Orbited, you can select the best existing server on a case-by-case basis, and then use Orbited to expose that server to the browser.

As an experiment, let's consider how to build a web mail application using standard practices. You would probably choose a web framework and implement various HTTP-facing methods that interact with a backend mail system. You would probably create a database schema for user accounts, and then implement logic to authenticate users against that database when they log in. Users would make an HTTP request to retrieve a list of new mail. Next you would implement logic that would query a mail server for their new mail. There are many more features you'd have to implement in your server-side logic, but they would follow this same basic pattern.

Now let's consider how you would do this with Orbited. First, set up an LDAP server as an address book and authentication server. Next, set up an IMAP and SMTP server for sending and receiving email. Then let the IMAP and SMTP server use the LDAP server for authentication. Next, set up Orbited and access your email directly in the browser using the IMAP protocol. Access your address book using the LDAP protocol directly in the browser, and send email using SMTP. Instead of writing code for the server-side, you simply configure existing components and write a GUI.

Now, if you want to add real-time chat to your webmail client, such as in Gmail, deploy an XMPP server and configure it to use the same LDAP server for authentication. Then have your web GUI connect to the XMPP server from the browser directly to access buddy list updates and send/receive chat messages in real time.

Let's say that you want to add a system for pushing email to the browser as soon as it's received. Instead of trying to create special "new mail" channels with a publish/subscribe Comet protocol, use the IMAP protocol's IDLE command, which causes the IMAP server to send a frame whenever new mail is received. You can see how Orbited is more than just a way to communicate with a browser in real time: it's also a way to reuse existing components by allowing these components to communicate "directly" with the browser. Simply put, Orbited lets you implement each use case with a communication protocol designed specifically for that use case.

■ 15.4 INDUSTRY PERSPECTIVE OF COMET BY MICHAEL CARTER

Comet is a technology that always seems to be on the edge of massive boom. We see more examples each year of big-name companies using push technology, like Facebook Chat, Gmail, or Google Wave, and with each successive year it feels like the Web is on the verge of a breakthrough. Comet, whose name was originally coined to describe this type of communication over HTTP, is starting to show its age as the HTTP layer is hidden further and further from developers. To put it plainly, Comet is becoming an implementation detail because of standardization and the need for a simpler programming model.

On standardization, the HTML5 specification puts forth two great additions to browsers: Server-Sent Events (SSE) and the WebSocket API and protocol. The main emphasis with this standardization is to move Comet from a "hack" to an explicitly supported communication mode. With SSE (which is only in Opera) the HTML5 specification lets a server provide a structured stream of data which is accessible in JavaScript via DOM events. This is good for all sorts of simple data-streaming applications, such as a casual news or stock ticker, or really any webpage that is mostly about content. WebSocket, on the other hand, appeals to application developers by providing a bidirectional stream. In particular, WebSocket provides a dead-simple API on the client, and an almost-trivially simple protocol to understand on the server. These facets of WebSocket, along with the reliability and ordering guarantees that are missing in raw Comet communication, make it an obvious replacement.

Another emerging standard is Comet Session Protocol (CSP), which provides the Comet-Session API to browsers. It is a very similar API to WebSocket, with the caveat that no native support is needed to implement CSP in browsers, so it works today. There are already OpenSource server implementations of CSP written in Python, Erlang, server-side JavaScript, and C, with Java and Ruby under active development. You can think of CSP as the simplest method for building a reliable network stream on top of HTTP for browsers. Exposing existing network applications to the browser is simple with a compliant server module and JavaScript client.

While the standardization is a nice confirmation that the general idea of tunneling real-time data transfers over HTTP is nice, standardization and the fact that Comet will be "built-in" to browsers will not increase usage. Instead, it is the way that Comet APIs are structured that makes the real difference. When the API for Comet is to "Just make long polling requests with an XHR," its easy to find yourself confined within HTTP. On the other hand, WebSocket, CometSession, or Orbited. TCP-Socket all provide a reliable, stream-like interface where two end points can communicate with each other.

This type of API is exactly what was used to create the first generation of network applications on a desktop, via TCP. Moving that paradigm to the browser lets developers use standard network-application development practices in browser-based applications. The fact that you can just "open a socket" to a remote mail, chat, game, or financial server means that we will see a rapid increase in libraries built around this concept. That is to say, the boom in OpenSource Comet development has so far been focused on all kinds of nasty transport-level concerns, such as intermediary tunneling and providing reasonable usability characteristics, but moving forward we can all stop reinventing the wheel and start writing protocols on top of standardized transport layers.

One such project that does exactly this is js.io, which is a JavaScript network library. Though most JavaScript developers are primarily concerned with the client-side of things, js.io lets you use the same set of APIs to write both clients and servers in JavaScript. In general, the rise of server-side JavaScript is something to keep an eye on, though that's a topic for another day. What makes js.io so relevant to this discussion on the future of Comet is that it seperates the transport layer from the application/protocol layer. Therefore, you could implement an XMPP protocol client once, and then use that code on top of WebSocket, CometSession, Orbited.TCPSocket, Flash Sockets (with a JS bridge), or any future transport layer that has characteristics similar to TCP.

The key here is that browsers provide building blocks rather than solutions. There have been discussions among developers to include XMPP as a basic client implementation in browsers. Although, it would be nice to have a native XMPP client accessible from JavaScript, it's not necessary—in fact, it would be detrimental to the Web. Implementing the protocol would be a waste of developers' time. If we have something like WebSocket native, then we can handle the rest in JavaScript. Putting an XMPP implementation into the browser feels just as wrong as putting an XMPP stack into the operating system. Let the browsers give us the "basic" building blocks, and JavaScript libraries will handle the rest.

If you think about it, this separation of transport and application protocols is precisely what made Internet applications so successful in the first place. We stopped worrying about re-implementing our TCP/IP stack long ago, and now there are hundreds of thousands of network client implementations for thousands of protocols that we simply take for granted. The barrier to entry is so much lower with a simpler programming model than Comet, and now that we have this new model, it won't be long before you'll take JavaScript/browser protocol implementations for granted.

■ 15.5 SUMMARY

Comet, often called Reverse Ajax, is a technique that allows web servers to push data to the browser. Real-time web applications are becoming increasingly popular, so Comet usage is steadily growing. CometD and Orbited are two stable frameworks that support Comet. CSP is an emerging standard that we can look forward to using in the future. As HTML 5 becomes a reality 'long polling and streaming hacks will be replaced by WebSockets. Server side enhancement for continuation and client side advances such as WebSockets have made it possible for Comet to become a major part of the future of Web 2.0.

## CHAPTER 16

Mobile Development Part I

In This Chapter:

- The Mobile Landscape
- Apple iPhone®
- Google Android™
- Palm Pre™
- Industry Perspective

This book contains two chapters on mobile application development because there are a lot of vendors that provide tools for developing mobile applications. The platform you choose for developing mobile applications depends on several factors, so we will give you a broad view of the tools that are available, along with some sample code.

In particular, this chapter discusses mobile development for several major platforms and the programming languages each platform uses.

The first part of this chapter gives you an overview of the mobile landscape in terms of the initial costs involved, support for web technologies (such as HTML5, XML, JSON, and OpenGL), and mobile-specific protocols.

The second part presents several major mobile platforms, including Apple iPhone, Google Android, and Palm Pre. This section also briefly discusses the application life cycle for some platforms and the tools that are available (such as plug-ins and IDEs), and provides sample code for each of these platforms.

There are several points to keep in mind as you read this chapter and the next. First, the primary purpose of these two chapters is to provide code samples to familiarize you with the development environment for mobile platforms that have significant differences. However, it's impossible to reduce the contents of an entire book dedicated to Android (or any other mobile platform discussed in this book) into a handful of pages. Thus, the focus of the two chapters is to demonstrate how to build simple applications in various mobile platforms.

Given the constraints involved, we believe that it is more beneficial for you to start your learning process by first seeing the steps for building mobile applications, and later you can learn the full details about important topics, such as the life cycle of mobile applications. On the other hand, if we provided an in-depth discussion about the details of the life cycle, we would need to omit other details, such as the process for creating mobile applications. With this rationale in mind, the life cycles of mobile applications will be very brief and limited to a couple of mobile platforms. You can search the Internet for articles or other books (most of which are entirely devoted to a single mobile platform) to help you with an in-depth look at the mobile platforms presented in this chapter.

Second, these two chapters are not designed to "promote" any specific mobile platform as superior to the others. You can make that determination yourself after reading the code samples and weighing the various factors involved, such as the amount of time you can devote to learning new languages.

Third, a comparison of the features of various mobile devices is necessary for end users and developers to determine what type of mobile applications that they want to develop and the target platforms for them. Since the programming-related information has higher priority, we will discuss a small set of device-specific features. If you want more information regarding feature comparisons, you can visit the websites of the mobile devices.

Fourth, the mobile landscape is changing very rapidly, so there is often a delay (measured in months) before you can find published books that discuss the newest features in the latest versions of tools. For example, Google Android version 1.6 contains significant new functionality, and it was released in September 2009. Obviously Android books published prior to October 2009 will not contain any material specific to version 1.6, which means that you will need to find other sources (articles, tutorials, documentation, or knowledgeable individuals) to learn about these new features.

Fifth, newly released software often contains bugs, some of which might prevent you from upgrading your existing code base. The sooner you discover software bugs that can affect your code, the sooner you can file bug reports, thereby initiating the bug resolution process.

After you finish reading these two mobile chapters, you will be able to make a more informed decision about the mobile platform that is best suited for your needs.

■ 16.1   THE MOBILE LANDSCAPE

The mobile device landscape is experiencing a boon in terms of the diversity of mobile applications and its growth potential (we believe that the mobile field is an integral and influential component in the future of the Web).

At the same time, there is a bewildering array of mobile devices available, with different sets of features, data plans, and operating systems (OS). Consider the variety of smartphones, some of which are more powerful than desktop computers from 10 years ago.

Most mobile devices support a browser (usually based on the open source project WebKit), email support, instant messaging, maps, music, games, search, social networking support (including Facebook, MySpace, and others), and widget support (including Yahoo, Nokia, and iPhone). Mobile devices also provide support for audio, video clips, and television. The largest category of mobile applications is games, with eBooks coming in second.

Some of the advantages of mobile devices include constant Internet connectivity and a Global Positioning System (GPS), but there are several disadvantages as well, such as limited memory, small resolution size, and keyboard "awkwardness."

■ 16.1.1   Initial Costs for Mobile-Based Development

Your initial cost depends on the platform, and you should consider the platform-specific costs for any of the following:

- SDK
- a mobile device
- a laptop
- monthly phone charges
- developer registration

In general, development tools, such as a SDK, are free, and the SDK either includes an emulator or a plug-in for an IDE. For example, Google provides a Google Android plug-in for Eclipse that has an embedded emulator. On the other hand, if you decide to develop FlashLite™-based applications for Nokia, you need to purchase the development tools from Adobe after the free trial period has expired.

In addition, if you want to develop iPhone applications, then you need a system that supports Objective-C, which means you need to purchase a Macbook® (or something comparable). Note that you have to register with Apple before you can put iPhone applications on the Apple iStore®, and the registration fee is USD $99 per year.

Another cost to consider is the additional monthly charges (and potential lock-in for your service plan) for your mobile device. Note that one alternative for testing your iPhone applications is the iPod Touch® (which is essentially an iPhone without the phone).

■ 16.1.2 Web Technologies for Mobile Devices

This section briefly discusses the following technologies (and the extent of their support) in relation to the mobile platform field:

- HTML5
- OpenGL
- Mobile-based protocols
- XML and JSON

This section also discusses some of the popular Web 2.0 products and services that are available on mobile devices.

16.1.2.1 HTML5 Support

The majority of the devices in this chapter (including iPhone, Google Android, Nokia, and the Palm Pre) are based on the open source WebKit browser, and since these phones account for roughly two-thirds of the smartphones sold today, their requirements can influence the extent to which HTML5 is implemented on mobile devices. Note that the two platforms that are not based on WebKit are Windows Mobile and RIM Blackberry®.

Several mobile browser vendors are involved in HTML5, and Opera is one of its leading developers. Although HTML5 has widespread support, one criticism is its lack of extensibility, which would let users define new semantic tags to provide additional information about a document.

Meanwhile, the success of the Apple iPhone (which is partially due to the visual experience) has probably influenced mobile OS vendors to upgrade their versions of WebKit. By the way, if you plan to work with SVG, keep in mind that SVG code that renders correctly in WebKit will also work correctly in the following:

- Google Chrome™
- Google Chrome Frame
- Google Earth™
- iPhone
- Konqueror™
- Safari®

16.1.2.2   OpenGL

OpenGL was introduced in 1992, and since then it has arguably become the most widely used graphics standard for developing portable graphics-oriented applications. The OpenGL Programming Guide is here: http://www.glprogramming.com/red/

OpenGL supports 2D and 3D graphics, which are suitable for high-performance application requirements, such as CAD/CAM, medical imaging, and even virtual role-playing systems.

The OpenGL Architecture Review Board is an independent consortium that guides the OpenGL specification. With broad industry support, OpenGL is the only truly open, vendor-neutral, multiplatform graphics standard.

Most mobile devices support OpenGL, which means that you can create graphics-based applications that combine 2D/3D effects, rendering images, and animation effects.

However, keep in mind that some features are generally unavailable on mobile devices, including image maps, nested tables, and pop-up windows.

16.1.2.3   Protocol Support

A number of different protocols for mobile-based applications have evolved since the 1990s, most of which are based on XML. The lone exception is iMode from Docomo (a Japanese company), which is based on a subset of HTML4. The following is a list of protocols for mobile applications:

- WML 1.x
- XHTML
- XHTML Basic
- XHTML Mobile Profile
- WCSS/WAP CSS
- WML 2.0
- iMode

XHTML is defined by the World Wide Web Consortium (W3C®), and as you might have guessed, XHTML documents are HTML documents that are also valid XML documents (see Chapter 3). XHTML Basic is a subset of XHTML designed for handheld devices (such as mobile phones, smart phones, and PDAs). XHTML Basic does not support CSS, frames, and scripting.

However, there are a couple of things to keep in mind: First, the XHTML 2 initiative was abandoned in 2009 in favor of HTML5; second, companies such as Google, Palm, and Apple are involved in providing HTML5 support for mobile applications on their platforms. Support for HTML5-based features on mobile devices is bound to continue for the foreseeable future, so it's worth your while to follow the specific feature support that is provided by your preferred vendor.

16.1.2.4 XML and JSON Support

There are several XML-based libraries available for mobile devices, such as kXML, which is an XML parser for J2ME applications that is here:
http://kxml.sourceforge.net/

kXML is a lightweight XML-based pull parser that is designed for limited computing environments, such as mobile devices. kXML 2 is based on the common XML Pull API, which is here:
http://xmlpull.org/

There are also several JSON-based libraries available for mobile devices. An article that describes how to use JSON on Android (JSON versus XML) is here:
http://www.moblitz.com/2009/02/consuming-json-response-in-android.html

16.1.2.5 Popular Web 2.0 Products and Services

Mobile-based applications have experienced a tremendous growth over the past several years. However, the GUI component of mobile application development differs from the GUI of desktop applications. In general, good mobile-based applications aim for simplicity, which means you should avoid complicated menu structures and navigation sequences that require numerous keystrokes. A consistent look and feel is important for applications, so if you decide on a particular design for one screen, try to use the same design for the other screens, and across different mobile devices. If you are developing computationally intensive games, battery life and power consumption are important considerations.

You can find suggestions and recommendations for mobile web design Best Practices here:

http://www.smashingmagazine.com/2009/01/13/mobile-web-design-trends-2009/

If you use a mobile device primarily as a telephone, consider other products and applications that are available, including Twitter, Facebook, YouTube, Flickr, and Google Maps. You can find many other Web 2.0 in oriented products and services that can help you find the information you need.

■ 16.1.3 Design Patterns and Best Practices

Mobile-based design patterns are solutions to well-known tasks in mobile applications. Design patterns can save you time and effort, let you benefit from other people's experience, and help you write better and more consistent code. You can find a set of design patterns here:

http://wiki.forum.nokia.com/index.php/Category:Mobile_Design_Patterns/

Mobile Best Practices consist of coding techniques and recommendations, which can help you write more consistent code. You can find a collection of Best Practices here:

http://www.w3.org/TR/mobile-bp/

Search the Internet for additional design patterns and Best Practices to help expand your knowledge of JavaScript.

Next, we'll take a closer look at developing mobile applications on some of the platforms we've discussed in this chapter. Each section contains subsections that provide additional information about the following:

• some language features
• source code format

- a simple application
- useful development tools

In addition, please check the appendices for additional links for more information about software, documentation, tutorials, and products for each of the respective platforms.

■ 16.2 APPLE IPHONE

The Apple iStore home page is: http://store.apple.com

In 2009, the Apple iPhone clearly dominated the mobile game development field. The Apple iStore had 500 applications available in mid-2008, which grew to 25,000 in early 2009, and over 65,000 by mid-2009, with more than a billion downloads. In addition, the number of registered applications on the Apple iStore surpassed 100,000 by the end of 2009, thereby surpassing Walmart® (the largest retailer in the world) in terms of the number of "items" in the store. Despite the perception of the Apple iPhone as a platform for games and entertainment, you can also find business applications for the iPhone.

The iPod Touch is also a popular product that has generated significant revenue, but recently sales have leveled off, and there has been speculation that Apple will discontinue the iPod®.

Although Apple does not have any official plans to support Java, SUN Microsystems announced plans to release a Java Virtual Machine (JVM) for the iPhone OS that will be based on the Java Micro Edition, thereby enabling Java applications to run on the iPhone. However, in view of the current licensing agreement for the iPhone SDK, such a scenario would probably require approval from Apple.

The iPhone OS does not have any support for Flash, but Adobe has announced that it will release a version of FlashLite that can run on the iPhone. Currently, Flash-based videos can be viewed by a "jailbroken" iPhone in conjunction with third-party applications.

The iPhone supports SVG (which appears to be a reversal of Apple's past position regarding SVG), but the iPhone lacks support for Flash. The absence of Flash on the iPhone may become a significant opportunity that can be exploited by competitors such as Google Android and Palm Pre, both of which have announced that they will support Flash before 2010. Note that

Mobile Safari supports much of SVG 1.1 and some SVG scripting, but there is no support for SMIL in SVG graphics.

Another point to remember is the importance of adhering to Apple's requirements for approving iPhone applications. One website that lists some potential reasons for rejection is: http://sqasolution.com/blog/2009/08/23/app-store-rejection-reasons/

One alternative to using Objective-C™ for iPhone applications is Adobe ActionScript™ (see Listing 2.10 for an example of ActionScript code). In September 2009, Adobe announced support for both iPhone and iPod Touch mobile applications in Adobe Flash Professional CS5 using Action-Script 3. In fact, CS5 will let developers build mobile applications for other platforms, including Google Android.

Apple does not allow virtual machines or just-in-time compilation of code, so the iPhone applications that are built from Flash-based tools are compiled into native code, and the executables that are just like those that are created from phone applications written in Objective-C, based on Objective-C code. However, these mobile applications cannot launch SWF files at run-time.

According to Adobe, iPhone applications that are built from Adobe Professional CS5 can be (and have been) accepted and delivered through Apple's App Store. Note that iPhone developers must still participate in Apple's iPhone Developer Program to submit their applications to the App Store. Some examples of iPhone applications built using an early version of Flash Professional CS5 are here:

http://labs.adobe.com/technologies/flashcs5/appsfor_iphone/

■ 16.2.1 Quick Platform Overview

Apple iPhone applications are written in Objective-C, which is a superset of C that resembles a hybrid of C and SmallTalk.

Apple provides an XCode-based IDE to develop iPhone applications. The GUI for iPhone mobile applications is Cocoa Touch, which is derived from Cocoa and only runs on the Mac OS. Apple also provides Interface Builder, which supports drag-and-drop functionality that makes it easier and quicker to develop iPhone applications. Apple iPhone applications are based on the Model-View-Controller (MVC) pattern, which originated in the SmallTalk programming language during the early 1980s in Xerox Parc.

■ 16.2.2 Overview of iPhone Applications

XCode is a project-oriented IDE that lets you create, develop, and test iPhone applications. XCode provides compilers for various languages, including C, C++, and Objective-C, and a GDB-like debugger for debugging mobile applications. An iPhone emulator is available to test your iPhone applications during the development cycle.

16.2.2.1 iPhone 3.0 OS Features

Apple's iPhone 3.0 added new features and improved upon features that were available in earlier releases of the OS. The new features include copy and paste and Spotlight, which provides better search capability for on-device content. Moreover, Spotlight can also search inside folders located on the server if you use Exchange 2007. Version 3.0 also provides support for Messaging and Notes, and improved support for calendar and mail. Two features that are unavailable include the ability to save attachments and encryption.

Open-Xchange is an open source collaboration vendor that launched a tool (in late 2009) called OXtender for Business Mobility, which supports "push" email for the iPhone and any other phone that uses the ActiveSync protocol from Microsoft. Apple iPhone 3.0 also provides support for MMS, but AT&T (the exclusive carrier for the Apple iPhone) did not support this service until October 2009. The Apple iPhone 3GS has been described as a "disruptive technology." You can get a guided tour of the Apple iPhone 3GS here: http://www.apple.com/iphone/guidedtour/

16.2.2.2 Brief Comparative Overview of Objective-C Code

This section compares Objective-C code with Java and C++. Your knowledge of either of these two languages will assist you in understanding Objective-C programs.

Objective-C is a superset of the C programming language that contains object-oriented features. However, Objective-C has a learning curve (even if you are familiar with C and C++), so it's important to write some Objective-C programs to help you become more comfortable with the language. So, if you have no knowledge of C or object-oriented languages (such as Java and C/C++), then consider searching the Internet for tutorials or books that provide a much more detailed explanation of the concepts that are contrasted in this section.

In Objective-C, all objects are allocated to the heap, and you must manually deallocate memory because Objective-C does not provide any garbage collection. Note that XCode does provide some assistance in finding memory leaks in your program.

Objective-C programs have "header" files with an ".h" extension and implementation files with an ".m" extension. By comparison, C programs have an ".h" file and a ".c" file; C++ programs have ".h" files and ".cpp" files. The "hello world" iPhone application (that we will create later in this section) contains a header file and the implementation file where you can add your custom code.

16.2.2.2.1 HOW OBJECTIVE-C DIFFERS FROM JAVA AND C/C++

If you have a Java or C background, there are several things about Objective-C code you need to keep in mind:

- Objective-C programs use the "@" symbol, which has nothing to do with annotations in Java
- Objective-C uses colons (:) to indicate subclasses, which is the same as C++ (but differs from Java and C#), and "protected" for protected members (which is the same as C++ and Java)
- Objective-C uses the minus (-) sign for instance methods and the plus (+) sign for class methods (comparable to a static method in Java)
- Objective-C uses pointers (*) which is the same as C, but different from C++ (which uses references) and Java and C# (no pointers are available)
- Some Objective-C types use the prefix NS, which is short for NextStep, including NSString and NSDictionary
- Objective-C uses "@implementation" for the implementation class, whereas Java uses the keyword "implements" (C++ uses a colon)
- Objective-C uses "self," which is similar to Python, but different from C++ and Java, which use "this"
- Header files in Objective-C have "@end" as the final statement, whereas C++ and Java have a curly bracket

- Objective-C programs use square brackets to indicate a method invocation. The main entry point in Objective-C programs is the `applicationDidFinishLaunching()` method, which you override with your application-specific code
- Objective-C handles object initialization as shown here:

```
MyClass *instance = nil;
instance = [[MyClass alloc] init];
```

Some additional concepts in Objective-C that you will need to learn (but are not covered in this chapter) include selectors, categories, autorelease pools, properties, protocols, and synthesize.

Now that you understand some of the differences between Objective-C and languages such as Java and C++, let's look at the Objective-C header file and implementation class, which are illustrated in the next section.

16.2.2.3 Structure of iPhone Source Files

Listing 16.1 shows the contents of the interface file `MyClass.h` and Listing 16.2 displays the contents of the implementation file `MyClass.m`.

Listing 16.1 MyClass.h

```
#include <UIKit/UIKit.h>
static int count;

@interface MyClass : MySuperclass<Protocol> {
@public
NSString *myVar;
@private
NSDictionary *myData;
@protected HelperClass *myhelper
}

+(void)classMethod;
-(void)instanceMethod;
@end
```

Listing 16.1 is a simple Objective-C header file that uses common C idioms (such as the `include` directive) and several of the Objective-C constructs that were described in the previous section, including `interface`, `public`, `NSString`, and `@private`.

Listing 16.2 MyClass.m

```
#include "MyClass.h"
@implementation MyClass
-(id)init{
// almost always do this
if(self =[super init]) {
// do stuff
}
return self;
}

+(void)classmethod {
// do something here
}
```

Listing 16.2 is an Objective-C implementation class that includes the header file `MyClass.h`, along with definitions for the private method `init()` that returns the `self` object and the public method `classmethod` (which does nothing).

The next two sections cover the two main types of iPhone applications: those for the iPhone and those for the Web.

■ 16.2.3   iPhone Applications for Mobile Devices

The iPhone SDK provides tools for creating applications for the iPhone OS, and sample code and documentation. After you create a free account, download the iPhone SDK from the members area of the iPhone Dev Center here: http://developer.apple.com/iphone

16.2.3.1   A Simple iPhone Application Using Xcode

This section shows you how to create an Apple iPhone application using the Xcode IDE, along with the structure of the project, followed by several code listings to help you understand iPhone application code.

Create a new iPhone "Hello World" application by performing the following steps:

Step 1: Launch Xcode (look in /Developer/Applications)

Step 2: Follow the menu path **File > New Project**

Step 3: Select Application under the iPhone heading

Step 4: Click the View–Based icon and then click the Choose button

Step 5: Enter "HelloWorld" to the right of the Save As: label

Step 6: Select a directory location and then click the Save button

XCode will create the `HelloWorld` project and then open a project window that contains a list of files, which is covered in the next section.

16.2.3.2 *Project Structure of an iPhone Application*

The iPhone project that you created in the previous section consists of 10 files and has a directory structure that is displayed in Listing 16.3.

Listing 16.3

```
Classes
  + HelloWorldAppDelegate.h
  + HelloWorldAppDelegate.m
  + HelloWorldViewController.h
  + HelloWorldViewController.m
HelloWorld.xcodeproj
  + project.pbxproj
HelloWorldViewController.xib
HelloWorld_Prefix.pch
icon.png
Info.plist
main.m
MainWindow.xib
```

In brief, the two files with `.h` extensions are Objective-C header files and the three files with `.m` extensions are Objective-C implementation files.

The file `HelloWorldController.xib` is called a xib file, and it contains information used by the Interface Builder (IB), which is discussed a bit later in this section.

The file `HelloWorld_Prefix.pch` is a precompiled header file that (conditionally) imports other Objective-C header files.

The binary file `icon.png` is an image file for this project.

The file `Info.plist` (displayed in Listing 16.5) is a file that contains additional project-related information.

The Objective-C implementation file `main.m` (displayed in Listing 16.4) contains the main entry point for this project.

The `MainWindow.xib` is another nib file for this project.

16.2.3.3   iPhone Project Files

Listing 16.4 displays the contents of the Objective-C implementation file main.m.

Listing 16.4 main.m

```
#import <UIKit/UIKit.h>

int main(int argc, char *argv[]) {
    NSAutoreleasePool * pool = [[NSAutoreleasePool alloc] init];
    int retVal = UIApplicationMain(argc, argv, nil, nil);
    [pool release];
    return retVal;
}
```

Listing 16.4 contains an import statement followed by a main method that allocates a pool, calls the Objective-C class that performs the real work, and then deallocates the memory pool.

Listing 16.5 shows a portion of the contents of the file Info.plist.

Listing 16.5 Info.plist

```
<?xml version="1.0" encoding="UTF-8"?>
<!DOCTYPE plist PUBLIC "-//Apple//DTD PLIST 1.0//EN"
          "http://www.apple.com/DTDs/PropertyList-1.0.dtd">
<plist version="1.0">
<dict>
    <key>CFBundleDevelopmentRegion</key>
    <string>en</string>
    <key>CFBundleDisplayName</key>
    <string>${PRODUCT_NAME}</string>
    <key>CFBundleExecutable</key>
    <string>${EXECUTABLE_NAME}</string>
    <key>CFBundleIconFile</key>
    <string>icon.png</string>
    <key>CFBundleVersion</key>
    <string>1.0</string>
</dict>
</plist>
```

Listing 16.5 contains an XML <dict> element with various child XML elements that are essentially name/value pairs for the HelloWorld application. For example, the language is English (en), and the values of several attributes are defined by referencing the values of variables that are defined elsewhere in this sample application.

Listing 16.6 displays a portion of the contents of the file HelloWorld-ViewController.xib.

Listing 16.6 HelloWorldViewController.xib

```
<?xml version="1.0" encoding="UTF-8"?>
<archive type="com.apple.InterfaceBuilder3.CocoaTouch.XIB"
version="7.02">
    <data>
        <int key="IBDocument.SystemTarget">512</int>
        <string key="IBDocument.SystemVersion">9D34</string>
        <string key="IBDocument.InterfaceBuilderVersion">667</string>
        <string key="IBDocument.AppKitVersion">949.33</string>
        <string key="IBDocument.HIToolboxVersion">352.00</string>
        <object class="NSMutableArray" key="IBDocument.EditedObject-
IDs">
            <bool key="EncodedWithXMLCoder">YES</bool>
            <integer value="1"/>
        </object>
        <int key="IBDocument.localizationMode">0</int>
        <string
key="IBDocument.LastKnownRelativeProjectPath">HelloWorld
.xcodeproj</string>
        <int key="IBDocument.defaultPropertyAccessControl">3</int>
    </data>
</archive>
```

Listing 16.6 is an XML document whose root node is the XML <archive> element, which contains an XML <data> element that consists of name/value pairs expressed as XML elements. As you can see, the names of many of the XML <string> elements indicate their purpose, such as System-Version, AppKitVersion, HIToolboxVersion, and so forth.

16.2.3.4 Interface Builder (IB)

IB is a very powerful and convenient visual tool that supports drag-and-drop functionality for managing any user interface (UI) widgets that you want to use in your iPhone applications.

For example, you can programmatically add a button to an application via the following code snippet:

```
UIButton *theButton = [[UIButton alloc] initWithFrame:myObj]
```

An easier way to produce the same result is by using IB to select a button from a set of existing UI objects, and then dragging that button onto the main window of your application.

Launch IB by double-clicking on `HelloWorldViewcontroller.xib`. In the right-side window is a palette of UI objects that you can drag and drop onto the main window. The available UI objects include buttons, lists, labels, date pickers, and text fields. Check the documentation for more details about these (and other) UI widgets and for detailed information about IB.

■ 16.2.4 iPhone Web Applications

The iUI project lets you develop web-based applications that resemble iPhone applications. However, these web applications do not require development for the Apple iStore and they are accessible from an iPhone simply by navigating to the URL of the iUI web application.

The iUI project is a JavaScript-based framework for developing native-looking applications for the iPhone. Its home page is:
http://code.google.com/p/iui

You can download the latest version of iUI from:
http://code.google.com/p/iui/downloads/list

Note that, in 2008, the Aptana plug-in for Eclipse provided support for iPhone development, but Aptana no longer provides iPhone support.

■ 16.2.5 Apple iPhone and Third-Party Tools

This section provides some information about iPhone applications that use other tools and technologies, including Google App Engine (GAE), Google Maps, and SVG.

16.2.5.1 *Zembly and iPhone*

In Chapter 7, you learned about Zembly as a social networking product, and in Chapter 9, you learned about the mash-up capabilities of Zembly. In this section, you will learn how you can use Zembly in conjunction with iPhone mobile applications.

The following steps illustrate how to clone and edit the iPhone Tree-Browser widget, which is a public Zembly widget available to everyone:

Step 1: Navigate to the Zembly home page at: https://zembly.com/

Step 2: Log in to your Zembly account

Step 3: Navigate to the iPhone TreeBrowser at:
https://zembly.com/things/5d06b103ecbd4a9997afd0a3195d6b4d

Step 4: Click the Clone and Edit button

Step 5: Rename this widget (optional)

Step 6: Click the Edit this Widget button

Listing 16.7 displays the contents of the HTML page for the cloned copy of the iPhoneTreeBrowser widget.

Listing 16.7 Cloned copy

```
<link rel="apple-touch-icon" href="${res('zembly_avatar_iphone
.png')}"/>

<meta name="viewport"
      content="width=320; initial-scale=1.0; maximum-scale=1.0;
      user-scalable=0;"/>

<div id="toolbar" class="toolbar">
    <!-- Note: pageTitle id is required by iUI -->
    <h1 id="pageTitle">iPhone Tree browser</h1>
    <!-- Note: backButton id and button class are required by iUI -->
    <a id="backButton" class="button" href="#"></a>
</div>

<div selected="true" class="panel" id="home">
    <p id="message" class="iPhoneTree-message">
    Loading ...
    </p>
</div>
```

As you can see, Listing 16.7 contains standard HTML code, including two HTML div elements with an HTML <h1> element and an HTML link element.

If you go to the Zembly home page and enter "iPhone" in the search box, Zembly will display a list of iPhone Zembly widgets, including iLoanPayment, iPhoneMovieFinder, and iLondonTube. You can clone and edit these (and other) Zembly widgets and add your own custom code.

16.2.5.2 Apple iPhone and Other Tools

A Python-based open source project with iPhone and GAE communication is here: http://code.google.com/p/touchengine/

You can read an associated IBM article here: http://www.ibm.com/developerworks/web//library/wa-aj-iphone/

An article describing the integration of Apple iPhone and Google Maps is here: http://code.google.com/apis/maps/documentation/v3/

You can also create interactive maps on the Apple iPhone with SVG as shown here: http://www.spatiallyadjusted.com/2008/09/18/using-svg-to-create-interactive-maps-on-the-apple-iphone/

■ 16.3 GOOGLE ANDROID

Google Android is an open source project that has limited support compared to the Apple iPhone, but a number of Android-based devices were released in 2009, which suggests that Google Android is growing in popularity. The Google Android home page is: http://code.google.com/android/

Although it's difficult to know for certain, Google may have plans to support Android on mobile devices, netbooks, and laptops, which would certainly make Android more scalable than any of its competitors in the mobile arena. At least 18 Android-based devices were in late 2009, which certainly bodes well for Google. In mid-2009, HTC released a powerful mobile device called Hero that runs on Android. The availability of such devices suggests that Google Android is becoming a viable alternative to the iPhone. Android supports animation, OpenGL, and Adobe Flash, which may be a big advantage for Android at some point. A useful set of Google applications for mobile phones is here: http://www.techbabu.com/2009/09/awesome-google-apps-for-mobile-phones/

The question now is whether or not Google and Apple are heading toward a "showdown."

The Android SDK (version 1.6 is the latest release) is available for download from: http://developer.android.com/sdk/1.6_r1/index.html

■ 16.3.1 Quick Platform Overview

Google Android applications are written in Java, and the application code is compiled into byte code with the Dalvik compiler (which is different from the Java compiler). Android applications are deployed as files with an `apk` extension, which can be opened via zip utilities (or the Java `jar` command). Google provides an Android plug-in for Eclipse to develop Android applications in the Eclipse IDE. Information about installing the Android plug-in for Eclipse is provided later in this chapter.

Google Android supports a network programming blocking model that is based on Java (`java.net.`), with one thread per connection. Android also uses the Java IO model (`java.nio.`), including the nonblocking IO from Java 1.4. Thus, read/write operations use buffer objects instead of input/output streams. Google Android also has support for TCP-based client-side and server-side sockets (by means of the classes `Socket` and `ServerSocket`, respectively), and one UDP-based socket (`DatagramSocket`).

Android tool support includes an emulator that is launched inside of Eclipse, and an Android Debug Bridge (ADB) utility for installing `.apk` files, which are the files created for Google Android applications. Other useful Android tools include Android Asset Packaging Tool (AAPT), Android Interface Description Language (AIDL), and `sqlite3`.

Check the appendices for links that provide additional information about the Android platform and Android tools.

■ 16.3.2 Overview of Android Applications

This section describes some of the features of Android, important notions (such as Intents and Views), and the methods that belong to the Android life cycle.

16.3.2.1 Android Features

Google Android version 1.5 provides support for the following functionality:

- creating and managing files on the filesystem
- storing data in a database
- web services
- telephony and messaging (SMS)
- graphics and animation effects
- audio and video

Google Android 2.0, which is the most recent version, supports some new functionality, such as a quick-search box and camera, camcorder, and gallery. Version 2.0 also supports a battery usage indicator and various Virtual Private Networks (VPNs).

16.3.2.2 Intents, Activities, and Views

The Android UI consists of Intents and Views. In abstract terms, an Android Intent represents the details regarding an action (often described by a verb) in an Android application.

An Android `Activity` is an Android base class that contains the Android methods described in the next section. An Activity contains one or more views that belong to an Android application.

An Android `View` is what users see on the screen, which includes the UI widgets of the Android application. The sample Android application in this chapter is an Android class that extends the Android `Activity` class and overrides the `onCreate()` method with custom code. Note that Android applications can also extend other Android classes (such as the `Service` class), and they can create threads.

The `onCreate()` method in the sample Android application is one of seven Android methods that make up the Android application life cycle, as described in the next section.

16.3.2.3 *Methods and Life Cycle of Android Applications*

A Google Android application contains the following methods, which are in the order they are called during the life cycle of an Android application:

- `onCreate()`
- `onRestart()`
- `onStart()`
- `onResume()`
- `onPause()`
- `onStop()`
- `onDestroy()`

The `onCreate()` method is called when an `Activity` is created, and its role is similar to `init()` methods in other languages. The `onDestroy()` method is called when an `Activity` is removed from memory, and its role is essentially that of a `destructor` method in C++. The `onPause()` method is called when an `Activity` must be paused (such as reclaiming resources). The `OnRestart()` method is called when an `Activity` is being restarted. The `OnResume()` method is called when an `Activity` interacts with a user. The `OnStart()` method is called when an `Activity` becomes visible on the screen. Finally, the `OnStop()` method is called to stop an `Activity`.

The methods `onRestart()`, `onStart()`, and `onStop()` are in the visible phase; the methods `onResume()` and `onPause()` are in the foreground phase. An Android application can pause and resume many times during the execution of an application; the details are specific to the functionality of the application (and possibly the type of user interaction as well).

■ 16.3.3   A Simple Android Application

This section provides you with the instructions and the code for creating a graphics-based Android application in Eclipse. You can use the NetBeans IDE to create Android applications. In both cases, there is an Android plug-in that facilitates developing Android applications using these two IDEs.

16.3.3.1   Downloading/Installing Software

Download and install NetBeans (as described in Chapter 6) and then install the Android plug-in for NetBeans from the following URLs:
http://kenai.com/projects/nbandroid/
http://kenai.com/projects/nbandroid/downloads

Download and install Eclipse 3.3 or higher (as described in Chapter 6) and then install the Android plug-in for Eclipse from:
http://dl-ssl.google.com/android/eclipse

16.3.3.2   A Simple Android Application in Eclipse

The example in this section explains how to create an Android project that renders graphics. Launch Eclipse and perform the following steps:

Step 1: Follow the menu path **File > New > Android Project**

Step 2: Enter Graphics1 for the Project name

Step 3: Enter Graphics1 for the Application name

Step 4: Enter graphics.oac for the Package name

Step 5: Enter DrawEllipses in the Create Activity input field

Step 6: Select the checkbox to the left of Android 1.5 for the Build Target

Step 7: Click the Finish button

Eclipse will generate a new Android project (whose structure is described in the next section). Next, launch this application by right-clicking on the project name Graphics, and then following the menu path: **Run As > Android Application**. The application will run after the Android emulator completes its initialization steps, which can take a minute or so (but each subsequent launch will be much faster).

16.3.3.3 Project Structure of an Android Application

The Graphics Android application contains several files with the structure shown in Listing 16.8, which is the type of structure that is automatically generated whenever you create an Android application in Eclipse.

Listing 16.8

```
Graphics
 + src
   + graphics.oac
     + DrawEllipses.java
 + gen (Generated Java Files)
   + graphics.oac
     + R.java
 + Android 1.5
   + android.jar
 + assets
 + res
   + drawable
     + icon.png
   + layout
     + main.xml
   + values
     + strings.xml
 + AndroidManifest.xml
 + default.properties
```

This Android application contains two Java files (DrawEllipses.java and R.java), a JAR file (android.jar), an image file (icon.png), three XML files (main.xml, strings.xml, and AndroidManifest.xml), and a text file default .properties.

You can add a second Java class to this Android application as follows:

Step 1: Right-click on graphics.oac (under src)

Step 2: Follow the menu path **New > Class**

Step 3: Enter MyCustomDrawableView in the Name input field

Step 4: Click the Finish button

16.3.3.4 Android Application Project Files

Listing 16.9 shows the contents of DrawEllipses.java, which is the main entry point for the Android application.

Listing 16.9 DrawEllipses.java

```java
package graphics.oac;

import android.app.Activity;
import android.os.Bundle;
import android.widget.TextView;

public class DrawEllipses extends Activity {
    MyCustomDrawableView myCustomDrawableView;

    /** Called when the activity is first created. */
    @Override
    protected void onCreate(Bundle savedInstanceState) {
        super.onCreate(savedInstanceState);
        myCustomDrawableView = new MyCustomDrawableView(this);

        setContentView(myCustomDrawableView);
    }
}
```

Listing 16.9 defines a DrawEllipses class that extends the Android Activity class. The DrawEllipses class calls the method onCreate(), which overrides the same method in the Activity base class. The onCreate() method sets the view based on the custom MyCustomDrawableView class whose contents are shown in Listing 16.10.

Listing 16.10 MyCustomDrawableView.java

```java
package graphics.oac;

import android.content.Context;
import android.graphics.drawable.ShapeDrawable;
import android.graphics.drawable.shapes.OvalShape;
import android.graphics.Canvas;
import android.view.View;

public class MyCustomDrawableView extends View {
    private ShapeDrawable drawable;

    public CustomDrawableView(Context context) {
        super(context);
    }

    protected void onDraw(Canvas canvas) {
        int basePointX = 0;
```

```
        int basePointY = 0;
        int maxCount   = 255;
        int rectWidth  = 80;
        int rectHeight = 50;
        int stripCount = 10;
        int hexColor   = 0x0;
        int Constant   = 256*256;

        for(int i=0; i<maxCount; i++)
        {
            drawable = new ShapeDrawable(new OvalShape());
            hexColor = (255*256 + (i%stripCount)*255)*Constant;
            drawable.getPaint().setColor(hexColor);

            drawable.setBounds(basePointX+i,
                               basePointY+i,
                               basePointX+i+rectWidth,
                               basePointY+i+rectHeight);

            drawable.draw(canvas);
        }
    }
}
```

Listing 16.10 contains the code for rendering a set of ellipses. The class MyCustomDrawableView extends the Android View class, and the constructor calls the constructor of the base class. Listing 16.10 also contains an onDraw() method that contains a for loop that renders a set of ellipses by means of the Android OvalShape() class.

Listing 16.11 displays the contents of R.java, which is automatically generated when you create a Google Android application.

Listing 16.11 R.java

```
/* AUTO-GENERATED FILE. DO NOT MODIFY.
 *
 * This class was automatically generated by the
 * aapt tool from the resource data it found. It
 * should not be modified by hand.
 */

package graphics.oac;

public final class R {
```

```
public static final class attr {
}
public static final class drawable {
    public static final int icon=0x7f020000;
}
public static final class layout {
    public static final int main=0x7f030000;
}
public static final class string {
    public static final int app_name=0x7f040001;
    public static final int hello=0x7f040000;
}
}
```

Listing 16.11 contains a set of UI element identifiers (specified as `int` variables) that are automatically generated for every Android application.

Listing 16.12 displays the contents of `main.xml`, which is another file that is automatically generated every time you create a Google Android application.

Listing 16.12 main.xml

```
<?xml version="1.0" encoding="utf-8"?>
<LinearLayout xmlns:android="http://schemas.android.com/apk/res/
android"
    android:orientation="vertical"
    android:layout_width="fill_parent"
    android:layout_height="fill_parent"
    >
<TextView
    android:layout_width="fill_parent"
    android:layout_height="wrap_content"
    android:text="@string/hello"
    />
</LinearLayout>
```

Listing 16.12 also contains a set of UI-related elements for the Android application, which in this case includes an XML `LinearLayout` element that specifies the layout and an XML `TextView` element for specifying the layout of the text. Note the @ symbol in the `android:text` attribute of the `TextView` element. The @ symbol is used for making the entries in the R.java class that were described earlier in this section.

Listing 16.13 shows the contents of `strings.xml`, which is the third file automatically generated when you create a Google Android application.

Listing 16.13 strings.xml

```
<?xml version="1.0" encoding="utf-8"?>
<resources>
    <string name="hello">Hello World, DrawEllipses!</string>
    <string name="app_name">Graphics</string>
</resources>
```

Listing 16.13 contains localization strings for the elements `hello` and `app_name`.

Listing 16.14 displays the contents of `AndroidManifest.xml`, which is automatically generated when you create a Google Android application.

Listing 16.14 AndroidManifest.xml

```
<?xml version="1.0" encoding="utf-8"?>
<manifest xmlns:android="http://schemas.android.com/apk/res/android"
      package="graphics.oac"
      android:versionCode="1"
      android:versionName="1.0">
    <application android:icon="@drawable/icon" android:label=
"@string/app_name">
        <activity android:name=".DrawEllipses"
                android:label="@string/app_name">
            <intent-filter>
                <action android:name="android.intent.action.MAIN" />
                <category android:name="android.intent.category.
LAUNCHER" />
            </intent-filter>
        </activity>
    </application>
    <uses-sdk android:minSdkVersion="3" />
</manifest>
```

Listing 16.14 is an XML document whose root node is the XML `<manifest>` element, which contains attributes that specify the Android namespace, the package for the Android application, and Android-specific details. The XML `<application>` element contains an XML `<activity>` element and an XML `<intent-filter>` element (neither of which is discussed in this section).

Listing 16.15 shows the contents of default.properties, which is automatically generated when you create a Google Android application.

Listing 16.15 default.properties

```
# This file is automatically generated by Android Tools.
# Do not modify this file -- YOUR CHANGES WILL BE ERASED!
#
# This file must be checked in Version Control Systems.
#
# To customize properties used by the Ant build system use,
# "build.properties", and override values to adapt the script to your
# project structure.

# Project target.
target=android-3
```

Listing 16.15 contains one line that specifies the value of the `target` property.

■ 16.3.4 Google Android Tool Integration

Google Android mobile applications can be integrated with several other tools and technologies, such as:

• Facebook
• Google Maps
• Simple programming language
• SVG
• uStream

The following is a link regarding Google Android and Facebook: http://content.techrepublic.com.com/2346-1035_11-341297.html?tag=nl.e106

You can find Android and uStream videos here: http://www.techcrunch.com/2009/09/17/ustreams-mobile-video-broadcasting-comes-to-android/

Additional information about Android and Google Maps is here: http://code.google.com/apis/maps/documentation/v3/

A live camera preview in Android is here: http://www.tomgibara.com/android/camera-source

In 2009, Google released the Simple programming language specifically for developing Android applications. The Appendix contains links about the Simple programming language, Google Android Projects, and other useful Android-related links.

This concludes our discussion on Google Android.

■ 16.4 PALM PRE

Palm released its Palm Pre in early 2008, and it looked promising because the Palm Pre supports features that other phones do not, such as multiple threads. The Palm home page is: http://www.palm.com/us/

However, Palm Pre faces at least two obstacles that may influence its popularity and eventual success.

First, Palm Pre does not support OpenGL, which means that graphic effects are handled via software rather than hardware. Even though the Palm Pre has a powerful graphics chip, there is no OpenGL graphics driver available. However, the absence of extensive graphics support for OpenGL is not entirely surprising, because Palm has targeted business-oriented applications rather than games. Palm is competing more directly with Blackberry rather than the iPhone, so graphics support is not as important as business applications.

Second, the iPhone has had a highly successfully marketing campaign that has helped Apple establish its dominance in the mobile application arena. The Palm Pre is a newer mobile device (although the difference is less than a year), and Palm does not have the resources to compete on the same level as Apple.

On the other hand, Palm is expected to support Adobe Flash (similar to Google Android), whereas Apple has not provided any indication that the iPhone will support Flash in the foreseeable future. Palm also joined Adobe's Open Screen Project, which is an initiative that provides Flash-based applications and web browsing support to a variety of devices, such as mobile devices, desktops, and televisions. Clearly this decision to join this initiative bodes well for the Palm Pre.

Palm made an other key decision in 2009, in addition to its decision to support Adobe Flash. In September, Palm announced that it would no longer support Windows Mobile, and instead focus future development on its WebOS operating system.

■ 16.4.1 Quick Overview of webOS and Mojo

Palm developed a platform called webOS, which is a Linux-based platform that uses WebKit (also used in Safari). WebOS was unveiled in January 2009, along with a presentation of webOS on the Palm Pre smartphone. WebOS provides multitask support, which is not available on the iPhone.

WebOS applications run in "cards", which are like small web pages made up of HTML, and native components let you switch between the cards, much like windows in a desktop environment. Screens in a card are called scenes, which are implemented as sibling DIV elements in the body of an HTML page.

WebOS applications also have something called a stage (implemented as an HTML document), and there are three types of stages: cards, dashboards, and alerts.

You can install Mojo (the installation steps are provided later in this section) to build applications in webOS. Mojo is analogous to the .NET framework on Microsoft Windows.

Mojo is strongly influenced by Ruby on Rails™ (RoR), whereby applications use an MVC pattern when you create applications in IDEs, such as Eclipse (Aptana support is available as well). In addition, Mojo provides UI widgets, system services, and support for HTML5 and CSS3. You can make Ajax-based calls, and you can even use jQuery™ (discussed in Chapter 3).

Applications use a scene stack designed like a deck of cards, and additional scenes are "pushed" onto the scene stack. Each time a scene is pushed onto the stack, `setup` and `activate` are called.

■ 16.4.2 Overview of Palm Applications

Palm Pre applications are based on a combination of HTML, JavaScript, and CSS. You can develop Palm applications in Eclipse after you install the Palm plug-in. The GUI for Palm Pre applications is webOS (which is exclusive to Palm). Every Palm Pre application is deployed as a file with an `.ipk` extension, which you can open using the Unix/Linux `ar` command. Note that Palm Pre applications contain text-based files (HTML, JavaScript, and CSS) and image files.

16.4.2.1 Downloading/Installing Software

First, follow the instructions in Chapter 11 to download and install the SUN Virtual Box software on your system, and then follow the instructions in Chapter 6 to install Eclipse.

Now complete the following steps to install the Palm plug-in for Eclipse:

Step 1: Follow the instructions in Chapter 6 to install Eclipse 3.4 (or higher)

Step 2: Start Eclipse and install the Palm plug-in with the following URL: https://cdn.downloads.palm.com/sdkdownloads/1.1/eclipse-plug-in/eclipse-3.4/site.xml

Note that Palm recommends installing the Palm plug-in for Aptana Studio. Its home page is: www.aptana.com

If you decide to use Aptana Studio, then install the Palm plug-in from: http://update.aptana.com/update/studio/3.4/

■ 16.4.3 A Simple Palm Pre Application

This section provides you with the instructions and code for creating a graphics-based Palm Pre application in Eclipse.

16.4.3.1 *Palm Pre Application in Eclipse*

This section explains how to create a webOS application with the Palm plug-in installed in Eclipse 3.4. You may need to make adjustments to the following steps if you are using a later version or Eclipse. In addition, you need to start the Palm emulator before you can launch the application you will create in this section.

After you have installed the Palm plug-in for Eclipse, create a webOS application in Eclipse by completing the following steps:

Step 1: Follow the menu path **Window > Open Perspective > Other** and then select webOS

Step 2: Follow the menu path **File > New Mojo Application**

Step 3: Specify a value for the input field Project Name, which automatically populates the fields Title, Vendor, ID, and Version

Step 4: Follow the menu path **File > New > Mojo Scene** and then type DrawRectangles in the Project input field and Scene1 in the Name input field, and then click the Finish button

Step 5: Follow the menu path **Run > Run > Mojo Application** and then click the OK button

Step 6: Select Palm Emulator and click on the OK button

16.4.3.2   *Project Structure of a Palm Pre Application*

Listing 16.16 displays the file and directory structure of the application that you created in the previous section.

Listing 16.16

```
DrawRectangles
  + app
    + stage-assistant.js
    + assistants stage-assistant.js
    + stylesheets
      + drawrectangles.css
  + appinfo.json
  + icon.png
  + index.html
  + sources.json
```

The app directory is the core directory that contains presentation logic. The app directory contains an `assistants` subdirectory (which contains the controllers for the applications) and a `views` subdirectory (which contains the HTML pages for the scenes in applications). The `views` subdirectory contains HTML files (which contain Mojo widgets) for scenes, with one subdirectory per scene.

The file `appinfo.json` contains metadata for applications, and the file `sources.json` allows for "lazy loading" of JavaScript that is automatically synchronized (but not for scenes).

16.4.3.3   *Palm Pre Project Files*

A Palm Pre application contains a number of files that Eclipse will automatically generate whenever you create a Palm Pre application. The following files are discussed in the order in which they appear in a Palm Pre application.

Listing 16.17 displays the contents of the JavaScript file `stage-assistant.js`, which is located in the `app/assistants` directory.

Listing 16.17 stage-assistant.js

```javascript
function StageAssistant() {
}

StageAssistant.prototype.setup = function() {
}
```

Listing 16.18 shows the contents of the file `appinfo.json`, which contains JSON-based information about the application you created earlier in this chapter.

Listing 16.18 appinfo.json

```
{
  "id": "com.mycompany.rectangles1",
  "version": "1.0.0",
  "vendor": "My Company",
  "type": "web",
  "main": "index.html",
  "title": "Rectangles1",
  "icon": "icon.png"
}
```

`appinfo.json` is similar to a manifest file that contains, such items as: `title`, `main`, ID, `version`, and `vendor` (other properties include `visible` and `nowindow`)

Listing 16.19 displays the contents of `index.html`, which illustrates how to render a set of rectangles.

Listing 16.19 index.html

```
<?xml version="1.0" encoding="UTF-8"?>
<!DOCTYPE html PUBLIC "-//W3C//DTD XHTML 1.1//EN"
        "http://www.w3.org/TR/xhtml11/DTD/xhtml11.dtd">
<html xmlns="http://www.w3.org/1999/xhtml" xml:lang="en">
  <head>
    <meta charset="utf-8">
    <title>Graphics Rectangles</title>
    <script type="text/javascript"><!--
window.addEventListener('load', function () {
  // Get the canvas element in the <body> tag
  var elem = document.getElementById('myCanvas');

  if (!elem || !elem.getContext) {
    return;
  }

  // Get the canvas 2d context
  var context = elem.getContext('2d');
  if (!context) {
    return;
  }
```

```
    var basePointX = 10;
    var basePointY = 10;
    var rectWidth  = 100;
    var rectHeight = 100;
    var rectCount  = 50;

    for(var i=0; i<rectCount; i++) {
      if(i % 2 == 0) {
        context.fillStyle = '#f00';
      }
      else {
        context.fillStyle = '#00f';
      }

      context.fillRect(basePointX+i, basePointY+i, rectWidth,
rectHeight);
    }
}, false);
    // --></script>
  </head>

  <body>
    <canvas id="myCanvas" width="400" height="500">
        Your browser does not support Canvas
    </canvas>
  </body>
</html>
```

Listing 16.19 starts with standard HTML content, followed by a JavaScript method that locates the HTML canvas element (whose id is myCanvas) in the HTML page with the following code snippet:

```
var elem = document.getElementById('myCanvas');
```

After determining that this element is non-null (which means that it has been defined in the HTML page), the next portion of the JavaScript locates the drawable graphics content of the HTML page with this code snippet:

```
var context = elem.getContext('2d');
```

The next section of Listing 16.19 initializes some JavaScript variables, and then a JavaScript loop computes the location of various rectangles and then renders each rectangle in the context with this code fragment:

```
context.fillRect(basePointX+i, basePointY+i, rectWidth,
                 rectHeight);
```

■ 16.5   TODAY'S MOBILE WEB

Over the last year, there has been an explosion of web-enabled phones. Smartphones are now part of our daily fashion statement rather than a tool used only by geeks and businessmen. Everywhere you go, people are using apps like Twitter and texting to keep in touch with friends. When you write web applications, you must keep this large explosion of mobile users in mind. In the past, writing web apps that support the mobile environment was a nightmare because mobile browsers were so far behind regular browsers. Today's mobile browsers are not only up to par with regular browsers, in many cases mobile browsers are leading the way in the adoption of HTML5. The good news is that, in most cases, your regular website can be used without modification by most high-end mobile browsers. The bad news is that mobile bandwidth has not kept up with standard home bandwidth. Because of the low bandwidth of many mobile devices, you should minimize the chattiness and packet size of your pages and Ajax calls. Decisions like choosing between JSON-based Representational State Transfer (REST) calls over Simple Object Access Protocol (SOAP) can make or break the success of your application.

Today's native mobile application market has been dominated by the iPhone. There are over 100,000 applications in the iPhone store. Over time, expect the iPhone to lose market share to other more developer-friendly devices. Today, developers are willing to learn and code in Objective-C because they see the great financial benefits in developing applications for the iPhone. However, expect Android and Palm Pre to emerge as leaders because their internal corporate applications focus on developer friendliness. Companies already have trained resources in Java, HTML, and JavaScript; so they probably won't retrain in Objective-C for internal apps. Frameworks like Appcelerator Titanium Mobile provide an interesting advantage because they lower the skill level needed for HTML/JavaScript/CSS and they let you deploy to all of the major platforms with a single code base. Expect their ability to adopt new enhancements in the platforms without delay to determine their success.

The future is always hard to predict, but one thing is for sure, as web developers, mobile considerations will become more of a consideration as time goes on. In the future, we will write offline mobile applications that use local databases and synch with servers when connectivity is available. New mobile browsers and faster mobile processors will eventually unite the mobile and desktop platforms. HTML5 brings new functionality, but with that functionality comes new challenges—and new frameworks to solve them.

■ 16.6   SUMMARY

This chapter explained some of the latest developments in the mobile arena. You learned about the Apple iPhone, and you saw how to create a simple iPhone mobile application, followed by a discussion of some of the project files in that application. Next, you learned about Google Android, the Android application life cycle, and you saw an Android-based code sample. Finally, you learned about Palm Pre and saw how to create Palm Pre mobile applications.

The next chapter discusses other significant mobile platforms, along with a number of start-up companies that are providing tools for creating mobile applications.

## CHAPTER 17

Mobile Development Part II

In This Chapter:

- Samsung
- SUN J2ME
- RIM Blackberry®
- Nokia
- JavaFX 1.2 for Mobile Applications
- MonoTouch™
- Motorola®
- Verizon® JIL Mobile
- Other Development Tools for Mobile Devices
- Companies for Mobile Development
- Mobile Trends in Other Technologies

This chapter provides an overview of mobile application development for several platforms. This chapter emphasizes a "cookbook" approach to developing mobile applications, focusing on the details of creating applications (usually in an IDE such as Eclipse or NetBeans), and letting you determine the mobile platform. This chapter tries to provide you with enough information (such as links and sample code) to minimize the amount of time it will take for you to start developing mobile applications on these platforms.

This chapter begins with a look at several important mobile platforms, including Samsung, J2ME, RIM Blackberry, Nokia, JavaFX 1.2, MonoTouch, Motorola, and Verizon. This section discusses the tools that are available (such as plug-ins and IDEs) and shows you how to create mobile applications for these platforms.

The next part of this chapter discusses tools that let you develop cross-platform mobile applications (such as XMLVM and Rhomobile™), and provides information about mobile-based companies that offer interesting products and tools for developing mobile applications.

The last section discusses some of the emerging trends in the mobile arena, such as mobile banking, cloud computing, and voice recognition.

The appendices contains useful links related to the material discussed in this chapter, and information about mobile-related initiatives for companies such as Microsoft, SalesForce, and Oracle.

■ 17.1 SAMSUNG

Samsung Mobile Innovator is a program which provides people with the resources for developing, testing and distributing their mobile applications and solutions. The program currently supports various platforms such as Windows Mobile, Symbian and Java:

http://innovator.samsungmobile.com/

Samsung currently supports Windows Mobile, Symbian, and Java, and there are plans to support other platforms in the future.

You can register for a free Samsung account (which is necessary to download software) here:

https://innovator.samsungmobile.com/mbr/individual.mbr.add.do

The following is a link to Caxixi, which is a drum application for Samsung Windows Mobile phone:

http://innovator.samsungmobile.com/caxixi/

You can find an overview of Symbian here:

http://www.embeddedstar.com/technicalpapers/content/s/embedded1013.html

The Symbian Operating System (OS) contains a kernel, middleware, support for graphics, and application engines. Symbian OS is the cornerstone of Symbian OS phones.

You can find an overview of Windows Mobile here:

http://developer.att.com/developer/index.jsp?page=toolsTechSection&id=2000049

Windows Mobile application development is based on C™/C++™ and development is often done in Visual Studio™. Developers can also use .NET

Compact Framework (CF), which is a version of the .NET for mobile devices. .NET CF provides support for all of the .NET languages.

■ 17.1.1 Quick Platform Overview

Material from Samsung reprinted with permission

Samsung provides assistance during the various stages of mobile development. Samsung provides a channel during the idea stage to hear ideas and business proposals. Proposals can be submitted via the "Market.Dev" link here: http://innovator.samsungmobile.com/mkt/bp/how.to.use.do?platformId=2

The Samsung business development team reviews the submitted proposals and then follows up with the submitters.

In the development stage, Samsung has a program that offers a number of APIs that are unique to Samsung mobile phones. For example, their current version of Windows Mobile SDK (v.2.1) provides 16 APIs, including Accelerometer, Haptics, Advance Camera API, and 3D Orientation/Compass. The specification for each set of APIs is included in the SDK.

The Samsung SDK is available here: http://innovator.samsungmobile.com/sm:WM_SDK2.1

During the testing phase, Samsung lets developers test their applications with the Samsung Virtual Device Lab. Samsung provides a set of phones (not emulators) that are connected to servers. They can be accessed from: http://innovator.samsungmobile.com/bbs/lab/view.do?platformId=2

Samsung also provides an app store (during the distribution phase) that is currently only available in the UK, France, and Italy (the store should be available in other countries in the upcoming months) that you can access here: http://www.samsungapps.com

In addition, there is a seller site that was made available in mid-2009 here: http://seller.samsungapps.com/login/signIn.as?returnURL=/main/sellerMain.as

17.1.1.1 Download/Installing Samsung Software

After you create a free Samsung account, download the following Samsung tools:

- Java SDK
- J2ME SDK
- Mobile Widget SDK
- Windows Mobile SDK

Download the Samsung SDK 1.1.2 beta for Java from: http://innovator.samsungmobile.com/down/cnts/toolSDK.detail.view.do? platformId=3&cntsId=5640

Launch the installer and follow the prompts to install the Samsung SDK.

Download the Samsung SDK for J2ME (which is an MSI installer) from: http://innovator.samsungmobile.com/down/cnts/toolSDK.detail.view.do? platformId=2&cntsId=4604

Launch the installer and follow the prompts to install the Samsung SDK for J2ME (note, this SDK requires configuration with Visual Studio).

The Samsung Mobile Widget SDK is an Eclipse plug-in that you can install using the following URL (try Internet Explorer if you encounter errors using Google Chrome): http://innovator.samsungmobile.com/downloads/widget/

Keep in mind that the Samsung Mobile Widget SDK also supports HTML5. For complete instructions and details, see the Samsung Mobile Widget SDK guide.

You can download the latest version of the Samsung Windows Mobile SDK (an MSI installer) from: http://innovator.samsungmobile.com/smi/WM_SDK2.1

Launch the installer and follow the prompts to complete the installation.

17.1.1.2 A Samsung J2ME Mobile Application

The J2ME file `Graphics1.java` for the Samsung project is identical to the J2ME code sample in the J2ME section of this chapter, so you can learn about the details of `Graphics1.java` in the J2ME section.

Now launch the Samsung SDK (which will appear in a web browser) and perform the following steps to create a new project:

Step 1: Click on New Project

Step 2: Specify `Graphics1` for the Project Name, `Graphics1` for the Package Name, and `Graphics1` for the Midlet Name.

Step 3: Click the Create Project button

Step 4: Click the OK button to accept the default APIs

Step 5: Expand the Source Files element, navigate to the `Graphics1.java` file, and double-click on it

Step 6: Replace the code in `Graphics1.java` with the code in Listing 17.3

Step 7: Click the Build icon to compile the code

Step 8: Click the Run icon to run the code

The Samsung SDK will generate a new J2ME Mobile Information Device Profile (MIDP) project, whose structure is described in the next section.

17.1.1.3 *Project Structure of a Samsung J2ME Application*

Listing 17.1 shows the structure of the Samsung mobile application that you created in the previous section.

Listing 17.1

```
Graphics1
 + Source Files
   + Graphics1.java
 + Resources
 + Binaries
   + MANIFEST.MF
   + Graphics1.jad
```

17.1.1.4 *Samsung J2ME Application Project Files*

As noted earlier, the J2ME file `Graphics1.java` is discussed in the J2ME section later in this chapter.

Check the appendices for Samsung links that provide additional information about Samsung tools, SDKs, and sample C# code.

■ 17.2   J2ME

SUN J2ME is a toolkit for creating Java-based mobile applications. Its home page is: http://java.sun.com/products/sjwtoolkit/

■ 17.2.1 Quick Platform Overview

SUN J2ME is available for Windows and Linux, and you can develop J2ME mobile applications in an IDE (such as Eclipse or NetBeans) or in stand-alone mode. J2ME applications are written in a version of Java for microdevices, and the source code is compiled into Java-based bytecode. J2ME applications are deployed as files with a `.jad` extension, which can be opened via zip utilities (and the Java `jar` command).

17.2.1.1   J2ME Features

SUN J2ME mobile applications can run on various mobile devices, including smartphones and PDAs. The J2ME toolkit provides various configurations, including Connected Limited Device Configuration (CLDC) and (MIDP). J2ME also supports various JSRs, such as:

- JSR 172 (web services)
- JSR 184 (3D graphics API)
- JSR 226 (SVG)
- JSR 238 (internationalization)
- 239 (Java bindings for OpenGL)

SUN J2ME also provides support for third-party emulation and customization. You can find additional information about the J2ME application life cycle here:
http://developers.sun.com/mobility/learn/midp/lifecycle/

■ 17.2.2   A Simple J2ME Application

This section provides you with the instructions and code for creating a graphics-based J2ME application using the J2ME SDK.

17.2.2.1   Downloading/Installing Software

Download and install NetBeans 6.5 (or higher) as described in Chapter 6, Debugging Tools. Next, install the J2ME plug-in for NetBeans here:
http://java.sun.com/downloads/

This Java ME 3.0 SDK is a Windows-only (116 MB) binary executable that is available from: http://java.sun.com/javame/downloads/sdk30.jsp

The EclipseME open source IDE lets you create J2ME-based mobile applications. Its home page is: http://eclipseme.org/

Mobile Tools for Java is a plug-in for Eclipse. Its home page is:
http://www.eclipse.org/dsdp/mtj/

You can install the MTJ plug-in for Eclipse using the following URL:
http://download.eclipse.org/dsdp/mtj/updates/1.0/stable/

17.2.2.2   A Simple J2ME Application in the ME 3.0 SDK

The example in this section is a graphics-based example for a J2ME application that you can create in the J2ME SDK as follows:

Step 1: Follow the menu path **File > New Project**

Step 2: Click the Next button

Step 3: Enter Graphics1 as the Project Name in the text input field

Step 4: Click the Finish button

The SDK will generate a new J2ME MIDP project whose structure is described in the next section.

17.2.2.3 *Project Structure of a J2ME Application*

The J2ME application that you created in the previous section contains one Java file and its structure is displayed in Listing 17.2.

Listing 17.2

```
Graphics1
 + Source Packages
   + graphics1
     Graphics1.java
```

This J2ME application contains the Java file Graphics1.java, which is discussed in the next section.

17.2.2.4 *J2ME Application Project Files*

Listing 17.3 shows the contents of Graphics1.java, which illustrates how to render a set of rectangles with a gradient color.

Listing 17.3 Graphics1.java

```
package graphics;

import javax.microedition.midlet.*;
import javax.microedition.lcdui.*;
import javax.microedition.lcdui.Graphics;

public class Graphics1 extends MIDlet implements CommandListener {
    private Command exitCommand; // The exit command
    private Display display;     // The display for this MIDlet

    public Graphics1() {
        display = Display.getDisplay(this);
        exitCommand = new Command("Exit", Command.EXIT, 0);
    }
```

```
        public void startApp() {
            Display.getDisplay (this).setCurrent (new DrawingCanvas ());
        }

        public void pauseApp() {
        }

        public void destroyApp(boolean unconditional) {
        }

        public void commandAction(Command c, Displayable s) {
            if (c == exitCommand) {
                destroyApp(false);
                notifyDestroyed();
            }
        }
    }
    class DrawingCanvas extends Canvas
    {
        public DrawingCanvas () {}

        public void paint(Graphics g)
        {
            int basePointX = 0;
            int basePointY = 0;
            int maxCount    = 200;
            int rectWidth   = 40;
            int rectHeight  = 20;
            int redWeight   = 0;

            for(int i=0; i<maxCount; i++)
            {
                redWeight = (int)(Math.floor(i*255/maxCount));
                g.setColor(redWeight, 0, 0);

                g.fillRect(basePointX+i,
                            basePointY+i,
                            rectWidth,
                            rectHeight);
            }
        }
    }
}
```

Listing 17.3 contains the code for rendering a set of gradient rectangles. The Java class Graphics1 extends the J2ME MIDlet class, and the constructor performs some simple initialization, as shown here:

```
public Graphics1() {
    display = Display.getDisplay(this);
    exitCommand = new Command("Exit", Command.EXIT, 0);
}
```

The `startApp()` method instantiates the `DrawCanvas` class (which contains the graphics-based code), as shown here:

```
public void startApp() {
    Display.getDisplay (this).setCurrent (new DrawingCanvas ());
}
```

The `DrawCanvas` Java class contains a `paint()` method that contains a `for` loop that renders a set of gradient rectangles by means of the J2ME Graphics class.

■ 17.3   RIM BLACKBERRY

The RIM Blackberry JDE is a Java-based IDE for developing applications for Blackberry devices. Its home page is: http://www.blackberry.com/

RIM Blackberry has targeted business-oriented mobile applications, which makes the Blackberry a direct competitor of the Palm Pre.

You can register for a free Blackberry account here: https://www.blackberry.com/CorpDevZone/register.do

■ 17.3.1   Quick Platform Overview

The Blackberry smartphone supports an extensive set of features, including Bluetooth, browser support, camera/video recording, email, GPS, IM, maps, text messaging.

Blackberry applications are written in JDE, which is a Java-based IDE developed by Blackberry. Blackberry applications are deployed as files with a `.jad` extension, which can be opened via zip utilities (and the Java `jar` command).

■ 17.3.2   A Simple Blackberry Application

Users can create Blackberry mobile applications either by installing the Blackberry plug-in for Eclipse or using the JDE. This section provides the location for both the Blackberry plug-in and the JDE, and then you will see an example of creating a Blackberry mobile application with the JDE.

17.3.2.1 *Downloading/Installing Software*

Complete the instructions described in Chapter 6 for downloading and installing Eclipse 3.4 (or higher).

Next, install the Blackberry plug-in for Eclipse using the following URLs:

http://www.blackberry.com/go/eclipseUpdate

http://na.blackberry.com/eng/developers/javaappdev/javaeclipseplug.jsp

Download the latest version (currently 4.7) of the Blackberry JDE from:

http://na.blackberry.com/eng/developers/javaappdev/javadevenv.jsp

17.3.2.2 *A Blackberry Application in the JDE*

Create a new Blackberry project by performing the following steps:

Step 1: Launch the Blackberry JDE

Step 2: Follow the menu path **File > New > Workspace**

Step 3: Enter `workspace1` as the name of the new workspace

Step 4: Click on `workspace1.jdw`

Step 5: Follow the menu path **File > New > Project**

Step 6: Enter `HelloWorld1` as the name of the new project

Step 7: Click the OK button

Step 8: Select the Template Midlet project

Step 9: Click the Finish button

The Blackberry JDE will create a new project as a subdirectory of `workspace1.jdw` (or wherever you clicked your mouse before creating this project).

17.3.2.3 *Project Structure of a Blackberry Application*

The Blackberry project that you created in the previous section has the following directory structure:

```
workspace1.jds
 + Graphics
   + MidletTemplate.java
```

As you can see, this is a very simple directory structure. The JDE lets you add as many additional files as you need for a project, but ours will consist of this single Java class.

17.3.2.4 *Blackberry Project Files*

The code for `MidletTemplate.java` is identical to the J2ME code in the Java class `GradientRectangles1.java`, which was discussed in the previous section.

■ 17.4 NOKIA

Nokia supports a tremendous variety of mobile devices, and recently formed a partnership with Adobe to promote the development of mobile applications based on FlashLite®. Nokia plans to focus on smartphones, which is where they believe they can establish a dominant position. The Nokia home page is: http://www.nokia.com and for Europe it is: http://europe.nokia.com/home

In mid-2009, Nokia also formed a partnership with Microsoft, which you can read about here: http://www.pcworld.com/article/170132/five_benefits_of_the_microsoftnokia_partnership.html

Nokia provides plug-in support for developing mobile applications in Eclipse, support for Web Runtime Widgets, and support for Qt, which was purchased by Nokia in 2008. Nokia also provides support for a C/C++ plug-in, the S60 browser, and netbook support.

The Nokia Ovi store (which is competing with the Apple store) is here: http://www.comms.ovi.com

Ovi for developers is here: http://www.forum.nokia.com/Ovi/

■ 17.4.1 Nokia Mobile Applications

This section shows you where to download Nokia software and how to create a Nokia Qt application in Eclipse.

17.4.1.1 *Downloading/Installing Nokia Software*

Download and install Eclipse 3.4 (or higher) by following the instructions in Chapter 6.

Install the Qt plug-in for Eclipse from: http://qt.nokia.com/developer/eclipse-integration

Download the Nokia Standalone Java ME Developer's Library from: http://www.forum.nokia.com/info/sw.nokia.com/id/3cfc525e-f0ec-491c-badd-085c0e2df8bf/Java_ME_Developers_Library.html

Expand the downloaded zip file in a convenient directory and launch Eclipse.

Download the Nokia Java ME Developer's Library for Eclipse from: http://www.forum.nokia.com/info/sw.nokia.com/id/3cfc525e-f0ec-491c-badd-085c0e2df8bf/Java_ME_Developers_Library.html

Install the plug-in for Eclipse as follows:

Step 1: Unzip the downloaded file

Step 2: Copy the included JAR file into the Eclipse/plug-ins subdirectory

Launch Eclipse and you will see the Java ME Developer's Library in the Eclipse Help Contents menu.

You can download the Nokia Web Developer's Library from: http://www.forum.nokia.com/info/sw.nokia.com/id/fd9cc12e-5eed-40ec-a439-c77f845fed73/Web_Developers_Library.html

Some additional Nokia downloads are here: http://www.forum.nokia.com/Tools_Docs_and_Code/Tools/Runtimes/

The open C/C++ plug-in is here: http://www.forum.nokia.com/Technology_Topics/Development_Platforms/Open_C_and_C++/

The Nokia S60 browser is here: http://opensource.nokia.com/projects/S60browser/

17.4.1.2 *A Nokia Qt Application in Eclipse*

Install the Qt plug-in for Eclipse (as described in the previous section), and then create a Nokia Qt application in Eclipse by performing the following steps:

Step 1: Follow the menu path **File > New > Other...**

Step 2: Follow the **Qt Designer > Qt Designer Form** menu path and click the Next button

Step 3: Select Dialog with Buttons bottom

Step 4: Specify `NokiaQt.ui` for the Source Folder and `Dialogue1.ui` for the file name

Step 5: Click the Finish button

Follow the **QtDesigner > Editor Mode > Preview in > Windows Vista** (other platforms can be selected) menu path to view the contents of this dialog window. Check the Qt documentation to learn how to create Qt applications using other Qt widgets.

17.4.1.3 *The Nokia Java ME Developer's Library for Eclipse*

You can import a Nokia Java ME mobile application in Eclipse by performing the following steps: In the standalone version that you installed in the previous section, download an SVG-based sample as follows:

Step 1: Expand the node Select Source codes for examples

Step 2: Click on Scalable 2D Vector Graphics…

Step 3: Click on the hyperlink in the text string this link

Step 4: Import the Java ME project into an Eclipse workspace

Step 5: Open the Java ME project in the Package Explorer

Step 6: Follow the menu path **Run > Run Configurations**

Step 7: Select Nokia SDK Plug-in from the configurations

Step 8: Select the MIDlet or JAD file you want to use

Step 9: Select the SDK (e.g., Prototype_4_0_S40_MIDP_Emulator)

Step 10: Click the Run button

■ 17.5 JAVAFX 1.2 FOR MOBILE APPLICATIONS

JavaFX is a scripting-based language that lets developers create cross-device applications for browsers, desktops, and mobile devices. SUN provides a JavaFX plug-in for Eclipse for developing JavaFX mobile applications. Keep in mind that the JavaFX plug-in for Eclipse is available for Windows and MacIntosh, but not on Linux. Note that JavaFX 1.3 is under development and you can expect its release in 2010–check the home page for information about features and official release dates.

■ 17.5.1 A Simple JavaFX Mobile Application

Install Eclipse (3.4 or higher) on your system and then install the JavaFX plug-in for Eclipse from: http://javafx.com/downloads/eclipse-plug-in/

17.5.1.1 A JavaFX Application in Eclipse

After you install the JavaFX 1.2 plug-in for Eclipse, perform the following steps to create a JavaFX mobile application:

Step 1: Follow the **File > New > Project... > JavaFX Project** menu path and click the Next button

Step 2: Type Graphics1 as the Project Name and select the Mobile radio button

Step 3: Click the Next button (twice)

Step 4: Follow the menu path **Building Blocks > Shapes > ShapePri-mitives**

Step 5: Click the Finish button

Eclipse will create a new JavaFX 1.2 mobile-based project called Graphics1, whose directory structure is discussed in the next section.

Launch this project by performing the following steps:

Step 1: Click on the Graphics1 project

Step 2: Follow the menu path **Run > Run As > JavaFX Application**

Step 3: Specify shapes.ShapePrimitives as the Main Class

Step 4: Click the Apply button and then click the Run button

After a few moments the DefaultFxPhone emulator will appear and display two triangles, one rectangle, one circle, and one trapezoid.

17.5.1.2 Project Structure of a JavaFX Mobile Application

The directory structure for the Graphics1 JavaFX1.2 mobile application is displayed in Listing 17.4.

Listing 17.4

```
Graphics1
+ src
   + shapes
     + ShapePrimitives.fx
+ JRE System Library
+ JavaFX System Library (mobile profile)
```

This project contains a single file ShapePrimitives.fx, whose contents are discussed in the next section.

17.5.1.3   JavaFX Project Files

Expand the Graphics1 project node until you locate the file ShapePrimitives.java, whose contents are displayed in Listing 17.5.

Listing 17.5 ShapePrimitives.java

```
/*
 * Copyright (c) 2007, Sun Microsystems, Inc.
 * All rights reserved.
 *
 * Redistribution and use in source and binary forms, with or without
 * modification, are permitted provided that the following condi-
   tions are met:
 *
 *   * Redistributions of source code must retain the above copyright
       notice,
 *     this list of conditions and the following disclaimer.
 *   * Redistributions in binary form must reproduce the above
       copyright
 *     notice, this list of conditions and the following disclaimer in
 *     the documentation and/or other materials provided with the
       distribution.
 *   * Neither the name of Sun Microsystems, Inc. nor the names of its
 *     contributors may be used to endorse or promote products derived
 *     from this software without specific prior written permission.
 *
 * THIS SOFTWARE IS PROVIDED BY THE COPYRIGHT HOLDERS AND CONTRIBUTORS
 * "AS IS" AND ANY EXPRESS OR IMPLIED WARRANTIES, INCLUDING, BUT NOT
 * LIMITED TO, THE IMPLIED WARRANTIES OF MERCHANTABILITY AND FITNESS
   FOR
 * A PARTICULAR PURPOSE ARE DISCLAIMED. IN NO EVENT SHALL THE COPY-
   RIGHT
 * OWNER OR CONTRIBUTORS BE LIABLE FOR ANY DIRECT, INDIRECT, INCI-
   DENTAL,
 * SPECIAL, EXEMPLARY, OR CONSEQUENTIAL DAMAGES (INCLUDING, BUT NOT
   LIMITED
 * TO, PROCUREMENT OF SUBSTITUTE GOODS OR SERVICES; LOSS OF USE,
   DATA, OR
 * PROFITS; OR BUSINESS INTERRUPTION) HOWEVER CAUSED AND ON ANY
   THEORY OF
```

```
 * LIABILITY, WHETHER IN CONTRACT, STRICT LIABILITY, OR TORT (IN-
   CLUDING
 * NEGLIGENCE OR OTHERWISE) ARISING IN ANY WAY OUT OF THE USE OF THIS
 * SOFTWARE, EVEN IF ADVISED OF THE POSSIBILITY OF SUCH DAMAGE.
 */
package transform;

import javafx.scene.shape.Rectangle;
import javafx.scene.paint.Color;
import javafx.stage.Stage;
import javafx.scene.Scene;
import javafx.animation.Timeline;
import javafx.animation.KeyFrame;
import javafx.animation.Interpolator;

import java.lang.Math;

/**
 * @author Michal Skvor
 */

var a : Number = 0.0;
// Size variable counted from changes angle variable
var s : Number = bind Math.sin( a ) * 2;

// Change a variable from 0 to 2*PI in 5 seconds
var timeline : Timeline = Timeline {
  repeatCount: Timeline.INDEFINITE
  keyFrames : [
    KeyFrame {
        time : 0s
        values : {
            a => 0.0 tween Interpolator.LINEAR
        }
    },
    KeyFrame {
        time : 5s
        values : {
            a => Math.PI tween Interpolator.LINEAR
        }
    }
  ]
};

Stage {
  scene : Scene {
```

```
      fill : Color.GRAY
      content : [
        Rectangle {
          // Bind size of rectangle to s variable
          transforms : [
            javafx.scene.transform.Translate {x : bind 100 - 40 * s / 2,
                              y : bind 100 - 40 * s / 2 },
            javafx.scene.transform.Scale { x : bind s, y : bind s }
          ]
          x : 0, y : 0
          width : 40, height : 40
          fill : Color.BLACK
        },
      ]
    }

    visible : true
    title : "Scale"
    width : 200
    height : 232
}

timeline.play();
```

The first part of Listing 17.5 contains Java-like import statements, followed by the definition of the variable type TimeLine for creating animation effects, as shown here:

```
var timeline : Timeline = Timeline {
    repeatCount: Timeline.INDEFINITE
    keyFrames : [
        KeyFrame {
            time : 0s
            values : {
                a => 0.0 tween Interpolator.LINEAR
            }
        },
        KeyFrame {
            time : 5s
            values : {
                a => Math.PI tween Interpolator.LINEAR
            }
        }
    ]
};
```

The `Timeline` variable contains two `KeyFrame` elements, each of which uses a `time` variable to specify the duration of the animation, based on linear interpolation.

The next section contains a `Scene` element that contains a `Rectangle` element for the animation effect. JavaFX will apply a translation and a scale transformation to this rectangle, as shown in this code fragment:

```
Rectangle {
  // Bind size of rectangle to s variable
  transforms : [
    javafx.scene.transform.Translate { x : bind 100 - 40 * s / 2,
                        y : bind 100 - 40 * s / 2 },
    javafx.scene.transform.Scale { x : bind s, y : bind s }
  ]
  x : 0, y : 0
  width : 40, height : 40
  fill : Color.BLACK
},
```

The final part of Listing 17.5 contains a code snippet that starts the animation effect, as shown here:

```
timeline.play();
```

As you can see, JavaFX provides a scripting language that lets you use a declarative style for specifying desired behavior. Check the appendices for links that describe how to create a wide variety of JavaFX applications.

■ 17.6 MONOTOUCH

In 2009, the Mono project created MonoTouch, which lets users create iPhone applications using C#. Its home page is:
http://monotouch.net/

MonoTouch is a commercial offering from Novell®. The pricing has not been finalized yet, but it should be similar to .NET components and .NET tools.

■ 17.6.1 MonoTouch Features

The beta is considered feature complete, but it will likely have bugs, and be missing some .NET bindings to the Objective-C APIs that are important.

Please notify Mono with a list of any incomplete bindings and they will release new versions/workarounds to aid your adoption of MonoTouch.

■ 17.6.2 A Simple MonoTouch Application

Although we do not discuss C# in this book, the MonoTouch example in this section is very straightforward and only requires rudimentary knowledge of C# (if you know Java you will understand the code).

17.6.2.1 Downloading/Installing Software

You can download the MonoTouch distribution from:
http://www.mono-project.com/MonoTouch_Installation
     You will need the following log in and password to download the MonoTouch beta. Please note that the username and password may have changed after this book was published.
     Username: monotouch-beta
     Password: eH3ootu2
     Read the following information here:
http://www.mono-project.com/MonoTouch_Beta

17.6.2.2 A Minimal MonoTouch Example

Listing 17.6 shows the contents of the C# class `HelloWorld.cs`, which demonstrates how to create a minimal MonoTouch "Hello, World" program here: http://monotouch.net/Tutorials/HelloiPhone

Listing 17.6 HelloWorld.cs

```
using System;
using MonoTouch.UIKit;

class Hello {
    static void Main (string [] args)
    {
        Console.WriteLine ("Hello World!");
    }
}
```

The first part of Listing 17.6 contains `using` statements (which are comparable to `import` statements in Java), followed by the definition of the `Hello` class, which contains a `Main` method that prints the message `Hello World!`.

Open a command shell and compile the code in Listing 17.6 as shown here:

```
$ smcs HelloWorld.cs -r:monotouch.dll
```

You can prepare the program for launch, as shown here:

```
mtouch -sim Hello.app HelloWorld.exe
```

Next, launch the program in the simulator, as shown here:

```
mtouch --launchsim=HelloWorld.exe --stdout=output
```

Listing 17.7 shows the contents of the class `AppController.cs`, which contains code that is frequently used in MonoTouch applications.

Listing 17.7: AppController.cs

```
public class AppController : UIApplicationDelegate {
  UIWindow window;

  public override void FinishedLaunching (UIApplication app)
  {
    var window = new UIWindow (UIScreen.MainScreen.Bounds) {
      new UILabel (new RectangleF (50, 50, 230, 100)) {
        Text = "Hello from MonoTouch"
      }
    };

    window.MakeKeyAndVisible ();
  }
}

class Demo {
  static void Main (string [] args)
  {
    UIApplication.Main (args, null, "AppController");
  }
}
```

The first part of Listing 17.7 defines an `AppController` class (which extends the MonoTouch `UIApplicationDeletgate` class) that contains the `FinishedLaunching()` method for defining and launching a `UIWindow` that contains a `UILabel` widget.

The next part of Listing 17.7 defines the `Demo` class with a `Main` method that instantiates the `UIApplication` class.

Check the appendices for additional useful links about MonoTouch.

■ 17.7 MOTOROLA

Motorola supports MOTODEV, which is an Eclipse-based development environment for developing mobile applications. Later in this section, you will see an example of creating a MOTODEV mobile application, and you will also learn how to set up a J2ME-based SDK from Motorola (along with some short code fragments).

In September 2009, Motorola announced the availability of Motorola CLIQ™, which you can read here:
http://wireless.sys-con.com/node/ 1102140

Moto CLIQ supports Android-based application development and provides development tools for creating mobile applications.

Recently, there has been some speculation that Motorola will focus on Android-based tools for primarily developing Android applications. By the time this book is published you will have a clearer picture in terms of how to invest your time using Motorola-based tools for creating mobile applications.

Motorola provides MOTODEV Studio (which uses the VMWare Player) for mobile application development. Motorola also provides support for J2ME and Android mobile applications, both of which are discussed later in this section.

■ 17.7.1 Overview of Motorola Mobile Applications

Motorola supports MOTODEV Studio, which is an Eclipse-based IDE for creating mobile and web-based applications. You must first install VMWare Player (which is described in the next section), and then install MOTODEV Studio.

17.7.1.1 Downloading/Installing Software

Follow the instructions in Chapter 6 to download and install Eclipse on your system.

Next, create a free VMWare account, sign in to your account, and download the VMWare Player from:

http://www.vmware.com/download/player/download.html

Then download the VMWare Player installer and follow the installation prompts.

Next, download the Motorola MOTODEV Studio for mobile applications and the installation guide (PDF file) from: http://developer.motorola.com/docstools/motodevstudio/webui/downloads/

After you download and install the VMWare Player from the previous section, follow the installation instructions in the accompanying PDF file to install the Motorola distribution.

You can download MOTODEV software for J2ME from:

http://developer.motorola.com/docstools/motodevstudio/javame/downloads/

You can download the MOTODEV tools for Android from:

http://developer.motorola.com/docstools/motodevstudio/download/

You can download MOTODEV CLIQ from:

http://wireless.sys-con.com/node/1102140

■ 17.7.2   A Motorola Mobile Application

After you install the software listed in the previous section, perform the following steps in the MOTODEV Studio to create a mobile application:

Step 1: Follow the menu path **File > New > Project > MOTODEV Studio for WebUI**

Step 2: Select WebUI Application (or Widget) Project and click the Next button

Step 3: Type `Motodev1` as the Project name

Step 4: Select the Contacts Search Sample checkbox

Step 5: Click the Finish button

Eclipse will create a new WebUI (Widget) application project called `Motodev1`, whose directory structure is discussed in the next section.

When you run this sample project, MOTODEV Studio will launch the VMWare Player (if it is not already running), after which the emulator will appear, and you can view the output from the sample project.

17.7.2.1 *Project Structure of a MOTODEV WebUI Application*

The directory structure for `Motodev1`, which you created in the previous section, is displayed in Listing 17.8.

Listing 17.8

```
Motodev1
+ src
   + ContactsSearch
      + scripts
      + resource
      + style
      + conteacts_search_app.descriptor
      + index.html
      + SKMenu.xml
+ dist
+ JavaScript Support
   + Script Language Libraries
   + ECMA 3 Browser Support Library
   + WebUI Support Library
```

This project contains several JavaScript files in the `scripts` subdirectory, but we will focus on the HTML file `index.html`, whose contents are discussed in the next section.

17.7.2.2 *MOTODEV Project Files*

Listing 17.9 shows the contents of the HTML file `index.html`, which was automatically generated when you created the `Motodev1` project in the previous section.

Listing 17.9 index.html

```
<!--
 Copyright (c) 2007-2009 Motorola, Inc. or its subsidiaries.
 All rights reserved.
 -->

<!DOCTYPE HTML PUBLIC "-//W3C//DTD HTML 4.01 Transitional//EN"
"http://www.w3.org/TR/html4/loose.dtd">
<html>
  <head>
        <title>Contacts Search</title>
```

```
    <meta http-equiv="Content-Type" content="text/html; charset=iso-
8859-1">

    <link href="style/style.css" rel="stylesheet" type="text/css">

    <script src="scripts/main.js" type="text/javascript"></script>
    <script src="scripts/search.js" type="text/javascript"></script>
    <script src="scripts/skMenu.js" type="text/javascript"></script>

  </head>
  <body id="body" onload="javascript:onLoad();">
    <div id="main">
    </div>
  </body>
</html>
```

The first part of Listing 17.9 contains several <script> elements in the HTML <head> element, as shown here:

```
    <script src="scripts/main.js" type="text/javascript"></script>
    <script src="scripts/search.js" type="text/javascript"></script>
    <script src="scripts/skMenu.js" type="text/javascript"></script>
```

These three JavaScript files are automatically included in the MOTO-DEV project you created.

The second part of Listing 17.9 contains an HTML <body> element that executes the onLoad() method when the sample application is launched.

■ 17.7.3 Motorola and J2ME

You can download the Motorola J2ME SDK from:
http://developer.motorola.com/docstools/motodevstudio/javame/down
loads/MOTODEV_SDK_for_Java_ME_3.0.0_Windows.exe/?return_to=
http://developer.motorola.com/docstools/motodevstudio/javame/down
loads/&download_page=1

If you have a Windows-based system you can launch the binary installer and follow the prompts to complete the installation.

17.7.3.1 J2ME Sample Applications

Perform the following steps to view the sample applications:

Step 1: Launch the SDK

Step 2: Click the Browse button and locate a JAD file under the Deployed subdirectory of the sample applications in the JMESDK/demos directory

Step 3: Click on the blue triangle (top of the screen) to launch the application

Because you have already seen J2ME-based mobile application code, the following code snippets for a "hello world" example should be familiar to you. First, the contents of the constructor:

```
myDisplay = Display.getDisplay(this);

titleScreen = new List("Hello World:", List.IMPLICIT);
titleScreen.append("Hello World!!!", null);
titleScreen.addCommand(exitCommand);
titleScreen.setCommandListener(this);
```

Next, the contents of the startApp() method:

```
myDisplay.setCurrent(titleScreen);
```

The GraphicsDemo sample application draws a rectangle by means of the following code fragment:

```
g.drawString("fillRect", (getWidth() / 2), 0,
       Graphics.HCENTER | Graphics.TOP);
g.drawString("drawRect", (getWidth() / 2),
       font.getHeight(),
       Graphics.HCENTER | Graphics.TOP);

g.fillRect(getWidth() / 6, font.getHeight() * 2,
       getWidth() / 3 * 2, 30);
g.setColor(0, 0, 255);
g.drawRect(getWidth() / 6, font.getHeight() * 2,
       getWidth() / 3 * 2, 30);
```

■ 17.7.4 Motorola and Android

Motorola supports Android-based mobile applications. You can download MOTODEV for Android from:

http://developer.motorola.com/docstools/motodevstudio/download/

Run the installer and follow the prompts to complete the installation.

Next, launch Eclipse and perform the following steps to create an Android mobile application:

Step 1: Follow the menu path **File > New > Other...**

Step 2: Select **Android > Android Project** using Studio for Android and click the Next button

Step 3: Type Android1 as the Project name and click the Finish button

Eclipse will create a new Android application project called Android1, whose directory structure is discussed in the next section.

When you run this sample project, MOTODEV Studio will launch the VMWare Player (if it is not already running), after which the emulator will appear and you can view the output from the sample project.

17.7.4.1 *Project Structure of a MOTODEV Android Application*

The directory structure for Motodev1, which you created in the previous section, is displayed in Listing 17.10.

Listing 17.10

```
Android1
+ src
   + com.android1
     + MainActivity.java
 + gen [Generated Java Files]
     + com.android1
        + R.java
  + Android 1.5
     + android.jar
+ res
+ assets
+ drawable
    + icon.png
+ layout
    + main.xml
+ values
    + strings.xml
+ AndroidManifest.xml
+ default.properties
```

As you can see in Listing 17.10, the Java class is called `MainActivity` `.java`, and it is located in the `src/com/android1` subdirectory of the `Android1` project. The next section discusses the code in `MainActivity.java`.

17.7.4.2 MOTODEV Android Project Files

Listing 17.11 displays the contents of the `MainActivity.java` file that was generated when you created the `Android1` project in the previous section.

Listing 17.11 MainActivity.java

```
package com.android1;

import android.app.Activity;
import android.os.Bundle;

public class MainActivity extends Activity {
    /** Called when the activity is first created. */
    @Override
    public void onCreate(Bundle savedInstanceState) {
        super.onCreate(savedInstanceState);
        setContentView(R.layout.main);
    }
}
```

The first part of Listing 17.11 starts with a `package` definition statement, followed by two `import` statements that reference Java Android classes. The next part defines the Java class `MainActivity` (which extends the Android `Activity` class) that contains the `onCreate()` method. This method overrides the `onCreate()` method in the base class with code that calls the `onCreate()` method of the base class and then sets the `view` object appropriately.

Listing 17.12 displays the contents of the `AndroidManifest.xml` file that was generated when you created the `Android1` project in the previous section.

Listing 17.12 AndroidManifest.xml

```
<?xml version="1.0" encoding="utf-8"?>
<manifest xmlns:android="http://schemas.android.com/apk/res/android"
      package="com.android1"
      android:versionCode="1"
      android:versionName="1.0">
```

```
    <application android:icon="@drawable/icon" android:label="@
string/app_name">
        <activity android:name=".MainActivity"
                android:label="@string/app_name">
            <intent-filter>
                <action android:name="android.intent.action.MAIN" />
                <category android:name="android.intent.category
.LAUNCHER" />
            </intent-filter>
        </activity>
    </application>
    <uses-sdk android:minSdkVersion="3" />
</manifest>
```

The content of Listing 17.12 is analogous to the AndroidManifest.xml that was discussed in the Android section in Chapter 16, (so we will skip the discussion of this file). In fact, Motorola-based Android mobile applications are identical to Android applications that are developed on any other mobile platforms.

■ 17.8   VERIZON JOINT INNOVATION LAB (JIL) MOBILE

Verizon supports mobile applications written in BREW, which also has integrated support for Flash.

In September 2009, there were some reports about Verizon's decision to abandon its support for the Palm Pre, citing poor sales as the reason for the decision (see the appendices for a link).

You can download BREW software from:
http://developer.verizon.com/jsps/devCenters/Brew/Landing_Pages/p_brew_sdk_tools_dtls.jsp

The Verizon Developer Community (VDC) is here:
http://developer.verizon.com/

■ 17.8.1   Verizon Mobile Applications in Eclipse

You can download the Verizon JIL SDK from:
http://developer.verizon.com/jsps/devCenters/JIL/Landing_Pages/jil_dwnlds_widget_sdk_dtls.jsp

Launch the JIL SDK to start an Eclipse session, and perform the following steps to create a Verizon mobile application:

Step 1: Follow the menu path **File > New > Widget Project**

Step 2: Type `MyWidget1` as the Project Name and click the Finish button

Eclipse will create a new widget application called `MyWidget1`.

Some additional links for developing Verizon applications on various platforms are available here:

http://developer.verizon.com/jsps/devCenters/wireless/index.jsp

You can submit your Verizon applications to the Verizon store here:

http://www.applyyourideas.com/default.aspx

■ 17.9   OTHER DEVELOPMENT TOOLS FOR MOBILE DEVICES

There are several open source frameworks and IDEs available for developing mobile devices, such as:

• Appcelerator
• XMLVM
• Rhomobile
• MonoTouch
• NetBeans 6.7.1/6.8 Mobility

■ 17.9.1   Appcelerator

Appcelerator is an open source framework that supports the development of mobile applications. Its home page is:

http://www.appcelerator.com/

Appcelerator provides support for Python and Ruby, and various Ajax toolkits, including JQuery, MooTools, Prototype, Scriptaculous, Dojo, and Yahoo YUI.

17.9.1.1 . Downloading/Installing Software

Follow the instructions in Chapter 6 for installing Eclipse on your system, and then download Titanium from:

http://www.appcelerator.com/products/download-titanium/download/

Launch the installer and follow the prompts to complete the Titanium installation on your system.

You can also read the Titanium quickstart guide here:

http://www.appcelerator.com/community/titanium-quick-start/

17.9.1.2 An Appcelerator Mobile Application in Eclipse

Launch Titanium and perform the following steps to create an Appcelerator mobile application:

Step 1: Launch the Titanium Developer executable and select an installation directory

Step 2: Click on the Create button

Step 3: Specify `MyTitanium` as the name of the project

Step 4: Provide values for the other input fields

Step 5: Select the jQuery toolkit

Step 6: Click the Create button

Eclipse will create a new Appcelerator mobile-based project called `MyTitanium`, whose directory structure is discussed in the next section.

17.9.1.3 Project Structure of an Appcelerator Mobile Application

Listing 17.13 shows the directory structure of the Appcelerator `MyTitanium` application you created in the previous section.

Listing 17.13

```
MyTitanium
+ dist
+ LICENSE.txt
+ manifest
+ Resources
+ tiapp.xml
+ Resources
  + index.html
  + jquery-1.3.2.js
```

This project contains the HTML file `index.html` and the XML configuration file `tiapp.xml`, whose contents are discussed in the next section.

17.9.1.4 Appcelerator Project Files

Listing 17.14 displays the contents of the HTML file `index.html` (from the resource subdirectory of the MyTitanium project).

Listing 17.14 index.html

```html
<html>
  <head>
    <script type="text/javascript" src="jquery-1.3.2.js"></script>
</head>

<body style="background-color:#1c1c1c;margin:0">
 <div style="border-top:1px solid #404040">
  <div style="color:#fff;;padding:10px">Welcome to Titanium</div>
 </div>
</body>
</html>
```

Listing 17.14 contains a `<script>` element that references the JQuery toolkit, which was selected when you created this project in a previous section.

Now launch the HTML file `index.html` and you will see the following message:

```
Welcome to Titanium
```

Listing 17.15 displays the contents of the XML file `tiapp.xml`, which was automatically generated when you created the MyTitanium project.

Listing 17.15 tiapp.xml

```xml
<?xml version='1.0' encoding='UTF-8'?>
<ti:app xmlns:ti='http://ti.appcelerator.org'>
<!-- These values are edited/maintained by Titanium Developer -->
<id>com.acme.app1</id>
<name>Mytitanium</name>
<version>1.0</version>
<publisher>Owner</publisher>
<url>http://www.yahoo.com</url>
<icon>default_app_logo.png</icon>
<copyright>2009 by Owner</copyright>
<!-- Window Definition - these values can be edited -->
<window>
<id>initial</id>
<title>Mytitanium</title>
<url>app://index.html</url>
<width>700</width>
<max-width>3000</max-width>
```

```
<min-width>0</min-width>
<height>800</height>
<max-height>3000</max-height>
<min-height>0</min-height>
<fullscreen>false</fullscreen>
<resizable>true</resizable>
<chrome scrollbars="true">true</chrome>
<maximizable>true</maximizable>
<minimizable>true</minimizable>
<closeable>true</closeable>
</window>
</ti:app>
```

As you can see in Listing 17.15, `tiapp.xml` is a simple XML-based configuration file containing various name/value pairs, such as `id`, `title`, and `url` for the associated Titanium application.

■ 17.9.2   Cross-Platform Development Tools

This section contains information about XMLVM and Rhomobile, which are two development tools for cross-platform mobile application development. Note that no sample code is provided for either of these tools, but you can navigate to the home page of these products and search those websites for sample code.

17.9.2.1   XMLVM

XMLVM is an open source cross-platform development framework for mobile devices that began in 2003. Its home page is:
http://www.xmlvm.org/

XMLVM facilitates the creation of mobile applications on different platforms. You can think of XMLVM as a tool that can "push" mobile applications to different mobile platforms. For example, developers start by creating a Google Android application, after which XMLVM can convert that application into corresponding iPhone and Palm Pre applications. XMLVM provides all of the Java tools for debugging and it cross-compiles Android applications from Java to Objective-C. In addition, XMLVM can generate mobile applications on the iPhone and Palm Pre.

XMLVM also provides two compatibility libraries, Android Compat-Lib and Cocoa Compat-Lib, that map Android API to the Cocoa API. Compat-Lib is written in Java and only uses Cocoa APIs. As an example, the Android button is in the package `android.widget`, which extends the `Android View` class, whereas the Android Button in Compat-Lib is a wrapper for the iPhone button.

Currently, XMLVM is licensed with GPL, and there is a possibility of dual licensing in the future (check the home page for more information).

Xokoban is an XMLVM tool that was developed for Android and cross-compiled to the iPhone and WebOS. Xokoban provides support for 2D animation, dialog boxes, accelerometer, and landscape full-screen mode.

You can download XMLVM from: http://www.xmlvm.org/download/

17.9.2.2 *Rhomobile*

Rhomobile is a Rails-based development platform for mobile devices. Its home page is: http://www.rhomobile.com/

You can develop Rhomobile applications online at Rhohub, which provides an online hosted environment that is available for public beta. The Rhohub home page provides free registration here:
http://www.rhohub.com/

Rhomobile uses GitHub to make code freely available from:
http://github.com/rhomobile/rhodes/tree/master

Check the appendices for additional links about developing mobile applications with Rhomobile.

17.9.2.3 *SVG and Mobile Applications in NetBeans*

In previous chapters, you learned how to create various types of projects using NetBeans IDE, and how to use NetBeans to develop mobile applications. NetBeans also supports SVG components, which includes buttons, labels, checkboxes, lists, sliders, and spinners. Additional information about NetBeans, SVG components, and the Mobility Visual Designer is here:
http://wiki.netbeans.org/MobilityDesignerRichComponents

■ 17.10 COMPANIES FOR MOBILE DEVELOPMENT

This section provides some information and links about several companies and tools that assist developers in creating mobile applications for various platforms. The companies in this section are:

• Agile Commerce
• Ansca

- PhoneGap
- Pivotal Labs

Agile Commerce is a start-up company that specializes in consulting services. Its home page is: http://www.agilecommerce.com

An Agile Commerce site with a Palm Pre application is here: https://agilecommerce.svn.beanstalkapp.com/flickr_search/trunk

Ansca (which uses the Lua programming language) lets you build iPhone applications using Flash-like functionality. Its home page is: http://www.anscamobile.com

You can register for an Ansca developer account to download the SDK at: http://developer.anscamobile.com

You can find Ansca sample code (also included in the SDK) here: http://developer.anscamobile.com/content/sample-code

PhoneGap is an open source device agnostic mobile application development whose home page is: http://phonegap.com

The latest version of the software is downloadable from: http://phonegap.com/download

Pivotal Labs provides a testing tool called Jasmine that is a unit test framework similar to JsUnit. You can download Jasmine from: http://github.cmo/pivotal/jasmine/tree/master

■ 17.11 MOBILE TRENDS IN OTHER TECHNOLOGIES

Recently we have seen the emergence of mobile applications in areas such as cloud computing, voice recognition, live streaming, social networks, and banking.

Mobile applications that provide cloud computing functionality are currently available on the iPhone, and you can expect to see more applications on other platforms as well.

For example, you can now manage your Amazon S3 via mobile applications here: http://cloudberrylab.com/?id=64

Another iPhone application is available for Rackspace, and Twilio provides functionality for Microsoft Azure.

Mobile applications are appearing for voice recognition, which is destined to become commonplace in our lives (and not just for mobile devices).

Mobile applications are available for Facebook, and some applications can provide real-time location-based functionality.

You can watch MP3 files on Google Android, view Flash-based applications, and even do your banking on a smartphone. Mobile browsers are becoming ever more powerful, and a jQuery plug-in was recently created for mobile development. Check the appendices for interesting links about these recent trends in the mobile application arena.

■ 17.12 SUMMARY

This chapter explained some of the latest developments in mobile devices, including Nokia, J2ME, RIM Blackberry, Verizon, Motorola, JavaFX 12, and MonoTouch.

You saw various examples of creating mobile applications on these platforms, and how J2ME is used. Next, you learned about tools that support cross-platform mobile development, including XMLVM and Rhomobile. You also learned about some recent trends, such as cloud computing, voice recognition, live streaming, social networks, and banking. Finally, you learned about various start-ups that have created mobile-related tools and services, such as Appcelerator, Agile Commerce, Ansca, PhoneGap, and Pivotal Labs.

## CHAPTER 18

Epilogue: The Future of the Web

In This Chapter:

- Current Major Trends
- Start-Up Innovators
- Future Trends for the Web
- Final Thoughts

This chapter begins with some of the major trends that we believe are important for the Web. We'll follow that by giving you some insight into the experiences of various start-up innovators from Silicon Valley, including tips and suggestions for creating your own start-up.

The next (and most extensive) part of this chapter contains opinions on the future of the Web from various industry figures and domain experts.

Note that this book contains a section with biographical information on each of the contributors to this book.

■ 18.1 CURRENT MAJOR TRENDS

There are several trends that will become significant in the near future:

- Mobile Technology
- HTML5
- The Real-Time Web
- Semantic Technology
- Social Networks

■ 18.1.1 Mobile Technology

The highly competitive mobile arena is continuing to grow at a significant pace, and currently the Apple iPhone offers the largest number of applications (both free and for pay), which are available for download at the online Apple store. The number of iPhone applications that were available on the Apple store reached 100,000 (with more than one billion downloads) by mid-2009, and this number is expected to increase well into 2010.

As you saw in Chapter 16, the number of Apple iPhone applications clearly dwarfs the number of applications of its competitors, such as Google Android, Nokia, and other mobile platforms. At the same time, the Apple iPhone market is crowded and very competitive, which means that developers are facing a huge challenge to gain traction with their mobile applications.

In less than a year, there has been a noticeable shift in focus for iPhone developers. For example, during 2008, developers could focus on implementing functionality for their iPhone applications; however, by early 2009, developers had become increasingly focused in the marketing aspects (rather than the technical details) of their iPhone applications.

This highly competitive landscape may push developers to other platforms because the alternatives offer greater visibility and perhaps better opportunities to sell mobile applications.

Another point to consider is that you need to learn Objective-C to write mobile applications for the Apple iPhone. On the other hand, Google Android applications are written in a Java-like language, and you can write mobile applications for Nokia using FlashLite, which (in some respects) resembles JavaScript or C#.

If you are trying to decide which platform to choose, the answer depends on your current level of programming expertise, the type of application that you want to develop, your target audience, and the expected number of downloads for your application, which will help you estimate your potential income.

While Google and Nokia do have online sites for selling mobile phone applications, currently there are few applications available; as a developer this may be advantageous to you, but keep in mind that you may also be competing with developers who are porting already-successful iPhone applications to other platforms to replicate their success.

■ 18.1.2   HTML5

In Chapter 2, you learned that several browsers provide some support for HTML5, and the level of support is expected to increase over time.

Google has adopted HTML5 as an important technology, and is developing tools, such as Native Client, that provide a "bridge" between JavaScript code and the large body of native code (written in languages such as C™) that is available in compiled libraries. In fact, some popular graphics-intensive games can run just fine in a browser with very smooth transition effects.

Another important point is the decision in mid-2009 by the World Wide Web Consortium (W3C) to abandon XHTML2 in favor of HTML5 (check the appendices for a link with details).

XForms is an XML-based technology that uses an Model-View-Controller (MVC) pattern to separate presentation logic, business logic, and data. Therefore, XForms makes it easier to write forms, reduces the need for handling events, and it is device independent. Unfortunately, XForms is part of the XHTML2 initiative, so the fate of XForms is uncertain.

■ 18.1.3   The Real-Time Web

When Twitter became available a few short years ago, its moniker "What are you doing now?" was viewed as whimsical and almost capricious. Recently, Twitter was described as a "new form of communication," and other companies seem to be scrambling to provide Twitter-like functionality. The Real-Time Web (which includes real-time search) make a formidable impact on the speed with which we can access information in real time, perhaps further exacerbating the challenge of information hyper-abundance (see the final section of this chapter for more discussion about this aspect of technology).

■ 18.1.4   Semantic Technology

Although the primary focus of this book concerns Web 2.0 technologies, there is also talk about the Semantic Web, Web 3.0, and even Web 4.0. One group perceives the evolution of the Web primarily from a quantitative viewpoint, which involves a mixture of new approaches to solving problems and continuous (yet fundamentally iterative) improvement of software. Another group perceives the evolution of the Web in terms of a qualitative change that will fundamentally affect the manner in which we benefit from new software technology.

■ 18.2   START-UP INNOVATORS

The "freemium" model provides users with a free service designed to be so compelling that the service will become an integral part of users' lives. The "base" service is free, and additional features are available at a nominal cost per user, thereby enticing large numbers of people to pay for premium services.

The economic downturn that began in 2007 made it difficult for start-ups to get venture capital funding, and gave rise to the terms Recession 2.0, Depression 2.0, and Web two-dot-over.

Investors told start-ups to reduce their burn rate, so they became "lean and mean" in a manner that vaguely resembled just-in-time manufacturing.

Consequently, the downturn spurred the creation of low-cost start-ups that only used open source software, paid people in sweat equity, and built a product that revolved around one core idea.

This section includes interviews with founders of at least one start-up company. They share their dos and donts and their opinions on how things have changed over the past 10 years in Silicon Valley. Hopefully, their experiences will give you insight into the rewards, challenges, and pitfalls you might face if you decide to launch your own start-up.

■ 18.3   VINCENT LAURIA

■ 18.3.1   Can you tell us about your background?

I graduated from Boston University with a degree in Computer Engineering and worked at IBM for 3 1/2 years before moving out west to Silicon Valley.

■ 18.3.2   What project(s) are you currently working on?

In 2007, I co-founded Lefora.com, a forum hosting service for communities on the Web. We've taken a technology that predates the Web—forums—and added a number of features commonly associated with Web 2.0. Some of these features include: hosting individual forums in the cloud (there's nothing for forum administrators to install), community ranking and moderation, integration with third-party services, such as Facebook, APIs, RSS feeds, and rich user profiles.

I'm also the organizer of the 4,700 member Silicon Valley New-Tech Meetup, which you can find at: www.newtechmeetup.org, where four companies get a chance to demo their services to a group of tech enthusiasts each month. I've been running this event since January 2006 and have reviewed hundreds of web companies. I've seen quite an evolution over the past few years. The biggest trend I've seen is that in '05 and '06, the primary focus on most services was social networking and connecting or sharing media with friends. Now this has faded to an underlying requirement for services built on top of somebody's social graph.

■ 18.3.3   How did you adjust your business as a result?

When we first started Lefora.com forum hosting, we wanted to make the sexiest forum product out there with slick interfaces for filtering and real-time interaction. What we quickly found out is that wasn't what customers wanted for a forum. We pared back our interface and made it our mission to improve forums and not shift into other community offerings. There are still a number of social and sharing features, but now they're woven into the product in such a way as to increase activity but not be distracting. These features are a key differentiator between us and traditional forums, yet they play a secondary role in the user experience.

■ 18.3.4   What significant changes do you think will happen in the Web in the next few years, and what will be the effect on start-ups?

What I see happening already, and what I think will only become more popular, will be consumer and enterprise services that fall under cloud computing. I'm referring to anything that is hosted in the cloud and stores all of your data there. Services will have richer APIs to interact on top of, or to the side of, other services. I think we'll see a number of new standard protocols to help facilitate this; from Single Sign-On (SOS), to sharing of your social graph, to updating your followers, I think different web companies will constantly be talking to each other on the back-end.

One of the biggest hurdles for this will be trust. The idea of hosting your data in the cloud has been marketed for years, but the trust factor has lead to slow adoption. How can I trust another company with my private data? I think just as we saw an explosion of services like wikis, blogs, and social networks in the consumer market before the enterprise market, the same will happen for cloud computing. Consumers will be ready to trust services with their private data for the value they get in return. As this mentality changes, it will shift into the enterprise with a bottom-up approach.

■ 18.3.5 How will this change in the near future?

We're already seeing a number of sites become platforms for other services, much like an Operating System (OS) platform. Examples of this are facebook, Twitter, OpenSocial, and the iPhone. The larger players will set the stage for APIs and how services will be built.

Additionally, mobile smartphones are quickly saturating the market and becoming a very solid alternative to using a full-blown computer. As cloud computing turns a web browser into a dumb terminal, mobile computing will be the preferred touch point for many services.

■ 18.3.6 What key factors should be considered when engaging in a new start-up?

I think the number one factor is to understand the problem you are solving. For any start-up, it's easy to want to add lots of features to attract a potentially larger audience. But as there are so many start-ups out there, you're much better playing to a niche and really hitting a homerun than trying to boil the ocean. Understand where your start-up fits in with other services and how you can complement each other.

Also, as a web start-up ultimately makes software, it is vital to have a strong technical team that works really well together. If you're starting a new company, you want people that have worked together before and can really click. And it's always a good idea to bring on a few advisers with specific expertise. No matter how much you may know, their outside perspective can help keep you in balance and save you time.

■ 18.3.7 What hard lessons have you learned that you wish you knew earlier?

A friend once said to me, "Jump and the net will appear" (which is also the title of a book). The biggest life lesson I've learned since coming out to Silicon Valley is that there is a world of opportunity out there. I was at IBM for almost four years, and the thought of leaving a comfortable job for the unknown was very scary to me. It wasn't until I actually took the leap that I realized how empowering it is to put yourself out there.

It was a valuable life lesson for me, to switch from employee to entrepreneur. Now I always know that there will be a place for me to land, and it's completely changed my thinking for the better.

■ 18.3.8 What are the primary factors for start-up success?

I think it's important to be flexible and realize you don't know all of the answers. The landscape on the Web is constantly evolving, so as long as you're willing to move with it, you should be in a good position. Mistakes will be made at any start-up—hopefully, you will learn from them. It also helps to be very optimistic and a little bit crazy.

■ 18.4 FUTURE TRENDS FOR THE WEB

When we started writing this book, we decided to include a final chapter containing predictions about the future of the Web. We have seen the Web evolve and change at an amazing pace over the past decade, and we all know that the Web will continue to evolve, perhaps even faster than today.

However, we soon realized that writing the chapter would be more challenging than we originally thought, partly because our lives are intensely focused on learning and working with the latest technologies in several important ways, including our day jobs, the user group meetings we attend, and the side projects we work on. While we believe that this intense work (in conjunction with our years of technical expertise) have made us experts in Web 2.0 technologies, we simply do not have the expertise to assess the future of the Web. Consequently, we recognized the value of gathering opinions from a variety of people in various industries, and the value of their varying opinions and experiences to our readers.

Therefore, we asked ourselves a simple question: who in the IT industry would be willing to collaborate with us and provide useful information regarding the future of the Web?

Oswald has met several industry leaders through many user group events he attends and Kevin knows several industry leaders through the three user groups he helps organize. At one point, we realized that many of our industry leader friends are very community oriented and would probably be willing to contribute a few pages to the book on what they felt was the direction of the future of the Web. We decided that inviting industry leaders to write small summaries about the future of the Web would be both interesting and valuable to the readers of this book.

We believe that the idea of crowd sourcing our future-of-the-Web chapter to industry leaders is valuable to. You we enjoyed working with our friends and industry leaders to put this chapter together. Since many of the topics covered in this book are constantly evolving, we sought industry leaders for their insight regarding the current and future trends in their area of interest. We hope that you benefit from reading these innovators' thoughts at the end of several of the chapters.

We gave our contributors guidelines for topics that we thought were relevant to the future of the Web, and more importantly, we gave them the freedom to express their viewpoint without requiring rigorous evidence to support it. Their comments cover an interesting spectrum, which might reaffirm your own viewpoint, or perhaps introduce ideas that you haven't thought about, or maybe even cause you to disagree with them. Although people may react in different ways to the material in this chapter, we believe that the ideas expressed by the contributors are useful to everyone.

We sincerely appreciate all of the contributions and we want to thank all of the contributors for their efforts, and we encourage everyone to thank them for their contributions to this book. We hope that you enjoy reading the rest of this chapter as much as we enjoyed putting it together. Indeed, the decision to share the knowledge of other people with our readers is a reflection of the collaborative spirit of this book.

■ 18.4.1 Andres Almiray

What does the future hold for the Web? Although nobody knows for certain, right now the future looks bright, very bright indeed.

The Web has become ubiquitous. You can find it on your desktop computer, on your mobile phone, on game consoles, and on broadcast program recorders; it is only a matter of time before you find it on your toaster. One of the key strengths of the Web is that it uses a standard User Interface (UI) "toolkit"[1] (as standard as HTML can be given the multitude of HTML renderer implementations). This toolkit is language agnostic, and virtually every programming language in existence can be used to create such content.

However, this key feature can also be seen as one of its weaknesses: HTML defines a small set of UI components that can be rendered natively by its host, such as text fields, buttons, and text regions; anything else requires additional capabilities on the host, usually provided by a scripting language. Although JavaScript (also known by its formal name: ECMAScript) is the de facto standard, not every host supports the same version of JavaScript. Therefore, web applications must handle incompatible features between versions, including the absence of a feature, which can trigger either a workaround or the exclusion of that particular feature.

Here is the key point: while it's true that the Web is everywhere, remember that it is also becoming increasingly difficult (with each passing day) to maintain web applications on different hosts that fulfill customers' expectations. This fact brings us to the challenges the Web must meet, from both the customer and developer points of view.

Customers want to run applications from everywhere. It is simply not enough to present a polished website with crystal clear graphics and friendly

---

1. Calling HTML a toolkit is a stretch, but it serves as a comparison to Java's Swing™, Adobe's Flash®, and Microsoft's Silverlight™, for example.

interaction: customers want to run applications on their smartphones (such as an iPhone). Screen real state poses a problem. Looking like a native application is often cited as a nice feature. Better yet, customers expect applications to interact with their data (as long as privacy concerns are honored and security access is granted). This means that web applications are not only expected to look like native applications, but also behave like native applications. With so many different hosts available it is simply not possible, and currently it would also be a maintenance nightmare for developers who can only choose a few targets and concentrate on them.

This fact leads us to application developers. We already established the limitations of HTML in terms of component diversity. Next, creating web applications that also look like native applications is difficult for developers. In addition, choosing the appropriate client library may be a complicated task for some of those developers. Finally, interacting with native facilities depends on the facilities and APIs exposed by the target host.

However, there are options available to solve these problems, and surely additional options will become available in the future. The Web software giants propose their own platform and solutions. For example, Google sticks to the tried-and-tested HTML plus scripting languages. Google has also dabbled in browser plug-ins that facilitate the task of talking to native services. After the first "dotcom" burst during the first part of this decade, when plug-ins ran amok without securing a market segment (only Flash managed to survive and grab most of the plug-in space), the existence of Google and its popularity certainly helps in promoting the use of a specific plug-in, such as Google Gears. We can only expect that, given Google's view of the Web as a platform, web applications will be found effectively everywhere, with the aid of targeted browser plug-ins.

Microsoft has its own platform based on Silverlight. You can expect it to play nice with every other software offering by Microsoft; however, there is also an open source implementation called Moonlight, fostered by the Mono project. Thus, developers can target all major operating systems, and hopefully a broad set of mobile devices, too.

The third major vendor is Adobe, with its combination of Flash/AIR. Flash has been the undisputed king for making interactive content for the Web, whether it is for online games, animated advertisements, or video. Adobe AIR lets Flash cross the browser boundary and go to the desktop.

In theory, developers can now write applications that target both the Web and the desktop, with few or no modifications at all to the Web version of the code. The mobile arena is catching up as well, and it is very likely you'll see Flash-powered applications running on your smartphone in the near future.

The latest newcomer to the "Web as a platform" battle is Sun, with its JavaFX platform. Unlike the previously discussed platforms, JavaFX targets online/offline, mobile, and consumer devices right from the start. During JavaOne 2009, we saw a glimpse of its future: JavaFX-powered applications running on a television screen, on a blue ray disc player, and on a smartphone. Again, the promise is that developers can write applications that target all of those hardware platforms without having to rewrite their applications from scratch to do so.

Although there is no clear winner on the "Web as a platform" battle yet, I would contend that the battle is beginning to heat up. In any case, customers will reap the benefits in the end, and web applications will eventually work seamlessly on every platform they target. Developers will have plenty of tools and options to create such applications. Who knows, we may even see a new operating system that lets you run a Web application as if it were a native one, with no distinction between native and online mode.

■ 18.4.2 Siamak Ashrafi

Web 1.0 was static web pages. Web 2.0 was exemplified by user-generated content as seen by Facebook, Twitter, MySpace, eBay, Blogger, and, most notably, Wikipedia. Wikipedia is using the worlds population to document all known information. As we look around, we see that almost every website allows user-generated data and some only exist because of user-generated content, e.g., YouTube. Even unlikely applications like Google Earth/Maps are accepting user-generated content to help enrich the application. Professional retired architects are using Sketch-Up to model entire towns and then place the models into Google Earth/Maps. You can final more information about this on the Google SketchUp blog here:
http://sketchupdate.blogspot.com/

I believe that the next big change on the Web will be device-generated content. This will occur because of the development of always-on, always-connected, intelligent, ubiquitous devices that will produce data published on the Web. This will lead to interesting device-device mash-ups, similar to the mash-ups we see today, e.g., Google Maps mashed-up with Housing Prices, but generated by devices.

For example, your cell phone GPS will tell your car that you are coming close to it. The car will determine you are coming from the grocery store and the car will automatically pop the trunk. Then, it will post your status and grocery list to your Facebook page so that your spouse will know you're on your way home and can review the grocery list and start preparing dinner.

The price of RFID, GPS, WiFi, Com, and environmental sensor chips is falling; they are getting smaller, and require almost no power. As manufactures build these devices and programmers start using them in interesting ways, we will see an accelerated adoption which will build on itself. This will allow even the smallest, cheapest devices to have intelligence. You will never have to look for your keys again, they will have WiFi and GPS, so they can send you a message and tell you where they are.

Your car will generate status updates for its location and mechanical condition and send them to the Web. Your house will publish updates to a website and can be monitored from anywhere in the world. It can even contact a carpenter if it needs repairs. A hospital room where every piece of medical equipment can communicate with every other device and adjust itself to the patient's changing situation, or as new medical information about the patient's condition added to NIH medical databases. Your car, house, and shoes will use Twitter and have followers—both human and otherwise.

With the proliferation of ubiquitous intelligent devices we will see even more real-time dynamic content on the Web. These devices will generate and post data that will make our lives easier, safer, and more efficient.

Kevin Nilson (one of the authors) gives a very interesting example of device-device mash-ups. As you are driving around town your refrigerator contacts your car and determines your location. Then it checks the Web and feeds the car's GPS the location of the closest place with the lowest price to pick up groceries. When you get to the grocery store, your prepaid groceries will be waiting for you.

This new Web will have to standardize on a set of protocols on which all devices can talk. Most vendors are interested in vendor lock-in and will try to push their own standards for ubiquitous connected devices. This will hinder adoption and slow down progress.

I believe JSONP will be the protocol of the future for the Web. It is more lightweight than XML and implemented in every known computer language. Devices could simply use web services with JSONP as a fast, clean communication protocol.

■ 18.4.3 Stephen Chin

18.4.3.1 Future of the Web

The growth of the World Wide Web has been dramatic and grandiose, but it is not without its tragedies. The debut of the Web as an Internet service available to the public was marked by a historic post by Tim Berners-Lee of CERN in 1991, which began as follows:

> The WorldWideWeb (WWW) project aims to allow links to be made to any information anywhere. The address format includes an access method (=namespace), and for most name spaces a host-name and some sort of path.[2]
>
> Tim Berners-Lee, Aug 6 1991, alt.hypertext

The Web was originally designed for physicists to share data, but quickly turned into a general purpose tool for law archives, digital images, movie databases, and other public knowledge bases. The subsequent commercialization of the Web opened up an even larger set of applications through the launch of e-commerce sites for the purchase of goods between businesses or directly to consumers. In turn, this led to the dot-com boom where traditional media channels started to get replaced with new, more direct mechanisms for marketing to the public.

As the Web took information exchange to new heights, there was a very sad technological saga going on in the background. Thin clients, built as web applications, started to rapidly overrun thick client technologies traditionally used to build desktop applications. Web applications had distinct advantages such as ease of deployment and operating system independence, but were comparatively lacking in terms of usability and power. The browser wars starting in the 90s further complicated things, making developing cross-browser

---

2. Full text available on Google Groups:
http://groups.google.com/group/alt.hypertext/msg/06dad279804cb3ba?hl=en&dmode=source

compartible web applications a painful endeavor, catering to the least common denominator. To this day, there are over 60^3 different web frameworks for the Java language alone, all of which try to solve the intractable problem of bringing rich application functionality to the browser.

The end result is that while information exchange, media distribution, and social betworking have advanced dramatically through the Web revolution, user interface technology is still struggling to recover from what some might consider a monumental and tragic setback.

The end result is that while information exchange, media distribution, and social networking have advanced dramatically through the Web revolution, user interface technology is still struggling to recover from what some might consider a monumental and tragic setback.

However, there is a silver lining through the birth of Rich Internet Application (RIA) technology. RIA frameworks have their roots in the thick client technologies of a decade past, but are dramatically easier to deploy and maintain, seamlessly span different operating systems and platforms, and leverage the full power of the Web to share and link data. They also inherited the best features of thick client technologies, such as robust controls and layouts, while adding rich animation and media support for building even more powerful user interface paradigms.

I see the RIA Revolution as the first step in a renaissance of user interface innovation. RIA platforms, such as Flex, JavaFX, and Silverlight have already started to challenge traditional UI paradigms, with dramatic advances in usability, navigation, and data visualization. With the introduction of 3D graphics there is an entire new set of UI possibilites to explore, including immersive virtual worlds, 3D data visualization, and Zommable UI.

The final frontier for the Web is to break free of the boundaries of the desktop, reaching new areas of our lives through embedded device integration. There are billions of mobile handsets in the world that have the potential to expand the Web's reach by several orders of magnitude. Similarly, televisions are the multimedia hub of households across the world, and the perfect stage for Web content distribution. In this new frontier, RIA technologies are leading the change by providing a common platform to expand the Web to mobile, TV, and beyond!

---

3. As listed on Java-Source.net: http://java-source.net/open-source/web-frameworks

■ 18.4.4 Aleksandar Gargenta

What are the most significant/important challenges facing the Web?
The most significant challenge to the Web has always been, and continues to be, the lack of standards-compliance among the major browser vendors, but most specifically Microsoft. Web developers perpetually deliver a substandard user experience to their audiences simply because they are forced to work with the lowest common denominator of web technologies. Alternatively, they resort to complex JavaScript frameworks or RIA plug-ins, further complicating their development efforts. Those alternative technologies typically impose a lot of limitations on the types of devices they can support. Think mobile web. Think semantic web.

What are some of the solutions that have been posed, and which ones are likely to be adopted?
While RIA technologies have their place on the Web, the only way we will see significant across-the-board improvements in the web user experience is through the evolution of web standards and a stricter compliance to the same.

The Web has already evolved. The next generation of web UIs is already partially here. It is called HTML5—and many believe that its amazing features make it a game-changer for the future of the Web, both for consumers and for developers.

While HTML5 is the next logical step in the evolution of the Web, it is frustrating to think that it may take years before its benefits will trickle down to the general public. Why? Old, archaic, incompatible browsers that many users hang on to and the lack of commitment to HTML5 from Microsoft.

What tools already exist, or need to be created, to address these challenges?
What's needed is a way to gently nudge both Microsoft and the general public to upgrade their browsers to support the existing standards and the new HTML5 features.

One of the solutions to this problem comes from Google, which coauthored HTML5. Their Google Chrome Frame plug-in for Microsoft's Internet Explorer (IE) expands the capabilities and the standards compliance of IE to better support HTML5. Many have rightly pointed out that it is ironic that a plug-in is needed for the standards support, but such is the state of the Web today.

While Google's solution is an ingenious hack, what is needed in the long run is a serious commitment from all browser vendors to make standards compliance a priority (at least the ACID test), because web standards do not commoditize the browsers, but rather empower the Web. How do we make the vendors see that insisting on the status quo is just delaying the inevitable? Do we need more creative solutions like Google's Chrome Frame? Do we tell web users to switch to an up-to-date standards-compliant browser (many are dropping support for IE6)? Do we just sit and wait?

Can you give a high-level roadmap of what significant events you think will happen in the next 5/10 years in the Web?

With an ever-expanding number of applications now being provided via the Software as a Service (SaaS) web model, no longer can the enterprises, and even the home users, ignore the lack of capabilities of their web browsers. It will take a few killer-web-apps (like Google Wave) to drive this point home, but users will expect (and therefore demand) that their browsers be up to the task. The Web was born from the standards and the future of the Web will be based on the standards.

■ 18.4.5 Ted Goddard

18.4.5.1 The Emergence of Web 3.0

The Web is many things: it is the ultimate repository for all human knowledge, it is the storefront for distributed commerce, it is the proxy for remote human interaction of nearly all kinds. It will certainly be difficult to foresee the future of the Web, but perhaps we can extrapolate a short distance based on some of the more interesting features that are emerging now.

18.4.5.2 Today's Challenges

The most significant challenges to the Web today are censorship and garbage. Restriction is failing on both ends: content that should get through for certain groups and certain parts of the world is blocked, and content that should never have existed is continually created.

Censorship is a societal problem, not a technological one (encryption techniques can only go so far when privacy is illegal). Can powerful search and indexing technologies eliminate garbage? Unfortunately, the motivation to create garbage is very strong: duplicating other parts of the Web to draw in ad revenue or responding to a forum just to be first are pervasive (this is only for illustration; it is not my desire to list all forms of garbage here). The arms race between search technologies and financially (or criminally) motivated garbage creation will be interesting to watch. Good will triumph over garbage in the end, but the battle is sure to be fierce.

Those are enormous challenges faced by society and the Web as a whole, though. What about challenges faced by web developers on the small part of the Web that they create? How can we make compelling, useful applications that work everywhere?

18.4.5.3 *Putting the A in Ajax*

We're always distracted by the next big thing, but now is the time to reap the benefits of Web 2.0, and this should occupy web developers for a number of years.

When we combine Ajax with a user-created web, we get a universal proxy for remote human interaction. What form that proxy takes is up to us. Every application is potentially a new unique communication tool in the language of whatever concepts the application already deals with. It's like a list containing telephone, fax, and email was suddenly expanded with an entry for each different web application.

But to understand why all this falls under Web 2.0, we need to extend Ajax to its natural limits.

With Web 1.0 applications, we are accustomed to clicking on hyperlinks or filling out forms to go to a new web page with the result of our requested batch operation. This corresponds to GET and POST operations respectively—how strange that the UI of the Web was essentially defined by RFC 1945 that defines HTTP 1.0.

In the most basic form of Ajax, we move away from batch operations to an event-based model, where user events can result in incremental page updates. Finally, we have decoupled the UI from the network protocol . . . or have we? If the entire process is still driven by HTTP requests from the user's browser, it's not fully asynchronous (what the A in Ajax supposedly stands for; nobody can agree on the other letters, though). For full decoupling, we need the ability to push updates from the server to the browser at any time. This technique is typically called Ajax Push or Comet to distinguish it from the most basic Ajax variant, but one day we will likely just call the entire set of techniques Ajax.

At last we have the key to bringing real-time communication to the Web: if we can push updates from the server to the browser, whenever we process user input in the application, we can immediately push arbitrary application-driven page updates to any of the users. The application has just become a new communication tool.

So we are on the cusp of a tremendous variety of new Web 2.0 applications that incorporate push. The Web becomes more than a vast network of hyperlinked documents, it is now a vast network of mutable hyperlinked documents. It's a small, but important, distinction. (Were the documents mutable under Web 1.0? Somewhat, but only in a weak sense from an application perspective.) How do we create applications that take advantage of Ajax Push?

Real-time communication on the Web is only just beginning, but technologies like Google Wave and ICEfaces have asynchronous capabilities at their core. Google Wave extends the idea of conversations to a full programming model with read/write access to the shared content (page updates are pushed when content is written). ICEfaces extend the rendering of dynamic pages to application initiated rendering (page updates are pushed when the application initiates a render pass).

Using a framework is the right way to develop commercial applications, but sometimes it seems like the view source has gone extinct. JavaScript is compressed and obfuscated, HTML is dynamically generated and obtuse, and Ajax Push implementation is complicated by browser connection limits. At the very least, we should be able to implement a push application just using `XMLHttpRequest` in a straightforward way. For that, we need full HTTP 1.1 support with control over pipelining and TCP connection use. Growing up, I always thought 1999 was a significant year in the future; it looks like it still is (the HTTP 1.1 specification was published in 1999, and without control over pipelining from JavaScript, we don't have HTTP 1.1).

However, it's not just the communication abstractions that have advanced along with Web 2.0; modern frameworks provide for extensive software re-use through component technologies (Google Gadgets and JavaServer Faces components, respectively, in the above examples). Open source component development will clearly be an important way to accelerate the development of Web 2.0 applications by spreading the effort across the community.

18.4.5.4 The Near Future

Plug-ins have never truly been part of the Web. At last, audio and video playback are first class in HTML5, but we're not done yet. To complete the picture in terms of human interaction over the Web, we also need audio and video input, accessible to web developers as simple form controls. There are important privacy concerns (similar to file uploads) but neither the technology nor the feature specification are difficult.

Since we're looking forward a little in time, how about in space? Location-aware browsing is a simple matter of obtaining a few coordinates (especially when browsing on a mobile device with GPS), but it is incredibly powerful, and the capability is available in most browsers now. (Note that, once again, there are important privacy concerns, so users need to know that their browser knows where they are right now.) The next step is really just for web developers to tailor the application to the user's physical location.

18.4.5.5 The Eternal Battle of Documents vs. Applications

Mighty forces are locked in an eternal battle for the web UI: is it a document, or is it a control panel? The same battle reaches deep into the applications themselves: is HTML served and immediately rendered, or is the view generated in the browser via JavaScript APIs?

This battle is a continuing source of innovation for the Web, so we can expect it to continue; but just in terms of the metaphor, consider that documents have a much longer recorded history than applications. Communication is the most important function of the Web and this is best served by language, and therefore, documents. Indeed, the forms of knowledge that we can capture in HTML must continually expand. Especially important are diagrams and formal notation (for science and mathematics). A big step will be to have inline SVG and MathML commonly available; at the very least, this helps to address the broken link problem for diagrams in technical documents.

18.4.5.6 Cyberspace

Is virtual reality a natural extension of the Web? Many virtual reality systems exist today (at least in the form of collaborative three-dimensional environments—or sometimes not so collaborative, because often the participants carry plasma weapons), so the problem is not that the basic technology is out of reach. Attempts were made early on with the Virtual Reality Modeling Language (VRML), but just having a rotatable teapot in your web page wasn't all that useful. Perhaps the difficulty is that for the virtual space to be interesting, it must be shared, but once it is shared, it is difficult for it to remain decentralized. Decentralization is vital to the scalability and autonomy of the Web. This will be an important area to watch, and it's certainly the next logical step for the Web if we try to extract a consensus from science fiction.

18.4.5.7   Web 2.0, Web 3.0, …

We're really not done with Web 2.0 yet: it includes push and advanced mark-up features that are not yet being taken advantage of on a large scale, and it always takes several years for fundamental innovations to propagate across browser versions and the development community.

Perhaps some simple extrapolation can give us a definition of Web 3.0. Web 1.0 was created by site owners and Web 2.0 was created by interactions between users. Web 3.0 must be created by the Web itself; in other words, an emergent consciousness from within the Web, capable of creating new content and new applications. Perhaps this new consciousness can at last answer the ultimate question: should we restrict mark-up to well-formed XML?

■ 18.4.6   Chett Haase

In the future I see two possibilities. The first is that the Web will be a happy place for all: safe for children to roam free, highly organized and easy to navigate, and chock-full of wonderful information—both useful and educational.

The other possibility is that the Web will continue to be the greatest festering cesspool of chaos since the Big Bang.

In this increasingly littered, content-full, and guidance-free virtual world, we have a greater need for methods of finding the information we're seeking and processing it quickly. Once upon a time, it was acceptable to use shopping sites that required lots of clicking, reading, browsing, and scrolling to buy each item. But those types of sites are now cumbersome and we find ourselves drawn toward other sites that make the experience quick and painless. The faster these vendors can separate you from the money in your account, the closer they are to profit, or at least solvency.

So what I actually predict, despite my utopian and possibly drug-addled ramblings in my introduction, is a web full of applications and sites that are increasingly rich (dare I say "filthy rich"?) and functional to make the vast amounts of content quickly digestible by a short-attention-span public.

We have already seen strides toward this rich future in various websites and web technologies. For example, Netflix now makes it easier to perform related tasks in the same screen, no longer taking you to a separate page for the details on *Hairball Express!*, or for suggestions on what other movies you may like now that you've added to your queue the blockbuster thrill ride *Vergil Head-Butts a Tractor III*.

Meanwhile, web technologies are making these rich applications more powerful and easier to develop. From Ajax to Flex to Silverlight, web application platforms are adding functionality that makes it easier to create rich, animated, and connected experiences that make online life easier and more enjoyable for users.

I expect this trend to continue, with websites and development platforms becoming increasingly rich to make the web viewing/browsing/purchasing experience faster and better for the user. Because if that user doesn't get what they want from one site, a competitor's site is just a Bing®, or Google, away.

■ 18.4.7 Yehuda Katz

Before Web 2.0, there was Dynamic HTML (DHTML). These terms began as attempts by the industry to describe trends that seemed larger than a single technology. The idea of DHTML described the movement of the Web from mostly static pages to dynamic, interactive pages. It described a bundle of technologies, and both Internet Explorer and Netscape pushed their browsers as *the* way to leap into the future of the dynamic Web.

Web 2.0 is an attempt by the industry to encapsulate a series of technical and nontechnical trends that are shaping the Web. There are certainly technologies that helped to shape Web 2.0, but those technologies aren't really at the core of those trends.

There is really only one major technology that enables the dynamic, social nature of the Web: JavaScript. What many people don't realize, though, is that JavaScript was released in late 1995, and Ajax was first released by Microsoft in 1999. While the term was first used in 1999, Web 2.0 did not rise in prominence until 2004, when O'Reilly® began publishing it.

While the technology of Web 2.0 existed as early as 1998, something changed in the half-decade that followed. Microsoft originally created Ajax as proprietary technology of Internet Explorer, to facilitate Outlook on the Web. It was not fully functional in Mozilla until 2002, and Safari did not support it until version 1.2 in 2004. This half-decade also witnessed the rise of web standards as the de facto mode of operation for browser vendors, a big change from the browser wars that spawned JavaScript and Ajax.

In fact, the standardization of the Web, more than any technology, defines the last five years. When Google released Chrome, the first big new browser since Safari, nobody asked whether or not it complied with web standards. Everyone assumed it did. And when jQuery and other libraries went looking for Chrome problems, they found virtually none. In effect, Web 2.0 has meant the maturing of the Web as a platform—a place where web developers can assume that anything new that calls itself the Web will support a common subset of features.

In the past few years, browser vendors have come together in fairly valiant efforts to build the next versions of JavaScript, HTML, and Cascading Style Sheets (CSS), as the technologies of the Web. As standards bodies go, they have managed to move rather quickly and get everyone (even the recalcitrant Microsoft) on board with rather helpful changes. While I fully anticipate to see vendors like Microsoft, Mozilla, and Apple drive innovation over the next five years, I also expect those efforts to be canonized in standards that will quickly make their way onto the Web as a platform.

In fact, that has already started to happen. The audio and video support in HTML5 originated in Opera, while the canvas tag, and CSS animations and transforms originated in Webkit. In all of those cases, the originators saw value in standardizing their invention rather than keeping it to themselves. This, to me, epitomizes the future of the Web.

■ 18.4.8 Van Riper

18.4.8.1 *Google Wave: A Peek into the Future of the Web*

Some of you may recall when Google Maps first introduced draggable web maps. At the time, it was truly innovative. Since then, the underlying Ajax techniques have propagated to the point that this type of interaction is now commonplace on the Web. Similar to when Google Maps was first introduced, I believe that Google Wave is today's leading indicator of the future direction of the Web. Regardless of whether Google Wave itself is a commercial success or not, I am confident that the vision it embodies will be realized over the coming years.

What are the core elements of the Google Wave vision? There are actually three main aspects to the vision: product, platform, and protocol. Many people are focusing on the initial Google Wave product: the web client first demonstrated at Google I/O 2009. However, it is important to note that the underlying protocol as an open standard will let others write their own Wave Clients. Even better, other companies will be able to build their own Wave Servers.

Starting with the product vision, the first key ingredient is the HTML5 Standard. The Google Wave product is placing a major bet on HTML5. Like many others, I was skeptical about the adoption of HTML5. Microsoft has been dragging its heels with respect to HTML5 support in Internet Explorer. This is why the recently announced open source Google Chrome Frame plug-in for Internet Explorer gives me new hope for broader adoption of HTML5. The second key ingredient is real-time web collaboration. Now, this is not a new technology by any means. However, Ajax was not a new technology either at the time Google Maps launched it into mainstream awareness. Similarly, I see Google Wave raising the bar such that any social site will need to do something similar or adopt Google Wave.

Next, I would like to talk about the Google Wave platform. As a platform, it embodies a vision that embraces third-party extension. Again, this is mostly familiar territory. Facebook was the real pioneer, and today OpenSocial™ is attempting to standardize the way social networks are extended by third-party applications. Google Wave takes this a step further though with the Wave Extension APIs for third parties. You extend at the platform level by writing Wave Gadgets and/or Wave Robots. Gadgets are nothing new, but the way they can be used collaboratively within Waves is new. Also, Wave Robots that can interact just like other participants within Waves opens up some really interesting possibilities.

Finally, crucial to the Google Wave vision is an open standard that supports third-party extension on the client and federated data on the server. There is no question that Facebook and Twitter have popularized open APIs that third parties leverage. However, your data resides on a single provider's system in both cases. The Google Wave Federation Protocol allows for multiple Wave Server providers to interoperate in a federated manner. If Google Wave succeeds, it will put an end to the current situation with walled gardens for user data. For developers, it will also mean writing your third-party extensions once and having them work across the federated network of Wave Servers and Wave Clients.

In conclusion, the future that I see for the Web is one where full HTML5 support, real-time collaboration, and federated data are ubiquitous. A future where third-party developers can add value to the entire federated network of Wave Servers by writing Wave Gadgets and Wave Robots once for deployment against any Wave Server and within multiple Wave Clients. I invite you to join me and ride Google Wave to the future of the Web.

■ 18.4.9 Alex Russel

18.4.9.1 The Stakes

It's easy to slip into hyperbole when talking about the Web, particularly if you're possessed of an optimistic disposition and a long view on history. After all, the Web is the largest single collection of distilled human knowledge ever assembled; an accomplishment of staggering proportions. Combined with systems that let us easily and cheaply search its entirety, today's Web forms a crucial link in the decision-making process for innumerable problems. Constructed of billions of small, uncoordinated points of data, the Web as a whole is incalculably valuable.

Several enabling properties have helped accelerate this trend:

- Plain text formats
- Declarative, semantic–ish content descriptions
- Reliable parsing (error tolerant)
- Coarse relationships described in a standard way (links)
- Configurability, not extensibility

These properties fly in the face of good engineering practice, and many continue to be controversial. Binary formats, generated and consumed by tools, provide unique performance advantages. Programmatic layout descriptions and built-in extensibility can provide much more control for developers and designers. In addition, error-tolerant parsing is difficult to implement, executes more slowly, and carries a nontrivial compatibility burden. The use of coarse relationships as the only way to describe content relationships feels artificially limiting and nonspecific. Most good engineers would design improvements to the current Web by reversing each of these design decisions, but they'd be wrong to do so. Changing any of them would severely limit the value of the entire system. But why?

The Web as we know it is a negotiation between web developers, end users, and outboard systems that operate by augmenting and observing what developers and end users have done (search engines, ad networks, etc.). All of the improbable features that enable the Web have proven critical in allowing each constituency to fully participate in the Web's evolution, even if their instantaneous results leave something to be desired. Reliable parsing and plain-text descriptions of content impose costs on developers and outboard systems, but form a critical bridge that allows nonprogrammers to participate in the creation of content for the system. Indeed, as developers who have worked with any large-scale network connected system will attest, being reliable instead of being strict is critical in the real world where humans (and the systems they build) inevitably make mistakes. Failing hard—the easy and correct thing to do—has the cumulative effect of reducing the amount of content available. A Web with less content is less valuable, so being forgiving toward content authors has made an enormous difference in the rate of expansion of the Web.

For proof, consider RSS and Atom, which are two XML-based systems for syndicating content. Because XML reversed several of HTML's core design principles, allowed built-in extensibility of the language, and encouraged hard failure (while retaining the plain-text nature of the system), RSS and Atom have proven the wisdom of HTML's permissiveness. Real-world implementors of outboard systems for consuming, re-using, and projecting RSS may have been surprised to find that they also needed to implement reliable, forgiving parsing. After all, the data was encoded in XML, so it should have been trivial for the publisher to validate that the XML-based data they were sending would not break a standards-compliant parser. But they don't. In the real world, even the most strictly specified formats are often broken, and consumers of those formats tend to find it more valuable to be forgiving of error than to ignore the message contained in the content, simply because a stamp was missing from the envelope. So the question for implementers of the future web is this: If we need to implement reliable parsing, no matter how strictly our standards tell implementers to deal with errors, why impose the cost on developers?

Similarly, we've learned the hard way that coarse relationships and post hoc organization of data is as (or more) powerful at scale than attempts to pre-categorize information will ever be. On a global scale it's simply impossible to agree on much of the terminology that would be required to understand the contents of the Web. Acolytes of the Semantic Web envision a day in which strictly (but locally) categorized data sets can be interchanged by ad hoc trans-formations of descriptions, with the promise of near zero loss of meaning as the incredible payoff for the effort. But it hasn't worked so far...at least not on a global scale. What has proven time and again to be valuable, though, is small interfaces consistently applied. Put another way, getting everyone to agree on a small, valuable (if vague) proposition is often more important than having smaller groups agree on everything. It's another frustrating lesson for systems designers looking to improve the Web because the lessons to date imply that our largest problems are largely political, not system oriented. Getting agree-ment in this sense is about enhancing the number and relative importance of clients that can understand the contract, and those clients win or lose based on the amount of potential content they can consume (reliable parsing, yet again!). Forging absolute agreement may indeed be more optimal, but if there's never any real possibility that everyone will adopt the same interpretations, is it better to be pervasive or to be right? The Web suggests the former.

Viewed from another angle, the success of the Web is the triumph of systems built to accommodate human frailties and forgive our predictable disagreements, both with each other and with our future selves. The Web has helped harness the collective memory and capacity of humanity to express itself. Our challenge, as those working to evolve the platform, is now to try to remember clearly how it got here because the costs of losing the open, flat, forgiving nature of the Web amidst a sea of short-term interests and optimal-but-impossible solutions. The Web has given our species the greatest gift of memory since the written word, but it's up to us to learn the lessons.

■ 18.4.10 Dylan Schiemann

18.4.10.1 Future of the Web

The Web and software evolve at extremely rapid rates and yet less quickly than we would like. It is often said that HTML succeeded because it has a low barrier to entry, is not controlled by one entity, and because it sucks less than the alternatives.

Several things are certain about the future of the Web:

1. We will continue to reinvent things. We just can't help ourselves. The constant re-invention of things user interface components and toolkits, as we've moved from desktop to the Web is one example. Ajax toolkits is another. The reinvention of the wheel is unavoidable, and probably even a good thing.

2. The real-time web will continue to evolve, with the goal to always be more real-time. In the early days of the Web, real-time meant that you could go to a web page with the latest information on a topic, rather than waiting until the next day to read the newspaper. Then RSS emerged as both a format listing recent updates and as the centerpiece for a collection of services that give you the most recent updates about a story. After that, services emerged to provide social news, whether in the form of Digg or Facebook, to give you the latest information as recommended by the world or details about your friends. Twitter then emerged as a service that is a more real-time, aggregated RSS. In many ways, though none of this is the real-time web I imagined when working with early implementations of Comet, the technology that powers popular services like Gmail Talk and Facebook Chat, or enterprise services such as real-time stock quotes. For me, the real-time web is about low-latency data transit between the browser and the data source. Of course, much of Comet is an outside the firewall reinvention of techniques used by organizations like Amazon® to provide real-time shopping recommendations.

3. Open and Closed. The Web has succeeded through a natural evolution from proprietary to standard to open as features have become commoditized. The rate at which this happens has become even faster with the rapid rise of distributed and open source development initiatives. In the early part of this decade, many of us forgot that standards couldn't exist until something had been tried in the wild, which stifled innovation for a while. Fortunately, companies like Apple and Opera have been allowed to experiment again in a way that is more open than what we see with platforms like Flash/Flex and Silverlight. I say fortunately because a world without the option to create anything that isn't already a standard

is one that will keep open platforms at a serious and growing disadvantage to closed platforms. Finally, the battle between the GPL and BSD visions of open source has and will continue to grow. Both philosophies are viable, but are appealing for very different reasons. In general, fanaticism and zealotry needs to be avoided to prevent handing the world to purely closed, walled garden platforms. In a world where the economic value of most things approaches zero, the livelihood of musicians, actors, and software engineers would be all under attack if we were to live in a world where GPL is the only option.

4. Cloud Platforms. A very interesting thing has happened with the emergence of cloud platforms. First, of course, is that it wasn't invented by Sun, who did popularize the concept that the network is the computer. But more importantly, the world was quickly moving to a place where the complexity in creating highly-scalable web applications was quickly becoming such an expensive proposition that start-ups would struggle to compete with the Googles and Amazons of the world. Instead, these two companies have led the change towards giving any developer access to the economies of scale previously enjoyed only by large organizations. The continued elimination of barriers to competition is to me the most impressive thing about cloud computing.

5. True commercial-open models. In the past, open source was generally a marketing gimmick or an act of desperation for companies. But the past few years has seen the emergency of many companies that have open-source as the DNA of their culture, my own company (SitePen) included. This fundamental change in mindset is one that places the needs of its customers and their users as the primary way to create a long-term sustainable business. The early goldrush of the Web was about getting funding and going public. After the dot-com bust, the model changed to getting funding and getting acquired by Google or Yahoo. Now, after the worldwide economic collapse, we're seeing the emergence of the micro-company that uses its marketing budget to create great open source or free lite versions of its products.

6. The behemoths strike back. Google, Yahoo, Microsoft, Apple, Facebook, MySpace, Sony, Amazon, and perhaps a few others are all attacking the same problem from different directions and with different strengths and weaknesses. And that is how to be a middleman that profits every time

you need access to content and media to inform and entertain you. From music to app stores to full-fledged platforms that build on and extend the Web, large companies can survive and make the Web a great place as well by taking advantage of their ability to simplify and streamline the world for you. As long as one of these companies doesn't win, this is in the best interest of the users of the Web.

The Web will evolve in a way that creates as little friction as possible towards creating open interfaces and great value for users, while finding a way to preserve a business model that makes it a way for people to derive value from their continued innovation.

■ 18.4.11 Greg Wilkins

To consider the future of the Web, we need to spend a little time analyzing its past.

The advantages of web applications over desktop applications was clear, even in the early days of the Internet and what has now become known as Web 1.0. For example, when banks initially made online banking available, they did so by sending their customers CDs that contained desktop applications with rich user interfaces, but there was little uptake among the non-computer-literate for such a service. In contrast, when banks started making banking available via web applications accessed via a browser, the uptake was huge and grew to become what is now the normal way for most people to access banking services.

The banking web applications were successful even though they lacked the rich user interfaces, functionality, and security of their desktop competition. Why? Because these web applications required no installation and provided ubiquitous access from any network-connected computer. Users loved the convenience of accessing their bank from anywhere in the world from almost any computer. Deployers loved the elimination of the need to maintain specific versions of native applications running on specific operating systems on inaccessible computers.

So when faced with a choice between rich UIs and zero install plus ubiquitous access, it was zero install with ubiquitous access that won the day!

But users still love rich UIs, and when given a choice between two equivalent web applications, the rich UI usually wins. The classic example of this came with the introduction of an Ajax interface to Google Maps.

Even though Google Maps was providing the same basic data that was available via several other free services, the rich UI quickly captured most of the market from the other servers and grew the user base enormously. Thus, the Web delivered another important message; namely, that market share is fickle and can be grown or captured easily with a rich UI that improves access to existing services.

So to be competitive on the Web, you now need to provide the trinity of zero install, ubiquitous access, and rich UIs. Web 2.0 applications are ones that take a no-compromise approach to achieving this trinity. They don't require plug-ins, they work with commonly available browsers, and they make no excuses for the usability of their UIs. To achieve the trinity, Web 2.0 applications typically use one or more of the open standard-based techniques: DHTML, Ajax, and Comet. DHTML has provided the rich presentation, and Ajax allows access to server-side data without a page-based UI paradigm. Comet allows applications to be dynamic and reactive to events on the server without user intervention. With Web 2.0, applications can now be delivered over the Web that in many cases are virtually indistinguishable from their desktop equivalents. There has been a move to an SaaS model where applications once thought of as desktop (e.g., email, calendar, and word processing) are now being offered over the Web. This move has only been encouraged by the fact that SaaS is a model that is often easier to monetize than software distribution or traditional web services. So is that the end of web development? Have we reached the end game? Unfortunately not.

Web 2.0 has also seen the application of good software engineering practice to web design. No longer is JavaScript treated as little more than an accessory to mark-up with small scriptlets scattered throughout the mark-up. Instead JavaScript libraries have been developed for presentation, portability, and application logic. Libraries now build on other libraries and the standing-on-the-shoulders-of-giants principle has come into play to allow developers to reach new heights.

One of the key benefits of the library/framework approach has been the shift of developer concerns from compatibility to capabilities. Initially, a primary concern of Web 2.0 developers was how to write code that would work on all of the available browsers, which was as if Java programmers needed to consider all available operating systems and CPU types. To a large extent the compatibility issues have now been solved by the JavaScript libraries and frameworks and the focus is now on browser capabilities rather than compatibilities. Now a web developer needs mostly to be concerned if a capability exists in the browser (e.g., graphics) rather than which implementation of that mechanism is provided (e.g., SVG vs. Canvas, etc.) as frameworks can solve the compatibility issues so that code can be written to work on any implementation.

The focus on capabilities has served to highlight what capabilities are currently lacking in commonly deployed browers:

- sound and video
- offline or persistent storage
- local peripherals (microphone, camera, printer)
- CPU-intensive tasks and multithreading
- streaming data
- cross-domain security

■ 18.4.12 Monica Anderson

In my view, Web 1.0 allowed the viewing of hyperlinked documents discovered by reference and browsing, and later by searching. Web 2.0 allows interaction with active and real-time content such as Google Maps and Twitter. Web 3.0 will again allow discovery of documents by topic-centric browsing rather than by searching, and will enable real-time Twitter-style information dissemination in many contexts using many different applications. Web 4.0 will allow document and information discovery by dialog-based interaction with problem domain, competent autonomous agents.

Among the most significant and important challenges facing the Web, I believe, is the declining signal-to-noise ratio. In the beginning, creating web-based content was difficult, which favored dedicated, educated, and technologically competent programmers who often published information of high quality of either general interest or of interest in some highly specific domain; therefore, the Web initially had a higher fraction of quality content. As web publishing becomes easier, it lets people publish whatever they want; much of which is of no interest to anyone outside of a narrow circle of friends of the publishers. It is difficult to automatically tell the difference between content only intended for an audience of immediate friends from topic-specific or general-interest quality content. The average quality of information discovered through web searches will continue to drop.

The Semantic Web only goes so far. Burdening the publishers, or even the readers, with the task of tagging is the wrong thing to do. Tagging is essentialist and therefore will fail for the same reasons all essentialist classification systems fail.

We need higher-level semantic tools to provide automatic and reasonably repeatable classification of documents to enable browsing the Web and true semantic search. These are a partial requirement for Web 3.0 and their unavailability will block reaching Web 4.0. The most promising approach is to use so-called Model Free Methods. Syntience Inc. has been developing these technologies since 2001.

In terms of the future changes in the Web that may occur, radical advances in technologies that understand text would be the most significant game changers. These advances would rapidly lead to good web-browsing systems; semantic search; and perfect spelling and grammar correction, including automatic copy editing, perfect automatic translation, perfect speech recognition, and perfect document summarization. Longer term we would get dialog-based systems that could be chat-based for the Web, telephone-based for traditional customer services, or voice-based on the Web.

If such a breakthrough is delayed, then we will see some number of spot technologies appear and grow. Many of them will come out of left field and will be hard to predict but real-time systems will certainly become important. People talk about "the next Twitter," and there will be many like that. For instance, there's value in moving telephone-based customer support to the Web, but to keep it voice-based with chat-like extensions rather than entirely chat based. Account numbers and personal data views, and data about the problem could be shared between customer service reps and the customer, which would increase effectiveness of the interaction.

Real-time search in all its forms will become very important. There are many real-time feeds besides Twitter, news feeds, stock feeds, chat rooms, and the like, which provide continuous text-based streams that need to be analyzed and displayed. We can do this to some degree using today's technologies; the challenge will be, like it always is today, to keep people from jamming the system by spamming advertising over it.

■ 18.5   FINAL THOUGHTS

■ 18.5.1   Web-Based Technology and Society

When Web 2.0 arrived, few people anticipated the extent to which it would transform our Web 1.0 view of the world. In the midst of this Web 2.0-based transformation, Web 3.0 is moving inexorably toward us, foreshadowing a disruption that, by comparison, could dwarf the changes wrought by Web 2.0 over Web 1.0.

Today, we possess the power to communicate with the world in a manner that was unparalleled just a few years ago, and the consequence is apparent: we feel overwhelmed as we struggle to manage the relentless stream of information. We easily forget that the volume of information that we are compelled to process vastly exceeds the needs of people who lived in earlier generations. As a simple yet illuminating example, every major newspaper in the U.S.A. publishes more information in a single day than was available during *an entire year* to the people in the early 1800s. Two centuries ago, the speed of new information was glacial, but today 20% of the information that Google finds during a 90-day period is new. Alas, we can only absorb new information at a linear rate, whereas new information is created at a geometric rate. The ever-widening gap between the creation and the absorption of information produces cognitive dissonance whose long-term effects should make us reflect on the imbalance in our lives.

■ 18.5.2   Everyone is Connected

Social networks give us the ability to connect with virtually anyone in the world, and yet the effort required to communicate with more than a few hundred people easily exceeds our capabilities. Nevertheless, what would be required to connect any two people on Earth? First, we would need a complete graph to represent each person, and a link between each pair of people in this graph. A complete graph consisting of n nodes contains $n \times (n - 1)/2$ connections. The Earth's population is approximately 7 billion people, which means that a complete graph involving everyone would contain approximately 25 billion connections, which is more than one million times greater than the number of stars in the Milky Way galaxy, and not too distant from the number of stars in the known universe.

If Facebook attempted such a phenomenal feat, then everyone's friend limit would be at least 1 million times larger than it is today, which would not take into account the time required to connect each person to every other person on Earth, or the various groups that have a Facebook presence (and also track the members of those groups).

New members of a network can leverage the knowledge and experience gained by their predecessors. In addition, people search for enablers and influencers, which are individuals who have a significant impact on many people. Neverthless, universal connectivity is highly impractical because it is inseparable from information hyper-abundance, which leads to the distressing loss of control that we feel because of our inability to absorb information quickly enough to satisfy our own needs and expectations.

What can help us solve the problem of hyper-abundance of information? How well can we adapt to decades of sustained and intensive connectivity? Will it be like the effects of an addiction? What are the limits of our individual capacity to connect with others, and in the future how will we manage multiple information streams simultaneously, and are there any effective alternatives? How will people manage a daily hyper-abundance of information relentlessly flowing from never-ending streams of data? How much can people absorb and retain on a daily basis? Do we have a collective consciousness, and if so, what is it?

■ 18.5.3 Transitive Trust

This principle is simple and obvious: if person A is a friend of B and person B is a friend of C, then person C is likelier to trust person A than a complete stranger. Sales and marketing people are acutely aware of this principle, which forms an important foundation for their ability to market and sell products and services. In social networks such as Facebook, the term "friend" is not interchangeable with the traditional meaning of the word. The word friend encompasses the following categories: family members, close friends, casual friends, acquaintances, and contacts.

Andrew Stone (creator of Twittelator) remarked that Facebook is about who you used to know; Twitter is about who you will know. Although Facebook and Twitter both involve transitive trust, there is a difference (even if it's only a perception). Twitter tweets feel like highly transient snippets of information, whereas a Facebook presence can be much more revealing of our private lives.

Even if we rely on transitive trust, how do we know that we are connected with all of the people who will be important to us? How do we find out what we don't know we need to know? How do we avoid the feeling that we are not receiving updates about important or significant events?

■ 18.5.4 Perfect Information for Everyone

In a world with perfect information that is freely available to everyone, financial pyramid schemes would undoubtedly be exposed before they had an opportunity to swindle the public, but there would be other important changes. For instance, the guilty would be apprehended and incarcerated, the judicial system would become increasingly efficient, and the innocent would be free. Political campaigns would become vastly simplified because politicians' statements would be instantly verified or discredited during speeches, debates, and advertisements.

Despite the appeal of perfect information, there is one crucial point that we cannot ignore: possessing information does not imply acting on that information; we do so primarily when it serves our interests, but our nature remains unchanged. Clearly, our individual limitations influence our goals, and our emotions, fears, and anxieties that collectively cause us to act in irrational ways. The theory of the rational consumer in a perfect marketplace was supplanted by the observation that we demonstrate irrational behavior in a consistent manner (and there is an element of irony to this point).

Unencumbered information has an amorphous quality that flows toward everyone, and yet an unlimited increase in information is like an increase in the money supply: its overall value diminishes when it's too plentiful. However, the concussive impact of market forces during the recession that began in 2007 still reverberates, and even the uber-rich have felt its adverse impact. This recession was caused by a mixture of information, misinformation, and opportunism, and perhaps our human nature prevented us from perceiving its obvious flaws and inevitable outcome.

If everyone had possessed perfect information, could we have averted the recession of 2007? What is the appropriate metaphor for the Web and its enormous supply of information: a rising tide that lifts all boats or a zero-sum game? Where are the boundaries between unlimited information and personal privacy?

■ 18.5.5 Intelligent Agents

The ceaseless flow of information has led to a heightened state of awareness whereby we measure our daily effectiveness by the extent to which we maintain constant connectivity. Although connectivity is highly satisfying, perhaps enabling us to ascend Maslow's hierarchy, the absence of connectivity causes withdrawal symptoms akin to a low-grade adrenaline bath. Technology improves relentlessly in terms of speed and capacity, but our brain cannot keep pace, and therefore we are likelier to feel increasingly overloaded with data in the coming years and decades.

Given the increasing hyper-abundance of information, we clearly can benefit from sophisticated intelligent agents working on our behalf to extract and deliver the information that is relevant to us. As our intelligent agents become more sophisticated, we will also become increasingly dependent on them for creating structure and order in our lives.

One currently popular and powerful technology is Twitter, which has been called a new form of communication that lets us be heard by vast numbers of people. With Twitter we can communicate and influence each other in a real-time fashion that is unmatched by the technology of five years ago. Twitter enables a community of participation yet allows—and encourages—our individuality, which gives us the best of the two things we crave the most.

Another interesting technology is Google Wave, which provides robots that can do anything that a human can do in a Google Wave. Perhaps Google robots are the early stage precursors of the future and more sophisticated intelligent agents that will help us filter out the noise so that we only receive the information that is relevant to us. Does Google Wave represent an early form of intelligent agents? Where will Facebook, Twitter, and Google Wave carry us in the next five years? Will Google Wave enable us to evolve from Marshall McLuhan's "the medium is the message" to (as someone remarked) "we are the message"?

How can we determine that information that we receive from intelligent agents is always correct, and who will determine the accuracy of that information? Is it feasible for someone to create viruses masquerading as intelligent agents? Will it be possible to create subversive intelligent agents that disseminate misinformation, and what tools do we need to assure that we can detect and prevent such behavior? If intelligent agents successfully meet the Turing test for sentience, who will be in control of our lives?

■ 18.5.6 Web 3.0 and Beyond

Although the first phase of Web 3.0 is closer to us than sophisticated intelligent agents, people do disagree about the nature of Web 3.0. For instance, developers think in terms of quantitative view: there will be more tools that are superior to their predecessors. Semantic technologists think in terms of levels of abstraction, and the type of metadata that will enable the transition to higher levels of abstraction. Casual end users think in terms of the new opportunities facilitated by more powerful connectivity.

Although Web 3.0 will not solve the challenges of information overload that we face on a daily basis, Web 3.0 will serve as a vitally important conduit that will establish more infrastructure and dismantle silos of information that exist throughout the world, and perhaps Web 4.0 will bring us much closer to the semantic technologists' vision of the Semantic Web.

In closing, we live in an amazing epoch of technological advances that affects people, companies, and even presidential candidates. Technology brings exciting and unexpected changes into our lives with ever-increasing frequency, making us adapt in ways in which we don't even recognize ourselves. Indeed, the relentless change and stimulation is exhilarating and intoxicating in a manner that somehow feels irresistibly addictive. Although we do not know what the future portends, we can be certain that Web 3.0 will usher in yet another exciting era of vibrant, powerful technological advances, and their associated social effects, that may take us closer to our collective destiny.

■ 18.6 SUMMARY

In this chapter, you learned about the experiences of a start-up innovators in Silicon Valley, and you also read the comments from well-respected members of the IT community regarding the future of the Web.

In closing, we believe that the material in this book gives you a very good starting point from which you can delve more deeply into tools, products, and technologies that will best serve your needs, be they your current job or your career development.

Trademark Acknowledgments

Adobe, Adobe AIR, Dreamweaver, Flex, Coldfusion, Flash, Flex and Flex Builder are either registered trademarks or trademarks of Adobe Systems Incorporated in the United States and/or other countries.

Agile Commerce and its logo are service marks of Agile Commerce, LLC.

AGWeb View, Allegro BTrees, Allegro Cache, Allegro CL, Allegro Graph, Gruff, Franz Semantic Technology, TopBraid, and Pepito are trademarks or registered trademarks or service marks or trade dress of Franz Inc.

AlertSite and DéjàClick are either trademarks or registered trademarks of Boca Internet Technologies, Inc.

Altova, Altova Map Force, Altova Mission Kit, and Semantic Works are either registered trademarks or common law trademarks of Altova GmbH in the U.S., the European Union and/or other countries.

Amazon, Amazon EC2, Amazon Elastic Map Reducer Amazon Web Services, Cloudberry Lab, Elastic Block Storage, Flexible Payments Service, Mechanical Turk, SimpleDB, and Simple Queue Service are trademarks, registered trademarks or trade dress of Amazon.com, Inc. in the U.S. and/or other countries.

Ansca is a trademark of Ansca, Inc.

Anthill, AnthillPro, and AnthillOS are trademarks of Urbancode, Inc.

Apache Geronimo, Apache Lucene, Apache Solr, Apache Tomcat, Ant, Hadoop, Hive, Jakarta JMeter, log4j, Maven, Struts, Tapestry, Tiles, Wicket, Xalan, and Xerces are registered trademarks or trademarks of The Apache Software Foundation.

Appcelerator is a registered trademark in the United States, Canada, and the European Union.

Appistry and CloudIQ are trademarks of Appistry, Inc.

Apple, Cocoa, iPhone, Leopard, Mac, Mac OS, Macintosh, Safari, and Tiger are registered trademarks of Apple Inc., registered in the U.S. and other countries.

Aptana, the Aptana logo, and Aptana Studio, are trademarks or registered trademarks of Aptana Inc. in the United States and/or other countries.

AspectJ is a trademark of Palo Alto Research Center Incorporated.

Bazaar (BZR), Cygwin, DbUnit, Gbuild, Hypertable, Inkscape, jQuery, Mercurial, Moodle, NAnt, NUnit, OCaml, rapidSVN, RCS, RestLet, Rife, Sphinx, TortoiseSVN, and Wordpress are GNU projects available under the GNU General Public License; version 2.0 or later.

Bazaar, BZR, Ubuntu, and Canonical are registered trademarks of Canonical Ltd.

Bebo is a trademark of AOL.

Bespin, Firefox, and Venkman are registered trademarks or trademarks of the Mozilla Foundation.

Bigdata is a registered trademark of SYSTAP, LLC.

Bitflash is a registered trademark of Open Text Corporation.

BlackBerry, RIM, Research In Motion, SureType and related trademarks, names and logos are the property of Research In Motion Limited and are registered and/or used in the U.S. and countries around the world.

Blueprint is a trademark of Blueprint Software Systems Inc.

Calais, Opencalais.com, Open Calais, Calais Document Viewer, Content Feed Explorer, and Gnosis, Tangaroo, are trademarks or registered trademarks of Thomson Reuters.

Cogito is a trademark and patent pending technology of Expert System S.p.A.

CometD, Dojo Toolkit, Bayeux Protocol are trademarks of The Dojo Foundation.

Compass and SiteMesh use the OpenSymphony Software License which is modified from, and fully compatible with the Apache Software License.

CRAIGSLIST is a registered mark in the U.S. Patent and Trademark Office.

Dapper is a trademark of Dapper, Inc.

Daylife API is owned by Daylife, Inc.

Dell Openmanage and Newservers are registered trademarks or trademarks of Dell Inc.

Denodo Technologies and Denodo are the registered trademarks of Denodo Technologies.

Django is a registered trademark of the Django Software Foundation.

Drive Score is a trademark of Fizber Inc.

eBay is a registered trademark of eBay Inc.

Eclipse and Babel Project are registered trademarks or trademarks of The Eclipse Foundation.

Eclipse and RestLet are available under the Eclipse Public License, version 1.0.

Engine Yard is a trademark of Engine Yard, Inc.

Facebook is a registered trademark or trademark of Facebook.

Firebug is a registered trademark of Parakey, Inc.

Freebase and all other Metaweb trademarks, service marks, product names, and trade names of Metaweb are owned by Metaweb.

GigaSpaces, GigaSpaces eXtreme Application Platform (XAP), GigaSpaces eXtreme Application Platform Enterprise Data Grid (XAP EDG), and GigaSpaces Enterprise are trademarks or registered trademarks of Giga Spaces Technologies.

Glassbox is a trademark of Glassbox Corporation.

Gluster and GlusterFS are all trademarks of Gluster, Inc. GlusterFS and Gluster Storage Platform are released under GNU General Public License v3 or later. Documentation is released under GNU Free Documentation License 1.2 or later.

GoGrid is a registered trademark of ServePath LLC.

Google, Blogger, Google Android, Google App Engine, Google Caffeine, Google Gears, Google Maps, GMail, iGoogle, Orkut, Jaiku OpenSocial, Picasa, and YouTube are registered trademarks or trademarks of Google.

GridGain is a registered trademark of GridGain Technologies LP.

hakia is a registered trademark of hakia, Inc.

hi5 is a registered trademark of hi5 Networks, Inc

Hyperic is a trademark of Hyperic, Inc.

IBM, IBM Blue Cloud, DB2, Infosphere, Tivoli, and WebSphere, are trademarks or registered trademarks of IBM in the United States; all others are trademarks or common law marks of IBM in the United States.

iCloud is a registred trademark of Xcerion AB.

Ikivo is a registered trademark of Ikivo AB. Ikivo Animator and Ikivo SVG Player are registered trademarks of Ikivo.

Intel and Intel Mash Maker are trademarks of Intel Corporation in the U.S. and other countries.

IntelliJ IDEA and JetBrains are registered trademarks of JetBrains.

JackBe and Presto are trademarks of JackBe Corporation.

JBars is available under the Mozilla Public License, version 1.1.

JBoss Application Server, JBoss Cache, JBoss Seam, and Hibernate are trademarks or registered trademarks of Red Hat, Inc. in the United States and other countries.

Jetty, Katta, Quartz, Subversion, vRaptor, and xindice are available under the Apache Software Foundation License, version 2.0.

JProbe is either a registered trademark or trademark of Quest Software, Inc. in the United States and other countries.

Juice is a either a registered trademark or trademark of Linkool International.

Juniper Networks is a registered trademark of Juniper Networks, Inc. in the United States and other countries.

Jython, modjy, and Python are available under the Python Software Foundation License, version 2.

Kayak, Kayak Network, and Kayak.com, are trademarks or registered trademarks of Kayak Software Corporation.

Kosmix.com is owned by or licensed to Kosmix and is subject to copyright, trademark, and other intellectual property rights under U.S. and international laws.

LinkedIn is a registered trademark of the LinkedIn Corporation.

Linux is the registered trademark of Linus Torvalds in the U.S. and other countries.

LongJump is a service and trademark of Relational Networks, Inc.

Meebo is a registered trademark of Meebo, Inc.

Meetup.com is a trademark of Meetup, Inc.

Microsoft, Azure, Bing, Excel, Expression, Hyper-V, Internet Explorer, Outlook, PowerPoint, SharePoint, Silverlight, SQL Server, Virtual PC, Visual Studio, Windows Mobile, Windows Vista, Windows XP, and Word are either registered trademarks or trademarks of Microsoft Corporation in the United States and/or other countries.

Moodle is a registered trademark of the Moodle Trust.

MOTOROLA and the Stylized "M" Logo are registered in the U.S. Patent & Trademark Office and are registered trademarks of Motorola, Inc.

MySpace is a registered trademark of MySpace, Inc.

NCSA Mosaic is a trademark of the National Center for Supercomputing Applications.

Netscape Navigator is a trademark of Netscape Communications Corporation.

NetSuite is a registered trademark of NetSuite, Inc.

Ning is a registered trademark of Ning, Inc.

Nokia is a registered trademark of Nokia Corporation.

OCaml is available under the Q Public License, version 1.0.

OMG CORBA is a registered trademark of Object Management Group, Inc. in the United States and/or other countries.

OpenID is a trademark of OpenID Foundation.

Opera is a trademark or registered trademark of Opera Software ASA.

Optimizeit is a trademark of Intuitive Systems, Inc.

Oracle, Oracle8i, Oracle9i, BEA webLogic, Coherence, JDeveloper, and TopLink, are registered trademarks or trademarks of Oracle Corporation and/or its affiliates.

Orbited is available under the MIT license.

Orbited is a trademark of Michael Carter.

Palm and Pre are trademarks of Palm, Inc.

PayPal is a registered trademark of PayPal, Inc.

PERFORCE is a registered trademark of Perforce Software, Inc.

Perl is a trademark or a registered trademark of The Perl Foundation.

Photobucket is a trademark of Photobucket, Inc

PHPUnit is available under the Berkeley Software Distribution License, version 1.0.

Pivotal Labs is a trademark of Pivotal Labs, Inc.

Post Rank is a trademark of Post Rank, Inc.

Python and PyCon are trademarks or registered trademarks of the Python Software Foundation.

RackSpace is a registered trademark of Rackspace US, Inc.

Rails and Ruby on Rails, and are registered trademarks of David Heinemeier Hansson.

Restlet is a registered trademark of Noelios Technologies.

Rhomobile is a trademark of Rhomobile, Inc.

RightScale is a registered trademark of RightScale, Inc.

Salesforce, Force.com, AppExchange, Face Connector and other marks of salesforce.com used on the AppExchange site are trademarks or service marks of salesforce.com, Inc.

Samsung is a trademark of Samsung in the United States or other countries.

ScaleOut StateServer and ScaleOut GeoServer are registered trademarks of ScaleOut Software Inc. ScaleOut SessionServer and ScaleOut StateServer Grid Computing Edition are trademarks of ScaleOut Software, Inc.

Prototype script.aculo.us is licensed under a Creative Commons Attribution-Share Alike 3.0 Unported License.

Serena and PVCS, are trademarks of SERENA Software, Inc.

Shibboleth is a registered trademark of Internet2.

Smalltalk is a trademark of ParcPlace Systems.

SmartClient is a trademark or registered trademark of Isomorphic Software, Inc.

SourceForge.net, Slashdot, ThinkGeek and freshmeat are registered trademarks and Geeknet is a trademark of Geeknet, Inc.

Spring and SpringSource are registered trademarks or trademarks of SpringSource, Inc.

Subversion is a registered trademark of Subversion Corporation.

Sun, Glassfish, Java, JavaBeans, JavaMail, JavaScript, JDBC, MySQL, Solaris, VirtualBox, and Zembly are trademarks or registered trademarks of Sun Microsystems, Inc. or its subsidiaries in the United States and other countries.

Terracotta and eHcache are trademarks of Terracotta, Inc.

The SproutCore name and logo are both trademarks of Sprout Systems, Inc.

TIBCO General Interface and TIBCO Software are the trademarks or registered trademarks of TIBCO Software Inc.

Topsy and the Topsy logo are trademarks or registered trademarks of Topsy, Inc.

TUMBLR is a registered trademark of Tumblr, Inc.

Twitter is a trademark of Twitter, Inc.

Unfuddle, Unfuddle.com, the Unfuddle.com logo, and all other trademarks, service marks, graphics and logos used in connection with Unfuddle.com are trademarks or registered trademarks of Unfuddle or Unfuddle's licensors.

UNIX is a registered trademark of The Open Group in the US and other countries.

VERISIGN is a registered trademark of VeriSign in the United States and/or other countries.

VMware is a registered trademark or trademark of VMware, Inc.

W3C, Cascading Style Sheets, SVG, XML, and XSL are a trademark (registered in numerous countries) of the World Wide Web Consortium; marks of W3C are registered and held by its host institutions MIT, ERCIM, and Keio.

Walk Score is a trademark of Front Seat Management, LLC.

webappVM is a trademark of OSS-1701, Inc.

WordPress and WordPress.com, are trademarks or registered trademarks of Automattic, Inc.

WSO2 is a trademark of WSO2.

XWiki is a registered trademark of XPertNet SARL.

Yahoo, De.licio.us, Flickr, Friends on Fire, Search Monkey, Yahoo Boss, Yahoo Meme, YOI, and Yahoo Pipes are trademarks or registered trademarks of Yahoo! Inc.

Yelp is a proprietary service mark of Yelp! Inc.

Zend is a registered trademark of Zend Technologies, Ltd.

Zoho and Zoho Cloud SQL are registered trademarks or trademarks of ZOHO Corporation.

GNU GENERAL PUBLIC LICENSE

Version 3, 29 June 2007

Copyright © 2007 Free Software Foundation, Inc. <http://fsf.org/>

Everyone is permitted to copy and distribute verbatim copies of this license document, but changing it is not allowed.

Preamble

The GNU General Public License is a free, copyleft license for software and other kinds of works.

The licenses for most software and other practical works are designed to take away your freedom to share and change the works. By contrast, the GNU General Public License is intended to guarantee your freedom to share and change all versions of a program—to make sure it remains free software for all its users. We, the Free Software Foundation, use the GNU General Public License for most of our software; it applies also to any other work released this way by its authors. You can apply it to your programs, too.

When we speak of free software, we are referring to freedom, not price. Our General Public Licenses are designed to make sure that you have the freedom to distribute copies of free software (and charge for them if you wish), that you receive source code or can get it if you want it, that you can change the software or use pieces of it in new free programs, and that you know you can do these things.

To protect your rights, we need to prevent others from denying you these rights or asking you to surrender the rights. Therefore, you have certain responsibilities if you distribute copies of the software, or if you modify it: responsibilities to respect the freedom of others.

For example, if you distribute copies of such a program, whether gratis or for a fee, you must pass on to the recipients the same freedoms that you received. You must make sure that they, too, receive or can get the source code. And you must show them these terms so they know their rights.

Developers that use the GNU GPL protect your rights with two steps: (1) assert copyright on the software, and (2) offer you this License giving you legal permission to copy, distribute and/or modify it.

For the developers' and authors' protection, the GPL clearly explains that there is no warranty for this free software. For both users' and authors' sake, the GPL requires that modified versions be marked as changed, so that their problems will not be attributed erroneously to authors of previous versions.

Some devices are designed to deny users access to install or run modified versions of the software inside them, although the manufacturer can do so. This is fundamentally incompatible with the aim of protecting users' freedom to change the software. The systematic pattern of such abuse occurs in the area of products for individuals to use, which is precisely where it is most unacceptable. Therefore, we have designed this version of the GPL to prohibit the practice for those products. If such problems arise substantially in other domains, we stand ready to extend this provision to those domains in future versions of the GPL, as needed to protect the freedom of users.

Finally, every program is threatened constantly by software patents. States should not allow patents to restrict development and use of software on general-purpose computers, but in those that do, we wish to avoid the special danger that patents applied to a free program could make it effectively proprietary. To prevent this, the GPL assures that patents cannot be used to render the program non-free.

The precise terms and conditions for copying, distribution and modification follow.

TERMS AND CONDITIONS

0. Definitions.

"This License" refers to version 3 of the GNU General Public License.

"Copyright" also means copyright-like laws that apply to other kinds of works, such as semiconductor masks.

"The Program" refers to any copyrightable work licensed under this License. Each licensee is addressed as "you". "Licensees" and "recipients" may be individuals or organizations.

To "modify" a work means to copy from or adapt all or part of the work in a fashion requiring copyright permission, other than the making of an exact copy. The resulting work is called a "modified version" of the earlier work or a work "based on" the earlier work.

A "covered work" means either the unmodified Program or a work based on the Program.

To "propagate" a work means to do anything with it that, without permission, would make you directly or secondarily liable for infringement under applicable copyright law, except executing it on a computer or modifying a private copy. Propagation includes copying, distribution (with or without modification), making available to the public, and in some countries other activities as well.

To "convey" a work means any kind of propagation that enables other parties to make or receive copies. Mere interaction with a user through a computer network, with no transfer of a copy, is not conveying.

An interactive user interface displays "Appropriate Legal Notices" to the extent that it includes a convenient and prominently visible feature that (1) displays an appropriate copyright notice, and (2) tells the user that there is no warranty for the work (except to the extent that warranties are provided), that licensees may convey the work under this License, and how to view a copy of this License. If the interface presents a list of user commands or options, such as a menu, a prominent item in the list meets this criterion.

1. Source Code.

The "source code" for a work means the preferred form of the work for making modifications to it. "Object code" means any non-source form of a work.

A "Standard Interface" means an interface that either is an official standard defined by a recognized standards body, or, in the case of interfaces specified for a particular programming language, one that is widely used among developers working in that language.

The "System Libraries" of an executable work include anything, other than the work as a whole, that (a) is included in the normal form of packaging a Major Component, but which is not part of that Major Component, and (b) serves only to enable use of the work with that Major Component, or to implement a Standard Interface for which an implementation is available to the public in source code form. A "Major Component", in this context, means a major essential component (kernel, window system, and so on) of the specific operating system (if any) on which the executable work runs, or a compiler used to produce the work, or an object code interpreter used to run it.

The "Corresponding Source" for a work in object code form means all the source code needed to generate, install, and (for an executable work) run the object code and to modify the work, including scripts to control those activities. However, it does not include the work's System Libraries, or general-purpose tools or generally available free programs which are used unmodified in performing those activities but which are not part of the work. For example, Corresponding Source includes interface definition files associated with source files for the work, and the source code for shared libraries and dynamically linked subprograms that the work is specifically designed to require, such as by intimate data communication or control flow between those subprograms and other parts of the work.

The Corresponding Source need not include anything that users can regenerate automatically from other parts of the Corresponding Source.

The Corresponding Source for a work in source code form is that same work.

2. Basic Permissions.

All rights granted under this License are granted for the term of copyright on the Program, and are irrevocable provided the stated conditions are met. This License explicitly affirms your unlimited permission to run the unmodified Program. The output from running a covered work is covered by this License only if the output, given its content, constitutes a covered work. This License acknowledges your rights of fair use or other equivalent, as provided by copyright law.

You may make, run and propagate covered works that you do not convey, without conditions so long as your license otherwise remains in force. You may convey covered works to others for the sole purpose of having them make modifications exclusively for you, or provide you with facilities for running those works, provided that you comply with the terms of this License in conveying all material for which you do not control copyright. Those thus making or running the covered works for you must do so exclusively on your behalf, under your direction and control, on terms that prohibit them from making any copies of your copyrighted material outside their relationship with you.

Conveying under any other circumstances is permitted solely under the conditions stated below. Sublicensing is not allowed; section 10 makes it unnecessary.

3. Protecting Users' Legal Rights From Anti-Circumvention Law.

No covered work shall be deemed part of an effective technological measure under any applicable law fulfilling obligations under article 11 of the WIPO copyright treaty adopted on 20 December 1996, or similar laws prohibiting or restricting circumvention of such measures.

When you convey a covered work, you waive any legal power to forbid circumvention of technological measures to the extent such circumvention is effected by exercising rights under this License with respect to the covered work, and you disclaim any intention to limit operation or modification of the work as a means of enforcing, against the work's users, your or third parties' legal rights to forbid circumvention of technological measures.

4. Conveying Verbatim Copies.

You may convey verbatim copies of the Program's source code as you receive it, in any medium, provided that you conspicuously and appropriately publish on each copy an appropriate copyright notice; keep intact all notices stating that this License and any non-permissive terms added in accord with section 7 apply to the code; keep intact all notices of the absence of any warranty; and give all recipients a copy of this License along with the Program.

You may charge any price or no price for each copy that you convey, and you may offer support or warranty protection for a fee.

5. Conveying Modified Source Versions.

You may convey a work based on the Program, or the modifications to produce it from the Program, in the form of source code under the terms of section 4, provided that you also meet all of these conditions:

  a) The work must carry prominent notices stating that you modified it, and giving a relevant date.

  b) The work must carry prominent notices stating that it is released under this License and any conditions added under section 7. This requirement modifies the requirement in section 4 to "keep intact all notices".

  c) You must license the entire work, as a whole, under this License to anyone who comes into possession of a copy. This License will therefore apply, along with any applicable section 7 additional terms, to the whole of the work, and all its parts, regardless of how they are packaged. This License gives no permission to license the work in any other way, but it does not invalidate such permission if you have separately received it.

  d) If the work has interactive user interfaces, each must display Appropriate Legal Notices; however, if the Program has interactive interfaces that do not display Appropriate Legal Notices, your work need not make them do so.

A compilation of a covered work with other separate and independent works, which are not by their nature extensions of the covered work, and which are not combined with it such as to form a larger program, in or on a volume of a storage or distribution medium, is called an "aggregate" if the compilation and its resulting copyright are not used to limit the access or legal rights of the compilation's users beyond what the individual works permit. Inclusion of a covered work in an aggregate does not cause this License to apply to the other parts of the aggregate.

6. Conveying Non-Source Forms.

You may convey a covered work in object code form under the terms of sections 4 and 5, provided that you also convey the machine-readable Corresponding Source under the terms of this License, in one of these ways:

a) Convey the object code in, or embodied in, a physical product (including a physical distribution medium), accompanied by the Corresponding Source fixed on a durable physical medium customarily used for software interchange.

b) Convey the object code in, or embodied in, a physical product (including a physical distribution medium), accompanied by a written offer, valid for at least three years and valid for as long as you offer spare parts or customer support for that product model, to give anyone who possesses the object code either (1) a copy of the Corresponding Source for all the software in the product that is covered by this License, on a durable physical medium customarily used for software interchange, for a price no more than your reasonable cost of physically performing this conveying of source, or (2) access to copy the Corresponding Source from a network server at no charge.

c) Convey individual copies of the object code with a copy of the written offer to provide the Corresponding Source. This alternative is allowed only occasionally and noncommercially, and only if you received the object code with such an offer, in accord with subsection 6b.

d) Convey the object code by offering access from a designated place (gratis or for a charge), and offer equivalent access to the Corresponding Source in the same way through the same place at no further charge. You need not require recipients to copy the Corresponding Source along with the object code. If the place to copy the object code is a network server, the Corresponding Source may be on a different server (operated by you or a third party) that supports equivalent copying facilities, provided you maintain clear directions next to the object code saying where to find the Corresponding Source. Regardless of what server hosts the Corresponding Source, you remain obligated to ensure that it is available for as long as needed to satisfy these requirements.

e) Convey the object code using peer-to-peer transmission, provided you inform other peers where the object code and Corresponding Source of the work are being offered to the general public at no charge under subsection 6d.

A separable portion of the object code, whose source code is excluded from the Corresponding Source as a System Library, need not be included in conveying the object code work.

A "User Product" is either (1) a "consumer product", which means any tangible personal property which is normally used for personal, family, or household purposes, or (2) anything designed or sold for incorporation into a dwelling. In determining whether a product is a consumer product, doubtful cases shall be resolved in favor of coverage. For a particular product received by a particular user, "normally used" refers to a typical or common use of that class of product, regardless of the status of the particular user or of the way in which the particular user actually uses, or expects or is expected to use, the product. A product is a consumer product regardless of whether the product has substantial commercial, industrial or non-consumer uses, unless such uses represent the only significant mode of use of the product.

"Installation Information" for a User Product means any methods, procedures, authorization keys, or other information required to install and execute modified versions of a covered work in that User Product from a modified version of its Corresponding Source. The information must suffice to ensure that the continued functioning of the modified object code is in no case prevented or interfered with solely because modification has been made.

If you convey an object code work under this section in, or with, or specifically for use in, a User Product, and the conveying occurs as part of a transaction in which the right of possession and use of the User Product is transferred to the recipient in perpetuity or for a fixed term (regardless of how the transaction is characterized), the Corresponding Source conveyed under this section must be accompanied by the Installation Information. But this requirement does not apply if neither you nor any third party retains the ability to install modified object code on the User Product (for example, the work has been installed in ROM).

The requirement to provide Installation Information does not include a requirement to continue to provide support service, warranty, or updates for a work that has been modified or installed by the recipient, or for the User Product in which it has been modified or installed. Access to a network may be denied when the modification itself materially and adversely affects the operation of the network or violates the rules and protocols for communication across the network.

Corresponding Source conveyed, and Installation Information provided, in accord with this section must be in a format that is publicly documented (and with an implementation available to the public in source code form), and must require no special password or key for unpacking, reading, or copying.

7. Additional Terms.

"Additional permissions" are terms that supplement the terms of this License by making exceptions from one or more of its conditions. Additional permissions that are applicable to the entire Program shall be treated as though they were included in this License, to the extent that they are valid under applicable law. If additional permissions apply only to part of the Program, that part may be used separately under those permissions, but the entire Program remains governed by this License without regard to the additional permissions.

When you convey a copy of a covered work, you may at your option remove any additional permissions from that copy, or from any part of it. (Additional permissions may be written to require their own removal in certain cases when you modify the work.) You may place additional permissions on material, added by you to a covered work, for which you have or can give appropriate copyright permission.

Notwithstanding any other provision of this License, for material you add to a covered work, you may (if authorized by the copyright holders of that material) supplement the terms of this License with terms:

a) Disclaiming warranty or limiting liability differently from the terms of sections 15 and 16 of this License; or

b) Requiring preservation of specified reasonable legal notices or author attributions in that material or in the Appropriate Legal Notices displayed by works containing it; or

c) Prohibiting misrepresentation of the origin of that material, or requiring that modified versions of such material be marked in reasonable ways as different from the original version; or

d) Limiting the use for publicity purposes of names of licensors or authors of the material; or

e) Declining to grant rights under trademark law for use of some trade names, trademarks, or service marks; or

f) Requiring indemnification of licensors and authors of that material by anyone who conveys the material (or modified versions of it) with contractual assumptions of liability to the recipient, for any liability that these contractual assumptions directly impose on those licensors and authors.

All other non-permissive additional terms are considered "further restrictions" within the meaning of section 10. If the Program as you received it, or any part of it, contains a notice stating that it is governed by this License along with a term that is a further restriction, you may remove that term. If a license document contains a further restriction but permits relicensing or conveying under this License, you may add to a covered work material governed by the terms of that license document, provided that the further restriction does not survive such relicensing or conveying.

If you add terms to a covered work in accord with this section, you must place, in the relevant source files, a statement of the additional terms that apply to those files, or a notice indicating where to find the applicable terms.

Additional terms, permissive or non-permissive, may be stated in the form of a separately written license, or stated as exceptions; the above requirements apply either way.

8. Termination.

You may not propagate or modify a covered work except as expressly provided under this License. Any attempt otherwise to propagate or modify it is void, and will automatically terminate your rights under this License (including any patent licenses granted under the third paragraph of section 11).

However, if you cease all violation of this License, then your license from a particular copyright holder is reinstated (a) provisionally, unless and until the copyright holder explicitly and finally terminates your license, and (b) permanently, if the copyright holder fails to notify you of the violation by some reasonable means prior to 60 days after the cessation.

Moreover, your license from a particular copyright holder is reinstated permanently if the copyright holder notifies you of the violation by some reasonable means, this is the first time you have received notice of violation of this License (for any work) from that copyright holder, and you cure the violation prior to 30 days after your receipt of the notice.

Termination of your rights under this section does not terminate the licenses of parties who have received copies or rights from you under this License. If your rights have been terminated and not permanently reinstated, you do not qualify to receive new licenses for the same material under section 10.

9. Acceptance Not Required for Having Copies.

You are not required to accept this License in order to receive or run a copy of the Program. Ancillary propagation of a covered work occurring solely as a consequence of using peer-to-peer transmission to receive a copy likewise does not require acceptance. However, nothing other than this License grants you permission to propagate or modify any covered work. These actions infringe copyright if you do not accept this License. Therefore, by modifying or propagating a covered work, you indicate your acceptance of this License to do so.

10. Automatic Licensing of Downstream Recipients.

Each time you convey a covered work, the recipient automatically receives a license from the original licensors, to run, modify and propagate that work, subject to this License. You are not responsible for enforcing compliance by third parties with this License.

An "entity transaction" is a transaction transferring control of an organization, or substantially all assets of one, or subdividing an organization, or merging organizations. If propagation of a covered work results from an entity transaction, each party to that transaction who receives a copy of the work also receives whatever licenses to the work the party's predecessor in interest had or could give under the previous paragraph, plus a right to possession of the Corresponding Source of the work from the predecessor in interest, if the predecessor has it or can get it with reasonable efforts.

You may not impose any further restrictions on the exercise of the rights granted or affirmed under this License. For example, you may not impose a license fee, royalty, or other charge for exercise of rights granted under this License, and you may not initiate litigation (including a cross-claim or counterclaim in a lawsuit) alleging that any patent claim is infringed by making, using, selling, offering for sale, or importing the Program or any portion of it.

11. Patents.

A "contributor" is a copyright holder who authorizes use under this License of the Program or a work on which the Program is based. The work thus licensed is called the contributor's "contributor version".

A contributor's "essential patent claims" are all patent claims owned or controlled by the contributor, whether already acquired or hereafter acquired, that would be infringed by some manner, permitted by this License, of making, using, or selling its contributor version, but do not include claims that would be infringed only as a consequence of further modification of the contributor version. For purposes of this definition, "control" includes the right to grant patent sublicenses in a manner consistent with the requirements of this License.

Each contributor grants you a non-exclusive, worldwide, royalty-free patent license under the contributor's essential patent claims, to make, use, sell, offer for sale, import and otherwise run, modify and propagate the contents of its contributor version.

In the following three paragraphs, a "patent license" is any express agreement or commitment, however denominated, not to enforce a patent (such as an express permission to practice a patent or covenant not to sue for patent infringement). To "grant" such a patent license to a party means to make such an agreement or commitment not to enforce a patent against the party.

If you convey a covered work, knowingly relying on a patent license, and the Corresponding Source of the work is not available for anyone to copy, free of charge and under the terms of this License, through a publicly available network server or other readily accessible means, then you must either (1) cause the Corresponding Source to be so available, or (2) arrange to deprive yourself of the benefit of the patent license for this particular work, or (3) arrange, in a manner consistent with the requirements of this License, to extend the patent license to downstream recipients. "Knowingly relying" means you have actual knowledge that, but for the patent license, your conveying the covered work in a country, or your recipient's use of the covered work in a country, would infringe one or more identifiable patents in that country that you have reason to believe are valid.

If, pursuant to or in connection with a single transaction or arrangement, you convey, or propagate by procuring conveyance of, a covered work, and grant a patent license to some of the parties receiving the covered work authorizing them to use, propagate, modify or convey a specific copy of the covered work, then the patent license you grant is automatically extended to all recipients of the covered work and works based on it.

A patent license is "discriminatory" if it does not include within the scope of its coverage, prohibits the exercise of, or is conditioned on the non-exercise of one or more of the rights that are specifically granted under this License. You may not convey a covered work if you are a party to an arrangement with a third party that is in the business of distributing software, under which you make payment to the third party based on the extent of your activity of conveying the work, and under which the third party grants, to any of the parties who would receive the covered work from you, a discriminatory patent license (a) in connection with copies of the covered work conveyed by you (or copies made from those copies), or (b) primarily for and in connection with specific products or compilations that contain the covered work, unless you entered into that arrangement, or that patent license was granted, prior to 28 March 2007.

Nothing in this License shall be construed as excluding or limiting any implied license or other defenses to infringement that may otherwise be available to you under applicable patent law.

12. No Surrender of Others' Freedom.

If conditions are imposed on you (whether by court order, agreement or otherwise) that contradict the conditions of this License, they do not excuse you from the conditions of this License. If you cannot convey a covered work so as to satisfy simultaneously your obligations under this License and any other pertinent obligations, then as a consequence you may not convey it at all. For example, if you agree to terms that obligate you to collect a royalty for further conveying from those to whom you convey the Program, the only way you could satisfy both those terms and this License would be to refrain entirely from conveying the Program.

13. Use with the GNU Affero General Public License.

Notwithstanding any other provision of this License, you have permission to link or combine any covered work with a work licensed under version 3 of the GNU Affero General Public License into a single combined work, and to convey the resulting work. The terms of this License will continue to apply to the part which is the covered work, but the special requirements of the GNU Affero General Public License, section 13, concerning interaction through a network will apply to the combination as such.

14. Revised Versions of this License.

The Free Software Foundation may publish revised and/or new versions of the GNU General Public License from time to time. Such new versions will be similar in spirit to the present version, but may differ in detail to address new problems or concerns.

Each version is given a distinguishing version number. If the Program specifies that a certain numbered version of the GNU General Public License "or any later version" applies to it, you have the option of following the terms and conditions either of that numbered version or of any later version published by the Free Software Foundation. If the Program does not specify a version number of the GNU General Public License, you may choose any version ever published by the Free Software Foundation.

If the Program specifies that a proxy can decide which future versions of the GNU General Public License can be used, that proxy's public statement of acceptance of a version permanently authorizes you to choose that version for the Program.

Later license versions may give you additional or different permissions. However, no additional obligations are imposed on any author or copyright holder as a result of your choosing to follow a later version.

15. Disclaimer of Warranty.

THERE IS NO WARRANTY FOR THE PROGRAM, TO THE EXTENT PERMITTED BY APPLICABLE LAW. EXCEPT WHEN OTHERWISE STATED IN WRITING THE COPYRIGHT HOLDERS AND/OR OTHER PARTIES PROVIDE THE PROGRAM "AS IS" WITHOUT WARRANTY OF ANY KIND, EITHER EXPRESSED OR IMPLIED, INCLUDING, BUT NOT LIMITED TO, THE IMPLIED WARRANTIES OF MERCHANTABILITY AND FITNESS FOR A PARTICULAR PURPOSE. THE ENTIRE RISK AS TO THE QUALITY AND PERFORMANCE OF THE PROGRAM IS WITH YOU. SHOULD THE PROGRAM PROVE DEFECTIVE, YOU ASSUME THE COST OF ALL NECESSARY SERVICING, REPAIR OR CORRECTION.

16. Limitation of Liability.

IN NO EVENT UNLESS REQUIRED BY APPLICABLE LAW OR AGREED TO IN WRITING WILL ANY COPYRIGHT HOLDER, OR ANY OTHER PARTY WHO MODIFIES AND/OR CONVEYS THE PROGRAM AS PERMITTED ABOVE, BE LIABLE TO YOU FOR DAMAGES, INCLUDING ANY GENERAL, SPECIAL, INCIDENTAL OR CONSEQUENTIAL DAMAGES ARISING OUT OF THE USE OR INABILITY TO USE THE PROGRAM (INCLUDING BUT NOT LIMITED TO LOSS OF DATA OR DATA BEING RENDERED INACCURATE OR LOSSES SUSTAINED BY YOU OR THIRD PARTIES OR A FAILURE OF THE PROGRAM TO OPERATE WITH ANY OTHER PROGRAMS), EVEN IF SUCH HOLDER OR OTHER PARTY HAS BEEN ADVISED OF THE POSSIBILITY OF SUCH DAMAGES.

17. Interpretation of Sections 15 and 16.

If the disclaimer of warranty and limitation of liability provided above cannot be given local legal effect according to their terms, reviewing courts shall apply local law that most closely approximates an absolute waiver of all civil liability in connection with the Program, unless a warranty or assumption of liability accompanies a copy of the Program in return for a fee.

END OF TERMS AND CONDITIONS

How to Apply These Terms to Your New Programs

If you develop a new program, and you want it to be of the greatest possible use to the public, the best way to achieve this is to make it free software which everyone can redistribute and change under these terms.

To do so, attach the following notices to the program. It is safest to attach them to the start of each source file to most effectively state the exclusion of warranty; and each file should have at least the "copyright" line and a pointer to where the full notice is found.

```
<one line to give the program's name and a brief idea of what it does.>
Copyright (C) <year>  <name of author>

This program is free software: you can redistribute it and/or modify
it under the terms of the GNU General Public License as published by
the Free Software Foundation, either version 3 of the License, or
(at your option) any later version.

This program is distributed in the hope that it will be useful,
but WITHOUT ANY WARRANTY; without even the implied warranty of
MERCHANTABILITY or FITNESS FOR A PARTICULAR PURPOSE. See the
GNU General Public License for more details.

You should have received a copy of the GNU General Public License
along with this program. If not, see <http://www.gnu.org/licenses/>.
```

Also add information on how to contact you by electronic and paper mail.

If the program does terminal interaction, make it output a short notice like this when it starts in an interactive mode:

```
<program>  Copyright (C) <year>  <name of author>
This program comes with ABSOLUTELY NO WARRANTY; for details type
'show w'.
This is free software, and you are welcome to redistribute it
under certain conditions; type 'show c' for details.
```

The hypothetical commands 'show w' and 'show c' should show the appropriate parts of the General Public License. Of course, your program's commands might be different; for a GUI interface, you would use an "about box".

You should also get your employer (if you work as a programmer) or school, if any, to sign a "copyright disclaimer" for the program, if necessary. For more information on this, and how to apply and follow the GNU GPL, see <http://www.gnu.org/licenses/>.

The GNU General Public License does not permit incorporating your program into proprietary programs. If your program is a subroutine library, you may consider it more useful to permit linking proprietary applications with the library. If this is what you want to do, use the GNU Lesser General Public License instead of this License. But first, please read <http://www.gnu.org/philosophy/why-not-lgpl.html>.

GNU LESSER GENERAL PUBLIC LICENSE

Version 3, 29 June 2007

Copyright © 2007 Free Software Foundation, Inc. <http://fsf.org/>

Everyone is permitted to copy and distribute verbatim copies of this license document, but changing it is not allowed.

This version of the GNU Lesser General Public License incorporates the terms and conditions of version 3 of the GNU General Public License, supplemented by the additional permissions listed below.

0. Additional Definitions.

As used herein, "this License" refers to version 3 of the GNU Lesser General Public License, and the "GNU GPL" refers to version 3 of the GNU General Public License.

"The Library" refers to a covered work governed by this License, other than an Application or a Combined Work as defined below.

An "Application" is any work that makes use of an interface provided by the Library, but which is not otherwise based on the Library. Defining a subclass of a class defined by the Library is deemed a mode of using an interface provided by the Library.

A "Combined Work" is a work produced by combining or linking an Application with the Library. The particular version of the Library with which the Combined Work was made is also called the "Linked Version".

The "Minimal Corresponding Source" for a Combined Work means the Corresponding Source for the Combined Work, excluding any source code for portions of the Combined Work that, considered in isolation, are based on the Application, and not on the Linked Version.

The "Corresponding Application Code" for a Combined Work means the object code and/or source code for the Application, including any data and utility programs needed for reproducing the Combined Work from the Application, but excluding the System Libraries of the Combined Work.

1. Exception to Section 3 of the GNU GPL.

You may convey a covered work under sections 3 and 4 of this License without being bound by section 3 of the GNU GPL.

2. Conveying Modified Versions.

If you modify a copy of the Library, and, in your modifications, a facility refers to a function or data to be supplied by an Application that uses the facility (other than as an argument passed when the facility is invoked), then you may convey a copy of the modified version:

    a) under this License, provided that you make a good faith effort to ensure that, in the event an Application does not supply the function or data, the facility still operates, and performs whatever part of its purpose remains meaningful, or

    b) under the GNU GPL, with none of the additional permissions of this License applicable to that copy.

3. Object Code Incorporating Material from Library Header Files.

The object code form of an Application may incorporate material from a header file that is part of the Library. You may convey such object code under terms of your choice, provided that, if the incorporated material is not limited to numerical parameters, data structure layouts and accessors, or small macros, inline functions and templates (ten or fewer lines in length), you do both of the following:

    a) Give prominent notice with each copy of the object code that the Library is used in it and that the Library and its use are covered by this License.

    b) Accompany the object code with a copy of the GNU GPL and this license document.

4. Combined Works.

You may convey a Combined Work under terms of your choice that, taken together, effectively do not restrict modification of the portions of the Library contained in the Combined Work and reverse engineering for debugging such modifications, if you also do each of the following:

    a) Give prominent notice with each copy of the Combined Work that the Library is used in it and that the Library and its use are covered by this License.

    b) Accompany the Combined Work with a copy of the GNU GPL and this license document.

    c) For a Combined Work that displays copyright notices during execution, include the copyright notice for the Library among these notices, as well as a reference directing the user to the copies of the GNU GPL and this license document.

    d) Do one of the following:

       0) Convey the Minimal Corresponding Source under the terms of this License, and the Corresponding Application Code in a form suitable for, and under terms that permit, the user to recombine or relink the Application with a modified version of the Linked Version to produce a modified Combined Work, in the manner specified by section 6 of the GNU GPL for conveying Corresponding Source.

       1) Use a suitable shared library mechanism for linking with the Library. A suitable mechanism is one that (a) uses at run time a copy of the Library already present on the user's computer system, and (b) will operate properly with a modified version of the Library that is interface-compatible with the Linked Version.

    e) Provide Installation Information, but only if you would otherwise be required to provide such information under section 6 of the GNU GPL, and only to the extent that such information is necessary to install and execute a modified version of the Combined Work produced by recombining or relinking the Application with a modified version of the Linked Version. (If you use option 4d0, the Installation Information must accompany the Minimal Corresponding Source and Corresponding Application Code. If you use option 4d1, you must provide the Installation Information in the manner specified by section 6 of the GNU GPL for conveying Corresponding Source.)

5. Combined Libraries.

You may place library facilities that are a work based on the Library side by side in a single library together with other library facilities that are not Applications and are not covered by this License, and convey such a combined library under terms of your choice, if you do both of the following:

    a) Accompany the combined library with a copy of the same work based on the Library, uncombined with any other library facilities, conveyed under the terms of this License.

    b) Give prominent notice with the combined library that part of it is a work based on the Library, and explaining where to find the accompanying uncombined form of the same work.

6. Revised Versions of the GNU Lesser General Public License.

The Free Software Foundation may publish revised and/or new versions of the GNU Lesser General Public License from time to time. Such new versions will be similar in spirit to the present version, but may differ in detail to address new problems or concerns.

Each version is given a distinguishing version number. If the Library as you received it specifies that a certain numbered version of the GNU Lesser General Public License "or any later version" applies to it, you have the option of following the terms and conditions either of that published version or of any later version published by the Free Software Foundation. If the Library as you received it does not specify a version number of the GNU Lesser General Public License, you may choose any version of the GNU Lesser General Public License ever published by the Free Software Foundation.

If the Library as you received it specifies that a proxy can decide whether future versions of the GNU Lesser General Public License shall apply, that proxy's public statement of acceptance of any version is permanent authorization for you to choose that version for the Library.

Index

D